T'S

h School?
2023

Adults, Wellbeing and Health
Libraries, Learning and Culture

Published in 2022 by
John Catt Educational Ltd,
15 Riduna Park,
Melton, Suffolk IP12 1QT UK
Tel: 01394 389850
Fax: 01394 386893
Email: enquiries@johncatt.com
Website: www.johncatt.com

A CIP catalogue record for this book is available from the British
Library.

ISBN: 978 1 915261 49 6

Contacts

Editor
Jonathan Barnes
Email: jonathanbarnes@johncatt.com

Advertising & School Profiles
Tel: +44 (0) 1394 389850
Email: sales@johncatt.com

Distribution/Book Sales
Tel: +44 (0) 1394 389863
Email: booksales@johncatt.com

Website: www.schoolsearch.co.uk

Contents

How to use this guide

Which School? has been specifically designed with the reader in mind. There are clearly defined sections providing information for anyone looking at independent education in the UK today.

Are you looking for help and advice? Take a look at our editorial section (pages 5-40). Here you will find articles written by experts in their field covering a wide variety of issues you are likely to come across when choosing a school for your child. Each year we try to find a differing range of topics to interest and inform you about the uniqueness of independent education.

Perhaps you are looking for a school or college in a certain geographical region? Then you need to look first in the directories, which begin on page D321. Here you will

find basic information about all the schools in each region complete with contact details. From this section you will be directed to more detailed information in the guide where this is available. An example of a typical directory entry is given below.

Are you looking for a certain type of school or college in your local area? Then you will need to look in the directories for your local area (see contents page for a list of all regions). Underneath each school you will find icons that denote the different types of schools or the qualifications that they offer.

Some of you may already be looking for a specific school or college. In which case, if you know the name of the school or college but are unsure of its location, simply

go to the index at the back of the guide where you will find all the schools listed alphabetically. Page numbers prefixed with the letter D denote the directory section; those without, a detailed profile.

If, however, you need to find out more information on relevant educational organisations and examinations, then you can look in the appendices where you will find up-to-date information about the examinations and qualifications available (page 419). There is also a section giving basic details about the many varied and useful organisations in the education field (page 441).

The profile and directory information in this guide is also featured on **www.schoolsearch.co.uk**, which also includes social media links, and latest school news.

Key to directory

County

Name of school or college

Indicates that this school has a profile

Address and contact number

Head's name

Age range

Number of pupils.
B = boys G = girls VIth = sixth form

Fees per annum.
Day = fees for day pupils.
WB = fees for weekly boarders.
FB = fees for full boarders.

Wherefordshire

College Academy

For further details see p. 12

Which Street, Whosville,
Wherefordshire AB12 3CD

Tel: 01000 000000

Head Master: Dr A Person

Age range: 11–18

No. of pupils: 660 B330 G330 VIth 200

Fees: Day £11,000 WB £16,000 FB £20,000

Key to directory icons

Key to symbols:
- (♦) Boys' school
- (♦) Girls' school
- (♦) International school
- (16·) Tutorial or sixth form college

Schools offering:
- (A) A levels
- (♠) Boarding accommodation
- (£) Bursaries
- (16·) Entrance at 16+
- (IB) International Baccalaureate
- (✐) Learning support
- (♠) Vocational qualifications

The questions you should ask

However much a school may appeal on first sight, you still need sound information to form your judgement

Schools attract pupils by their reputations, so most go to considerable lengths to ensure that parents are presented with an attractive image.

Modern marketing techniques try to promote good points and play down (without totally obscuring) bad ones. But every Head knows that, however good the school prospectus is, it only serves to attract parents through the school gates. Thereafter the decision depends on what they see and hear.

When you choose a school for your son or daughter, the key factor is that it will suit them. Many children and their parents are instinctively attracted (or otherwise) to a school on first sight. But even if it passes this test, and 'conforms' to what you are looking for in terms of location and academic, pastoral and extracurricular aspects, you will need to satisfy yourself that the school does measure up to what your instincts tell you.

Research we have carried out over the years suggests that in many cases the most important factor in choosing a school is the impression given by the Head. As well as finding out what goes on in a school, parents need to be reassured by the aura of confidence which they expect from a Head. How they discover the former may help them form their opinion of the latter.

So how a Head answers your questions is important. Based on our research, we have drawn up a list of 24 points on which you may need to be satisfied. The order in which they appear below does not necessarily reflect their degree of importance to each parent, but how the Head answers them may help you draw your own conclusions:

- How accessible is the Head, whose personality is seen by most parents as setting the 'tone' of the school?
- Will your child fit in? What is the overall atmosphere?
- To which organisations does the school belong? How has it been accredited?
- What is the ratio of teachers to pupils?
- What are the qualifications of the teaching staff?
- How often does the school communicate with parents through reports, parent/teacher meetings or other visits?
- What is the school's retention rate? Do larger lower classes and smaller upper classes reflect a school's inability to hang on to pupils?
- What are the school's exam results? What are the criteria for presenting them? Are they consistent over the years?
- How does the school cope with pupils' problems?
- What sort of academic and pastoral advice is available?
- What is the school's attitude to discipline?
- Have there been problems with drugs or sex? How have they been dealt with?
- What positive steps are taken to encourage good manners, behaviour and sportsmanship?
- Is progress accelerated for the academically bright?
- How does the school cope with pupils who do not work?
- What is the attitude to religion?
- What is the attitude to physical fitness and games?
- What sports are offered and what are the facilities?
- What are the extracurricular activities? What cultural or other visits are arranged away from the school?
- What steps are taken to encourage specific talent in music, the arts or sport?
- Where do pupils go when they leave – are they channelled to a few selected destinations?
- What is the uniform? What steps are taken to ensure that pupils take pride in their personal appearance?
- What are the timetable and term dates?
- Is it possible to speak to parents with children at the school to ask them for an opinion?

The most important challenges for independent schools

Barnaby Lenon, chair of ISC, provides an overview of the independent sector and why a focus on a broad education remains essential

There are about 609,000 pupils in independent schools in the UK, 6% of the total. Most of these would be eligible for a free state school place so these pupils save the British taxpayer a huge amount.

Many are on means-tested fee reductions: fee assistance runs at more than £1.2bn a year.

About 65,000 are boarders.

The average independent school is quite small – about 392 pupils. The majority of the schools are junior schools, preparing pupils well for the senior school they are going onto.

Many independent schools contribute to the local community through partnerships with state schools. This can include sharing classrooms, sharing IT, sports and catering facilities, seconding teaching staff, and sponsoring state academies.

Many independent schools have set up campuses abroad in order to raise money for bursaries. There are about 100 such campuses, many in China, and they educate over 65,000 pupils.

Independent schools face a number of challenges in 2023. Most immediate is the rising cost of energy and most other products which will drive school fee inflation.

This comes on top of the huge cost of the teachers' pension scheme which is causing many schools to move to a less expensive, private pension system. More small schools are merging with other schools in the face of these budget difficulties.

Looking further ahead, independent schools are aware of the implications of a Labour Party victory in a 2024 election. They seem committed to two different policies – removal of charitable status and charging VAT on school fees. These two changes would cause some schools to fail, would hasten mergers, and would require most schools to cut costs so the full weight of VAT does not fall on parents and fees. Schools are planning ahead now in order to minimise the impact of these changes, changes which are not inevitable but perfectly possible.

The good news for independent schools has been great GCSE and A-level results and the proportion gaining entry to top universities in the UK and USA. In 2022 exam grades nationally were set at a midpoint between the grades in 2019 and 2021. But many independent schools did not see this level of deflation. Entry to Oxford, Cambridge and other good universities has remained high despite all the media hype.

For me, the important thing is for governors and bursars to get a firm grip on financial projections and for head teachers to focus on a broad education and academic success. There has been a greater focus on pastoral care and pupil well-being in school inspections recently. These things are important but it is essential not to lose focus on the main purpose of school.

For more information about the Independent Schools Council see page 34

The good news for independent schools has been great GCSE and A-level results and the proportion gaining entry to top universities in the UK and USA.

Setting children up for success at school in the early years

Jane O'Brien, Head of Nursery at King's House School in Richmond, reflects on the importance of an excellent early years education

A high-quality early years education is one of the most important factors in a child's development, and sets them up to have the best start in life.

At King's House Nursery we aim to foster a happy and relaxed atmosphere where children learn to relate to one another and to adults through play-based activities, laying the foundations for independence and learning.

We offer a free-flow provision with a balance of adult-led and child-initiated activities. In both Caterpillar Class (rising 3s) and Butterfly Class (rising 4s) the focus is on developing the three primary areas and four specific areas of learning.

We are lucky to have highly experienced staff, many who have been with us since the Nursery first opened in 2009. With a staff ratio of 1:6 and small group activities, teachers know each child and communication between home and nursery is excellent. Our staff work hard to create a curriculum which promotes curiosity and independence: the class theme changes each week, varying from 'under the sea' to 'people who help us'. It is wonderful to see the boys and girls engaging with the topics, and 'animals' is always hugely popular! The children love talking about their pets and learning about farm animals.

The children also love being visited by different people to enrich their learning, such as groups who teach Makaton. A huge range of specialist teaching develops specific skills, from PE lessons to weekly yoga sessions to promote gross motors skills. In Butterfly Class children are introduced to French in weekly circle time as well as having sessions from music and drama teachers. Technology also plays a key role in understanding the world, and children are introduced to a range of simple equipment and early coding toys.

Literacy and maths form a key part of the early years. Early mark-making skills and fine motor control are promoted through a wide range of activities, and we teach the anima phonics programme in Butterfly Class and Reception to introduce children to the 42 phonic sounds of the English language through a multi-sensory approach.

We have a maths mastery approach ensuring children learn the essential problem solving skills needed as they move through their time at school.

Developing social skills is a vital aspect of a child's early years development. We are a polite, courteous and kind community, placing a great emphasis on how to share, take turns, listen to and be kind to others. The boys and girls love caring for the sunflowers and seeds they have planted in the playground, creating a space that everyone respects. Butterfly Class are also able to enjoy the school's 35-acre sports ground on Sports Day: it is a real privilege to have access to this outdoor space in London. A highlight for Reception is their weekly visits to Forest School in Ham Woods, developing children's appreciation for nature.

We love seeing how far our boys and girls come from their first day in Caterpillars to the end of Butterfly Class, ready to start in Reception. With the Nursery and School linked at King's House, the transition is helped by the boys participating in whole school events and being familiar with the 'big school'. We also enjoy excellent relationships with future schools for our girls. The children move on having developed essential life skills throughout their time at Nursery.

Our first children who started in King's House Nursery in 2009 are now finishing their time at school, and it is wonderful to see how they have grown into resilient, happy and confident young people.

> Developing social skills is a vital aspect of a child's early years development. We are a polite, courteous and kind community, placing a great emphasis on how to share, take turns, listen to and be kind to others.

For more information about King's House School, see page 118

Fostering independence at boarding schools

Sam Cooper, Head of Boarding at Gordon's School, shares how he and his wife Daisy engender independence in a supportive environment

Boarding schools have come a long way since the tales of cold showers, uncaring, strict staff and huge dormitories filled with rows of home sick children. These days we peddle patience, guiding students as they navigate social interactions, mental health issues and meeting the high expectations of the school, all that while being away from home for the first time, starting in a new school and living with 30 other peers. For most, mixed Year 7 boarding works, providing a balanced, consistent constant, based on what guides us.

Nowadays, boarding is often described as 'one big sleepover' by students, who regard it as very much a 'home from home': secure, friendly places where children not only flourish academically, but also learn tolerance, resilience, discipline, independence - and make life-long friends in the process.

Evenings and weekends are packed with activities, both external and in house, and as well as large grounds and facilities, children can enjoy the company of perhaps hundreds of others every day and weekend. With the right culture, the older students become older sibling figures who guide the younger ones in the ways of boarding.

As Head of Boarding at Gordon's and a joint Houseparent of Woolwich House, alongside my wife Daisy, the work of settling in our new charges begins months before they actually arrive. During in-person meetings or Zoom calls with overseas parents, we try and glean as much information as we can about their child so we can help them settle in as quickly as possible. We feel we know them before they arrive!

Communication with the parents helps build trust between us and we notice a sense of relief from them that not only will Gordon's provide stability for their children but some of the military values on which the school is built, camaraderie and a sense of being the best one can be for something bigger than oneself, in the form of House identity and eventually living the school's motto *Semper Fidelis*.

Parents can help their children by increasing independence, reducing their dependence on mobile phones and prompting them to carry out practical tasks and chores such as making their own bed.

The use of mobiles is limited throughout their year in our junior House and are removed from students for their first three weeks (although they are permitted to use the House phone to speak to their parents during this time). The vast majority of parents support this policy.

The reasoning behind their removal is to encourage friendships - it's easy to sit in a corner with their phone if they're feeling self-conscious but without one, they are making friends and learning how to gel with those in their House.

Phone usage is gradually increased but we find that often when these once much sought-after privileges arrive, they are ignored in favour of spending time playing with their friends!

Almost as soon as the new 11 year old boarders are dropped off, they are packing for a night's camping. High wires, rock climbing and marshmallows around campsite fires help break down any barriers and start cementing friendships with others beyond their boarding House.

The Boarding House is run as an extension of our home – the kitchen door is always open and our children and dog running around. Saturday morning pancakes in our kitchen are a weekly treat! Students feel comfortable, safe and secure - it's their term time home and our aim is to make them feel that way.

In the early stages the children are kept busy with many activities. If they're playing rounders or 'capture the flag' then they won't be feeling homesick! However, home sickness is always going to crop up and it usually happens at bed time. Then they come downstairs and are on the sofa drinking hot chocolate and talking it through. They also support each other in their bunk beds really early on – that is how they develop those lasting friendship bonds.

Each new boarder is assigned a carefully selected buddy – a boarder from a year above them with a similar background, to guide them through their first year and on to their senior boarding houses.

We really push independence and organisation from the start and try and get them to realise that if they can get tidiness and organisation sorted this year, it will be easier in the long run and allow them to focus on their academics and sports.

They are all ready to go on to their senior houses at the end of the year here, looking forward to more independence and with the skills and maturity to deal with the next stage of their boarding journey. Then it's our turn to release our fledglings and have another empty nest ready for the next year's cohort. Exhausting? Yes. Fun? The best. Worth it? More than anything.

Sam and Daisy Cooper are both Houseparents of the Year 7 Boarding House at Gordan's, Tes Boarding School of the Year.

For more information about Gordon's School, see page 222

Why choose a boarding school?

Chris Coetzee & Elizabeth Hanson, Heads of House for boys and girls boarding at King's School Rochester, share some of the opportunities available when attending a boarding school

At King's School Rochester, we have two boarding houses offering a boutique boarding experience where no-one is a number. The second oldest boarding school in the world, King's was founded in 604 AD. As the centuries have ticked over, the boarding community has changed to reflect the society we live in and today our boarding family has pupils from both the UK and 20 different countries including Brazil, Malaysia, Germany, Spain and the Ukraine.

We are proud to provide a warm, home from home, family experience to all our boarders and to facilitate that, we limit boarding numbers to 55 pupils, split into a boys' house (School House) and a girls' house (St Margaret's). The houses are just that, modernised large Victorian homes and are just a stone's throw from the school itself, the second oldest school in the world, one of the most vibrant high streets in the South East of England and just over half an hour away by train to the bright lights of London.

The reasons for boarding in the 21st century are as diverse as the flags we fly on our mantlepieces.

For many UK based pupils, staying at school during the week and going home on a weekend allows them to participate fully in the multitude of after school activities. We encourage everyone to get 'stuck in' and as a result, making friends becomes effortless. Music scholars can stay late and take part in regular concerts and open mic nights. When taking part in Sport, many pupils stay over to attend after school matches and to represent the school on a Saturday at fixtures, whilst for Drama it gives pupils the flexibility to throw themselves into rehearsals ready for Opening Night. During public exam times, many of our day pupils take up flexi boarding, only staying a few nights a week to help them focus on revision. Having tutors on hand, quiet spaces for study, and eliminating the stress of a commute really has its benefits.

Service families entrust us with their children, safe in the knowledge we provide a stable and nurturing environment, allowing them to form and build friendships that will last a lifetime. Working alongside the day staff, we create strong pastoral systems around all our boarders to help them navigate the ups and downs teenage life brings.

International boarders join us to experience a British boarding school, just like in Harry Potter. Some pupils can only join the boarding community for a term due to the arrangements of absence in their country of origin, and some fall in love with the school and it's traditions and end up staying for their whole school career.

Boarding life teaches pupils the importance of good routines and positive habits. More and more Sixth Form parents and pupils are using boarding as a prelude to university life. It is a far cry from the Victorian images of boarding with gruel and angry housemasters stomping around the house. All the rooms are decorated to a high modern standard and equipped with ultra-high speed wireless connections, making a video call home or a quick online game with friends an enjoyable experience. There are multiple common rooms where pupils can socialise, watch movies, play video games or enjoy a fierce game of cards - just like they would at home.

Boarders at King's also have top quality dining and our very own Italian chef prepares two course meals for lunch and dinner every day. There is always a range of healthy options to choose from and pupils with special dietary needs are expertly catered for. Out of set meal times, pupils have access to their own mini-kitchens to make food and enjoy snacks with friends.

On weekends, some boarders return to their parents and some stay in the boarding house. For those staying, there's always an activity to get involved in, be it a trip to the beach, a pottery or cookery class, horseriding, a West End show in London or a visit to the local shopping centre for some retail therapy.

There are many reasons why families choose boarding and for those that choose King's, the family-focused boarding community we have here ensures that everybody settles in quickly, makes friends and has fun. We find the hardest part of boarding is often saying goodbye to friends and teachers after what many pupils call 'the most unforgettable experience of their lives'.

Boarding life teaches pupils the importance of good routines and positive habits. More and more Sixth Form parents and pupils are using boarding as a prelude to university life.

For more information about King's School Rochester, see page 230

Choosing a senior school for your child

Ipswich School staff offer their advice and some questions to consider when choosing a senior school for your child

What facilities should be top of the list at senior school level?

Nicholas Weaver, Headmaster at Ipswich School, advises parents not to be overly swayed by facilities.

The simple answer here is that this is less important than the people. We are blessed with some outstanding facilities - for example a state of the art music school, excellent science labs and some of the best sports facilities in the region, if not the country. But without the quality and care of the teachers who use those facilities, children will not flourish. So, yes, you do want to see a school which is investing in all areas, maintaining an up to date environment and moving with the times, but make sure that you focus on the staff who inhabit that environment, as we do at Ipswich School.

What questions should parents be asking about the pastoral care/ wellbeing offerings?

Audrey Cura, Senior Deputy Head Pastoral says that there are three questions that matter here:

1. Who looks after my child on a daily basis, getting to know them and us as parents? At Ipswich School a child will have a tutor, a Head of Year and a Head of Section so there is always someone to turn to.

2. What support systems are in place pastorally and academically for when things might get a bit off track for my child? As well as the tutors and Heads of Year and Section we have another layer of support which includes our School Nurse, Chaplain and Deputy Head.

3. And finally how does the school work with families to ensure good communication? A good school should have teachers that are approachable and both parents and children should know exactly who to turn to with any concerns.

What sort of things should you be looking for in the curriculum of a senior school?

Tom Allen, Deputy Head Academic is clear that knowledge still plays an important role: how else are students able to know which questions to ask, or where to look for information?

It is important that students gain a solid and broad foundation in STEM, Languages, Humanity and Arts subjects to give them the flexibility to meet the requirements of future employment.

It's useful to understand if the school prioritises choice or setting? You can't have both in the timetable. We prioritise student choice, although, as a selective school we know that all of our students will be able to do well. Scale can also help: larger schools offer a broader range of subjects (we offer 27 A Level options) and employ specialist subject teachers throughout the school - beware small Sixth Forms!

Just as important, does the school's approach to the curriculum encourage students to develop self-awareness, to enhance their digital literacy and to collaborate effectively with others? These are questions worth asking. Our regular Learning Scores reward these attributes and encourage pupils to take academic risks and to draw connections across disciplines.

How much weight should you give to the co-curricular offerings?

Tracy Boyle, Director of Co-Curriculum is convinced that a full and varied co-curricular offer brings long term benefits - and enhances academic performance.

A weekly comprehensive and varied co-curricular provision is hugely important. Whether they are on the sports field, on stage or in the concert hall, pupils learn to take risks in a supportive environment, how to recover from setbacks, how to collaborate in a team-setting and how to become effective leaders.

Do you need to consider your child's personality when it comes to the type of school/ size of the cohort?

Anna Caston, Head of Year 7-8 at Ipswich School says larger schools offer more opportunity but small tutor groups help a child to settle.

Whatever the personality of your child, super outgoing or quiet and shy, the best for all children is for them to be part of a safe, small group where they feel secure. But don't assume this means they should be in a smaller school. Larger schools mean that there will be lots of different personality types within the year group and that makes it easier for children to find those that they connect with. What's important is to understand how schools manage the cohort so that children feel secure. At Ipswich School, in Years 7-8, we have tutor groups of about 20 children, in which they remain for the first two years, with the same tutor and Head of Year. I always say not to worry about coming from a small primary school into a year group that is sometimes bigger than their whole school because they only need to concentrate on those 20 in their form to begin with. The form groups become really tight teams, helped by our Cardinal Cup competitions and a trip to Cumbria together at the start of Year 8.

However, if your child enjoys sport or music or drama, at any level, then having a larger cohort is vital. Being able to have fixtures with A, B, C and D teams playing means nearly everyone who wants to play will get a match. Watching a play with a cast of 100 is quite something and hearing a full orchestra made up of school children or a choir of 80 is spine tingling.

Whatever the personality of your child, they will need to feel safe but have the opportunity to meet a variety of people who they can make their friends for life.

For more information about Ipswich School, see page 78

Why GCSEs are no longer fit for purpose

Caroline Jordan, Headmistress at Headington School, questions whether we should be seeking an alternative

This summer, there were tears of happiness and some of disappointment as we welcomed back our GCSE cohort to collect their results. Good news and a sign of things going back to how they should be – except, I am beginning to wonder if this is one thing we should be relegating to the past.

GCSEs don't make sense. Why test children when they are still required to complete another two years of study? While your university or employer will likely want to see you've achieved a pass in Maths and English, very few are likely to pore over the results of your extra subjects and decide that this – rather than the extra-curricular activities another candidate brings to the table – is what differentiates you. With such a large portfolio of subjects, it's simply not possible to study them all in the necessary depth while also maintaining a healthy attitude towards your learning. At Headington we've already taken steps to reduce the number of subjects sat by our pupils, with the majority taking nine GCSEs and encouraged to take an additional one-year qualification (we offer the Higher Project Qualification, School Certificate in Philosophy and Award in Financial Education) as a tenth subject. However, I don't think this goes far enough.

Any parent of a 16 year old will tell you about the toll that our current system takes upon them. Learning new material must stop earlier to ensure an opportunity for mock examinations, to practise being tested and ascertain what is known. Holidays are dominated by revision. So much revision! Children with no natural aptitude or interest in a subject will find themselves hating it all the more for having to go over it again and again in the hope they can regurgitate that information on the exam day. While schools offer varying degrees of choice, most mandate that courses are chosen from a range of different blocks. The English Baccalaureate, a measure which state schools are assessed upon, means many will consider English, Maths, Science, a humanity and a language subject a must. Great for breadth, less good for the child for whom, for example, language learning takes twice as long and is half as successful. So much assessment leaves so little opportunity for creativity, for enrichment and for learning for learning's sake. Where is the time to go into greater depth – to unlock unexpected interests and light a spark of passion as you delve into new territory?

> So much assessment leaves so little opportunity for creativity, for enrichment and for learning for learning's sake.

It is of course possible for a school to help its pupils achieve good results without teaching to the test, drilling facts mercilessly and sucking all the joy out of a subject. But it's not easy when some of those more innovative and exciting approaches risk children not 'reaching their academic potential' based on a final exam. It's a risk many schools, judged on their results by families, the media and indeed the Department for Education, cannot afford to take under the current climate. It's a system which sets up a vast swathe for failure. If you have a bad day, if you are unwell, or have a crisis of confidence or suffer a family emergency, this could happen even to high achievers.

Exams are expensive too. There are entry costs for each subject, invigilators are required, then there's the marking and moderation and any remarks. The greatest expense, though, over and above financial concerns, is one of time. Think what more could be achieved if we considered how better we could use those hours to enrich and enhance learning!

There are certain skills and knowledge that all young people should strive to acquire and I would not argue that a degree of assessment is unnecessary but this kind of high stakes, summative assessment tells us little. How can a single, stark number improve someone's comprehension or shape their further study? If we are not able to use the information GCSEs give us then what value do they have?

We need to find a novel method of assessment which does not pose undue stress on these young people but instead helps them identify their strengths and weaknesses and supports them in finding what they want to pursue from a position of information and confidence. We can't just throw out GCSEs overnight, much as I might like to. We need to know sixth formers are suitably prepared and will cope with the academic workload of A Levels or their alternatives. It is also important that schools can be held to account so parents can make an informed decision on who they entrust their children's education to. What we need to do is open the conversation and have a real discussion about the purpose and future of GCSEs and find a better alternative that works for everyone.

For more information about Headington
School, see page 52

Taking charge of your learning – the path to independent learning

Mr Matthew Godfrey, Deputy Head of Downe House, on how to help inspire a more independent approach to learning

Independent learning is often seen as the holy grail of education. For a teacher, it is hugely rewarding when a pupil takes the initiative to read or research beyond the curriculum simply because they feel motivated to do so. But school life is busy, and pupils cannot always prioritise learning for learning's sake.

It is a common misconception that independent learning is simply working on your own without any supervision. It does not necessarily mean less teacher guidance and it certainly does not mean using technology without a clear sense of focus and direction; rather, it means receiving specific, smart guidance with independence as an end-goal.

So, what encourages independent learning? Downe House School's pupils and teachers provide an insightful, first-hand point of view on how to become an independent learner.

Two Sixth Formers – both called Louisa – felt that at GCSE, there is so much material to get through that there isn't the time or opportunity to look beyond the academic curriculum. Louisa A, who is going on to study English Literature, Biology and Chemistry at A Level and hopes to progress on to medical school, said: "GCSEs helped me with self-discipline and being able to prioritise. But those skills are pretty much taken for granted at A Level: now we can take charge of our own learning with the bonus that we have selected subjects we want to study."

Louisa B, who is taking A Levels in German, Spanish and English Literature, pointed out that the ability to critique yourself is a key part of being an independent learner. "I feel I am getting better at assessing my own progress. But this is, in part, a result of a genuine desire to learn more."

This desire is fuelled by focusing on subjects that are of genuine interest. A strong teacher-pupil relationship is also key. It was clear, too, how important other aspects of school life were to both pupils in their journeys towards independent learning.

"When I was younger, I identified role models in the years above me. I remember listening to the Global Ambassadors talking about current events during assemblies and thinking that I would like to do that one day," said Louisa B.

Louisa A added: "It helps younger girls to see behaviour modelled by the older pupils. There is a culture of academic aspiration in the school. There are many Sixth Form girls in leadership positions and running school societies, and I think that does inspire younger girls to aim high and get involved."

Sophia, a Lower Fifth (Year 10) pupil, talked about the academic mentoring scheme within the boarding houses at Downe House. "It's a good idea because you get to talk to older students and to see how you can develop as a student and a person. My mentor is in the Lower Sixth (Year 12) and she helps me by explaining things and sharing some of the notes she made when she was my age."

Sophia touched on how older pupils can help with another important element of independent learning – metacognition. "Talking to other pupils about how they learn best helps me to understand how my own mind works and how I can improve the way I learn."

Isadora, a Lower Fifth (Year 10) pupil and an academic scholar, said that she enjoyed taking part in extracurricular activities, such as the Downe House Elective Programme because it enabled her to explore areas outside the curriculum. "It was really interesting! I loved Mr Breeze's course on 'The Power of China'. I don't think it really counts as independent learning because I wasn't really directing the learning myself, but it broadened my knowledge and mind."

Dr Andy Atherton, English teacher and Director of Research and Academic Enrichment at Downe House, explained how the Elective Programme has helped to enhance the academic spirit of the school. "The Electives are an opportunity for our teachers to model their own academic interests and enthusiasms outside the conventional classroom. Our pupils get to witness how animated they are by their subjects - and this is infectious. Listening to Mrs Henson talking about how mathematics has helped us to navigate the globe, or to Dr Jones as he explains the chemistry behind everyday objects is eye-opening for the girls. It's very important for our pupils to see that learning isn't just for exams – it's an enjoyable, lifelong process that provides ongoing intellectual nourishment."

Ms Maria Reichardt, Head of Academic Scholars and a Teacher of French at Downe House, said that the school's super-curricular programme, which includes a wide range of teacher-led and pupil-led societies and activities, helps the girls to see how they can become better versions of themselves: "These opportunities help them to see intellectual endeavours in a similar light to physical ones: if you want to run a marathon, you don't do it straight away; rather, you work at it gradually and improve over time."

For more information about Downe House, see page 50

Music in independent schools – full of opportunities for all

How Durlston Court School embraces the power of music and the benefits it has for students and the wider community

With a purpose-built Music School and dedicated staff, musical opportunities at Durlston Court School offer all children from Pre-Prep through to Senior the chance to find a love of music and to share the joy.

The music department headed by Director of Music, Caroline Moss, is a welcoming hub of learning, laughter, and creativity. From the age of four, Reception children receive weekly class music lessons with specialist staff and Pre-Prep children have their own orchestra. Run by the Head of Strings alongside senior pupils, the younger children relish the opportunity to listen to and play alongside the older pupils.

With a team of ten peripatetic staff teaching a full range of individual lessons it is no wonder that most Durlston children play an instrument ranging from piano to cello, to drums and electric guitar. It is the mission, however, of the music department that music is for all, regardless of age or ability, working hard to make music accessible.

In the classroom projects are designed to ensure that everyone, regardless of ability, can access the benefits of music. Creating protest songs to highlight plastic pollution, composing music for short stories, writing music for a film trailer, and generating a podcast are just some of the projects. Class concerts run every term, and every child is involved in some way.

Getting the older students more involved in the running of the department is important. A pupil prefect team have taken an active role in decision making. One of their ideas was to create a 'Musical Mindfulness Room' where students can book the small room and listen to classical music in a calming environment. Addressing mental health is more crucial than ever in the current climate, and music is a powerful tool in meditation and calming the brain. The Music Committee is a group voted in by the peers from Year 3–8. They meet together and discuss how to keep the music department moving forward. They are also in control of the last ten minutes of some lessons, where they bring a project to the class and Mrs Moss joins in as a student rather than a teacher. One of these projects involved Mrs Moss learning how to play the cello in front of Year 3 and 4 so they could see that everybody can learn something new, regardless of age!

Addressing mental health is more crucial than ever in the current climate, and music is a powerful tool in meditation and calming the brain.

Children have regular opportunities to perform throughout the year from informal concerts including 'bands' that have been created by the children in their break and lunch times to the more formal opportunities. There is a myriad of choirs, an orchestra, samba band, jazz band, various ensembles, and a ukulele band which have completed a tour of the local area raising money for charity.

Concerts at Durlston offer talented musicians the chance to shine, as well as music scholarships offered alongside senior responsibilities. There is an excellent record in examination results too. It is, however, music for the whole community which brings the added joy. As musicians performed in the grounds of a local care home, one resident said: "I look out of my window every day and see beautiful flowers, today I look out and see beautiful faces making beautiful music." There wasn't a dry eye in the house!

A further demonstration of the power of music was during the school's 'Big Gig' – a concert to raise funds for Ukraine charities. The event saw pupils, staff, parents, family and neighbours gather with picnic blankets and camping chairs as they settled to watch a music concert. Children from Years 3 to 8 sang and played their instruments, the Durlston Jazz Band, Samba Band, and Orchestra took to the stage to perform tracks old and new. The Choir Engine, a community choir, led by Caroline, also joined the school to perform and support the event. Mrs Moss had further challenged the children to raise money in their year groups and the children made crafts to sell and games to play and circulated the field with their buckets on the night. Mrs Moss explained proudly: "Every child worked extremely hard to learn music for the evening and to contribute in their own way. They have done it all with enthusiasm and passion and I have been humbled by their commitment." In total £4048 was raised as part of this event, a long way from the initial £1000 target!

Whilst a music department might be found in one area of the grounds, the enthusiasm, positivity, and joy are certainly felt across the school and continues to extend to the local community – a true demonstration of the power of music.

For more information about Durlston Court School, see page 216

The vital role of technology in a holistic approach to wellbeing

Caldicott share how their recently developed 'Wellbeing Survey' helps to monitor the happiness of their students

In a fast-paced, evolving world where our children are facing challenges unique to their generation, does it not make sense that the ways in which we support them must also modernise?

Nothing will ever replace the effectiveness of a one-on-one chat between a student and a trusted mentor, but in many cases, by the time this chat comes around, the child has already spent some time struggling in silence. That's why at Caldicott, under the leadership of Sarah Bisschop, our Deputy Head (Pastoral), we are constantly looking for new ways to monitor our boys' wellbeing and happiness. The weekly 'Wellbeing Survey' is our bespoke system that analyses and tracks the mental wellbeing of each child and identifies individual trends as well as patterns across year groups (and the whole school). Critically, the Wellbeing Survey enables early intervention as and when it's needed, and can even lead to structural change, if we notice that a year group's happiness is dipping at certain times of the year, for instance. Being able to add quantitative data to a school's repertoire of pastoral tools, helps spot early warning signs and make decisions about whether a child might need a one-on-one chat, or some other kind of intervention.

A sceptic might (fairly) suggest that if children are made to do the survey every week, then nine times out of ten they're not engaging with it. We count on that, and the point is, the one time out of ten when they actually are feeling unhappy or need help, they can very easily reach out. Using the 'black box' or directly talking to a teacher about a problem, can seem like simple solutions, but if a child doesn't want to reach out in such a direct way, the survey allows them to still be heard.

Mr Legge, our Designated Deputy Safeguarding Lead runs the Wellbeing Survey, and agrees with the principles of Dr Roger Morgan, who originally completed the research that underpins our survey. Mr Legge thinks of it as an 'unhappiness survey'; rather than showing how happy the boys are, it highlights when they are unhappy. The questions are rotated to avoid overfamiliarity, and an algorithm has established a benchmark score to define 'happy' and 'unhappy'. In weeks where scores dip, tutors use their views as experts in pastoral care, and their unique relationship with their tutee to identify why the score has changed, and if necessary, they will escalate and intervene. There are also 'red flag' questions, which, if answered a certain way, alert the tutor that they need to investigate immediately.

Recently, a boarder was experiencing homesickness and as such his scores in the Wellbeing Survey were slightly lower than usual one week. The tutor spoke with him and found out the root of the problem was stress due to not having enough time to prepare for pre-tests and carry out his extra-curricular activities. The tutor sat him down and they created a plan for the week which broke up the spare time he had; it ultimately showed that he actually had more free time than he thought. Early intervention in low-level wellbeing issues such as this are vital for a boy's overall happiness, and in ensuring they don't develop into a bigger issue down the line.

Over the last couple of years, the Wellbeing Survey has taught us that relying solely on traditional methods when it comes to pastoral care is not enough – we must strive to uncover new approaches that give children easier ways to express themselves.

For more information about Caldicott, see page 48

Relying solely on traditional methods when it comes to pastoral care is not enough – we must strive to uncover new approaches that give children easier ways to express themselves.

Promoting a values-based education

Mr Mark Turnbull, Head of Kent College, Canterbury talks about the significance of values at the school

The speed of change

Some now refer to the lockdowns of covid as something of a 'great acceleration'. It certainly felt like it at the time. As with all rapid changes there are often consequences that emerge in quieter times. If such times as these present us all with uncertainties, then it is all the more important that schools understand and live in a values-based culture.

In March 2020, schools in the UK were forced to adapt in an instant to online learning. Many achieved this brilliantly, and thereby allowed parents far more insight into the learning of their children. Quite often this also revealed a newfound respect for the creativity of the teachers who delivered it. Such a shift in perception occurred alongside an awakening of our attitudes towards each other through Black Lives Matter and Everyone's Invited. And since the return to on-campus learning it has become even more apparent that all schools need to further address the crisis of teenage mental health. Facts also recognised by the government.

> We believe every child will thrive if they are able to develop confidence in their own identity and abilities from a foundation of fundamental values.

Preparing students for the future

The overall effect is that it is now so much clearer to many that the role that schools perform in preparing children for their adult lives stretches far wider than ensuring academic progress and achievement. One look at the job titles of senior leaders in more progressive schools will start to show any parent how the nature of education has changed significantly.

At Kent College we believe every child will thrive if they are able to develop confidence in their own identity and abilities from a foundation of fundamental values. Like many schools, KC has a religious foundation, and ours is in Methodism. John Wesley, the founding father of Methodism is often attributed with saying 'Do all the good you can, by all the means you can, in all the ways you can..' Powerful, and to some self-evident, words that provide a strong starting point. What we want to do at KC is to provide a translation of these words that shows students how they can not only live by our founding principles but how these also support their own wellbeing and personal fulfilment.

Our KC values

We began a process that consulted all our stakeholders, along with employers accessed through our parent body. From this we have distilled eight core values that are both true to our foundation and which are relevant to supporting access to the progressive curriculum we want to deliver.

RESPECT: Value oneself, others and the world around you.
OPENNESS: Embrace equality, diversity and inclusion.
ACT JUSTLY: Work for good through service to others.
KINDNESS: Be considerate and compassionate towards others.
AMBITION: Engage positively with all learning opportunities.
RESILIENCE: Build the courage to take risks and to forgive others.
HUMILITY: Walk humbly.
CURIOSITY: Inquire actively.

Going through such a process has been so important in ensuring that we engage our whole community. For when we are all committed to the same values, every person knows that they can stand on a foundation that is supported by everyone around them; and on such sure footing, confidence in who they are can grow and each member of the community has the opportunity to thrive.

If our children are going to be genuinely ambitious in their learning, and their wellbeing is going to be effectively supported, then every school has to start with how it lives out its values.

For more information about Kent College, see page 224

Embracing the great outdoors

Stroud School believes that outdoor learning has huge benefits for children

At Stroud School, King Edward VI Preparatory in Romsey, it has been a year like no other for outdoor provision – its children have been learning outside more than ever before!

In particular, the school was delighted to bring its summer residentials back into the school programme this year with school groups in Scotland, on the south coast, the wilds of Dartmoor and Ironbridge to name a few! This was not only the first residential trip for its younger children, but the first residential trip for many of the older children who have missed out on the last few years of shorter residentials, and acclimatising to time away from families.

Following this, Stroud embraced its second 'Intrepidus week': where the whole school enjoyed a week of adventures and bravery. Intrepidus Week included a bespoke timetable of events in each year group, designed to excite, challenge and broaden the children's experiences. These events were run alongside the school's normal English and Maths curriculums to ensure it continued its normal, rigorous learning alongside the extra adventures.

Stroud was also delighted to welcome 'Campfire Wild Adventures' back, allowing all children to enjoy a bushcraft session during the week. Children also undertook a range of activities including orienteering, dancing, art, swimming and a nature walk. This all being a part of its drive to embed and further develop outdoor learning. Following the National Lockdowns, last September 2021 also saw the introduction of Mr Caie as Outdoor Education Leader and Wildlife Ranger, a new role for the school. Mr Caie has spent the last year focussing on unlocking the potential of the school's extensive outdoor areas, whilst developing the curriculum of outdoor learning across all year groups.

This new momentum has been clear from the start, with the school's introduction of new Outdoor Learning sessions built into each half term for Years 3-8. Some highlights of these new sessions included: a rewilding study with Year 3, forest bathing with Year 4, Year 5 undertaking the RFS Junior Forester Award, orienteering challenges with Year 6, and ropework and weather systems with Years 7 and 8. The school's new outdoor provision also supported its STEAM week and World Book Day; there were space themed challenges to build students' teamwork and problem-solving abilities as part of our World Book Day, and sessions

> The true potential of the school's surroundings is being unleashed for the benefit of its children, community and natural environment!

looking at planetary rovers and lunar craters in STEAM week.

Stroud has also begun the re-development of its outdoor spaces, with several areas of woodland getting a new lease of life with pathway restoration, seating areas and hedgerows. Other areas are being left to recover organically as part of a wider rewilding effort. Mr Caie has also constructed a wildlife hide nestled into a forgotten corner of the grounds, in which children have been able to get closer to wildlife and also have an outdoor hub to use in wetter weather. Many other exciting projects are on the horizon!

Alongside offering new opportunities to its children, Stroud School has begun developing ways in which its facilities and staff can support the local community. To kick this off, 2022 has seen Stroud working with the brilliant team at Romsey Young Carers to offer outdoor experiences and events, including Easter egg hunts, as part of the charity's support for young carers and their families. With success and enjoyment already felt by all involved, we are looking forward to developing and expanding this outreach next year.

As a whole, this year has seen our outdoor spaces come alive with activity. The true potential of the school's surroundings is being unleashed for the benefit of its children, community and natural environment!

It is this, along with a combination of passion for being with friends, having new adventures and learning within a different context, combined with determination to live the school's motto of being forever undaunted – In Aeternum Intrepidus – that Stroud sees its children push themselves out of their comfort zones and embark on activities and endeavours that sometimes feel quite challenging.

Stepping out of our comfort zone, as we all know, is the way in which we learn. We are all here for that single purpose of flourishing and growing together, and with grit and determination Stroud School believes its children have shown that we can all do hard things and have a fabulous time, pushing our limits and enjoying that little bit of independence from the security of our known environment. Stroud is very excited to see what the future holds…

For more information about Stroud School, King Edward VI preparatory, please visit the school website https://stroud.kes.school or call on 01794 513231.

For more information about Stroud School, see page 258

Going from strength to strength

Maltman's Green School is delighted to achieve 'Excellent' in all areas in its latest ISI Inspection

Maltman's Green girls' school delivers an outstanding academic and extra-curricular programme from our 400-year-old malting house in the heart of the home counties green-belt. On a beautiful 12-acre site in leafy Gerrards Cross, Maltman's girls can enjoy some of the best facilities around, from flood lit sports courts and playing fields to a heated six lane 25m swimming pool. We provide a nurturing environment from age 2 through to 11 when our happy and confident girls progress to senior school. Throughout their time at Maltman's, each girl is treated as an individual and given the opportunity to find her passions and unlock her talents.

Maltman's Green may be non-selective but our outcomes and pupil achievements mirror those of highly selective schools – as proven by our recent 81% Secondary Transfer Test (11+) qualification rate and twenty scholarships awarded to independent senior schools. Maltman's girls progress to some of the best senior schools in the country – both grammar and independent – including Wycombe Abbey, Cheltenham Ladies College, Downe House and Dr Challoner's High School. How do we achieve this? Through an ambitious and dynamic curriculum, a nurturing environment and dedicated staff, meaning that our pupils are supported, inspired and encouraged to achieve their very best.

This rigorous approach and excellent teaching were highlighted by the Independent Schools Inspectorate (ISI) at their most recent inspection in February 2022, when Maltman's Green was awarded 'excellent' in all areas – an outstanding achievement. Some of the comments made by the inspectors highlight both the quality of education we provide and the personal development we promote in our pupils:

"The quality of the pupils' academic and other achievements is excellent. Pupils of all ages and abilities make excellent progress over time because of the systematic use of the assessment framework in planning for individual needs. Pupils' linguistic and other mathematical skills are outstanding, and pupils apply these with great confidence to other areas of learning. Pupils demonstrate excellent attitudes to learning when the curriculum creates opportunities for them to develop independence in their learning. Pupils readily think for themselves and acquire higher-order thinking skills which they instinctively apply to all areas of learning.

"The quality of the pupils' personal development is excellent. Pupils' self confidence and self-esteem are outstanding. Pupils' social development and collaboration are extremely strong; they undertake positions of responsibility with great pleasure and success. Pupils make an excellent contribution to the school and the wider community. Pupils show great respect, and interest, in each other's cultural beliefs and values.

"Pupils of all ages make excellent progress over time, as a result of the many opportunities provided for them to succeed.

"Pupils' social development and collaboration are extremely strong; they undertake positions of responsibility with great pleasure and success. Pupils make an excellent contribution to the school and the wider community. Pupils show great respect, and interest, in each other's cultural beliefs and values."

The Maltman's girls continue to impress beyond the school gates. Girls compete in a host of national sporting competitions, most recently being crowned U11 National Champions at the Independent Schools Gymnastics Association (ISGA) Championship and the British Schools Gymnastics Association (BSGA) Milano Team National Finals. The girls also scooped U10 team Silver and U9 team Bronze at the ISGA championships as well as a number of individual medals, including National Champion Gold at the BSGA Championships. There were also huge successes at the Independent Association of Prep Schools (IAPS) National Gymnastics Championship in November 2021. This academic year alone, girls have had sport masterclasses from former England international netball star, Tracey Neville, and the inspiring footballer, Charlie Fogarty. They compete in national swimming galas, netball tournaments and cricket and tennis festivals.

In 2022, 123 girls from Years 1-6 took part in LAMDA Acting exams, and there is opportunity for girls to learn instruments including the saxophone and harp, and take part in language lessons, such as Spanish, French, German and Mandarin. Ballet has also been provided at Maltman's Green for over 25 years and has a 100% pass rate in ballet exams. The Royal Academy of Dancing syllabus is taught from Pre-Primary upwards.

In their final year at Maltman's Green, the Year 6 girls enjoy a full programme of enriching experiences to give them a final year of fun memories with their peers and to teach valuable life skills that will set them in good stead as they move onto their senior schools.

With no signs of slowing down, Maltman's Green really is going from strength to strength, and with no barriers to success for these fortunate girls, the future certainly is bright.

Find out more at www.maltmansgreen.com.

For more information about Maltman's Green School, see page 232

'We must not stop moving forward'

Headmaster Mr Daniel Berry explains what makes Kirkham Grammar School so unique

Located in Lancashire in the heart of the North-West, Kirkham Grammar School continues to remain an extremely popular choice for large numbers of families. We are within easy access of Manchester, the Lake District and the seaside resorts of the Fylde coast.

The longer you spend at Kirkham Grammar School, the more you begin to understand what clearly makes it such a unique school. We are about so much more and continue to thrive in a challenging market. The life of a school is a busy one. As Headmaster of Kirkham Grammar School, this experience continues to be filled with wonderful opportunities. So, when choosing a school for a child, it is so important to understand what makes it so unique and ultimately a perfect environment for your child to excel in.

We are convinced that in an environment that currently has a high reputation, we must not stop moving forward. When one stands still, one is in effect, going backwards. KGS is a remarkable school within the North-West educational landscape. In nurturing well-qualified, compassionate, self-assured members of the community, our vision sets out the opportunity to look forward and plan without losing sight of what has come before. Every child comes through the school only once and deserves the best.

> The family ethos of the school is fundamental and is a key factor in driving our future plans for growth and expansion.

Our seven-year vision for the school will see improved and additional teaching, boarding and pastoral facilities. This will be known as 'Project 480' and coincides with the foundation date of the school in 1549. The school has a particular niche within the marketplace and we are extremely proud of our global reputation for sport, alongside a strong measure of normality and humility. The expectation for any potential family joining KGS is to join us as early as possible due to increased demands for places. The journey begins from 3 – 18 years. Therefore, all the facilities we provide and develop are of equal importance. The family ethos of the school is fundamental and is a key factor in driving our future plans for growth and expansion.

So what is it that makes such a school so special and unique? The range of opportunities given to our pupils is the main reason for such an envious reputation. The school has three values which uphold all we strive to achieve. These are a strong family ethos, inspirational teaching and for each child to fulfil their potential. Our aim is just as simple: to provide an excellent education that continues to develop the whole child.

As I have firmly believed in my years as a Headmaster, it is the breadth and balance of the provision that helps pupils become the best they can possibly be. That must incorporate both the aspiration to succeed to the very highest levels, but also an opportunity to find an activity within the school which gives all pupils the chance to shine. I have been overwhelmed at how much co-curricular provision goes on in the school; the diversity and range of clubs or societies that take place weekly is outstanding and a true testament to our staff and pupils.

The virtue of a school does not depend entirely on its classrooms; the equipment in its laboratories; the number of its pupils; nor even the success of its exam results. There is an unseen influence that is exerted by buildings and surroundings that are beautiful and dignified, and in keeping with fine honourable traditions and high ideals embedded at Kirkham Grammar School. We are proud of our school. There is something at Kirkham Grammar that is intangible but very real; the atmosphere in which we dwell, that pervasive spirit which surrounds us and influences all of which we strive to achieve. It is a great heritage at Kirkham Grammar and one which will stay with you for life.

The recent inspection has confirmed what we all knew about Kirkham Grammar School: it is the best kept educational secret in Lancashire. However, it is extremely pleasing that it has been officially acknowledged against national criteria that we are working hard to ensure our pupils get the finest education. The inspection found that the quality of the pupils' academic and other achievements is excellent and the quality of the pupils' personal development is excellent. Pupils reflect the strong family ethos of the school and demonstrate excellent collaboration in and out of lessons. Pupils develop excellent levels of confidence at all ages, supported by the strong personal, social, health and educational (PSHE) and enrichment programmes. Pupils show a clear respect for different faiths and diversity, demonstrating excellent levels of empathy and tolerance towards others. Pupils make informed choices, empowered and supported by their teachers.

As the school motto clearly states, 'Ingredere Ut Proficias'.

For more information about Kirkham Grammar School, see page 194

Help in funding the fees

Chris Procter, Managing Director of SFIA Wealth Management, outlines a planned approach to funding your child's school fees

Despite the challenges of the Covid-19 pandemic and, more recently, the conflict between Russia and Ukraine the independent education sector remains resilient, according to the latest Independent Schools Council (ISC) survey, conducted in January 2022. The number of pupils in ISC schools stood at 544,316, a new record high.

Average school fee increases were 3% between the 2020/21 and 2021/22 school years, the second lowest annual rise ever recorded in the ISC Census. The average day school fees were £5,218 which is an increase of 3.1%. The average boarding school fees were £12,344 per term, an increase of 2.9%.

Fees charged by schools vary by region – for example, the average day school fees per term ranged from £4,500 in the North West to £6,250 in London.

Over £1.2bn of fee assistance was provided in the 2021/22 school year, of which £960m came from schools themselves. Over a third of pupils in ISC schools received at least one type of fee support.

£480m of means-tested fee assistance was provided, an increase of £25m on the previous year. The average means-tested bursary stood at over £10,840. Nearly half of all pupils on means-tested bursaries had more than half of their fees remitted.

The overall cost of school fees (including university fees) might seem daunting: the cost of educating one child privately could well be very similar to that of buying a house but, as with house buying, the school fees commitment for the majority of parents can be made possible by spreading it over a long period rather than funding it all from current resources.

It is vital that parents do their financial homework, plan ahead and start to save early. Grandparents who have access to capital could help out; by contributing to school fees they could also help to reduce any potential future inheritance tax liability.

Parents would be well-advised to consult a specialist financial adviser as early as possible, since a long-term plan for the payment of fees – possibly university as well – can prove very advantageous from a financial point of view and offer greater peace of mind. Funding fees is neither science, nor magic, nor is there any panacea. It is quite simply a question of planning and using whatever resources are available, such as income, capital, or tax planning opportunities.

The fundamental point to recognise is that you, your circumstances and your wishes or ambitions, for your children, or grandchildren are unique. They might well appear similar to those of other people but they will still be uniquely different. There will be no single solution to your problem. In fact, after a review of all your circumstances, there might not be a problem at all.

So, what are the reasons for seeking advice about education expenses?

- To reduce the overall cost
- To get some tax benefit
- To reduce your cash outflow
- To invest capital to ensure that future fees are paid
- To set aside money now for future fees
- To provide protection for school fees
- Or just to make sure that, as well as educating your children, you can still have a life

Any, some, or all of the above – or others not listed – could be on your agenda, the important thing is to develop a strategy.

At this stage, it really does not help to get hung up on which financial 'product' is the most suitable. The composition of a school fees plan will differ for each family depending on a number of factors. That is why there is no one school fees plan on offer.

The simplest strategy but in most cases, the most expensive option, is to write out a cheque for the whole bill when it arrives and post it back to the school. Like most simple plans, that can work well, if you have the money. Even if you do have the money, is that really the best way of doing things? Do you know that to fund £1,000 of school fees as a higher rate taxpayer paying 40% income tax, you currently need to earn £1,667, this rises to £1,818 if you are an additional rate taxpayer where the rate is 45%.

How then do you start to develop your strategy? As with most things in life, if you can define your objective, then you will know what you are aiming at. Your objective in this case will be to determine how much money is needed and when.

You need to draw up a school fees schedule or what others may term a cash flow forecast. So, you need to identify:

- How many children?
- Which schools and therefore what are the fees? (or you could use an average school fee)
- When are they due?
- Any special educational needs?
- Inflation estimate?
- Include university costs?

With this basic information, the school fees schedule/cash flow forecast can be prepared and you will have defined what it is you are trying to achieve.

Remember though, that senior school fees are typically more than prep school fees – this needs to be factored in. Also, be aware that the cost of university is not restricted to the fees alone; there are a lot of maintenance and other costs involved: accommodation, books, food, to name a few. Don't forget to build in inflation, I refer you back to the data at the beginning of this article.

You now have one element of the equation, the relatively simple element. The other side is the resources you have available to achieve the objective. This also needs to be identified, but this is a much more difficult exercise. The reason that it is more difficult, of course, is that school fees are not the only drain on your resources. You probably have a mortgage, you want to have holidays, you need to buy food and clothes, you may be concerned that you should be funding a pension.

This is a key area of expertise, since your financial commitments are unique. A specialist in the area of school fees planning can help identify these commitments, to record them and help you to distribute your resources according to your priorities.

The options open to you as parents depend completely upon your adviser's knowledge of these complex personal financial issues. (Did I forget to mention your tax position, capital gains tax allowance, other tax allowances, including those of your children and a lower or zero rate tax paying spouse or partner? These could well be used to your advantage.)

A typical school fees plan can incorporate many elements to fund short, medium and long-term fees. Each plan is designed according to individual circumstances and usually there is a special emphasis on what parents are looking to achieve, for example, to maximise overall savings and to minimise the outflow of cash.

Additionally, it is possible to protect the payment of the fees in the event of unforeseen circumstances that could lead to a significant or total loss of earnings.

Short-term fees

Short-term fees are typically the termly amounts needed within five years: these are usually funded from such things as guaranteed investments, liquid capital, loan plans (if no savings are available) or maturing insurance policies, investments etc. Alternatively, they can be funded from disposable income.

Medium-term fees

Once the short-term plan expires, the medium-term funding is invoked to fund the education costs for a further five to ten years. Monthly amounts can be invested in a low-risk, regular premium investment ranging from a building society account to a friendly society savings plan to equity ISAs. It is important to understand the pattern of the future fees and to be aware of the timing of withdrawals.

Long-term fees

Longer term funding can incorporate a higher element of risk (as long as this is acceptable to the investor), which will offer higher potential returns. Investing in UK and overseas equities could be considered. Solutions may be the same as those for medium-term fees, but will have the flexibility to utilise investments that may have an increased 'equity based' content.

Finally, it is important to remember that most investments, or financial products either mature with a single payment or provide for regular withdrawals; rarely do they provide timed termly payments.

Additionally, the overall risk profile of the portfolio should lean towards the side of caution (for obvious reasons).

There are any number of advisers in the country, but few who specialise in the area of planning to meet school and university fees. SFIA is the largest organisation specialising in school fees planning in the UK.

This article has been contributed by SFIA and edited by Chris Procter, Managing Director.

Chris can be contacted at:
SFIA, 27 Moorbridge Road,
Maidenhead,
Berkshire, SL6 8LT
Tel: 01628 566777
Email: enquiries@sfia.co.uk
Web: www.sfia.co.uk

33

The Independent Schools Council

The Independent Schools Council (ISC) works with its members to promote and preserve the quality, diversity and excellence of UK independent education both at home and abroad

What is the ISC?

The ISC brings together seven associations of independent schools, their heads, bursars and governors. Through our member associations we represent approximately 1,400 independent schools in the UK and overseas, which educate more than half a million children.

The ISC's work is carried out by a small team of dedicated professionals in central London. We are assisted by contributions from expert advisory groups in specialist areas. Our priorities are set by the board of directors led by our chairman, Barnaby Lenon.

ISC schools

Schools in membership of the ISC's constituent associations offer a high quality, rounded education. Whilst our schools are very academically successful, their strength also lies in the extra-curricular activities offered, helping to nurture pupils' soft skills. There are independent schools to suit every need, whether you want a day or boarding school, single-sex or co-education, a large or a small school, or schools offering specialisms, such as in the arts.

Our schools are very diverse: some are selective and highly academic, while others have very strong drama or music departments full of creative opportunities. For children with special needs there are many outstanding independent schools that offer some of the best provision in the country.

Many schools have high levels of achievement in sport, offering a wide range of facilities and excellent coaches. Independent schools excel at traditional sports like football and rugby, but also offer more unusual sports like rowing and fencing.

There is also a wealth of co-curricular opportunities available. Whether your child is into debating, sailing, or the Model United Nations, most schools offer numerous clubs and activities.

Academic results

Typically, the ISC publishes a sector-wide analysis of Year 11 and Year 13 exam results for independent schools every August. However, due to the ongoing impact of the pandemic on grading, the ISC did not conduct an external analysis of member schools' results in 2022. There was no sector-wide ISC publication of results in 2020 or 2021 because exams were temporarily replaced by different assessment processes created in response to the crisis.

Looking back to 2019, 45.7% of Year 13 exam entries at independent schools were graded A*/A, compared to the national average of 25.5%. That year 95.6% of Year 11 exams at independent schools were graded C/4 or higher, compared to the national average of 67.3%.

Fee assistance

Schools take affordability very seriously and are acutely aware of the sacrifices families make when choosing an independent education. Schools work hard to remain competitive whilst facing pressures on salaries, pensions and maintenance and utility costs. They are strongly committed to widening access and many schools have extended their bursary provision – this year, the amount of means-tested fee assistance has risen to a total of £480m. Over 180,000 pupils currently benefit from reduced fees, representing over a third of pupils at our schools.

School partnerships

Independent and state schools have been engaged in partnership activity for many years, with the majority of ISC schools currently involved in important cross-sector initiatives. These collaborations involve the sharing of expertise, best practice and facilities, and unlock exciting new opportunities for all involved. To learn more about these valuable partnerships, visit the Schools Together website: https://www.schoolstogether.org/

ISC Associations

There are seven member associations of the ISC, each with a distinctive ethos in their respective entrance criteria and quality assurance:

Girls' Schools Association (GSA)
Headmasters' and Headmistresses' Conference (HMC)
Independent Association of Prep Schools (IAPS)
Independent Schools Association (ISA)
The Society of Heads
Association of Governing Bodies of Independent Schools (AGBIS) – www.agbis.org
Independent Schools' Bursars Association (ISBA) – www.isba.org.uk

Further organisations who are affiliated to the ISC: Boarding Schools Association (BSA), Council of British International Schools (COBIS), Scottish Council of Independent Schools (SCIS) and Welsh Independent Schools Council (WISC).

The Independent Schools Council can be contacted at:
First Floor,
27 Queen Anne's Gate,
London,
SW1H 9BU
Telephone: 020 7766 7070
Website: www.isc.co.uk

 independent schools council

Choosing a school initially

Educational institutions often belong to organisations that guarantee their standards. Here we give a brief alphabetical guide to what the initials mean

BSA

The Boarding Schools' Association

Since its foundation in 1965-6, the Boarding Schools' Association (BSA) has promoted boarding education and the development of quality boarding through high standards of pastoral care and boarding accommodation. So parents and prospective pupils choosing a boarding school can be assured that more than 600 member schools in nearly 40 countries worldwide are committed to providing the best possible boarding environment for their pupils.

A UK boarding school can only be a full member of the BSA if it is also a member of one of the Independent Schools Council (ISC) constituent associations, or in membership of the BSA State Boarding Forum (SBF). These two bodies require member schools to be regularly inspected by the Independent Schools' Inspectorate (ISI) or Ofsted. Other boarding schools who are not members of these organisations can apply to be affiliate members. Similar arrangements are in place for overseas members. Boarding inspection of ISC-accredited independent schools has been conducted by ISI since September 2012. Ofsted retains responsibility for the inspection of boarding in state schools and non-association independent schools.

Boarding inspections must be conducted every three years. Boarding in England is judged against the National Minimum Standards for Boarding Schools which have been newly updated for September 2022.

Relationship with government

BSA is in regular communication with the Department for Education (DfE) on all boarding matters in England and also with devolved governments for other parts of the UK. The Children Act (1989) and the Care Standards Act (2001) require boarding schools in England to conform to national legislation. The promotion of this legislation and the training required to carry it out are matters on which the DfE and BSA work together. BSA worked especially closely with the DfE and other government departments during the coronavirus pandemic, supporting the safety and continuity of education for its member schools' pupils and staff.

Boarding training

BSA delivers the world's largest professional development programme for boarding staff. It offers:

- Two-year courses for graduate and non-graduate boarding staff – these involve eight study days and two assignments, each about 4,000 words long. This is the flagship training opportunity for staff seriously interested in boarding excellence

- A Diploma course for senior experienced boarding staff, involving three study days and two assignments spread between March and October

- A broad range of day seminars and webinars on topics of particular interest to boarding/pastoral staff – e.g. Essentials of Boarding, Leading a Boarding Team,

- Meeting the Needs of Overseas Boarders

- Specialists one or two-day conferences for Boarding Staff, Heads, Health & Wellbeing staff**, Marketing and Admissions staff* and State Boarding Schools staff and Safeguarding Leads**

- Basic training online, for those very new to boarding.

*With SACPA (Safeguarding and Child Protection Association), part of the BSA Group
**With HIEDA (Heath in Education Association) part of the BSA Group
**With BAISIS (British Association of Independent Schools with International Students), part of the BSA Group

In 2022, BSA Group also launched a new association, The Institute of Boarding (TIOB), which aims to be the world's first professional association for boarding school staff.

State Boarding Forum (SBF)

BSA issues information regards its state boarding school members and BSA should be contacted for details of these schools. In these schools, parents pay for boarding but not for education, so fees are substantially lower than in an independent boarding school.

Chief Executive: Robin Fletcher
Deputy Chief Executive and Chief Operating Officer: Aileen Kane

Boarding Schools' Association
Unit 11/12
Manor Farm
Cliddesden
Basingstoke
Hants
RG25 2JB
Tel: 020 7798 1580
Email: bsa@boarding.org.uk
Website: www.boarding.org.uk

GSA

The Girls' Schools Association, to which Heads of independent girls' schools belong

The Girls' Schools Association helps girls and their teachers to flourish. It represents the Heads of a diverse range of independent UK girls' schools (day & boarding), among which are some of the top-performing schools in the country.

The GSA encourages high standards of education and promotes the benefits of being taught in a largely girls-only environment. GSA schools are internationally respected and have a global reputation for excellence. Their innovative practice and academic rigour attract pupils from around the world. Students at GSA schools enjoy abundant extra- and co-curricular opportunities. Academically, they thrive in the humanities and do disproportionately well in 'difficult' modern languages and STEM (science, technology, engineering, maths) subjects. A high percentage – 93% – progress to higher education.

GSA schools share experience, specialisms, opportunities and facilities with state sector schools in a wide range of partnerships. Many also provide means-tested bursaries for families of limited financial means.

The GSA is also committed to research projects which unite both state and independent girls' schools.

Twenty first century girls' schools come in many different shapes and sizes. Some cater for 100% girls, others provide a predominantly girls-only environment with boys in the nursery and/or sixth form. Some follow a diamond model, with equal numbers of boys but separate classrooms between the ages of 11 to 16. Educational provision across the Association offers a choice of day, boarding, weekly, and flexi-boarding education. Schools range in type from large urban schools of 1000 pupils to small rural schools of around 200. Many schools have junior and pre-prep departments, and can offer a complete education from age 3/4 to 18. Some also have religious affiliations. Heads of schools in the Girls' Day School Trust (GDST) are members of the GSA.

The Association aims to inform and influence national and international educational debate and is a powerful and well-respected voice within the educational establishment, advising and lobbying educational policy makers on core education issues as well as those relating to girls' schools and the education of girls. The Association has strong links with the Department for Education, OFQUAL, Awarding Bodies and Higher Education institutions.

The GSA also provides its members and their staff with professional development courses, conferences, advice and opportunities to debate and share best practice, ensuring that they have every opportunity to remain fully up-to-date with all aspects of their profession.

As the GSA is one of the constituent bodies that make up the Independent Schools' Council (ISC), its schools are required to undergo a regular cycle of inspections to ensure that these rigorous standards are being maintained. Most GSA schools also belong to the Association of Governing Bodies of Independent Schools, and Heads must be in membership of the Association of School and College Leaders (ASCL) or the National Association of Headteachers (NAHT). Early Career Teachers take part in the Induction Programme overseen by ISTIP.

The Association's secretariat is based in Leicester.

Suite 105, 108 New Walk, Leicester LE1 7EA
Tel: 0116 254 1619
Email: office@gsa.uk.com
Website: www.gsa.uk.com
Twitter: @GSAUK

President 2022/3: Heather Hanbury, LEH
President 2023/4: Marina Gardiner Legge, Oxford High School for Girls
Chief Executive: Donna Stevens

HMC

The Headmasters' and Headmistresses' Conference, to which the Heads of leading independent schools belong

Founded in 1869 the HMC exists to enable members to discuss matters of common interest and to influence important developments in education. It looks after the professional interests of members, central to which is their wish to provide the best possible educational opportunities for their pupils.

The Heads of some 296 leading independent schools are members of The Headmasters' and Headmistresses' Conference, whose membership now includes Heads of boys', girls' and coeducational schools. International membership includes the Heads of around 56 schools throughout the world.

The great variety of these schools is one of the strengths of HMC but all must exhibit high quality in the education provided. While day schools are the largest group, about a quarter of HMC schools consist mainly of boarders and others have a smaller boarding element including weekly and flexible boarders.

All schools are noted for their academic excellence and achieve good results, including those with pupils from a broad ability band. Members believe that good education consists of more than academic results and schools provide pupils with a wide range of educational co-curricular activities and with strong pastoral support.

Only those schools that meet with the rigorous membership criteria are admitted and this helps ensure that HMC is synonymous with high quality in education. There is a set of membership requirements and a Code of Practice to which members must subscribe. Those who want the intimate atmosphere of a small school will find some with around 350 pupils. Others who want a wide range of facilities and specialisations will find these offered in large day or boarding schools. Many have over 1000 pupils. 32 schools are for boys only, others are coeducational throughout or only in the sixth form. The first girls-only schools joined HMC in 2006. There are now 39 girls-only schools.

Within HMC there are schools with continuous histories as long as any in the world and many others trace their origins to Tudor times, but HMC continues to admit to membership recently-founded schools that have achieved great success. The facilities in all HMC schools will be good but some have magnificent buildings and grounds that are the result of the generosity of benefactors over many years. Some have attractive rural settings, others are sited in the centres of cities.

Pupils come from all sorts of backgrounds. Bursaries and scholarships provided by the schools give about a third of the 240,000 pupils in HMC schools help with their fees. These average about £35,000 per annum for boarding schools and £15,000 for day schools. About 190,000 are day pupils and 45,000 boarders.

Entry into some schools is highly selective but others are well-suited to a wide ability range. Senior boarding schools usually admit pupils after the Common Entrance examination taken when they are 13.

Most day schools select their pupils by 11+ examination. Many HMC schools have junior schools, some with nursery and pre-prep departments. The growing number of boarders from overseas is evidence of the high reputation of the schools worldwide.

The independent sector has always been fortunate in attracting very good teachers. Higher salary scales, excellent conditions of employment, exciting educational opportunities and good pupil/teacher ratios bring rewards commensurate with the demanding expectations. Schools expect teachers to have a good education culminating in a good honours degree and a professional qualification, though some do not insist on the latter especially if relevant experience is offered. Willingness to participate in the whole life of the school is essential.

Parents expect the school to provide not only good teaching that helps their children achieve the best possible examination results, but also the dedicated pastoral care and valuable educational experiences outside the classroom in music, drama, games, outdoor pursuits and community service. Over 89% of pupils go on to higher education, many of them winning places on the most highly-subscribed university courses.

All members attend the Annual Conference, usually held in a large conference centre in September/October. There are ten divisions covering England, Wales, Scotland and Ireland where members meet once a term on a regional basis, and a distinctive international division.

The chair and committee, with the advice of the general secretary and membership secretary, make decisions on matters referred by membership-led sub-committees, steering groups and working parties. Close links are maintained with other professional associations in membership of the Independent Schools Council and with the Association of School and College Leaders.

Membership Secretary: Dr Simon Hyde
Tel: 01858 469059

12 The Point
Rockingham Road
Market Harborough
Leicestershire LE16 7QU
Email: office@hmc.org.uk
Website: www.hmc.org.uk

Leading Independent Schools

IAPS

The Independent Association of Prep Schools (IAPS) is a membership association representing leading headteachers and their prep schools in the UK and overseas

With around 660 members, IAPS schools represent a multi-billion pound enterprise, educating more than 170,000 children and employing more than 15,000 staff. As the voice of independent prep school education, IAPS actively defends and promotes the interests of its members.

IAPS schools must reach a very high standard to be eligible for membership, with strict criteria on teaching a broad curriculum, maintain excellent standards of pastoral care and keeping staff members' professional development training up-to-date. The head must be suitably qualified and schools must be accredited through a satisfactory inspection. IAPS offers its members and their staff a comprehensive and up-to-date programme of professional development courses to ensure that these high professional standards are maintained.

Member schools offer an all-round, values-led broad education which produces confident, adaptable, motivated children with a passion for learning. The targets of the National Curriculum are regarded as a basic foundation which is greatly extended by the wider programmes of study offered. Specialist teaching begins at an early age and pupils are offered a range of cultural and sporting opportunities.

IAPS organises a successful sports programme where member schools compete against each other in a variety of sports. In 2019-20, over 17,000 competitors took part in 119 events across 7 sports.

Our schools are spread throughout cities, towns and the countryside and offer pupils the choice of day, boarding, weekly and flexible boarding, in both singe sex and co-educational schools. Most schools are charitable trusts, some are limited companies and a few are proprietary. There are also junior schools attached to senior schools, choir schools, those with a particular religious affiliation and those that offer specialist provision as well as some schools with an age range extending to age 16 or above.

Although each member school is independent and has its own ethos, they are all committed to delivering an excellent, well-rounded education to the pupils in their care, preparing them for their future.

IAPS
Bishop's House
Artemis Drive
Tachbrook Park
CV34 6UD
Tel: 01926 887833
Email: iaps@iaps.uk
Website: iaps.uk

ISA

The Independent Schools Association (ISA) is a family of over 590 Headteachers who represent the diverse range of independent education practised across the UK and overseas

The Independent Schools Association (ISA), established in 1878, is one of the oldest of the Headteachers' Associations for schools that make up the Independent Schools Council (ISC).

ISA exists to provide professional support, fellowship and opportunity to their 595 Members who nurture and develop over 120,000 pupils within their schools. Promoting best practice and fellowship remains at the core of the ISA, as it did when it began over 140 years ago.

ISA celebrates a wide-ranging membership, not confined to any one type of school, but including all: nursery, pre-preparatory, junior and senior, all-through schools, coeducational, single-sex, boarding, day, as well as performing arts and specialist provision schools.

As well as the support and specialist professional development opportunities for ISA's Members through their programme of courses and conferences, pupils in ISA schools benefit from their Head's membership with access to the extensive ISA Sport and Arts programmes.

ISA Sport champions inclusion in physical activity through positive experiences for young people across a programme of 58 national (and over 140 regional) events at venues such as St George's Park.

ISA Arts helps schools inspire creativity, expression and individuality across the arts through both virtual and in-person events.

Membership is open to any Head or Proprietor, provided they meet the necessary accreditation criteria, including inspection of their school by a government-approved inspectorate.

The ISA President, Lord Lexden, represents the Association in the House of Lords and seeks to join discussions of education when they take place and welcomes further collaboration between the independent and maintained sectors.

ISA is supported by a number of committees, comprised of serving Heads and Honorary Members, who meet regularly to consider the issues that affect independent education. Some committee areas include education, monitoring developments in education and formulating responses to Government, and EDI, developing and promoting the principles of inclusion within the Association and supporting Members in promoting Equality, Diversity and Inclusion (EDI) in their schools.

President: Lord Lexden
Chief Executive: Rudolf Eliott Lockhart

ISA House, 5-7 Great Chesterford Court, Great Chesterford, Essex CB10 1PF
Tel: 01799 523619
Email: isa@isaschools.org.uk
Website: www.isaschools.org.uk

ISA celebrates a wide-ranging membership, not confined to any one type of school, but including all: nursery, pre-preparatory, junior and senior, all-through schools, coeducational, single-sex, boarding, day and performing arts and special schools

The Society of Heads

The Society is an Association of Heads of just over 130 well-established independent schools

The Society is an Association of Heads of just over 130 well-established independent schools. It was founded in 1961 when a group of Heads decided they needed a forum in which to share ideas and experience. Since then the Society has grown substantially in size, reputation and effectiveness and represents a vibrant community of independent schools throughout England and Wales with some additional overseas members.

The Society's policy is to maintain high standards in member schools, to promote independent education, to provide an opportunity for the sharing of ideas and common concerns, to foster links with the wider sphere of higher education and to strengthen relations with the maintained sector by promoting partnerships.

Within the membership there is a wide variety of educational experience. Some schools are young, some have evolved from older foundations, some have behind them a long tradition of pioneer and specialist education; a number are at the leading edge of education in music, dance and the arts; and several are well known for their effective support for those with specific learning difficulties. The great majority are co-educational but we also have some all-boys and all-girls schools. Many have a strong boarding element; others are day only. All offer a stimulating sixth-form experience and give a sound and balanced education to pupils of widely varying abilities and interests.

The Society is one of the constituent Associations of the Independent Schools Council. Every Full Member school has been accredited through inspection by the Independent Schools Inspectorate (or Estyn in Wales and HMIE in Scotland) and is subject to regular visits to monitor standards and ensure that good practice and sound academic results are maintained. The Society is also represented on many other educational bodies.

All members are in membership of the Association of School and College Leaders (ASCL) or other union for school leaders and Full Member schools belong to AGBIS or an equivalent professional body supporting governance.

There are also categories of Alliance and Alliance Overseas Membership to which Heads are elected whose schools do not fulfil all the criteria for Full Membership but whose personal contribution to the Society is judged to be invaluable.

The Society hosts the autumn meeting, summer meeting and the annual conference for members. The Society also provides an extensive professional development programme.

The Society of Heads Office,
Office 101B, Harborough Grow-On Centre, Compass Point Business Park, Market Harborough, Leicestershire LE16 9HW
Tel: 01858 433760
Email: info@thesocietyofheads.org.uk
Website: www.thesocietyofheads.org.uk

The Society has grown substantially in size, reputation and effectiveness and represents a vibrant community of independent schools throughout England and Wales with some additional overseas members.

Profiles

Channel Islands

St Michael's Preparatory School

St. Michael's Preparatory School is situated in a unique educational setting on Jersey in the Channel Islands. A forward thinking IAPS prep school preparing pupils for the rigours of secondary school education both on and off island. We place great emphasis upon the traditional values of care, consideration and courtesy.

The staff and pupils are justifiably proud of the School, and work together to create and maintain a high-achieving, well-organised and friendly environment in which every child is encouraged to do 'a little bit better' than anyone thought possible.

The curriculum is designed to give all children a broad, balanced and relevant education, which enables them to develop as enthusiastic, active and competent learners acquiring the knowledge, skills and understanding to allow them to grow up in today's world leading a full and active life. The school's ethos places emphasis on the individual and aims to encourage development in academic, physical, spiritual, moral and cultural aspects of the 'whole child'.

The teaching is multi-sensory, allowing children of all abilities and learning styles to be able to make progress in their learning. Differentiation is integral to the curriculum and children with special needs are well supported, as are the gifted and talented, who go on to achieve scholarship success.

The schemes of work are based upon the National Curriculum, the Jersey Curriculum and the requirements of the ISEB Common Entrance and Scholarship syllabuses. The curriculum is enriched and enhanced by numerous trips and visits as Jersey has an array of museums, cultural sites of interest and environmental locations.

The school prepares children for Common Entrance and Scholarships to English boarding secondary schools as well as entry to local Jersey establishments. We also offer a Shell Year (pre-GCSE) specifically to provide a bridging opportunity for Year 10 entry to our island state schools. Classes are small and there is a very low pupil to teacher ratio. All expected subjects are taught and there are flourishing and well-equipped Art, Music, Science, Design Technology and ICT departments as well as a custom built Sports Hall, Dance/Drama Studio, Gymnasium and indoor Swimming Pool, as well as new state of the art cricket facilities, including a double-aspect pavilion and soon to be completed, all-weather (Astro) hockey pitch.

As well as providing a wide range of academic subjects, the school seeks to introduce each child to a large variety of sports, performing arts, activities and challenges enabling him or her to discover, through experience, hidden talents and preferences with a view to future specialisation.

I hope St. Michael's pupils will leave us having achieved the very best they are capable of, having found out what it is that they love and are good at, having learned to challenge themselves and to value other people.

I.S.I. Inspection (Oct 2017) Key findings:
- The quality of the pupils' learning and achievements is excellent
- The quality of the pupils' personal development is excellent

"St Michael's makes ordinary children special, and special children extra-ordinary." A parent quote.

ST MICHAEL'S
PREPARATORY SCHOOL

(Founded 1949)

La Rue de la Houguette, Five Oaks, St Saviour, Jersey JE2 7UG UK

Tel: 01534 856904

Email: office@stmichaels.je

Website: www.stmichaels.je

Headmaster: Mr Mike Rees

Appointed: 2014

School type: Co-educational Day

Age range of pupils: 3–14 years

No. of pupils enrolled as at 01/09/2022: 319

Boys: 172 *Girls:* 147

Fees as at 01/09/2022:

Day: £11,730–£18,450

Average class size: 19 max

Teacher/pupil ratio: 1:9

Central & West

Caldicott

Caldicott is a day and boarding country prep school for boys aged 7 – 13 in South Buckinghamshire. Situated in a beautiful 40-acre site, we are just 15 miles from Heathrow Airport and 30 minutes from London. Our expansive, growing daily bus service currently operates from Chiswick, Brook Green, Notting Hill, Marlow and the local area. We pride ourselves on our warm community where our pupils are happy and grow into confident all-rounders who have the grit and determination to succeed. Caldicott is a special place with a strong community spirit and sense of social responsibility. We encourage teamwork, intellectual curiosity and a love of learning in an atmosphere where creativity flourishes.

We have the reputation as one of the best prep schools in the UK with an excellent record in preparing boys for scholarships and Common Entrance to top UK public schools including Eton, Harrow, Radley and Wellington. Two years in a row, our leavers have attained a 'full house' of scholarships – meaning boys have excelled across art, sport, music, drama and academia. We have a strong and dynamic staffroom of dedicated and inspirational teachers and professionals – highly qualified academic teachers, expert sports coaches and musicians and drama specialists. Our recently commended pastoral care and wide range of extra-curricular activities mean boys get a full and enriching experience. Despite being successful across the major sports, our underlying philosophy is 'sports for all'; every week we have a mixture of external and House matches, giving every boy the opportunity to play in competitive fixtures week in, week out.

Boarding, compulsory in Years 7 and 8 and optional (in the form of flexi and occasional boarding) for Years 3 – 6, is caring, fun, and an integral part of the school community. Following our first year offering flexi boarding, we were proud to win BSA's 'Supporting Junior Boarders' Award. Boys live and work together in a friendly, supportive environment, build life-long friendships and develop independence before they go on to their senior schools at 13+.

We endeavour to harness the best of the school's traditions and values within a forward-looking and innovative approach all within a caring and supportive environment. Senior schools commend us for our well-mannered, considerate, confident boys who have high personal, moral and spiritual values and are striving to become their very best.

Crown Lane, Farnham Royal,
Buckinghamshire SL2 3SL UK

Tel: 01753 649301

Email: admissions@caldicott.com

Website: www.caldicott.com

Headmaster: Mr Jeremy Banks BA (Hons) QTS, MEd

Appointed: 2018

School type: Boys' Day & Boarding Preparatory

Age range of boys: 7–13 years (flexi boarding from 7)

No. of pupils enrolled as at 01/09/2022: 250

Fees as at 01/09/2022:

£6,527 – £12,170 per term

Average class size: 15

Downe House School

What makes Downe House special? The answer is in the Downe House DNA: Collaboration, Resilience, Creativity, Aspiration, Compassion, Communication, being Outward looking and Digital Ready.

In the classroom, on the pitch, on stage and everywhere in between, these values are the hope, aim and aspiration for every pupil in the school. Upon stepping through the school gates, every pupil is treated and celebrated as an individual. Whether she is an artist with an aptitude for mathematics, a scientist with a love of music, or an athlete with an interest in politics, Downe House will introduce, nurture and encourage every student's passion. The dynasty of Downe House women who preceded, and the sheer variety of the career paths and achievements of our alumnae is testimony to our ethos. They all carry with them the imprint of the Downe House DNA.

Downe House honours an exceptional programme to nurture global citizens and expands the pupils' cultural horizons. Every pupil in the Lower Fourth (Year 8) spends a term at our school in France, the Downe House Sauveterre, a beautiful chateau that allows the students to experience French life, language and culture. Older pupils have the opportunity to take part in the Global Schools' Exchange Programme, studying abroad in one of 15 partner schools across 6 continents. There is also a Global Internship Programme as well as DH LINKS, the School's comprehensive networking and careers initiative, along with our World Ready Programme, which is layered into every aspect of School life, tailored for every stage of development as pupils progress up through the year groups, to prepare them for the wider world.

Although personal triumphs and individual achievements are the most celebrated within School, the foundation of academic success is evident from the GCSE and A Level statistics. In 2022, at I/GCSE 88% of grades were awarded at 9-7 (A*-A) and and an amazing 34% of all our pupils achieved 9 or more grade 9-8s (A*). 74% of the A Levels taken by our students were graded A*-A and 91% were graded A*-B. These outstanding results ranked Downe House as the fourth best Girls Boarding School in the UK, and achieved places at some of the world's top universities for our graduates.

"Downe House was everything we hoped for in the next step for our daughter's education. You have evidently done a wonderful job of creating the right environment to foster achievement and happiness." (New parent, 2021)

Downe House was founded as 'a school where every individual within the community matters', and this has not changed. We work in partnership with parents to ensure that every Downe House pupil leaves School with a lifelong intellectual curiosity, the confidence that she can face life's challenges, and a steadfast place in a lively school community.

Downe House offers idyllic accommodation onsite, with a wealth of activities as part of our boarding model. So well-suited to the needs of a busy modern family that over 90% of pupils are boarding students. Offering both boarding and day places, Downe House provides every pupil with the gift of time and space for extra-curricular activities balanced with important family time.

Downe House

(Founded 1907)

Downe House, Cold Ash, Thatcham,
West Berkshire RG18 9JJ UK

Tel: +44 (0)1635 200286

Email: registrar@downehouse.net

Website: www.downehouse.net

Headmistress: Mrs Emma McKendrick BA(Liverpool)

Appointed: September 1997

School type: Girls' Day & Boarding Senior & Sixth Form

Age range of girls: 11–18 years (boarding from 11)

No. of pupils enrolled as at 01/09/2022: 590

No. of boarders: 565

Fees as at 01/09/2022:

Day: £10,960 per term

Full Boarding: £14,740 per term

Average class size: 15-20

Headington School Oxford

Headington is a highly successful day and boarding school in Oxford for 800 girls aged 11-18 with a Preparatory School for 250 girls aged 3-11 occupying its own site just across the road. The School offers girls an unrivalled opportunity to pursue academic, sporting and artistic excellence in a caring and nurturing environment.

Founded in 1915 and set in 23 acres of playing fields and gardens, the superb facilities provide the perfect backdrop for teaching and learning that extends way beyond the classroom and curriculum. Headington encourages participation in all aspects of sport and culture, teamwork and leadership, challenging girls to discover and explore their own potential and achieve more than they thought possible.

Consistently in the premier league of academic schools in the UK, life at Headington is about much more than exam results. Through the sheer breadth of subjects and activities at Headington, the School aims to educate the complete individual, giving girls the confidence and self-awareness to compete, contribute and succeed at school, university and in their adult lives.

Facilities

Headington offers a superb range of facilities to support and enhance learning.

These include a state-of-the-art Music School complete with recording studio, 240-seat professional theatre, light and airy Art School, Dance and Fitness Centre, Swimming Pool and award-winning Library. The School recently completed an update to our Sixth Form Centre. A new Creativity and Innovation Centre opened in September 2021 and a state of the art Food and Nutrition Centre opened in April 2022.

Outside the classroom

Around 120 extra-curricular activities take place every week. A wide choice of subjects, sports, interests and hobbies including such diverse pastimes as Debating and Robotics, Cheerleading and CCF.

Headington offers a genuinely inclusive approach to sport and encourages each girl to enjoy sport at the level that suits her. Girls can choose from more than 30 different sporting activities, from Athletics to Zumba. The School enjoys national success in a wide range of sports including Fencing, Rowing, Cross Country, Swimming and Equestrian.

Around 450 individual music lessons take place each week while the School has four orchestras, three choirs and numerous ensembles.

There is a busy programme of productions in our Theatre each year and girls become involved in all aspects of theatre, from writing and producing their own plays, to lighting, costume and make up.

A huge range of dance options are on offer, from Ballet to Street Dance and Contemporary. As well as annual Dance Shows, the Headington Dance Company competes in local and national competitions.

Boarding

Headington has always been a boarding school and just over a quarter of the School board with us today. The four boarding houses provide the girls with a 'home from home' where, supported by a team of highly experienced staff, they learn to develop into mature and independent young people. Many boarders come from the UK and the School is also very proud of its international boarding community, made up of more than 30 nationalities from all over the world. Girls can choose between full, weekly or half-weekly boarding.

(Founded 1915)

London Road, Oxford, Oxfordshire OX3 7TD UK

Tel: +44 (0)1865 759100

Fax: +44 (0)1865 760268

Email: admissions@headington.org

Website: www.headington.org

Headmistress: Mrs Caroline Jordan MA(Oxon)

School type: Girls' Day & Boarding

Age range of girls: 11–18 years

Fees as at 01/09/2022:

Day: £6,580–£7,160 per term

Boarding: £8,815 – £14,415 per term

Prep: £3,450 – £5,275 per term

Average class size: Depends on age

Teacher/pupil ratio: 1:8

Marlborough College

Marlborough College provides an exceptional, contemporary full-boarding education set in a beautiful environment steeped in history. It is a welcoming community where ambition and scholarship are highly valued, creativity is celebrated, diversity is embraced and where each pupil is encouraged and challenged to be the best that they can be.

There is no "right" path through Marlborough College. Indeed, we celebrate and take pride in the fact that each young person's journey might be different. The children who thrive here take responsibility for their own journey, responding to the amazing opportunities and support available to them, and they want to be the best that they can be.

Founded in 1843, Marlborough College is the UK's largest co-educational full-boarding school. The College is academically ambitious, offering a progressive, challenging and enriching education both on and off the formal curriculum. Our co-curricular provision is second to none and all pupils become involved in a wide range of sporting and cultural activities. More than 80% of our pupils gain places at Russell Group Universities or Oxbridge, our sports teams regularly reach the latter stages of national competitions, our Symphony Orchestra plays in partnership with the Southbank Sinfonia and our artists exhibit in the Mount House Gallery.

Located in beautiful Wiltshire, in one of the most attractive market towns in the country, the College benefits from a 286-acre site, stunning period buildings including a Gothic Revival chapel and the neo-classical Memorial Hall, which is also a world class concert hall, as well as university-quality sporting facilities. The campus is centred around a four thousand year old Neolithic mound, reputedly the burial place of Merlin.

Marlborough College welcomes pupils from the UK and overseas. We have six girls' houses, six boys' houses and four mixed houses of 13-16 year old boys with mixed Sixth Forms of girls and boys. The pastoral care delivered through our 16 boarding houses is unrivalled, ensuring each child is known and cared for individually. The greatest strength of our school is the quality of the human relationships throughout our community. Full boarding fosters independence and interdependence. Pupils form friendships for life and develop the social and leadership skills needed to flourish in adult life.

We are a genuine community which seeks for everyone to benefit and contribute. The house and tutor systems and the great range of learned societies in the school make sure that the intellectual and emotional development of each child is nurtured, and further education and careers after school are planned carefully. We place an ethos of service to others and a love of learning at the heart of everything we do and whilst we are proud of our Anglican heritage, ours is an inclusive ethos, welcoming pupils of all faiths and none.

Connections with the College's alumni within the UK and internationally are exceptionally strong and valued. Our wholly owned subsidiary, Marlborough College Malaysia, provides an important global aspect to the Marlborough family. We are committed to access and outreach and there is a well-developed partnership with Swindon Academy and involvement with local and international schools and institutions. Our pupils are encouraged to be outward facing and to aspire to change things for the better – ultimately, we would like to be judged by the contributions made by past, present and future Marlburians to the health of wider society throughout the course of their lives.

(Founded 1843)

Bath Road, Marlborough, Wiltshire SN8 1PA UK

Tel: 01672 892200

Email: admissions@marlboroughcollege.org

Website: www.marlboroughcollege.org

Master: Mrs Louise Moelwyn-Hughes

School type:
Co-educational Boarding Senior & Sixth Form

Age range of pupils: 13–18 years

No. of pupils enrolled as at 01/09/2022: 1012

Boys: 569 **Girls:** 443

Fees as at 01/09/2022:

Full Boarding: £14,310 per term

Shiplake College

Shiplake College is a thriving boarding and day school for boys aged 11-18, with girls joining in the Sixth Form. In September 2023 the College will begin the transition to being fully co-educational and welcome girls into Year 7. Overlooking the River Thames, two miles upstream of the famous Henley Royal Regatta stretch, students enjoy an inspirational 45-acre rural site. Flexi, weekly and full boarding is available from Year 9 (age 13) with some flexi-boarding available from Year 7 (age 11).

Every pupil is placed at the heart of Shiplake life and the College's ethos is underpinned by the three Is – Inclusive, Individual and Inspirational. All pupils are valued regardless of academic prowess, artistic flair or sporting ability, with opportunities for all to join in and try new things.

Shiplake provides a friendly, supportive and structured environment to bring out the best in each and every pupil and aims to equip them with the skills they need to enter the next stage of their lives as confident, personable and talented young adults. Academically ambitious and renowned for outstanding pastoral care and personal development, the College welcomes pupils with wide-ranging skills and talents, who will make the most of the many opportunities offered to them.

Every pupil becomes well-known to their House's pastoral team, especially the Housemaster, personal tutor and matron. Each pupil's best method of learning is identified and catered for by their teachers, with high-achieving pupils continually stretched while those requiring additional support can access it in a variety of ways. There is a wide range of A Level and BTEC subjects available, with all Sixth Formers also undertaking either a EPQ or CoPE.

Interpersonal skills, confidence and talents are also discovered outside the classroom. Two afternoons are reserved for an array of clubs and activities, including a comprehensive outdoor education programme, with pupils encouraged to extend their horizons and experience new challenges and responsibilities. Sports training takes place on three afternoons a week, with the majority of fixtures on Saturday mornings.

The College recruits highly motivated teaching staff with an ability and passion to inspire future generations and we ensure pupils have the best possible learning resources and facilities at their disposal. The environment we provide encourages pupils to take inspiration from their teachers, their surroundings, and each other.

The Sixth Form Centre includes a café where Year 12 and 13 girls and boys can socialise and work independently. The Davies Centre, opened in 2020, includes storage for rowing boats and other watersports, mountain biking and outdoor education, CCF and DofE equipment, and incorporates an indoor archery/rifle range, a climbing wall, weights room and an ergo room, which transforms into a function room with a balcony overlooking the river.

Academic, Art, Music, Drama and Sport Scholarships, and means-tested bursaries, are available. The College is also offering one 100% All-Rounder scholarship to a boy or girl currently at a state-maintained primary school who would be looking to join Year 7 each September, who would not be able to attend Shiplake without substantial financial support.

Entry points are normally at Year 7 (11+), Year 9 (13+) and Year 12 (16+). Prospective families are encouraged to arrange an individual visit or attend an open morning, which take place in the Autumn Term and March each year. Please go to www.shiplake.org.uk to book your attendance, complete a registration form and explore the whole site, which includes details of admissions processes, fees, bus routes and answers to most academic, co-curricular and pastoral questions that prospective parents may have.

SHIPLAKE COLLEGE
HENLEY-ON-THAMES

(Founded 1959)

Henley-on-Thames, Oxfordshire RG9 4BW UK

Tel: +44 (0)1189 402455

Fax: +44 (0)1189 405204

Email: registrar@shiplake.org.uk

Website: www.shiplake.org.uk

Headmaster: Mr T G Howe MA, MSt, MBA

Appointed: 2019

School type:
Co-educational Day & Boarding Senior & Sixth Form

Religious Denomination: Church of England

Age range of pupils: 11–18 years

No. of pupils enrolled as at 01/09/2022: 524

Boys: 456 *Girls:* 68 *Sixth Form:* 213

No. of boarders: 126

Fees as at 01/09/2022:

Day: £20,850–£26,508

Weekly Boarding: £29,229–£37,173

Full Boarding: £39,591

Flexi Boarding (2 nights per week): £24,618 – £31,017

Average class size: 16

Teacher/pupil ratio: 1:6

St Mary's Calne

St Mary's (founded in 1873) is an independent boarding and day school for girls aged 11-18, a happy, purposeful and flourishing community of around 360 pupils with an 80% to 20% boarding-to-day ratio. St Mary's welcomes cultural diversity and around 15% of the students come from overseas.

The school is located in the market town of Calne and amidst the Wiltshire Downs, an area of stunning natural beauty and historical significance. The school is within easy reach of the university towns of Bath, Bristol and Oxford and just over an hour by train from London. This ideal location means that the girls benefit from a huge range of co-curricular opportunities.

Focus on the individual

Small by design, St Mary's provides exceptional all-round education in a warm, nurturing environment. It is the individualised approach to every aspect of school life that makes St Mary's Calne special.

The pastoral care is outstanding. Every girl has a Tutor to support her through aspects of school life, from organisational skills and subject choices through to university application.

High Achievers

St Mary's Calne has a well-deserved reputation for academic excellence and is committed to providing an education that will challenge and inspire its pupils. In the Sunday Times Parent Power Schools' Guide 2022, St Mary's was ranked 1st independent school in Wiltshire and 2nd in the South West. St Mary's is also the first independent school in the UK to be awarded the Platinum Science Mark Award.

In 2021, the girls went on to study at a range of leading universities including Oxford, Cambridge, Durham, Edinburgh, Exeter, King's College London (KCL), London School of Economics (LSE) and University College London (UCL). Several girls were also successful in gaining places at prestigious universities in the USA.

Outside the Classroom

Opportunities in sport, music, art and drama abound and the facilities are superb, including a £2.55 million sports complex and full-size astro, theatre, a Sixth Form Centre and a state-of-the-art new library, overlooking the orchard.

Almost 80% of girls play musical instruments and take part in a wide variety of ensembles. The girls perform at many events, both in the local community and further afield.

Drama productions in the purpose-built theatre are of the highest standard and have transferred to the London stage. The Drama Department has a unique relationship with RADA, offering a course in advanced communication skills and girls also perform annually at the Edinburgh Fringe.

In Art, in addition to holding a triennial exhibition in London, the girls have received numerous awards, including having artwork selected for the Young Artists' Summer Show at the Royal Academy of Arts. The girls are also very active in the local community and have helped in local hospitals, residential care homes, the community library and in local schools.

Sport plays a very important part in school life and all the students are encouraged to participate, whatever their ability. Several girls represent the county in Lacrosse and Athletics and many have gone through the county development system in Netball and Hockey. Girls have represented England and Wales in Lacrosse, trained for the GB Pony Eventing Teams and competed in the English Nationals for swimming. The Tennis Academy was a National Finalist in the LTA's prestigious 2021 'School of the Year' Awards. In addition, a huge range of co-curricular sports, such as ski racing, climbing, golf and ultimate frisbee are available.

For further information, or to book onto one of our Open Days, please visit: www.stmaryscalne.org

ST MARY'S CALNE

(Founded 1873)

Curzon Street, Calne, Wiltshire SN11 0DF UK

Tel: 01249 857200

Fax: 01249 857207

Email: office@stmaryscalne.org

Website: www.stmaryscalne.org

Headmistress: Dr Felicia Kirk BA (University of Maryland), MA & PhD (Brown University)

Appointed: January 2013

School type: Girls' Day & Boarding Senior & Sixth Form

Religious Denomination: Church of England

Age range of girls: 11–18 years (boarding from 11)

No. of pupils enrolled as at 01/09/2022: 360

Sixth Form: 119

Fees as at 01/09/2022:

Day: £32,280

Full Boarding: £43,260

Average class size: Max 17, smaller in the Sixth Form

Teacher/pupil ratio: 1:5

Thornton College

Thornton College day and boarding school for girls, located between Milton Keynes and Buckingham, is set in 25 acres of beautiful grounds. The main school building is a manor house dating back to the 14th century and it became a school in 1917, founded by the Sisters of Jesus and Mary. The school is very proud of its rich history, exceptional pastoral care for the individual and its strong emphasis on core Christian values, though it is also proud of the fact that it is a forward looking school, with exciting opportunities both in and outside the classroom, and where girls of all faiths and no faith are equally welcome and equally valued.

Thornton College is part of an international family of J&M schools in twenty eight countries around the world. This gives our students the best of opportunities for student international partnership programmes, celebrations, projects and exchanges, enabling each student to grow a unique global outlook and cultural intelligence.

Boarding is 'upstairs' in our main manor house offering a home from home experience. The boarding bedrooms and common areas are bright and spacious. We offer flexi, weekly and termly boarding for domestic and international students with a dense programme of exciting evening activities and weekend trips.

Thornton College is a one site school ensuring that there is smooth transition for students throughout pre-prep, prep, senior and sixth form and lots of leadership and role modelling opportunities.

Our academic results are comparable with high achieving competitive schools whilst having a varied ability intake and Thornton consistently ranks as one of the top non-selective schools in the UK. Girls can join us at three years old into our Pre-Reception class offering families the very best start to their daughter's education. Woodland walks, cookery, ballet, French, music and movement, library time and a host of other weekly activities excite their young minds. As a Forest School, girls at Thornton excel inside and outside the classroom with our Prep school children enjoying our outdoor classroom in our woodlands and exploring and pond dipping in our eco habitat park. Thornton College is leading the introduction of robotics into Prep school curriculum and won the Independent School of the Year Award 2020 for our Student Careers Programme and was a finalist school in the ISA Awards 2020 for Outstanding STEAM Provision. Students in Senior and Sixth Form enjoy overseas sporting tours, World Challenges, Duke of Edinburgh (with sixth formers achieving their Gold Awards); EPQs; UCAS and careers events and debating. Our Sixth Form, which opened in 2016, offers a wide subject choice, small class sizes and individual attention with future pathway support. In 2020 and 2021 100% of Sixth Formers achieved their first choice universities.

Thornton College is an incredibly diverse and multi-talented community where each girl can thrive to be the best version of herself, to know her own strengths, to recognise her own challenges and to pursue with confidence the next stages of her life.

THORNTON

(Founded 1917)

College Lane, Thornton, Milton Keynes, Buckinghamshire MK17 0HJ UK

Tel: 01280 812610

Email: admissions@thorntoncollege.com

Website: www.thorntoncollege.com

Headteacher: Dr Louise Shaw

Appointed: November 2021

School type: Girls' Day & Boarding

Age range of girls: 3–18 years (boarding from 8)

No. of pupils enrolled as at 01/09/2022: 402

No. of boarders: 60

Fees as at 01/09/2022:

Day: £11,190–£17,835 per annum

Weekly Boarding: £19,830–£25,095 per annum

Full Boarding: £24,660–£30,585 per annum

Average class size: 14

Teacher/pupil ratio: 1:20

Wycombe Abbey

Wycombe Abbey is a modern, full boarding school committed to creating tomorrow's female leaders. It has a long tradition of academic excellence, it is consistently one of the country's top performing schools.

Our learning environment is supportive, yet challenging, with a sense that pupils and their teachers are on an educational journey together. We pride ourselves on the outstanding teaching provided by our specialists who communicate a genuine love of their subject and serve to inspire the girls they teach.

We believe that education should not simply be about delivering a curriculum and examination syllabus, but that real learning stems from stimulating intellectual curiosity and nurturing a love for the subjects being taught, which will stay with our girls throughout their lives.

In all we do, boarding is the key to our continued success. The School has a culture that inspires throughout the day, seven days a week, empowering girls to achieve their best, academically and socially. Our happy and close community is a truly global one, with 29 countries represented. Each girl is known, and cherished, as an individual. Consequently, every girl's potential, whatever that might be, is explored and fulfilled.

Girls learn to be independent, to value and support others, and to develop the skills needed for future challenges in a global workplace. Given the nature of boarding life, girls are able to enjoy a wealth of co-curricular opportunities. Each and every girl carves out a unique learning path according to her interests and has the space to thrive within our magnificent grounds. Our approach to boarding is also sympathetic to the needs of today's families and pupils have the opportunity to go home regularly and parents are actively involved in the numerous School events and activities.

The School is an oasis of calm, set in 170 acres of magnificent, conservation-listed grounds and woodland. Modern, state-of-the-art facilities include the Sports Centre, with a 25-metre indoor pool, the Performing Arts Centre with a theatre and recital hall, an atrium café, dance and fitness studios, and extensive sports pitches. Two new Boarding Houses opened in September 2017 and a refurbishment of all the boarding accommodation is ongoing.

Wycombe Abbey is easily accessible with excellent transport links. It is about 35 miles west of London and 30 miles east of Oxford. It is a 30-minute journey from Heathrow Airport and a 90-minute journey from Gatwick Airport by road.

To find out more about gaining a place at Wycombe Abbey, please visit our website at www.wycombeabbey.com or contact our Admissions Team on (+44) (0) 1494 897008 or by emailing admissions@wycombeabbey.com.

WYCOMBE ABBEY

(Founded 1896)

Frances Dove Way, High Wycombe, Buckinghamshire HP11 1PE UK

Tel: +44 (0)1494 520381

Email: admissions@wycombeabbey.com

Website: www.wycombeabbey.com

Headmistress:
Mrs Jo Duncan MA (St Andrews), PGCE (Cantab)

Appointed: September 2019

School type: Girls' Day & Boarding

Religious Denomination: Church of England

Age range of girls: 11–18 years

No. of pupils enrolled as at 01/09/2022: 660

Fees as at 01/09/2022:

Day: £33,150

Full Boarding: £44,100

East

Abbot's Hill School

Abbot's Hill is a school where one size does not fit all. We know and value everyone: we know that pupils do better when they are happy and so their wellbeing is our central focus. We know that every pupil will find their own path and so we help them to navigate it alongside dedicated and expert staff, committed to ensuring that each individual thrives.

The School was founded on the present site in 1912 by sisters Alice, Katrine and Mary Baird, who founded the school to educate young women of character. Set in 76 acres of grounds within easy reach of St Albans, Berkhamsted, Kings Langley and the surrounding villages, and with excellent transport links to the M25 and the Euston train line, we pride ourselves on the broad and stimulating education we provide. One foot is firmly rooted in our heritage but the other strides forwards into the future.

The school's founding motto was *Vie et Virtute* – meaning 'Strength and Power' – and this spirit lives on through our values, which underpin all that we do. Diverse pupils with wide-ranging talents and backgrounds come together in a close community that is large enough to offer choice and flexibility but compact enough to ensure that no child is overlooked.

At Abbot's Hill, academic excellence goes hand in hand with pastoral excellence. We are ambitious for all our pupils and offer exceptional learning opportunities to stretch, challenge and support the individuals in our care.

Self-belief and happiness, alongside a 'can-do' approach to every aspect of school life, enable our pupils to thrive and succeed. We are especially proud of the confidence which typifies our Year 11 leavers: they are the 'top' of the school and this means they have leadership opportunities beyond those of their contemporaries. As a result, they leave us equipped with the skills and confidence to prosper in their future lives.

We believe our pupils enjoy inspirational learning opportunities alongside challenging and enriching co-curricular activities, in a safe environment where they can be themselves and learn to be independent, resilient and confident. Beyond the classroom, our pupils' experiences are vast and varied. From our many co-curricular clubs to a comprehensive schedule of day trips and residential visits, the opportunities are endless. It is through this wealth of opportunity that each pupil finds what sparks her curiosity and love of learning.

"Fifty or so clubs, from Young Engineers to Origami, are run by the girls wherever possible. 'Whatever your interest, there's something for you', said one cheery student. If there isn't a club that appeals, there's no obstacle, indeed every encouragement, to start one." The Good Schools Guide, 2021

Our growing pupil mentoring and community partnership programmes ensure that each pupil knows she is part of something bigger and develops her sense of self by giving back to others. Our pupils are independent thinkers, have a strong, moral compass alongside a social conscience, and are accepting and respectful of themselves and others. They have been described as 'authentic, not arrogant' which perfectly describes an Abbot's Hill pupil.

Abbot's Hill

(Founded 1912)

Bunkers Lane, Hemel Hempstead, Hertfordshire HP3 8RP UK

Tel: 01442 240333

Email: registrar@abbotshill.herts.sch.uk

Website: www.abbotshill.herts.sch.uk

Headmistress: Mrs K Gorman BA, MEd (Cantab)

Appointed: January 2020

School type: Girls' Day

Age range of girls: 4–16 years

No. of pupils enrolled as at 01/09/2022: 482

Fees as at 01/09/2022:

Prep School: £4,056 – £5,162 per term

Senior School (Years 7-11): £6,984 – £7,026 per term

Average class size: 12–18

Brentwood School

Brentwood School shines out as a beacon of excellence. Our students are happy individuals who thrive on the high standards which are expected of them. They benefit from state-of-the-art facilities, set in the heart of Brentwood in Essex, and surrounded by 75 acres of green playing fields and gardens.

Academically, we sit comfortably alongside the best day and boarding schools in the country, and we enjoy an unparalleled local reputation.

We celebrate a 466-year history and take our heritage seriously. We are a Christian School with a chapel and a chaplain, and our School values, encapsulated in our motto "Virtue, Learning and Manners", have as much resonance today as they did when written by English poet John Donne in 1622. Our pupils are expected to have self-respect, to exhibit pride in their appearance and embrace values such as courtesy, consideration for others, kindness, looking after each other, honour, courage, sportsmanship, duty and selflessness.

Brentwood School pupils achieve excellent academic standards that rank among some of the best in the country. Our track record of exam results shows consistent high grades are achieved by all our pupils. They work exceptionally hard and are supported by highly professional and inspiring teachers to achieve excellent results at both GCSE level and in Sixth Form, whether studying A levels or the IB Diploma. An average of eight students per year are offered places at Oxford or Cambridge and over 80% of offers are from Russell Group universities.

We offer both GCSEs and IGCSEs; A Levels, the BTEC National Extended Diploma in Sport or Business, and the IB Diploma. More recent curriculum developments include the introduction of a Human Universe course in Years 10 and 11, which examines critical thinking and global issues.

Brentwood was the first school in Essex, and one of the first in the country, to adopt the Diamond Model: single-sex classes from the age of 11-16 within an overall mixed gender environment.

From an early age, we encourage pupils to aim high, think creatively and develop independence, so by the time they leave Sixth Form, they are well prepared for the expected, but can also tackle the unknowns. A flourishing Old Brentwoods community keeps thousands of alumni connected across the globe.

Our vast and exciting co-curricular programme enjoys national prominence, and we focus on providing opportunities for all to participate, as well as the pursuit of excellence for the most able.

Our Combined Cadet Force is one of the oldest and largest in the country, we offer The Duke of Edinburgh's Award and Outdoor Learning to pupils who want to satisfy their taste for adventure, and a Voluntary Service in Action Unit which raises tens of thousands of pounds every year to help specific charitable organisations.

Our sports centre houses a 25-metre swimming pool, glass-backed squash courts, fencing salle and dance studio and pupils achieve top sporting honours both nationally and internationally.

We are proud to be a Steinway School, enabling our pupils to learn on the very best-made pianos in the world, as well as some rare instruments otherwise unavailable to them.

Our musicians have played in the National Youth Orchestra, and our actors have gained places in the National Youth Theatre, RADA and other top Drama schools.

The lessons pupils learn at Brentwood will last for a lifetime. Integrity, initiative, a spirit of enterprise and an international mind-set help our pupils to thrive in the twenty-first century.

Brentwood School

(Founded 1557)

Middleton Hall Lane, Brentwood, Essex CM15 8EE UK

Tel: 01277 243243

Fax: 01277 243299

Email: headmaster@brentwood.essex.sch.uk

Website: www.brentwoodschool.co.uk

Headmaster: Mr Michael Bond

Appointed: September 2019

School type: Co-educational Day & Boarding

Religious Denomination: Church of England

Age range of pupils: 3–18 years

No. of pupils enrolled as at 01/09/2022: 1968

Fees as at 01/09/2022:

Day: £21,783

Full Boarding: £42,687

Average class size: 20 in Prep & Senior; 8 in Sixth Form

Teacher/pupil ratio: 1:9

Framlingham College

Framlingham College is a co-educational boarding and day school for children aged 3-18, set in the beautiful surroundings of rural Suffolk. Founded in 1864 as a memorial to Prince Albert, the College was established to reflect and support the prince's interest in British educational development.

Today this legacy continues, through the College's celebration of a forward-looking and ambitious learning culture that encourages curiosity and enquiry. A school that is aspirational for every pupil, the College's vision, structure and size places emphasis on understanding, guiding and inspiring each child individually – so they can discover and develop their talents, find their own voice, confidence, self-belief and create their own life-story.

When a young person joins Framlingham College, they are welcomed because of who they are. They are valued for their experience, their history, their ambition and their belief in their future.

The school's educational approach allows teaching to go beyond textbook learning and 'learning to test'. Instead, it prepares pupils for a constantly evolving world, by providing a rigorous and challenging knowledge-rich curriculum, focussing on skills and connectivity between subjects and fostering a culture of high aspiration.

By encourage pupils to seek out challenge, to embrace opportunity and to give them the time to reflect and learn from each experience, the school supports pupils to better understand themselves and the world around them. Pupils leave with an appreciation of the education they have experienced and an awareness of the issues facing society, inspired to give back to their community.

A focus on each child's wellbeing is paramount because a happy child will thrive. The integrated house structure at Framlingham College is an integral part of the school's pastoral care. Surrounding every pupil is the support of their House Mistress or Master, their Tutor, their teachers, the chaplain, and their peer mentors getting to know them and what makes them tick.

As a result of the House community pupils develop their deepest friendships, find their confidence and ignite sparks of admiration for the older pupils that lead to application and fulfilment in the larger community of the school.

The full, part and flexible boarding options available at the school empower pupils to grow in confidence and maturity and enables a strong sense of community. Boarding offers pupils the opportunity to further develop social and emotional skills and independent learning, whilst also enhancing each individual's understanding of their personal attributes and characteristics, their appreciation of their place as global citizens and their realisation of the importance of health and wellbeing.

The idyllic backdrop of 110 acres of bucolic Suffolk countryside – set across two sites at the Senior School and the Prep School – provides an inspiring and invigorating environment where pupils have the freedom to think and room to grow. And from here, pupils' horizons are global.

There is no typical Framlinghamian, no singular path that pupils take. Framlinghamians are academics, actors, musicians, expeditioners, sports people, innovators, scientists, ruminators, decision makers, storytellers, teammates, artists, fun lovers, nurturers and thought provokers. Often pupils are many things within one. But they are all individual with their own story to tell.

To find out more about the school, book a private tour or register for an upcoming open day please visit www.framlinghamcollege.co.uk/join/visit-us, contact the admissions team at admissions@framlinghamcollege.co.uk or ring 01728 723789.

WHERE EVERY PUPIL CREATES THEIR OWN STORY

(Founded 1864)

Framlingham, Suffolk IP13 9EY UK

Tel: +44 (0)1728 723789

Email: admissions@framlinghamcollege.co.uk

Website: www.framlinghamcollege.co.uk

Principal and Head of the Senior School: Mrs Louise North

Head of the Prep School: Mr Jonathan Egan

School type: Co-educational Day & Boarding Prep & Senior, Nursery & Sixth Form

Religious Denomination: Church of England, but all faiths are welcome

Age range of pupils: 3–18 years

No. of pupils enrolled as at 01/09/2022: 640

Fees as at 01/09/2022:

Day: £10,110–£23,064

Full Boarding: £26,499–£35,865

Haberdashers' Boys' School

Haberdashers' Boys' School is a leading independent day boys' school for students aged 4 to 18. Situated in an idyllic 100-acre co-educational campus in Hertfordshire, Habs Boys shares its wonderful location with its sibling school, Haberdashers' Girls' School. From September Habs Boys and Habs Girls will teach A Levels in co-educational classes, with students sitting a minimum of one A Level in mixed gender classes across at the other school.

At Habs Boys, our academic performance speaks for itself. At GCSE, 61% were 9 and 95% were 7 to 9. At A Level, 52% of the grades awarded were A* and 86% were A* to A.

Whilst outstanding outcomes remain a priority at Habs, great exam results are just one part of the educational journey at Habs and is not possible without the other academic and extensive co-curricular opportunities on the campus, creating relevant life skills and character development opportunities for all our students. We encourage all our students to make full use of the incredible campus, exploring their individual interests and passions, in and beyond the classroom.

As a school, our purpose is to empower our young people to make a profound and positive impact on society. This requires personal adaptability and resilience, curiosity, genuine empathy and a sense of responsibility for the people and the world around them.

We are a diverse community with a strong global perspective. Our roots are firmly in our philanthropic founding principles and this guides our deep sense of responsibility in the world. This environment, combined with our innovative teaching approach, prepares our students for the fast-moving world.

Admissions

We offer places to bright and ambitious students who are courageous and curious in all aspects of life.

At 4+ pupils are invited to the school and will participate in a series of activities. Some will then be invited back for a second stage. Our 7, 11, 13 and 16+ process involves one or multiple entrance assessments and an invitational second round interview. Our 16+ entry is also contingent on GCSE results the August before a student joins us.

Those pupils already in our Preparatory School are offered unconditional places as they move up from Year 6 to Year 7 in the Senior School.

Bursaries

At Habs, we are working to ensure every curious and ambitious child can access a Habs education. Our bursaries are means-tested and determined by a family's financial situation. The assistance provided can range from partial to full bursaries, with approximately 10% of our students currently receiving a free school place.

Scholarships

We offer a variety of different scholarships at the school from 11+. Academic, Art, Design and Technology, Drama, Music and Sport scholarships are available across our different entry levels and can offer 10-20% fee remission.

HABERDASHERS' BOYS' SCHOOL

(Founded 1690)

Butterfly Lane, Elstree, Borehamwood, Hertfordshire WD6 3AF UK

Tel: 020 8266 1700

Email: office@habsboys.org.uk

Website: www.habsboys.org.uk

Headmaster: Mr Gus Lock

Appointed: 2018

School type: Boys' Day Preparatory, Senior & Sixth Form

Age range of boys: 4–18 years

No. of pupils enrolled as at 01/09/2022: 1500

Fees as at 01/09/2022:

Pre-Prep: £17,352 (including school lunches)

Prep: £21,687 (including school lunches)

Senior School: £22,659

Haberdashers' Girls' School

Haberdashers' Girls' School is a leading independent day girls' school for students aged 4 to 18. Situated in an idyllic 100-acre co-educational campus in Hertfordshire, Habs Girls shares its wonderful location with its sibling school, Haberdashers' Boys' School. From September Habs Girls and Habs Boys will teach A Levels in co-educational classes, with students sitting a minimum of one A Level in mixed gender classes across at the other school.

At Habs Girls, our academic performance speaks for itself. At GCSE 54% of the grades awarded were 9 and 91% 7 to 9 and at A Level, 52% of the grades awarded were A* and 85% A*.

Whilst outstanding outcomes remain a priority at Habs, great exam results are just one part of the educational journey at Habs and is not possible without the other academic and extensive co-curricular opportunities on the campus, creating relevant life skills and character development opportunities for all our students. We encourage all our students to make full use of the incredible campus, exploring their individual interests and passions, in and beyond the classroom.

As a school, our purpose is to empower our young people to make a profound and positive impact on society. This requires personal adaptability and resilience, curiosity, genuine empathy and a sense of responsibility for the people and the world around them.

We are a diverse community with a strong global perspective. Our roots are firmly in our philanthropic founding principles and this guides our deep sense of responsibility in the world. This environment, combined with our innovative teaching approach, prepares our students for the fast-moving world.

Admissions
We offer places to bright and ambitious students who are courageous and curious in all aspects of life.

At 4+ pupils are invited to the school and will participate in a series of activities. Some will then be invited back for a second stage. Our 7, 11 and 16+ process involves one or multiple entrance assessments and an invitational second round interview.

We also offer Occasional Places as spaces become available in Year 4, 5, 8, 9 and 10. The availability of these places are confirmed in February; full details can be found n our website.

Those pupils already in our Junior School are offered unconditional places as they move up from Year 6 to Year 7 in the Senior School.

Bursaries
At Habs, we are working to ensure every curious and ambitious child can access a Habs education. Our bursaries are means-tested and determined by a family's financial situation. The assistance provided can range from partial to full bursaries, with approximately 10% of our students currently receiving a free school place.

Scholarships
We offer a variety of different scholarships at the school from 11+. Academic, Art, Creative Writing, Drama, Music and Sport scholarships are available across our different entry levels and can offer 10-20% fee remission.

Habs

HABERDASHERS' GIRLS' SCHOOL

(Founded 1875)

Aldenham Road, Elstree, Borehamwood, Hertfordshire WD6 3BT UK

Tel: 020 8266 2300

Email: office@habsgirls.org.uk

Website: www.habsgirls.org.uk

Headmistress: Mrs Rose Hardy

Appointed: 2019

School type: Girls' Day Preparatory, Senior & Sixth Form

Age range of girls: 4–18 years

No. of pupils enrolled as at 01/09/2022: 1200

Fees as at 01/09/2022:

Reception to Year 2: £18,909 (including school lunches)

Year 3 to Year 6: £19,719 (including school lunches)

Year 7 to Year 11: £21,516

Year 12 to Year 13: £21,636

Haileybury

Haileybury is a leading independent co-educational boarding school, situated on 500 acres of beautiful Hertfordshire countryside, just 20 miles north of London.

Haileybury's spectacular grounds are home to outstanding facilities, excellent teaching and superb pastoral care for its community of boarding and day pupils.

Academic opportunity

The school offers a dedicated Lower School for Years 7 and 8 and a wide range of GCSEs and IGCSEs. In the Sixth Form, pupils can select to study for A levels or the International Baccalaureate (IB) Diploma.

Haileybury is ranked Top 10 in The Times league table for co-ed independent schools which offer the IB.

Its unrivalled curriculum allows pupils to select personal pathways, such as coding and global civilisations, based on their individual passions. In the Sixth Form, electives include criminology, geopolitics and music technology.

Boarding and day

More than two-thirds of pupils are boarders and school life is centred around 12 boarding houses, Lower School benefitting from having their own house. Pupils join at 11+, 13+ or 16+ entry points. For Lower School pupils, flexiboarding is available which means families do not have to commit to full boarding at this stage and pupils can return home for the weekend. From Year 9 onwards, there is the additional flexibility of pupils being able to return home after sporting commitments on Saturday afternoons.

Exceptional opportunities

Beyond the academic curriculum, pupils benefit from a vast array of activities, including professional sports coaching and regular visits from speakers and performers from the arts, sporting and academic worlds.

The co-curricular programme is packed with opportunities, from Climbing and Scuba Diving to Film Making and the Model United Nations – and countless activities in between.

Haileybury also encourages pupils to immerse themselves in the Creative Arts both academically and as part of their co-curricular options. Drama, Music, Dance, LAMDA and Art are at the heart of school life. The School takes pride in hosting spectacular arts productions with multiple showcases per term and pupils are able to take part in music concerts, drama productions and public performances throughout the year.

The first school to do so in the UK, Haileybury is taking part in the global Stan-X programme, a pioneering study of genetics. Working from a pupose-built lab, Haileybury pupils are contributing to efforts to find cures for diseases such as pancreatic cancer and diabetes.

Supportive environment

At Haileybury, a caring environment is crucial to a pupil's happiness and fulfilment. There is an emphasis on pastoral care with around-the-clock support from housemasters and housemistresses, the chaplain and tutors, as well as an onsite health centre providing a circle of care. The school is a home-from-home, with a warm and friendly feel. Every child is given the confidence to find their identity on a personal journey of discovery.

A warm welcome

Our open days and taster events take place throughout the year and families are warmly invited to come along and discover what life at Haileybury has to offer and why its pupils flourish. For further information, please contact our Admissions Department on 01992 706353 or at admissions@haileybury.com

Haileybury

(Founded 1862)

Haileybury, Hertford, Hertfordshire SG13 7NU UK

Tel: +44 (0)1992 706353

Email: uk.admissions@haileybury.com

Website: www.haileybury.com

The Master: Mr Martin Collier MA BA PGCE

Appointed: September 2017

School type:
Co-educational Day & Boarding Senior & Sixth Form

Age range of pupils: 11–18 years (boarding from 11) (entry at 11+, 13+ and 16+)

No. of pupils enrolled as at 01/09/2022: 908

Boys: 464 **Girls:** 444 **Sixth Form:** 362

No. of boarders: 542

Fees as at 01/09/2022:

Day: £6,595–£9,920 per term

Full Boarding: £8,615–£13,580 per term

Teacher/pupil ratio: 1:7

Ipswich School

Ipswich School is a top ten independent school in East Anglia and one of the top 200 schools in the UK (Sunday Times Parent Power).

Founded circa 1399, it is one of the oldest schools in England with a rich heritage – it is the only school to be mentioned in a play by Shakespeare and has one of the longest-standing school newsletters. The student-led weekly newsletter continues to be a popular read for all in the school community to this day.

Ipswich School has a strong and consistent academic reputation. Students achieve excellent examination results and progress to the best universities, including Oxbridge and top Russell Group. In 2022 over a third of pupils achieved at least three A grades. 18 pupils achieved three or more A* grades and 8 pupils achieved all A* grades. Popular university destinations include Durham University, Kings College London, University of Exeter, University of Warwick and the University of Edinburgh. 92% of students secured their choice of university. Two-thirds of GCSE exams were graded 9-7 and 41 pupils achieved 9-7 grades in all their exams – nearly a third of pupils.

Above all, life at Ipswich School is busy and fun; students develop a spirit of service and an understanding of their role as global citizens. Every Thursday afternoon is dedicated to activities that expand horizons such as helping in the local community, CCF or environmental work.

Lessons are dynamic and interactive, with small class sizes and a broad curriculum that offers nearly 30 A Level options. Life Skills are an important part of the curriculum, which start in the lower years and progress to 'The Edge' programme at Sixth Form – a series of multi-disciplinary lessons that includes an ILM certification in Leadership and Management.

Music, sport and drama provision are extensive and inclusive and see dedicated performers compete at national level. Music is a very popular activity with over half the school taking part in one or more of the ensembles. The orchestra performs at the world-renowned Aldeburgh Festival – the event founded by famous local composer Benjamin Britten – and the annual Festival of Music, hosted at the school, brings the school and local community together.

Sport is taught by a team of highly qualified coaches and team achievements span all ages. Teams are regular National Cup finalists for both hockey and rugby from U13 upwards; the U15 Girls Cricket team are national runners-up and the U18 Boys Hockey team are indoor hockey champions.

Ipswich is less than an hour from London but is surrounded by seaside, forests and rivers. The school is just a few minutes from the heritage Suffolk Coast and 'Constable Country' – protected areas of outstanding natural beauty.

'... commitment to the development of personal skills that will help take these able students a lot further than exam results alone.' Good School Guide

2022 GCSE results: Grade 9: 21%, Grade 9-8: 43%, Grades 9-7: 66%
2022 A level results: A*: 28%, A* – A: 57%, A* – B: 83%

IPSWICH SCHOOL

(Founded before 1390)

Henley Road, Ipswich, Suffolk IP1 3SG UK

Tel: 01473 408300

Email: admissions@ipswich.school

Website: www.ipswich.school

Headmaster: Mr Nicholas Weaver MA

Appointed: 2010

School type: Co-educational Day & Boarding Prep & Senior, Nursery & Sixth Form

Religious Denomination: Church of England

Age range of pupils: 0–18 years

Fees as at 01/09/2022:

Day: £18,261

Full Boarding: £37,410

Teacher/pupil ratio: 1:20

King's Ely

Nestled in the beautiful cathedral city of Ely, King's Ely is a leading independent co-educational day and boarding school located just 15 minutes from Cambridge. As one of the oldest schools in the country, King's Ely nurtures the academic and pastoral needs of around 1,000 pupils from the age of 2 through to 18. We are proud to have received an 'excellent' rating in all areas following our latest ISI Inspection, recognising the highest levels of pastoral care, academic rigour and extra-curricular activity. Ely Cathedral serves as our school chapel and makes the perfect setting for assemblies and concerts.

The ethos of a King's Ely education enables pupils of all ages to flourish, from the children in King's Ely Acremont Pre-Prep to the young men and women in our Sixth Form. The progress young people make throughout their King's Ely journey is astounding and accounts for our high placement in local and national added-value rankings, including the top five in Cambridgeshire. Whether a student shines in a classroom, in a laboratory, on a stage, on a pitch or on a mountainside, we promise an abundance of opportunity for personal development, both academically and socially.

Innovative approaches to teaching and learning are the hallmark of every section of King's Ely. Through a broad and balanced curriculum, pupils develop the self-knowledge and inner-resilience to enable them to face the challenges of an ever-changing world. 85% of students secure places at first-choice universities, including Oxford and Cambridge. However, our aim is for students to develop learning habits that successfully prepare them for life, not just exams. As reported in the Good Schools Guide, we *"turn out well-rounded, likeable individuals who attain academically but who also realise there is more to life than just results."*

Music, Drama and Theatre, Art, Fashion and Textiles, Photography and Dance are each embedded in the culture of King's Ely, with vast opportunities for pupils of all aspirations. All major sports are offered, along with an impressive array of other activities, helping every pupil to realise their sporting potential. Rowing, athletics, golf, cricket, hockey, tennis, rugby, netball, equestrian and football – the choices are endless. Our Boat Club is located just a short walk from school, providing an uninterrupted stretch of water that runs for over 15 miles in each direction.

From the high peaks of the Himalayas to the gushing torrents of the rivers in the Alps, our unique Ely Scheme Programme also offers boundless opportunities for pupils to learn through outdoor education. We give students the chance to undertake their Duke of Edinburgh's Award at all three levels.

The range of clubs and activities on offer to pupils, both during and after school, is vast. Pre-Prep children enjoy things like Forest School and Engineering Club; Junior children enjoy clubs like Archery and Pottery, and Senior pupils enjoy clubs like Clay Pigeon Shooting and Language Leaders. There really is something for everyone.

We were delighted to be a finalist in the 2020-21 Independent Schools of the Year Awards. However, King's Ely is more than a school. We are a community, a family. We take each child on a seamless journey, travelling from one section to the next, whilst welcoming newcomers at key transition stages, giving support and adapting the offering to the needs of every child in our care. With over 45 nationalities represented at King's Ely, students enjoy their schooldays in the company of friends from a range of cultures and backgrounds.

"King's Ely is a happy place. My children genuinely enjoy going to school and, as parents, we could not ask for anything more." King's Ely parents, Mr and Mrs Warriner.

(Founded 970 AD)

Ely, Cambridgeshire CB7 4EW UK

Tel: 01353 660707

Fax: 01353 667485

Email: admissions@kingsely.org

Website: www.kingsely.org

Principal: Mr John Attwater MA (Oxon)

Appointed: September 2019

School type: Co-educational Day & Boarding Prep & Senior, Nursery & Sixth Form

Age range of pupils: 2–18 years

No. of pupils enrolled as at 01/09/2022: 1023

Fees as at 01/09/2022:

Day: £11,607–£24,729

Full Boarding: £26,268–£35,958

Average class size: Max 20

Teacher/pupil ratio: 1:9

Mander Portman Woodward – MPW Cambridge

Cambridge is where the MPW success story began. Nearly 50 years ago, three Cambridge graduates – Messieurs Mander, Portman and Woodward came together with an ambition to create a unique secondary education experience. They focused on several elements, based on their great Alma Mater, which they considered significant to the overall learning experience. Amongst these were the following: small class sizes, a strong tutorial system and superb teaching – and all of these within an informal atmosphere, which would allow creative minds to flourish.

Move the clock forward to the present day and these elements are still very much the hallmark of an MPW education. With fewer than 10 students per class for GCSE and A level, (though in fact the college average is closer to 6 in a class), the learning experience is truly personalised. As well as simulating the small class size at Oxbridge our students experience the privilege of being treated as an individual and not a number. Small classes mean our students know their questions will be answered and that they will have genuine contact time with their tutors in every lesson. With more than 30 A level subjects on offer and no restrictions on combinations, our students can choose subjects that suit them. Whilst Maths, Business, Economics and of course the Sciences remain popular choices, less well known subjects such as Ancient History and Classical Civilisation are also available.

With a current cohort of 60% British and 40% International, MPW Cambridge offers a world-class education to all. Education, however, is much more than what happens in the classroom. Preparation for life after secondary education is important too. Students need to be especially well-informed when they begin their UCAS application. The support provided by the personal tutors to each tutee is immense. From initial, informal discussion on determining the most suitable university course, through several drafts of the personal statement, often through BMAT or other entrance tests, for some even through daunting interview prospects, the MPW Personal Tutor is there. Their mandate is to 'hold the student's hand' throughout, providing encouragement and support.

We're also proud to assist those who might not have done so well the first time around. Our weekly assessments provide diagnostics where we can see which elements require further support. They also ensure that all of our students are fully prepared for the actual exam and properly understand critical success factors such as timing and weighting.

We'll leave the final words to Ofsted, taken from our college report: 'Pupils and sixth-form students say that Mander Portman Woodward (MPW) is 'amazing' and a great place to study. They know what they want to get out of their studies and are exceptionally well motivated to learn. Staff have high expectations. Most pupils and students respond to these expectations by working hard, so they achieve very well. They are confident that the support they get from their teachers will help them to be 'the best that they can be'.'

M|P|W

(Founded 1987)

3-4 Brookside, Cambridge, Cambridgeshire CB2 1JE UK

Tel: 01223 350158

Fax: 01223 366429

Email: cambridge@mpw.ac.uk

Website: www.mpw.ac.uk

Principal: Mr Tom Caston

School type:
Co-educational Day & Boarding Senior & Sixth Form

Age range of pupils: 15–19 years

Average class size: 6

Teacher/pupil ratio: 1:5

Orwell Park School

Developing a life-long love of learning in a magical setting...

Orwell Park, established in 1868, is a co-educational prep school for day pupils and boarders from 2 1/2 to 13. The outstanding beauty of the grounds and the historic 18th century buildings contribute to an inspiring experience which combines the legacy and the traditions of the past with the dynamism and energy of the present and future. Outstanding facilities include a working Victorian observatory, a walled garden with outdoor pool, a nine-hole golf course, floodlit sports facilities, a library in the mansion house, as well as a state of the art outstanding Pre-Prep facility, which was opened in 2013, set in the shadow of the main building among woods full of opportunities for outdoor learning.

Boys and girls are given every opportunity to be the best they can be, both in and outside the classroom. High expectations, and learning strategies tailored to the individual child, lead to high levels of attainment. Pupils progress to a wide range of senior schools both local and national, with all of our Year 8s achieving entry to their 23 chosen senior schools this year (Oundle, Uppingham, Marlborough, Stowe, Gresham's, Ipswich School , King's Ely, The Leys, RHS, Ampleforth, Benenden, Brighton College, Cheltenham Ladies' College, Eastbourne College, Framlingham College, Harrow, Ipswich High, King's Canterbury, King's Worcester, Norwich, Queen Ethelburga's, Rugby and Westminster). Our leaving year group in 2022 also achieved 25 scholarships in art, academic, drama, music, DT, sport and allrounder.

Whilst we value greatly the past, we also embrace technology and, as such, every child in Years 3-8 has their own ipad in order to enhance learning in the classroom and beyond. The ipads allow pupils to learn in a way that they are used to, fostering collaboration between pupils, whilst providing portability.

In addition to the traditional curricular subjects, Orwell Park pupils are involved in a comprehensive activity programme, including: orchestra and various ensembles, chess, Astronomy club in our own 19th century observatory, community service, skiing, equestrianism, climbing on the bouldering wall, OPS Challenge (a two-year mini D of E course), camping and campfire fun in the School's woodlands, Art and DT clubs, Goldies and Blueys (boys' and girls' clubs), as well as numerous large scale theatrical productions. The school achieves success in all the major sports and recently introduced cricket for all girls as the summer sport. In addition, Orwell Park is linked with Mayo College in Rajasthan, India and Year 7 pupils have the opportunity to visit India and sample the Taj Mahal, Jaipur and spend time at one of India's most famous boarding schools.

Boarding is extremely popular at Orwell Park and takes the form of flexible boarding, weekly boarding and full boarding, which incorporates a comprehensive programme of weekend activities. Pupils choose to board, driven by a desire to enjoy the company of friends once the normal school day is over. Dormitories are bright, spacious and clean and a dedicated team of boarding staff and school matrons are totally committed to the health and welfare of the boys and girls in their care.

Join us at an Open Event to see for yourself what makes Orwell Park such a special and inspirational place to be.

For more information contact our Registrar on 01473 653224 or email admissions@orwellpark.org.

ORWELL PARK SCHOOL

(Founded 1868)

Nacton, Ipswich, Suffolk IP10 0ER UK

Tel: 01473 659225

Fax: 01473 659822

Email: admissions@orwellpark.org

Website: www.orwellpark.co.uk

Headmaster: Mr Adrian Brown MA(Cantab)

Appointed: September 2011

School type:
Co-educational Day & Boarding Preparatory & Nursery

Religious Denomination: Interdenominational

Age range of pupils: 2.5–13 years

No. of pupils enrolled as at 01/09/2022: 270

Fees as at 01/09/2022:

Pre-Prep Day: £3,139 – £4,465 per term

Prep Day: £6,352 – £7,039 per term

Prep Boarding: £8,669 – £10,337 per term

Average class size: 12-14

Teacher/pupil ratio: 1:12

St Cedd's School

St Cedd's School is a co-educational 3-11 Charitable Trust School offering pupils the opportunity to aspire and achieve in a caring environment that nurtures talent and supports individual endeavour. This is a school in which every child matters. We value and celebrate their many diverse talents and qualities and the grounded confidence the pupils develop results in great personal achievement.

Individual Pupil Progress

The progress of pupils, of all abilities, throughout the school is rapid. Our standardised assessment results and 11+ scores far exceed national averages and annually we celebrate an unrivalled success rate to selective grammar and independent senior schools with an impressive track record of scholarship awards. This level of achievement is significant given that the school is academically non-selective. Assessments on entry are designed to capture the strengths and areas for development of each child so that the education is tailored to the needs of the individual.

Centre of Excellence

The Independent Schools Inspectorate (ISI) placed St Cedd's School at the top level in every category of inspection in March 2022 which places the school amongst the very best 3-11 preparatory schools in the country. The accolade confirms what we witness every day; high academic achievement, outstanding records of attainment in music, an inclusive sporting ethos and successes at national tournaments, a sense of purpose and ambition that shows itself in the attitude and actions of the pupils and staff, and a very effective pastoral care system.

In December 2021, the academic excellence of the school, and our provision for the most able, was recognised by the National Association for Able Children in Education through the reaccreditation of our NACE Challenge Award.

Broad and Balanced Curriculum

With over 80 clubs and activities to choose from, extra-curricular opportunities are balanced with a firm focus on academic work. This synergy supports the development of confident self-assured pupils ready for the challenges ahead. PE, music, art, French and science are taught by specialists with the teaching of PE, music and French starting in the Pre-School. Acknowledging the breadth of talents of pupils is an important aspect of life at St Cedd's School. To this end, our baccalaureate-style Year 6 curriculum, HOLDFAST, leads to awards in recognition of 'Holistic Opportunities to Learn and Develop, Furthering Achievement, Service and Talent'.

As a member of the Choir Schools Association our Choristers sing in the Cathedral Choir and the Junior and Senior Chamber Choirs sing at Evensong in Chelmsford Cathedral.

Nurturing the Future

For over 90 years, boys and girls at St Cedd's School have been enjoying a quality of education that is among the very best you will find. We provide the best start in our vibrant Pre-School where the children thrive in a colourful and nurturing environment that widens their horizons and instils in them a love of learning.

Breakfast Club operates from 7:30am-8:00am and a wrap-around care programme is open until 6:00pm. Fees include curriculum-linked extra-curricular activities, 1-1 learning support, lunch and the majority of after-school clubs.

To attend an open day or to arrange an individual tour, please contact Mrs Abbott on 01245 392810 or email admissions@stcedds.org.uk.

St Cedd's School

(Founded 1931)

178a New London Road, Chelmsford, Essex CM2 0AR UK

Tel: 01245 392810

Email: info@stcedds.org.uk

Website: www.stcedds.org.uk

Head: Mr Matthew Clarke

Appointed: September 2018

School type:
Co-educational Day Preparatory & Nursery

Age range of pupils: 3–11 years

No. of pupils enrolled as at 01/09/2022: 400

Boys: 200 **Girls:** 200

Fees as at 01/09/2022:

Day: £3,200-£4,100 per term

Average class size: 23; maximum 24

St Columba's College

St Columba's College and Preparatory School is an independent Catholic day school for pupils aged 4-18 in St Albans, Hertfordshire. We provide a high-quality education to young people of all faiths and of no particular persuasion.

Our Columban ethos and values guide all that we do, allowing us to provide an education of the head and heart that places academic success, happiness and confidence at the centre of our mission. We have created a nurturing environment where each student is challenged to achieve their own best academic standard, while becoming confident, resilient and compassionate individuals.

Teaching the Columban values of courage, courtesy and compassion enables our students to become confident and well-rounded individuals, with the skills to enter an ever-changing and complex world.

Our moral education is based on the educational tradition of the Brothers of the Sacred Heart. We support each student's development in a community where they are known, valued and treasured, through a well-structured pastoral system.

We strive for academic excellence whilst realising that it is a well-rounded education that best prepares our young people for the world and workplace of tomorrow. As a result, our young people are academically successful, intellectually curious, happy and empathetic. The world needs leaders with these qualities, who can connect with people and respond wisely to the many complex challenges we face in an ever-changing society.

St Columba's College has moved to co-education! In 2021, we welcomed girls into Lower Prep (Reception, Year 1 and Year 2) and the Lower Sixth Form (Year 12).

From September 2022, girls are being welcomed into Form 1/Year 7. This will be followed by a phased transition, which will eventually see St Columba's offering its unique, high-quality Catholic educations to both boys and girls from ages 4-18.

In recent years we have invested millions of pounds in new facilities including a fitness suite, science and D&T labs, and a modern IT suite in the Prep School. We have refurbished our Sixth Form Centre, Senior School Music Department, Art Department, and IT Suites, and the Lower Prep facilities in the Prep School. Plans are underway to upgrade our sports pitches, for use by the whole school.

During the pandemic in 2020 and 2021, our remote learning programme was a great success with parents and pupils. Our dedicated staff utilised a range of resources, including Microsoft Teams, to deliver interactive and engaging lessons, following the normal timetables. We continued our provision of strong pastoral support through regular communication with parents and students. The Heads of House and Tutors maintained ongoing contact with the students and their families as they adapted to remote learning.

In the ISI Inspection of St Columba's College in May 2022, the school was recognised as fully compliant and 'Excellent' in all areas. The ISI report stated that pupils have an excellent attitude towards their learning, and that their knowledge, understanding and skills are highly developed. Pupils were found to have a high level of social awareness and valued diversity within the school community.

St Columba's pupils continue to be recognised nationally for their academic and extra-curricular achievements, including the Big Bang (STEM) Competition Finals, Biology and Physics Olympiads, and the British Education Awards. They continue to be accepted onto prestigious programmes such as the Royal College of Music Junior Department.

(Founded 1939)

King Harry Lane, St Albans, Hertfordshire AL3 4AW UK

Tel: 01727 892040

Email: admissions@stcolumbascollege.org

Website: www.stcolumbascollege.org

Head: Mr David Shannon-Little

Appointed: 2022

School type: Co-educational Day & Sixth Form

Religious Denomination: Catholic

Age range of pupils: 4–18 years

No. of pupils enrolled as at 01/09/2022: 805

Fees as at 01/09/2022:

Reception, Prep 1, 2: £11,883

Prep 3: £13,986

Prep 4, 5, 6: £15,426

Senior: £17,949

Average class size: 10-24

St Faith's

Bright Beginnings – Exciting Futures

St Faith's is a Prep School for boys and girls aged 4-13 located in a green, spacious site in the heart of Cambridge.

We believe in providing a future-focused education, preparing our pupils for the needs of the modern world. Pupils need the skills of team work, an understanding of how a computer works and of the engineered world around them, and a strong grounding in Science and Maths, the Humanities and Languages as the foundation stones for virtually every path their future lives might take.

Across our wide-ranging curriculum each child is taught, developed and nurtured, to equip them well for life. Our teachers are passionate about sharing their knowledge, exploring new ideas, challenging the status quo and instilling a life-long passion for learning. We provide a tailored education to our pupils to ensure they are supported to fulfil their potential. Top-down excellence in all lessons enables our pupils to achieve more then they thought possible. With small class sizes, exceptional teachers and excellent facilities, all subjects follow an accelerated curriculum and the vast majority of pupils work at a higher level commensurate with their age.

A leader in the early introduction of Computing to the curriculum, we now support over 25 schools in their development of Computing. In 2015 we became the first, and still only, Prep school to teach Engineering as a core curriculum subject for all children from age seven. Our curriculum explores all forms of engineering; chemical, mechanical, robotics, structural, civil, electrical and aeronautical. In 2018 The Times awarded us 'Strategic Education Initiative of the Year' for our introduction of Engineering to the curriculum. Furthermore, The Week Independent Schools Guide named us 'The Best of the Best' for STEM education in 2019.

Sport is a conduit for developing mental and physical fitness, team spirit and resilience. Twenty different individual and team sports are taught at St Faith's. Our 'Sport for All' culture ensures that all pupils, irrespective of ability, receive specialist sports teaching from the age of five. In 2018/19 11 team and 9 individual national titles were awarded to St Faith's in Gymnastics, Trampolining, Hockey and Athletics. The 2019/20 season was suspended but by March we held national titles in girls and boys hockey, netball and gymnastics. Drama, Music and Art are tools not only for teaching children a life-long love of the arts but for promoting self-belief and confidence.

Our green and spacious 9-acre site, located in the heart of Cambridge, together with extensive playing fields a two-minute walk away, provide some of the best facilities of any prep school in the UK. The shelves in our library are crowded with over 12,000 works of fiction and non-fiction. Engineering suites provide access to tools and equipment beyond many inventor's wildest dreams. Fully-equipped science laboratories and computer suites are used by all year groups. The Hub provides flexible large indoor spaces for interdisciplinary projects, a roof-top night sky viewing platform and a virtual reality suite allows all children to explore the universe around them in the most exciting ways.

St Faith's pupils are confident, articulate, grounded and courteous, attributes which will stand them in good stead for their futures. In 2021/2022, a record number of scholarships, 38 in total, were awarded to Year 8 pupils as they moved to senior schools, with over 90% of leavers gaining a place at their first choice school.

(Founded 1884)

Trumpington Road, Cambridge, Cambridgeshire CB2 8AG UK

Tel: 01223 352073

Email: admissions@stfaiths.co.uk

Website: www.stfaiths.co.uk

Headmaster: Dr C Hyde-Dunn

Appointed: September 2021

School type: Co-educational Day Preparatory

Age range of pupils: 4–13 years

No. of pupils enrolled as at 01/09/2022: 571

Boys: 310 **Girls:** 261

Fees as at 01/09/2022:

Day: £14,505–£18,270

Average class size: 16-18

St Margaret's School, Bushey

St Margaret's School in Bushey, Hertfordshire, is an independent day and boarding school for pupils aged 2 to 18. Founded in 1749, we are one of the oldest independent schools in the UK. As well as day places for all ages, we offer a range of flexible boarding options for both UK and international pupils from the age of 11.

We are a school with a proven record of academic success in public examinations and our pupils move onto competitive courses at leading universities and institutions both here in the UK and around the world. In 2020 86% of our A-level results were A*-B grades, with 72% of all GCSE results at 9-7 grades.

Our outward looking ethos aims to encourage a genuine enthusiasm for learning and an ability to independently explore subjects beyond the classroom. Our curriculum addresses a rapidly changing world filled with complex challenges as well as exciting new possibilities.

In January 2020, we began our transition to co-education, with St Margaret's School starting the journey from being an all girls school to providing education to both girls and boys.

The pastoral care at St Margaret's is the central pillar upon which the success of the school is based and we are proud of the quality of care and opportunity given to every one of our pupils no matter what stage of their education. We offer a rich programme of extra-curricular activities and pupils are encouraged to find their talent whatever that may be.

There is no typical St Margaret's pupil; all are valued individually by our qualified and committed staff. However, they are all dedicated young people who strive to succeed in all that they do and are passionate about topics facing them today. The quality of care at St Margaret's School enables pupils to grow in an atmosphere of tolerance and understanding and leave equipped with the confidence, aptitude and skills they need for life and for work.

Our beautiful 60 acre site boasts a combination of superbly resourced historic and modern buildings and we are easily accessible from both London, the Home Counties and all the major London airports. If you have not yet visited us, please do and we will show you the love of learning, culture of achievement and relish of challenge that is the essence of St Margaret's.

ST MARGARET'S

SCHOOL

(Founded 1749)

Merry Hill Road, Bushey, Hertfordshire WD23 1DT UK

Tel: +44 (0)20 8416 4400

Email: admissions@stmargarets-school.org.uk

Website: www.stmargarets-school.org.uk

Headteacher: Lara Péchard

Appointed: January 2020

School type: Co-educational Day & Boarding

Age range of pupils: 2–18 years

No. of pupils enrolled as at 01/09/2022: 650

Fees as at 01/09/2022:

Nursery (full-time): £3,920 per term

Junior: £4,395 – £5,367 per term

Senior Day: £6,423 per term

Senior Full Board: £12,225 per term

Average class size: 20

The Leys School

Founded in 1875 The Leys School is Cambridge's leading co-educational boarding school for children aged 11 – 18. Unusually for a city school, it is situated within a leafy 50 acre campus, close to the banks of the River Cam, yet only a 10 minute walk from the buzz of the city centre. Our ethos is simple – to provide an excellent, all-round education for our pupils, combining the traditional values of tolerance, respect and decency with a forward-looking and collaborative approach to teaching and learning.

Our Unique Location; the Cambridge Experience
The university of Cambridge provides the kind of enrichment opportunities most schools can only dream of. Links with the University are strong and we take full advantage of this; we host world-renowned speakers in our Great Hall and attend academic lectures within university departments. Our Chapel Choir regularly joins forces with the College choirs, singing in some of the most stunning College Chapels in the world. We share our award-winning Boathouse with 3 university colleges and compete in many of their sporting fixtures. Our superb location truly does offer a world of exceptional opportunities.

Academic Life
Through the provision of a broad and balanced curriculum Leys pupils develop into articulate, confident and well-rounded individuals. Their timetables are tailored to their aptitudes, needs and interests. As pupils move up through the school they take on increased responsibility for planning their workloads, with support from a coordinated tutorial system. Class sizes are small and the school's academic results reflect the expertise, vitality and enthusiasm of its teachers.

Beyond the Classroom
Pupils at The Leys are encouraged to take part in as many wider-curricular activities as they can realistically manage. Over 100 clubs, societies and groups take place every week. 26 sports are offered from Athletics to Water Polo, alongside CCF, Duke of Edinburgh and Community Service groups. The opportunities for outdoor pursuits are endless and, combined with first class performance facilities, the school exudes an air of purposefulness and busyness.

Support and Wellbeing
The Leys is a close-knit community, based on mutual respect and shared values. Its backbone is the House system where our pupils are assured of a supportive and caring environment. Their wellbeing is at the heart of what The Leys stands for; it is a happy, inspiring and unique place.

Joining The Leys
Girls and boys join The Leys in Years 7, 9 and 12 and may either sit the school's own tests, obtain places via pre-assessment in Year 7 or apply for one of a range of scholarships, bursaries or exhibitions.

Visit The Leys
Open Mornings are held on a termly basis alongside Small Group Visits whereby up to 6 families may visit the school together. The Admissions Team is also happy to arrange Private Visits when required. To find out what makes The Leys such a special place contact The Admissions Team on 01223 508904 or email admissions@theleys.net to arrange to come and visit.

THE Leys
CAMBRIDGE

(Founded 1875)

Trumpington Road, Cambridge,
Cambridgeshire CB2 7AD UK

Tel: 01223 508900

Fax: 01223 505303

Email: admissions@theleys.net

Website: www.theleys.net

Headmaster: Mr Martin Priestley

Appointed: September 2014

School type:
Co-educational Day & Boarding Senior & Sixth Form

Age range of pupils: 11–18 years

No. of pupils enrolled as at 01/09/2022: 567

Fees as at 01/09/2022:

Day: £18,240–£25,260

Full Boarding: £27,525–£37,740

Average class size: 15-20

Teacher/pupil ratio: 1:8

The Peterborough School

The Peterborough School is the city's only independent day school for boys and girls from Nursery to Sixth Form.

Situated on one beautiful, leafy campus in the heart of Peterborough, the Nursery, Prep and Senior Schools enjoy excellent transport links and shared facilities.

The combined campus means the School is a vibrant place with small classes providing boys and girls with the individual attention, opportunities, confidence and ability to exploit fully their natural potential within a happy, caring and friendly community.

The 56-place Nursery has been rated Outstanding in its last five ISI Inspections. It enjoys an excellent location in a separate building on the School site, with ample gardens and outside spaces, and is close enough to Peterborough station, with its high-speed train services to London, to make it highly attractive for working families.

In the Preparatory School (4 to 11 years), the children are encouraged to be independent and inquisitive learners and develop many important skills through the extended curriculum and numerous extra curricular clubs and activities available.

In the Senior School and Sixth Form, students' unique talents are identified and developed, whether they are in the classroom, in the creative arts or on the sports field. Closely monitored academic performance means students usually achieve levels higher than those originally expected.

The Sixth Form is going from strength to strength with consistently impressive A Level results and is an area of focus for development, with a new bespoke Sixth Form block now in place. This facility has a large, wi-fi enabled Study Room, including a student meeting space, offices and a large, well-facilitated Common Room with kitchen. This development has also created a new state-of-the art Senior Library.

Our pastoral support is extremely strong and we passionately believe that children cannot learn well unless they are happy.

Headmaster, Adrian Meadows, is proud that the long-standing traditions of the school, which was founded in 1895, remain but at the same time it is a forward-looking, progressive place where children continually surprise and delight him. *"I have seen students winning a national STEM award on the same day that the Reception Classes and Pre-schoolers enjoyed a Teddy Bear's Picnic. Being amongst children of such a wide age range is fascinating, entertaining and always interesting but overall it is incredibly rewarding and humbling to be part of such an amazing school and community."*

Visitors to the School and Nursery are very welcome. We have Open Days on Saturdays in October and May each year when appointments are not necessary. There is also a Sixth Form Open Evening in October. Alternatively individual visits can be booked by calling the School on 01733 343357 or by visiting the website and completing the online form: www.thepeterboroughschool.co.uk/admissions

(Founded 1895)

Thorpe Road, Peterborough, Cambridgeshire PE3 6AP UK

Tel: 01733 343357

Fax: 01733 355710

Email: office@tpsch.co.uk

Website: www.thepeterboroughschool.co.uk

Headmaster: Mr A D Meadows BSc(Hons)

Appointed: September 2007

School type: Co-educational Day Preparatory & Senior, Nursery & Sixth Form

Age range of pupils: 6 weeks–18 years

No. of pupils enrolled as at 01/09/2022: 480

Fees as at 01/09/2022:

Day: £11,250–£17,829

Average class size: 15

The Royal Hospital School

Royal Hospital School is set in 200 acres of stunning Suffolk countryside overlooking the River Stour and about an hour from London. It is a leading independent, co-educational boarding and day school providing a full and broad education, fit for the modern world. The School's ethos is understanding each young person's strengths, to help them to make the right choices at the right time, navigating through their critical formative years and ensuring their education becomes the foundation for their happiness and success.

With 400 boarders making up the pupil body of approximately 700 pupils, the School's extensive grounds and boarding houses allow pupils to thrive in an exceptional environment. Pupils entering at age 11 join our coeducational Junior House, a chance to get to know the whole year group and settle into life at senior school. Pupils then move into either a boys' or girls' boarding house, before joining our co-education house, Nelson House, in Year 13. At this stage single studies and more independent living is encouraged in preparation for life beyond school.

Facilities include a state-of-the-art music school with recital hall, recording studio and specialist rooms, drama and dance studios, an art and design technology centre, science laboratories, a well-stocked reference and multimedia library and ICT suites. There are over 96 acres of sports fields, an all-weather pitch, extensive courts, and a golf course as well as indoor facilities including a large swimming pool, squash courts, a climbing wall, gymnasium, martial arts studio, strength and conditioning room and fitness suite. All pupils take part in traditional team sports such as rugby, cricket, netball, and hockey, but there is also the opportunity to try a diverse range of over 100 cocurricular activities such as sailing, water polo, mountain biking, climbing, canoeing, horse riding, dry skiing, shooting and kick boxing. The School is an RYA training centre and has a world-renowned Sailing Academy, home to the current World Sailing Youth Champion.

RHS was recently shortlisted for the ISP Co-educational School of the Year and Best International Student Experience Awards, alongside being re-awarded with the Edtech 50 School Award for inspirational technology-led learning. A recent ISI inspection also rated RHS 'Excellent' in all areas, quoting; *"The School realises its aim to enable pupils to grow into the person they wish to become, fulfilling their potential and leaving very well prepared for life."*

Headmaster, Simon Lockyer, explains the School's aims and ethos: *"We inspire our pupils to have the courage to be ambitious for their futures and the commitment to pursue whichever path they choose. We challenge pupils of all academic abilities, steering them to look beyond the moment and beyond the confines of the classroom, and to approach life with an open and receptive mind.*

"Everyone can achieve the most exceptional things, but we are all different. That is why we focus on the individual, getting to know every one of our pupils and finding out what motivates them. It is this focus on personal challenge and individual guidance that enables our pupils to develop into self-reliant, socially responsible adults with enviable open mindedness and resilience, so sought-after by employers and important in life."

ROYAL HOSPITAL SCHOOL

(Crown Charity, founded 1712)

Holbrook, Ipswich, Suffolk IP9 2RX UK

Tel: 01473 326136

Email: admissions@royalhospitalschool.org

Website: www.royalhospitalschool.org

Headmaster: Mr Simon Lockyer BSc MEd

Appointed: September 2016

School type:
Co-educational Day & Boarding Senior & Sixth Form

Religious Denomination: Christian

Age range of pupils: 11–18 years

No. of pupils enrolled as at 01/09/2022: 730

Fees as at 01/09/2022:

Day: £18,207–£20,253

Weekly Boarding: £27,825–£34,542

Full Boarding: £29,211–£37,614

3-Night Boarding: £24,999 – £29,982

International: £30,927 – £39,381

Average class size: 15-20

Teacher/pupil ratio: 3.75:1

East Midlands

Fairfield Prep School

Fairfield Prep School is a top-performing, independent school for boys and girls aged 3-11. It is part of the Loughborough Schools Foundation which is a charity committed to providing an education to cherish through a Nursery; two complementary Prep Schools and three high achieving Senior Schools: The Grammar School for boys, The High School for girls and The Amherst School, a non-selective co-education school. Uniquely the Schools share a beautiful campus and exceptional resources in many fields including Music, STEM and Sport.

Originally founded in 1929 as part of Loughborough High School, Fairfield Prep became an autonomous school within the Foundation in 1969. It is now a flourishing school of over 500 pupils and is perfectly situated to provide a first-class 21st Century Primary education.

A new chapter for each child

Fairfield Prep School is committed to the development of every pupil; the priority is to ensure that each child enjoys and benefits from their time at the School. That means a friendly and supportive community and endless exciting experiences, all backed by high academic standards.

Every pupil at Fairfield has many opportunities to thrive and to find a passion for things that matter to them. Therefore, success and achievement are both found through the inspiring and lively academic environment, as well as numerous extra-curricular activities which take place outside the classroom.

Fairfield was judged 'Excellent' across all eight categories by the Independent Schools Inspectorate in both 2016 and 2021 and everyone at Fairfield works together to create positive experiences for each and every child. The children continually achieve at the very highest level and thoroughly enjoy everything that the School has to offer and pupils move onto the next stage of their educational journey within the Foundation as happy, confident and well-rounded individuals, ready to face the wealth of challenges ahead.

Excellent ways of understanding

The pastoral care at Fairfield is excellent and all staff work hard to bring out the best in each and every child. Each child benefits from effective, sensitive and well-coordinated pastoral care that enables academic achievement with individual care and focus, alongside an excellent holistic foundation for future learning.

Excellent experiences and opportunities

From Kindergarten to Year 6, the opportunities are vast and varied. There are over 40 clubs and activities available at lunchtime and after school encompassing Sport, Music, Drama and Art. From Origami to Music Theory, these include a Running Club, Rainbows and Dance. Most importantly, each child is encouraged and given the confidence to participate and enjoy success whatever their interests.

Charity and community work are also part of the School ethos. The School Council decides upon the charity focus for each term and fundraise for a rota of local, national, overseas and animal focused causes.

Excellent spaces and facilities

In 2016, Fairfield opened a new state-of-the-art building which provides new high-tech, light and airy classrooms with access to outdoor space, a large gymnasium and performance hall, specialist Art, Science and Food Technology rooms and a purpose-built Kindergarten. There is also a Forest School in a half-acre of woodland on the campus where children can safely explore the outdoor environment and develop an appreciation of the natural world.

FAIRFIELD
Prep School

(Founded 1969)

Leicester Road, Loughborough, Leicestershire LE11 2AE UK

Tel: 01509 215172

Email: fairfield.admissions@lsf.org

Website: www.lsf.org/fairfield

Headmaster: Mr Andrew Earnshaw

Appointed: January 2013

School type: Co-educational Day Preparatory

Age range of pupils: 3–11 years

No. of pupils enrolled as at 01/09/2022: 505

Fees as at 01/09/2022:

Kindergarten: £4,010 per term

Pre-Prep (Reception to Year 2): £4,120 per term

Upper Prep (Years 3 to 6): £4,220 per term

Loughborough Amherst School

Loughborough Amherst School is an independent co-educational school for ages 4-18. It is part of the Loughborough Schools Foundation which is a charity committed to providing an education to cherish through a Nursery; two complementary Prep Schools and three high achieving Senior Schools: The Grammar School for boys, The High School for girls and The Amherst School, a non-selective co-education school. Uniquely the Schools share a beautiful campus and exceptional resources in many fields including Music, STEM and Sport.

Loughborough Amherst School became Loughborough's new co-educational independent school in September 2019, however the foundations were laid 170 years ago when the school was founded as a Catholic school for girls.

Ambitious for your child

Staff at Amherst, see their role as not just to help each child realise their academic potential. They also want to help every child in the School find a profound sense of self-belief. Amherst believes that young people with self-belief are not only happier in themselves, but are more able to show compassion to others, and to use their talents to make the world a better place.

Loughborough Amherst School is dedicated to creating an environment where every pupil has the opportunity for long-term spiritual and moral growth, not to mention long-term happiness.

When pupils leave the School, the aim is for them to be confident and successful. But, equally importantly, the staff want them to be caring and empathetic young people; equipped to face the best and worst that life offers. The kind of young person you'll be proud of.

At the heart of the School's ethos is the philosophy of their founder, Blessed Antonio Rosmini, that a 'pupil must be allowed to grow and develop as an integrated human person'.

A new and exciting phase in the history of the School was embarked on when boys were welcomed into the Senior School and Sixth Form in September 2019, making Loughborough Amherst School co-ed from 4 to 18 years. Amherst staff were also excited to welcome their first elite sports Boarders, thanks to their partnership with the Lawn Tennis Association and the Loughborough University National Tennis Academy.

Thanks to the Nursery and Sixth Form, children can develop at Amherst from infancy to adulthood. Together with the small size of the School, it creates a distinctively close school community with a family atmosphere. That's what makes Amherst so warm and welcoming.

With a teacher to pupil ratio of 1:8 enabling exceptionally high levels of individual academic support, each child has every chance of realising their goals. So, whether a child is a high flyer or someone who might benefit from extra educational input, the caring and holistic approach at Amherst will help them grow as a well-rounded individual.

Beyond the Timetable

There is a rich and engaging range of enrichment opportunities at Amherst to encourage the wider development of each child. Activities are offered for every age range during lunchtimes and after school, ranging from dance and football to public speaking, chess and debating. Above all, it is hoped that these opportunities encourage each child to discover life-long passions, interests and skills.

LOUGHBOROUGH
Amherst School

(Founded 1850)

Gray Street, Loughborough, Leicestershire LE11 2DZ UK

Tel: 01509 263901

Email: amherst.admissions@lsf.org

Website: www.lsf.org/amherst

Headmaster: Dr Julian Murphy

Appointed: September 2016

School type:
Co-educational Day Preparatory, Senior & Sixth Form

Age range of pupils: 4–18 years

No. of pupils enrolled as at 01/09/2022: 335

Fees as at 01/09/2022:

Day Fees (Reception to Year 2): £3,740 per term

Day Fees (Years 3 to 6): £3,850 per term

Day Fees (Years 7 to 9): £4,780 per term

Day Fees (Years 10 to 11): £4,840 per term

Day Fees (Years 12 to 13): £4,880 per term

Loughborough Grammar School

Loughborough Grammar School is a top-performing, independent day and boarding school for boys aged 10-18. It is part of the Loughborough Schools Foundation which is a charity committed to providing an education to cherish through a Nursery; two complementary Prep Schools and three high achieving Senior Schools: The Grammar School for boys, The High School for girls and The Amherst School, a non-selective co-education school. Uniquely the Schools share a beautiful campus and exceptional resources in many fields including Music, STEM and Sport.

Loughborough Grammar School is one of the oldest independent schools in the country, able to trace its origins back to 1495.

A passion for life & learning

Loughborough Grammar School is a school where academic achievement is at the centre of everything. Dedicated staff and outstanding resources enable Loughborough Grammar School boys both to fulfil their potential in examinations and to embark on intellectual adventures beyond the classroom.

However, the boys encounter far more than is required for academic success. Staff at the Grammar School understand that they will only succeed if they feel happy and contented. Considerable focus is therefore placed on the development of a strong moral compass where kindness towards others and a commitment to fairness and equality are valued as key personal attributes.

So that each boy can enjoy his time at Loughborough Grammar School, there is an attentive system of pastoral care that ensures that each boy is supported by pastoral staff who fully know him, his interests and his worries, so that they can both monitor his progress and guide him towards areas in which he will feel challenged and fulfilled.

Each boy is an individual and staff want him to feel totally at ease within himself, whatever his unique interests or pursuits. The Grammar School strongly believes that pupils benefit from a well-rounded education, which is why it is so important that every boy at Loughborough Grammar School has the opportunity to discover passions that he will retain beyond his school days and into adult life.

In the early years, boys are encouraged to try as many experiences as possible, gradually finding their unique niche as they progress through the School. These activities beyond the classroom play a major part in helping boys to develop into resilient young men, who are confident yet sensitive and aware of their responsibilities to others.

The Grammar School provides a myriad of opportunities through an extensive extra-curricular programme which offers Sport, Music and Drama as well as over 100 clubs and societies. Boys are expected to take advantage of the activities and clubs that are on offer and to show pride in representing the School outside its walls.

A Loughborough Grammar School education is therefore a busy one, where each boy thrives through engaging in a broad range of activities that will complement his academic achievement, and help him to develop into a well-rounded and happy young man.

Boarding at the Grammar School

The success of the boarding community has been an enriching part of Loughborough Grammar School for much of its long history. With an active community of some 75 boarders, the boarding is like a concentration of the very best that the School offers, condensed into two wonderfully welcoming Houses within the campus.

Just like the Day pupils, Boarders are supported, individually known, cared for and cared about and encouraged to make the most of all the opportunities such a high achieving School provides.

LOUGHBOROUGH
Grammar School

(Founded 1495)

Buckland House, Burton Walks, Loughborough, Leicestershire LE11 2DU UK

Tel: 01509 233233

Email: grammar.admissions@lsf.org

Website: www.lsf.org/grammar

Headmaster: Dr Daniel Koch

Appointed: September 2022

School type: Boys' Day & Boarding Senior & Sixth Form

Age range of boys: 10–18 years

No. of pupils enrolled as at 01/09/2022: 890

Fees as at 01/09/2022:

Day Fees (Years 6-9): £4,900 per term

Day Fees (Years 10-11): £4,980 per term

Day Fees (Years 12-13): £4,990 per term

Full boarding and tuition with EAL:
£12,490 – £12,580 per term

Loughborough High School

Loughborough High School is a top-performing, independent school for girls aged 11-18. It is part of the Loughborough Schools Foundation which is a charity committed to providing an education to cherish through a Nursery; two complementary Prep Schools and three high achieving Senior Schools: The Grammar School for boys, The High School for girls and The Amherst School, a non-selective co-education school. Uniquely the Schools share a beautiful campus and exceptional resources in many fields including Music, STEM and Sport.

Founded in 1850, the High School is one of the country's oldest Grammar Schools for girls. Most of the values that are upheld and the traditions that are celebrated have been established in the ensuing years, always with the goal of creating a wonderfully welcoming community within which every pupil is supported and encouraged to become all that they can be.

Achievement comes from a sense of wellbeing

Everyone is someone at Loughborough High School: whether competing on the sports field, performing with our world-class Music department or volunteering to help others, the individual talents of every student are nurtured in a warm and supportive community that enjoys all the advantages of a single-sex environment within a Foundation of four closely-linked Schools.

The High School takes great pride in their pupils' academic achievements but also believe that education is about so much more than excellent examination results. This is a school with a love of learning at its heart and where there are no limits placed on female aspiration: whether a pupil wants to be an astrophysicist, an actress or an anthropologist, the teachers help and encourage all the girls to achieve success. The aim is to develop adaptable, independent and socially responsible young women, who approach their learning with imagination, energy and a sense of adventure.

At the heart of everything lies the wellbeing of each pupil: diversity and difference are celebrated and the caring, committed staff support each girl in developing the self-awareness, courage and resilience needed to negotiate the challenges of modern life. As part of the Loughborough Schools Foundation, each pupil will be a lifelong member of a vibrant and happy family.

Remarkable Results

Pupils are encouraged to be enthusiastic about learning and the girls are supported by dedicated teachers who will encourage them to be curious, and question and debate in the classroom and beyond to help them develop key learning skills.

The smaller class sizes, superb teaching and well-resourced departments, and an overall environment that's ideal for learning, create the conditions where each girl can do her very best.

Remarkable Choices

The enrichment programme is extensive and constantly evolving – ranging from numerous sporting and musical pursuits to hobbies such as chess and gardening.

Activities are offered for every age range during lunchtimes and after school. This includes opportunities for the Adventure Service Challenge (Years 7 to 9) and the Duke of Edinburgh's Award Scheme (Years 9 to 13) which help girls to push boundaries and acquire new skills. Girls can also join the Combined Cadet Force where cadets not only follow the ethos of the School, but also develop core values of loyalty, integrity, courage, respect for others and selfless commitment. All High School girls are encouraged to express themselves and enjoy as wide a range of school experiences as possible.

LOUGHBOROUGH
High School

(Founded 1850)
Burton Walks, Loughborough, Leicestershire LE11 2DU UK

Tel: 01509 212348

Email: high.admissions@lsf.org

Website: www.lsf.org/high

Head: Dr Fiona Miles

Appointed: April 2019

School type: Girls' Day Senior & Sixth Form

Age range of girls: 11–18 years

No. of pupils enrolled as at 01/09/2022: 545

Fees as at 01/09/2022:

Day Fees (Years 7 to 9): £4,900 per term

Day Fees (Years 10 to 11): £4,980 per term

Day Fees (Years 12 to 13): £4,990 per term

Oakham School

Oakham School is a vibrant co-educational independent boarding and day school for pupils aged between 10 and 18. Founded in 1584, its uniquely structured population of 50:50 boarders and day pupils and 50:50 girls and boys create a genuinely inclusive school community.

Set in the heart of rural England close to Rutland Water, Oakham offers full boarding, weekly boarding and day options that fit around busy family life.

Oakham aims to provide an education for children that recognises that these School years are precious and should be joyful, memorable and transformative.

The School combines its exceptional pastoral care with academic excellence and outstanding co-curricular opportunities, underpinned by its core values, to enable its pupils to flourish at school and long into the future.

The connected curriculum means each individual pupil is given the opportunity to excel in what they love the most and experience new things.

Pastoral care lies at the heart of Oakham School. All pupils – day and boarding – belong to a House, where they are part of a larger community of pupils and staff. Led by a Housemaster or Housemistress, and supported by a team of Tutors, Prefects and a Matron, each House community is filled with people who care for all aspects of our pupils' wellbeing.

Our unique Boarding House structure ensures that staff are expertly versed and trained to the needs of their specific age group. Pupils will primarily go to their Housemaster/ Housemistress if there is a problem but there is a large wider network of adults, who can offer support, for example our Chaplain, our Medical Centre staff, our counsellor, our mental health practitioner, and our catering team. The Barraclough Dining Hall serves an extensive choice of nutritious and freshly prepared food. The School's state-of-the-art Medical and Pastoral Centre offers a dedicated space to promote wellbeing, as well as offering medical support 24 hours a day, 7 days a week.

Over many years, the School has received national recognition for its outstanding achievements in sport, music, drama and the Duke of Edinburgh Scheme.

Our genuinely holistic approach to education means that students leave Oakham as intellectually ambitious thinkers, who are effective and independent learners, well equipped with the skills and habits of mind to thrive in tomorrow's world.

There are five major drama productions every year and we teach over 500 individual music lessons each week. Oakham also has a national reputation for Sport, offering 30 different sports to students of all levels – from enthusiasts to elite athletes.

Students can choose from over 130 activities to take part in every week to discover and develop their interests and talents and provide service to others. In addition to CCF, Duke of Edinburgh and Voluntary Action, options range from dance to robotics, e-textiles to sailing – there really is something for everyone.

Above all, Oakham is a welcoming community that values learning and human relationships, which are the bedrock of a successful and happy life.

A series of Open Events are being held across October and November. For more information and to book a place, please call the Admissions team on 01572 758758 or visit oakham.rutland.sch.uk.

(Founded 1584)

Chapel Close, Oakham, Rutland LE15 6DT UK

Tel: 01572 758758

Email: admissions@oakham.rutland.sch.uk

Website: www.oakham.rutland.sch.uk

Headmaster: Mr Henry Price MA (Oxon)

Appointed: September 2019

School type:
Co-educational Day & Boarding Senior & Sixth Form

Religious Denomination: Church of England

Age range of pupils: 10–18 years

No. of pupils enrolled as at 01/09/2022: 1040

Boys: 537 **Girls:** 503 **Sixth Form:** 376

No. of boarders: 516

Fees as at 01/09/2022:

Day: £6,580–£8,140 per term

Full Boarding: £10,100–£13,550 per term

Average class size: 20

Teacher/pupil ratio: 1:7

Greater London

Elmhurst School

Elmhurst is more than a school. It is a community who come together for the good of the pupils and work tirelessly to support them in their endeavours; something we have been doing for over 150 years. Many of our pupils continue to visit us and even rejoin the community as parents, such is the warmth and affection that the school holds. Today we focus on nurturing the brilliance in every boy through partnerships, inspiring spaces and a focus on what is best for boys.

From our youngest pupils in our Little Elms nursery, staff encourage curious, brave and determined learners to blossom. Little Elms' pupils benefit from contact with specialist teachers in Art, Music, IT, Drama and French which ensures the boys are very much a part of the school. Routines are established that continue throughout their time here and this builds a familiarity supporting pupils' transition at each stage. Parent partnerships are formed and continuity between home and school approaches, optimises learning.

As a boys' school, we understand the importance of a curriculum with literacy at its heart, driving a love of reading and learning. We also value each individual, provide a broad, challenging curriculum to enable pupils to thrive and to support each boy in his preparations for 11+ entry to local grammar and independent schools.

Sport, Drama and outdoor learning together with Art and Music ensure life at Elmhurst is always varied and performance opportunities plentiful. Boys are encouraged to take part in a range of activities through our curriculum and extensive extra-curricular clubs programme.

Responsibility too is encouraged. Our eldest pupils are asked to buddy up with our nursery pupils, writing to them to introduce themselves at the start of the year and then meeting up with them weekly for lunch and spending play times together throughout the term. These relationships are beneficial to both the older and younger pupils and become a very important part of their school life. School voice is active in Elmhurst and our school council meets regularly to feedback ideas and feelings about the community. In a similar way, our active parents association come together to share ideas with the Head and collectively ambitious school development plans are shaped.

As part of the Bellevue family of schools, we have the additional opportunity to take part in group wide initiatives and our Y6 debaters are often successful in the Prep School debating competition amongst other things. As an ISA school, we are regular participants in regional and national sports competitions, with many of our teams and pupils enjoying great success on the sporting front.

Visit us

Nestled in the heart of South Croydon with excellent transport links (adjacent to South Croydon railway station and bus stops serving no 64 and 433 routes) and a generous car park for easy pick up and drop off, we are a school proud of its local area and our pupils regularly take advantage of the excellent facilities in South Croydon as well as support local charities and initiatives.

We host regular open events and taster sessions throughout the year. Why not pop in and see why an Elmhurst education is the right one for your son?

For more information or to sign up to visit us, go to www.elmhurstschool.net

(Founded 1869)

44-48 South Park Hill Road, South Croydon, Surrey CR2 7DW UK

Tel: 020 8688 0661

Email: admissions@elmhurstschool.net

Website: www.elmhurstschool.net

Head of School: Mrs Sara Marriott

School type: Boys' Day Preparatory & Nursery

Age range of boys: 3–11 years

No. of pupils enrolled as at 01/09/2022: 140

Fees as at 01/09/2022:

Day: £3,680–£4,290 per term

Kew College Prep

Set in leafy South-West London, Kew College Prep provides a small, supportive and vibrant school community. The minute you walk through the door, the ethos of the school is apparent; it is a friendly and caring environment which is relaxed but purposeful. The relationship between staff and pupils is warm and open and there is a tangible buzz of creativity in the air. The children are respectful, responsible, hard-working, and fun-loving individuals who thrive given opportunities to take risks in their learning and set challenges for themselves.

The curriculum is designed to provide pupils with opportunities to create, connect and collaborate both within and beyond the classroom. Children are encouraged to ask questions and think creatively. Technology is used to enhance learning across all subject areas, and sports and arts feature prominently in school life. The school's Junior House (Years 3-6) is also the springboard for our unique 11+ programme. From Year 5 onwards, each child is provided with a tailored learning plan. The results of entrance exams to secondary schools are excellent with numerous scholarships attained.

The children display an overwhelming desire to achieve and are inspired by staff who work with boundless energy, dedication and determination. No stone is left unturned as they strive to support and nurture every child to achieve their full potential. A strong moral value system is embedded from an early age so that, by the time the pupils leave Kew College Prep, they can think independently and critically. They are inquisitive, reflective and well-rounded; true individuals who are prepared for the rigours of secondary school and for the changing world in which they live.

"Both of our boys joined the school in the Nursery and have flourished in the nurturing and caring environment the school provides. The children are all confident, articulate, well-mannered, and thoroughly nice kids who are comfortable in the company of adults. Our boys have thrived at Kew College Prep and always raced enthusiastically into school each day. The teaching and school philosophy is very much focused on helping each child to achieve their best in a happy environment. As parents, we really couldn't ask for more." The Stewart family

"We chose Kew College Prep for our four daughters for its warm atmosphere and its happy, friendly, and well-mannered pupils. We feel fortunate to have also found a school which fulfils its promise of educating our children to their highest potential. We have children with differing abilities and personalities, but Kew College Prep has provided support and education for all of them. Every child at this school is unique, but one thing that every child here has in common is that they will leave strengthened by their experience." The Ahmed Family

Registrar: Mwarburton@kewcollege.com

Potential unlocked.

(Founded 1927)

24-26 Cumberland Road, Kew, Surrey TW9 3HQ UK

Tel: 020 8940 2039

Email: enquiries@kewcollege.com

Website: www.kewcollege.com

Head: Mrs Jane Bond BSc, MA(Ed), PGCE

School type:
Co-educational Day Preparatory & Nursery

Age range of pupils: 3–11 years

No. of pupils enrolled as at 01/09/2022: 284

Fees as at 01/09/2022:

Nursery: £2,690 per term

Kindergarten – Year 6: £4,725 per term

Average class size: 20

King's House School

King's House School is an independent day prep school for boys aged 3 to 13 with a co-educational Nursery for 3- and 4-year-olds. Founded in 1946, we offer each child a high-quality, broad academic and co-curricular education where they can discover their unique talents and passions, and the needs of each individual are truly catered for.

King's House provides a happy, supportive, and safe environment for our pupils, where the boys – and girls in our wonderful nursery – thrive and flourish. Pupils are cherished as individuals and provided with the skills and mental resilience to succeed in whatever path they choose in life.

Here at King's House, we aim to ensure that the school keeps pace with global developments so that pupils are ready to take their place in an ever-changing world. When pupils leave us, they are not only armed with outstanding academic results, but also with a sense of self-awareness, respectfulness, and independence. Academic success is a result of the happy, relaxed atmosphere at KHS, which allows pupils to simply be themselves. Pupils benefit from our 35-acre multi-use sports ground in Chiswick, located on the banks of the River Thames and steeped in history since its official opening in 1926.

At King's House Nursery children are taught and supported by a team of highly experienced staff, who strive to give every child the opportunity to flourish and grow. The nursery opened in January 2009 just around the corner from King's House School and benefits from light, spacious and inspiring facilities. Nestled in The Alberts, in the heart of the community, you will find an oasis of warmth, laughter and a wealth of resources to inspire little minds and create a love of learning. Children move up to school as happy, thoughtful children ready for their next journey: girls move onto a wide range of schools, both state and independent.

King's House is a mixed-ability inclusive school at our two main entry points, Nursery and Reception. Applications can be made anytime from birth onwards, and about half of our Reception intake is made up of boys coming from our Nursery. We believe in the importance of a full preparatory education, with the boys progressing onto Senior Schools at 13+. Their final two years here allow them to take on leadership roles within a small year group, giving them the space to develop academically and emotionally. Boys move onto to a wide range of day, boarding, co-ed and single sex senior schools, with many achieving scholarships.

We warmly invite you to visit us and get in touch at admissions@kingshouseschool.org or 020 8940 1878.

(Founded 1946)

68 King's Road, Richmond, Surrey TW10 6ES UK

Tel: 020 8940 1878

Email: admissions@kingshouseschool.org

Website: www.kingshouseschool.org

Head: Mr Mark Turner BA, PGCE, NPQH

Appointed: 2011

School type: Boys' Day Preparatory, Co-ed Nursery

Age range of boys: 3–13 years

Age range of girls: 3–4 years

No. of pupils enrolled as at 01/09/2022: 425

Fees as at 01/09/2022:

Day: £2,720–£6,530 per term

Laleham Lea School

Laleham Lea School was recently awarded the highest possible rating of 'Excellent' across Focused Compliance and Educational Quality Inspection including Academic Achievement following a full inspection from the Independent Schools Inspectorate. The Inspection reported that *'The quality of the pupils' academic and other achievements is excellent'* and, *'The quality of the pupils' personal development is excellent'*.

The inspectors reported that, *'Pupils make excellent progress, achieving at levels in advance of expectations for their age and ability'*, *'Pupils are outstanding communicators'*, *'Pupils develop highly effective study skills (and) are highly enthusiastic learners'*.

Along with excellent academic results and an impressive list of Senior School destinations and Scholarship Awards, Laleham Lea Catholic School is also known for and is proud of its pastoral care which was praised by the inspectors who commented that, *'The quality of the pupils' personal development is excellent'*, *'Pupils have high levels of self-understanding for their age and show notable resilience'*, *'Pupils show outstanding respect for each other and are highly inclusive'* and *'Pupils develop good relationships and demonstrate excellent social skills'*.

The Catholic life of the school was also recognised by the Inspection team who reported that, *'Pupils show excellent development of their spiritual understanding in their everyday lives'*.

Head Teacher Ms Barry said, *"I am delighted with the findings of the Inspection Report which validates the tremendous hard work of our students, Staff and Governors. We work alongside all our families and our whole community to provide an excellent education for each child in our school where children love to learn with their friends. This further builds on our Denominational Inspection report of October 2019 where Laleham Lea was also deemed to be 'Outstanding'."*

At Laleham Lea we firmly believe in putting the child at the centre of everything we do. From the warm welcome as you walk through the door in the morning to the playground where all ages play, run and socialise together as one happy family. Bright, light filled classrooms and enthusiastic, experienced teachers engage young minds' thirst for knowledge, helping each developing individual to reach their full potential and ultimately move on to the school of their choice. Our pupils become happy, confident, fulfilled young people through both academic and extra-curricular activities.

Every child takes part in team sports and every child is involved in school productions and concerts. Our greatest pleasure is to watch a once shy child blossom into the confident soloist, take a leading role in school assembly or simply help a fellow pupil through a challenging moment. A high standard of teaching and learning is central to our success. Your son or daughter will be taught in well equipped classrooms and our teachers hold specialist qualifications and have experience in specific areas of the curriculum such as Science, Modern Languages, Computer Studies (ICT), Art, Music and Sports.

Together with parents, who are the first educators, we aim to lead our children towards tolerance, understanding and sensitivity to the needs of others so that they may grow up as well balanced individuals with a strong sense of personal identity and an awareness of God's love.

Our outstanding pastoral care provides for a happy, caring community for all and we invite you to come and visit Laleham Lea; we can assure you of a very warm welcome.

Contact Mrs Edwards in the School Office to book your tour and secure your child's place for 2023 and beyond. 0208 660 3351. www.lalehamlea.co.uk

(Founded 1965)

29 Peaks Hill, Purley, Surrey CR8 3JJ UK

Tel: 020 8660 3351

Email: secretary@lalehamlea.co.uk

Website: www.lalehamlea.co.uk

Headteacher: Ms K Barry

School type:
Co-educational Day Preparatory & Nursery

Age range of pupils: 3–11 years

No. of pupils enrolled as at 01/09/2022: 131

Fees as at 01/09/2022:

Day: £9,576

Average class size: 17

St Helen's College

Nestled on the edge of Court Park in a quiet corner of Hillingdon, St. Helen's College is a family-run independent school for boys and girls aged 3 to 11, with a separate, thriving Kindergarten for boys and girls aged 2-3.

The school has a real family feel and has been described by inspectors as a 'haven of harmony'. Indeed, the most recent ISI quality inspection judged St. Helen's College outstanding, the quality of teaching excellent, the pupils' personal development outstanding and pupils' achievements, both academic and extra-curricular, excellent.

The report said: *'Pupils achieve high standards in academic work and a wide range of other activities. They are extremely successful in all aspects of learning…this is reflected in their success in entrance examinations both to maintained grammar and independent schools'.*

The school's values and ethos set it apart. Led by the Head, Shirley Drummond, staff create a harmonious, loving environment, nurture the individual qualities of every pupil and ensure that children develop a lifelong love of learning, find out where their talents and interests lie, and leave school with traditional values and strength of character, ready to face the challenges of adult life with confidence, resilience and joy!

The children enjoy lessons taught by highly qualified specialist teachers right from the start, allowing them to study at a high level led by teachers with a real passion for their subject. There is also an extremely wide-ranging and quite unique range of 70+ co-curricular activities available, with superb music, drama and sports provision and clubs including cookery, gardening, yoga, taekwondo, ceramics, dance and many, many more.

The school benefits from specialist modern facilities and is strongly rooted in its local community, enjoying links with local churches, Brunel University and local theatres.

The safe, loving, encouraging environment at St. Helen's College fosters excellent academic achievement and well-rounded, confident pupils. Inspectors noted, *'Pupils' personal development is outstanding, well supported by excellent pastoral care. The overall feeling is of a warm, friendly community where everyone knows each other and feels safe and secure'.*

St. Helen's College operates a flexible year-round extended care provision, with Breakfast Club from 7.30 a.m. and after school care until 6 p.m. daily during term time, and Holiday Club running during school holidays to assist working parents.

Parents may register children for entry to the school at 2+ (Kindergarten) or 3+ (Nursery). This is an extremely popular school and early registration is advisable. Prospective parents may register online using the online registration form or by contacting the school using the details below.

Online and in-school open mornings are held regularly. The Head, Head of Lower School and Director of Admissions are available to answer questions and take registrations at these events.

Alternatively, prospective parents may book an individual tour one morning during term time by telephoning 01895 234371 or emailing info@sthelenscollege.com.

(Founded 1924)

Parkway, Hillingdon, Uxbridge, Middlesex UB10 9JX UK

Tel: 01895 234371

Email: info@sthelenscollege.com

Website: www.sthelenscollege.com

Head: Ms Shirley Drummond BA, PGCert, MLDP, FCCT

Appointed: 2016

School type: Co-educational Day

Age range of pupils: 2–11 years

No. of pupils enrolled as at 01/09/2022: 380

Boys: 188 *Girls:* 192

Fees as at 01/09/2022:

Day: £10,560–£13,020

Average class size: 22

Teacher/pupil ratio: varies

St Catherine's School

St Catherine's is a vibrant and caring Catholic school that welcomes girls of all faiths and backgrounds. Our friendly community helps each pupil develop confidence as she explores her gifts and talents, and is inspired to meet challenges creatively. The School proudly combines excellent pastoral care with an innovative and ambitious curriculum that prepares girls for the 21st century.

Our recent excellent inspection reports from the Independent Schools Inspectorate and the Diocese of Westminster note that 'teaching at St Catherine's is more than the sum of its classroom parts...pupils have a wrap-around experience that leads them to learn exceptionally well' and that 'pupils flourish because of the secure, caring ethos of the School'. We see these features in the achievements of our girls and in their readiness to learn.

In the Prep Department, which welcomes girls from 5 to 11 years of age, an emphasis on curiosity and discovery establishes firm foundations that later lead to success in the Senior School (where each pupil has a guaranteed place). Girls enjoy a wide range of subjects and benefit from passionate and experienced teachers who know them well, offer support and challenge at all stages, and are in regular contact with parents.

The Senior School girls certainly rise to the challenges posed by public examinations. St Catherine's is proud of its value added at GCSE and A Level, and we enjoy seeing our young women go on to university courses and careers of their choice, and to bright futures.

Those who visit St Catherine's often remark on the warm and genuine enthusiasm of our pupils. The school's Christian ethos and emphasis on values helps girls to engage with the world around them, while open discussion, time for reflection, pupil-led committees and a wide range of opportunities create a lively environment where they can feel a sense of belonging. Our emphasis on character,

and on the deeper values of compassion, integrity and resilience, is also developed through a comprehensive co-curricular programme.

St Catherine's is committed to developing its facilities and over recent years we have been pleased to see girls enjoying new buildings and refurbishments, like the Science Block and Sixth Form Centre, which are designed to enhance their curriculum and social experiences. We also provide exciting trips, competitions and school events throughout the year; whether it is a trip to Iceland, regional athletics finals or a part in the latest school musical, there are plenty of opportunities for girls to develop their skills and their friendships within the school community.

Information about public examination results, co-curricular opportunities and wrap-around care can all be found on the school website: www.stcatherineschool.co.uk

ST CATHERINE'S SCHOOL
—— TWICKENHAM ——

(Founded 1914)

Cross Deep, Twickenham, Middlesex TW1 4QJ UK

Tel: 020 8891 2898

Fax: 020 8744 9629

Email: info@stcatherineschool.co.uk

Website: www.stcatherineschool.co.uk

Headmistress: Mrs Johneen McPherson MA

Appointed: September 2018

School type: Girls' Day Preparatory, Senior & Sixth Form

Age range of girls: 5–18

No. of pupils enrolled as at 01/09/2022: 434

Fees as at 01/09/2022:

Day: £13,395–£16,875

Average class size: 15-20

Teacher/pupil ratio: 1:11

Staines Preparatory School

We are a happy, welcoming and non-selective school that prides itself on creating a genuine family atmosphere alongside a first rate education. Our ethos of 'educating today's children for the challenges of tomorrow' is more than academics, we will be with you and your child every step of the way throughout their first stage of education.

The pupils at Staines Prep learn the value of commitment to successful learning, develop discipline and a sense of responsibility. This supportive and nurturing environment enables pupils to fulfil their potential and become more confident, independent lifelong learners across all areas of the curriculum and well–adjusted, global citizens.

As a school we adopt a 'Growth Mindset' culture. Growth Mindset is a programme which looks to empower pupils with the core belief that abilities, rather than being fixed, can be developed over time. Research shows that this powerful belief leads to an increased focus on learning, greater resilience, and superior achievement. The ISI inspectors were particularly impressed by the personal development of pupils, noting in their report that "pupils display high levels of self-esteem due to the nurturing environment of the school".

Our school facilities not only include inspiring classrooms but a science lab and art, design and technology suite which many senior schools would be envious of. We have a large sports hall and theatre space which all pupils take advantage of from nursery upwards. This year we have added a state of the art home economics room.

We are very proud to have been awarded the School Games Gold award which, along with our wide range of extra-curricular activities, shows our commitment to sport and promoting a healthy lifestyle for all our pupils across all year groups. Our playgrounds are full of activities that get the pupils moving and developing a Growth Mindset outside of the classroom, from a trim trail and climbing wall for the older years through to an array of playground games for the lower school and nursery.

Our Environmental Area, The Sanctuary, allows the children to bring science to life whilst learning to safely explore the great outdoors. We use Forest School principles to teach skills that can be used in the classroom and beyond, encouraging team work, responsibility and communication as well as building self-esteem and independence. The children are not limited in what they can do but instead are taught how to access and manage the risks in nature.

We understand how hard our parents work and we aim to support them by providing wraparound care from 7.30am until 6pm. We are less than 5 minutes' walk from Staines railway station, making pick-up and drop-off that little bit easier. We also operate a bus service from surrounding areas.

We are delighted to have been shortlisted for the Independent School Awards 3 years in a row, in addition to our ISI 'excellent in all areas' rating following a full inspection in 2019. We are proud to have received a Primary Quality mark accreditation for our curriculum and practice.

To come and experience the school first hand, you can arrange a private tour to fit in around your commitments or visit us at one of our popular open events which run throughout the year.

(Founded 1935)

3 Gresham Road, Staines-upon-Thames, Surrey TW18 2BT UK

Tel: 01784 450909

Email: admissions@stainesprep.co.uk

Website: www.stainesprep.co.uk

Head of School:
Ms Samantha Sawyer B.Ed (Hons), M.Ed, NPQH

Appointed: September 2014

School type:
Co-educational Day Preparatory & Nursery

Religious Denomination: Non-denominational

Age range of pupils: 3–11 years

No. of pupils enrolled as at 01/09/2022: 298

Boys: 157 **Girls:** 141

Fees as at 01/09/2022:

Day: £11,250–£13,500

Average class size: 16 (max 20)

Whitgift School

Whitgift is one of Britain's finest independent day and boarding schools, offering a friendly, vibrant and inclusive environment for 10-18-year-old boys. Our core purpose is to educate bright and talented young men to become independent learners and thinkers, to achieve beyond what they believed they could, and to leave the School ready to give back to the society in which they will be leaders.

The School offers a variety of pathways to qualifications, including the A Levels, Pre U and the International Baccalaureate, and consistently ranks as a top 15 world IB school. Alongside exceptional academic standards, the co-curricular activities feature more than 100 clubs & societies, more than 40 sports and an active Outdoor Education programme that takes students worldwide. A packed Performing Arts programme performs regularly, staging first-class musicals and plays. Orchestras and choirs play at major venues, including the Royal Albert Hall, Cadogan Hall and locally the Fairfield Halls.

The School's Boarding House, which opened in 2013, is superbly-equipped and offers full, weekly and flexi-boarding to boys aged 13-18. This option allows students to make the most of their time at Whitgift without distractions or a lengthy commute. Structured homework and free time sessions, as well as organised evening and weekend activities, ensure that boarders build a strong balance between their academic studies and their co-curricular interests. For those who live further afield, there are 12 dedicated bus routes covering routes across London, Surrey, Kent and Sussex.

Whitgift takes pride in being a diverse student body and global citizenship and digital literacy are key areas of focus for the entire school community. Pastoral support is the foundation of our provision, with each pupil and his parents guaranteed a friendly face to turn to for advice and guidance. The latest ISI Report states, "*The quality of pastoral care is outstanding... a calm courteous approach pervades the School, indicated by highly civilised and positive relationships between staff and pupils.*"

In 2020 Whitgift was awarded the title of Independent Boys' School of the Year and the judges said it was "*a compelling entry that radiated the school's inclusive and collaborative values in the context of an all-boys school.*" In 2022, Whitgift has been shortlisted for the Community and Partnership award by Independent School Parent for our work with Primary age children throughout the academic year and during Summer School.

Open Events

We encourage you to come and visit us on one of our Open Events to get a true feel for our inspiring school community.

WHITGIFT

(Founded 1596)

Haling Park, South Croydon, Surrey CR2 6YT UK

Tel: +44 20 8633 9935

Email: admissions@whitgift.co.uk

Website: www.whitgift.co.uk

Headmaster: Mr Christopher Ramsey

Appointed: September 2017

School type: Boys' Day & Boarding Senior & Sixth Form

Religious Denomination: Accepting of all faiths

Age range of boys: 10–18 years

No. of pupils enrolled as at 01/09/2022: 1550

Fees as at 01/09/2022:

Day: £22,269

Weekly Boarding: £35,973

Full Boarding: £43,629

Average class size: 20

Teacher/pupil ratio: 1:7

London

Bassett House School

Bassett House School is a traditional prep school with an innovative soul, nestled in leafy Notting Hill. Our small size means that each child is known and nurtured by every member of staff, and each is provided with an educational journey bespoke to their strengths and needs. Committed, inspirational teachers stretch pupils who are excelling as well as providing those who require extra help, the support and tools they need to achieve their goals. Continued provision after school allows pupils the freedom to stay behind to complete homework with the help of their teachers, which has proven effective in priming a positive attitude toward learning. A plethora of clubs is on offer after this time, with wrap around care available to support busy working parents.

No two days are alike and a Bassett House pupil benefits from learning across three world-class learning spaces, complete with state of the art Performing Arts Studio, library, stage and Scandinavian inspired Montessori Early Years spaces, and all within walking distance from one another. Every child spends quality time outside every day, whether that's pursuing our sustainability curriculum in our urban garden, playing in nearby Kensington 'Rocket' Memorial Park, or partaking in sports fixtures.

With the help of expert specialist teachers, pupils are encouraged in a variety of enriching learning including entrepreneurial challenges and musical performances such as Battle of the Bands. During Art lessons, pupils learn about modern and classic artists such as Damien Hirst and Van Gogh, refining their eye for detail and manipulating a wide range of media. Pupils' artwork is proudly displayed around the school and during the annual Art Exhibition. Music classes include genres covering the popular to the gothic, fine-tuning auditory and performing skills with peripatetic lessons readily available. Pupils are encouraged to express themselves freely during end of year performances –

ranging from Chitty Chitty Bang Bang to School of Rock. Teachers harness the alchemy of learning and teach a future-proof curriculum, so that pupils leave Bassett House bold and brave enough to be fearless with their dreams, in order to embark upon remarkable futures.

Residential trips are a particular highlight for Bassett children, who have recently been measuring river velocities and learning about Constable at Flatford Mill, ordering in French in a market in Normandy, and considering the Viking architecture of York (to name but a few). These experiences help to develop rounded, outward looking, tenacious pupils, which serves them well in their Senior School interviews.

Our most recent ISI report rated our outcomes as outstanding across the board, and of 16 Year 6 pupils, two thirds were awarded scholarships, with over 70 offers of a place within some of London's most superior Senior Schools.

As a member of the Dukes Education group of schools, Bassett House benefits from the sharing of best practices across the group and potential all-through schooling options. Teachers are provided with world-class Professional Development, guidance, and support from the Governing Body.

Catering for Nursery (aged 3+) to Year 6, pupils learn through our values of Courage, Compassion and Commitment. As one school leaver put it, *"At Bassett House, you learn Maths and English but more than that, you learn how to be yourself."*

Bassett House is proud to be the best small school in Notting Hill. We are small enough to be bespoke, yet big enough to thrive.

BASSETT HOUSE
SCHOOL

(Founded 1947)

60 Bassett Road, Notting Hill, London, W10 6JP UK

Tel: 020 8969 0313

Email: info@bassetths.org.uk

Website: www.bassetths.org.uk

Headmistress: Mrs Kelly Gray

School type:
Co-educational Day Preparatory & Nursery

Age range of pupils: 3–11 years

No. of pupils enrolled as at 01/09/2022: 120

Fees as at 01/09/2022:

Day: £9,954–£20,742

Average class size: 18

Teacher/pupil ratio: 1:5

City of London School
A rounded education in the Square Mile

There is no such thing as a typical CLS pupil. What characterises the education offered is a true preparation for life.

City of London School is a truly unique independent school, not least because of its unrivalled location on the banks of the Thames, between St. Paul's Cathedral and the Tate Modern. We are at the heart of the capital and our pupils benefit enormously from all that is on offer on our doorstep. Our location allows us to attract the very best outside speakers, offer top-class work shadowing placements and visit the many places of interest in this world-class city. We are a modern and forward-looking institution drawing on clever pupils from all social, economic and ethnic backgrounds and, in so doing, truly reflect the diversity of the capital in the 21st century. Pupils come from a huge number of both state primary and independent preparatory schools and, once here, receive an academic yet liberal education. Our central location allows pupils to travel to CLS from all over London, encouraging resourcefulness and self-reliance in their journey to school, and in their wider life.

Our examination results are excellent, but, more importantly, pupils leave us ready for life beyond school, with a sense of identity and an independence of thought and action which are rare among leavers from independent schools; it is significant that the vast majority of pupils go on to their first choice of university, with a large number attending Oxford and Cambridge universities, and various medical schools. Facilities are outstanding (the school moved downstream to its new buildings in 1986) and are continually updated. The state-of-the-art Winterflood Theatre and refurbished Science laboratories provide a first-rate environment in which our pupils learn and thrive. We are generously endowed with academic, music and sports scholarships and, in addition, the bursary campaign has raised significant funding for a number of full-fee places to be awarded each year to those who could not otherwise afford the fees. In this way, the school seeks to maintain the socio-economic mix which has always been its tradition and strength. Admission at 10+, 11+, 13+ and 16+ is by entrance examinations, followed by interviews for those candidates who complete their examination papers to a satisfactory standard.

For dates and to book onto one of our open days please visit our website.
Tel: 020 3680 6300
Email: admissions@cityoflondonschool.org.uk
twitter.com/@CityofLdnSchool

City of London School

(Founded 1442)

Queen Victoria Street, London, EC4V 3AL UK

Tel: 020 3680 6300

Email: admissions@cityoflondonschool.org.uk

Website: www.cityoflondonschool.org.uk

Head: Mr A R Bird MSc

Appointed: January 2018

School type: Boys' Day Senior & Sixth Form

Age range of boys: 10–18 years

No. of pupils enrolled as at 01/09/2022: 950

Sixth Form: 250

Fees as at 01/09/2022:

Day: £21,057

Devonshire House Preparatory School

Academic and leisure facilities

The school is situated in fine premises in the heart of Hampstead with its own walled grounds. The aim is to achieve high academic standards whilst developing enthusiasm and initiative throughout a wide range of interests. It is considered essential to encourage pupils to develop their own individual interests and a good sense of personal responsibility.

Curriculum

Early literacy and numeracy are very important and the traditional academic subjects form the core curriculum. The younger children all have a class teacher and classroom assistant and their day consists of a mixture of formal lessons and learning through play. Whilst children of all ages continue to have a form teacher, as they grow older an increasing part of the curriculum is delivered by subject specialists. The combined sciences form an increasingly important part of the timetable as the children mature. The use of computers is introduced from an early stage, both as its own skill and as an integrated part of the pupils' education.

Expression in all forms of communication is encouraged, with classes having lessons in art, music and drama, and French. Physical exercise and games also play a key part of the curriculum. Much encouragement is given to pupils to help widen their horizons and broaden their interests. The school fosters a sense of responsibility amongst the pupils, and individuality and personal attention for each pupil is considered essential to make progress in the modern world.

The principal areas of the National Curriculum are covered, though subjects may be taken at a higher level, or at a quicker pace. For the girls approaching the 11+ senior schools' entry examinations, special emphasis is given to the requirements for these, and in the top two years for the boys, Common Entrance curriculum is taught. The pupils achieve great success in these examinations and a number also sit successfully for senior school scholarships.

The school has its own nursery, The Oak Tree Nursery, which takes children from two-and-a-half years of age.

Entry requirements

The Oak Tree Nursery: For children entering the Oak Tree Nursery, places are offered on the basis on an informal assessment made at the nursery. Children in The Oak Tree Nursery transfer directly to the Junior School.

The Junior School: For children entering the junior school from the ages of three to five, places are offered on the basis of assessment made at the school. From the age of six, places are usually subject to a written test taken at school. At eight, children transfer directly into the upper school. Parents and their children are welcome to visit for interview and to see around the school.

The Upper School: Entry to the upper school is principally from the junior school. For pupils seeking to join the school from elsewhere places are normally subject to a written entrance test.

(Founded 1989)

2 Arkwright Road, Hampstead, London, NW3 6AE UK

Tel: 020 7435 1916

Email: enquiries@dhprep.co.uk

Website: www.devonshirehouseschool.co.uk

Headmistress: Mrs S. Piper BA(Hons)

School type:
Co-educational Day Preparatory & Nursery

Religious Denomination: Non-denominational

Age range of boys: 2.5–13 years

Age range of girls: 2.5–11 years

No. of pupils enrolled as at 01/09/2022: 543

Boys: 317 **Girls:** 226

Fees as at 01/09/2022:

Day: £9,870–£20,475

Durston House

Durston House is a leading London prep school which has a fine record of preparing boys for Senior School. Our pupils leave at 13 heading to top Independent London schools such as St Pauls, Merchant Taylors, Hampton and Harrow. Durston House places an emphasis on high standards of work and targets that are commensurate with each pupil's personal development.

We believe that it is hugely important to create an educational environment that encourages all pupils to be curious and enthusiastic about their opportunities to learn and grow. At Durston House, the manner in which this growth is guided is one of relaxed, quiet integrity of purpose, allowing boys the freedom to develop themselves. This is the essence of our ongoing success.

A boy's education here is shaped by the development of his character, his curiosity to learn and discover more, and his expanding capability. The curriculum we offer is very broad, deep and rigorous, allowing ample opportunity for boys to question and explore. Independent learning is valued and encouraged by our well-qualified staff, always keen to inspire and engage boys beyond the lesson objective. A particular interest in an idea or a subject is fostered and nurtured by teachers, who themselves are enthusiasts for learning.

In essence, here at Durston House, we are all learners, old and young; this positive interaction is supported by small class sizes, where individuality and independence can flourish. Full specialist teaching is introduced at Year 5, with some specialism occurring in specific subjects lower down the school. Boys with specific needs are offered Learning Support. Lessons are delivered in a range of ways, taking account of different learning styles and preferences, and the certainty that boys should explore and experience practically, not just from a textbook. Workshops, Outings, Trips and outdoor adventures complement the classroom experience across all year groups.

Throughout the school there is an Enrichment Programme, offering a wide range of activities from yoga, engineering, debate, chess, cooking and philosophy to name a few. The aim of the Enrichment programme is to enhance the boys' critical thinking and develop life skills. Extensive use is made of local facilities, especially for drama and swimming.

Sport is strong, with both of the school's playing field sites having floodlit, all-weather facilities; fixtures against other schools are common and there has been much sporting success in recent years.

Entry into the Reception year is in order of registration and is non-selective. For all other years, entry assessment procedures are in place. We take pride in the true and visible diversity of our community and embrace pupils and staff from all ethnic, cultural and religious backgrounds. We have built a community in which mutual respect and understanding, fairness and opportunities for all are promoted.

DURSTON HOUSE

(Founded 1886)

12-14 Castlebar Road, Ealing, London, W5 2DR UK

Tel: 020 8991 6530

Email: info@durstonhouse.org

Website: www.durstonhouse.org

Headmaster: Mr Giles Entwisle

Appointed: September 2020

School type: Boys' Day Preparatory (Co-ed from September 2023)

Age range of boys: 4–13 years

No. of pupils enrolled as at 01/09/2022: 326

Fees as at 01/09/2022:

Day: £4,470–£5,720 per term

Average class size: 10-16

Ealing Independent College

We prepare students aged 13 to 19 from the UK and worldwide for university entry through the GCSE and A level programmes, providing expert teaching, supportive individual help and guidance.

The College offers a friendly and personalised learning environment with small class sizes, where students have a strong support system in place, both through the teachers as well as their peers.

With an average class size of ten, it gives our staff the chance to fully understand each individual student – to get to know how they best make progress – and to make a bespoke learning programme for them, geared towards ensuring that they perform to the very best of their abilities.

Ealing Independent College is a wonderful place to learn and grow, supported by passionate and dedicated staff who ensure each and every student reaches their potential and leave with grades and university destinations that they could only have dreamed of. We encourage our students to develop confidence and resilience to succeed as they forge their own path in life. We aim to empower our students to make courageous decisions that are right for them.

We encourage our students to be resourceful, analysing the options in front of them and making informed decisions about choices that impact them. We teach our students to be persistent, to push through and not to settle. We are a diverse community, where everyone has the freedom to be themselves and learn from each other.

The individual is at the core of all elements that make up our unique approach to teaching and learning. As a College we are not satisfied with just teaching the curriculum; we want to help students become the best version of themselves. We want to help them celebrate and develop their individuality and to achieve their true potential.

The learning extends beyond the classrooms, with a selection of clubs and societies available to enrich and enhance the College experience.

Physical fitness activities are some of the extra-curricular activities on offer for the students. Running club and football training take place every week, as well as a "Talk Sports Club", where students can watch and discuss sports competitions and events. Other societies include Metaphysics and Folklore society, Biomedical Society, Debating Society, Engineering Society, and a Medicine and Dentistry Interview Practice weekly session.

Finally, Ealing Independent College takes pride in giving the students opportunities to lead some of the societies themselves. The student-led clubs include Student Council and the Student Magazine Committee.

It only takes a visit to fully appreciate the unique atmosphere we provide. We encourage you to book an individual visit and tour to experience the College in action, meet relevant teachers, and speak to some of our students.

83 New Broadway, Ealing, London, W5 5AL UK

Tel: 020 8579 6668

Email: admissions@ealingindependentcollege.com

Website: www.ealingindependentcollege.com

Headteacher: Allan Cairns

School type: Co-educational Day Senior & Sixth Form

Age range of pupils: 13–19 years

No. of pupils enrolled as at 01/09/2022: 96

Average class size: 10

Eaton House Belgravia

Eaton House Belgravia is an outstanding independent school and Nursery, educating boys between the ages of 2 and 11. Founded in 1897, the school has become part of the very fabric of Chelsea and Belgravia, offering a diverse and intellectually stimulating education in the heart of London. The school is notably non-selective at entry to reception. Small class sizes and an individual learning plan for each pupil ensure that each boy is stretched and supported according to their individual needs. The school is ambitious for its pupils, committed to igniting each boy's potential beyond academic excellence, into the realms of first-rate music, drama, creative arts and sport. Headmaster, Mr Huw May, is passionate about the importance of learning fluid intelligence, which is enhanced by the critical thinking taught as part of the academic timetable.

The boys benefit from an excellent network of pastoral care, in which it is emphasised not only that the staff look after the boys, but that the boys look after each other. On joining the school, new pupils are assigned an older boy to act as a 'buddy', guiding them through the start of their journey at Eaton House Belgravia. This, in addition to dedicated form teachers and an extensive wellbeing hub, ensures that every child can flourish emotionally as well as academically. Pupils are therefore well prepared to go on to their senior schools, which consistently include a range of top schools, such as St Paul's, Westminster, Dulwich College, King's College Wimbledon and Summer Fields.

Alumni that have passed through Eaton House Belgravia include many great talents, such as Sir Laurence Olivier, Eddie Redmayne OBE, Bear Grylls OBE, Anthony Asquith and Philip Pullman CBE FRSL. The schools' most important legacy, however, continues to be the many happy children who have left Eaton House Belgravia with a passion for learning. Mr May, says, *"We want all Eaton House Belgravia boys to discover a love of learning early.*

We achieve this by igniting the spark of their interest and prompting them to think about what they are learning in a wider context."

Entrance procedure

Nursery and Reception: Entrance to our Nursery and Reception is non-selective. Registration is accepted from birth and early application is advised. We welcome boys to our co-ed Nursery in the September following their second birthday. The majority of our Nursery pupils go on to attend Reception, where they are joined by those who register for 4+ entry.

Years 1 to 6: Children registered to join Eaton House Belgravia after the initial Reception entry point will be invited to visit the school for an admissions assessment before a place can be offered (subject to availability). Prospective pupils are asked to complete a formal 8+ assessment for external entry into Year 4.

EATON HOUSE BELGRAVIA

Providing an outstanding education since 1897

3-5 Eaton Gate, London, SW1W 9BA UK

Tel: 0203 917 5050

Email: admissions@eatonhouseschools.com

Website: www.eatonhouseschools.com

Headteacher: Mr Huw May

School type: Boys' Day Preparatory, Co-ed Nursery

Age range of boys: 2–11 years

Age range of girls: 2–4 years

No. of pupils enrolled as at 01/09/2022: 320

Fees as at 01/09/2022:

Reception to Year 3: £7,235 per term

Year 4 to Year 6: £8,015 per term

Average class size: 16

Eaton House The Manor Boys' School

Eaton House The Manor Boys' School is an outstanding independent school and Nursery, set opposite the leafy green stretches of Clapham Common. The school offers an academically thorough, dynamic education to boys between the ages of 2 and 13 and is notably non-selective at its reception entry point. A broad range of specialist subject teaching promotes intellectual curiosity and encourages each pupil to pursue his interests.

The school is committed to the individual learning of the boys, instilling in them an academic and social confidence that they carry through life. Eaton House The Manor has sent many generations of boys to Eton, Westminster, St. Paul's, King's College Wimbledon, Dulwich College and other top secondary schools. Pupils achieve scholarships every year, including, in 2022, academic scholarships to King's College Wimbledon and Dulwich College. A wide range of sporting and artistic opportunities are available to the boys, with extra-curricular activities making the most of the school's high-quality facilities and access to the Common.

Pupil wellbeing is incredibly important to all at Eaton House The Manor; staff prioritise the mental health of their pupils, as happy children achieve great results. The House system, dedicated form tutors, and an extensive wellbeing hub, contribute to a strong framework of pastoral care – ensuring that every child is championed and supported.

Eaton House The Manor Boys' School is located on the same extensive premises as Eaton House The Manor Girls' School, making it the ideal place for siblings to enjoy the benefits of a single sex education on one site.

In their 2022 report, the Independent Schools Inspectorate found both Eaton House The Manor Boys' School and Eaton House The Manor Girls' School to be 'excellent' in all areas, which include *"the quality of pupils' academic and other achievements"* and *"the quality of pupils' personal development"*. Headmistress, Mrs Sarah Segrave, says, *"A school is not a building, a curriculum or a timetable. Rather, it is a place where children grow intellectually and emotionally, guided by teachers who are determined that children succeed and are happy."*

Entrance procedure

Nursery and Reception: Entrance to our Nursery and Reception is non-selective. Registration is accepted from birth and early application is advised. We welcome boys to our co-ed Nursery in the September following their second birthday. The majority of our Nursery pupils go on to attend Reception, where they are joined by those who register for 4+ entry.

Years 1 to 8: Children registered to join Eaton House The Manor Boys' School after the initial Reception entry point will be invited to visit the school for an admissions assessment before a place can be offered (subject to availability). Prospective pupils are asked to complete a formal 8+ assessment for external entry into Year 4.

EATON HOUSE THE MANOR

Boys' School

58 Clapham Common North Side, London, SW4 9RU UK

Tel: 0203 917 5050

Email: admissions@eatonhouseschools.com

Website: www.eatonhouseschools.com

Head of Prep: Mrs Sarah Segrave

Head of Pre-Prep: Mr David Wingfield

School type: Boys' Day Preparatory, Co-ed Nursery

Age range of boys: 2–13 years

Age range of girls: 2–4 years

No. of pupils enrolled as at 01/09/2022: 510

Fees as at 01/09/2022:

Reception to Year 3: £6,300 per term

Year 4 to Year 8: £7,560 per term

Average class size: 20

Eaton House The Manor Girls' School

Eaton House The Manor Girls' School is an outstanding independent school and Nursery, set opposite the leafy green stretches of Clapham Common. The school offers a balanced, highly academic education to girls between the ages of 2 and 11 and is non-selective at its reception entry point. A philosophy of 'the sky is the limit learning' allows each girl to reach her fullest potential, supported by specialist subject teaching and excellent pastoral care. Consequently, pupils leave for a range of top secondary schools each year, including St Paul's Girls' School, JAGS, Alleyn's, Woldingham and Wycombe Abbey.

Academic exploration and risk-taking are two essential ingredients in Eaton House The Manor Girls' School teaching. The girls thrive in a relaxed but highly stimulating classroom environment that promotes intellectual curiosity. Beyond an excellent core curriculum of literacy and numeracy, an equal emphasis is given to the arts and STEM subjects. Each girl is also encouraged to pursue her interests through an increasingly co-curricular attitude to learning and a sophisticated range of extracurricular activities. The school's well rounded curriculum is reflected in the diversity of the record 30 scholarships won by their 30 outgoing pupils for 2022. These included Academic Art, Dance, Drama, Sport and Music scholarships.

Pupils benefits from an exceptional wellbeing network. Form tutors provide ongoing support for each girl in their care, getting to know them on an individual level, whilst new pupils are helped to settle in by their individual 'big sisters', a role that the older girls take great pride in playing. As one parent commented *"There is a lovely feeling of girl power about the place!"* (The Good Schools Guide, 2022).

Eaton House The Manor Girls' School is located on the same extensive premises as Eaton House The Manor Boys' School, making it the ideal place for siblings to enjoy the benefits of a single sex education on one site.

In their 2022 report, the Independent Schools Inspectorate found both Eaton House The Manor Girls' School and Eaton House The Manor Boys' School to be 'excellent' in all areas, which include *"the quality of pupils' academic and other achievements"* and *"the quality of pupils' personal development"*. Headmistress, Mrs Claire Fildes, says, *"I want the girls to achieve their full academic potential whilst allowing them the space to become confident and kind, ready to take the next steps on their journey as strong, impressive and independent-minded young women."*

Entrance procedure

Nursery and Reception: Entrance to our Nursery and Reception is non-selective. Registration is accepted from birth and early application is advised. We welcome girls to our co-ed Nursery in the September following their second birthday. The majority of our Nursery pupils go on to attend Reception, where they are joined by those who register for 4+ entry.

Years 1 to 6: Children registered to join Eaton House The Manor Girls' School after the initial Reception entry point will be invited to visit the school for an admissions assessment before a place can be offered (subject to availability). Prospective pupils are asked to complete a formal 8+ assessment for external entry into Year 4.

EATON HOUSE THE MANOR

Girls' School

58 Clapham Common North Side, London, SW4 9RU UK

Tel: 0203 917 5050

Email: admissions@eatonhouseschools.com

Website: www.eatonhouseschools.com

Headteacher: Mrs Claire Fildes

School type: Girls' Day Preparatory, Co-ed Nursery

Age range of boys: 2–4 years

Age range of girls: 2–11 years

No. of pupils enrolled as at 01/09/2022: 260

Fees as at 01/09/2022:

Reception to Year 3: £6,300 per term

Year 4 to Year 6: £7,360 per term

Average class size: 20

Heathside School Hampstead

Welcome to Heathside

Children come first at Heathside. We help each child find their own path to learning so they can fulfil their unique potential. The result is young people who are happy, articulate, independent, confident in their abilities and keen to find their place in the world. This is the time when your child will start to define their interests, open up their horizons and discover the educational pathway that will lead to their future. Our approach is to offer the level of academic challenge that will encourage your child to be the best they can possibly be.

Your child will receive an exceptional degree of support, so they gain confidence and grow – emotionally, socially and academically. Day by day, we will show your child the steps they need to take to get to where they want to be. Every aspect of our teaching builds their confidence, respects their progress, and acknowledges where they are before helping them go further.

English and maths are taught each morning, with additional attention given to children who benefit from a slower pace or thrive on greater challenge. From an early age, your child will learn the traditional skills of handwriting, spelling and times tables. Through art, music, STEM subjects and humanities we delve into topics, exploring them from every avenue, making our curriculum rich and rewarding.

Children thrive in a relaxed environment where they call their teachers by their first name. Working in small groups, teachers know each child extremely well so are able to provide precisely the right amount of support or challenge at precisely the right time.

For many, the right educational pathway means the traditional 11+ route to senior school. In Years 5 and 6, your child will have access to outstanding 11+ tuition, including early morning and holiday preparation classes, as well as specialist interview guidance. Outcomes for Heathside pupils are consistently high, with most Year 6 pupils gaining places at their first choice senior school in London or beyond. For others, the 13+ route is preferred, and this small group of students receive specialist support and tuition in our 'Prometheans' group. Heathside has an excellent record of achieving academic scholarships at both 11+ and 13+ including the prestigious Queens Scholarship at Westminster.

Throughout their time at Heathside, your child will have the chance to take part in a range of sporting and outdoor activities both on Hampstead Heath and in other local facilities. Our long-term relationship with Hampstead Heath enables us to capitalise on the value of outdoor play and Forest School. A recent study from Hasselt University in Belgium found that growing up in a greener urban environment boosts children's intelligence. Add to this an extensive array of after school clubs, and your child will have every opportunity to stretch themselves and broaden their interests.

HEATHSIDE SCHOOL
HAMPSTEAD

(Founded 1993)

84a Heath Street, Hampstead, London, NW3 1DN UK

Tel: +44 (0)20 3058 4011

Email: info@heathsideschoolhampstead.com

Website: www.heathsideschoolhampstead.com

Headteacher: Katherine Vintiner

Appointed: 2019

School type:
Co-educational Day Preparatory & Nursery

Age range of pupils: 2–13 years

No. of pupils enrolled as at 01/09/2022: 230

Fees as at 01/09/2022:

Day: £17,642–£19,974

Average class size: 16

ICS London

ICS London is a co-educational international day school in the heart of central London. We are one of only two IB World Schools in the city offering the full International Baccalaureate (IB) programme for learners aged 3 to 18 years.

Providing an inclusive and international community for early years, primary, secondary and high school students, our children and young people study on two close-by locations at our primary and secondary school sites in elegant Marylebone and Paddington.

Diversity

With over 40 years' experience, we are a truly international school where diversity is celebrated with around 65+ different nationalities represented each year. Our multicultural values combined with our international outlook give the school an open-minded perspective that welcomes diversity, encourages cultural connections and brings rich international influences into our classrooms.

Personalised Learning

At ICS London, we strive to create a home from home for students. It's a welcoming environment where the whole community comes together to shape students into well-rounded people.

Our family of passionate and attentive teachers take a personalised approach to learning with small class sizes and individual support that nurture and develop students. Building lessons around the specific needs of students has the advantage of identifying the potential and strengths of each student – and then creating the right environment for these talents to grow. It means we're producing well-rounded students – but also well-rounded people, who believe in the value of their abilities to contribute to the world. Having strong relationship with their teachers gives students real, personalised support throughout their time at ICS London.

Quality Assurance and Accreditation

Quality is assessed, recognised and assured at ICS London through accreditation with the:

- IB World School: ICS London is authorised and accredited by the International Baccalaureate. This is subject to a strict accreditation process monitored by the IB which ensures our education provision is of the highest quality.
- Independent Schools Inspectorate: This is a government approved inspectorate for independent schools which ensures quality on behalf of the UK Department for Education (DfE).

Key Fast Facts

ICS London also prides itself on offering a holistic and personalised learning experience:

- Class sizes: Between 6 and 18 students
- Teacher to student ratio: 1 to 5
- In Secondary School each student is assigned a mentor
- Individual study plans can be tailored to meet students' needs

Admissions Process

As a rolling admissions policy is in place, students can join anytime throughout the year. Students can also easily transfer from other curriculums, such as the UK or US and join the IB programme at ICS London.

For further information please visit www.icschool.co.uk or call +44 (0)20 7298 8800.

ICSLONDON
INTERNATIONAL SCHOOL
Shaping the world

(Founded 1979)

Early Years & Primary Campus:
7B Wyndham Place, London, W1H 1PN UK

Secondary & Diploma Campus:
21 Star Street, London W2 1QB UK

Tel: +44 (0)20 729 88800

Email: admissions@ics.uk.net

Website: www.icschool.co.uk

Head of School: David Laird

School type: Co-educational Day

Age range of pupils: 3–19 years

No. of pupils enrolled as at 01/09/2022: 175

Fees as at 01/09/2022:

Day: £19,770–£28,920

Average class size: Av 12, Max 16

Teacher/pupil ratio: 1:5

Kensington Park School

Kensington Park School is an independent, co-educational day and boarding school for students aged 11 to 18. Founded in 2017, the school prides itself on a culture which defines excellence by the individual student, not by the cohort, and which seeks, above all, to realise and release potential. Both inside and outside the classroom, KPS students are excited, challenged, and inspired to become the best possible version of themselves.

Split across two teaching sites on either side of Kensington Gardens, the Lower School (Years 7 to 11) is situated on leafy Bark Place, while the Sixth Form overlooks the Natural History Museum on Queen's Gate. Transition through KPS is not, therefore, simply 'more of the same'. As students move through the school, they are presented with exciting new opportunities and responsibilities, and given the space to develop the independence they need to become successful life-long learners, at university and beyond. The school's boarding house, located within easy reach of both school buildings in Earl's Court, gives students in Year 9 and above the opportunity to live and study in the heart of cosmopolitan central London.

An academically purposeful school, a personalised delivery is one of the core pillars of a KPS education. Small class sizes at every level ensure teaching is tailored to students' individual needs and goals, and as students begin to select their subjects for study at GCSE and A level, the timetable is structured to allow them the flexibility to pursue their academic interests, unconstrained by set option blocks. A broad and balanced 21st century curriculum, which includes Computer Science and Mandarin introduced from Year 7, means KPS students are well-prepared for the fast-paced and ever-changing world around them.

Underpinned by an integrated personal tutor and house system, an attentive and discerning system of pastoral care not only supports students, but fosters a palpable sense of community in which all students are individually known, valued, and affirmed. Tutors play a key role in building the warm relationships between student, home, and the school, maintaining regular communication with parents and guardians on their child's personal and academic development.

An extensive sport and co-curricular programme complements the academic curriculum, enabling students to become well-rounded, balanced, and resilient individuals. The school partners with a number of local facilities, such as the Porchester Centre, Will To Win, and the Old Football Pitches in Hyde Park, for activities including netball, football, swimming, rock climbing and even ice-skating. A state-of-the art theatre and creative suite offer exceptional facilities for music, drama and the arts.

A combination of academic and personal enrichment, individualised support, and outstanding pastoral care ensures KPS students achieve exceptional academic results, and every year the school's A Level graduates secure places on competitive undergraduate courses at universities including Oxford, Cambridge, and many in the Russell Group and US.

The school's selection process, which is written in-house, seeks to identify not only academic potential, but also individuals who will thrive in and contribute to the school's vibrant, diverse, and inclusive community. Academic, sport, music and art scholarships are available at 11+ and 13+, while the Kensington Scholars programme supports academically ambitious students applying to join the Sixth Form.

We welcome all prospective students and their families to join one of our Open Days, or arrange an individual visit to the School through our Admissions team.

Kensington Park
SCHOOL

KPS Lower School (Years 7 to 11):
40-44 Bark Place, Bayswater, London, W2 4AT UK

Tel: +44 (0)20 7616 4400

KPS Sixth Form:
59 Queen's Gate, South Kensington, London, SW7 5JP UK

Tel: +44 (0)20 7225 0577

Email: admissions@kps.co.uk

Website: www.kps.co.uk

Headmaster: Mr Stephen Mellor

School type:
Co-educational Day & Boarding Senior & Sixth Form

Age range of pupils: 11–18 years

Fees as at 01/09/2022:

Tuition (Years 7-11): £26,300

Tuition (Sixth Form): £27,350

Boarding (Single, Twin & Triple en-suite):
£19,000 – £30,000

Lloyd Williamson School Foundation

Introduction

The Lloyd Williamson Schools Foundation has grown in both size and reputation to become the established schools they are today. The main departments are: a Nursery, a Transition School for 5-7 year olds, a Senior School for 7-11 year olds and an Upper School for 11-16 year olds. The names Lloyd and Williamson are family names that belong to the founder. We believe they convey one of the main points of ethos at the school: that we are a family – and a strong one at that! To ensure the schools' future success, we have recently become a charitable foundation. We have an excellent reputation for strong academic standards and personalised, holistic learning for individual children. We are based in W10 in the Royal Borough of Kensington and Chelsea, with small classes to a maximum of 16 in Primary and 18 in Secondary. The schools have extended opening hours, competitive, realistic fees and all-year-round provision, including Holiday Clubs.

Mission Statement and Ethos:

- Lloyd Williamson School Foundation believes that each child is an individual.
- We create the conditions for that child to reach their own unique potential.
- Teachers build positive relationships, working with each pupil to be curious, intellectual and creative. Fear of failure is banished.
- Equality and diversity permeate the fabric of our school – we are a family where everyone belongs.
- We have small class sizes with individual, tailored teaching. Children come from a wide range of backgrounds and abilities, but they are all motivated.
- We help them develop resilience, creativity and purpose. They feel safe, creative and curious, and are not stressed by education. Happy, confident students develop a rich and positive sense of who they are and can be.

Admissions

The school is open from 8:00am-5:30pm (main school hours from 8:30am-3:30 or 4:00pm).

Parents are invited to meet the Co-Principals for a personal tour of the school during school hours in order to gain a real flavour of how the school operates on a daily basis. After that, we invite the child to join us for a day. There is no formal entrance examination, but we are looking for aptitude and a positive attitude.

As a small school, everyone knows everyone from the babies up to our oldest member of staff! We cherish individuality and self-confidence and our aim is that every child will develop an organic and strong positive sense of self. We enable this through the development of positive relationships so that all our children can learn to be strong and independent.

Contact Information

www.lws.org.uk
Admissions: admin@lws.org.uk
Main School and Nursery: 020 8962 0345

LLOYD WILLIAMSON
—— SCHOOLS ——

12 Telford Road, London, W10 5SH UK

Tel: 020 8962 0345

Email: admin@lws.org.uk

Website: www.lloydwilliamson.co.uk

Co-Principals: Ms Lucy Meyer & Mr Aaron Williams

Appointed: December 1999

School type: Co-educational Day

Age range of pupils: 4 months–16 years

Fees as at 01/09/2022:

Day: £18,000

Nursery: £100 per 10.5 hours day

Average class size: 12-16

Teacher/pupil ratio: 1:12

Newton Prep

In a London landscape crowded with prep schools, Newton Prep stands out. The school has an unbeatable combination of size and eclecticism, coupled with extraordinary facilities and outside spaces. Its position at the heart of Central London's most burgeoning development, Newton is a short walk away from the Nine Elms to Battersea riverfront. This hosts the bustling new 'town' around the rebuilt Battersea Power Station; a new extension of the Northern Line tube now means the school is within five minutes of three stations.

When arriving, visitors and prospective parents always comment on Newton Prep children: they are well-educated, of course, but noticeably curious, kind and articulate. Above all, in this modern world, they are equipped with the best of British values: pupils are encouraged to think for – and be – themselves.

Academic success is central to all that is taught. More than that, however, the school ensures children are equipped with a sense of self, resilience and hopefulness. We encourage children to think outside the curriculum. Whether it's piano lessons, judo or Boggle, children need ways of engaging: we aim for our Newton Prep children to enter adolescence feeling that they already have more to contribute than just academic achievements. Yes, we need to get them into the right schools, but not at the total expense of their well-being, character and love of learning.

Inspiring a love of learning is central to Newton Prep's offering. With a huge all-weather pitch capable of supporting four fixtures at a time, a 120-seat recital hall, a music technology suite, recording studio, 300 seat auditorium, three gymnasiums, bustling art studios, dance studios, two libraries and three hands-on science labs, children are encouraged to "do" as well as "learn". We have an oasis of a garden where our children perform Shakespeare, hunt for mini-beasts and conduct scientific experiments.

Despite the excellence of their education, Newton Prep children are notable for their lack of arrogance; there is no sense of entitlement here. The kindness and generosity shown by the pupils towards their peers is remarkable; we are particularly proud of the engagement between the older children and our youngest pupils.

This spirit of community is also built into the Newton Diploma, our revolutionary humanities curriculum for Years 7 and 8. This is a cross-curricular, rigorous and exciting programme which allows pupils to explore links between subjects, extend initiatives for service and leadership, and breathe real fire into their intellectual curiosity.

We are not a blazers-and-boaters kind of school. As a school only thirty years young, we are not limited to looking back at the past to inform what we do in the future. We focus all our present energies on ensuring a bright future for our bright children. We want Newton Prep children to enjoy their precious childhood years.

(Founded 1991)

149 Battersea Park Road, London, SW8 4BX UK

Tel: 020 7720 4091

Email: enquiries@newtonprep.co.uk

Website: www.newtonprepschool.co.uk

Headmistress: Mrs Alison Fleming BA, MA Ed, PGCE

Appointed: September 2013

School type:
Co-educational Day Preparatory & Nursery

Age range of pupils: 3–13 years

No. of pupils enrolled as at 01/09/2022: 646

Boys: 346 **Girls:** 300

Fees as at 01/09/2022:

Day: £10,575–£22,395

Average class size: 19 (smaller in Years 7 & 8)

Norfolk House School

A small school with a big, beating heart.

Norfolk House School and Nursery is a leading London preparatory school for boys and girls aged 2-11. Our Nursery is located in a beautifully converted three-storey Victorian house in Princes Avenue, Muswell Hill. In Form 2, our pupils move from our Princes Avenue PrePrep site into the Junior Prep department in our school on Muswell Avenue and join our Form 3 pupils.

We are proud of the outstanding quality of education and pastoral care programmes for our children. The school takes great pride in its happy and warm environment, where each pupil is valued and supported. Pupils at Norfolk House are nurtured and guided through school life; we aim to stimulate and inspire our children, develop their interests and equip them with lifelong learning skills.

Our latest school inspection said that *"exceptionally positive attitudes to learning are evident across the school."* It went on to state that *"the quality of the pupils' academic and other achievements is excellent"* and that our *"pupils are exceptionally well prepared for the next stage of their education"* at the end of their time at Norfolk House.

We are committed to ensuring that your child thrives, enjoys school to the fullest, and realises their potential. Their experience at Norfolk House, from the small class sizes to the highly personalised learning provision, has been carefully curated to nurture and grow the unique person within.

At Norfolk House, we view academic excellence and personal growth not as competing priorities but as profoundly interdependent outcomes of quality education. A glance at our leavers' destinations demonstrates that London's leading senior schools consistently see the contribution and potential that Norfolk House pupils offer.

Though the prospect may seem distant now, we know that our pupils today will become the adult role models of tomorrow. To equip them for the fast-changing world in which they will grow up is a duty in which we take great pride. Our future-facing curriculum and time-tested values support pupils to develop into flourishing individuals, developing both self-efficacy and a life-long curiosity about the world and those with whom they share it.

Junior Prep & Senior Prep:
10 Muswell Avenue, Muswell Hill, London, N10 2EG UK

Tel: +44 (0)2088 834584

Nursery and Pre Prep:
5 Princes Avenue, Muswell Hill, London, N10 3LS UK

Tel: +44 (0)2084 444399

Email: office@norfolkhouseschool.org

Website: www.norfolkhouseschool.org

Headteacher: Mr Tej Lander

Appointed: September 2022

School type:
Co-educational Day Preparatory & Nursery

Age range of pupils: 2–11 years

North Bridge House

North Bridge House (NBH) prides itself on its impressive results and academically non-selective co-education, challenging and inspiring pupils throughout every stage of their school career. With specialist expertise at the Early Years Foundation Stage all the way through to A Level, we are on a constant journey of getting to know every learner as a unique individual, helping them to find and realise their true academic and personal potential.

Celebrating results well above the national average, the Nursery and Pre-Prep Schools develop the fundamental skills upon which pupils' future successes are built. The nurturing environment combined with a broad and forward-thinking curriculum allows children to develop a genuine love of learning without the added pressure of entrance exams; pupils automatically progress to NBH Prep School at 7+. As well as specialist teaching in French, Italian, music and sport, progress-enhancing initatives such as Philosophy for Children and Forest School promote children's all-important social and emotional development.

NBH Prep School excellently prepares happy, confident pupils for entry to the UK's leading senior schools – often with prestigious scholarship places. Pupils are taught entirely by subject specialists from Year 5, benefiting from an outstanding academic and co-curricular offering that encompasses everything from PPE to the Arts. Celebrating top results in the various 11+, Consortium, Common Pre-Test and Common Entrance examinations, while providing highly sought-after entry to our own Senior School campuses, NBH Prep individually prepares pupils for the school best suited to their talents and interests – bespoke preparation for every path to success.

Preparing pupils for university and the world of work with unrivalled UCAS and careers support, NBH Senior Schools continue to build on their highly successful track records, progressing students to top Russell Group and Oxbridge destinations. 2022 saw 54% of all GCSE grades awarded at 7+, with NBH Senior Canonbury scoring 67% A*-B grades at A Level. The expert teaching teams harness research into teen development and learning patterns to further understand and maximize pupils' potential. For example, using evidence-based research, we have implemented a later (midweek) start time for teens, which reflects current findings regarding the teenage brain and sleeping patterns, and continue to work with the Institute of Education on developing metacognition in our students.

PE is essential to our school group's offering and our prime north London location sees us benefit from the best facilities for track and field, outdoor adventure, and water sports. From Bushcraft to the DofE Award, there is also a busy schedule of enrichment activities and school trips, all centred around our aim to cultivate character and promote wellbeing. This, together with our outstanding pastoral support, sees our students leave as articulate, confident, determined young people, proud to be themselves.

School locations:
North Bridge House Nursery School
33 Fitzjohn's Avenue, Hampstead, London NW3 5JY
North Bridge House Pre-Prep School
8 Netherhall Gardens, Hampstead, London NW3 5RR
North Bridge House Nursery & Pre-Prep West Hampstead
85-87 Fordwych Road, West Hampstead, London NW2 3TL
North Bridge House Prep School
1 Gloucester Avenue, Regent's Park, London NW1 7AB
North Bridge House Senior Hampstead
65 Rosslyn Hill, Hampstead, London NW3 5UD
North Bridge House Senior & Sixth Form Canonbury
6-9 Canonbury Place, Islington, London N1 2NQ

North Bridge House

(Founded 1939)
65 Rosslyn Hill, London, NW3 5UD UK
Tel: 020 7428 1520
Email: admissionsenquiries@northbridgehouse.com
Website: www.northbridgehouse.com
Executive Headteacher: Mr Brendan Pavey
Head of Nursery School: Mrs Nishi Kapoor
Head of Pre-Prep School: Ms Michelle Blaber
Head of Nursery & Pre-Prep West Hampstead: Mrs Eilish Sleator
Head of Prep School: Mr Tom Le Tissier
Head of Senior Hampstead: Mr Christopher Jones
Head of Senior Canonbury: Mrs Charlotte Tassell-Dent
School type: Co-educational Day Preparatory & Senior, Nursery & Sixth Form
Age range of pupils: 2–18 years
No. of pupils enrolled as at 01/09/2022: 1400
Fees as at 01/09/2022:
Day: £8,676–£23,148
Average class size: 20

Orchard House School

All children can learn to thrive, regardless of early learning ability. At Orchard House School, we believe tailor-made teaching opens young minds to endless possibilities, encouraging them to think creatively and form their own ideas. In addition to guiding pupils to high academic achievement, our programme of learning celebrates personal strengths, builds confidence from an early age and recognises the importance of self-esteem, self discipline and sensitivity to others. Our pupils mostly call it having fun. We call it; being the best they can be.

Complementing our outstanding teaching, the school is equipped with an abundance of specialist teaching facilities which has resulted in a number of awards in recent years, including; the NAACE Mark for excellence in Education Technology, and the TES Independent Schools Award for Sport. Music and Drama play a key role at Orchard House, with pupils of all ages participating in drama and musical productions, clubs, concerts, and assemblies. Specialist coaching and teaching in Sport and Music are available to all, not just to the sporting or musical 'elite'. Our Sports facilities at Rocks Lane feature football, cricket, rugby and hockey pitches, netball courts, all-weather pitches for lacrosse and a sports field for athletics and Sports Days. Our pupils benefit from nearby access to swimming facilities to ensure the breadth of sporting activities are offered.

While our school is renowned for academic excellence, pastoral care comes first. Children blossom when they feel secure, happy, and valued. No child has any doubt that teachers will lend a safe and sympathetic ear to their issues. Each child has a Pupil Pastoral Care Plan where they can note any private worries so that teachers may monitor their happiness and well-being, and our buddy system helps newcomers through their early days.

The school's House system encourages teamwork and a competitive spirit, allowing children to celebrate their own success as well as the achievements of others.

Our Year 6 pupils are uniquely prepared for entrance to a senior school which is best suited to their abilities, character and interests. We prepare children for senior school life, of which the 11+ assessments are just one part. As part of their preparation, parents and pupils will attend Senior School Open Days, have individual meetings with the Form teachers and Deputy Head to discuss choices and meet with the Headteacher about all options. Our children also benefit from priority entry into Dukes Education senior schools: Hampton Court House, Eaton Square Senior and from September 2023, Kneller Hall in Twickenham.

Exciting times lie ahead for Orchard House School. Plans are in motion for a multimillion pound redevelopment, in partnership with neighbouring Chiswick & Bedford Park Preparatory School. In 2023, the nurseries will come together, and from 2024 a new combined school will come into existence under the Orchard House name. This new school will benefit from a full refurbishment of all three school sites as well as additional specialist teaching space in the form of a new Science, Technology and Computing Centre, additional spaces for Art, Music and Drama, a fuller timetable of enrichment and clubs, and expert subject teaching. As a thriving three form entry school, all of our children in the lower school will benefit from a full time teaching assistant and throughout the school there will be specialist teaching staff across the curriculum, ensuring academic excellence alongside outstanding pastoral care. This investment from Dukes Education will put Orchard House School squarely on the map as one of London's premier preparatory schools.

ORCHARD
HOUSE SCHOOL

(Founded 1993)

16 Newton Grove, Bedford Park, London, W4 1LB UK

Tel: 020 8742 8544

Email: info@orchardhs.org.uk

Website: www.orchardhs.org.uk

Headmaster: Mr Kit Thompson

Appointed: September 2021

School type:
Co-educational Day Preparatory & Nursery

Age range of pupils: 3–11 years

No. of pupils enrolled as at 01/09/2022: 273

Fees as at 01/09/2022:

Day: £10,158–£21,159

Average class size: 21

Teacher/pupil ratio: 1:7

Prospect House School

At Prospect House School, we focus on making each child feel valued and secure and on making their educational experience both challenging and fun. This allows us to develop every child to their fullest potential, as our outstanding results demonstrate. Our school was inspected by the ISI in February 2022 and we are thrilled to say that we have been judged as excellent in all areas, the highest possible achievement.

Prospect House's superb teachers provide a supportive and encouraging academic environment in which children excel. The sound of laughter is never far away, as Prospect House children discover their aptitude for sport, music, art, computing, drama or a whole host of other opportunities both within the curriculum or before or after school. Whether taking up the trombone, building a go-cart or orienteering on Putney Heath, our children relish each new challenge and emerge better able to face the next challenge that comes their way.

Music is an important part of life at Prospect House. We have over 200 individual music lessons taking place each week and a school orchestra, chamber choir and senior and junior choirs, as well as a number of ensembles. All children act in assemblies, school plays, musical productions and concerts throughout the year. Children in Years 1 to 6 enjoy drama lessons and our high-quality staging, lighting, sound and props give every production a professional feel.

Physical activity promotes wellbeing, so we offer a busy sports programme. This includes football, netball, hockey, running, cross country, athletics, cricket, swimming, dance and gymnastics. Our approach to fixtures and tournaments successfully balances participation for everyone with letting our sports stars shine.

Residential trips thrill the children with the sense of adventure, encouraging risk-taking and building self-reliance, whether on a history expedition, a bushcraft adventure, a week in the Isle of Wight engaging in a wide range of adventure activities or a week in Poole filled with sun, sea, sand and a whole lot of watersports.

We encourage our children to think for themselves, to be confident and to develop a sense of responsibility for the world in which they live. By the time they leave us aged 11, Prospect House children are ready to thrive at London's best senior schools. This is reflected in our impressive 11+ results. Every year, a notable proportion of our children win scholarships to leading senior schools.

Prospect House School is proudly non-selective. True to our belief, children are not tested and judged at the tender age of 3 or 4 years. Our stellar results repeatedly show all children can fulfil their potential, regardless of early learning ability. We encourage our high-flyers to soar, whilst children who need a little extra help are given the support they need to reach their fullest potential. At Prospect House, every child is helped to achieve a personal best.

PROSPECT HOUSE
SCHOOL

(Founded 1991)

75 Putney Hill, London, SW15 3NT UK

Tel: 020 8246 4897

Email: info@prospecths.org.uk

Website: www.prospecths.org.uk

Headmaster: Mr Michael Hodge BPED(Rhodes) QTS

Appointed: September 2017

School type:
Co-educational Day Preparatory & Nursery

Age range of pupils: 3–11 years

No. of pupils enrolled as at 01/09/2022: 310

Fees as at 01/09/2022:

Day: £9,954–£20,742

Average class size: 20

Teacher/pupil ratio: 1:7

Queen's Gate School

Queen's Gate School is an independent day school for girls between the ages of 4 and 18 years. In 2021, we celebrated our 130th anniversary, having been founded in 1891. The school is an Educational Trust, situated in five large Victorian Houses within easy walking distance of Kensington Gardens, Hyde Park, South Kensington and Gloucester Road tube stations and the South Kensington museums.

The School offers an education for life in a challenging environment where sound values and individuality are nurtured within a supportive atmosphere. Our aim is to create a secure, happy, yet stimulating environment in which each girl can realise her academic and personal potential and make full use of individual interests and talents. We encourage the development of self-discipline and create an atmosphere where freedom of thought and ideas can flourish.

The Principal, Miss Amy Wallace, joined Queen's Gate in September 2022 and continues to build on the existing strengths of the School, whilst enabling girls to enjoy new opportunities in and out of the classroom.

In the Senior School, girls follow as wide a curriculum as possible and generally take GCSEs in ten subjects that must include English, Mathematics, at least one science and a modern language. A full range of A Level subjects is offered. In the Lower Sixth girls normally take three/four subjects and in addition many complete the Extended Project Qualification (EPQ). The girls are offered excellent careers advice to assist in their UCAS and US applications.

Sport is highly valued at Queen's Gate with two compulsory sessions for all girls each week. A whole range of sports are available during the School day including netball, athletics, basketball, hockey, fencing, swimming, rowing, cross-country, biathlon and dance. Girls achieve much success, with some earning national and international status.

Co-curricular activities at Queen's Gate see girls taking part in Model United Nations conferences throughout the year, become part of clubs including the horticultural society, STEM club and Cosmetics club and experience trips around the UK and abroad to enhance their learning experience.

Music plays a large role in the School life, with concerts and recitals throughout the School year both in and out of school, and Drama productions across both the Junior and Senior schools see girls performing at venues including RADA Studios and the Chelsea Theatre.

The Junior School is situated just a few yards down the road from the Senior School at 125 and 126 Queen's Gate. The beautifully restored buildings boast spacious form rooms, three fully equipped laboratories, a state-of-the-art STEAM (Science, Technology, Engineering, Art and Mathematics) Room and an elegant Assembly Hall. Junior pupils also use Senior School facilities and benefit from specialist subject teaching from Senior School staff. Senior girls often visit the Junior School to assist with activities, thus reinforcing the continuity of education from 4-18 available at the School.

Admission is by test and interview in the Junior School. Entrance to the Senior School is by the London 11+ Consortium entrance examination. Applicants for the Sixth Form must achieve six GCSEs at Grade 7 or above with Grade 8 or 9 (or their equivalent) required in those subjects they wish to pursue at A Level.

In addition to the Open Events in the Senior and Junior Schools throughout the year, parents are always welcome to make a private visit to see the schools at work. Appointments can be made by contacting the Registrar on 0207 594 4982 or by email registrar@queensgate.org.uk.

(Founded 1891)

133 Queen's Gate, London, SW7 5LE UK

Tel: 020 7589 3587

Email: registrar@queensgate.org.uk

Website: www.queensgate.org.uk

Principal:
Miss Amy Wallace MA MPhil (Cantab), PGCE (Oxon)

Appointed: September 2022

School type: Girls' Day & Sixth Form

Age range of girls: 4–18 years

No. of pupils enrolled as at 01/09/2022: 500

Sixth Form: 81

Junior School: 116

Senior School: 384

Fees as at 01/09/2022:

Junior School: £21,285

Senior School & Sixth Form: £23,580

Average class size: 23

Teacher/pupil ratio: 1:10

Rosemary Works Independent School

Rosemary Works School is a non-selective independent co-educational primary school, with a pre-school nursery class, taking children from the age of 3 to 11 years old.

Our key aims are Challenge, Innovate and Nurture. We provide an aspirational and inspirational education to our pupils, in an environment of warmth and security. We have a strongly nurturing ethos that runs through everything that we do, and the personal development of our pupils is excellent. At the core of Rosemary Works School is the belief that primary school should be a place of happiness and safety, where children are eager to learn and have the space to thrive.

Our curriculum is innovative and exciting, and our skilled teachers are dedicated to finding the 'superpower' inside every one of our pupils. We provide a broad indoor and outdoor curriculum, designed to inspire our pupils with a life-long love of learning. We provide pupils with the skills that will enable them to embrace confidently the opportunities and challenges that life will bring to them. Modern foreign language, music, and Forest School are taught by subject specialists, and our pupils benefit from weekly swimming lessons in the nearby sports centre.

Working alongside our subject specialists, our Headteacher strives to ensure that each child is regarded as an individual, and that lesson plans are developed meticulously to ensure each child's particular educational needs are fulfilled, whether they require additional support in order to master a tricky concept, or they require more challenging work to meet the potential of their ability.

Our Headteacher works personally with each of our families to ensure that pupils are guided in their journeys to the secondary schools of their choice, and are supported with exam prep, mock interviews, and booster clubs.

We provide wraparound care for our children, 49 weeks a year. Our extra-curricular clubs and holiday play-schemes offer an array of activities to enrich the pupils' experience at Rosemary Works. These include musical instrument tuition, arts and crafts, sports, performing arts, and an array of outings.

We are based on the border of Islington and Hackney, alongside the Regent's Canal. We occupy a bright 2-story building, with two playgrounds, a ball pitch, and garden. We are just a couple of minutes' walk from the new Britannia Leisure Centre, Shoreditch Park and Rosemary Gardens, and we make good use of the sporting facilities that they provide. Our proximity to the City and the centre of London gives us excellent access to a vast array of institutions, such as The Royal Institution, London Zoo, and the many museums and arts centres that provide excellent programmes designed for schools.

1 Branch Place, London, N1 5PH UK

Tel: 02077 393950

Email: info@rosemaryworks.com

Website: www.rosemaryworks.com

Headteacher: Ms Amanda Parker NPQH, MPhil

School type:
Co-educational Day Preparatory & Nursery

Age range of pupils: 3–11 years

St Paul's Cathedral School

Governed by the Dean and Chapter and seven lay governors, the original residential choir school, which can date its history back to the 12th century, has, since the 1980s, included non-chorister day boys and girls aged 4-13. The number of pupils is currently 260.

In its 2017 inspection, the ISI awarded the School its highest accolade of 'Excellent' in both educational attainment and pupil progress.

A broad curriculum prepares all pupils for 11+ and 13+ examinations including scholarship and Common Entrance examinations. The school has an excellent record in placing pupils in outstanding senior schools, many with scholarships. With its unique and central location, the school is able to make the most of what London can offer culturally and artistically in particular. A wide variety of sports and musical instrument tuition is offered: the school has an exceptional record in preparing pupils for ABRSM exams. Choristers receive an outstanding choral training as members of the renowned St Paul's Cathedral Choir.

The life of the school is based on the following aims and principles:

St Paul's Cathedral School is a Christian, co-educational community which holds to the values of love, justice, tolerance, respect, honesty, service and trust in its life and practice, to promote positive relationships throughout the school community and where the safety, welfare and emotional well-being of each child is of the utmost importance.

The school aims to instil a love of learning through a broad curriculum. It aims to give each pupil the opportunity to develop intellectually, socially, personally, physically, culturally and spiritually. All pupils are encouraged to work to the best of their ability and to achieve standards of excellence in all of their endeavours.

Through the corporate life of the school, and through good pastoral care, the school encourages the independence of the individual as well as mutual responsibility. It aims to make its pupils aware of the wider community, espouses the democratic process and encourages a close working relationship with parents and guardians.

Facilities: the school is situated on one site to the east of St Paul's Cathedral. It has a separate Pre-Prep department, excellent Science lab and ICT room. It has two outside play areas and a hall.

Entry is at 4+ and 7+ years. 4+ entry is held in the November preceding the September a child will enter the school and 7+ entry is held in the January preceding the September a child will enter the school. At 7+, pupils are given a short test and spend a day in school. Chorister voice trials are held throughout the year for boys between 6 and 8 years old. Occasional places in other year groups sometimes become available and, at 11+, the school now offers scholarship awards in music, the arts, sport and academics. Further information can be found on the school's website www.spcslondon.com

St Paul's Cathedral School is a registered charity (No. 312718), which exists to provide education for the choristers of St Paul's Cathedral and for children living in the local area.

ST PAUL'S CATHEDRAL SCHOOL

(Founded 12th Century or earlier)

2 New Change, London, EC4M 9AD UK

Tel: 020 7248 5156

Fax: 020 7329 6568

Email: admissions@spcs.london.sch.uk

Website: www.spcslondon.com

Headmaster: Simon Larter-Evans BA (Hons), PGCE, FRSA

Appointed: September 2016

School type: Co-educational Pre-Prep, Day Prep & Boarding Choir School

Religious Denomination:
Church of England, admits pupils of all faiths

Age range of pupils: 4–13 years

No. of pupils enrolled as at 01/09/2022: 270

Fees as at 01/09/2022:

Day: £5,348–£5,759 per term

Full Boarding: £3,235 per term

Average class size: 15-20

Teacher/pupil ratio: 1:10

The Hampshire School, Chelsea

The Hampshire School, Chelsea, London, is an independent school for boys and girls aged 3-11. Sheltered beneath the architectural grandeur of the former Chelsea Public Library, this historic setting just off King's Road, with its expansive library, plays host to an enviable amount of space, with a desirable play area and impressive climbing structure.

As you walk through the halls of The Hampshire School, you will grasp how academically rigorous and community-focused the school is, with brilliant pupil work on display, in all subjects, where children are free to flourish at their own pace.

This September, after being awarded an ISI Inspection of the highest honour, the Hampshire School has been fortunate enough to appoint new Head, Richard Lock. Richard is ambitious about the future of the school. With a focus on providing high-quality teaching and learning, outstanding co-curricular provision and raising ambition for each child at every stage.

Richard comments: *"It is wonderful to take the reins of a particularly wonderous school. Aim high (our school motto) is a fundamental element of the broad and rigorous academic curriculum at the Hampshire School. I look forward to leading the school forward over the coming years"*

The Hampshire School Chelsea is a school with unparalleled joy, with children seizing their opportunities to be recognised for achievements, whether on the stage, on the sports field, in lessons or more. The school boasts brilliant facilities, with specialist science lessons in the extensively resourced science laboratory. The school also has a purpose-built Music and Drama room, fittingly named after the founders of the School known as 'The Anne and Susan Hampshire Music and Drama room' with their distinguished careers in the performing arts.

At The Hampshire School, we want children to flourish, that's why we offer extracurricular clubs, allowing pupils to further their talents, learn hidden skills and develop themselves in the school setting. We also provide wrap-around care to give parents extra flexibility with their child's provision.

The Hampshire School
CHELSEA

15 Manresa Road, Chelsea, London, SW3 6NB UK

Tel: +44 (0)2073 527077

Email: info@thehampshireschoolchelsea.co.uk

Website: www.thehampshireschoolchelsea.co.uk

Headteacher: Mr Richard Lock

Appointed: September 2022

School type:
Co-educational Day Preparatory & Nursery

Age range of pupils: 3–11 years

The Merlin School

Choosing a school for your child at the age of four is an important decision providing a significant first opportunity to inspire a little learner and prepare them for the next stage of their education. At Merlin we specialise in these precious early years. The Merlin, established in 1986, is a creative and nurturing co-educational pre-prep which does not assess on entry. You'll find us in the heart of Putney, in a beautiful Victorian house. We offer a warm and homely atmosphere where all staff take time to engage with our children, supporting the development of their independence and confidence. There is a vibrant buzz about the school, where the children thrive as part of a caring community. Corridors and classrooms teem with life and practical activities enhance learning and stimulate pupils' imagination.

Our school motto is 'have a go', and we aim to evoke a thirst for learning, encouraging curiosity in the world around us. Whilst Maths and English underpin our syllabus, we pride ourselves on the depth and breadth of our curriculum. We believe in the importance of delivering a range of subjects and experiences, providing children with crucial and exciting opportunities and encouraging a love of learning.

Each term, a new topic is taught and many aspects of History, Geography, Art/Design & Technology are woven together under that chosen theme. This cross-curricular approach to teaching puts learning into context and encourages the children to make connections; it captures the children's imagination, fires their enthusiasm, and inspires them to want to learn. A wander around our classrooms will take you on a journey through various topics from Gods and Monsters to The Seven Wonders of The World.

Over half of our timetable is taught by specialist teachers including Science, Drama, Music, Computing, French and PE/Games with both our Deputy and Head being actively involved in the teaching of all year groups. Pupils relish the challenge of their first formal sports lessons, learning about teamwork and sportsmanship alongside the specific sports skills, gearing them up to find their own sporting pathway. Our children bounce into Science lessons wondering what practical activity awaits, they master the skills of thinking and creating in Computing lessons, and build confidence through giving presentations and taking part in assemblies and innovative drama productions.

At the end of their school journey with us, we send our children off to their next schools with the confidence to build new relationships, the enthusiasm to learn, instilled with a positive attitude towards new challenges. Despite being a non-selective school, Merlin children make excellent progress from their individual starting points, and go on to a range of prestigious schools.

Please do book on to one of our school tours to see for yourself – we look forward to welcoming you!

(Founded 1986)

4 Carlton Drive, London, SW15 2BZ UK

Tel: 020 8788 2769

Email: admissionenquiries@merlinschool.net

Website: www.merlinschool.net

Headteacher: Miss Violet McConville

Appointed: September 2021

Principal: Mrs Kate Prest

School type: Co-educational Day Pre-Preparatory

Age range of pupils: 4–8 years

No. of pupils enrolled as at 01/09/2022: 130

Fees as at 01/09/2022:

Day: £5,510 (Inclusive)

Average class size: 15

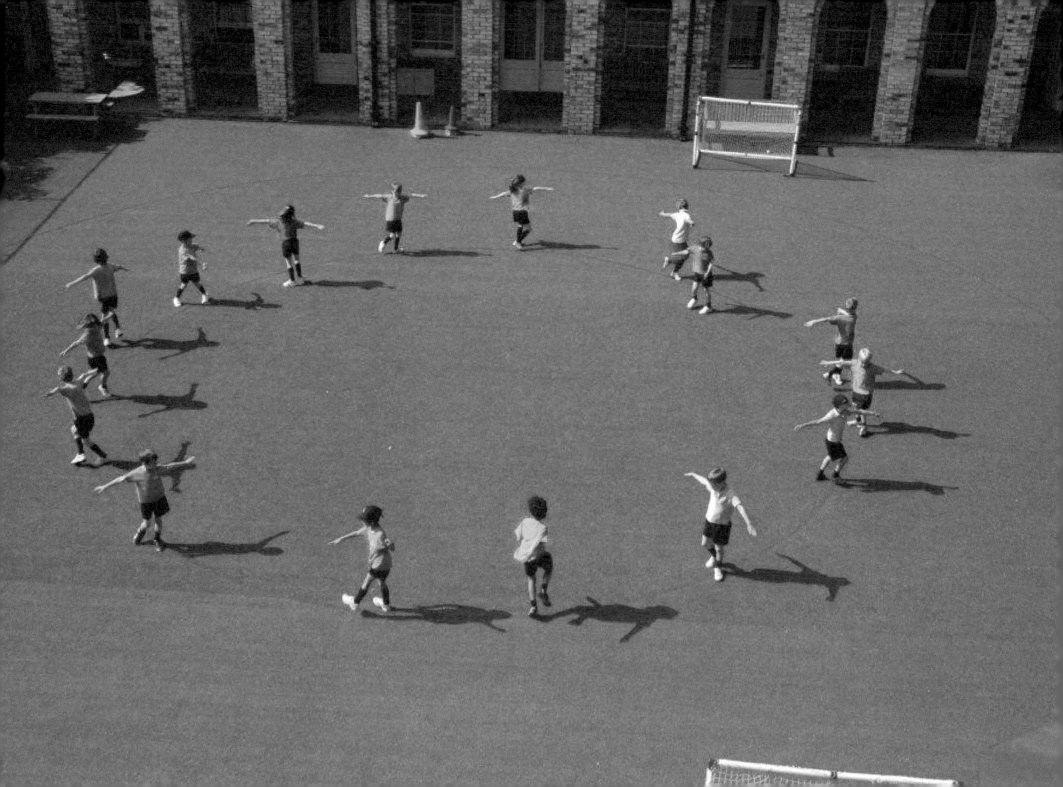

Ursuline Preparatory School

Ursuline Preparatory School is a Roman Catholic school that welcomes children of all faiths and none. Non-selective by choice, the school offers a values-driven, academic education to girls from 3-11 years of age and to boys in the Nursery class.

Established in 1892 to promote the values of St Angela Merici OSU, Ursuline Preparatory School places equal value on the education of heart, mind and soul in the certain knowledge that only through the equal development of all three can a child truly excel. The school's mission is to develop a community that lives each day working together (Insieme) and united in harmony, valuing the contributions of all and championing the virtues of love, compassion, kindness and generosity. The children are encouraged to be grateful for the gifts they have been given and to develop these gifts to the full, in generous service to others. The school seeks to pass on the living and faith-filled tradition of Jesus Christ by having unswerving faith in every single one of our pupils and by encouraging them, in turn, to have faith and hope in others. A keen focus is to educate and create future leaders in the spirit of Serviam (I will serve), keeping justice at the centre of their lives.

The core provision of this school is three-fold:

* A strong Ursuline ethos;

* An academic provision, whether in the classroom or online, that prepares children fully for secondary school;

* A strong partnership between pupils, parents and staff.

Our children enjoy a rich diversity of experiences, both inside and outside of the classroom. Our 11+ preparation curriculum, full sporting programme, and developed range of extra-curricular activities, provides an enriching and engaging provision.

The girls at Ursuline Preparatory School follow an academic curriculum and are fully supported, securing places in their senior school of choice. As a result of the Ursuline ethos, and the academic preparation put in place, the girls here can face the 11+ process with confidence. Last year girls received offers from the following schools: City of London, Claremont Fan Court, Emanuel, Guildford High School, Kingston Grammar, Lady Eleanor Holles, Marymount, Notre Dame, Putney High, Surbiton High, Sutton High, St John's Leatherhead, St Paul's Girls School, Ursuline High School and Wimbledon High.

While we are a non-selective school our girls exceed expectations at 11+ with many scholarships offered.

An Ursuline education seeks to help the young people here grow and flourish in an environment in which every child is loved and valued. On such sure foundations, we help them become the very best that they can be. Please do come and visit; you will be made most welcome.

(Founded 1892)

18 The Downs, Wimbledon, London, SW20 8HR UK

Tel: 020 8947 0859

Email: headteachersoffice@ursulineprep.org

Website: www.ursulineprep.org

Head Teacher: Mrs Caroline Molina BA (Hons)

Appointed: January 2020

School type: Girls' Day Preparatory, Co-ed Nursery

Religious Denomination: Roman Catholic

Age range of boys: 3–4 years

Age range of girls: 3–11 years

No. of pupils enrolled as at 01/09/2022: 145

Fees as at 01/09/2022:

Nursery Mornings: £2,625 per term

Nursery – Year 6 Full Time: £4,275 per term

Average class size: 18

Teacher/pupil ratio: 1:5

Wandsworth Preparatory School

We work hard. We dream big. We achieve the extraordinary
Wandsworth Preparatory School is a co-educational independent day school for children aged 4-11. Part of the Bellevue Education group of schools, Wandsworth Prep is a school that provides an outstanding educational environment, with a broad and exciting curriculum that stimulates imagination, encourages independent learning and provides pupils with the tools to thrive.

Wandsworth Prep treats every pupil as an individual, helping each child to discover their unique talents and build their confidence in learning. Our pupils benefit from a first-class holistic education built on vital pastoral care rooted in academic excellence. Our creative curriculum brings learning to life through our engaging, thematic approach. Lessons are interactive and full of memorable experiences that inspire a love of learning, encourage curiosity, and promote independence and collaborative learning skills.

We provide classes from Reception to year 6, giving our children solid foundations for learning, with the curriculum carefully designed to ensure that each child can fulfil their individual potential. Our curriculum is challenging, diverse and engaging. We are proud of our excellent academic results, with each child reaching their goal and enabling them to attend the best schools in the area.

This term, we welcome our new Head, Laura Nike. Formerly Head of Prep at the Old Palace School based in Croydon, Laura brings experience, educational vision and exceptional commitment to high-quality, academically rigorous teaching and learning to the role. Laura comments: *"The strong sense of shared values within the school community allows the children here to thrive with confidence in an academic setting. Our high calibre specialist teachers enable the pupils to achieve the highest outcomes in all areas of the curriculum. Every child in our school is known and seen for who they are, and we draw alongside each child to nurture their talents, ambitions and interests."*

WANDSWORTH PREPARATORY SCHOOL

The Old Library, 2 Allfarthing Lane, London, SW18 2PQ UK

Tel: +44 (0)2088 704133

Email: office@wandsworthprep.com

Website: www.wandsworthprep.com

Headteacher: Ms Laura Nike

Appointed: September 2022

School type: Co-educational Day Preparatory

Age range of pupils: 4–11 years

North-East

Barnard Castle School

Barnard Castle School is a leading independent day and boarding school set amid stunning countryside in Northern England.

'Barney', as it is affectionately known, provides an exceptional all-round education, with a broad and balanced curriculum, first class facilities and excellent pastoral care within a happy, family environment for boys and girls aged between 4 and 18.

Through creating an inspirational, compassionate and unpretentious environment, the School develops young adults with character, where each child is nurtured and encouraged to develop their full potential.

'Barnardians' are happy, confident, resilient, intellectually curious, tolerant and driven, with an undercurrent of humility, who are ready and prepared to face, embrace and lead in an ever-changing world.

Barnard Castle School's ethos of openness means that it welcomes parents, former pupils and friends of Barney to join its community, and encourages families to visit and experience for themselves the welcoming and happy atmosphere.

Situated in an excellent rural environment, Barnard Castle School is well served by a range of transport links, with several airports and railway stations close by.

Furthermore, Barney has educated many notable former students (known as 'Old Barnardians'), counting professional athletes, television personalities as well as entrepreneurs and business leaders among its alumni.

BARNARD CASTLE SCHOOL

(Founded 1883)

Barnard Castle, Durham DL12 8UN UK

Tel: +44 (0)1833 696030

Email: admissions@barneyschool.org.uk

Website: www.barnardcastleschool.org.uk

Headmaster: Mr Tony Jackson

Appointed: March 2017

School type: Co-educational Day & Boarding Preparatory, Senior & Sixth Form

Age range of pupils: 4–18 years

No. of pupils enrolled as at 01/09/2022: 736

Fees as at 01/09/2022:

Day: £7,626–£15,498

Full Boarding: £22,362–£31,659

Average class size: 18

Teacher/pupil ratio: 1:18

North-West

Beech Hall School

Beech Hall is a non-selective school for boys and girls aged 6 months to 16 years situated in a beautiful sixteen-acre site on the edge of the Peak District. The school prides itself on providing a truly child-centred approach to education and pushing the boundaries of what is possible – as was recently demonstrated by a team of six from the school swimming the English Channel to raise money for Mencap.

A balanced focus on academic attainment, sporting opportunities, emphasising individual strengths and celebrating traditional values is at the heart of Beech Hall. The school believes that opportunities beyond the curriculum are just as important as those in the classroom and aims to provide a truly unique curriculum for every child. Small classes and a focus on the individual child as well as quality teaching and exceptional facilities all make this possible.

Beech Hall is a small school and this ensures staff can evaluate and prioritise the needs of every individual pupil. Staff not only monitor the academic progress and pastoral welfare of each individual child from an early stage in his or her career but also put in place an individually devised academic pathway through to 16 – that evolves as children's capacities and interests develop. Beech Hall is a school with a family feel where pupils who might struggle to flourish in larger schools thrive and realise their potential.

Pupils benefit from a team of expert specialist teachers and dedicated learning support staff as well as the opportunities offered in terms of extracurricular activities outside scheduled lessons. The school believes that young people benefit greatly from contributing to the ethos of the community and encourage every pupil to participate in the sporting and cultural life of the school, as well as assuming a variety of positions of responsibility.

Sport underpins the extra curriculum programme at Beech Hall and the PE department is well resourced with a gym, Astro-turf, playing fields and a heated swimming pool. The school has a long and proud history of sporting achievement and plays all the major team sports including Football, Rugby, Cricket, Netball, Hockey and Rounders. Pupils also have the opportunity to represent the school in sporting activities such as Cross Country, Athletics and Swimming.

Small class sizes and excellent communication between staff and families ensure that the Beech Hall staff focus on every child as an individual. It also enables the school to provide a mainstream educational environment for all pupils, including those (around a third) who have an additional educational need, such as dyslexia or autism. This approach, fully supported by the highest levels of pastoral care is, the school believes the best way to support children with learning needs and help them reach their full potential. As part of this approach, the school groups children by ability for the core subjects and start the GCSE programme a year early, in Year 9. Talented and experienced teaching staff are also supported by a learning support team, who include a full time SENCO and school counsellor.

Beech Hall children work hard, play hard and achieve great results. The school is proud of pupils academic success, particularly being a non-selective school and in 2021 there was a 92% pass rate of GCSE exams.

Beech Hall School knows what makes children happy, knows how to help them achieve academically and knows how to provide them with opportunities to shine. This ensures children leave Beech Hall hugely confident in who they are as individuals and ready for their next step.

Beech Hall School

Beech Hall Drive, Tytherington, Macclesfield, Cheshire SK10 2EG UK

Tel: 01625 422192

Email: secretary@beechhallschool.org

Website: www.beechhallschool.org

Headmaster: Mr James Allen

School type:
Co-educational Day Preparatory, Senior & Nursery

Age range of pupils: 6 months–16 years

Brabyns Preparatory School

Nestled in the heart of picturesque Cheshire countryside in the small town of Marple, Brabyns Preparatory School is a co-educational independent day school for children aged two to eleven.

Our unique surroundings and warm family ethos provide a peaceful and nurturing environment for the positive development and growth of all children at the school. Children are engaged with learning and given the support, encouragement and freedom they need to develop through exploring new opportunities.

We acknowledge and appreciate each child's individual strengths and characteristics. They are instilled with confidence in our happy, caring environment whilst developing excellent life values and skills. This sits alongside their educational development to ensure every child is inspired to reach their potential.

We pride ourselves on our warm family atmosphere in which all children are valued as individuals and are encouraged and inspired to reach their full potential within a disciplined yet caring environment.

We are committed to offering a first-class academic education within a forward-thinking and dynamic curriculum, in a way that is rewarding and engaging for children, parents and staff.

We offer a rich and diverse experience for the whole school community including a wide range of academic, sporting, language and performing arts opportunities, plus an extensive extra-curricular programme. Our 'Forest School' provides a lovely bridge between formal and informal learning, equipping the children with the skills they need to face uncertainty and change with courage and resilience.

Enjoyment and excellence are at the heart of an education that encompasses academic study, leadership, cultural pursuits, communication and excellent pastoral care.

Our aim is to develop confident individuals and to enable them to realise their potential and contribute fully to the world in which they grow. We nurture every child's individual talent and celebrate their achievements. Brabyns values its close partnership with parents; through working collaboratively we identify each child's strength to assist in the pursuit of excellence.

Each and every child has a part to play in Brabyns' life and every child is respected. By the time children leave us at the end of Year 6 they have built firm foundations not only for secondary school but for life ahead and move on with countless life-long memories.

34-36 Arkwright Road, Marple, Stockport, Cheshire SK6 7DB UK

Tel: 0161 427 2395

Email: admin@brabynsprepschool.co.uk

Website: www.brabynsprepschool.co.uk

Headteacher: Mrs Lindsay McKenna

School type:
Co-educational Day Preparatory & Nursery

Age range of pupils: 2.5–11 years

Fees as at 01/09/2022:

Day: £1,974–£2,719 per term

Forest Park Preparatory School

Forest Park Preparatory School provides an excellent educational start for your child. It is a unique school underpinned by core values that support the development of every child.

Rated 'Excellent' in all areas within our most recent Inspection Report (2019), this is a school where children are inspired and challenged from their very first day with us. Challenged to think independently and creatively, to enjoy and participate fully in their learning, and to achieve their full potential.

There is a real sense of belonging and family at Forest Park. From their first days in Pre Prep, children encourage one another to live the school motto, 'I can and I will'. In our warm and supportive environment, children learn to value themselves and each other, to take risks and responsibility, to learn from their mistakes and build on their successes year by year.

With a broad and exciting curriculum, and supported and encouraged by excellent specialist teachers, our children steadily build knowledge and understanding, key skills and a robust work ethic year on year. When the time comes, they are able to take senior school entrance exams for the local state and independent grammar schools comfortably in their stride, without the pressures of intensive preparation.

We are dedicated to ensuring our children succeed with their 11+ examinations, without undue pressure.

As a result, our pupils gain places in the region's top grammar schools, with 85% recently passing for a school of their choice last year. Most importantly, every child is ready for the next step, confident, optimistic, and ready and willing to make the most of all the opportunities life presents.

Parents choose Forest Park Preparatory School because they want their children to be happy and to develop in a dynamic and challenging, yet caring environment.

FOREST PARK
PREPARATORY SCHOOL

Lauriston House, 27 Oakfield, Sale, Greater Manchester M33 6NB UK

Tel: 0161 973 4835

Email: office@forestparkprep.co.uk

Website: www.forestparkprep.co.uk

Headteacher: Mr Nick Tucker

School type:
Co-educational Day Preparatory & Nursery

Age range of pupils: 3–11 years

Forest Preparatory School

Situated in the attractive suburb of Timperley, Forest Preparatory School is a co-educational, independent day school for children aged two to eleven.

At Forest, staff provide a happy, stimulating and well-disciplined environment, and encourage each child to strive for excellence, and reach their full potential in all areas of school life.

Excellent pastoral care is built on knowledge of every child as an individual, and with an 'open door' policy strong links are formed with parents, allowing for excellent communication between home and school. In our most recent Early Years Inspection Report, inspectors noted that "nurturing and supportive staff have successfully created a homely and welcoming environment that contributes positively to children's achievements." This is something we feel very passionate about at Forest. In addition, our Wraparound Care enables children from the age of three to be safely looked after in school from 7:30am until 5:55pm each day.

Our vision is embedded in putting pupil success at the heart of every decision. We believe in developing pupils' self-esteem so that they have the confidence to use their individual talents, skills and knowledge effectively and leave Forest equipped to be lifelong learners.

We value the partnership which exists between school, parents and community and the part it plays in realising this vision.

Though the school is not selective at infant level, Forest has great expectations, resulting in high aspirations from the children, and great achievements occurring both in and out of the classroom

Parents at Forest Preparatory School are very fortunate with the extensive choice of highly respected secondary schools available in the area and we aim to help them choose the right school for their child.

Our curriculum goes beyond the demands of the National Curriculum; it is personally structured and, in the later years, there is a clear focus placed on the requirements of the Independent and State Grammar Schools entrance examinations at 11+. The curriculum remains broad and balanced with a continued emphasis on creativity, questioning, and independent thinking. A priority for Forest is to help guide and prepare our children for their future schools.

The Early Years Foundation Stage comprises the Pre-Prep Nursery (2-3 year olds), Kindergarten (3-4 year olds) and Reception. Our Early Years department provides a stimulating, caring and vibrant environment where children aged 2-5 years of age learn important social skills and thrive on the planned learning opportunities, particularly in early reading, writing, mathematics, technology and creativity.

Children feel happy, secure and valued. They gain a wealth of learning experiences including Computing, PE, French and Music tuition from specialist teachers. There is also the opportunity for children to attend a range of after-school activities including Yoga, Spanish, Dance and Kiddy Cook.

Nursery children may start with their academic year group from the September after their second birthday and they may attend for any combination of mornings, afternoons or full days. Reception is a natural progression from Kindergarten, combining a warm, welcoming atmosphere with a bright, spacious and stimulating environment, which provides a wide variety of learning areas. The children are well-motivated learners, who continue to work within the seven areas of learning from the Foundation Stage curriculum, with an increased focus on the teaching of reading, writing and numeracy.

We believe that Forest is a great place to be and we would love to help your children learn. We hold a number of events for prospective parents throughout the year and our next Open Morning is Saturday 5th March 10.00am – 12.00pm.

FOREST PREPARATORY SCHOOL

ANIMO ET FIDE

(Founded 1924)

Moss Lane, Timperley, Altrincham, Greater Manchester WA15 6LJ UK

Tel: 0161 980 4075

Email: office@forestschool.co.uk

Website: www.forestschool.co.uk

Headmaster: Mr Graeme Booth

School type:
Co-educational Day Preparatory & Nursery

Age range of pupils: 2–11 years

Kirkham Grammar School

At Kirkham Grammar School, we believe in the values of a traditional education alongside a drive towards modern ambition. It is our intention to continue to build upon our history as a recognised centre of excellence for academic attainment and the holistic development of the learner. We believe everyone has a place in our community including our parents, pupils, staff, governors and alumni alike; we all have a part to play in the drive for continued excellence.

Kirkham Grammar School is an Independent Co-educational Day and Boarding School for pupils aged 3-18. The school prides itself on its warm, family atmosphere. Academic success remains at the heart of the school's aims.

The Senior School has undergone a transformation over the last decade and boasts a host of magnificent new facilities. Recent developments have included four new classrooms, additional upgraded boarding accommodation and a new Pastoral Hub.

Our excellence in sport has been acknowledged as one of only two schools in the North West of England to be ranked in the top twenty in the world. Recent successes include LTA National Tennis Champions, National Schools Cup U18 Rugby Finalists and Sedbergh National Super Tens Champions. Sporting facilities are outstanding with a floodlit all-weather surface and Lawrence House Pavilion.

The Junior, Infant and Pre-School is situated opposite the Senior School and has a roll of 250 pupils aged from 3-11 years. As well as enjoying its own on-site state of the art facilities, it also has access to the Senior School facilities, including an Astroturf pitch and multi-purpose hall.

Our newly designed Pre-School has now fully opened. The setting has been thoughtfully designed to meet the needs and requirements of children from rising 3s to 4 years old. The Pre-School offers a wide range of exciting activities and resources, which promote each child's learning across all areas of the Early Years Foundation Stage framework. The setting is a welcoming 'home-from-home' where children feel relaxed and happy, whilst being guided and nurtured by our dedicated Pre-School team. As always at Kirkham Grammar Junior, Infant and Pre-School, our fundamental aim is to offer the best possible environment in which children can flourish and naturally love learning forever.

Our most recent inspection again recognised the School as 'excellent across all areas' – the highest grading possible within the independent sector. During the inspection, lessons were observed, meetings undertaken and every aspect of the school's infrastructure and life inspected. The inspection found that the quality of the pupils' academic and other achievements is excellent, saying: *"Pupils are articulate and display excellent verbal and communication skills."* The report added: *"Pupils are ambitious learners, eager to respond to challenging opportunities in lessons and clear target setting in marking."* The quality of the pupils' personal development was also deemed excellent: *"Pupils reflect the strong family ethos of the school and demonstrate excellent collaboration in and out of lessons."* Following the inspection, Headmaster, Mr Daniel Berry said: *"The inspection re-confirmed what was already known: Kirkham Grammar School is the best-kept educational secret in Lancashire. However, it was pleasing for everyone that it has been officially acknowledged once again, against national criteria, that we are working hard to ensure our pupils receive the finest education."*

We believe Kirkham Grammar School exists for our children and therefore they must have the best! This is reflected in the school continuing to be oversubscribed in all year groups.

KIRKHAM
GRAMMAR SCHOOL

(Founded 1549)

Ribby Road, Kirkham, Preston, Lancashire PR4 2BH UK

Tel: 01772 684264

Fax: 01772 672747

Email: info@kirkhamgrammar.co.uk

Website: www.kirkhamgrammar.co.uk

Headmaster: Mr Daniel Berry

Appointed: 2016

Head of Junior School: Mrs Kirsten O'Donoghue

School type: Co-educational Day & Boarding Prep & Senior, Nursery & Sixth Form

Age range of pupils: 3–18 years

No. of pupils enrolled as at 01/09/2022: 930

Boys: 460 **Girls:** 470 **Sixth Form:** 180

No. of boarders: 90

Fees as at 01/09/2022:

Junior School (4–11 years) Day: £3,287 per term

Senior School (11-18 years) Day: £4,399 per term

Senior School (11-18 years) Boarding:
£4,182 per term (in addition to the Day fee)

Pre-School (3-4 years): £260.82 (Full week) – £57.96 (Full day)

Average class size: 12.5

Teacher/pupil ratio: 1:9

Lime House School

"Fun,Fab, Fair", Lime House School is a great place to learn to be your best self.

Lime House School – www.limehouseschool.co.uk – just south of Carlisle on the edge of the Lake District National Park, is an independent, co-educational boarding and day school which welcomes pupils, aged seven to 18, from all over the world.

Lime House School offers a rigorous academic and intellectual education which will challenge and engage your child. Supportive and nurturing in approach, the school empowers pupils to establish secure foundations for independent learning from which to launch their futures in tertiary education, and the careers of their choice.

The school has a wide and varied curriculum at both Primary and Secondary levels, with a dynamic range of subjects offered to Sixth Form. Pupils of all abilities are welcome, those with Special Education Needs are supported by a dedicated team of professionals.

Headteacher, Mr Andy Guest, says: *"It is a privilege to lead a school of such vibrancy. The academic programme is rich and fulfilling, with pupils benefiting from tailored programmes, delivered by subject specialists, who enthuse our learners with their passion. The super-curricular opportunities inform the academic life of the school with a range of cultural, performance, and sporting activities.*

"Pupils are guided in their growth as future global citizens and custodians, by their personal development tutors, and are encouraged to explore their dreams and define their path. Lime House School is a joyous and enriching place for all who are involved in our community."

The school's ethos is that learning should be integrated and fun, extending beyond the classroom and informing all we do.

The activities programme includes: sporting; music; art; photography; debating; environmental and strategic thinking. Pupils engage wholeheartedly with their beautiful surroundings with Forest School enhancing wellbeing and resilience. Weekends are structured, with pupils exploring diverse educational, cultural and fun filled experiences.

Lime House is a school of outstanding potential, its vibrancy and tolerance reflected in each of its pupils. Why not arrange a visit to see what we can offer your child?

(Founded 1899)

Holm Hill, Dalston, Carlisle, Cumbria CA5 7BX UK

Tel: 01228 710225

Email: office@limehouseschool.co.uk

Website: www.limehouseschool.co.uk

Headteacher: Mr Andy Guest

Appointed: September 2022

School type: Co-educational Day & Boarding Preparatory, Senior & Sixth Form

Age range of pupils: 7–18 years

No. of pupils enrolled as at 01/09/2022: 170

Fees as at 01/09/2022: £35,550

Average class size: 15

Teacher/pupil ratio: 1:20

Rossall School

The Good Schools Guide describes Rossall as 'A warm, happy and inclusive environment energised by a vision and challenge that is clearly helping all pupils to meet their potential.'

Set on a historic 160-acre campus, Rossall is one of the country's leading independent co-educational boarding and day schools, where boys and girls aged 0–18 are nurtured in a safe, secure and supportive environment.

Rossall currently provides one of the broadest curriculum programmes available in the UK independent school market. Rossall Preparatory School has a bespoke curriculum whilst the Senior School continues to follow the British National Curriculum, culminating with GCSE/iGCSE examinations at the end of Year 11. In the Sixth Form, pupils then have the choice to study either A levels or the globally recognised IB Diploma Programme.

In 2021, the IB cohort's average point score of 35 placed Rossall firmly amongst the premier league of IBDP schools within the UK. At A-Level, over 2/3s of all grades awarded either A*-A. GCSE pupils also achieved excellent GCSE results. Over 55% of all entries awarded this summer were a grade 7 or above, with an astounding fifth of all grades achieving the coveted grade 9.

Small class sizes and a rigorous tutorial system ensures academic excellence, with 95% of Rossall pupils entering higher education at universities around the world. This year, over 60% of students progressed to Russell Group/ Top 20 universities including Imperial College London, King's College London, University of Bristol and University of Warwick.

Rossall's enviable on-campus facilities include 150 acres of outdoor grassed sports pitches, floodlit all-weather surfaces, a gymnasium, heated indoor swimming pool, Fives courts, a shooting range and a multi-use-games-area (MUGA).

In September 2019, Rossall opened its brand new £4 million Sports Centre, boasting a 50m sprint track and multiple indoor courts.

The School also has its very own Golf Academy (currently ranked Number 1 in England for senior students) which includes an indoor golf studio equipped with the latest video analysis equipment and GC3 launch monitor/ simulator, as well as an indoor putting lab and short game facility.

Rossall also boasts its own Elite Football Academy for boys and girls in partnership with the English League One football club, Fleetwood Town FC, and is home to the Lawrence House Astronomy & Space Science Centre, the only centre of its kind in Britain, specialising in astronomy education.

In September 2021, Rossall became an All-Steinway School and already has its own International Piano Academy.

A huge range of extracurricular activities is offered to all pupils throughout the school. Pupils can join everything from the award-winning Chapel Choir to The Combined Cadet Force (the oldest CCF in the country!). The diverse range of clubs at Rossall ensures that there is something for everybody.

Admitting boarders as young as seven years old, Rossall's 'family structure' provides the framework for its exceptional standards of pastoral care. With major investments recently ploughed into its 10 boarding houses, each house is a well-equipped and comfortable home, which are in the process of being sensitively modernized to the highest standard.

Rossall School is a registered charity (No. 526685) that exists to provide education for children.

Rossall
INSPIRING EXCELLENCE

(Founded 1844)

Broadway, Fleetwood, Lancashire FY7 8JW UK

Tel: +44 (0)1253 774201

Email: admissions@rossall.org.uk

Website: www.rossall.org.uk

Head: Mr Jeremy Quartermain

Appointed: August 2018

School type: Co-educational Day & Boarding

Religious Denomination:
Church of England but accept all religions

Age range of pupils: 0–18 years

No. of pupils enrolled as at 01/09/2022: 855

Boys: 488 *Girls:* 367 *Sixth Form:* 220

No. of boarders: 350

Fees as at 01/09/2022:

Day: £3,145–£5,050 per term

Weekly Boarding: £5,350–£8,695 per term

Full Boarding: £7,955–£12,895 per term

Average class size: 16

Teacher/pupil ratio: 1:11

South-East

Bethany School

Set on a 60 acre rural campus in the beautiful Kent countryside, Bethany School is a flourishing co-educational day, full and weekly boarding School that provides a welcoming and caring environment for pupils between the ages of 11 and 18.

Bethany enjoys an excellent reputation as a particularly friendly and happy community. It is a strong, thriving School with an enviable building programme, including recent and regular upgrading of boarding School facilities; a fantastic six lane 25 metre indoor swimming pool, state-of-the-art fitness suite, a sixth form centre with excellent facilities and an expansive outdoor high ropes course.

Location
Situated in Kent, known as the 'Garden of England', Bethany has an idyllic location with easy accessibility. London is less than an hour by train, Gatwick Airport one hour by taxi and Heathrow an hour and a half. The Eurostar terminal at Ashford International is just 30 minutes away.

The very best academic education
As a mainstream School, Bethany prides itself on nurturing academic excellence while catering for pupils with a broad range of abilities. The School offers a wide variety of subjects in modern classrooms with specialist facilities, including a Science Centre with modern laboratories.

The entire campus is served by a wireless network and all pupils have their own laptop. Much of the curriculum is delivered through ICT and pupils gain important digital skills. Almost all of our sixth formers progress on to university courses, leaving Bethany with a mature, self-confident sense of purpose.

CReSTeD registered since 1994, Bethany's Learning Support department enjoys an international reputation for its success in giving specialist help to dyslexic pupils within the mainstream curriculum. In addition, for those pupils who require it, we offer support for English as an Additional Language.

Boarding life and overseas pupils
Our boarding community brings great diversity to Bethany. We are a small School and yet we have boarders coming from over 20 different countries, enriching our education with a variety of experiences and backgrounds.

We aim to inspire individual excellence in every pupil and this approach underlies everything we do at Bethany. Its success is evidenced by the excellent transition from School to university made by our pupils each year. Sixth form boarders benefit from single bedrooms with en suite bathrooms, all with easy access to kitchens and laundry rooms. This experience, combined with our Body for Life programme, is designed to be a stepping stone to life at university, all within the supportive environment of the School.

Outside the classroom
At Bethany, we believe that pursuits outside the classroom are very important in developing pupils' personalities. Everyone takes part in sport at least three times a week, and chooses from a huge array of extra-curricular activities including horse riding, chef school, golf, fishing, clay pigeon shooting, archery, orchestra and country pursuits. The Duke of Edinburgh's Award is hugely popular and very successful at Bethany.

The Headmaster firmly believes that School should be enjoyed rather than endured and it is the positive and nurturing atmosphere and the level of focus given to each individual pupil, that helps makes Bethany 'refreshingly different'.

Bethany since 1866

(Founded 1866)

Curtisden Green, Goudhurst, Cranbrook, Kent TN17 1LB UK

Tel: 01580 211273

Email: registrar@bethanyschool.org.uk

Website: www.bethanyschool.org.uk

Headmaster: Mr Francie Healy BSc, HDipEd, NPQH

Appointed: 2010

School type: Co-educational Day & Boarding

Age range of pupils: 11–18 years

No. of pupils enrolled as at 01/09/2022: 346

Boys: 221 *Girls:* 125 *Sixth Form:* 77

No. of boarders: 83

Fees as at 01/09/2022:

Day: £18,795–£20,760

Weekly Boarding: £29,175–£32,205

Full Boarding: £31,455–£35,400

Average class size: 15-17

Teacher/pupil ratio: 1:8

Brighton College Nursery, Pre-Prep & Prep School

The Nursery at Brighton College sees its young learners start their educational journey at just three years old, taught by qualified teachers. They attend five mornings a week and many enjoy staying for a flexible afternoon offering themed learning time in French, yoga, beach school, art and movement, which can be followed by the in-house after-school care group which runs until 5.45pm. The Nursery day is a highly flexible offering which suits the school's many types of parent. The curriculum has been developed to place an emphasis upon play-based learning and on supporting the individual interests and abilities of the children. Its innovative approach incorporates a programme of fine motor skill development and an emphasis on role-play in teaching, alongside an embedded use of technology including classroom CTouch screens, remote controlled devices and simple coding software and tablets.

Each year the Nursery pupils move on to Reception classes, fully prepared for their first year of school. They take with them a strong foundation and which ensures that they are keen learners who are ready to flourish. Alongside French and Mandarin teaching, the curriculum in Reception includes specialist art, PE, games and music lessons. Pupils from Reception upwards also benefit from weekly lessons in computing, teaching vital IT literacy and e-safety, and library lessons aimed at inspiring all pupils to read and learn about a range of literacy genres from the earliest age. At six years, children are given the opportunity to take up individual instrumental lessons taught by music specialists and become confident performers in weekly assemblies and annual concerts. Swimming lessons start when the children are five, adding to their action packed week of learning.

As the children progress into Year 4, their world of learning expands to incorporate curriculum drama, home economics, design and technology and Latin, alongside the traditional maths, English, science and humanities subjects. The co-curricular provision is also extended, incorporating LAMDA courses, choirs, music ensembles and orchestras. Over 50 clubs and activities are offered to the children during lunchtimes and after school, ranging from sewing or chess to debating or hockey. A programme of residential trips also begins in Year 5 which assists pupils to gain vital team-building and independence skills learnt in experiences outside of the classroom.

As the main feeder school into Year 9 at Brighton College, pupils here look forward to moving across from Year 8. They are well prepared for the next chapter in their education, having enjoyed a full programme of transition during their final term, 'Chapter IX', which, in liaison with the College, ensures that they are fully prepared. Many are successful in taking with them scholarship awards in both academic and co-curricular subjects.

BRIGHTON COLLEGE
NURSERY, PRE-PREP & PREP SCHOOL

Walpole Lodge, Walpole Road, Brighton, East Sussex BN2 0EU UK

Tel: 01273 704343

Email: prepadmissions@brightoncollege.net

Website: www.brightoncollege.org.uk

Headmaster: Mr Ant Falkus

Appointed: August 2022

School type:
Co-educational Day Preparatory & Nursery

Age range of pupils: 3–13 years

No. of pupils enrolled as at 01/09/2022: 512

Fees as at 01/09/2022:

Day: £4,400–£7,430

Burgess Hill Girls

"The community at Burgess Hill Girls is very special. The way we bond with our teachers is not something you come across every day. I feel very lucky to be a part of this school."

Laura, Year 10, Burgess Hill Girls

A transformative education

Burgess Hill Girls is an Excellent rated independent school in Sussex for girls aged 2 to 18 years of age.

Whatever the stage at which your daughter joins Burgess Hill Girls you can be confident of two things: that she will be known for who she is as an individual and she will be provided with an outstanding, transformative education of the whole person.

I am, I can, I should, I will

Our school motto, 'I am, I can, I should, I will', conveys and underpins our whole approach, identifying and realising the potential of your daughter as she proceeds, giving her the very best possible opportunities to become a successful women of the future.

As parents, success will be having a happy and healthy daughter who loves going to school, loves to learn, loves participating, and is able to make friends for life. For the girls, success may be doing well in lessons and tests, being part of a team, playing a musical instrument and having fun with friends.

At Burgess Hill Girls we pride ourselves on unlocking the academic talent that is found within our girls and strongly believe each individual will thrive in our high-achieving environment. Whilst Burgess Hill Girls aims to provide the very best opportunities for everyone to excel, we believe that success is more than obtaining the highest marks and grades. We recognise just as much all those fantastic qualities that are not materialistic or target driven. Success at our school is when we produce bright, confident and independent young women who have and will continue to achieve great things.

Perfectly located

Burgess Hill Girls stands in 14 acres of beautiful grounds within a conservation area close to Burgess Hill's town centre in the centre of Sussex. All aspects of the school are located on this one campus; Nursery, Pre-Prep & Prep, Senior, Sixth Form and Boarding Houses. The school is only a five minute walk from the railway station (on the London to Brighton line) and close to excellent road networks (10 miles from Brighton and only 20 miles from Gatwick); the school is easily accessible for local and international students. A flexible, daily minibus service is provided for girls across Sussex and beyond.

Visit Burgess Hill Girls

We would be very pleased to meet you, put a name to a face and show you round our school. Please get in touch to arrange a visit.

BURGESS HILL
— GIRLS —
Tomorrow's Women

(Founded 1906)

Keymer Road, Burgess Hill, West Sussex RH15 0EG UK

Tel: 01444 241050

Email: admissions@burgesshillgirls.com

Website: burgesshillgirls.com

Head of School: Lars Fox

Appointed: 2022

School type: Girls' Day & Boarding, Co-ed Nursery

Religious Denomination: Interdenominational

Age range of boys: 2.5–4 years

Age range of girls: 2.5–18 years

No. of pupils enrolled as at 01/09/2022: 557

Boys: 30 **Girls:** 527 **Sixth Form:** 70

No. of boarders: 50

Fees as at 01/09/2022:

Day: £9,825–£22,410

Full Boarding: £34,560–£39,900

Average class size: Max 20

Teacher/pupil ratio: 1:11

Churcher's College

Churcher's College is an Independent day school for boys and girls from 3-18 years of age offering Nursery, Junior, Senior and Sixth Form education. With around 950 pupils in the Senior School and 235 pupils in the Junior School (excluding the Nursery) of approximately equal numbers of boys and girls, Churcher's College enjoys recognition as one of the most accomplished independent, co-educational day schools in the country.

Location
The school is hosted on two campus sites in Hampshire enabling the Junior School and Nursery pupils to flourish in their own beautiful grounds in Liphook, whilst maintaining close links to the Senior School and Sixth Form located in nearby Petersfield. Both sites offer on-site playing fields and unrivalled facilities, providing the comfort and opportunities of an open, green environment.

Limitless Potential
We seek to give the widest range of experiences and the opportunity to excel. The children at Churcher's College thrive in an atmosphere of high expectation but even higher achievement in a happy, well-disciplined and caring environment.

Excellent examination results are clearly important; the achievement of these forms a core element in a child's time here. Equally, the development of self-esteem, moral values and leadership are vitally important parts of a child's education.

By developing the full academic, creative and sporting talents of the girls and boys, within the context of social awareness, our aim is to fully prepare them for all they will face in the dynamic and challenging world in which we live. The pupils of Churcher's College become confident, responsible, respected and selfless citizens in a world which will require gifted, flexible young people of character, dedication and compassion.

An inclusive school
Churcher's is an inclusive school where parents, children, staff and friends all contribute to the rich and broad education provided.

"We love all the variety, there really is something for everyone. It really is a place for both my son and daughter to find their niche and fly." Parent

"Pupils personal development is excellent. The pastoral systems provide a secure base where pupils can feel confident and can flourish." ISI Inspection

"The extra-curricular provision is excellent." ISI Inspection

"Teachers have a strong knowledge which they present enthusiastically to their pupils; this acts as a stimulus for increasingly sophisticated thinking." ISI Inspection

Visit us to discover more
You are warmly invited to join us and explore our school to find out more. Open events are held throughout the year, simply visit the website or contact the Admissions Team for more details. We look forward to meeting you soon.

Please visit ChurchersCollege.com for details of Open Events or contact our Admissions Team on 01730 263033 or admissions@churcherscollege.com.

CHURCHER'S COLLEGE
NURSERY·JUNIOR·SENIOR & SIXTH FORM

(Founded 1722)

Petersfield, Hampshire GU31 4AS UK

Tel: 01730 263033

Email: admissions@churcherscollege.com

Website: www.ChurchersCollege.com

Headmaster: Mr Simon Williams , MA, BSc

Appointed: September 2004

School type: Co-educational Independent Day

Age range of pupils: 3–18 years

No. of pupils enrolled as at 01/09/2022:

Senior School: 950

Junior School: 235

Fees as at 01/09/2022:

Day: £11,535–£17,265

Average class size: 22

Teacher/pupil ratio: 1:12

Claremont Fan Court School

Word of mouth will tell you we are the hidden gem of North Surrey and South West London. With 100 acres of beautiful landscaped grounds in which to learn and develop, build friendships and ambition, we are recognised by families as a medium-sized school with strong academic ambition for our pupils, but not at the expense of wellbeing for and attention to the individual child.

As a co-educational school where you can pursue the sports, subjects and activities that suit you, not just your gender, we believe that when pupils truly understand both themselves and the world around them, they can achieve what perhaps seems impossible. If a pupil says 'I can't do it', Claremont will add a 'yet' to the end of that statement. This critical positive thinking creates a robust strength of character to take them through into the adult world, embracing all the challenges that come with it.

Claremont is proud to be neither too big, nor too small. When combined with our gently selective admissions process, we create the space for children to find their niche and thrive within it. We invest in pupils' character, so they can unlock the potential they didn't even know they had and explore opportunities they had never tried before. Both staff and pupils flourish in an atmosphere of respect, courtesy, friendship and a love of learning.

Each month we focus on a different character quality, such as confidence, courage or responsibility, and incorporate it into everything from assemblies, discussions, activities and curriculum work. The academic programme then ensures that pupils attain the highest qualifications of which they are capable. Behavioural standards are high because pupils develop and value respect for peers, teachers, the school and greater society.

We believe in investing in teaching and learning, and have implemented important steps to ensure the school feels smaller as it grows, through smaller classes, forms and houses, yet richer in subject and co-curricular opportunities. Many praise the immersive experience of learning history and literature in rooms once home to royalty, and mathematics, science and technology in stunning and spacious new facilities, but we believe it is in combining pastoral and academic support that pupils best succeed. Our pupils typically pursue traditional courses and universities, but in offering over 60 co-curricular activities with everything from dissection to dragon's den, lacrosse to Lego clubs, there are opportunities to open our pupils' eyes to the careers of tomorrow as well as today.

To see what being confident in character, limitless in potential and strong in understanding could mean for your child, please visit our website for more information or sign up to one of our regular open events.

CLAREMONT FAN COURT SCHOOL

(Founded 1922)

Claremont Drive, Esher, Surrey KT10 9LY UK

Tel: 01372 473794

Email: admissions@claremont.surrey.sch.uk

Website: www.claremontfancourt.co.uk

Head: Mr William Brierly

Appointed: September 2018

School type: Co-educational Day Preparatory & Senior, Nursery & Sixth Form

Religious Denomination: Non-Denominational

Age range of pupils: 2.5–18 years

No. of pupils enrolled as at 01/09/2022: 1100

Fees as at 01/09/2022: Please see website

Average class size: 15

Teacher/pupil ratio: 1:10

Claremont School

Claremont Senior School and Sixth Form

Founded in 2011, Claremont Senior School is situated in the heart of historic Bodiam, famous for its picturesque 14th Century castle. With 'student voice' at its heart, the school has an unrelenting focus on attitude and activism as the central pillars of its holistic educational philosophy and offers a dynamic learning environment where young people consistently say they can be themselves. Never before has there been so many career paths, university courses and avenues for teenagers to explore, as the forces of technological change transform our world. By presenting students with challenge, opportunity and experimentation the school seeks to give them the confidence to fulfil their individual potential and face their futures with self-assurance, optimism and a boundless drive to be the best version of themselves. Relaxed, but ambitious and rigorous in approach, Claremont is a local school with an international perspective. It is a special place to work and a unique place to learn.

An extensive extra curricular, enrichment and service programme recognises that, for many young people, the greatest learning experiences can come from outside the classroom. The Co Curricular programme is inspired by the eight core skills valued by universities, apprenticeship courses and ultimately future careers, with the aim of giving students opportunities to explore new talents as well as become masters of the things they love. Student outcomes are outstanding with over 80% of Sixth Form students able to access their first choice of university, of which a third are Russell Group institutions.

Claremont has been judged 'Outstanding' by Ofsted in its last 3 consecutive inspections and in October 2021, was named Independent School of the Year for the Performing Arts.

'*Being able to prepare young people for Maths degrees at Harvard as effectively as for Fashion courses in London is something all our staff are deeply proud of.*' Ed Dickie, Head of Senior School

Claremont Prep School

Founded in 1925, Claremont Prep is a magical place to learn and grow. It's a joyful environment where children feel happy, secure and valued, where they further skills and knowledge and start to learn to adapt to the ever changing demands of the modern world. The school is based in rural St Leonards just 5 miles from the seaside and surrounded by over 100 acres of wonderful grounds to include extensive sports and playing fields and a locally renowned cross county track, alongside some truly magnificent woodlands. The main house is steeped in history, with curious winding corridors and beautiful spaces to learn in. There is even an icehouse hidden in the forest.

In lessons, the approach to learning is all about 'getting better', that it is good to aim high and there are no limits to furthering skills and knowledge in and outside the classroom. Many teachers are secondary school trained so are very knowledgeable about senior school life and how best to prepare children for GCSEs and all the challenges and opportunities that come with this next crucial stage in their education. All this, whilst nurturing an environment of friendship and kindness where children can most definitely still be children.

Green Flag and BBC Young Reporter School status

Environmental consciousness is firmly embedded in the School's culture, so children of all ages regularly learn about eco issues on a global scale but are also empowered to make real change. The Prep School holds the much coveted Green Flag and BBC Reporter school status. The children write and publish their own magazine The Arrow. The School is one of the first (if not the first) schools to have its own Eco Store.

Bodiam, Nr Robertsbridge, East Sussex TN32 5UJ UK

Tel: 01580 830396

Email: enquiries@claremontschool.co.uk

Website: www.claremontschool.co.uk

Principal: Mr Giles Perrin

School type: Co-educational Day & Boarding Prep & Senior, Nursery & Sixth Form

Age range of pupils:
3 months–18 years (boarding from 10)

Cranleigh School

Cranleigh is Surrey's leading co-educational independent school offering both day and boarding education for children aged 7-18, enabling siblings to be educated together.

Set on adjacent hills, the Preparatory School and the Senior School enjoy a spectacular 280-acre rural setting on the Surrey/West Sussex border, by the Surrey Hills, an Area of Outstanding Natural Beauty; yet they are conveniently situated close to the mainline city of Guildford, roughly equidistant between Gatwick and Heathrow, and only an hour's drive from London, where Cranleigh pupils regularly visit professional exhibitions and performances.

Both the Prep and the Senior Schools are proud of their excellent academic track records, culminating in outstanding performances at Common Entrance, GCSE and A-level. 99% of pupils go on to Higher Education, and Cranleigh also has a consistently strong Oxbridge contingent.

Such academic excellence does not come at the expense of co-curricular success at Cranleigh and the Schools currently boast national and county level representatives in a wide range of sports, including cricket, riding, hockey, rugby and swimming.

Pupil participation in sport, music and drama is actively encouraged at all levels; most Saturdays see every pupil playing sport for the school. More than 10 dramatic productions each academic year provide acting opportunities for all and the hugely popular Technical Theatre encourages the development of backstage skills.

Around 40 per cent of pupils play at least one musical instrument. Many take the opportunity to perform in more than 30 concerts a year, with over 10 musical groups, including symphony orchestra, wind band, chapel choir, big band, strings, trios, quartets and several other choirs.

The Schools offer outstanding facilities alongside new academic blocks. Sports facilities enjoyed by both the Prep and the Senior School include a double-sized indoor sports centre, four artificial playing surfaces, full equestrian centre, two expansive hard court areas for netball and tennis, a generous array of rugby and cricket pitches, a three-par, nine-hole golf course and an indoor pool. Equally outstanding sports staff includes former England players, an England national coach and an Olympic Gold Medallist (Hockey).

The Schools also boast professional-standard theatre facilities, rehearsal rooms, beautiful art studio spaces and a modern design centre fully equipped with 3D printers. The students have the opportunity to showcase their work in professional exhibitions several times a year.

Most importantly, Cranleigh prides itself on providing a happy, nurturing environment, founded upon an extremely supportive pastoral system (every pupil has their own tutor) and a high staff to pupil ratio, underscored by an invariably passionate house spirit. In such an environment, pupils can flourish into the well-rounded, self-motivated and confident individuals Cranleighans are famed for becoming, well prepared for life after school and invariably blessed with a circle of lifelong friends.

Pupils enter Cranleigh following a process of holistic review, at the main entry points of 13 and 16, and in other years where places are available. Regular Welcome Mornings are held and a wide range of academic and non-academic Scholarships are available.

CRANLEIGH
EX CULTU ROBUR

(Founded 1865)

Horseshoe Lane, Cranleigh, Surrey GU6 8QQ UK

Tel: +44 (0) 1483 273666

Fax: +44 (0) 1483 267398

Email: admissions@cranleigh.org

Website: www.cranleigh.org

Headmaster: Mr Martin Reader MA, MPhil, MBA

Appointed: September 2014

School type:
Co-educational Day & Boarding & Sixth Form

Age range of pupils: 7–18 years (including Prep School)

No. of pupils enrolled as at 01/09/2022: 683

Boys: 397 *Girls:* 286 *Sixth Form:* 256

No. of boarders: 485

Fees as at 01/09/2022:

Day: £35,175

Full Boarding: £42,720

Average class size: 20 (9 in Sixth Form)

Teacher/pupil ratio: 1:7

Durlston Court

Children are able to join Durlston at any point – whenever they join Durlston Court you can be assured they will be welcomed, supported, challenged, motivated and happy.

Learning in Durlston Pre-Prep is vibrant, interactive and fun. Small class sizes with high adult ratios ensure that every child is nurtured – socially and academically. The children have a myriad of opportunities and develop the confidence to embrace challenge in the classroom and in music, sport, drama and dance as well. Outdoor challenges in the Forest School develop resilience and perseverance, and experiences like dancing the Charleston at a 1920s afternoon tea dance, really bring learning to life.

In Middle School, children continue to make amazing progress inside and outside the classroom. They are encouraged to participate in the range of new and exciting experiences such as: starting a band; learning to sail; growing vegetables in the Middle School Garden; representing the school in a team, and the list goes on. Middle School teachers and specialist staff inspire a passion for learning, encourage the children to be the best they can be and help the pupils find what they love through the amazing opportunities and facilities on offer.

The adventure continues in the senior years with the children at Durlston challenged and supported by specialist, inspirational teachers in wonderful purpose built facilities. We encourage the children to take advantage of all the opportunities on offer from competing in sailing to taking the lead in a charity music concert.

Extending to GCSE from September 2023
From September 2023, Durlston Court School will welcome Year 9 pupils as we extend our provision to allow pupils, current and new, to continue their education to Year 11 and GCSE examinations.

In order to retain the family environment, we will phase expansion plans welcoming Year 9 pupils from September 2023, Year 10 from September 2024 and the first Year 11 cohort in September 2025.

"With our nurturing and supportive environment and all the advantages that provides, parents have increasingly been asking me whether we could consider taking Durlston Court to GCSE. Our Common Entrance curriculum has always provided an excellent foundation for future study and as the nature of senior schools is changing, we felt it was the right time for us to extend our provision. After extensive research, consultations and planning, we are confident that we can successfully balance the Durlston ethos of a supportive family environment with extending our exceptional teaching and learning opportunities to Year 11." Richard May, Headmaster

Whilst we hope that Durlston will be the natural choice for our pupils' GCSE education, we accept that this may not be the right decision for every family and are therefore also committed to continuing to prepare pupils for whatever school their parents choose.

DURLSTON COURT
Prep & Senior School

(Founded 1903)

Becton Lane, Barton-on-Sea, New Milton, Hampshire BH25 7AQ UK

Tel: 01425 610010

Email: registrar@durlstoncourtco.uk

Website: www.durlstoncourt.co.uk

Headmaster: Mr Richard May

Appointed: 2015

School type: Co-educational Day & Nursery

Age range of pupils: 2–16 years (Year 9 from 2023)

No. of pupils enrolled as at 01/09/2022: 260

Fees as at 01/09/2022: Please see website

Average class size: 15

Eagle House School

Eagle House is a coeducational, boarding and day Prep, Pre-Prep and Nursery located in Berkshire and only 50 minutes from London, benefitting from a close relationship with Wellington College. The school's superb grounds and excellent facilities are the background to an experience where success, confidence and happiness are paramount. The school is proud of its academic record, preparing children for a host of top independent schools and boasting a diverse and robust curriculum.

In December 2022 Andrew Barnard retires as Head after 16 years of excellent leadership. His successor will be Mrs Jane Jones.

Younger pupils follow the International Primary Curriculum and our older children have embarked on a new 'Curriculum 200', specially created for Years 5 to 8 that links subjects through topics and themes. Great teaching, new technology and a focus on the basics mean that children make good progress and love to be in the classroom. Independent learning is a focus for all children and our Extended Project programme helps drive inquisitive minds.

We unashamedly offer lots as part of our Golden Eagle activities experience. Children benefit from a huge range of opportunities in sport, music, drama, art, outward bound and community programmes. Busy children are happy and fulfilled children and we like to think that all pupils are Learning for Life.

Learning for Life means that children benefit from the best all-round education. They can feel confident in the classroom, on the games field, on stage, in the concert hall and in the community. Everyone is given the chance to stretch themselves in every area. Challenge is an important part of growing up and at Eagle House we learn that success and failure are both positive experiences.

Bright learning environments, outdoor learning areas and wonderful sporting facilities are important, but it is the community that shapes a young person. Through the excellent pastoral care and tutor system, coupled with a buddy structure, ensuring children have an older pupil to support them, Eagle House seeks to develop wellbeing from the youngest to the oldest.

Recognising how to be a positive influence within a community is also part of the Eagle House journey. Our wonderful Learning for Life programme teaches children about themselves and the wider community. Through community service we aim to make all our pupils responsible and independent as well as able to show empathy and understanding towards others. Time for reflection in chapel and assemblies also improves the way we look at the world and mindfulness sessions help us all take stock.

Boarding is a popular option and allows children to experience a varied evening programme of activities as well as being part of a vibrant and caring community. Boarding encourages independence but it is also great fun and whether full, weekly or flexi, boarders have the most wonderful time.

We often say that Eagle House children have the time of their lives and we firmly believe this. Learning for Life at Eagle House opens the doors to all sorts of opportunities and this results in children who are highly motivated and enthusiastic in all they do.

Eagle House buzzes with achievement and laughter – not a bad way to grow up!

Eagle House is a registered charity (No 309093) for the furtherance of education.

(Founded 1820)

Sandhurst, Berkshire GU47 8PH UK

Tel: 01344 772134

Email: info@eaglehouseschool.com

Website: www.eaglehouseschool.com

Headmaster: Mr A P N Barnard BA(Hons), PGCE

Appointed: September 2006

Head from January 2023: Mrs Jane Jones MA (Cantab)

School type:
Co-educational Day & Boarding Preparatory & Nursery

Age range of pupils: 3–13 years

No. of pupils enrolled as at 01/09/2022: 388

Boys: 220 **Girls:** 168

No. of boarders: 50

Fees as at 01/09/2022:

Day: £13,035–£20,385

Full Boarding: £27,390

Average class size: 17

Teacher/pupil ratio: 1:10

Farlington School

About Farlington School

Located in Horsham, West Sussex, Farlington School is a co-educational independent day and boarding school for pupils aged 4 to 18. Set within 33 acres of parkland on the borders of Sussex and Surrey, Farlington offers a perfect rural backdrop with plenty of space to grow. Formerly an all-girls' school, Farlington began welcoming boys in 2018 and has been fully co-educational since September 2021.

At Farlington, we strive to help our students develop confidence and self-belief, both inside and outside the classroom. Our core values constantly seek to develop Individuality, Opportunity and Community. **Individuality** is about recognising and celebrating each student's voice. Our constant aim is to enable **opportunities** for our pupils to learn across our full and extensive curriculum. As a true 'through school', we provide a caring and cohesive **community**, in which each student is recognised as a valued and valuable member.

Pastoral care, wellbeing and fun are at the heart of a Farlington education, and we passionately believe that happiness enables success. Here, friendships are forged for life, and our emphasis is on promoting respect for others, celebrating teamwork, and developing collective responsibility.

Extra-Curricular Provision

Farlington offers an extensive extra-curricular provision, incorporating sporting, creative and enrichment options. Our twice daily activities programme allows every pupil to be involved in an enrichment activity – outdoors or indoors; practical, intellectual or unusual. We offer a range of extra-curricular art, music, dance and drama clubs, and provide a varied and inclusive extra-curricular sports programme.

Academic Success

Farlington students consistently achieve outstanding results at GCSE and A-Level. In 2022, our A-Level results were exceptional: 45% of grades awarded to Farlington students were A*-A; 81% were grades A*-B; and 92% were grades A*-C. Impressively, 88% of Farlington students achieved at least one A or A* at A-Level. Indeed, The Sixth Form at Farlington is a very successful place academically – in 2019, our Value Added results placed us in the top 1% of schools nationally. Our GCSE results in 2022 were equally as impressive: 77% of grades awarded to Farlington students were 9-6; 52% were grades 9-7; and 95% were grades 9-4. Overall, 28% of all GCSE grades awarded to Farlington students were 9-8.

Alumni & Awards

Notable Farlington alumni include Olivier Award-winning actor and puppeteer Romina Hytten, and Issy Hayes, now a successful triathlete and part of the England Next Generation talent squad. Over recent years, Farlington Art students have triumphed in prestigious art competitions, including the ISA National Art Competition and the RBA's Rising Stars and Star Students Competitions. Farlington was shortlisted for the Outstanding Response to Covid-19 Award at the Independent Schools of the Year Awards 2021.

Recent Developments

Following the arrival of Headmaster James Passam in 2021, exciting developments at Farlington have included a stylish new Sixth Form Refectory, and the introduction of Design & Technology, together with a brand new DT Workshop. Farlington has also improved its Dance offering, with the subject now available to students both as part of the curriculum and in the form of extra-curricular examination and non-examination classes.

FARLINGTON School

(Founded 1896)

Strood Park, Horsham, West Sussex RH12 3PN, UK

Tel: 01403 254967

Email: office@farlingtonschool.com

Website: www.farlingtonschool.com

Headmaster: Mr James Passam

Appointed: September 2021

School type: Co-educational Day & Boarding Preparatory, Senior & Sixth Form

Age range of pupils: 4–18 years

No. of pupils enrolled as at 01/09/2022: 340

Fees as at 01/09/2022:

Day: £2,050–£6,350 per term

Weekly Boarding: £10,500 per term

Full Boarding: £11,300 per term

Flexi Boarding from: £65 per night

Average class size: 16

Gordon's School

Built by public subscription over a century ago at the insistence of Queen Victoria, Gordon's School is the national monument to General Charles Gordon of Khartoum, is listed as one of Britain's outstanding schools by Her Majesty's Chief Inspector and Tes Boarding School of the Year for 2022.

A non-selective, co-educational residential and day boarding school, while Gordon's School embraces modern ideas, General Gordon's legacy of traditional values remains. The School's ethos is that high performance without good character is not true success.

To this end, it's not just in the classrooms where students excel. Successes are achieved in drama and the arts; debating and public speaking; dance and sport. The School also boasts an enviable record in attaining Duke of Edinburgh awards.

While the individual is celebrated, the whole School unites for parades. Since its inception, students have marched and there has always been a Pipes and Drums band. Dressed in their Blues uniform, the students parade around eight times a year and the school is the only one permitted to march along Whitehall – an annual tradition in remembrance of General Gordon.

Set in over 50 acres of beautiful Surrey countryside within easy access of major airports and roads, the School is home to some 950 students and offers Day and Residential (weekly and termly) Boarding.

At the start of September 2020, Gordon's School entered one of the most exciting chapters in its 135 year history. A new sports hub and additional all-weather pitch was added to the already extensive facilities on the Surrey site and the school announced its partnership with Harlequins. As a result of the partnership, promising rugby players can now follow a pathway to a career in the game while receiving a first class education.

Each Student is assigned to one of the ten Houses – four residential boarding and six day boarding. Recently opened has been a dedicated Year 7 bespoke Residential Boarding House for our youngest students. Inter-House competitions are fiercely contested.

Spiritual guidance and support is given through chapel services and informal worship. And Houseparents provide a 'home from home', lending special atmosphere to each Boarding House and ensuring that free time off for students is fun, with numerous activities.

There are three main admission points – at 11 years old; 13 years old and for Sixth Form.

Scholarships are offered for those coming into the Sixth Form. The scholarships enable those awarded to benefit from a programme to enhance their development and give them wider opportunities to progress in their field. Bursaries are also available.

The real judgement of Gordon's is the students. All who visit are struck by the friendliness, discipline and vibrancy throughout the school and by the family atmosphere, exemplified by the special rapport between staff and students. This is borne from a community that strives to live with integrity, to be courteous, enthusiastic and diligent, even in adversity.

Gordon's School is unique. Please book a visit and find out why.

(Founded 1885)

West End, Woking, Surrey GU24 9PT UK

Tel: 01276 858084

Fax: 01276 855335

Email: registrar@gordons.school

Website: www.gordons.school

Head Teacher: Andrew Moss MEd

Appointed: September 2010

School type:
Co-educational Day & Boarding Senior & Sixth Form

Age range of pupils: 11–18 years

No. of pupils enrolled as at 01/09/2022: 938

Boys: 492 **Girls:** 446 **Sixth Form:** 317

Fees as at 01/09/2022:

Day: £9,081

Weekly Boarding: £18,222

Full Boarding: £19,446

Average class size: 22

Teacher/pupil ratio: 1:12

Kent College, Canterbury

Kent College is an outstanding day and boarding school that celebrates both its 130 years of history and tradition, and its forward-looking, innovative approach to education. It has a reputation as a friendly school, and is most definitely a place where teachers really get to know the pupils, with the time and space to give individual attention, both academically and pastorally. Music, drama and sport all play central roles in the life of the School, and many pupils also enjoy the opportunities provided by the School's Farm and Riding Centre.

Part of the Methodist Schools group, Kent College is deeply rooted in the Methodist tradition that welcomes all pupils of every faith and none. 'Do all the good you can' is a guiding principle, and one that allows pupils to develop into confident young adults, aware of their responsibilities and their place in the world.

Location

The School's location, on the outskirts of the historic city of Canterbury, provides a safe, healthy and beautiful environment for pupils to grow up. The School sits in 80 acres (32 hectares) of land with extensive sports fields, as well as the Farm and Riding Centre. Yet the centre of Canterbury, with its wide selection of shops, restaurants, theatres, cinemas and world-heritage site, within which sits Canterbury Cathedral, is only a 5-minute journey by car. A high-speed train service links Canterbury to London, and the School is within 100 minutes of Gatwick, Heathrow, Stansted and City of London airports.

Boarding

Kent College has a long history of welcoming boarding pupils from abroad, as well as from British families resident in the UK or working overseas. Boarders make up around one third of pupils, and there are over 42 countries represented in the boarding community. The five friendly and comfortable Senior boarding houses truly become a 'home away from home'. The School also offers weekly and occasional boarding.

Academic Success

The bespoke approach to the curriculum differentiates the college's approach and ensures highly personalised teaching resulting in excellent results. The school regularly ranks in the top 10 small cohort schools for the International Baccalaureate with an average score of 37 for the last 7 years. 75% of students achieve A* – B at A Level and 98% of students regularly go to their first university of choice.

Beyond the classroom

The performing arts are a particular strength at Kent College, with an impressive line-up of vocal and instrumental ensembles, and many opportunities to perform for all ages and abilities. The Great Hall is an impressive 600-seat auditorium that allows students to gather for worship and to showcase their musical, theatrical and performance talents within a world-class theatre. In sport, the aim is to provide something for every pupil, from recreational sport and promoting fitness to top-level coaching for our elite players. Kent College teams make formidable competitors in any sport. Hockey and cricket are a particular strength with regular representation by our pupils in county, regional and national squads. The School's scholarship programme offers talented individuals individual support in art, design, drama, music and sport. There is also a wide-ranging list of activities and clubs on offer for all pupils, including a full Duke of Edinburgh programme, horse riding and Farm Club at the School Farm.

KENT COLLEGE
CANTERBURY

(Founded 1885)

Whitstable Road, Canterbury, Kent CT2 9DT UK

Tel: +44 (0)1227 763 231

Email: admissions@kentcollege.co.uk

Website: www.kentcollege.com

Head of Kent College: Mr Mark Turnbull

School type: Co-educational Day & Boarding Prep & Senior, Nursery & Sixth Form

Religious Denomination: Methodist

Age range of pupils:
3 months–18 years (boarding from 8 years)

Garden Cottage Nursery: 3 months–3 years

No. of pupils enrolled as at 01/09/2022: 818

Fees as at 01/09/2022:

Day: £3,855–£6,932 per term

Full Boarding: £9,326–£12,883 per term

Average class size: 15, max 18

King Edward VI School

King Edward VI School, Southampton, has been at the heart of the city for over 460 years and is one of the UK's leading independent 11-18 co-educational day schools.

As a leading co-educational Independent day School, King Edward's undoubtedly has high academic standards and expectations. Under the guidance of an expert teaching staff, our pupils perform at the highest levels in public examinations, and both GCSE and A level outcomes are consistently exceptional.

With a reputation for academic excellence, the School boasts a thriving Sixth Form that produces consistently excellent A Level examination results ensuring students continue on to a range of competitive institutions, most to one of the UK's top 25 universities and, on average, approximately 10% of students proceed to Oxford or Cambridge. Results at GCSE and IGCSE are equally outstanding.

Outside of the academic, King Edward's also aims to foster a sense of personal worth in every pupil through a wide range of co-curricular activities, particularly with an active engagement in community work, so that every individual emerges as a fully responsible member of society. In the last year alone the student Charities Commission has raised over £27,000 for local and national charitable causes.

Each year students can be found taking part in excursions to worldwide destinations. The most recent co-curricular trips have included a technology trip to Tokyo, a biology field trip to Ecuador and the Galapagos Islands, a cultural exchange with a school in North Carolina, and a trekking expedition in Vietnam. Language students regularly participate in the exchange programmes on offer to Germany, France and Spain as well as in cultural visits to schools in the USA and Prague. Closer to home the School also organises an annual summer camp to Swanage for local young carers, run by our Sixth Formers.

Sport and the arts are an integral part of school life. Students are given the opportunity to represent the School across the major team games as well as individual sports. Overseas tours, regular fixtures, tournaments and school events offer a competitive sporting environment and King Edward's boasts 33 acres of sports ground, a fully equipped gym and multiple all weather pitches. The Creative Arts Faculty offers an amazing array of facilities from recital rooms, a recording studio and music technology suite to a custom-built dance studio. The state-of-the-art Dobson Theatre has a capacity for 400 seats and provides a superb venue for our talented dramatists and musicians. An array of public performances throughout the year allow King Edward's performers to showcase their talents, whatever their ability level.

Students are actively encouraged to become involved in fund-raising and community work and take part in some of the 150 clubs and societies that are available outside of lesson time. King Edward's also runs a well-established Duke of Edinburgh's Award Scheme that makes use of the school's Rural Studies Centre in Dartmoor.

King Edward's strives to ensure that all pupils reach and fulfil their full potential. A happy atmosphere amongst first-class teaching facilities provide exceptional academic stimulus alongside an extraordinary breadth of co-curricular opportunities. Seventeen bus routes extend throughout south Hampshire, allowing students from the New Forest, Salisbury, Winchester and east of Southampton easy and direct access to the School.

KING EDWARD VI SCHOOL

(Founded 1553)

Wilton Road, Southampton, Hampshire SO15 5UQ UK

Tel: 023 8070 4561

Fax: 023 8070 5937

Email: registrar@kes.hants.sch.uk

Website: https://kes.school/

Head Master: Mr N T Parker

Appointed: August 2019

School type: Co-educational Day Senior & Sixth Form

Age range of pupils: 11–18 years

No. of pupils enrolled as at 01/09/2022: 965

Fees as at 01/09/2022:

Day: £18,645

Average class size: 22

Teacher/pupil ratio: 1:10

King Edward's Witley

Pupils thrive at King Edward's. We encourage them to be the best versions of themselves because individual achievement and personal growth count for more than league tables. Our unique heritage and place among British co-educational independent schools means that we can provide the best preparation for adult life to a wider range of young people than almost any other institution.

King Edward's offers your son or daughter a school that can feel as warm and welcoming as home. A springboard to a lifelong love of learning which can nurture confidence, foster collaboration and prepare them for life in a multicultural world. Most of all it can help them discover who they are. This is a school shaped by generosity of spirit, not by background.

Academic focus

A King Edward's education is a rounded education. All academic staff are subject specialists, GCSE/IGCSE in Year 11 followed by a choice of A-level courses or the IB Diploma programme in the Sixth Form. Young people discover skills, talents and enthusiasms they never knew they had and are encouraged to set their sights high and be ambitious in their learning. Our rich co-curricular programme broadens their horizons.

Pastoral

All our pupils benefit from small class sizes and our House system with its supportive pastoral networks at the heart of school life. Each House is committed to strong connections uniting and blending boarders and day pupils into a single team. Diversity has been a strength since our foundation in 1553 and while most of our 440 pupils are local, we attract international pupils from more than 30 countries. They help teach us what it means to be part of the wider human family.

Boarding

King Edward's is a thriving community with four senior boys and two senior girls Houses for day, weekly and flexi boarders. Lower School pupils in Years 7 and 8 reside in Queen Mary House, an impressive family-oriented building steeped in history. Each House has a pastoral team consisting of a House parent and assistant House parent, Matron and an academic tutor. Additionally, there is a 24-hour Medical Centre and an on-site chaplain.

Mindful of our responsibility to prepare our pupils for the next stage in their educational journey, in September 2022 we opened an impressive Upper Sixth Form House that represents a stepping-stone to the independence and the full university experience. The House provides a unique opportunity, allowing pupils to study independently while honing important life skills, in a vibrant, communal environment consistent with student campus accommodation.

Hobbies and activities

On our leafy, 100-acre site amid the Surrey Hills we have space for all the sport, drama, music, hobbies, and intellectual pursuits a young mind can take. King Edward's is a wonderfully safe place for youthful adventure and curiosity.

The School creates a foundation for life both now and for the future. Our timeless education reaches far beyond the exciting and challenging academic curriculum and the broad range of opportunities in all areas of school life – sporting, artistic, social and cultural.

Pupils leave as independent free-thinkers – agile, motivated, and self-disciplined. The creative, entrepreneurial thinking they develop here gives the next generation of inventors, designers and problem-solvers the ability to grasp life with both hands.

King Edward's
W I T L E Y

Petworth Road, Godalming, Surrey GU8 5SG UK

Tel: 01428 686735

Email: admissions@kesw.org

Website: www.kesw.org

Head: Mrs Joanna Wright

School type: Co-educational Day & Boarding

Religious Denomination: Christian

Age range of pupils: 11–18 years

No. of pupils enrolled as at 01/09/2022: 440

Fees as at 01/09/2022:

£5,960 – £12,250 per term

Average class size: 15

King's School Rochester

King's School Rochester is a remarkable school with a rich and diverse heritage, where pupils have been educated here for over 1,400 years under the watchful gaze of Rochester Cathedral and Rochester Castle. Founded in 604AD, King's is the second oldest school in the world and the world's oldest Cathedral Choir School.

While a sense of place is bound to have an impact on the development of the children learning here, it is the skills, experiences and opportunities provided to them, both within and outside the classroom, that will enable them to thrive in an uncertain and fast-changing world.

At King's, we believe in preparing children for the 21st Century through educating the whole child. Our priority though, is ensuring that happy children perform to their best and the school is an exceptionally happy and friendly place where moral values, self-discipline, emotional intelligence and a Christian spirit underpin our family community.

Our academic results are excellent at all levels but we believe that building a love of learning and developing independent thinking skills are just as important as achieving the best grades. We keep our class sizes small so that teachers know their pupils as individuals and can help each of them shine. We are a school where all are cared for and where links between home and school are a real strength.

We offer and encourage pupils to take part in a huge range of co-curricular opportunities to ignite and nurture their interests, providing experiences which will develop confidence in them for life. Sport, Music, Drama, Outdoor Pursuits, CCF and a range of clubs and societies are integral to the school's commitment to provide a broad educational experience.

Music is a huge strength and we are privileged to use Rochester Cathedral as our chapel. We hold seasonal concerts throughout the year in the Nave and the Cathedral.

Choristers are educated in our Preparatory School. Music Scholars go on to leading international conservatoires.

Under the refurbished Vines Church is our Drama studio, equipped with digital sound and lighting. We are a proud Royal Shakespeare Company Associate School and our pupils have staged productions across Kent. King's has a strong reputation for exceptional drama performances and productions of "Titanic the Musical" and "Fiddler on the Roof" have been comparable to the standard of productions in the West End.

Our coaches and many of our pupils play at County, National and International level. The King's School Rochester Sports Centre provides pupils with extensive facilities to train, in addition to playing fields, a heated indoor swimming pool and boat house situated on the bank of the River Medway, while the Paddock is regarded as one of the finest cricket fields in the county.

The boarding community at King's reflects the personal approach of the school. Boarding starts from age 11 and we have 55 beds across our two Boarding Houses, St Margaret's House for girls and School House for boys. The small boarding community ensures a real boutique and family-feel to both Houses which are comprised of both British and international students.

We offer co-education from 3 to 18 and our structure of Pre-Prep, Prep and Senior Schools enables us to offer a tailor-made experience for each age group while giving access to the excellent facilities of the whole school.

King's School Rochester is in every sense a school for life.

(Founded 604 AD)

Satis House, Boley Hill, Rochester, Kent ME1 1TE UK

Tel: 01634 888555

Email: admissions@kings-rochester.co.uk

Website: www.kings-rochester.co.uk

Principal: Mr B Charles

Appointed: 2019

School type: Co-educational Day & Boarding Prep & Senior, Nursery & Sixth Form

Age range of pupils: 3–18 years

No. of pupils enrolled as at 01/09/2022: 638

Sixth Form: 101

No. of boarders: 55

Fees as at 01/09/2022:

Day: £3,770–£7,175 per term

Full Boarding: £8,175–£11,775 per term

Average class size: 18

Teacher/pupil ratio: 1:18

Maltman's Green School

Our Approach

At Maltman's Green we believe in the pursuit of excellence with a sense of fun. Girls are inspired to do their best inside and outside of the classroom through an ambitious and dynamic curriculum, extensive extra-curricular opportunities, a nurturing environment and dedicated staff. We prepare girls for the modern world through a relevant, adaptable and innovative approach that is supported by a foundation of traditional values. Our girls are given every opportunity to succeed across multiple disciplines, fostering confidence and self-belief, and empowering them for whatever future awaits.

We believe that the emotional, social and physical wellbeing of our girls is paramount. By providing a personalised learning experience in an encouraging and nurturing environment, we ensure our girls feel happy, confident and valued – a perfect foundation from which children can flourish.

Games and The Arts

Our sports provision is an outstanding feature of the School, with dedicated facilities and daily lessons. All girls enjoy friendly tournaments between houses and within year groups where those with the talent and inclination can progress to squad level to compete locally, regionally or nationally, usually with exceptional results.

Music is a very important part of life at Maltman's Green. Specialist teaching, exceptional facilities and lots of choice give our girls plenty of opportunity to explore and showcase their musical talents. Many of our girls participate in various choirs and we have a wide choice of musical instrument lessons available as well as a variety of instrumental ensemble groups to join. Drama too has a big part to play in school life where regular performances and workshops give girls a strong sense of confidence and creative expression. Our dedicated performance space with high-quality staging, lighting, costumes and props give our shows a professional feel.

Achievements

Our girls are encouraged to be independent thinkers, to challenge themselves and to always try their best. Maltman's Green provides a firm foundation, preparing girls to face senior school and beyond with confidence, determination and a lifelong love of learning. This is reflected in our impressive Bucks Secondary Transfer Test (11+) results, 81% qualification rate for 2021/22, and twenty scholarships awarded to Independent Senior Schools. This, combined with our girls' impressive achievements across sport, music and drama, affirm our position as one of the foremost prep schools in the country.

Outstanding Characteristics

Our rigorous approach and excellent teaching were highlighted by the Independent Schools Inspectorate (ISI) at their most recent inspection in February 2022, when Maltman's Green was awarded "excellent" in all areas – an outstanding achievement. *"The quality of the pupils' academic and other achievements is excellent. Pupils of all ages and abilities make excellent progress over time because of the systematic use of the assessment framework in planning for individual needs. Pupils' linguistic and other mathematical skills are outstanding, and pupils apply these with great confidence to other areas of learning. Pupils demonstrate excellent attitudes to learning when the curriculum creates opportunities for them to develop independence in their learning. Pupils readily think for themselves and acquire higher-order thinking skills which they instinctively apply to all areas of learning."*

MALTMAN'S GREEN SCHOOL

(Founded 1918)

Maltmans Lane, Gerrards Cross, Buckinghamshire SL9 8RR UK

Tel: 01753 883022

Email: registrar@maltmansgreen.com

Website: www.maltmansgreen.com

Headmistress: Mrs Jill Walker BSc (Hons), MA Ed, PGCE

Appointed: 2020

School type: Girls' Day Preparatory & Nursery

Age range of girls: 2–11 years

No. of pupils enrolled as at 01/09/2022: 315

Fees as at 01/09/2022:

Day: £2,595 Nursery (5 mornings & 1 afternoon)–£5,700 Year 6 (per term)

Manor House School, Bookham

Founded in 1920 and having celebrated its Centenary Year in 2020-2021, Manor House School can be found nestled amidst seventeen acres of gardens, woodland and sports fields in the village of Bookham, Surrey.

Manor House School is a selective Independent Day School for girls aged 4-16 with a Co-Educational Nursery and Lower Prep. It provides a smaller, nurturing learning environment producing consistently great academic results in a happy, friendly, and caring school environment. An individual approach to teaching and learning enables each pupil at the School to achieve their personal best, both academically and personally. Our staff are passionate about laying strong foundations for the children in Nursery and Lower Prep. As a member of the GSA (Girls' Schools Association) our aim is to support and develop happy young women in the Prep School and the Senior School, who love coming to school and believe in their abilities to learn and succeed.

There is an extensive co-curricular enrichment programme with up to 50 extra-curricular clubs and activities operating across the school each term. Girls are encouraged to seek out new experiences and try something new. Manor House achieves excellent Key Stage 2 and GCSE results. For more information on their latest results, please visit www.manorhouseschool.org/academic-results/gcseresults.

Seven school values form the foundations of school life and the school motto 'To Love is to Live' was chosen in 1921 by the Bishop of Plymouth. Dr. Masterman, who was a close friend of one of the school's original founders.

Manor House girls enjoy high levels of success in all areas of Sport boasting some future world class soccer players, cyclists, triathletes and tennis stars in its midst. There is a popular Senior Scholarships Programme from Year 7 (application in Year 6) offering Major and Minor Academic Scholarships at up to 50% and 40% of the basic annual tuition fee and up to 10% for an Art, Drama or Music award.

Facilities include an award-winning Nursery, Forest School, indoor sports hall which transforms into a seated theatre space for professional productions, outdoor swimming pool, a Tennis Academy, tennis and netball courts and purpose-built science blocks. Girls enjoy many opportunities in the creative and expressive arts, with additional music, singing and drama lessons a popular choice.

The School day operates from 7.45am to 6pm to accommodate working and/or busy parents. Fees include a daily hot lunch and there is a local minibus service in the mornings and afternoons and a late bus to Effingham train station which is serviced by good rail connections. The School bus routes service Ashtead, Dorking, Claygate, Cobham, Epsom, Esher, Fetcham, Hinchley Wood, Guildford, Kingswood, Walton-on-Thames, Weybridge, Wimbledon/Kingston, West Byfleet and surrounding areas.

For more information visit www.manorhouseschool.org. There are three main Open Morning events per year in October, March and May. For more information, contact:admissions@manorhouseschool.org.

(Founded 1920)

Manor House Lane, Little Bookham, Leatherhead, Surrey KT23 4EN UK

Tel: 01372 457077

Email: admin@manorhouseschool.org

Website: www.manorhouseschool.org

Headteacher: Ms Tracey Fantham BA (Hons) MA NPQH

School type:
Girls' Day, Co-ed Pre-Preparatory & Nursery

Age range of boys: 2–6 years

Age range of girls: 2–16 years

No. of pupils enrolled as at 01/09/2022: 300

Fees as at 01/09/2022:

Day: £9,747–£18,315

Average class size: 15-20

Northbourne Park School

Northbourne Park School is an independent day and boarding school for children from 2 to 13. Set in over 100 acres of beautiful park and woodland in rural Kent, the school is within easy reach from central London, Eurostar and Gatwick Airport. Northbourne Park School provides children with a first-class education focusing on the individual needs of every child, inspiring them to succeed across a wide range of learning experiences. Our setting offers each child a safe environment with freedom and space and countless opportunities to grow in confidence and succeed.

Academic

Northbourne Park School is an environment where each and every child can flourish. Pupils gain confidence in their learning and through inspirational teaching from dedicated staff and an engaging and stimulating curriculum, their results are phenomenal. We focus on individual needs and consistently achieve academic excellence, with many of our pupils gaining scholarships to top Senior Schools. The school's Language Programme helps every child develop foreign languages in an integrated learning environment. The result is a clear advantage when they move on to Senior Schools.

Sport

We are passionate about sport and through an excellent sports programme the pupils develop key skills and learn the importance of teamwork and leadership. We coach traditional sports as well as more diverse such as archery. The school has excellent facilities including a brand new all-weather sports pitch.

Creative Arts

We nurture a love for all the Arts. Many pupils learn one or more instruments in our purpose-built Music suite. They have the opportunity to take part in the choir, band, orchestra, string and brass groups performing regularly within the school and in the local area. Other opportunities include LAMDA lessons, regular drama productions and Public Speaking that ensure the pupils are articulate and confident in their performances. Artistic talents are encouraged through a range of media including sculpture, costume design, 3D printing and pottery.

Community

Pupils are provided with a first-class level of pastoral care in a safe and nurturing environment with a real family atmosphere. Our welcoming boarding community provides a home-from-home environment and a continuous boarding service at weekends throughout the term. Boarders enjoy regular excursions and activities, and the accompanied services to London and Paris provide opportunities for weekends at home. Northbourne Park School holds Tier 4 Status for non-European pupils requiring visas under the UK Visa and Immigration Service scheme.

Extra Curricular

We provide the pupils with a fun and extensive programme of afternoon clubs that help develop their interests and skills. Love of the outdoors and respect for the environment begins in the Pre-Prep and develops through into the Prep School with fun physical adventures. Whether they are playing in the woods, camping out overnight or following our Outdoor Education Programme, children love Northbourne Park life.

The children are at the heart of everything we do and it is important to us that they learn with confidence and enjoy each and every day at school. All prospective pupils are welcome and we offer a wide range of scholarships.

Every day is an Open Day at Northbourne Park School, come and visit us!

(Founded 1936)

Betteshanger, Deal, Kent CT14 0NW UK

Tel: 01304 611215

Email: admissions@northbournepark.com

Website: www.northbournepark.com

Headmaster: Mr Sebastian Rees BA(Hons), PGCE, NPQH

Appointed: September 2015

School type: Co-educational Day & Boarding

Age range of pupils: 2–13 years (boarding from 7)

No. of pupils enrolled as at 01/09/2022: 188

Boys: 95 *Girls:* 93

No. of boarders: 45

Fees as at 01/09/2022:

Day: £9,243–£17,607

Weekly Boarding: £22,161

Full Boarding: £25,659

Average class size: 15

Parkside School

Whilst Parkside's rich history has its roots steeped in tradition, the boys and girls (in Nursery) enjoy a hugely diverse and exciting curriculum which embraces and prepares them for the future. The strong values and family ethos are clearly at the heart of this energetic and ambitious School.

It is a wonderful environment where the children's curiosity is awakened. Their journey is one of discovery; where talents and passions are nurtured and developed, and the pupils are taught to take responsibility for their learning. There is a genuine pride in every pupil at Parkside; all successes are celebrated for excellence in academic, creative and sporting achievements. This, coupled with firm foundations of instilling courage, confidence, and character leads to the development of respectful young gentlemen.

The Class of 2021/2022, celebrated 100% pass rate in their Common Entrance exams, as well as 27% of the Year securing Scholarships to their chosen Senior School. The Maths results saw an incredible 85% of the Year achieving A* – A; with continued success in English and Science, whereby 90% and 80% respectively achieved A* – B. As well as this, Year 6 achieved an outstanding number of offers for Senior School places at Year 9 entry, following our successful Pre-Test Programme (PTP). This is a direct result of a unique and innovative curriculum delivered through the inspired teaching of a passionate and dedicated staff team; underpinned by the 'make it happen' mantra led by the Head.

Being part of the 'Parkside Family' is a privilege, but not one which is taken for granted. The importance of recognising the wider community and world we live in, serves to teach valuable life lessons about appreciation and gratitude rather than entitlement. This, as a result, means that Parkside boys leave as well rounded, exceptional individuals with respect, humility, integrity and outstanding moral fibre.

Ms Janssen states *"(the children) develop the courage to rise to each challenge, persevere when the going gets tough and face their fears with confidence. Success comes from experiencing failure."*

Further developments during 2022/23 include a fully restored 22m indoor swimming pool, a fully floodlit all-weather pitch and an additional three outdoor cricket nets. A diverse and extensive Extracurricular Club Programme includes Coding, Yoga, Trail Biking, Target Shooting, Golf and Knitting.

Parkside has been shortlisted as one of the Best Independent Boys' Schools in 2022 by the Independent School Parent Magazine as well as for the Best Performing Arts Department, which pays testament to the School's ethos, culture and dedication to its whole community.

PARKSIDE
SCHOOL

(Founded 1879)

The Manor, Stoke d'Abernon, Cobham, Surrey KT11 3PX UK

Tel: 01932 862749

Email: office@parkside-school.co.uk

Website: www.parkside-school.co.uk

Headteacher: Ms Nicole Janssen

Appointed: January 2019

School type: Boys' Day Preparatory, Co-ed Nursery

Age range of boys: 2–13 years

Age range of girls: 2–4 years

No. of pupils enrolled as at 01/09/2022: 270

Fees as at 01/09/2022: Please enquire

Average class size: 14-18

Ryde School with Upper Chine

A Breath of Fresh Air Every Day

Ryde aims to provide world class education on the Isle of Wight. As a Round Square, PSB and IB World School Ryde nurtures pupils' character and skills, helping them to make a positive difference and embrace the opportunities of the wider world.

Situated in a safe and idyllic island setting, just off the South Coast of England, Ryde School with Upper Chine (known locally as Ryde School) has been inspiring pupils for one hundred years. The only independent day and boarding school on the Isle of Wight, boys and girls aged 2 1/2 to 18 enjoy excellent academic teaching alongside a wide range of extra-curricular activities, in a nurturing environment – helping them to be resourceful and resilient in the face of challenge and change.

We pride ourselves on aiming high for our pupils and offering many diverse activities alongside our academic teaching to build resilient, confident pupils ready to embrace the wider world. Main sports, such as netball, cricket, rugby and hockey are played against schools on and off island with football, athletics, croquet and riding also on offer. Sailing is built into the curriculum with beginner to elite sailors thriving at Ryde. The school has an excellent record of academic achievement throughout all age groups and was the first independent school in the UK to offer the IB Career-related Programme alongside the IB Diploma Programme and our A Level Plus Programme, through which pupils study for A Levels but also take advantage of the IB courses on offer and add them as enrichment options. We also offer a one year GCSE and Pre-Sixth Form course providing excellent preparation for entry into the Sixth Form.

Pupils leave to go on to study at Oxbridge, medical schools, other Russell Group Universities and Art, Music and Drama colleges. Pupils succeed academically and are well-mannered, characterful, happy and independent; a result of Ryde School's dynamic yet welcoming environment.

Boarding pupils live in two new boarding houses within the 17 acres of School grounds: Millfield, a sensitively renovated Victorian villa for the younger boarders or the new purpose-built Centenary House, with stunning sea views, designed to prepare older students for university and adult life. Both houses have multiple common rooms, study areas and single and twin bedrooms, mostly en-suite. Weekends are spent learning to paddle board, go-karting or simply enjoying long walks on the beaches with a boarding house dog. Barbecues and football are regular pursuits as well as cooking and now latterly bee keeping! The beehives are situated in the gardens of the School and pupils are looking forward to trying Ryde School honey.

Day pupils range from local Island families to those travelling to the school daily from Portsmouth and the surrounding areas via the 10 minute hovercraft service. Boarding options include full, weekly and flexi with a diverse boarding community including around 13 different nationalities. Ryde is only 90 minutes from Heathrow and parents embrace the weekly and flexi boarding option to enable them to live on the island or nearby and commute more widely to work, on the mainland and further afield. Breakfast and supper clubs and school buses across the island augment that flexibility for our pupils.

Our Open Mornings each term are a great time to view the school as is our annual Summer School during four weeks of July and August. We also offer individual tours throughout the year and will work with you to find a suitable time if you are visiting the Island for a short period.

RYDE SCHOOL
WITH UPPER CHINE

(Founded 1921)

Queen's Road, Ryde, Isle of Wight PO33 3BE UK

Tel: 01983 562229

Email: admissions@rydeschool.net

Website: www.rydeschool.org.uk

Headmaster: Mr Will Turner

Appointed: August 2022

School type: Co-educational Day & Boarding Prep & Senior, Nursery & Sixth Form

Age range of pupils: 2.5–18 years (boarding from 10)

No. of pupils enrolled as at 01/09/2022: 795

Fees as at 01/09/2022:

Day: £2,780 – £4,970 per term

Weekly boarding: £9,600 – £9,765 per term

Full boarding: £10,780 – £10,945 per term

Average class size: 15-22

Teacher/pupil ratio: 1:10

Seaford College

Seaford College is a coeducational independent day and boarding school for pupils aged 5 to 18, situated amid 400 acres of picturesque parkland in West Sussex. The College, with its excellent amenities and outstanding panoramic views, offers an inspirational environment that nurtures academic excellence, sporting success and creative talent.

The college uses its resources to provide and enhance educational, cultural, spiritual and social opportunities so that students leave school as confident, articulate and well-rounded individuals.

Pupils in the Preparatory School at Seaford College share the superb facilities with the Senior School and enjoy a seamless education from 5 to 18. The Prep School prides itself on its friendly atmosphere.

Boarding is offered to students from the age of 10 and many pupils elect to board in order to take full advantage of the social, sporting and extracurricular activities on offer. The College offers full boarding, weekly and flexible boarding in order to meet the needs of pupils and their parents.

A new boys' boarding house, has individual and twin bedrooms opened in 2011. Girls board in the historic Mansion house. Recent developments include a new music suite, which consists of individual teaching and practice rooms, a computer and keyboard room, a sound-proofed band practice room and outdoor concert arena.

A state-of-the-art maths and science block offers the latest technologies and facilities, while the College has long been recognised as a centre of excellence for art and design. A large exhibition gallery is incorporated into the purpose-built arts faculty.

Seaford College offers outstanding sports facilities, including an all-weather water-based Astroturf hockey pitch, golf course and driving range. Students regularly play at county level. A state-of-the-art sports centre was opened in 2017.

Overseas students are expected to study English as a foreign language and study for the International Language Testing System, which is a requirement for UK university entrance.

Seaford opened an impressive Sixth Form centre in September 2019. They have their own social areas, study areas and cafe. Seaford sees its Sixth Form very much as a transitional stage. They have their own social centre, which has facilities for individual study, a lounge area and several classrooms where subjects such as Economics, Business Studies and Media Studies are taught.

Sixth Form boarders have study bedrooms, as well as their own common room. Students are divided into small tutor groups, but most commonly meet on a 1-to-1 basis with their tutors to discuss aspects of their work and progress.

Many of Seaford's Sixth Formers go on to university or higher education – all are equipped with self-confidence, as well as a passion for life and a willingness to succeed.

Entry to the College is by test and Trial Day and, although intake is non-selective, expectations are high. If your child is talented and enthusiastic, the College offers a range of scholarships at 11+, 13+ and Sixth Form, including Academic Studies, Music, Art and Sport.

The college has its own dedicated learning support unit, catering for pupils with dyslexia, dyscalculia and dyspraxia.

Whatever their chosen path, Seaford College seeks to prepare young people for adult life so that they have the personal skills and confidence to make it a success. The school allows its pupils to achieve their potential and beyond, inspiring personal ambition and success so that personal ambitions are achieved inside and outside the classroom.

(Founded 1884)

Lavington Park, Petworth, West Sussex GU28 0NB UK

Tel: 01798 867392

Fax: 01798 867606

Email: headmasterpa@seaford.org

Website: www.seaford.org

Headmaster: J P Green MA BA

School type: Co-educational Day & Boarding Preparatory, Senior & Sixth Form

Age range of pupils: 5–18 years

No. of pupils enrolled as at 01/09/2022: 943

Boys: 560 **Girls:** 383 **Sixth Form:** 264

No. of boarders: 214

Fees as at 01/09/2022:

Day: £11,880–£24,630

Weekly Boarding: £24,735–£33,345

Full Boarding: £38,070

Average class size: 15-20

Teacher/pupil ratio: 1:9

Sherborne House School

Sherborne House School is a small co-ed day school just outside of Chandlers Ford. Sitting in four acres of woodland, in the quiet village of Hiltingbury, it caters for 272 pupils between the ages of 6 months and 11 years, with average class sizes of just twelve.

Under the Headship of Mark Beach, the school was inspected by the Independent Schools Inspectorate in July 2021, which rated it 'excellent in all areas'. Being part of Bellevue Education, a world-class group of exceptional schools, Sherborne House remains dedicated to providing the best possible education to their children.

In addition, personal development at the school was ranked Excellent in the last ISI report and something Mark says he is particularly proud of. "We tell the children all the time to make the most of every opportunity they're given. That really does prepare them for the future in which they can embrace and explore everything that comes their way."

The nursery provision from 6 months to 4 years is award winning. Fully renovated in 2020, the nursery takes children aged between 6 months to 3 years. Close, nurturing attention is paid to the small classes and weekly specialist French, music and P.E. lessons for those aged two upwards.

Through the purposeful and busy atmosphere within the school gates, it is evident that each child at Sherborne House is encouraged to explore. The children learn by pursuing their own interests, cultivating their curiosity, developing tenacity and providing the confidence to own their own voice.

The school's language of learning encourages children to reflect on the mental processes and the skills they use and apply in their self-driven learning journey. Rather than simply praising success (or a final outcome), they celebrate effort, persistence and positive attitudes to the frequent challenges in the process of learning. By empowering their children to develop their 'learning to learn' skills, the school aims to improve outcomes for all.

Sherborne House boasts a curriculum which is irresistible; allowing children to embrace challenges with resilience and to enjoy the effort and mistakes that come with learning. Indeed, children at Sherborne House are evidently intrigued by the how and why of mistakes made; acting on constructive feedback and offering praise for a job well done. This visibly consistent approach was articulated most profoundly to us by children during our visit. When talking about their learning, the children spoke proudly about the focus their teachers have on relevance, on their interests and on fun; 'Our teachers listen to us and we lead our learning with their support.'

This is mirrored in Mark's aim; 'to engender confidence in exploration entwined with awe about learning – to sew a golden thread which interweaves throughout a child's life enabling their enquiring mind, to go on to write their own extraordinary story.

39 Lakewood Road, Chandlers Ford, Eastleigh, Hampshire SO53 1EU UK

Tel: 02380 252440

Email: info@sherbornehouse.co.uk

Website: www.sherbornehouse.co.uk

Headmaster: Mr Mark Beach

School type:
Co-educational Day Preparatory & Nursery

Age range of pupils: 6 months–11 years

Sherfield School

Sherfield School is a leading co-educational independent day and boarding school for children from 3 months to 18 years. It offers an outstanding, all-round academic, active and creative environment where children of all ages have the opportunity to thrive and flourish as they experience the excitement and enjoyment of learning.

Set in 76 acres of idyllic parkland in Hampshire, the 12th Century manor house is at the heart of Sherfield school and boasts a wealth of history linked to the local community. Sherfield School lies nestled in beautiful countryside between Reading and Basingstoke. With good public transport links and its own minibus service, Sherfield is set in a safe, semi-rural setting, yet within close proximity to London.

Pupils at Sherfield benefit from rich and diverse learning experiences, both within and outside the classroom. There are a range of high quality facilities including indoor sports hall, drama studio, two synthetic all-weather surfaces, fitness suite, recording studio and extensive woodland. The state of the art boarding house offers full, weekly and flexi boarding options, in a vibrant and engaging environment offered to domestic and international pupils.

The co-curricular provision is extensive, with provision from 7.30am to 6pm for day pupils and evening and weekend activities for boarders. Sherfield runs an extraordinary enrichment programme which promotes the life-skills needed for everyday life, develop "soft-skills" that employers and universities look for, while also giving pupils the opportunity to find out more about their interests and passions. Outdoor learning is embedded in the ethos of the school, providing opportunities for pupils to learn in different contexts and develop a blend of academic and non-academic experiences.

At Sherfield, we strongly believe in a holistic approach to learning, and one that results in continued development, unleashing the true potential of passionate and creative problem solvers that make up this vibrant school. Children are ready to continue their journey long after leaving Sherfield and contribute to an ever changing global society.

An education at Sherfield is unique, as every pupil receives personalised support and guidance, identifying their individual talents and nurturing their potential. The Sherfield experience enables young people to thrive and flourish as they experience the excitement and enjoyment of learning. Pupils at Sherfield are ambitious, enterprising, inventive, thoughtful, inquisitive and supportive of each other. As a close knit community, they develop the confidence and desire to be the best they can possibly be as they take control of their futures. In an ever changing and evolving society, Sherfield pupils are adept at developing the necessary skills, qualities and experiences to meet the challenges of the future.

At Sherfield great academic results are just a by-product of something even bigger, a brilliant, well-rounded education that identifies and celebrates every child's strengths, and teaches them how to become the best version of themselves. As our Latin motto 'Ad Vitam Paramus' suggests, Sherfield prepares children for life.

SHERFIELD
S C H O O L
Nursery· Junior-Prep· Senior-Prep· Senior· Sixth Form

South Drive, Sherfield-on-Loddon, Hook, Hampshire RG27 0HU UK

Tel: 01256 884800

Email: admissions@sherfieldschool.co.uk

Website: www.sherfieldschool.co.uk

Headmaster: Mr Nick Brain BA(Hons), PGCE, MA, NPQH

School type: Co-educational Day & Boarding Prep & Senior, Nursery & Sixth Form

Age range of pupils:
3 months–18 years (boarding from 9)

No. of pupils enrolled as at 01/09/2022: 625

Fees as at 01/09/2022: Please see website

Sir William Perkins's School

Making your mark on the world begins on day one at Sir William Perkins's School.

We are an independent day school for girls aged 11 to 18 where great things are expected, and where generosity, curiosity and ambition thrive. We are home to approximately 600 students who join us from independent and maintained schools, and who flourish within a diverse, vibrant and happy community.

At SWPS, students are at our heart. We expect the best from them, and in return they can expect the best from us; both in terms of teaching of the highest quality – where everyone is stretched and challenged – and in receiving the tailored support and attention they need to achieve. SWPS is a warm and friendly school: the staff know our students, their talents, hopes and aspirations, and we work with them to develop innate confidence, leadership skills and an ability to perform well with others.

Set in 13 acres of attractive green-belt grounds in Surrey, Sir William Perkins's School is a beautiful environment in which every student can flourish. With first-rate facilities equipped to the highest standard, students have space in which to study, relax, exercise and express themselves.

Academic success is always the priority at SWPS and we are delighted that the 2022 A Level and GCSE results are the best in the School's history. Students consistently achieve outstanding results in STEM subjects – Chemistry, Biology, Maths, Further Maths, Physics and Computer Science. However, the culture is such that education is about far more than achieving top grades. Students are encouraged to become involved in many of the 150 co-curricular activities on offer, with clubs as diverse as Sewing and Dissection. Almost all our students take part in the Duke of Edinburgh Award Scheme, with the number taking the Gold Award among the highest in Surrey.

We pride ourselves on our commitment to pastoral care, with a fully staffed wellbeing room and even a visiting therapy dog. Music, Art and Drama permeate through the school with concerts, productions and exhibitions throughout the year. Sport is high on the agenda and students play competitive fixtures in netball, hockey, tennis, cricket and athletics. Other activities are available such as football, trampolining and dance. We are an elite rowing school – currently ranked in the top 5 girls' schools in the country and this year have achieved notable successes at, among others, the National Schools Regatta and the Henley Regatta.

The school's Sixth Form Centre offers education to the highest standard, as well as welcoming spaces for students to study or relax. Sir William Perkins's School's UCAS preparation programme starts mid-way through Year 12 and continues to the end of Year 13. This focused approach also includes a Higher Education Fair featuring 50 of the most prestigious learning establishments, and a UCAS conference day with specialist speakers providing advice on a wide range of subjects.

SWPS students are prepared for all aspects of life beyond school – and their educational journey continues in Sixth Form, where they are empowered to become confident and successful young adults.

(Founded 1725)

Guildford Road, Chertsey, Surrey KT16 9BN UK

Tel: 01932 574900

Fax: 01932 574901

Email: reg@swps.org.uk

Website: www.swps.org.uk

Head: Mr C C Muller

Appointed: September 2014

School type: Girls' Day Senior & Sixth Form

Age range of girls: 11–18 years

No. of pupils enrolled as at 01/09/2021: 600

Fees as at 01/09/2022:

Day: £6,246 per term

Average class size: Senior School: 24, Sixth Form: 10

Teacher/pupil ratio: 1:8

Skippers Hill Manor Preparatory School

"Skippers is a magical school. A place where every child can be the child they want to be. The school caters brilliantly for all three of my very different children who are happy and thriving. It's a gem of a place with a fab reputation, I wouldn't hesitate recommending Skippers." Current parent 2022

The children at Skippers Hill are at the heart of the school and ensuring their happiness and wellbeing is key. The high academic achievement, broad range of talents and impressive social confidence that the children show year after year is embedded in the school's core ethos. Their smiles speak for themselves!

An excellent team of specialist staff provide exciting opportunities for the children to achieve to the best of their abilities in all areas. Whether they thrive on academic challenge, feel a burning desire to perform, are bursting with creative spirit or can't wait to hit the sports field, the children are encouraged to make the most of every opportunity.

The strong academic results speak for themselves, with children consistently performing above national and local averages at every stage of their education. For a mixed ability school, Skippers has an excellent reputation for gaining significant numbers of scholarships for entry to top senior schools at 13+ across a range of disciplines. The school has strong, long-standing relationships with the senior schools in the area and Skippers children are highly sought-after for their sound academic grounding, strong sense of community spirit and overall zest for life.

Skippers is privileged to enjoy a stunning rural setting in 22 acres of beautiful Sussex countryside that truly enables the all-round development of the children in their care. Children are provided with the space to flourish in every sense and the bespoke programme of outdoor learning is interwoven throughout the curriculum for all ages.

Skippers is a warm and welcoming community; a visit to the school would be strongly advised in order to experience the energy for yourself and to gain a deeper understanding of what a special place Skippers is.

"I was completely blown away by how happy everyone was! The atmosphere was calm and extremely happy and I loved the relationship that has so clearly been built up between all the adults and the children." Prospective parent 2022

After a recent visit the headmaster of Tonbridge, James Priory commented:

"I was really impressed by their gentle confidence, the enthusiasm they showed for academic subjects and co-curricular pursuits, and the extent to which they knew and encouraged each other in their interests."

Skippers Hill Manor Preparatory School

Five Ashes, Mayfield, East Sussex TN20 6HR UK

Tel: 01825 830234

Email: info@skippershill.com

Website: www.skippershill.com

Headmaster: Mr Phillip Makhouli

School type: Preparatory School & Nursery

Age range of pupils: 2–13

Fees as at 01/09/2022:

Day: £2,932–£5,062 per term

St Lawrence College

Founded in 1879, St Lawrence College is a thriving independent day and boarding school, providing a first class education for boys and girls from 3 to 18 years. Currently, we have approximately 585 pupils – 145 in the Junior School and 438 in the Senior School, of which 135 are boarders (boarding from 7 years of age).

Located in the Kent coastal town of Ramsgate, and within easy walking distance of the sea, the school is set in 45 acres of safe and spacious grounds, housing both beautiful historic architecture and outstanding contemporary facilities.

In the Classroom

Academic standards are high across the school, which offers an extensive choice of GCSEs and A-levels, with an excellent success rate of pupils going on to their first choice of university. We ensure pupils attain their personal best academically, whilst preparing them for life in a rapidly changing global society. Modern facilities combined with traditional values, based on our Christian roots, draw out the talents of each pupil, whilst our policy for keeping class sizes small ensures that our teachers can look after the individual needs of each pupil.

Outside the Classroom

Sporting facilities are exceptional, and expert coaching is provided at all levels in a variety of disciplines, including rugby, netball, hockey and cricket. We were national champions in boys' indoor hockey and girls' outdoor hockey last year. The magnificent sports centre houses a fitness suite, squash courts, climbing wall, dance studio and a large sports hall for activities such as badminton and basketball.

Music and drama flourish, enhanced by the school's 500-seat theatre, and there are many opportunities for pupils to perform. All pupils benefit from an extensive activities programme which in the Senior School includes the CCF (Combined Cadet Force) and a thriving Duke of Edinburgh's Award Scheme, as well as chess, archery, golf, fencing, football, sailing, horse riding, swimming, table tennis, musical theatre and many more activities.

Boarding at St Lawrence

Strong pastoral care, high quality teaching and a great emphasis on extra-curricular activity make this a very special community in which to live and learn. Boarding is central to the school's life and is one of our great strengths. A wide range of evening and weekend activities are provided for boarders, along with additional events and fun day trips. We offer full time and weekly boarding options, and we aim to provide a 'home-from-home' for our boarding pupils, both in terms of comfort and atmosphere. In recent years, a substantial programme of investment has created exceptional boarding facilities, with all rooms en-suite.

Location

The self-contained campus is situated within easy walking distance of the historic seaside town of Ramsgate. It has excellent transport links to the continent, being near to both Dover and the Channel Tunnel. London is only 75 minutes away by high-speed rail link to St Pancras International. Gatwick and Heathrow are under two hours away.

St Lawrence College

(Founded 1879)

College Road, Ramsgate, Kent CT11 7AE UK

Tel: 01843 572931

Email: admissions@slcuk.com

Website: www.slcuk.com

Head of College: Mr Barney Durrant

School type: Co-educational Day & Boarding Prep & Senior, Nursery & Sixth Form

Age range of pupils: 3–18 years

No. of pupils enrolled as at 01/09/2022: 585

Fees as at 01/09/2022:

Day: £8,394–£18,558

Full Boarding: £29,454–£38,952

Teacher/pupil ratio: 1:8

St Swithun's School

Compassion, integrity, and a quiet sense of self-confidence
St Swithun's School is a renowned independent day, weekly and full-boarding school for girls set in 45 acres overlooking the Hampshire Downs on the outskirts of Winchester, yet only 50 minutes by train from central London. It offers excellent teaching, sporting and recreational facilities.

Boarding at St Swithun's is designed with the modern family in mind. The range of boarding options allows parents to balance the demands of a busy lifestyle, reassured that their daughter has access to a huge breadth of opportunities, first class academic and pastoral support, further education expertise and the secure, homely atmosphere of a contemporary British boarding house.

The school has a long-standing reputation for academic rigour and success. Girls are prepared for public examinations and higher education in a stimulating environment in which they develop intellectual curiosity, independence of mind and the ability to take responsibility for their own learning. They achieve almost one grade higher at GCSE than their already significant baseline ability would suggest, and approximately half a grade higher at A level. St Swithun's offers a comprehensive careers and higher education support service throughout the school years. Its Oxbridge preparation is part of a whole-school academic enrichment programme providing additional challenge and stimulation.

St Swithun's describes itself as an 'appropriately academic' school, celebrating intellectual curiosity and the life of the mind, but not to the exclusion of all else. They expect their pupils to develop individual passions and through them to acquire a range of skills and characteristics. These characteristics will include a willingness to take risks, to question and to debate, and to persevere in the face of difficulty. In the words of Samuel Beckett: *"Ever tried. Ever failed. No matter. Try again. Fail again. Fail better."*

Whilst achieving academic excellence, girls also have the opportunity to do 'something else'. There is an extensive co-curricular programme of over 100 weekly and 50 weekend activities to choose from. As well as academic classrooms and science laboratories, there is a magnificent performing arts centre with a 600-seat auditorium, a music school, an art and technology block, a sports hall and a full-size indoor swimming pool. There is an impressive library and ICT facility. The grounds are spacious and encompass sports fields, tennis courts and gardens.

With kindness and tolerance at the heart of its community, St Swithun's provides a civilised and caring environment in which all girls are valued for their individual gifts. By the time a girl leaves she will be courageous, compassionate, committed and self-confident with a love of learning, a moral compass and a sense of humour.

Open days provide an excellent introduction to the school and include a student-led tour, an opportunity to meet the staff and a presentation from the head giving an overview of the unique atmosphere and opportunities at St Swithun's. To book a place on an open day, or to arrange an individual visit at a more convenient time, please contact Kate Cairns on 01962 835703 or email registrar@stswithuns.com. Keep up to date with latest news by visiting www.stswithuns.com, or on Twitter @StSwithunsGirls.

St Swithun's
WINCHESTER

(Founded 1884)

Alresford Road, Winchester, Hampshire SO21 1HA UK

Tel: 01962 835700

Fax: 01962 835779

Email: office@stswithuns.com

Website: www.stswithuns.com

Head of School: Jane Gandee MA(Cantab)

Appointed: 2010

School type: Girls' Day & Boarding Senior & Sixth Form

Age range of girls: 11–18 years

No. of pupils enrolled as at 01/09/2022: 505

Sixth Form: 137

No. of boarders: 214

Fees as at 01/09/2022:

Day: £22,794

Full Boarding: £38,340

St. Andrew's School

St. Andrew's School was founded in 1937 and is a respected and thriving coeducational prep school, of around 300 children. Set in 11 acres of grounds approximately half a mile from Woking town centre, the School seeks to create a nurturing and happy environment of trust and support in which all pupils are encouraged and enabled to develop their skills, talents, interests and potential to the full – intellectually, physically and spiritually.

At St. Andrew's children feel secure and confident and are highly motivated to perform to the best of their ability in all aspects of school life. They are competitive without losing sight of their responsibility to share and they are justifiably proud of their school and their own personal achievements. We also place great emphasis on consideration for others. Courtesy and mutual respect underpins the behaviour policy at St. Andrew's and we aim to teach children about patience, empathy and unselfishness, whilst encouraging them to use their time wisely in an independent and self-reliant manner.

St. Andrew's School prides itself in providing a broad based curriculum that focuses on enabling our children to enjoy a full range of subjects. Educating the whole child is central to our ethos and, whilst academic standards are high, there are also real opportunities to develop their skills in art, music and sport together with a fantastic programme of after school activities. This is supported by specialist teaching facilities for all subjects including science, ICT, music and art. In our latest ISI inspection (Jan 2016) the school was rated 'excellent' in all areas and, with the benefit of individual attention and specialist teachers in all areas of the curriculum, the children are able to reach their full potential in a happy, caring and supportive environment.

When it is time to move on to senior schools at the end of Year 8, the children are prepared for entrance and scholarship exams to a wide range of independent senior schools and the school provides guidance and advice to parents on the senior school choices that best suit each individual child.

St. Andrew's is very proud of its excellent on-site facilities including a brand new theatre, food tech room, classrooms, library and changing rooms together with excellent sports pitches, all weather sports surface, tennis courts, cricket nets and a swimming pool. We are very fortunate to enjoy the benefits of carefully designed school grounds that meet the needs of the children's physical and social development. Main school games are football, hockey, cricket and netball. Other activities include cross-country running, swimming, tennis and athletics.

Children can be supervised at school from 8am and, through our extensive after-school activities programme for Year 3 and above, until 6pm most evenings during the week. An after-school club is available from 4.15pm to 6pm (chargeable) for Pre-Prep, Year 3 and Year 4 children.

Children are assessed for entry into Year 2 and above. The school has a number of scholarships and bursaries available.

Don't just take our word for it, come and visit the school to see for yourself! We have three open days, one per term, but you are also welcome to visit the school at other times. Please contact the Head of Marketing & Admissions for more information and to arrange a visit. We look forward to welcoming you.

ST. ANDREW'S

SCHOOL · WOKING

(Founded 1937)

Church Hill House, Horsell, Woking, Surrey GU21 4QW UK

Tel: 01483 760943

Email: admissions@st-andrews.woking.sch.uk

Website: www.st-andrews.woking.sch.uk

Headmaster: Mr D Fitzgerald

Appointed: 2020

School type:
Co-educational Day Preparatory & Nursery

Age range of pupils: 3–13 years

No. of pupils enrolled as at 01/09/2022: 310

Fees as at 01/09/2022:

Day: £4,392–£17,280

Teacher/pupil ratio: 1:10

Stroud School, King Edward VI Preparatory

Stroud School is an exciting, independent preparatory school where boys and girls aged 3 to 13 thrive in its unique family environment. With an ISI Excellent rating, it is the preparatory school for King Edward VI School, Southampton.

Highwood House is an impressive Victorian building standing in 22 acres of beautiful rural countryside. With only six former heads since its foundation in 1926, Stroud has always been a school that values the family ethos. It is a school with a strong academic record, fantastic sports facilities and links to strong academic secondary schools. Stroud's curriculum achieves the highest academic standard without compromising the key skills its children need to be successful in the workplace and generally in life.

The school ethos and curriculum is centred around the Stroud Spirit values, which provide pupils with a strong sense of community; this character curriculum not only fosters creativity and curiosity, but it equips its children with empathy, celebrates individuality and encourages its children to live up to the school motto, in aeternum intrepidus – Forever Undaunted – every day.

Specialist teaching begins in Nursery with specialist sport, music, languages and computing, and this develops along with the children, until they receive a curriculum that is entirely specialist taught from the beginning of Year 6. With small classes, dedicated teachers and an exciting extra-curricular clubs and activities programme, children are exposed to many activities which will hopefully ignite their passions. Additionally, there's an outdoor pool, huge sports hall, riding paddock, dance studio, music practice rooms, a science lab, dedicated ICT suites for both KS1 and KS2/3 plus a brand new Masterchef-style food tech kitchen and a newly-expanded Wellbeing centre.

Stroud has always been a school that believes in children thriving when they are happy and have plenty of access to the great outdoors. In a world where education is increasingly digitised, Stroud wants its children to flourish outside, whether that's during Forest School sessions in the woods, conducting science experiments down by the ponds or caring for the school farm animals. Its farm is home to chickens (fed by the little ones), beehives and pygmy goats, which live alongside three ponies. There are large ponds used for pond dipping and ecology studies, and a newly-built bird hide nestled into their woodland to allow children to get closer to nature. Veg boxes sit just outside the classrooms and the school has held an Eco School Green Flag for more than 10 years, recognising our commitment to sustainability.

Sport assumes an inclusive approach at Stroud and the school regularly uses the pitches at its Wellington Sports Ground, its Outward Bound Centre in the Dartmoor National Park, and facilities at its senior school King Edward VI. Traditional sports are part of school life: boys play rugby, football, hockey and cricket, while girls take on netball, hockey and cricket.

Stroud was, in fact, one of the first schools to offer cricket to all boys and girls from Year 3 upwards, suggesting a willingness to embrace new ideas. Certainly, alternative sports play a big part in the curriculum, such as handball, ultimate Frisbee and lacrosse, alongside athletics and swimming in the Summer Term.

Several new initiatives over the last two years have been demonstrative of how well Stroud is moving forward. And further planned developments allow for new facilities that will keep pace with a 21st Century educational need. What has not changed at Stroud, however, is the opportunities that it provides for its pupils.

STROUD SCHOOL
King Edward VI Preparatory

(Founded 1926)

Highwood House, Highwood Lane, Romsey, Hampshire SO51 9ZH UK

Tel: 01794 513231

Email: registrar@stroud-kes.org.uk

Website: stroud.kes.school

Headmistress: Mrs Rebecca Smith

School type:
Co-educational Day Preparatory & Nursery

Age range of pupils: 3–13 years

Fees as at 01/09/2022:

Day: £4,060–£6,515 per term

Average class size: 16-18

The Abbey School

One of the country's foremost independent girls' schools from 3-18 The Abbey is a place where academic excellence becomes a natural process of growth and curiosity at every stage of the journey, from the age of 3 to 18. We are a school that celebrates success in all its forms, and every girl is encouraged to explore her own unique strengths and discover her passions through a vast choice of opportunities – both inside and outside the classroom.

For many years The Abbey Junior School has been developing a leading system of inquiry-based study where students are in charge of their own learning. We help them to cover topics with active, questing intelligence, led by questions, finding their own answers. Our teachers support, encourage and guide so that students have the confidence to make discoveries of their own.

From September 2021, we embraced the internationally recognised and renowned Primary Years Programme (PYP) as an IB Candidate School, combining it with our own Abbey Ideas and Passion (Abbey IP). Together they support our theme of Human Intelligence.

The programme is academically challenging, robust, supporting curriculum milestones and going far beyond them. It is innovative and outward-looking, prioritising creativity and connections. It is full of joy, reward and illumination. Simply put: it is the most exciting, innovative and rigorous curriculum available anywhere in the country.

Throughout the Senior School, we seek to provide a 'real-world' education that goes outside the classroom to offer a myriad of opportunities for students to explore, identify and cultivate their passions. Far from being a blank canvas, every individual arrives with a rich palette of her own unique colours – and we encourage them to embrace them in all their glory. Our exceptional co-curricular provision sets us apart: whatever your daughter's enthusiasm, there will be an activity just right for her and lots of new things to try.

Sixth Form provides a pathway to suit each student through our A Level and IB curriculum offerings. Our internationally-minded ethos means that we collaborate across divides and strive to provide an education that prepares students to step out into an uncertain world with confidence, empathy, and at ease with those from all cultures. Our pioneering methods put the 'why' back at the heart of learning and our holistic approach places equal emphasis on academic achievement, intellectual agility and emotional wellbeing.

The academic results attained speak for themselves. The A Level cohorts regularly achieve upwards of 70% A*-A grades – enabling them to move on to study at the university that is right for them. The School is also one of the top performing IB schools academically – not only in the UK, but globally. In 2022, our students achieved an average of 40 points, compared to the global average of 30, placing The Abbey as one of the leading IB Schools in the World.

Above all, The Abbey is passionate about creating a learning experience that is joyful and meaningful. Our self-regulating culture helps us all to look after each other, and our inspiring teachers are dedicated to fostering a special relationship with each and every individual.

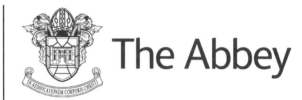

(Founded 1887)

Kendrick Road, Reading, Berkshire RG1 5DZ UK

Tel: 0118 987 2256

Email: admissions@theabbey.co.uk

Website: www.theabbey.co.uk

Head: Mr Will le Fleming

Appointed: September 2020

School type:
Girls' Day Preparatory & Senior, Nursery & Sixth Form

Age range of girls: 3–18 years

No. of pupils enrolled as at 01/09/2022: 1000

Fees as at 01/09/2022:

Day: £13,185–£19,830

The New Beacon School

The New Beacon is a place of energy and success, for individual boys and for the entire school community. We know what makes boys tick – from the sensitive to the ebullient – and I have no doubt they achieve more here than in any school I have led. A clear mission, high expectations and excellent teaching lead to achievement: they can all be found in this Prep School.

In the classroom, on the sports field, in the music room, the art, design and technology departments, or even in the way members of the school community support each other, New Beacon boys strive for personal excellence. It is our ambition to help them in this and in reaching their full potential.

We aim to stimulate every part of the boy's brain – academic, intellectual, creative, cultural, spiritual and physical. Music is a great strength of the school – three former pupils are current organ scholars at Oxford / Cambridge. There is sport for all with our top teams competing at the highest national level – and four current international sportsmen in modern pentathlon, England rugby and two playing in the same test match earlier in 2022.

In 2021 The New Beacon formed a closer association with Tonbridge School: two like-minded boys' schools with remarkably similar mission. Traditionally, many boys leave The New Beacon for Tonbridge but, equally, a central part of our mission is to work with parents in finding the best secondary school for each individual boy. They are all unique! The Kent 11+ test has seen an 86% pass rate in the last five years. Boys at 13 have proceeded to 23 different independent day and boarding schools in the last six years with Sevenoaks School being another popular option.

The New Beacon
Ex Fumo · Dare · Lucem

Brittains Lane, Sevenoaks, Kent TN13 2PB UK

Tel: 01732 452131

Email: admin@newbeacon.org.uk

Website: www.newbeacon.org.uk

Headmaster: Mr Mike Piercy

School type:
Boys' Day & Boarding Preparatory, Co-ed Nursery

Age range of boys: 3–13 years

Age range of girls: 3–4 years

No. of pupils enrolled as at 01/09/2022: 350

Fees as at 01/09/2022:

£3,550 – £5,995 per term

Average class size: 15

The Oratory Prep School

The Oratory Prep School is a leading independent day and boarding Catholic school for children aged 2 – 13, set within 65 acres of South Oxfordshire countryside.

Pupils benefit from an excellent education enriched by outstanding facilities including extensive woodland, ponds and adventure playgrounds; a learner pool and a 25 metre heated indoor swimming pool; a full size 3G pitch; and a raked 300-seater auditorium with state-of-the-art sound and lighting systems.

Our impressive scholarship record and consistently high grades provides testament to the hard work of the whole school family and, whilst our vision is to provide outstanding learning opportunities for all, we are conscious of the importance to strike the right educational balance, so that our children are prepared for their future endeavours, whilst very much enjoying the journey that they are embarking on. This is crucial in our every-changing global climate.

At The Oratory Prep School, we are proud of the work of all our children and are passionate about ensuring their emotional and social wellbeing. Our commitment to excellent pastoral support, with an emphasis on Catholic values, is central to all aspects of school life.

Beyond the classroom, we provide a wealth of opportunities enabling pupils to thrive in a variety of fields, whether in orchestra, choir, on the stage or on the rugby field. Our action-packed Activity Programmes offer activities ranging from fencing to cookery alongside our diverse Saturday Enrichment Programme including modules in debating, interview and presentation skills, orienteering and beekeeping. Outstanding Performing Arts opportunities are also available, through LAMDA from Year 1, instrument and vocal tuition, and musical and drama productions.

Little Oaks Nursery is where the journey begins. We welcome children from two years of age where we instil a spirit of exploring and discovery and an appetite for trying out new things.

We nurture aspiration from the earliest age through an excited and varied curriculum that challenges and extends our children academically and is rich in music, art, sport and outdoor learning.

In Junior Prep (Reception to Year 4) and Senior Prep (Year 5 to 8), our pupils achieve academic success through a well-rounded, hands on education that brings out the best in each child.

We balance academic rigour with fostering a continuous love for learning, making it fresh and fun and engendering a raft of skills and attitudes – such as being inquisitive, creative and adventurous.

Alongside this, we offer a wealth of extra-curricular trips and activities to enrich learning and provide a breadth of experience that enables each child to discover talents and passions that prepare them for senior school and for life beyond.

Boarding is an integral part of school life. We provide full, weekly and flexi-boarding to children from the time that they enter Year 3 upwards with many taking advantage of our weekly flexi-boarding programmes. Boarders enjoy a full and varied calendar of activities throughout the year – from our Saturday Enrichment Programme and sports matches to various outings and cultural trips.

Here at The Oratory Prep School, our focus is to work with you and your child to ensure that his or her learning journey continues – not only in a way that challenges them intellectually, but in a manner that inspires their curiosity and enables them to dream.

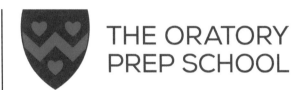

THE ORATORY PREP SCHOOL

Great Oaks, Goring Heath, Reading, Berkshire RG8 7SF UK

Tel: 0118 984 4511

Email: office@oratoryprep.co.uk

Website: www.oratoryprep.co.uk

Headteacher: Mr Andrew De Silva

Appointed: September 2022

School type:
Co-educational Day & Boarding Preparatory & Nursery

Age range of pupils: 2–13 years (boarding from 7)

No. of pupils enrolled as at 01/09/2022: 330

Fees as at 01/09/2022:

Day: £3,600–£6,200 per term

Full Boarding: £7,790–£9,050 per term

Average class size: 16-18

The Royal School, Haslemere

Excellence, Future Ready, A Sense of Fun

The Royal is a vibrant, co-educational all-through school located on a safe and idyllic 26-acre site in the historic, charming market town of Haslemere, Surrey, yet only 50 minutes by train from central London. As an organisation that embraces modern ideas but is steeped in tradition and history, we are proud of our 180 years of history and privileged to have HRH The Princess Royal as our President.

Excellence

Excellent teaching and outstanding pastoral care underpin everything we do. It is a powerful combination in enabling happiness and success. Pupils leave us with the qualifications and experience they need to take up places at the highest-performing universities. The different courses Royal students go on to read at University reflect a school culture that celebrates individuality and diversity. Courses range from traditional academic degrees such as History and English to highly specialist degrees such as Software Engineering and Medical Sciences to vocational degrees like Journalism & Communications.

Future Ready

Our commitment is to ensure pupils are future ready to thrive in this rapidly changing world. In a time when artificial intelligence is growing at such a rate, developing character and the skills that make us uniquely human is even more important. Our Future Ready Programme, with facilities to match, runs from Reception to Upper Sixth and provides opportunities beyond the traditional curriculum to develop future skills. The programme focuses on three key areas, helping pupils become: Practically Ready, Emotionally Ready and Intellectually Ready. In addition to the curriculum, our new facilities, such as our state-of-the-art Royal TV studio, podcast room, and editing suite, nurture and harness skills such as creativity, collaboration and digital literacy in our pupils.

A Sense of Fun

Royal pupils are engaged, interested and good-humoured; they are quick to encourage and congratulate each other, whatever their strengths and achievements. An extensive extra-curricular programme offers endless opportunities to get involved and try something new, whether on the sports pitch, stage, or even racetrack! Nurturing pupils' willingness to step outside their comfort zone often leads to their greatest achievements.

Home from Home Boarding from age 11+

Our happy, home-from-home boarding environment allows for a sense of community and belonging, where each child is known and nurtured. The rapport between staff and pupils is excellent. Many of our boarders establish life-long friendships across the globe.

High Achievers Programme

The Royal Scholarship Programme is a fantastic opportunity for those who excel academically or possess exceptional talent in Art, Music, Performing Arts and Sports to develop their skills and passions whilst making a powerful contribution to our vibrant and forward-looking school.

Experience The Royal

As soon as visitors come to The Royal, they are struck by the warmth and family feel of the place where pupils are happy and successful. Open Events are the perfect opportunity to experience what makes The Royal the ideal place to thrive. Visit our website www.royal-school.org and register to attend an Open Morning. For more information about our admissions process, email admissions@royal.surrey.sch.uk or call our admissions team on 01428 603 051.

The Royal School

(Founded 1840)

Farnham Lane, Haslemere, Surrey GU27 1HQ UK

Tel: 01428 605805

Email: admissions@royal.surrey.sch.uk

Website: www.royal-school.org

Head: Mrs Pippa Smithson BA (Hons), PGCE, MEd

Appointed: February 2020

President: HRH The Princess Royal

School type: Co-educational Day & Boarding Prep & Senior, Nursery & Sixth Form

Religious Denomination: Church of England

Age range of pupils:
6 weeks–18 years (boarding from 11)

No. of pupils enrolled as at 01/09/2022: 315

No. of boarders: 45

Fees as at 01/09/2022:

Day: £3,681–£6,414 per term

Weekly Boarding: £9,435 per term

Full Boarding: £10,731 per term

Average class size: 15-20

Teacher/pupil ratio: 1:10

Upton House School

Upton House is a progressive and highly regarded Nursery, Pre-Prep and Prep school educating boys and girls from aged 2–11 years. Located in the heart of Windsor, Upton boasts excellent academic standards, high calibre staff and a warm and nurturing environment where children blossom and are prepared with confidence for the very best senior schools. Individual talent is developed, and a progressive curriculum offers a balanced co-education ensuring children are equipped with vital life skills for the future.

"Our children progress to their next schools as confident, successful and independent individuals. We were delighted to be awarded 'Excellent' in all areas in our recent Independent Schools Inspection Report." Rhian Thornton, Headmistress

Although non-selective, 30% of pupils in the past 3 years have achieved one or more scholarships to their chosen senior school. Details of scholarships and next schools can be found on the website.

Little Upton Pre-Nursery and Nursery is a very special environment where children begin their Upton journey from as young as age 2. Little Upton is open a flexible 48 weeks a year should parents require and benefits from being in a beautiful whole school setting. Staff are highly qualified, experienced practitioners and engage the children in stimulating, challenging and exciting activities that enable them to develop their love of learning within the Early Years Foundation Stage. Specialist subjects include French from 2 years old and Mandarin from 3 years old as well as regular PE and music lessons.

Facilities in the Pre-Prep and Prep departments at Upton House include a newly opened arts block housing music rooms, an art and DT studio and a media room with green screen filming facilities. A vibrant and creative technology curriculum which is embedded into all areas of the curriculum. A brand new recording studio enables all the children to create and record as part of our newly introduced music technology lessons. All classrooms are furnished with interactive white boards and iPads are used daily by pupils to support learning throughout the school. Facilities also include a kitchen for Food Technology lessons, a drama and dance studio, gymnasium, two libraries and a delightful Nursery music room. Diverse sporting activities include netball, rugby, hockey, cricket and athletics as well as rowing, judo, fencing and ballet. A wide range of individual musical instrument lessons are also available.

Children at Upton House enjoy breakfast club from 7.45am, healthy meals prepared on site and a wide range of after school extra-curricular activities until 6pm. Holiday clubs are run on site outside of term time.

To book for an open morning, or to arrange a personal tour of the school, please register online or contact Miss Deborah Bates: registrar@uptonhouse.org.uk. We look forward to welcoming you!

We look forward to welcoming you!

(Founded 1936)

115 St Leonard's Road, Windsor, Berkshire SL4 3DF UK

Tel: 01753 862610

Email: registrar@uptonhouse.org.uk

Website: www.uptonhouse.org.uk

Head: Mrs Rhian Thornton BA (Hons) NPQH LLE PGCE

Appointed: September 2016

School type: Co-educational Prep, Pre-Prep & Nursery

Age range of pupils: 2–11 years

No. of pupils enrolled as at 01/09/2022: 299

Boys: 100 **Girls:** 199

Fees as at 01/09/2022:

Day: £3,383–£5,615 per term

Average class size: 16

Wellington College

Wellington College is a vibrant and inspiring coeducational boarding and day school set in 400 acres of parkland, 40 minutes from Heathrow. The College, whose educational philosophy is based on values of kindness, courage, respect, integrity and responsibility, is celebrated not only for its academic achievements but also for its sporting, artistic and dramatic provision which are second to none. Stellar examination results, outstanding provision across all co-curricular areas, and a raft of national accolades contribute to the College's national and international reputation. Wellingtonians study GCSEs, followed by the IB Diploma or A Levels and, whichever route they take, results are superb: in 2022, 75% of grades achieved at A Level were A*/A (with 38% A* and 95% A*-B), while the College's incredible IB average of 41.3 yet again made Wellington one of the UK's highest achieving boarding schools offering the IB Diploma. 75% achieved 40 points or above and 12 students achieved the maximum 45 points. On average 20 of the cohort gain places at Oxford or Cambridge every year and, in 2022, 21 students went on to US universities, many to Ivy League institutions.

The College has an outstanding reputation for sport, with over 30 different activities offered with emphasis equally placed on both performance and participation. Last year Wellington was represented in 12 national finals, with wins or placings in Netball, Hockey, Golf, Rugby, Rackets, Climbing and Fencing, and fielded over 200 teams across all sports, with nearly 2,000 fixtures played. A strategic focus in 2021/22 to raise the profile of girls' sport led to the addition of Friday evening showpiece sporting events in Hockey and Netball, played under lights.

Performing Arts are equally strong. Music and Drama are stunning, with 60% of pupils taking music or LAMDA lessons. Recently, our choir has been to Northern France and recorded and videoed an anthem for the Diamond Jubilee. There have been orchestral and a cappella recordings, two musicals, a student-written play, Shakespeare productions and imaginative and inclusive junior plays as well as a bumper-packed Arts festival, with a spectacular film-music concert. Dance thrives with two spectacular shows each year, as well as many smaller performances and individual lessons. House competitions are popular with the House Singing competition a student highlight. Indeed, student-run events are an important feature of the arts provision and a feature of the student ambassador and scholarship programme.

Leadership and service to others are central: co-curricular activities include its outward-facing Global Citizenship programme in which pupils create and run innovative social action projects, as well as the CCF and Duke of Edinburgh's Award. Over 70 clubs and societies provide unique opportunities, from WTV (Wellington's own television company) to the pupil-run radio station, DukeBox, which broadcasts 24/7, reaching listeners in 41 countries across the globe.

Wellington builds strong external partnerships to broaden impact in education. Wellington was the first HMC school to be accorded Teaching School status and continues its close and mutually beneficial partnership with 58 state schools. The Wellington family of schools includes Eagle House prep school and seven schools in China and Thailand, with new schools in development. This network supports opportunities for cultural dialogue and understanding and broadens access to world-class education including through bursaries and regional education initiatives.

Further information including details about Visitors Days can be found on the website and the Admissions Office can be contacted on +44 (0)1344 444013.

WELLINGTON COLLEGE

(Founded 1853)

Duke's Ride, Crowthorne, Berkshire RG45 7PU UK

Tel: +44 (0)1344 444000

Email: admissions@wellingtoncollege.org.uk

Website: www.wellingtoncollege.org.uk

Master: Mr James Dahl

Appointed: September 2019

Director of IB: Mr Richard Atherton

School type:
Co-educational Day & Boarding Senior & Sixth Form

Religious Denomination: Church of England

Age range of pupils: 13–18 years

No. of pupils enrolled as at 01/09/2022: 1100

Boys: 600 **Girls:** 500 **Sixth Form:** 485

No. of boarders: 865

Fees as at 01/09/2022:

Day: £32,940–£35,760

Full Boarding: £45,090

Average class size:
Lower + Middle = 20 Upper School = 12

Teacher/pupil ratio: 1:7

Weston Green School

Inspiring individuals and nurturing potential for a successful future

A warm welcome to Weston Green School!

As you step through the doors of our wonderful school we hope that you will soon feel part of this special place where children thrive within wonderful surroundings. From age 2-11, our children grow to become independent and confident young people, achieve exceptionally well academically and most of all enjoy their experiences through the immense joy and wonder of learning.

We were recently awarded 'Excellent' in all areas by the Independent Schools Inspectorate (ISI) for the academic achievement and personal development of our pupils, reinforcing our objectives to celebrate childhood and give pupils a breadth of enrichment opportunities to achieve individual success.

Weston Green takes pride in its well-regarded reputation for being a warm and welcoming school where children secure high academic achievement and successfully go on to attain their choices of future schools.

From Nursery and Early Years though to when they leave us at Year 6, every individual is nurtured so that they will not only develop and achieve academically, but also personally, socially and emotionally. Our academic excellence is founded on a focus on the development of the whole person, that each child is provided with the opportunities to enable them to flourish and our partnership with you is key in delivering this successfully.

Our pupils are happy and confident and as a result are successful learners. We guide them through every step to ensure they are well prepared personally, socially and academically for their next phase of education. We call this our Future Schools Programme. Feeding into a broad range of schools, we work closely with families to identify and support the preparation and application for the school that is the right fit for your child.

Our dedicated and specialist teachers have a wealth of experience, expertise and curriculum knowledge, having aspirations for each child to become inquisitive and creative learners, undaunted by their mistakes and eager to face increasingly complex challenges. You will see a school day which places a high priority on the core areas of reading, writing, mathematics and science, yet engages a child in learning these in a highly imaginative and innovative curriculum. In this way children develop crucial skills for learning which then benefits the broad, diverse and rich thematic curriculum we offer.

If you're looking for a school place (for boys and girls aged 2 – 11 years), please come along for a personal tour – contact info@westongreenschool.org.uk to book your place. We look forward to welcoming you soon.

Weston Green School

Weston Green Road, Thames Ditton, Surrey KT7 0JN UK

Tel: 020 8398 2778

Email: info@westongreenschool.org.uk

Website: www.westongreenschool.org.uk

Head Teacher: Mrs Sarah Evans BA Hons, NPQH

School type:
Co-educational Day Preparatory & Nursery

Age range of pupils: 2–11 years

No. of pupils enrolled as at 01/09/2022: 195

Fees as at 01/09/2022: Please see website

South-West

Kingsley School

Welcome to Kingsley School

There are many reasons students could fall in love with Kingsley School, an independent co-educational boarding and day school located in Bideford on the banks of the River Torridge in North Devon.

One reason could be location – Kingsley is set in 25 acres of playfields and woodland, surrounded by stunning countryside, and just five minutes from popular surfing beaches. And another reason could be the school's strong academic tradition – at Kingsley every sixth form student typically goes on to university, including top-tier higher education institutes like Oxford and Cambridge.

But ultimately our students rate the opportunity to find their place, the exceptional support they receive and the welcome as the prime reasons they just can't see themselves going anywhere else but Kingsley.

Kingsley School is an inclusive day and boarding school where every child is important and is treated with dignity and respect. As a relatively small school of around 400 boys and girls, Kingsley's atmosphere is like that of a large family where everybody knows each other well.

The school's philosophy encourages personal qualities such as courage, generosity, honesty, imagination, tolerance and kindness. In addition, we develop the students' wider interests and skills in sport, music, art, and drama. Kingsley also has a national reputation for its Learning Development Centre which provides additional support for students with moderate learning needs. Overall, a Kingsley education develops the individual character and talents of each and every student both inside and outside the classroom.

Becoming part of the family: The boarding houses at Kingsley help form part of the family atmosphere at the school. Students live in three comfortable and well-equipped houses in the school's grounds; two for boys and one for girls. Each house has 30-40 students who are supervised by two teachers and their families who live in the houses as well.

Kingsley School Earth Centre: Kingsley is located within the UNESCO North Devon biosphere and the school's Earth Centre is a unique and very exciting ongoing project for all pupils at school. In response to the challenges of our time, the Earth Centre puts the natural world and environmental sustainability at the core of education here at Kingsley. Kingsley is very proud to be named ISA Sustainability and Environmental Education School of the Year 2020, and a finalist for the Green Award in the Independent School of the Year Awards 2021.

Sport and Clubs: Sport includes traditional sports plus judo, handball and gymnastics squads competing at a National level. As part of the National Theatre Connections programme, the school drama cast performed at the Theatre Royal, Plymouth and the National Theatre, London this year. Popular extra-curricular clubs include the Duke of Edinburgh's Award Scheme, orchestra, computing, art, film making, choir and surfing.

Transport: we run an accompanied coach service to and from Heathrow Airport and Bristol Airport at the beginning and end of each term. Weekly boarding options with transport to London and the South East.

Do follow us on social media

Facebook: Kingsley School Bideford
Instagram: Kingsley School
Twitter: @KSBideford
YouTube: Kingsley School Bideford
www.kingsleyschoolbideford.co.uk

(Founded 1884)

Northdown Road, Bideford, Devon EX39 3LY UK

Tel: 01237 426200

Fax: 01237 425981

Email: admissions@kingsleyschoolbideford.co.uk

Website: www.kingsleyschoolbideford.co.uk

Headteacher: Mr Robert Pavis

Appointed: February 2022

Head of the Prep School: Mr Andrew Trythall

School type: Co-educational Day & Boarding Prep & Senior, Nursery & Sixth Form

Age range of pupils: 0–18 years (boarding from 9)

No. of pupils enrolled as at 01/09/2022: 395

No. of boarders: 100

Fees as at 01/09/2022:

Day: £2,180 per term

Weekly Boarding: £6,135 per term

Full Boarding: £8,775 per term

Average class size: 14

Teacher/pupil ratio: 1:9

Yarrells School & Nursery

About Yarrells

Yarrells School and Nursery provides excellent opportunities for children to enjoy their learning in an enriching environment both indoors and outdoors. We promote high academic standards, integrating the performing & visual arts and sport within a dynamic and extensive curriculum.

Head's Welcome

Yarrells is a gorgeous school, full of happy children who love to learn. Our relationships with the young people we teach are so important. We work really hard to foster happiness, self-confidence and aspiration for life in every individual here.

My absolute passion is to provide an outstanding educational environment for children; one that is warm, nurturing and provides space for a broad curriculum. All the doors of opportunity are open for our young people and the children at Yarrells are able to explore their identities and their talents fully so that they grow both their confidence and their skills to meet life's challenges with relish.

We are incredibly proud of our academic record (91% success rate at 11+ grammar entry in 2020-21) and equally proud of our commitment to non-selective entry to Yarrells at all ages. We work hard to support and challenge our pupils so that their learning is exciting, stimulating and makes their brains ache – in a good way! This gives them a strong sense of achievement, whether they are striving for a grammar school place at 11+, a scholarship award or overcoming a curriculum area of genuine personal difficulty.

We are truly individual in our approach and seeing the commitment and passion within our community every day makes me beam with pride.

(Founded 1927)

Yarrells House, Upton, Poole, Dorset BH16 5EU UK

Tel: 01202 622229

Email: office@yarrells.co.uk

Website: www.yarrells.co.uk

Head: Mrs Sally Moulton

Appointed: September 2012

School type:
Co-educational Day Preparatory & Nursery

Age range of pupils: 2–11 years

No. of pupils enrolled as at 01/09/2022: 257

Boys: 129 **Girls:** 128

Fees as at 01/09/2022: Please enquire

West Midlands

Edenhurst Preparatory School

Edenhurst Preparatory School is an independent, co-educational day school located in Newcastle under Lyme, Staffordshire for pupils aged three months to eleven years.

Our aim is to inspire and support pupils in their learning, and to build a solid foundation for future success. Our dedicated staff and small class sizes help us to achieve this by creating a positive learning environment, with a healthy mix of play, discovery and responsibility.

When the time comes for our pupils to leave Edenhurst, we take pride in their confidence and individuality, their passion for learning, and their ability to embrace all challenges they may encounter in later life.

We are very mindful of the importance of developing a partnership between school and home, maintaining regular contact between teaching staff and parents in order to best serve the needs of each child.

We have a vision to equip children with the necessary skills and attributes to thrive in a rapidly changing world which give our children the 'Edenhurst Edge' – that little bit extra that sets them above their peers.

Our core values are clearly understood and shared by every member of the Edenhurst school community and we:

- nurture – developing children's individual talents and gifts by providing an appropriate level of challenges.
- inspire – using the latest technology to provide a broad and balanced curriculum delivered by Specialist teachers.
- achieve – fostering a love of learning and equip children with the necessary skills to succeed, achieving excellent results in all areas of school life.

The Edenhurst Nursery caters for children from the age of three months to four years, offering the highest quality care in a safe, engaging and nurturing environment. Our qualified, friendly staff are dedicated to providing each child with all the support and encouragement they need to learn and grow.

In Edenhurst Pre-Prep we work closely with each and every child, in order to support them in developing the skills and interests cultivated in the Early Years Foundation Stage. As well as English and Maths, pupils in Pre-Prep study Science, Geography, History and Religious Studies. In addition, children benefit from specialist teaching in Music, Art, ICT, French and P.E., which includes Swimming.

Upon entering the Prep Forms, a specialist subject-based approach is adopted. Each subject is led by a teacher who is a specialist in their own field, allowing the children to benefit from expertise and an enthusiasm derived from a genuine interest in each subject.

Pupils in the Prep Forms continue to build on their skills in English and Maths, as well as other core subjects, and preparation for entrance examinations at 11+ is an ongoing process at Edenhurst. Small class sizes of 20 or below are maintained to allow for the most advantageous pupil to adult ratio.

Children benefit from a careful and sensitive familiarisation with the demands of examinations, and parents are also invited to join the Head or Deputy Head for a discussion on future schooling. Edenhurst has an excellent record in preparing children for transfer to senior school at age 11, and each year a number of children gain scholarships to a range of schools.

Westlands Avenue, Newcastle-under-Lyme, Staffordshire ST5 2PU UK

Tel: 01782 619348

Email: office@edenhurst.co.uk

Website: www.edenhurst.co.uk

Headteacher: Mr Michael Hibbert (Emma Mousley from January 2023)

School type:
Co-educational Day Preparatory & Nursery

Age range of pupils: 3 months–11 years

Fees as at 01/09/2022:

Day: £3,019–£3,655 per term

Ellesmere College

Since its founding in 1884, Ellesmere College has become renowned for its individual focus on student's academic and personal success. An incredibly friendly co-ed boarding, weekly and day school, 600 students from ages 7 to 18, and from all across the globe, are encouraged to explore, engage and evolve to the best of their potential through the College's innovative, dynamic and world class academic and co-curricular opportunities.

At every entry point to the College students are offered a broad choice of academic subjects as well as a vast range of co-curricular activities (DofE, CCF, ESB, EPQ, ILM, Survive and Thrive with the John Muir Award, expeditions, career conventions, affiliations, etc) that develop essential life skills – leadership, initiative, confidence, teambuilding, and above all a belief in themselves that they can achieve if they try their best – the ethos at the heart of the school – to be 'Life:Ready'.

Academic
Ellesmere College has recently been accredited as a High Performance Leaning (HPL) World Class School – one of only 39 in the world. At Key Stages 2 & 3 we offer a wide curriculum preparing them for their choice of i/GCSEs as they move up to Middle School at age 13. Our award winning Support for Learning department supports those students with diverse academic needs including dyslexia, dyspraxia and dyscalculia.

In Sixth Form, students choose A Levels, BTEC or International Baccalaureate (IB), and our students regularly gain entrance to their first-choice university including Oxford, Cambridge and Russell Group institutions. We are ranked in the top 20 British schools offering the IB and are launching our International Foundation Programme (IFP) in the Autumn.

Pastoral Care
All students at the College – whether day pupils or boarders – are assigned to a House, under which they compete in termly House Competitions. Our student accommodation provides a high-quality, comfortable and secure environment for our students from Year 8, with residential staff on site to tend to the pupils' personal and pastoral needs 24 hours a day.

Drama, Music and the Arts
The College was the first independent school to be awarded Artsmark Platinum by the Arts Council of Great Britain for its commitment and delivery of the arts from the traditional to more modern media. Singing is an area of real excellence with four award winning choirs and a wide range of ensembles with opportunities to perform. Participation at every level is encouraged and supported by ESB, LAMDA, ballet & dance classes, and individual tuition.

Sports
We are immensely proud of our sporting tradition at Ellesmere College and physical education is an integral part of the curriculum – playing for ones' house or school, or at national, international and Olympic level. We are an accredited WAoS (World Academy of Sport) Athlete Friendly Education Centre (AFEC), allowing students to balance their studies with demanding training and competition schedules. There are seven distinct Sports Academies – rugby, cricket, tennis, swimming, shooting, football and golf – as well as a High Performance Hockey Programme and many other sports.

We believe very strongly that the foundations for a successful adult life are built at a young age – and at Ellesmere College we empower and enrich our students to become confident, strong and exceptional young adults – truly 'Life Ready'.

(Founded 1884)

Ellesmere, Shropshire SY12 9AB UK

Tel: 01691 622321

Fax: 01691 623286

Email: registrar@ellesmere.com

Website: www.ellesmere.com

Head of School: Mr Brendan Wignall MA, FRSA, MCMI

School type: Co-educational Day & Boarding Preparatory, Senior & Sixth Form

Age range of pupils: 7–18 years (boarding from 12)

No. of pupils enrolled as at 01/09/2022: 600

Fees as at 01/07/2022:

Day: £6,960 per term

Weekly Boarding: £9,035 per term

Full Boarding: £12,655 per term

Teacher/pupil ratio: 1:8

Mander Portman Woodward – MPW Birmingham

MPW Birmingham was founded in 1980 with the goal of ensuring that students experience an education based on the Oxford and Cambridge tutorial system. This means that lessons are more relaxed and informal than a typical school, but are also academically stimulating and demanding. With fewer than ten students in any class, lessons are intensive but rewarding with plenty of opportunity for individual attention and personalised teaching.

MPW Birmingham guides students in their learning by encouraging them to focus on our model of success: aspiration, attitude, attendance, application and achievement. We help students obtain results that all too often they never thought were possible. With almost 30 subjects to choose from at A level and many at GCSE, MPW Birmingham provides a breadth of study opportunity that is unique for a small college. MPW helps students demystify the examination process and develop both the technical skills and academic knowledge needed to perform well under timed conditions. We offer all of our students the opportunity to sit weekly assessments enabling students to perfect examination technique.

We run a university support programme that values every student in equal measure regardless of aspiration; we treat all students as though they are elite. We prepare students for a range of courses including medicine, dentistry and Oxbridge and ensure that they are well equipped to cope with the demands of university life.

Students benefit from outstanding pastoral care with each student being allocated a Personal Tutor. This builds upon our core values of diligence, respect, tolerance and care. We expect our students to work hard but we also expect to provide more support to our students than they would receive at other schools. Our culture is one based on high expectations but one that is both nurturing and unpretentious. We run a non-compulsory enrichment programme in which many students participate, developing both sporting and cultural interests. There is no glass ceiling in MPW Birmingham and we strive to enable all students to reach their potential and use their talents without inhibition.

Our mission is to be one of the leading colleges of its type within the country, enabling students to develop confidence, maturity, knowledge and skills, turning academic aspirations into reality. MPW helps build the character of students enabling them to develop good self-discipline regarding work, intellectual curiosity and a sense of duty regarding community. Our best ambassadors are our students and we are rightly proud of what they achieve with us and what they go on to achieve afterwards. We change lives for the better and help bring about progress and success. Irrespective of where a student is starting from, MPW helps young people achieve special things.

(Founded 1980)

16-18 Greenfield Crescent, Edgbaston, Birmingham, West Midlands B15 3AU UK

Tel: 0121 454 9637

Fax: 0121 454 6433

Email: birmingham@mpw.ac.uk

Website: www.mpw.ac.uk

Principal: Mr Mark Shingleton

School type: Co-educational Day Senior & Sixth Form

Age range of pupils: 14–19 years

Average class size: 8

Shrewsbury School

Located on a beautiful 110-acre site, perched above the historic town of Shrewsbury and the banks of the River Severn, Shrewsbury School has a world-class reputation for all-round excellence. Fully co-educational, with a seven-day boarding heartbeat and an integral day community, we deliver a dynamic education that develops the abilities and enthusiasms of every individual girl and boy.

School should be serious fun. Learning and enjoyment go hand in hand: in the classroom, through a vibrant cocurricular programme and in the communal life of the School. At Shrewsbury, we aim to provide the most diverse, challenging and supportive environment in which all our children can thrive and exceed their own expectations.

A good education opens doors. This means getting the best possible examination results and qualifications. Academic excellence is achieved through a wide-ranging curriculum that uncovers and encourages a genuine love of learning, alongside inspirational teaching that challenges each pupil to strive for her or his personal best.

In 2022, both A Level and GCSE results have been determined by teachers rather than examination. Although the headline A Level figures make for excellent reading (30% A*, 81% A*-B), what has mattered more than ever has been the transition of pupils to their chosen universities and over 90% of Shrewsbury School pupils have been confirmed in their first choice places with 78% attending World Top 200 universities. At GCSE level, 50% of grades were awarded at 9 or 8 (an A* on the old system) and 73% at 9 to 7. Pupils now have an excellent base from which they can move forward with confidence towards their A Level studies.

However, examination certificates are just one product of education. Many skills, values and aptitudes do not come with a piece of paper, but they are nonetheless vital for happy and purposeful living. A great education nurtures character; and it lasts a lifetime.

We want all our pupils to enjoy their life beyond the classroom and Shrewsbury has a long-standing reputation for musical, dramatic and sporting excellence. We compete internationally in cricket and rowing and, on a national level, we are one of the strongest schools for football, cross-country and fives. Facilities and coaching are first-rate across each of these sports, as well as a host of others, including rugby, hockey, netball, lacrosse, fencing, swimming and tennis.

The breadth and quality of drama and music-making at Shrewsbury is remarkable. Shrewsbury School plays and musicals have regularly drawn praise at the Edinburgh Fringe Festival and each year our pupils have the opportunity to perform at prestigious venues, such as London's Cadogan Hall and Birmingham Town Hall. A number of our pupils win places at top music colleges year-on-year.

The Barnes Theatre opened in 2020 by Old Salopian Sir Michael Palin, providing a fantastic home for Drama and Dance at Shrewsbury. The building houses an intimate 230-seat auditorium, two drama studios, a fully equipped dance studio and a state-of-the-art technical workshop.

Shrewsbury pupils also enjoy an extraordinary variety of clubs, societies and co-curricular activities, many of which take place on a dedicated weekly basis. Surrounded by glorious unspoilt countryside, the School makes the most of its close proximity to the Shropshire hills and Snowdonia.

The Shrewsbury School motto gets to the heart of our vision: *Intus Si Recte Ne Labora* – 'if all is right within, trouble not'. Ours is not a superficial, skin-deep education but one that seeks to develop the whole person. If our values are true, and we live by them with honesty and conviction; if we look beyond the surface of things to question and champion independence of mind; and if we learn deeply in order to lead lives of meaning, generosity and purpose, then we will see the full fruits of a Shrewsbury education.

Shrewsbury School

(Founded 1552)

The Schools, Shrewsbury, Shropshire SY3 7BA UK

Tel: 01743 280552

Fax: 01743 243107

Email: admissions@shrewsbury.org.uk

Website: www.shrewsbury.org.uk

Headmaster: Mr. Leo Winkley

Appointed: 2018

School type: Co-educational Day & Boarding Senior & Sixth Form

Religious Denomination: Anglican

Age range of pupils: 13–18 years

No. of pupils enrolled as at 01/09/2022: 845

Boys: 558 **Girls:** 287

No. of boarders: 616

Fees as at 01/09/2022:

Day: £27,930

Full Boarding: £42,210

Average class size: GCSE: 18; A level: 10

Teacher/pupil ratio: 1:9

Tettenhall College

A quintessentially British boarding school, nestled in the leafy English village of Tettenhall, yet within proximity of Wolverhampton and the UK's second city, Birmingham. Tettenhall College provides a safe, and inspiring learning environment which nurtures each child's natural gifts and guides them to reach their true potential, encompassed within 33 acres of protected, ancient woodland.

Tettenhall College is a 'home from home'; boarders are welcomed into modern, newly renovated, well equipped single-sex boarding houses, each with its own dedicated House Parent who live in School with their own families. Round the clock medical and pastoral care ensures that each child feels happy and secure, and our in-house catering team serves a wide variety of tasty and healthy cuisines for breakfast, lunch and dinner. Each boarding house has its own kitchen in which students can prepare their own meals and snacks.

The seven-day boarding activity programme is busy and diverse and encourages each child's immersion into school life, including: trips to historic towns and locations, visits to museums and theme parks and activities such as mountain biking and indoor climbing.

Tettenhall College believes that extracurricular activities are the cornerstone of a well-rounded education and that it fosters social and team working skills. Every child is certain to find activities which will suit them; from our own heated, indoor swimming pool, to squash courts, rugby, cricket and football pitches, extensive music department, art studio and our Victorian-era performance theatre at the heart of the school site. The theatre underpins the ethos of expression and personality that the school encourages. Tettenhall College believes that creative and expressive arts truly inform and foster learning, whilst developing key life skills such as public speaking and improvisation. There's also a multitude of clubs to join, from orchestras, bands, and language clubs to film society, fencing, drama, and chess.

Attainment is consistently high, with over 50% of A level students earning grades A* to A and a high proportion attending the country's most sought after British Russell Group universities, as well as those abroad. Each student in Senior School partakes in the 'Pathways Programme' which introduces them to a wide variety of career and educational opportunities and helps them set out their own career path.

Joining Tettenhall College welcomes you to the global 'TC Family', an international network of former pupils located in the UK and everywhere from Australia to the United States, working in countless industries and professions. Many students return to the School for the annual alumni events and are keen to share their advice and expertise at our career events.

A LEADING DAY & BOARDING SCHOOL FOR BOYS AND GIRLS, AGED 2 - 18

(Founded 1863)

Wood Road, Tettenhall, Wolverhampton, West Midlands WV6 8QX UK

Tel: 01902 751119

Email: admissions@tettcoll.co.uk

Website: www.tettenhallcollege.co.uk

Headteacher: Mr Christopher McAllister

Appointed: January 2020

School type: Co-educational Day

Age range of pupils: 2–18 years

No. of pupils enrolled as at 01/09/2022: 440

Fees as at 01/09/2022:

Day Fees: £2,740 – £5,180 per term

Weekly Boarding Fees from: £6,139 per term

Full Boarding Fees: £7,998 – £11,615 per term

Average class size: 16

Teacher/pupil ratio: 1:8

The Royal School, Wolverhampton

The building works continue! After opening as a Free school/ State Boarding School in 2016, and following the ambitious and successful growth programme in pupil numbers over the past five years, The Royal School's exciting building programme is now well under way to develop first class teaching facilities for pupils from five to 19. Phase one of the school's development plan saw a new Sixth Form Centre and refurbished classrooms. Phase two starts in the summer with renovation and more classrooms coming on line.

At the centre of all that we do is our inclusive community where students study, play and live together harmoniously. The Royal is a small, cohesive community with a friendly atmosphere for both day pupils and boarders alike. Our strong academic tradition is based upon individual attention and encouragement, as well as excellent pastoral care founded on respect, tolerance and understanding of others. Students achieve their full academic potential, whilst a wide range of extended-day activities is available to develop character and leadership. We prepare pupils for Oxbridge and other top universities while also catering to pupils of all abilities. The School regularly achieves high standards in both A-Level and GCSE results, particularly in STEM subjects of mathematics and the sciences. The Royal combines traditional values with a modern outlook and a 'real-world' attitude. At The Royal, education is about developing the whole individual.

Developing the 'whole person' in sport, drama, music and adventurous activity, young people at The Royal are also better placed to make the best of their opportunities to become well-rounded individuals with confidence and empathy for those around them.

The Royal School
Wolverhampton

Penn Road, Wolverhampton,
West Midlands WV3 0EG UK

Tel: +44 (0)1902 341230

Email: info@theroyal.school

Website: theroyalschool.co.uk

Principal: Mr Mark Heywood

School type: Co-educational Day & Boarding

Age range of pupils: 4–19 years (boarding from 11)

No. of pupils enrolled as at 01/09/2022: 1476

Fees as at 01/09/2022:

Full Boarding: £14,580

Average class size: 25

West House School

Situated in the leafy oasis of the Calthorpe Estate, West House School has occupied the same site since its foundation in 1895. Since that time, the school has evolved significantly to become an independent preparatory school for boys aged 4-11 years, with a co-educational Early Years Department offering care and education for children aged from 6 months. West House is a member of The Independent Association of Preparatory Schools and, as such, upholds the requirement to provide a 'world class education'.

Set within five acres of beautiful grounds, less than two miles from Birmingham city centre, the school lies at the heart of a thriving community. Pupils of all ages benefit from two all-weather playing surfaces, a nature reserve and the multi-functional Duce Hall, providing indoor sporting and theatrical facilities. The school is also surrounded by many outstanding cultural and recreational amenities which enrich the lives of all pupils and allow them to explore and extend their talents in numerous curricular and extra-curricular pursuits.

West House is a non-denominational school, guided by Christian principles. It is divided into three departments – Prep (Years 3-6), Pre-Prep (Years 1 & 2) and the Early Years Foundation Stage (Nursery – Reception). From their earliest years, children are encouraged to adopt the core values of the school which are actively promoted throughout the working day and frequently form the focus of assemblies and PSHE lessons.

The school continues to boast a unique family atmosphere of which founding Headmaster, Arthur Perrott Cary Field, would have been proud. In the spirit of combining the best of its traditions with an education that prepares pupils for life in the middle part of the twenty first century, it remains determined to be at the forefront of innovation. This is reflected in the delivery of an ambitious curriculum which complements academic rigour with significant opportunities for pupils to explore personal interests in sport, art, music and drama.

Employing 45 full-time and part-time academic staff, many of whom are subject specialists, West House has grown considerably during the last five years to accommodate approximately 330 pupils, with 130 attending the EYFS Department.

Pupils are prepared for a wide range of senior schools, and standards at 11+ are consistently high, with most Year 6 boys transferring to local grammar schools, King Edward's School, Birmingham and Solihull School. A number of pupils are awarded academic and sporting scholarships and the school also enjoys outstanding success in academic challenges, quizzes and competitions at regional and national level.

Further details about the school can be found at www.westhouseprep.com

West House
INDEPENDENT PREPARATORY SCHOOL FOR BOYS

(Founded 1895)

24 St James's Road, Edgbaston, Birmingham, West Midlands B15 2NX UK

Tel: 0121 440 4097

Fax: 0121 440 5839

Email: secretary@westhouseprep.com

Website: www.westhouseprep.com

Headmaster:
Mr Alistair M J Lyttle BA(Hons), PGCE, NPQH

School type: Boys' Day Preparatory, Co-ed Nursery

Age range of boys: 6 months–11 years

Age range of girls: 6 months–4 years

No. of pupils enrolled as at 01/09/2022: 350

Fees as at 01/09/2022:

Day: £2,200–£4,226 per term

Average class size: 17 (two form entry)

Teacher/pupil ratio: 1:12

Yorkshire & Humberside

Pocklington School

Pocklington is an inclusive, family focussed and academic school that offers incredible experiences inside and outside the classroom. We believe in encouraging pupils to seize opportunities from the broad range of activities we offer. Along with our approach to teaching and learning, these help to form our young Pocklingtonians' character and grow the qualities that support our values. Our sense of community, care for each other and pride in the school is tangible. This is no more evident than in our outstanding boarding provision. At the heart of this ethos lie our Values and Virtues. They guide us at Pocklington and mean our pupils leave with a deep sense of social responsibility and the ability to shape their own future.

Pocklington School lies 12 miles east of York on the edge of a vibrant, friendly market town, on a 50-acre campus with good public transport links and its own bus service. The school, founded in 1514, blends strong traditions with innovation and flexibility, encouraging pupils to have the courage to take chances with their learning and achieve the best that they can.

Numerous co-curricular activities for day and boarding pupils take place every day until 5pm, and each pupil is encouraged to pursue their own interests to help develop the depth of character and self-awareness to tackle life's challenges on their own terms. Facilities include a 300-seat theatre, an indoor sports hall, strength and conditioning room and swimming pool, plus 21-acres of grass sports pitches and two full-sized synthetic pitches.

Full, weekly and part-time boarding options are available, in outstanding boarding houses that create a home from home for all our boarders.

Right through from Prep School, where the Curiosity Project curriculum enables children to expand their critical thinking skills through structured and creative enquiry, to the Sixth Form where independent thought is prized, our pupils are encouraged to be resilient, resourceful learners. To support the school's strategic goal of further improving academic performance, increasing pupils' independence and meeting the needs of modern family life, pupils engage in a 5-day academic week, Monday to Friday. Saturdays are reserved for sports fixtures, and boarders enjoy a full weekend programme of activities and trips.

We employ the best educational tools and new technology to ensure youngsters are enthused and inspired by the world of knowledge available to them. Our Art and Design Technology Centre has every facility to encourage the pursuit of traditional arts and crafts, as well as providing cutting-edge equipment for digital and computer design, and manufacturing technology. An individual approach, supported by flexible learning platforms allows each pupil to progress at their own pace, boosting their confidence and self-esteem so they often exceed their expectations.

Our Sixth Form has spacious communal areas, a study centre, and a comprehensive library. Students are encouraged to work both collaboratively and independently as they begin to make the transition to university study and/or workplace success.

Recent former pupils who retain links with the school include Davis Cup winner Kyle Edmund, England rugby star Rob Webber and world-renowned concert pianist Alexandra Dariescu.

We aim to instil the Pocklington Values and Virtues into all our pupils, to engage with our families and support them in raising the Pocklingtonians of tomorrow and to be open to innovation, conscious of tradition and so secure our Foundation's future.

POCKLINGTON SCHOOL
Ages 2 to 18

(Founded 1514)

West Green, Pocklington, York, North Yorkshire YO42 2NJ UK

Tel: 01759 321200

Fax: 01759 306366

Email: admissions@pocklingtonschool.com

Website: www.pocklingtonschool.com

Headmaster: Mr Toby Seth MA (Cantab)

Appointed: January 2019

School type: Co-educational Day & Boarding Prep & Senior, Nursery & Sixth Form

Religious Denomination:
Christian ethos welcoming all faiths and none

Age range of pupils: 2–18 years

No. of pupils enrolled as at 01/09/2022: 775

Boys: 387 **Girls:** 388 **Sixth Form:** 180

No. of boarders: 80

Fees as at 01/09/2022:

Day: £17,127

Weekly Boarding: £27,321

Full Boarding: £31,434
(See website for full range of boarding options)

Queen Ethelburga's Collegiate

Students and staff at Queen Ethelburga's College and Faculty are celebrating another successful year, following the publishing of the 2022 A level and BTEC examination results. In 2022, students in the academically focused College achieved 96% A*/B at A Level. The Faculty, which offers a wider range of academic, creative and vocational courses, achieved 86% A*/B. The percentage of D*/D grades in The Faculty was 81%.

QE is an Excellent rated Collegiate (ISI 2019), known locally, nationally, and internationally as a group of four schools that promotes the highest standards in all that it does. The Collegiate welcomes girls and boys from 3 months and supports them through four schools – Chapter House (3 months to Year 5), King's Magna (Year 6 to 9), The College and The Faculty (both Year 10 to 13).

QE also places great emphasis on our students growing into resilient, caring, compassionate and confident adults, who develop independence and initiative, and who can take responsibility for their own learning and futures. We provide opportunities for students to take part in a range of wider enrichment and extra-curricular activities to help them to gain skills in leadership, teamwork and collaboration, and decision making.

Students at QE have access to an impressive 150 sports and activities each week, including popular sports such as rugby, hockey, football, netball, cricket, swimming, basketball, rounders, tennis, dance, gymnastics, trampolining, climbing, athletics, badminton, and volleyball. Our team of sports staff cater for all abilities and encourage each student to make the most of all the fantastic opportunities on offer during their time here. We have a well-honed mix of physical education teachers and specialist sports coaches, many of whom are ex-professional sportspeople themselves. This means there really is no limit to the level our students can train to. Health and fitness is so central to school life for students that many continue with sport and exercise, either recreationally or as a route of study, that it continues to be a key part of their lives long after they have left us for the next step in their education or career.

What enables us to deliver all of this sporting activity so successfully of course is the outstanding range of high quality facilities on campus. We're pretty unique in that we have a dedicated Sports Village to which all students have access to inside and outside of formal school hours. The Village is home to a 25-metre swimming pool, triple court sports hall, 100 station fitness suite and free weights centre. Outside we have a four-lane synthetic cushioned running track and over 30 acres of both grass and artificial 3G pitches. We also have a number of specialist studios used for; martial arts, wrestling, dance, gymnastics, table tennis, cycling, archery, fencing and boxing.

In addition to all this, the students can make use of an eight-metre climbing wall at the campus activity centre, which also houses an assault course and additional tennis courts. There really is something for everyone and for all abilities.

Care is the most important element within the QE community; every member of the Collegiate, staff and student, is responsible for the pastoral care and happiness of the site. QE offers support and guidance to all students and parents to ensure that we are all working to support individual students needs and equipping them with the right skills, not only to be successful in education, but to excel in their chosen career and life in general. Our dedicated THRIVE@QE programme offers all students a huge range of activities to support their positive mental health and wellbeing.

QE's Hill Standard is 'To be the best that I can with the gifts that I have' providing every child with a springboard to their individual successes, whichever pathway they choose.

(Founded 1912)

Thorpe Underwood Hall, Ouseburn, York, North Yorkshire YO26 9SS UK

Tel: 01423 33 33 30

Email: admissions@qe.org

Website: www.qe.org

Principal: Dan Machin

School type: Co-educational Day & Boarding Prep & Senior, Nursery & Sixth Form

Religious Denomination: Multi-Denominational

Age range of pupils: 3–19 years (boarding from 7)

No. of pupils enrolled as at 01/09/2022: 1400

Average class size: 18

Teacher/pupil ratio: 1:10

Rishworth School

Adventure awaits at Rishworth School. After all, this is a school whose past teachers included the real James Bond himself. Patrick Dalzel-Job was "an unusual officer who possesses no fear of danger," the kind who would evacuate all civilians from a large town called Narvik just before it was destroyed by German bombers — courage and charisma that would inspire a decades-long blockbuster series.

At Rishworth School, Dalzel-Job taught Chemistry and ran the Combined Cadets Force (CCF). His legacy prevails. At any given day, life at the school is action-packed — the kind that would lead to an excellent education both in and out of the classroom.

Each week, there are over 90 enrichment and extension activities available to students. From skiing and rock climbing to astronomy and mystery solving, these let students live the school's motto "Res Non Verba" (Deeds Not Words).

Such spirit and adventure are found from the nursery room through to Sixth Form. They start young exploring the great outdoors during forest school. By the time they reach the end of their schooling journey, students are bold and courageous in their academic achievements. Many set off to top universities such as Cambridge to study law, or even to taking exciting routes such as commercial pilot training.

Founded in 1724, Rishworth School has been around for almost 300 years. It offers a curriculum designed to cater to every child's needs. Small classes — 15 on average at the Senior School and eight on average in the Sixth Form — allow teachers to understand each child's character and talents. It's an approach that's led to outstanding exam results. Based on the 2022 summer A Level examinations, students of Rishworth School achieved a 100% pass rate, and 80% of students scored A* to C.

Located in the countryside within Ryburn Valley, the 140-acre campus overlooks moors, fields, hills and the reservoir — the perfect backdrop for the spirit of community and the sense of belonging every students feels here.

It is a home away from home with a blend of people, practices, provisions, and place where students can thrive. Boarders feel happy, cared for, healthy and secure. "Rishworth School taught independence and gave me confidence. Boarding at Rishworth solidified these attributes," says former student Andy McPhail.

Still, academic excellence is only one aspect of success Rishworth School students achieve. Self-discovery, finding new passions, trying new things and learning new skills outside of the classroom are some achievements a student will experience during their years here.

Understanding the role that learning outside the classroom plays in students' development, Rishworth introduced enrichment programmes that range from music and sports to photography and film.

Fancy learning to Kayak or learn how to code? Rishworth School has both a kayaking club and a coding programme for students. On top of that, F1 remote control, cooking club, orchestra and community projects are some of the other options available

RISHWORTH
SCHOOL

(Founded 1724)

Oldham Road, Sowerby Bridge, Halifax, West Yorkshire, HX6 4QA UK

Tel: +44 (0)1422 822217

Email: admissions@rishworth-school.co.uk

Website: www.rishworth-school.co.uk

Head: Dr Anthony Wilkins

Appointed: November 2020

School type: Independent Boarding and Day School

Age range of pupils: 3–18

Fees as at 01/09/2022:

Available online

Average class size: 14-18 (8-12 in Sixth Form)

The Froebelian School

The Froebelian School in Horsforth is a thriving and dynamic independent prep school, which places children at the very heart of all it strives to achieve. From the age of three we seek to equip our children with a lifelong thirst for and love of learning and the school continually achieves impressive levels of academic success, preparing them for the next stage in their educational journey.

The children and staff work harmoniously together creating a nurturing environment, with a uniquely happy atmosphere.

Children are at the heart of everything we do and we are passionate that they enjoy a positive experience, in a caring, structured and secure environment. To ensure we are laying solid foundations for a lifelong love of learning, to gain knowledge and skills, and develop personal attributes, relevant to their futures, we have made significant investment in our early years provision creating bespoke-designed classrooms and continuous access to an exceptional outdoor space.

"We knew from our first visit to the school that it was perfect. Every day our instincts are justified, as we watch our little girl blossom into a confident, delightful and happy little person." A Parent

With 51 weeks a year provision for all children and 30 hours funding available for our youngest children, our plans for further investment and development in STEAM and Sport, balance both academic and co-curricular spheres of school life and honour our school motto – 'Giving a flying start to the citizens of tomorrow.'

Our aim is to provide a first-class all-round education and committed pastoral care in which we celebrate uniqueness where the needs, abilities, interests and aspirations of each of our bright, inquisitive children are met and their talents can flourish in a caring, structured and secure environment. As a result, our children regularly secure a place at their first-choice senior school and we enjoy an excellent scholarship success rate.

Throughout the year extensive learning opportunities are balanced by a wide range of co-curricular activities in sport, music, art and technology and events. We foster our children's curiosity and imagination at every stage of school life and the children are nurtured and supported by an excellent staff: pupil ratio of 1:10.

Welcoming pupils between the ages of 3 and 11, we set the highest standards and expectations and as one of the North's leading Independent prep schools we also have one of the most flexible fee scales in the region.

The latest Independent Schools Inspectorate report judged The Froebelian School as 'excellent' for the quality of the pupils' achievements and the quality of pupils' personal development – this is the highest judgement available.

"The pupils' attitudes to learning are exceptional" ISI Inspectorate

Awarded 'Outstanding' in all areas by Ofsted once again, in their recent inspection, our private day nursery, First-Steps at Froebelian, follows the school's ethos closely and offers younger children the opportunity to start realising their full potential at an earlier age.

Situated in Horsforth, a pleasant and vibrant suburb of Leeds near to the ring road, the school is easily accessible from most areas of Leeds, Bradford and Harrogate. Our site is very secure with a wooded area offering delightful views over the Aire valley.

The school is an educational charity where ultimate responsibility rests with a School Council (governors). The day-to-day running of the school is delegated to the Headteacher, supported by a Senior Leadership Team.

We would love you to experience life at Froebelian – come and visit us and find out more.

Visit www.froebelian.com to find out more.

THE FROEBELIAN SCHOOL
GIVING A FLYING START TO THE CITIZENS OF TOMORROW

(Founded 1913)

Clarence Road, Horsforth, Leeds, West Yorkshire LS18 4LB UK

Tel: 0113 2583047

Email: office@froebelian.co.uk

Website: www.froebelian.com

Head Teacher: Mrs Catherine Dodds BEd (Hons), PGCE

Appointed: 2015

School type:
Co-educational Day Preparatory & Nursery

Age range of pupils: 3–11 years

No. of pupils enrolled as at 01/09/2022: 160

Fees as at 01/09/2022:

Day: £5,850–£8,700
(compulsory school lunches £705 per annum)

Teacher/pupil ratio: 1:10

Scotland

Loretto School

Our changing world is full of challenges and opportunities for young people. Finding a school that can provide an all-round education to fully prepare them for what lies ahead is vital. Loretto is that school.

Founded in 1827, Loretto is Scotland's first boarding school. Today an independent, private, boarding and day school, it welcomes girls and boys, from 3 to 18 years.

Set in a safe, leafy 85-acre campus just six miles from Edinburgh, Loretto enjoys all the advantages of this rural setting while being globally connected – the School is just nine kilometres/six miles from Scotland's capital city, its international airport, rail, and road networks.

Welcoming just over 500 pupils, the first thing you notice when you enter Loretto's campus is the warmth and energy of both pupils and staff. Relationships are marked by kindness, care and respect; a truly special environment for providing the confidence and know-how to thrive in life beyond Loretto. More than nine pupils out of ten achieve places at their chosen onwards destination, many attending top universities such as, Oxford, Cambridge, St Andrews, Newcastle, and Durham, as well as American universities.

Loretto, with its superb location on Scotland's Golf Coast, also has a strong tradition of top-level golf. The school's surrounding area of East Lothian offers a choice of magnificent links courses, and in 2002 this tradition blossomed into The Golf Academy. The Academy is now regarded as one of Europe's leading golf academies where pupils can develop their sporting talent in tandem with an exceptional education.

Directed by a team of top-class PGA Professional coaches, Loretto offers golfers access to state-of-the-art practice centres, and an abundance of local, accessible golf courses. With innovative practice facilities, including a nine-hole artificial putting green, several driving bays, bunker and chipping areas, and a putting studio with video analysis and Trackman.

From day one, Loretto's founder was dedicated to blending academic excellence with a wealth of experiences beyond the classroom. The enormous range of co-curricular activities offered ensures that each pupil can grow and develop wherever their interests and talents may lie. The School's achievements in music, art, drama and its strong reputation in sporting endeavours – both in major team sports and other sports, are testament to that.

Ultimately, to really understand the warm and welcoming atmosphere that makes Loretto different, you have to experience the School in person. So please come along for a visit – you will soon see why our pupils are so proud to be called Lorettonians.

Loretto

(Founded 1827)

Pinkie House, Linkfield Road, Musselburgh, East Lothian EH21 7RE UK

Tel: +44 (0)131 653 4455

Email: admissions@loretto.com

Website: www.loretto.com

Head of School: Dr. Graham R. W. Hawley

Appointed: 2014

School type: Co-educational Day & Boarding Prep & Senior, Nursery & Sixth Form

Age range of pupils: 3–18 years

No. of pupils enrolled as at 01/09/2022: 520

Fees as at 01/09/2022:

Day: £2,933–£8,385 per term

Full Boarding: £8,020–£12,315 per term

Flexi Boarding: £6,830 – £10,220 per term

Average class size: Junior 14; Senior 17; Exam Years 15

Teacher/pupil ratio: 1:7

Wales

Westbourne School

Westbourne has a proud tradition of academic excellence, as cited by the Sunday Times 2021 Schools Guide: **'Westbourne is one of the most consistently high-achieving independent schools in Britain.'**

Ranked 1st in the UK league tables for smaller schools since 2015, named 'IB School of the Year' by the Sunday Times Best Schools 2019 Guide and recently shortlisted for both Independent School of the Year 2021 and The Week's 'Best of the Best', Westbourne''s award-winning approach centres upon providing a highly supportive learning environment, exceptional leadership opportunities and a focus on turning career aspirations into reality.

Nationally recognised excellence

- 1st in the UK League Tables since 2015 (Daily Telegraph/Best-Schools; smaller schools)
- IB School of the Year 2019 (Sunday Times Schools Guide)
- 1st IB Sixth Form (Sunday Times Schools Guide) / 3rd Overall in the UK (Sunday Times Schools Guide)
- Awarded 'excellent' in all 5 inspection categories (Estyn National Inspectorate)

Exceptional Results

IB Diploma: 100% Pass, 39 Point average, 85% of Higher Levels at Grade 7/6 (A*/A equivalent), Over 50% of students achieved 40+ Points putting them in the top 2% world-wide. **GCSE/IGCSE:** 100% A*-C, 86% A*/A, Full course and 1 year GCSE/IGCSE programmes offered.

Certainty of university entry

90% Russell Group University average. Westbourne graduates progress to study highly competitive courses including Medicine, Engineering, Economics, Computer Science, Business and Law.

Outstanding teachers and unparalleled support

Offering individualised academic excellence, Westbourne has a warm and highly supportive culture. Small class sizes, an 8:1 pupil-to-teacher ratio and a tutorial style ensures every student excels.

More than 50% of teachers at Westbourne have a PhD or Masters and more than 50% have taught internationally, so can quickly relate with local and international students alike.

Boarding environment

Located in the safe seaside town of Penarth, ranked as one of the Top 10 best places to live in the UK, also just minutes from the vibrant capital city of Cardiff, Westbourne is a resoundingly British school. A student body of 72% British students, complemented by 16% European, 12% Asian students drawn from 24 different countries; no one nationality dominates.

Boarding students live within 2 minutes-walk of the main school building, in a modern fully-equipped boarding house, supported by live in, caring and professional House Parents.

Co-curricular activities and world-class facilities

Westbourne runs an expansive co-curricular programme, enriched with opportunities for students to test themselves through competitions, Olympiads and Duke of Edinburgh Awards.

Entrepreneurship, debating and drama clubs, Scientific Research and Philosophy societies, critical thinking classes and a wealth of local facilities make full use of the seaside location. Including tennis courts, gym, sailing, playing and athletics fields, an Olympic pool, white water rafting and two ice rinks to name just a few.

WESTBOURNE SCHOOL

(Founded 1896)

Hickman Road, Penarth, Glamorgan CF64 2AJ UK

Tel: 029 2070 5705

Email: admissions@westbourneschool.com

Website: www.westbourneschool.com

Headteacher: Dr GW Griffiths BSc, PhD, ARCS, PGCE

School type: Co-educational Day & Boarding Prep & Senior, Nursery & Sixth Form

Age range of pupils: 2–18 years

No. of pupils enrolled as at 01/09/2022: 351

Fees as at 01/09/2022:

Day: £8,520–£14,975

Full Boarding: £35,850–£37,950

Average class size: 16

Teacher/pupil ratio: 1:8

Overseas

École Jeannine Manuel – Lille

École Jeannine Manuel Lille is a non-profit coeducational school founded in 1992 and welcomes students from nursery to 12th grade. As the sister campus of École Jeannine Manuel Paris, the school has the same educational project and mission: promoting international understanding through bilingual education. An associated UNESCO school, École Jeannine Manuel Lille is the only non-denominational independent school in Nord-Pas-de-Calais, with over 900 pupils representing 40 nationalities and every major cultural tradition. The school's academic excellence matches it diversity: École Jeannine Manuel Lille is regularly ranked among the best French high schools (ranked first for four consecutive years). The school is accredited by the French Ministry of Education, the International Baccalaureate Organization (IBO), the Council of International Schools (CIS), and the New England Association of Schools and Colleges (NEASC).

Ecole Jeannine Manuel Lille's campus extends over 8.5 acres. It includes a boarding house, a restaurant, and state-of-the-art sports facilities including a 1600 m2 gym with its own climbing wall, a 300m racing track, and two outdoor playing fields. The boarding house currently welcomes 120 pupils from 6th to 12th grade.

Each year, École Jeannine Manuel Lille welcomes non-French speaking students. These students integrate the school through the adaptation program, which provides intensive instruction in French, support in English as needed, help in understanding and adjusting to French culture, and differentiated coursework and assessment during their adaptation period. The lower and middle school follow the French national curriculum with several exceptions: English is taught every day and, in middle school, experimental sciences, history and geography are taught in English. The curriculum is enriched at all levels, not only with a more advanced English language and literature curriculum, but also, for example, with Chinese language instruction (compulsory in grades 3-4-5), an integrated science program in lower school, and independent research projects in middle school.

In upper school, tenth graders follow the French national curriculum, albeit taught 50% in French and 50% in English. In 11th grade, pupils choose between the French track (*Baccalauréat Français International*, BFI) and the International Baccalaureate Diploma Programme (IBDP). Approximately 25% of our pupils opt for the IBDP.

Admission

Although admission is competitive, the school makes every effort to reserve space for international applicants, including children of families who expect to remain in France for a limited period of time and wish to combine a cultural immersion in French education with the ability to re-enter their own school systems and excel.

International understanding through a bilingual education

(Founded 1992)

418 bis rue Albert Bailly, Marcq-en-Baroeul, 59700 France

Tel: +33 3 20 65 90 50

Fax: +33 3 20 98 06 41

Email: admissions-lille@ejm.net

Website: www.ecolejeanninemanuel.org

Head of School: Constance Devaux

School type: Co-educational Day & Boarding

Age range of pupils: 3–18 years

No. of pupils enrolled as at 01/09/2022: 980

Fees as at 01/09/2022:

Day: €6,225

Full Boarding: €15,985–€24,285

IB Classes: €21,495

Average class size: 25 (15 in IBDP)

École Jeannine Manuel – Paris

École Jeannine Manuel is a non-profit pre-K-12 coeducational school founded in 1954 with the mission to promote international understanding through bilingual (French/English) education. An associated UNESCO school, École Jeannine Manuel welcomes pupils representing 80 nationalities and every major cultural tradition. The school's academic excellence matches its diversity: École Jeannine Manuel is regularly ranked among the best French high schools (state and independent) for its overall academic performance (ranked first for ten consecutive years). The school is accredited by the French Ministry of Education, the International Baccalaureate Organization (IBO), the Council of International Schools (CIS) and the New England Association of Schools and Colleges (NEASC).

Each year, the school welcomes more than 100 new non-French speaking pupils. These students integrate the school through our adaptation program, which provides intensive instruction in French, support in English as needed, help in understanding and adjusting to French culture, and differentiated coursework and assessment during their adaptation period.

The lower and middle school follow the French national curriculum with several exceptions: English is taught every day and, in middle school, experimental sciences, history and geography are taught in English. The curriculum is enriched at all levels, not only with a more advanced English language and literature curriculum, but also, for example, with Chinese language instruction (compulsory in grades 3-4-5), an integrated science program in lower school, and independent research projects in middle school.

In upper school, tenth graders follow the French national curriculum, albeit taught 50% in French and 50% in English. In 11th grade, pupils choose between the French track (*Baccalauréat Français International*, BFI) and the International Baccalaureate Diploma Programme (IBDP). Approximately 25% of our pupils opt for the IBDP.

Over the past three years, approximately 13% of our graduating students attended US colleges or universities, 41% chose to study in the UK, and 29% entered the French higher education system. Around 7% of graduating students go on to study in countries all over the world such as the Netherlands, Switzerland, Belgium, Germany, Spain, Italy, and Australia.

Admission:

Admission is competitive and applications typically exceed available spaces by a ratio of 7:1. The school nonetheless makes every effort to reserve space for international applicants, including children of families who expect to remain in France for a limited period of time and wish to combine a cultural immersion in French education with the ability to seamlessly re-enter the school system in their home country.

ÉCOLE Jeannine Manuel
International understanding through a bilingual education

(Founded 1954)

70 rue du Théâtre, Paris, 75015 France

Tel: +33 1 44 37 00 80

Fax: +33 1 45 79 06 66

Email: admissions@ejm.net

Website: www.ecolejeanninemanuel.org

Principal: Jérôme Giovendo

School type: Co-educational Day

Age range of pupils: 4–18 years

No. of pupils enrolled as at 01/09/2022: 2400

Fees as at 01/09/2022:

Day: €7,450–€8,215

IB Classes: €26,350

Average class size: 25

Geographical directory of schools

Channel Islands

Guernsey D324

Jersey D324

KEY TO SYMBOLS

- ⊕ *Boys' school*
- ⊛ *Girls' school*
- 🌐 *International school*
- 16⁺ *Tutorial or sixth form college*
- Ⓐ *A levels*
- ⬛ *Boarding accommodation*
- £ *Bursaries*
- IB *International Baccalaureate*
- ✎ *Learning support*
- 16⁺ *Entrance at 16+*
- 🎓 *Vocational qualifications*
- IAPS *Independent Association of Preparatory Schools*
- HMC *The Headmasters' & Headmistresses' Conference*
- ISA *Independent Schools Association*
- GSA *Girls' School Association*
- BSA *Boarding Schools' Association*
- S *Society of Heads*

Unless otherwise indicated, all schools are coeducational day schools. Single-sex and boarding schools will be indicated by the relevant icon.

Guernsey

Blanchelande College
Les Vauxbelets, St Andrews,
Guernsey GY6 8XY
Tel: 01481 237200
Principal: Mr Robert O'Brien
Age range: 2–18 years

Elizabeth College
The Grange, St Peter Port,
Guernsey GY1 2PY
Tel: 01481 726544
Principal: Ms Jenny Palmer
Age range: 2–18 years
Ⓐ Ⓔ ✎ ⑯

Elizabeth College Junior School
Beechwood, Queen's Road, St
Peter Port, Guernsey GY1 1PU
Tel: 01481 722123
Headteacher: Mr Richard Fyfe
Age range: 2–11 years
✎

The Ladies' College
Les Gravées, St Peter Port,
Guernsey GY1 1RW
Tel: 01481 721602
Principal: Ms Ashley Clancy
Age range: G2–18 years
🧍 Ⓐ ⑯

Jersey

Beaulieu Convent School
Wellington Road, St Helier,
Jersey JE2 4RJ
Tel: 01534 731280
Executive Headmaster: Mr Chris Beirne
Age range: B16–19 years G3–19 years
🧍 Ⓐ Ⓔ ✎ ⑯

De La Salle College
Wellington Road, St Saviour,
Jersey JE2 7TH
Tel: 01534 754100
Head of College: Mr Jason Turner
Age range: B3–18 years
🧍 Ⓐ ⑯ 🐾

FCJ Primary School
Deloraine Road, St Saviour,
Jersey JE2 7XB
Tel: 01534 723063
Headteacher: Ms Donna Lenzi
Age range: 4–11 years
✎

Helvetia House School
14 Elizabeth Place, St
Helier, Jersey JE2 3PN
Tel: 01534 724928
Headmistress: Mrs Lindsey
Woodward BA, DipEd
Age range: G4–11 years
🧍

Jersey College For Girls
Le Mont Millais, St Saviour,
Jersey JE2 7YB
Tel: 01534 516200
Principal: Mr Carl Howarth
Age range: G11–18 years
🧍

**St Christopher's
Preparatory School**
1901 Building, Rue De La Chapelle,
St Clement, Jersey JE2 6LN
Tel: +44 (0)1534 724758
Age range: 3–11 years

St George's Preparatory School
La Hague Manor, Rue de la
Hague, St Peter, Jersey JE3 7DB
Tel: 01534 481593
Headmaster: Mr Cormac Timothy
Age range: 2–11 years
Ⓔ ✎

**ST MICHAEL'S PREPARATORY
SCHOOL**
For further details see p.44
La Rue de la Houguette, Five
Oaks, St Saviour, Jersey JE2 7UG
Tel: 01534 856904
Email: office@stmichaels.je
Website: www.stmichaels.je
Headmaster: Mr Mike Rees
Age range: 3–14 years
No. of pupils: 319
Fees: Day £11,730–£18,450
Ⓔ ✎

Victoria College
Mont Millais, St Helier, Jersey JE1 4HT
Tel: 01534 638200
Head Teacher: Dr Gareth Hughes
Age range: B11–18 years
🧍 Ⓐ ✎ ⑯

**Victoria College
Preparatory School**
Pleasant Street, St Helier, Jersey JE2 4RR
Tel: 01534 723468
Head Teacher: Mr Dan Pateman
Age range: B7–11 years
🧍 ✎

Central & West

KEY TO SYMBOLS

- ⚹ *Boys' school*
- ⚹ *Girls' school*
- 🌐 *International school*
- 16· *Tutorial or sixth form college*
- Ⓐ *A levels*
- ⚏ *Boarding accommodation*
- £ *Bursaries*
- IB *International Baccalaureate*
- ✐ *Learning support*
- 16· *Entrance at 16+*
- ✿ *Vocational qualifications*
- IAPS *Independent Association of Preparatory Schools*
- HMC *The Headmasters' & Headmistresses' Conference*
- ISA *Independent Schools Association*
- GSA *Girls' School Association*
- BSA *Boarding Schools' Association*
- Ⓢ *Society of Heads*

Unless otherwise indicated, all schools are coeducational day schools. Single-sex and boarding schools will be indicated by the relevant icon.

Buckinghamshire

Akeley Wood School
Akeley Wood House, Buckingham,
Buckinghamshire MK18 5AE
Tel: 01280 814110
Headmaster: Mr Simon Antwis
Age range: 12 months–18 years
No. of pupils: 700 VIth100
Fees: Day £10,665–£15,900
Ⓐ £ 16⃝

Ashfold School
Dorton House, Dorton, Aylesbury,
Buckinghamshire HP18 9NG
Tel: 01844 238237
Headmaster: Mr Colin MacIntosh
Age range: 3–13 years
♙

**Broughton Manor
Preparatory School**
Newport Road, Broughton, Milton
Keynes, Buckinghamshire MK10 9AA
Tel: 01908 665234
Heads: Mr J Smith & Mrs R Smith
Age range: 2 months–11 years
£

CALDICOTT
For further details see p.48
Crown Lane, Farnham Royal,
Buckinghamshire SL2 3SL
Tel: 01753 649301
Email: admissions@caldicott.com
Website: www.caldicott.com
Headmaster: Mr Jeremy
Banks BA (Hons) QTS, MEd
Age range: B7–13 years
(flexi boarding from 7)
No. of pupils: 250
♙ ♙ ✎

Chesham Preparatory School
Two Dells Lane, Chesham,
Buckinghamshire HP5 3QF
Tel: 01494 782619
Headmaster: Mr Jonathan Beale
Age range: 3–13 years
✎

Child First Aylesbury Pre-School
35 Rickfords Hill, Aylesbury,
Buckinghamshire HP20 2RT
Tel: 01296 433224
Age range: 3–5 years

Crown House Preparatory School
Bassetsbury Manor, Bassetsbury
Lane, High Wycombe,
Buckinghamshire HP11 1QX
Tel: 01494 529927
Headteacher: Mrs Sarah Hobby
Age range: 3–11 years
✎

Dair House School
Bishops Blake, Beaconsfield
Road, Farnham Royal,
Buckinghamshire SL2 3BY
Tel: 01753 643964
Headmaster: Mr Terry Wintle BEd(Hons)
Age range: 3–11 years
£ ✎

Davenies School
Station Road, Beaconsfield,
Buckinghamshire HP9 1AA
Tel: 01494 685400
Headmaster: Mr Carl
Rycroft BEd (Hons)
Age range: B4–13 years
No. of pupils: 337
Fees: Day £12,105–£18,255
♙ £ ✎

Gateway School
1 High Street, Great Missenden,
Buckinghamshire HP16 9AA
Tel: 01494 862407
Head of School: Mrs Cath
Bufton-Green
Age range: 2–11 years
✎

Godstowe Preparatory School
Shrubbery Road, High Wycombe,
Buckinghamshire HP13 6PR
Tel: 01494 529273
Headmistress: Ms Sophie Green
Age range: B3–7 years G3–13
years (boarding from 7)
♙ ♙ £ ✎

Griffin House Preparatory School
Little Kimble, Aylesbury,
Buckinghamshire HP17 0XP
Tel: 01844 346154
Headmaster: Mr Tim Walford
Age range: 3–11 years
✎

Heatherton School
10 Copperkins Lane, Amersham,
Buckinghamshire HP6 5QB
Tel: 01494 726433
Headteacher: Mrs Nicola Nicoll
Age range: B3–4 years G3–11 years
No. of pupils: 144
Fees: Day £3,240–£14,595
♙ ✎

High March
23 Ledborough Lane, Beaconsfield,
Buckinghamshire HP9 2PZ
Tel: 01494 675186
Head of School: Mrs Kate Gater
Age range: B3–4 years G3–11 years
No. of pupils: 280
Fees: Day £5,850–£16,185
♙ £ ✎

Milton Keynes Preparatory School
Tattenhoe Lane, Milton Keynes,
Buckinghamshire MK3 7EG
Tel: 01908 642111
Head of School: Mr Simon Driver
Age range: 2 months–11 years
£

Pipers Corner School
Pipers Lane, Great Kingshill, High
Wycombe, Buckinghamshire HP15 6LP
Tel: 01494 718 255
Headmistress: Mrs H J Ness-
Gifford BA(Hons), PGCE
Age range: G4–18 years
♙ Ⓐ £ 16⃝ ❀

Stowe School
Buckingham, Buckinghamshire
MK18 5EH
Tel: 01280 818000
Headmaster: Dr Anthony Wallersteiner
Age range: 13–18 years
♙ Ⓐ ♙ £ ✎ 16⃝

Swanbourne House School
Swanbourne, Milton Keynes,
Buckinghamshire MK17 0HZ
Tel: 01296 720264
Head of School: Mrs Jane Thorpe
Age range: 4–13 years
♙ £ ✎

The Beacon School
15 Amersham Road, Chesham Bois,
Amersham, Buckinghamshire HP6 5PF
Tel: 01494 433654
Headmaster: Mr William Phelps
Age range: B3–13 years
✎

**The Chalfonts Independent
Grammar School**
19 London Road, High Wycombe,
Buckinghamshire HP11 1BJ
Tel: +44 (0)1494 875502
Principal: Mr David Shandley
Age range: 11–18 years
♙ IB

The Grove Independent School
Redland Drive, Loughton, Milton
Keynes, Buckinghamshire MK5 8HD
Tel: 01908 690590
Principal: Mrs Deborah Berkin
Age range: 3 months–13 years

The Webber Independent School
Soskin Drive, Stantonbury Fields, Milton
Keynes, Buckinghamshire MK14 6DP
Tel: 01908 574740
Principal: Mrs Hilary Marsden
Age range: 6 months–16 years
Ⓐ ✎

THORNTON COLLEGE
For further details see p.60
College Lane, Thornton, Milton
Keynes, Buckinghamshire MK17 0HJ
Tel: 01280 812610
Email: admissions@
thorntoncollege.com
Website: www.thorntoncollege.com
Headteacher: Dr Louise Shaw
Age range: G3–18 years
(boarding from 8)
No. of pupils: 402
Fees: Day £11,190–£17,835 WB
£19,830–£25,095 FB £24,660–£30,585
♙ ♙ Ⓐ ♙ ✎

**Walton Pre-Preparatory
School & Nursery**
The Old Rectory, Walton Drive, Milton
Keynes, Buckinghamshire MK7 6BB
Tel: 01908 678403
Head of School: Mrs
Chantelle McLaughlan
Age range: 2 months–5 years

WYCOMBE ABBEY
For further details see p.62
Frances Dove Way, High Wycombe,
Buckinghamshire HP11 1PE
Tel: +44 (0)1494 520381
Email: admissions@
wycombeabbey.com
Website: www.wycombeabbey.com
Headmistress: Mrs Jo Duncan MA
(St Andrews), PGCE (Cantab)
Age range: G11–18 years
No. of pupils: 660
Fees: Day £33,150 FB £44,100
♙ ♙ Ⓐ ♙ £ ✎ 16⃝

Gloucestershire

Al-Ashraf Primary School
Al-Ashraf Cultural Centre,
Stratton Road, Gloucester,
Gloucestershire GL1 4HB
Tel: 01452 503533
Head Teacher: Mr Abdullah Patel
Age range: 2–11 years

**Al-Ashraf Secondary
School for Girls**
Sinope Street, off Widden Street,
Gloucester, Gloucestershire GL1 4AW
Tel: 01452 300465
Head Teacher: Abdullah Patel
Age range: G11–16 years

Beaudesert Park School
Minchinhampton, Stroud,
Gloucestershire GL6 9AF
Tel: 01453 832072
Headmaster: Mr C D Searson
Age range: 3–13 years
(boarding from 8)

Berkhampstead School
Pittville Circus Road, Cheltenham,
Gloucestershire GL52 2QA
Tel: 01242 523263
Headmaster: Richard Cross
Age range: 3 months–11 years
No. of pupils: 254
Fees: Day £2,820–£4,045

Bredon School
Pull Court, Bushley, Tewkesbury,
Gloucestershire GL20 6AH
Tel: 01684 293156
Headmaster: Mr Nick Oldham
Age range: 7–18 years

Cheltenham College
Bath Road, Cheltenham,
Gloucestershire GL53 7LD
Tel: 01242 265600
Head of School: Mrs Nicola Huggett
Age range: 13–18 years

**Cheltenham College
Preparatory School**
Thirlestaine Road, Cheltenham,
Gloucestershire GL53 7AB
Tel: 01242 522697
Head of School: Mr Tom O'Sullivan
Age range: 3–13 years

Cheltenham Ladies' College
Bayshill Road, Cheltenham,
Gloucestershire GL50 3EP
Tel: +44 (0)1242 520691
Principal: Eve Jardine-Young MA
Age range: G11–18 years
(boarding from 11)
No. of pupils: 876
Fees: Day £26,700–£30,390
FB £39,780–£44,790

Dean Close Airthrie
27-29 Christ Church Road,
Cheltenham, Gloucestershire
GL50 2NY
Tel: 01242 512837
Headmaster: Mr Jason Dobbie
Age range: 3–11 years

**Dean Close Pre-Preparatory
& Preparatory School**
Lansdown Road, Cheltenham,
Gloucestershire GL51 6QS
Tel: +44 (0)1242 512217
**Headmaster Preparatory
School:** Mr Paddy Moss
Age range: 2–13 years
(boarding from 7)

Dean Close School
Shelburne Road, Cheltenham,
Gloucestershire GL51 6HE
Tel: +44 (0)1242 258000
Headmaster: Mr Bradley
Salisbury MEd, PGCE
Age range: 13–18 years
(boarding from 13)
No. of pupils: 490
Fees: Day £8,470–£8,980
FB £12,625–£13,150

Dean Close St John's
Castleford Hill, Tutshill,
Gloucestershire NP16 7LE
Tel: 01291 622045
Head: Mr Nick Thrower
Age range: 3–13 years
(boarding from 7)

Edward Jenner School
The Elms, 44 London Road, Gloucester,
Gloucestershire GL1 3NZ
Tel: 01452 380808
Head Teachers: Ms. Manda
& Mr. Phil Brookes
Age range: 5–16 years

Hatherop Castle School
Hatherop, Cirencester,
Gloucestershire GL7 3NB
Tel: 01285 750206
Headmaster: Mr Nigel Reed
M.Ed, B.Sc (Hons), PGCE
Age range: 2–13 years

Hopelands Preparatory School
38/40 Regent Street, Stonehouse,
Gloucestershire GL10 2AD
Tel: 01453 822164
Heads: Mrs Sonja Jones
& Mrs Maria Boix
Age range: 3–11 years

Immanuel Christian School
Rodford Tabernacle, Westerleigh Road,
Westerleigh, Gloucestershire BS37 8QG
Tel: 01454 311710
Head Teacher: Ms Joanna Gulliford
Age range: 4–16 years

Kitebrook Preparatory School
Kitebrook House, Moreton-in-
Marsh, Gloucestershire GL56 0RP
Tel: 01608 674350
Headmistress: Mrs Susan McLean
Age range: 3–13 years

**OneSchool Global UK
Bristol Campus**
Station Road, Wanswell, Berkeley,
Gloucestershire GL13 9RS
Tel: 01453 511282
Age range: 7–18 years

**OneSchool Global UK
Gloucester Campus**
Eastbrook Road, Gloucester,
Gloucestershire GL4 3DB
Tel: 01452 417722
Age range: 7–18 years

Rendcomb College
Rendcomb, Cirencester,
Gloucestershire GL7 7HA
Tel: 01285 831213
Head of School: Mr Rob Jones
Age range: 3–18 years

St Edward's Preparatory School
London Road, Charlton
Kings, Cheltenham,
Gloucestershire GL52 6NR
Tel: +44 (0)1242 388550
Head of Prep School: Mr Paul
Fathers BA (Hons) PGCE
Age range: 1–11 years

**St Edward's Senior
School & Sixth Form**
Cirencester Road, Charlton Kings,
Cheltenham, Gloucestershire GL53 8EY
Tel: +44 (0)1242 388555
Principal: Mr Matthew Burke BA
(Hons), PGCE, Ad dip Ed, NPQH
Age range: 11–18 years

The Acorn School
Church Street, Nailsworth, Stroud,
Gloucestershire GL6 0BP
Tel: 01453 836508
Headmaster: Mr Graeme E B Whiting
Age range: 6–18 years

The King's School
Gloucester, Gloucestershire GL1 2BG
Tel: 01452 337337
Headmaster: Mr David Morton
Age range: 3–18 years

The Richard Pate School
Southern Road, Leckhampton,
Cheltenham, Gloucestershire GL53 9RP
Tel: 01242 522086
Headmaster: Mr Robert MacDonald
Age range: 3–11 years

Westonbirt Prep School
Westonbirt, Tetbury,
Gloucestershire GL8 8QG
Tel: 01666 881400
Headmaster: Mr Sean Price
Age range: 2–11 years

Westonbirt School
Westonbirt, Tetbury,
Gloucestershire GL8 8QG
Tel: 01666 880333
Headmistress: Mrs Natasha
Dangerfield
Age range: 11–18 years

Wotton House International School
Wotton House, Horton Road,
Gloucester, Gloucestershire GL1 3PR
Tel: +44 (0)1452 764248
Principal: Dr Daniel Sturdy
Age range: 7–16 years

Wycliffe College
Bristol Road, Stonehouse,
Gloucestershire GL10 2AF
Tel: 01453 822432
Senior School Head: Mr
Nick Gregory BA, MEd
Age range: 3–19 years
(boarding from 7)
No. of pupils: 696
Fees: Day £9,675–£20,985
FB £20,625–£38,115

Oxfordshire

Abingdon Preparatory School
Josca's House, Kingston Road,
Frilford, Oxfordshire OX13 5NX
Tel: +44 (0)1865 391570
Headmaster: Mr Craig Williams
Age range: B4–13 years

Abingdon School
Park Road, Abingdon,
Oxfordshire OX14 1DE
Tel: +44 (0)1235 849029
Headmaster: Mr Michael Windsor
Age range: B11–18 years

Bloxham School
Bloxham, Banbury,
Oxfordshire OX15 4PE
Tel: 01295 720222
Headmaster: Mr Paul Sanderson
Age range: 11–18 years

Carfax College
39-42 Hythe Bridge Street,
Oxford, Oxfordshire OX1 2EP
Tel: +44 (0)1865 200676
Principal: Carl Morris
Age range: 11–21 years
No. of pupils: 24

Carrdus School
Overthorpe Hall, Banbury,
Oxfordshire OX17 2BS
Tel: 01295 263733
Head: Mr Edward Way
Age range: 3–11 years

Chandlings
Bagley Wood, Kennington,
Oxford, Oxfordshire OX1 5ND
Tel: 01865 730771
Head: Christine Cook
Age range: 2–11 years

Cherwell College Oxford
St George's Mansion, George Street,
Oxford, Oxfordshire OX1 2AR
Tel: 01865 953362
Principal: Mr Stephen Clarke
Age range: 12–18 years

Christ Church Cathedral School
3 Brewer Street, Oxford,
Oxfordshire OX1 1QW
Tel: 01865 242561
Headmaster: Mr Richard Murray
Age range: B3–13 years
(boarding from 7) G3–4 years

Cokethorpe School
Witney, Oxfordshire OX29 7PU
Tel: 01993 703921
Headmaster: Mr D Ettinger
BA, MA, PGCE
Age range: 4–18 years

Cothill House
Cothill, Oxfordshire OX13 6JL
Tel: 01865 390800
Headmaster: Mr D M Bailey
Age range: B8–13 years

Cranford House School
Moulsford, Wallingford,
Oxfordshire OX10 9HT
Tel: 01491 651218
Headmaster: Dr James Raymond
Age range: 3–18 years
No. of pupils: 525
Fees: Day £3,650–£6,175

d'Overbroeck's
333 Banbury Road, Oxford,
Oxfordshire OX2 7PL
Tel: 01865 688 600
Principal: Mr Jonathan Cuff
Age range: 11–18 years

Dragon School
Bardwell Road, Oxford,
Oxfordshire OX2 6SS
Tel: 01865 315405
Head: Emma Goldsmith
Age range: 4–13 years
No. of pupils: 798
Fees: Day £7,473 FB £10,931

EF Academy Oxford
Pullens Lane, Headington,
Oxfordshire OX3 0DT
Tel: +41 (0) 43 430 41 00
Head of School: Mr. Mark
Fletcher-Single
Age range: 16–19 years
Fees: Day £29,500 FB £44,500

Emmanuel Christian School
Sandford Road, Littlemore,
Oxford, Oxfordshire OX4 4PU
Tel: 01865 395236
Principal: Mrs Elizabeth Nesbitt
Age range: 3–11 years

Greene's College Oxford
45 Pembroke Street, Oxford,
Oxfordshire OX1 1BP
Tel: 01865 664400
Principal: Mrs. Carmen Dare
Age range: 16–18 years
No. of pupils: VIth60

Headington Preparatory School
26 London Road, Oxford,
Oxfordshire OX3 7PB
Tel: +44 (0)1865 759400
Head: Mrs Jane Crouch BA (Hons), MA
Age range: G3–11 years

HEADINGTON SCHOOL OXFORD
For further details see p.52
London Road, Oxford,
Oxfordshire OX3 7TD
Tel: +44 (0)1865 759100
Email: admissions@headington.org
Website: www.headington.org
Headmistress: Mrs Caroline
Jordan MA(Oxon)
Age range: G11–18 years
Fees: Day £6,580–£7,160

Kingham Hill School
Kingham, Chipping Norton,
Oxfordshire OX7 6TH
Tel: 01608 658999
Acting Headmaster: Ms Magnus Eyles
Age range: 11–18 years

Magdalen College School
Cowley Place, Oxford,
Oxfordshire OX4 1DZ
Tel: 01865 242191
Master: Miss Helen Pike
Age range: B7–18 years G16–18 years

Moulsford Preparatory School
Moulsford-on-Thames,
Oxfordshire OX10 9HR
Tel: 01491 651438
Headmaster: Mr B Beardmore-Gray
Age range: B4–13 years
(boarding from 9)
No. of pupils: 372
Fees: FB £7,850

New College School
2 Savile Road, Oxford,
Oxfordshire OX1 3UA
Tel: 01865 285 560
Head of School: Dr Matthew Jenkinson
Age range: B4–13 years
No. of pupils: 156
Fees: Day £11,100–£17,700

Our Lady's Abingdon School
Radley Road, Abingdon-on-
Thames, Oxfordshire OX14 3PS
Tel: 01235 524658
Principal: Mr Stephen Oliver
Age range: 7–18 years
No. of pupils: 374 VIth61
Fees: Day £11,280–£16,815
Ⓐ Ⓔ ⌀ ⑯

Oxford High School GDST
Belbroughton Road, Oxford,
Oxfordshire OX2 6XA
Tel: 01865 559888
Headmistress: Ms Marina
Gardiner Legge
Age range: G4–18 years
👤 ⑯

Oxford International College
1 London Place, Oxford,
Oxfordshire OX4 1BD
Tel: +44 (0)1865 203988
Principal: Ms Kim Terrar
Age range: 14–19 years
🌐 ⌀ ⑯

Oxford Montessori School
Forest Farm School, Elsfield,
Oxford, Oxfordshire OX3 9UW
Tel: 01865 352062
Age range: 2–16 years

Oxford Sixth Form College
12 King Edward Street, Oxford,
Oxfordshire OX1 4HT
Tel: +44 (0)1865 793233
Principal: Mr Mark Love
Age range: 15–19 years
⑯ Ⓐ ⌀ ⌀

Radley College
Radley, Abingdon,
Oxfordshire OX14 2HR
Tel: 01235 543000
The Warden: Mr J S Moule
Age range: B13–18 years
👤 🌐 ⌀ ⑯

Rupert House School
90-92 Bell Street, Henley-on-
Thames, Oxfordshire RG9 2BN
Tel: 01491 574263
Head: Mr Nick Armitage
Age range: 3–11 years
⌀

Rye St Antony
Pullen's Lane, Oxford,
Oxfordshire OX3 0BY
Tel: 01865 762802
Head of School: Ms Joanne Croft
Age range: B3–11 years G3–18
years (boarding from 9)
👤 🌐 ⌀ ⌀ ⑯

SHIPLAKE COLLEGE
For further details see p.56
Henley-on-Thames,
Oxfordshire RG9 4BW
Tel: +44 (0)1189 402455
Email: registrar@shiplake.org.uk
Website: www.shiplake.org.uk
Headmaster: Mr T G
Howe MA, MSt, MBA
Age range: 11–18 years
No. of pupils: 524 VIth213
Fees: Day £20,850–£26,508 WB
£29,229–£37,173 FB £39,591

🌐 Ⓐ ⌀ Ⓔ ⌀ ⑯

Sibford School
Sibford Ferris, Banbury,
Oxfordshire OX15 5QL
Tel: 01295 781200
Head: Mr Toby Spence
Age range: 3–18 years
🌐 ⌀ ⌀ ⑯ 🐾

St Clare's, Oxford
139 Banbury Road, Oxford,
Oxfordshire OX2 7AL
Tel: +44 (0)1865 552031
Head of School: Mr Duncan Reith
Age range: 15–19 years
No. of pupils: 280
Fees: Day £21,196 FB £44,118
🌐 ⑯ ⌀ Ⓔ Ⓘ⒝ ⌀

St Edward's, Oxford
Woodstock Road, Oxford,
Oxfordshire OX2 7NN
Tel: +44 (0)1865 319200
Warden: Alastair Chirnside
Age range: 13–18 years
No. of pupils: 775
Fees: Day £10,794 FB £13,489
🌐 Ⓐ ⌀ Ⓔ Ⓘ⒝ ⌀ ⑯

St Helen and St Katharine
Faringdon Road, Abingdon,
Oxfordshire OX14 1BE
Tel: 01235 520173
Headmistress: Mrs Rebecca
Dougall BA MA
Age range: G9–18 years
👤 ⌀ ⑯

St Hugh's School
Carswell Manor, Faringdon,
Oxfordshire SN7 8PT
Tel: 01367 870700
Headmaster: Mr James Thompson
Age range: 3–13 years
Fees: Day £12,285–£21,195
WB £23,655–£25,350
⌀ ⌀

St John's Priory School
St John's Road, Banbury,
Oxfordshire OX16 5HX
Tel: 01295 259607
Headmistress: Mrs Tracey Wilson
Age range: 3–11 years
⌀

St Mary's Preparatory School
13 St Andrew's Road, Henley-on-
Thames, Oxfordshire RG9 1HS
Tel: 01491 573118
Headmaster: Mr Rob Harmer (BA)Hons
Age range: 2–11 years
No. of pupils: 129
Fees: Day £4,010

Summer Fields
Mayfield Road, Oxford,
Oxfordshire OX2 7EN
Tel: 01865 454433
Headmaster: Mr David
Faber MA(Oxon)
Age range: B4–13 years
(boarding from 8)
👤 ⌀ ⌀

The King's School, Witney
New Yatt Road, Witney,
Oxfordshire OX29 6TA
Tel: 01993 778463
Principal: Mr Matthew Cripps
Age range: 3–16 years
⌀

The Manor Preparatory School
Faringdon Road, Abingdon,
Oxfordshire OX13 6LN
Tel: 01235 858458
Headmaster: Mr Alastair Thomas
Age range: 2–11 years
No. of pupils: 372
Ⓔ ⌀

The Unicorn School
20 Marcham Road, Abingdon,
Oxfordshire OX14 1AA
Tel: 01235 530222
Headteacher: Mr. Andrew Day BEd
(Hons)University of Wales (Cardiff)
Age range: 7–16 years

Tudor Hall School
Wykham Park, Banbury,
Oxfordshire OX16 9UR
Tel: 01295 263434
Headmistress: Ms Julie Lodrick
Age range: G11–18 years
(boarding from 11)
👤 🌐 ⌀ ⌀ ⑯

Windrush Valley School
The Green, London Lane,
Ascott-under-Wychwood,
Oxfordshire OX7 6AN
Tel: 01993 831793
Headteacher: Mrs Amanda Douglas
Age range: 3–11 years
No. of pupils: 120
Fees: Day £7,005–£7,341
⌀

Wychwood School
74 Banbury Road, Oxford,
Oxfordshire OX2 6JR
Tel: +44 (0)18655 57976
Headmistress: Mrs A K
Johnson BSc (Dunelm)
Age range: G11–18 years
(boarding from 11)
👤 🌐 ⌀ ⌀ ⑯

West Berkshire

Brockhurst & Marlston House Schools
Hermitage, Newbury, West Berkshire RG18 9UL
Tel: 01635 200293
Headmaster: Mr David Fleming MA (Oxon), MSc
Age range: 2–13 years
(boarding from 7)

Cheam School
Headley, Newbury, West Berkshire RG19 8LD
Tel: +44 (0)1635 268242
Headmaster: Mr William Phelps
Age range: 2–13 years
(boarding from 8)

DOWNE HOUSE SCHOOL
For further details see p.50
Downe House, Cold Ash, Thatcham, West Berkshire RG18 9JJ
Tel: +44 (0)1635 200286
Email: registrar@downehouse.net
Website: www.downehouse.net
Headmistress: Mrs Emma McKendrick BA(Liverpool)
Age range: G11–18 years
(boarding from 11)
No. of pupils: 590
Fees: Day £10,960 FB £14,740

Horris Hill
Newtown, Newbury, West Berkshire RG20 9DJ
Tel: 01635 40594
Headmaster: Mr Rob Stewart
Age range: B2–13 years
(boarding from 8)

St Gabriel's
Sandleford Priory, Newbury, West Berkshire RG20 9BD
Tel: 01635 555680
Principal: Mr Ricki Smith
Age range: 6 months–18 years

St. Michael's School
Harts Lane, Burghclere, Newbury, West Berkshire RG20 9JW
Tel: 01635 278137
Headmaster: Rev. Fr. John Brucciani
Age range: B4–18 years (boarding from 11) G4–11 years

Wiltshire

Avondale School
High Street, Bulford, Salisbury, Wiltshire SP4 9DR
Tel: 01980 632387
Head of School: Mr Ben Coombes
Age range: 2–11 years

Bishopstrow College
Bishopstrow, Warminster, Wiltshire BA12 9HU
Tel: +44 (0)1985 219210
Principal: Ms Lorraine Atkins
Age range: 7–17 years

Chafyn Grove School
33 Bourne Avenue, Salisbury, Wiltshire SP1 1LR
Tel: 01722 333423
Headmaster: Mr Simon Head
Age range: 3–13 years
No. of pupils: 265

Cricklade Manor Prep
The Manor House, Calcutt Street, Cricklade, Wiltshire SN6 6BB
Tel: 01793 750275
Headmaster: Mr Guy Barrett
Age range: 2–11 years

Dauntsey's
High Street, West Lavington, Devizes, Wiltshire SN10 4HE
Tel: 01380 814500
Head Master: Mr Mark Lascelles
Age range: 11–18 years
No. of pupils: 820 VIth270
Fees: Day £19,650 FB £32,550

Emmaus School
School Lane, Staverton, Trowbridge, Wiltshire BA14 6NZ
Tel: 01225 782684
Head: Mrs M Wiltshire
Age range: 5–16 years
No. of pupils: 75
Fees: Day £3,500–£4,400

Godolphin Preparatory School
Laverstock Road, Salisbury, Wiltshire SP1 2RB
Tel: +44 (0)1722 430545
Head: Ms Julia Miller
Age range: G3–11 years
(boarding from 7)

Godolphin School
Milford Hill, Salisbury, Wiltshire SP1 2RA
Tel: +44 (0)722 430545
Head: Ms Emma Hattersley
Age range: G11–18 years
(boarding from 11)

Heywood Prep
The Priory, Priory Street, Corsham, Wiltshire SN13 0AP
Tel: 01249 713379
Headmistress: Ms Rebecca Mitchell
Age range: 2–11 years
No. of pupils: 200
Fees: Day £9,525–£10,755

Leehurst Swan School
Campbell Road, Salisbury, Wiltshire SP1 3BQ
Tel: 01722 333094
Headteacher: Mrs Mandy Bateman
Age range: 4–16 years
Fees: Day £8,985–£15,300

Maranatha Christian School
Queenlaines Farm, Sevenhampton, Swindon, Wiltshire SN6 7SQ
Tel: 01793 762075
Headteacher: Mr Tom Price
Age range: 3–18 years

MARLBOROUGH COLLEGE
For further details see p.54
Bath Road, Marlborough, Wiltshire SN8 1PA
Tel: 01672 892200
Email: admissions@marlboroughcollege.org
Website: www.marlboroughcollege.org
Master: Mrs Louise Moelwyn-Hughes
Age range: 13–18 years
No. of pupils: 1012
Fees: FB £14,310

OneSchool Global UK Salisbury Campus
The Hollows, Wilton, Salisbury, Wiltshire SP2 0JE
Tel: 01722 741910
Age range: 7–18 years

Pinewood School
Bourton, Shrivenham, Swindon, Wiltshire SN6 8HZ
Tel: 01793 782205
Headmaster: Mr Neal Bailey
Age range: 3–13 years
(boarding from 9)

Salisbury Cathedral School
The Old Palace, 1 The Close, Salisbury, Wiltshire SP1 2EQ
Tel: 01722 555300
Head Master: Mr Clive Marriott BEd MA
Age range: 3–13 years

Sandroyd School
Rushmore, Tollard Royal, Salisbury, Wiltshire SP5 5QD
Tel: 01725 516264
Headmaster: Mr Alastair Speers
Age range: 2–13 years

St Francis School
Marlborough Road, Pewsey,
Wiltshire SN9 5NT
Tel: 01672 563228
Headmaster: Mr David Sibson
Age range: 0–13 years
Fees: Day £4,821–£12,571
(£)(🐭)

St Margaret's Preparatory School
Curzon Street, Calne, Wiltshire SN11 0DF
Tel: 01249 857220
Head of School: Mr Luke Bromwich
Age range: 2–11 years
No. of pupils: 180
(£)(🐭)

ST MARY'S CALNE
For further details see p.58
Curzon Street, Calne,
Wiltshire SN11 0DF
Tel: 01249 857200
Email: office@stmaryscalne.org
Website: www.stmaryscalne.org
Headmistress: Dr Felicia Kirk
BA (University of MD), MA &
PhD (Brown University)
Age range: G11–18 years
(boarding from 11)
No. of pupils: 360 VIth119
Fees: Day £32,280 FB £43,260
(🧍)(🌍)(A)(🎓)(£)(🐭)(16+)

Stonar School
Cottles Park, Atworth, Melksham,
Wiltshire SN12 8NT
Tel: 01225 701740
Head of School: Mr Matthew Way
Age range: 2–18 years
No. of pupils: 370
Fees: Day £9,120–£17,715
FB £24,450–£36,960
(🌍)(A)(🎓)(£)(🐭)(16+)

Warminster School
Church Street, Warminster,
Wiltshire BA12 8PJ
Tel: +44 (0)1985 210100
Headmaster: Mr Matt Williams BA MA
Age range: 2–18 years
(boarding from 7)
No. of pupils: 550
Fees: Day £5,740 FB £11,770
(🌍)(A)(🎓)(£)(IB)(🐭)(16+)

East

*See also Greater London (D347)
for schools in Essex and Hertfordshire

KEY TO SYMBOLS
- 🔹 *Boys' school*
- 🔹 *Girls' school*
- 🔹 *International school*
- 16 *Tutorial or sixth form college*
- Ⓐ *A levels*
- 🔹 *Boarding accommodation*
- £ *Bursaries*
- IB *International Baccalaureate*
- 🔹 *Learning support*
- 16 *Entrance at 16+*
- 🔹 *Vocational qualifications*
- IAPS *Independent Association of Preparatory Schools*
- HMC *The Headmasters' & Headmistresses' Conference*
- ISA *Independent Schools Association*
- GSA *Girls' School Association*
- BSA *Boarding Schools' Association*
- S *Society of Heads*

*Unless otherwise indicated, all schools are coeducational day schools.
Single-sex and boarding schools will be indicated by the relevant icon.*

Bedfordshire

Al Hikmah Boys School
145 High Street, Luton,
Bedfordshire LU4 9LE
Tel: 01582 594885
Acting Headteacher: Maulana
Abdul Muhit
Age range: B11–16 years
(symbol)

Al Hikmah Girls School
82-86 Dunstable Road, Luton,
Bedfordshire LU1 1EH
Tel: 01582 728196
Acting Headteacher: Maulana
Abdul Muhit
Age range: G9–19 years
(symbol)

Bedford Girls' School
Cardington Road, Bedford,
Bedfordshire MK42 0BX
Tel: 01234 361900
Headmistress: Ms Gemma Gibson
Age range: G7–18 years
(symbols)

**Bedford Greenacre
Independent School**
58-60 Shakespeare Road, Bedford,
Bedfordshire MK40 2DL
Tel: 01234 352031
Principal: Mr Ian Daniel
Age range: 3–18 years
(symbol)

Bedford Modern School
Manton Lane, Bedford,
Bedfordshire MK41 7NT
Tel: 01234 332500
Headmaster: Mr Alex Tate
Age range: 7–18 years
No. of pupils: 1289
Fees: Day £10,528–£14,443
(symbols)

Bedford Preparatory School
De Parys Avenue, Bedford,
Bedfordshire MK40 2TU
Tel: 01234 362274
Headmaster: Mr Ian Silk
Age range: B7–13 years
(symbols)

Bedford School
De Parys Avenue, Bedford,
Bedfordshire MK40 2TU
Tel: 01234 362200
Head Master: Mr James Hodgson BA
Age range: B7–18 years
(symbols)

King's House School
33-43 High Street, Leagrave,
Luton, Bedfordshire LU4 9JY
Tel: 01582 491430
Head of School: Ms Jade Pawaar
Age range: 2–11 years

**OneSchool Global UK
Biggleswade Campus**
The Oaks, Potton Road, Biggleswade,
Bedfordshire SG18 0EP
Tel: 01767 602800
Age range: 7–18 years

**OneSchool Global UK
Dunstable Campus**
Ridgeway Avenue, Dunstable,
Bedfordshire LU5 4QL
Tel: 01582 665676
Age range: 7–18 years

Orchard School & Nursery
Higham Gobion Road, Barton le Clay,
Bedford, Bedfordshire MK45 4RB
Tel: 01582 882054
Headmistress: Mrs Anne Burton
Age range: 0–9 years

Pilgrims Pre-Preparatory School
Brickhill Drive, Bedford,
Bedfordshire MK41 7QZ
Tel: 01234 369555
Head: Mrs J Webster BEd(Hons), EYPS
Age range: 3 months–7 years

Polam School
45 Lansdowne Road, Bedford,
Bedfordshire MK40 2BU
Tel: 01234 261864
Head: Darren O'Neil
Age range: 1–7 years
No. of pupils: 110
Fees: Day £10,080

St George's School
28 Priory Road, Dunstable,
Bedfordshire LU5 4HR
Tel: 01582 661471
Head of School: Mr Stuart Compton
Age range: 3–11 years
(symbol)

Cambridgeshire

Abbey College Cambridge
Homerton Gardens, Purbeck Road,
Cambridge, Cambridgeshire CB2 8EB
Tel: 01223 578280
Principal: Dr Julian Davies
Age range: 13–21 years
(symbols)

Cambridge Seminars College
87-89 Cherry Hinton Road, Cambridge,
Cambridgeshire CB1 7BS
Tel: +44 (0)1223 300 123
Principal: Mr Phil Scherb
Age range: 16–20 years
(symbols)

Cambridge Steiner School
Hinton Road, Fulbourn, Cambridge,
Cambridgeshire CB21 5DZ
Tel: 01223 882727
Education Manager: Ms Sarah Fox
Age range: 2–16 years
(symbol)

CATS College Cambridge
Elizabeth House, 1 High Street,
Chesterton, Cambridge,
Cambridgeshire CB4 1NQ
Tel: +44 (0)1223 314431
Principal: Mr Dominic Tomalin
Age range: 14–19+ years
(symbols)

Heritage School
17-19 Brookside, Cambridge,
Cambridgeshire CB2 1JE
Tel: 01223 350615
Headmaster: Mr Jason Fletcher
Age range: 4–16 years

Kimbolton School
Kimbolton, Huntingdon,
Cambridgeshire PE28 0EA
Tel: 01480 860505
Headmaster: Mr Jonathan Belbin
Age range: 4–18 years
(symbols)

King's College School
West Road, Cambridge,
Cambridgeshire CB3 9DN
Tel: 01223 365814
Head: Mrs Yvette Day
BMus, MMus, GDL
Age range: 4–13 years
(symbols)

KING'S ELY
For further details see p.80
Ely, Cambridgeshire CB7 4EW
Tel: 01353 660707
Email: admissions@kingsely.org
Website: www.kingsely.org
Principal: Mr John
Attwater MA (Oxon)
Age range: 2–18 years
No. of pupils: 1023
Fees: Day £11,607–£24,729
FB £26,268–£35,958
(symbols)

Landmark International School
The Old Rectory, 9 Church
Lane, Fulbourn, Cambridge,
Cambridgeshire CB21 5EP
Tel: 01223 755100
Headteacher: Gareth Turnbull-Jones
Age range: 4–16 years
No. of pupils: 100
(symbols)

**Magdalene House
Preparatory School**
Chapel Road, Wisbech,
Cambridgeshire PE13 1RH
Tel: 01945 583631
**Senior Deputy Head, Prep
School:** Mrs Keryn Neaves
Age range: 3–11 years
(symbol)

MANDER PORTMAN WOODWARD – MPW CAMBRIDGE
For further details see p.82
3-4 Brookside, Cambridge,
Cambridgeshire CB2 1JE
Tel: 01223 350158
Email: cambridge@mpw.ac.uk
Website: www.mpw.ac.uk
Principal: Mr Tom Caston
Age range: 15–19 years

Oaks International School
Cherry Hinton Road, Cambridge,
Cambridgeshire CB1 8DW
Tel: +44 (0) 1223 416938
Headteacher: Ms Amanda Gibbard
Age range: 2–11 years

Sancton Wood School
2 St Paul's Road, Cambridge,
Cambridgeshire CB1 2EZ
Tel: +44 (0)1223 471703
Head of School: Mr Richard Settle
Age range: 1–16 years

St Andrew's College Cambridge
13 Station Road, Cambridge,
Cambridgeshire CB1 2JB
Tel: +44 (0)1223 903048
Principal: Wayne Marshall
Age range: 14–19 years

ST FAITH'S
For further details see p.90
Trumpington Road, Cambridge,
Cambridgeshire CB2 8AG
Tel: 01223 352073
Email: admissions@stfaiths.co.uk
Website: www.stfaiths.co.uk
Headmaster: Dr C Hyde-Dunn
Age range: 4–13 years
No. of pupils: 571
Fees: Day £14,505–£18,270

St John's College School
73 Grange Road, Cambridge,
Cambridgeshire CB3 9AB
Tel: 01223 353652
Headmaster: Mr N. Chippington
MA(Cantab), FRCO
Age range: 4–13 years
No. of pupils: 464

St Mary's School
Bateman Street, Cambridge,
Cambridgeshire CB2 1LY
Tel: 01223 353253
Headmistress: Ms Charlotte Avery
Age range: G3–18 years
(boarding from 9)

Stephen Perse Junior School, Fitzwilliam Building
Shaftesbury Road, Cambridge,
Cambridgeshire CB2 8AA
Tel: 01223 454700 (Ext:2000)
Age range: 5–11 years

Stephen Perse Nurseries & Early Years
Cambridge Road,
Madingley, Cambridge,
Cambridgeshire CB23 8AH
Tel: 01223 454700 (Ext:5000)
Age range: 1–5 years

Stephen Perse Senior School
Union Road, Cambridge,
Cambridgeshire CB2 1HF
Tel: 01223 454700 (Ext:1000)
Age range: 11–16 years

THE LEYS SCHOOL
For further details see p.94
Trumpington Road, Cambridge,
Cambridgeshire CB2 7AD
Tel: 01223 508900
Email: admissions@theleys.net
Website: www.theleys.net
Headmaster: Mr Martin Priestley
Age range: 11–18 years
No. of pupils: 567
Fees: Day £18,240–£25,260
FB £27,525–£37,740

The Perse Pelican Pre-Prep & Nursery
92 Glebe Road, Cambridge,
Cambridgeshire CB1 7TD
Tel: 01223 403940
Head: Ms Francesca Heftman
Age range: 3–7 years

The Perse Prep School
Trumpington Road, Cambridge,
Cambridgeshire CB2 8EX
Tel: 01223 403920
Head: Mr James Piper
Age range: 7–11 years

The Perse Upper School
Hills Road, Cambridge,
Cambridgeshire CB2 8QF
Tel: 01223 403800
Head: Mr Ed Elliott
Age range: 11–18 years

THE PETERBOROUGH SCHOOL
For further details see p.96
Thorpe Road, Peterborough,
Cambridgeshire PE3 6AP
Tel: 01733 343357
Email: office@tpsch.co.uk
Website:
www.thepeterboroughschool.co.uk
Headmaster: Mr A D
Meadows BSc(Hons)
Age range: 6 weeks–18 years
No. of pupils: 480
Fees: Day £11,250–£17,829

Whitehall School
117 High Street, Somersham,
Cambridgeshire PE28 3EH
Tel: 01487 840966
Head of School: Chris Holmes
Age range: 6 months–11 years

Wisbech Grammar School
Chapel Road, Wisbech,
Cambridgeshire PE13 1RH
Tel: 01945 583631
Head of School: Mr Barnaby Rimmer
Age range: 11–18 years

Essex

Alleyn Court School
Wakering Road, Southend-on-Sea, Essex SS3 0PW
Tel: 01702 582553
Headmaster: Mr Rupert
W.J. Snow B.Ed, NPQH
Age range: 2–11 years

Apex Primary School
60-62 Argyle Road, Ilford, Essex IG1 3BG
Tel: 020 8554 1208
Head Teacher: Ms Meherun Hamid
Age range: 3–11 years

Brentwood Preparatory School
Shenfield Road, Brentwood,
Essex CM15 8BD
Tel: +44 (0)1277 243300
Headmaster: Mr Jason Whiskerd
Age range: 3–11 years
No. of pupils: 591

BRENTWOOD SCHOOL
For further details see p.68
Middleton Hall Lane,
Brentwood, Essex CM15 8EE
Tel: 01277 243243
Email: headmaster@
brentwood.essex.sch.uk
Website:
www.brentwoodschool.co.uk
Headmaster: Mr Michael Bond
Age range: 3–18 years
No. of pupils: 1968
Fees: Day £21,783 FB £42,687

Colchester High School
Wellesley Road, Colchester,
Essex CO3 3HD
Tel: 01206 573389
Headteacher: Ms Karen
Gracie-Langrick
Age range: 2–16 years
No. of pupils: 320
Fees: Day £9,465–£13,620
£ ✎

Coopersale Hall School
Flux's Lane, off Stewards Green
Road, Epping, Essex CM16 7PE
Tel: 01992 577133
Headmistress: Ms Moreen Barnard
Age range: 2–11 years

Elm Green Preparatory School
Parsonage Lane, Little Baddow,
Chelmsford, Essex CM3 4SU
Tel: 01245 225230
Principal: Ms Ann Milner
Age range: 4–11 years

Felsted Preparatory School
Felsted, Great Dunmow, Essex CM6 3JL
Tel: 01371 822610
Headmaster: Mr Simon James
Age range: 4–13 years
⚕ ✎

Felsted School
Felsted, Great Dunmow, Essex CM6 3LL
Tel: +44 (0)1371 822600
Headmaster: Mr Chris Townsend
Age range: 4–18 years
⚽ Ⓐ ⚕ £ ⒾⒷ ✎ ⑯

Gosfield School
Cut Hedge Park, Halstead Road,
Gosfield, Halstead, Essex CO9 1PF
Tel: 01787 474040
Head of School: Mr Rod Jackson
Age range: 2–18 years
Fees: Day £7,680–£17,250
⚽ ✎

Heathcote School
Eves Corner, Danbury,
Chelmsford, Essex CM3 4QB
Tel: 01245 223131
Head of School: Mrs Samantha Scott
Age range: 2–11 years
No. of pupils: 105
Fees: Day £9,450
£ ✎

Holmwood House School
Chitts Hill, Lexden, Colchester,
Essex CO3 9ST
Tel: 01206 574305
Headmaster: Mr Edward Bond
Age range: 6 months–16 years
⚕ ✎

Littlegarth School
Horkesley Park, Nayland,
Colchester, Essex CO6 4JR
Tel: 01206 262332
Head of School: Ms Kathy Uttley
Age range: 2–11 years

Maldon Court Preparatory School
Silver Street, Maldon, Essex CM9 4QE
Tel: 01621 853529
Headteacher: Elaine Mason
Age range: 1–11 years
✎

New Hall School
The Avenue, Boreham,
Chelmsford, Essex CM3 3HS
Tel: 01245 467588
Principal: Mrs Katherine Jeffrey MA,
BA, PGCE, MA(Ed Mg), NPQH
Age range: 1–18 years
No. of pupils: 1400
Fees: Day £9,621–£20,502 WB
£18,234–£28,026 FB £21,177–£32,472
⚽ ⚕ £ ✎ ⑯

**OneSchool Global UK
Colchester Campus**
Sudbury Road, Stoke By Nayland,
Colchester, Essex CO6 4RW
Tel: 01206 264230
Age range: 7–18 years

Oxford House School
2-4 Lexden Road, Colchester,
Essex CO3 3NE
Tel: 01206 576686
Head Teacher: Mrs Sarah Leyshon
Age range: 2–11 years

Saint Nicholas School
Hillingdon House, Hobbs Cross
Road, Harlow, Essex CM17 0NJ
Tel: 01279 429910
Headmaster: Mr Terence Ayres
Age range: 2–16 years
£

Saint Pierre School
16 Leigh Road, Leigh-on-Sea,
Southend-on-Sea, Essex SS9 1LE
Tel: 01702 474164
Headmaster: Mr Peter Spencer-Lane
Age range: 2–11 years

ST CEDD'S SCHOOL
For further details see p.86
178a New London Road,
Chelmsford, Essex CM2 0AR
Tel: 01245 392810
Email: info@stcedds.org.uk
Website: www.stcedds.org.uk
Head: Mr Matthew Clarke
Age range: 3–11 years
No. of pupils: 400
Fees: Day £3,200–£4,100
✎

St John's School
Stock Road, Billericay, Essex CM12 0AR
Tel: 01277 623070
Headteacher: Mr A. Angeli BA (Hons)
Age range: 2–16 years

St Margaret's Preparatory School
Hall Drive, Gosfield, Halstead,
Essex CO9 1SE
Tel: 01787 472134
Headteacher: Mrs Carolyn Moss
Age range: 2–11 years
Fees: Day £3,240–£4,055
£ ✎

St Mary's School
91 Lexden Road, Colchester,
Essex CO3 3RB
Tel: 01206 572544
Principal: Mrs Nicola Griffiths
Age range: B3–4 years G3–16 years
⚕ £ ✎

**St Michael's Church Of
England Preparatory School**
198 Hadleigh Road, Leigh-on-Sea,
Southend-on-Sea, Essex SS9 2LP
Tel: 01702 478719
Headmaster: Mr James Mobbs
Age range: 3–11 years

St Philomena's Catholic School
Hadleigh Road, Frinton-on-
Sea, Essex CO13 9HQ
Tel: 01255 674492
Head of School: Mrs P Mathews
ACIS, BA Hons, PGCE, MA, NPQH
Age range: 4–11 years
✎

St. Anne's Preparatory School
154 New London Road,
Chelmsford, Essex CM2 0AW
Tel: 01245 353488
Head of School: Valerie Eveleigh
Age range: 3–11 years

**Stephen Perse Junior School,
Dame Bradbury's School**
Ashdon Road, Saffron
Walden, Essex CB10 2AL
Tel: 01223 454700 (Ext: 4000)
Age range: 1–11 years
✎

Thorpe Hall School
Wakering Road, Southend-
on-Sea, Essex SS1 3RD
Tel: 01702 582340
Headmaster: Mr Stephen Duckitt
Age range: 2–16 years
✎

Ursuline Preparatory School
Old Great Ropers, Great Ropers Lane,
Warley, Brentwood, Essex CM13 3HR
Tel: 01277 227152
Headmistress: Mrs Pauline Wilson MSc
Age range: 3–11 years
✎

Widford Lodge Preparatory School
Widford Road, Chelmsford,
Essex CM2 9AN
Tel: 01245 352581
Headteacher: Miss Michelle
Cole A.C.I.B. – P.G.C.E.
Age range: 2–11 years

Woodlands School, Great Warley
Warley Street, Great Warley,
Brentwood, Essex CM13 3LA
Tel: 01277 233288
Head: Mr David Bell
Age range: 2–11 years

Woodlands School, Hutton Manor
428 Rayleigh Road, Hutton,
Brentwood, Essex CM13 1SD
Tel: 01277 245585
Head: Ms Paula Hobbs
Age range: 3–11 years

Hertfordshire

ABBOT'S HILL SCHOOL
For further details see p.66
Bunkers Lane, Hemel Hempstead,
Hertfordshire HP3 8RP
Tel: 01442 240333
Email: registrar@abbotshill.
herts.sch.uk
Website:
www.abbotshill.herts.sch.uk
Headmistress: Mrs K Gorman
BA, MEd (Cantab)
Age range: G4–16 years
No. of pupils: 482

Aldenham School
Elstree, Hertfordshire WD6 3AJ
Tel: 01923 858122
Headmaster: Mr James Fowler
Age range: 3–18 years

Aldwickbury School
Wheathampstead Road,
Harpenden, Hertfordshire AL5 1AD
Tel: 01582 713022
Headmaster: Mr Paul Symes
Age range: B4–13 years

Beechwood Park School
Markyate, St Albans,
Hertfordshire AL3 8AW
Tel: 01582 840333
Headmaster: Mr E Balfour
BA (Hons), PGCE
Age range: 3–13 years

Berkhamsted School
Overton House, 131 High Street,
Berkhamsted, Hertfordshire HP4 2DJ
Tel: 01442 358001
Principal: Mr Richard
Backhouse MA(Cantab)
Age range: 3–18 years
No. of pupils: 1883 VIth422
Fees: Day £6,750–£23,175
WB £31,500 FB £37,575

Bishop's Stortford College
School House, Maze Green
Road, Bishop's Stortford,
Hertfordshire CM23 2PQ
Tel: +44 (0)1279 838575
College Head: Ms Kathy Crewe-Read
Age range: 13–18 years

Bishop's Stortford College Prep School
School House, Maze Green
Road, Bishop's Stortford,
Hertfordshire CM23 2PQ
Tel: +44 (0)1279 838583
Head of the Prep School: Mr
Bill Toleman
Age range: 4–13 years

Charlotte House Preparatory School
88 The Drive, Rickmansworth,
Hertfordshire WD3 4DU
Tel: 01923 772101
Head: Miss P Woodcock
Age range: G3–11 years

Duncombe School
4 Warren Park Road, Bengeo,
Hertford, Hertfordshire SG14 3JA
Tel: 01992 414100
Headmaster: Mr Jeremy
Phelan M.A. (Ed)
Age range: 2–11 years
No. of pupils: 301
Fees: Day £10,380–£14,565

Edge Grove School
Aldenham Village, Watford,
Hertfordshire WD25 8NL
Tel: 01923 855724
Head of School: Miss Lisa McDonald
Age range: 3–13 years
No. of pupils: 501

Egerton Rothesay School
Durrants Lane, Berkhamsted,
Hertfordshire HP4 3UJ
Tel: 01442 865275
Headteacher: Mr Colin Parker
BSc(Hons), Dip.Ed (Oxon),
PGCE, C.Math MIMA
Age range: 6–19 years

Gurukula – The Hare Krishna Primary School
Hartspring Cottage, Elton Way,
Watford, Hertfordshire WD25 8HB
Tel: 01923 851 005
Head of School: Ms Gunacuda
Dasi (Gwyneth Milan)
Age range: 4–12 years

HABERDASHERS' BOYS' SCHOOL
For further details see p.72
Butterfly Lane, Elstree,
Borehamwood,
Hertfordshire WD6 3AF
Tel: 020 8266 1700
Email: office@habsboys.org.uk
Website: www.habsboys.org.uk
Headmaster: Mr Gus Lock
Age range: B4–18 years
No. of pupils: 1500

HABERDASHERS' GIRLS' SCHOOL
For further details see p.74
Aldenham Road,
Elstree, Borehamwood,
Hertfordshire WD6 3BT
Tel: 020 8266 2300
Email: office@habsgirls.org.uk
Website: www.habsgirls.org.uk
Headmistress: Mrs Rose Hardy
Age range: G4–18 years
No. of pupils: 1200

HAILEYBURY
For further details see p.76
Haileybury, Hertford,
Hertfordshire SG13 7NU
Tel: +44 (0)1992 706353
Email: uk.admissions@
haileybury.com
Website: www.haileybury.com
The Master: Mr Martin
Collier MA BA PGCE
Age range: 11–18 years
(boarding from 11)
No. of pupils: 908 VIth362
Fees: Day £6,595–£9,920
FB £8,615–£13,580

Heath Mount School
Woodhall Park, Watton-at-Stone,
Hertford, Hertfordshire SG14 3NG
Tel: 01920 830230
Headmaster: Mr Chris Gillam BEd(Hons)
Age range: 3–13 years
No. of pupils: 492 B270 G222
Fees: Day £12,435–£19,185

Howe Green House School
Great Hallingbury, Bishop's
Stortford, Hertfordshire CM22 7UF
Tel: 01279 657706
Headmistress: Ms Deborah
Mills BA (Hons) Q.T.S
Age range: 2–11 years
No. of pupils: 177
Fees: Day £433–£4,313

Immanuel College
87/91 Elstree Road, Bushey,
Hertfordshire WD23 4EB
Tel: 020 8950 0604
Head: Mr Mike Buchanan
Age range: 4–18 years

Kingshott
Stevenage Road, St Ippolyts,
Hitchin, Hertfordshire SG4 7JX
Tel: 01462 432009
Headmaster: Mr David Weston
Age range: 3–13 years
No. of pupils: 400
Fees: Day £6,555–£14,115

Little Acorns Montessori School
Building 19 & 21, The Lincolnsfield
Centre, Bushey Hall Drive, Bushey,
Hertfordshire WD23 2ES
Tel: 01923 230705
Age range: 3 months–5 years

Lochinver House School
Heath Road, Little Heath, Potters
Bar, Hertfordshire EN6 1LW
Tel: 01707 653064
Headmaster: Mr Ben Walker BA(Hons)
Age range: B4–13 years
No. of pupils: 345
Fees: Day £12,060–£15,840

Lockers Park
Lockers Park Lane, Hemel
Hempstead, Hertfordshire HP1 1TL
Tel: 01442 251712
Headmaster: Mr Gavin Taylor
Age range: B4–13 years
No. of pupils: 171
Fees: Day £11,505–£18,225 WB £26,325

Longwood School
Bushey Hall Drive, Bushey,
Hertfordshire WD23 2QG
Tel: 01923 253715
Headteacher: Ms Claire May
Age range: 3 months–11 years

Manor Lodge School
Rectory Lane, Ridge Hill, Shenley,
Hertfordshire WD7 9BG
Tel: 01707 642424
Head Teacher: Mrs A Lobo BEd(Hons)
Age range: 3–11 years

Merchant Taylors' Prep
Moor Farm, Sandy Lodge Road,
Rickmansworth, Hertfordshire WD3 1LW
Tel: 01923 825648
Head of School: Dr Karen McNerney
Age range: B3–13 years

Queenswood
Shepherd's Way, Brookmans Park,
Hatfield, Hertfordshire AL9 6NS
Tel: 01707 602500
Principal: Mrs Jo Cameron
Age range: G11–18 years
(boarding from 11)
No. of pupils: 418
Fees: Day £7,115–£8,440 WB
£7,325–£10,615 FB £8,395–£11,810

Radlett Preparatory School
Kendal Hall, Watling Street,
Radlett, Hertfordshire WD7 7LY
Tel: 01923 856812
Principal: Mr M Pipe BA Hons, QTS
Age range: 4–11 years

Sherrardswood School
Lockleys, Welwyn, Hertfordshire AL6 0BJ
Tel: 01438 714282
Headmistress: Mrs Anna Wright
Age range: 2–18 years

St Albans High School for Girls
Townsend Avenue, St Albans,
Hertfordshire AL1 3SJ
Tel: 01727 853800
Head: Ms Amber Waite
Age range: G4–18 years

St Albans Independent College
69 London Road, St Albans,
Hertfordshire AL1 1LN
Tel: 01727 842348
Principals: Mr. A N Jemal
& Mr Elvis Cotena
Age range: 14–19 years

St Albans School
Abbey Gateway, St Albans,
Hertfordshire AL3 4HB
Tel: 01727 855521
Headmaster: Mr JWJ Gillespie
MA(Cantab), FRSA
Age range: B11–18 years G16–18 years

St Christopher School
Barrington Road, Letchworth
Garden City, Hertfordshire SG6 3JZ
Tel: 01462 650 850
Head of School: Ms Emma-Kate Henry
Age range: 3–18 years

ST COLUMBA'S COLLEGE
For further details see p.88
King Harry Lane, St Albans,
Hertfordshire AL3 4AW
Tel: 01727 892040
Email: admissions@
stcolumbascollege.org
Website:
www.stcolumbascollege.org
Head: Mr David Shannon-Little
Age range: 4–18 years
No. of pupils: 805

**St Edmund's College
& Prep School**
Old Hall Green, Nr Ware,
Hertfordshire SG11 1DS
Tel: 01920 824247
Headmaster: Mr Matthew
Mostyn BA (Hons) MA (Ed)
Age range: 3–18 years
(boarding from 11)

St Francis' College
Broadway, Letchworth Garden
City, Hertfordshire SG6 3PJ
Tel: 01462 670511
Headmistress: Mrs B Goulding
Age range: G3–18 years
(boarding from 10)

St Hilda's School
28 Douglas Road, Harpenden,
Hertfordshire AL5 2ES
Tel: 01582 712307
Headmaster: Mr Dan Sayers
Age range: B2–4 years G2–11 years
No. of pupils: 150
Fees: Day £3,285–£4,260

St Hilda's School, Bushey
High Street, Bushey,
Hertfordshire WD23 3DA
Tel: 020 8950 1751
Headmistress: Miss Sarah-
Jane Styles MA
Age range: B2–4 years G2–11 years

St Joseph's In The Park
St Mary's Lane, Hertingfordbury,
Hertford, Hertfordshire SG14 2LX
Tel: 01992 513810
Head of School: Mr Douglas Brown
Age range: 2–11 years

**ST MARGARET'S
SCHOOL, BUSHEY**
For further details see p.92
Merry Hill Road, Bushey,
Hertfordshire WD23 1DT
Tel: +44 (0)20 8416 4400
Email: admissions@
stmargarets-school.org.uk
Website:
www.stmargarets-school.org.uk
Headteacher: Lara Péchard
Age range: 2–18 years
No. of pupils: 650

St. John's Prep School
The Ridgeway, Potters Bar,
Hertfordshire EN6 5QT
Tel: +44 (0)1707 657294
Head Teacher: Mrs C Tardios
Age range: 3–11 years

Stanborough Primary School
Appletree Walk, Watford,
Hertfordshire WD25 0DQ
Tel: 01923 673291
Head of School: Mrs T Madden
Age range: 3–11 years

Stanborough Secondary School
Stanborough Park, Garston,
Watford, Hertfordshire WD25 9JT
Tel: 01923 673268
Interim Head: Mr K. James
Age range: 11–18 years

Stormont
The Causeway, Potters Bar,
Hertfordshire EN6 5HA
Tel: 01707 654037
Head Teacher: Miss Louise Martin
Age range: G4–11 years

The Christian School (Takeley)
Dunmow Road, Brewers End,
Takeley, Bishop's Stortford,
Hertfordshire CM22 6QH
Tel: 012/9 871182
Headmaster: Mr M E Humphries
Age range: 3–16 years

The King's School
Elmfield, Ambrose Lane, Harpenden,
Hertfordshire AL5 4DU
Tel: 01582 767566
Headteacher: Mr Andy Reeves
Age range: 2–16 years

The Purcell School, London
Aldenham Road, Bushey,
Hertfordshire WD23 2TS
Tel: 01923 331100
Principal: Mr Paul Bambrough
Age range: 10–18 years

**Tring Park School for the
Performing Arts**
Mansion Drive, Tring,
Hertfordshire HP23 5LX
Tel: 01442 824255
Principal: Mr Stefan Anderson
MA, ARCM, ARCT
Age range: 8–19 years
No. of pupils: 370 VIth171
Fees: Day £15,405–£24,885
FB £26,190–£37,605

Westbrook Hay Prep School
London Road, Hemel Hempstead,
Hertfordshire HP1 2RF
Tel: 01442 256143
Headmaster: Mark Brain
Age range: 3–13 years
No. of pupils: 340
Fees: Day £10,905–£15,690
£ ✎

York House School
Sarratt Road, Croxley Green,
Rickmansworth, Hertfordshire WD3 4LW
Tel: 01923 772395
Headmaster: Mr Jon Gray BA(Ed)
Age range: 3–13 years
No. of pupils: 395
Fees: Day £3,876–£5,164
✎

Norfolk

All Saints School
School Road, Lessingham,
Norwich, Norfolk NR12 0DJ
Tel: 01692 582083
Head of School: Samantha
Dangerfield
Age range: 7–16 years
✎

Beeston Hall School
Beeston Regis, West Runton,
Cromer, Norfolk NR27 9NQ
Tel: 01263 837324
Headmaster: Mr Fred de
Falbe BA(Hons) PGCE
Age range: 4–13 years
⊞ ✎

**Downham Preparatory School
& Montessori Nursery**
The Old Rectory, Stow Bardolph,
Kings Lynn, Norfolk PE34 3HT
Tel: 01366 388066
Principal: Mrs E J Laffeaty-Sharpe
Age range: 3 months–13 years

Glebe House School & Nursery
Cromer Road, Hunstanton,
Norfolk PE36 6HW
Tel: 01485 532809
Headmaster: Mr Louis Taylor
Age range: 0–13 years
(boarding from 7)
⊞ ✎

**Gresham's Nursery and
Pre-Prep School**
Market Place, Holt, Norfolk NR25 6BB
Tel: 01263 714575
Head: Ms Sarah Hollingsworth
Age range: 2–7 years
🌐

Gresham's Prep School
Holt, Norfolk NR25 6EY
Tel: 01263 714600
Head: Mrs Cathy Braithwaite
Age range: 7–13 years
🌐 ⊞ ✎

Gresham's Senior School
Cromer Road, Holt, Norfolk NR25 6EA
Tel: 01263 714500
Headmaster: Mr Douglas
Robb MA, MEd
Age range: 13–18 years
No. of pupils: 540
Fees: Day £27,450 FB £39,345
🌐 Ⓐ ⊞ £ ⒤ ✎ ⒃

Langley Pre-Prep & Prep School
Taverham, Norwich, Norfolk NR8 6HU
Tel: 01603 868206
Head of Prep: Mr Mike A
Crossley NPQH, BEd(Hons)
Age range: 6 months–13 years
⊞ ✎

Langley Senior School & Sixth Form
Langley Park, Loddon,
Norwich, Norfolk NR14 6BJ
Tel: 01508 520210
Headmaster: Mr Jon Perriss
Age range: 10–18 years
🌐 ⊞ ✎ ⒃

Norwich High School for Girls GDST
95 Newmarket Road, Norwich,
Norfolk NR2 2HU
Tel: 01603 453265
Head: Ms Alison Sefton
Age range: G3–18 years
⊞ ✎ ⒃

Norwich School
71a The Close, Norwich,
Norfolk NR1 4DD
Tel: 01603 728430
Head: Mr Steffan D A Griffiths
Age range: 4–18 years
⒃

Norwich Steiner School
Hospital Lane, Norwich,
Norfolk NR1 2HW
Tel: 01603 611175
Age range: 3–19 years
✎

Notre Dame Preparatory School
147 Dereham Road, Norwich,
Norfolk NR2 3TA
Tel: 01603 625593
Headmaster: Mr Rob Thornton MA
Age range: 2–11 years
✎

**OneSchool Global UK
Swaffham Campus**
Turbine Way, Swaffham,
Norfolk PE37 7XD
Tel: 01760 336939
Age range: 7–18 years

**Riddlesworth Hall
Preparatory School**
Hall Lane, Diss, Norfolk IP22 2TA
Tel: 01953 681246
Head: Mrs V White
Age range: 2–13 years
⊞ ✎

Thetford Grammar School
Bridge Street, Thetford, Norfolk IP24 3AF
Tel: 01842 752840
Head: Mr Michael Brewer
Age range: 3–19 years
⊞ ✎ ⒃

Town Close School
14 Ipswich Road, Norwich,
Norfolk NR2 2LR
Tel: 01603 620180
Headteacher: Mr Chris Wilson
Age range: 3–13 years
No. of pupils: 450
Fees: Day £3,081–£4,673
£ ✎

Wymondham College Prep School
Golf Links Road, Wymondham,
Norfolk NR18 9SZ
Tel: 01953 609000 (option 3)
Headteacher: Mr Jon Timmins
Age range: 4–11 years
No. of pupils: 150
Fees: FB £12,165
⊞

Suffolk

**Barnardiston Hall
Preparatory School**
Hall Road, Barnardiston, Nr
Haverhill, Suffolk CB9 7TG
Tel: 01440 786316
Headmaster: Lt Col K A
Boulter MA(Cantab)
Age range: 6 months–13 years
⊞ ✎

Brookes UK
Flempton Road, Risby, Bury St
Edmunds, Suffolk IP28 6QJ
Tel: 01284 760531
Principal: Ms Natalie Taylor
Age range: 2–16 years
⊞

Culford School
Bury St Edmunds, Suffolk IP28 6TX
Tel: +44 (0)1284 728615
Headmaster: Mr J F Johnson-
Munday MA, MBA
Age range: 1–18 years
🌐 Ⓐ ⊞ £ ✎ ⒃

Fairstead House School
Fairstead House, Fordham Road,
Newmarket, Suffolk CB8 7AA
Tel: 01638 662318
Head of School: Mr Michael Radford
Age range: 3 months–11 years
No. of pupils: 95
Fees: Day £10,704–£11,934
£ ✎

Finborough School
The Hall, Great Finborough,
Stowmarket, Suffolk IP14 3EF
Tel: +44 (0)1449 773600
Headmaster: Mr Steven T. Clark
Age range: 2–18 years
Fees: Day £9,630–£14,880 WB
£18,030–£24,150 FB £22,440–£30,090
🌐 Ⓐ ⊞ ✎

FRAMLINGHAM COLLEGE
For further details see p.70
Framlingham, Suffolk IP13 9EY
Tel: +44 (0)1728 723789
Email: admissions@
framlinghamcollege.co.uk
Website:
www.framlinghamcollege.co.uk
**Principal and Head of the Senior
School:** Mrs Louise North
Age range: 3–18 years
No. of pupils: 640
Fees: Day £10,110–£23,064
FB £26,499–£35,865

Ipswich High School
Woolverstone, Ipswich, Suffolk IP9 1AZ
Tel: 01473 780201
Head of School: Mr Mark Howe
Age range: 3–18 years
No. of pupils: 450
Fees: Day £10,710–£16,935
WB £28,500 FB £38,200

IPSWICH SCHOOL
For further details see p.78
Henley Road, Ipswich, Suffolk IP1 3SG
Tel: 01473 408300
Email: admissions@ipswich.school
Website: www.ipswich.school
Headmaster: Mr Nicholas
Weaver MA
Age range: 0–18 years
Fees: Day £18,261 FB £37,410

Old Buckenham Hall School
Old Buckenham Hall, Brettenham
Park, Ipswich, Suffolk IP7 7PH
Tel: 01449 740252
Headmaster: Mr David Griffiths
Age range: 3–13 years
No. of pupils: 242
Fees: Day £6,947 FB £9,052

ORWELL PARK SCHOOL
For further details see p.84
Nacton, Ipswich, Suffolk IP10 0ER
Tel: 01473 659225
Email: admissions@orwellpark.org
Website: www.orwellpark.co.uk
Headmaster: Mr Adrian
Brown MA(Cantab)
Age range: 2–13 years
No. of pupils: 270

Saint Felix School
Halesworth Road, Southwold,
Suffolk IP18 6SD
Tel: +44 (0)15027 22175
Headmaster: Mr. James Harrison
Age range: 2–18 years
(boarding from 7)

South Lee Preparatory School
Nowton Road, Bury St
Edmunds, Suffolk IP33 2BT
Tel: 01284 754654
Acting Head: Mrs Sarah Catchpole
Age range: 4 months–13 years

St Joseph's College
Belstead Road, Ipswich, Suffolk IP2 9DR
Tel: +44 (0)1473 690281
Principal: Mrs Danielle Clarke
Age range: 2–18 years

Stoke College
Ashen Lane, Stoke by Clare,
Sudbury, Suffolk CO10 8JE
Tel: +44 (0)1787 278141
Principal: Dr. Gareth P. Lloyd
Age range: 11–18 years

Summerhill School
Westward Ho, Leiston, Suffolk IP16 4HY
Tel: 01728 830540
Principal: Mrs Zoe Readhead
Age range: 5–18 years

The Meadows Montessori School
32 Larchcroft Road, Ipswich,
Suffolk IP1 6AR
Tel: 01473 233782
Headteacher: Ms Samantha Sims
Age range: 3–16 years

The Old School Henstead
Toad Row, Henstead, Beccles,
Suffolk NR34 7LG
Tel: 01502 741150
Head: Mr W J McKinney
Age range: 2–11 years

THE ROYAL HOSPITAL SCHOOL
For further details see p.98
Holbrook, Ipswich, Suffolk IP9 2RX
Tel: 01473 326136
Email: admissions@
royalhospitalschool.org
Website:
www.royalhospitalschool.org
Headmaster: Mr Simon
Lockyer BSc MEd
Age range: 11–18 years
No. of pupils: 730
Fees: Day £18,207–£20,253 WB
£27,825–£34,542 FB £29,211–£37,614

Woodbridge School
Burkitt Road, Woodbridge,
Suffolk IP12 4JH
Tel: +44 (0)1394 615000
Head of School: Miss Shona Norman
Age range: 4–18 years
Fees: Day £11,148–£18,885 WB
£26,844–£29,178 FB £34,998

East Midlands

KEY TO SYMBOLS
- 🕇 *Boys' school*
- 🕇 *Girls' school*
- 🌐 *International school*
- 16 *Tutorial or sixth form college*
- Ⓐ *A levels*
- ♨ *Boarding accommodation*
- £ *Bursaries*
- IB *International Baccalaureate*
- ✐ *Learning support*
- 16 *Entrance at 16+*
- ❀ *Vocational qualifications*
- IAPS *Independent Association of Preparatory Schools*
- HMC *The Headmasters' & Headmistresses' Conference*
- ISA *Independent Schools Association*
- GSA *Girls' School Association*
- BSA *Boarding Schools' Association*
- Ⓢ *Society of Heads*

Unless otherwise indicated, all schools are coeducational day schools.
Single-sex and boarding schools will be indicated by the relevant icon.

Derbyshire

Barlborough Hall School
Park Street, Barlborough,
Chesterfield, Derbyshire S43 4ES
Tel: 01246 810511
Headteacher: Mrs Karen Keeton
Age range: 3–11 years

Dame Catherine Harpur's School
Rose Lane, Ticknall, Derby,
Derbyshire DE73 7JW
Tel: 01332 862792
Headteacher: Lorna Harvey
Age range: 3–11 years

Derby Grammar School
Rykneld Hall, Rykneld Road, Littleover,
Derby, Derbyshire DE23 4BX
Tel: 01332 523027
Head: Mr Paul Logan
Age range: 4–18 years
(£)(✎)

Derby High School
Hillsway, Littleover, Derby,
Derbyshire DE23 3DT
Tel: 01332 514267
Headteacher: Mrs Amy Chapman
Age range: 3–18 years
(✎)

Emmanuel School
Juniper Lodge, 43 Kedleston Road,
Derby, Derbyshire DE22 1FP
Tel: 01332 340505
Headteacher: Mr Ben Snowdon
Age range: 3–11 years
(✎)

Mount St Mary's College
College Road, Spinkhill, Near
Sheffield, Derbyshire S21 3YL
Tel: 01246 433388
Headmaster: Dr Dan Wright
Age range: 11–18 years
No. of pupils: 350
Fees: Day £12,870–£14,790 WB
£20,220–£25,980 FB £24,780–£32,445
(✈)(A)(宿)(£)(✎)(16+)

Normanton House School
Normanton House, Village Street,
Derby, Derbyshire DE23 8DF
Tel: 01332 769333
Head of School: Ms A Ahmed
Age range: 5–16 years

Old Vicarage School
11 Church Lane, Darley Abbey,
Derby, Derbyshire DE22 1EW
Tel: 01332 557130
Head of School: Mrs Kerry Wise
Age range: 3–13 years
(✎)

Repton Prep
Milton, Derby, Derbyshire DE65 6EJ
Tel: 01283 707100
Head of School: Mrs Vicky Harding
Age range: 3–13 years
(宿)(£)(✎)

Repton School
The Hall, Repton, Derbyshire DE65 6FH
Tel: 01283 559200
Head of School: M J
Semmence MA, MBA
Age range: 13–18 years
(✈)(A)(宿)(£)(✎)(16+)

S. Anselm's School
Stanedge Road, Bakewell,
Derbyshire DE45 1DP
Tel: 01629 812734
Headmaster: Mr Frank Thompson
Age range: 2–13 years
(宿)(✎)

St Peter & St Paul School
Brambling House, Hady Hill,
Chesterfield, Derbyshire S41 0EF
Tel: 01246 278522
Headteacher: Mrs Jill Phinn
Age range: 3 months–11 years
(✎)

St Wystan's School
High Street, Repton,
Derbyshire DE65 6GE
Tel: 01283 703258
Head Teacher: Ms Kara Lebihan
Age range: 2–11 years
(✎)

Watchorn Christian School
Watchorn Church, Derby Road,
Alfreton, Derbyshire DE55 7AQ
Tel: 07387 721877
Age range: 3–11 years

Leicestershire

Al-Aqsa Schools Trust
The Wayne Way, Leicester,
Leicestershire LE5 4PP
Tel: 01162 760953
Headteacher: Arafat Q Hingora
Age range: 4–16 years
(✎)

Brooke House College
12 Leicester Road, Market
Harborough, Leicestershire LE16 7AU
Tel: 01858 462452
Principal: Mr Ian Smith
Age range: 11–19 years
(✈)(宿)

Brooke House Day School
Croft Road, Cosby, Leicester,
Leicestershire LE9 1SE
Tel: 0116 286 7372
Head: Mrs Joy Parker
Age range: 3–16 years

Darul Uloom Leicester
119 Loughborough Road,
Leicester, Leicestershire LE4 5LN
Tel: 0116 2668922
Principal: Moulana Ishaq Boodi
Age range: B11–23 years
(boarding from 11)
(✈)(宿)

**Emmanuel Christian
School, Leicester**
Didsbury Street, Braunstone,
Leicester, Leicestershire LE3 1QP
Tel: 0116 222 0792
Age range: 4–16 years

FAIRFIELD PREP SCHOOL
For further details see p.102
Leicester Road, Loughborough,
Leicestershire LE11 2AE
Tel: 01509 215172
Email: fairfield.admissions@lsf.org
Website: www.lsf.org/fairfield
Headmaster: Mr Andrew Earnshaw
Age range: 3–11 years
No. of pupils: 505
(✎)

Jameah Boys Academy
33 Wood Hill, Leicester,
Leicestershire LE5 3SQ
Tel: 01162 927746
Age range: B5–16 years
(✈)

Jameah Girls Academy
49 Rolleston Street, Leicester,
Leicestershire LE5 3SD
Tel: 0116 262 7745
Age range: G5–16 years
(✈)

Leicester Grammar Junior School
London Road, Great Glen,
Leicester, Leicestershire LE8 9FL
Tel: 0116 259 1950
Head of School: Mrs S Ashworth Jones
Age range: 3–11 years
No. of pupils: 391
Fees: Day £11,493–£12,212
(✎)

Leicester Grammar School
London Road, Great Glen,
Leicester, Leicestershire LE8 9FL
Tel: 0116 259 1900
Headmaster: Mr John Watson
Age range: 10–18 years
No. of pupils: 856
Fees: Day £14,130
(A)(£)(✎)(16+)

Leicester High School for Girls
454 London Road, Leicester,
Leicestershire LE2 2PP
Tel: 0116 2705338
Headmaster: Mr Alan Whelpdale
Age range: G3–18 years
(✈)(16+)

Leicester Islamic Academy
320 London Road, Leicester,
Leicestershire LE2 2PJ
Tel: 01162 705343
Headteacher: Mrs T. Jakhura
Age range: 3–11 years

Leicester Preparatory School
2 Albert Road, Leicester,
Leicestershire LE2 2AA
Tel: 01162 707414
Headmistress: Ms Claudette Salmon
Age range: 2–11 years

LGS Stoneygate
London Road, Great Glen,
Leicester, Leicestershire LE8 9DJ
Tel: 01162 592282
Headmaster: Mr J F Dobson
Age range: 4–16 years

**LOUGHBOROUGH
AMHERST SCHOOL**
For further details see p.104
Gray Street, Loughborough,
Leicestershire LE11 2DZ
Tel: 01509 263901
Email: amherst.admissions@lsf.org
Website: www.lsf.org/amherst
Headmaster: Dr Julian Murphy
Age range: 4–18 years
No. of pupils: 335

**LOUGHBOROUGH
GRAMMAR SCHOOL**
For further details see p.106
Buckland House, Burton
Walks, Loughborough,
Leicestershire LE11 2DU
Tel: 01509 233233
Email: grammar.admissions@lsf.org
Website: www.lsf.org/grammar
Headmaster: Dr Daniel Koch
Age range: B10–18 years
No. of pupils: 890

LOUGHBOROUGH HIGH SCHOOL
For further details see p.108
Burton Walks, Loughborough,
Leicestershire LE11 2DU
Tel: 01509 212348
Email: high.admissions@lsf.org
Website: www.lsf.org/high
Head: Dr Fiona Miles
Age range: G11–18 years
No. of pupils: 545

Ratcliffe College
Fosse Way, Ratcliffe on the Wreake,
Leicester, Leicestershire LE7 4SG
Tel: +44 (0)1509 817000
Headmaster: Mr Jon Reddin
BSc, MSc, NPQH
Age range: 3–18 years
(boarding from 11)

St Crispin's School
6 St Mary's Road, Stoneygate,
Leicester, Leicestershire LE2 1XA
Tel: 01162 707648
Headmaster: Mr Andrew Atkin
Age range: 2–16 years

The Dixie Grammar School
Market Place, Market Bosworth,
Leicestershire CV13 0LE
Tel: 01455 292244
Headmaster: Mr Richard Lynn MA
Age range: 3–18 years

Lincolnshire

Ayscoughfee Hall School
Welland Hall, London Road,
Spalding, Lincolnshire PE11 2TE
Tel: 01775 724733
Headteacher: Ms Theresa Wright
Age range: 3–11 years

**Bicker Preparatory
School & Early Years**
School Lane, Bicker Bar, Boston,
Lincolnshire PE20 3DW
Tel: 01775 821786
Head of School: Ms Anne
Daynes BEd Hons
Age range: 3–11 years

Burton Hathow Preparatory School
Odder Farm, Saxilby Road, Burton,
Lincoln, Lincolnshire LN1 2BB
Tel: 01522 274616
Head Teacher: Ms Penny Ford
Age range: 2–11 years

Copthill School
Barnack Road, Uffington,
Stamford, Lincolnshire PE9 3AD
Tel: 01780 757506
Headmaster: Mr J A Teesdale
BA(Hons), PGCE
Age range: 2–11 years

Dudley House School
1 Dudley Road, Grantham,
Lincolnshire NG31 9AA
Tel: 01476 400184
Headteacher: Ms Jenny Johnson
Age range: 3–11 years

**Grantham Preparatory
International School**
Gorse Lane, Grantham,
Lincolnshire NG31 7UF
Tel: +44 (0)1476 593293
Headmistress: Mrs K A Korcz
Age range: 3–11 years

**Greenwich House
Independent School**
106 High Holme Road, Louth,
Lincolnshire LN11 0HE
Tel: 01507 609252
Headmistress: Mrs J Brindle
Age range: 9 months–11 years

Handel House Preparatory School
The Northolme, Gainsborough,
Lincolnshire DN21 2JB
Tel: 01427 612426
Headteacher: Mr Mark Raisborough
Age range: 3–11 years

Kirkstone House School
Main Street, Baston, Peterborough,
Lincolnshire PE6 9PA
Tel: 01778 560350
Headteacher: Mr Stuart Judge
Age range: 5–18 years

Lincoln Minster School
The Prior Building, Upper Lindum
Street, Lincoln, Lincolnshire LN2 5RW
Tel: 01522 551300
Headmistress: Mrs Maria Young
Age range: 4–18 years
No. of pupils: 500

**St George's Preparatory School
& Little Dragons Nursery**
126 London Road, Boston,
Lincolnshire PE21 7HB
Tel: 01205 317600
Directors: Mark & Sarah Whelan
Age range: 3–11 years

St Hugh's School
Cromwell Avenue, Woodhall
Spa, Lincolnshire LN10 6TQ
Tel: 01526 352169
Headmaster: Mr Jeremy Wyld
Age range: 2–13 years

Stamford High School
St. Martin's Street, Stamford,
Lincolnshire PE9 2LL
Tel: 01780 484200
Head of School: Mrs Vicky Buckman
Age range: G11–18 years
(boarding from 11)

Stamford Junior School
Kettering Road, Stamford,
Lincolnshire PE9 2LR
Tel: 01780 484400
Headteacher: Mr Matthew O'Reilly
Age range: 2–11 years
(boarding from 7)

Stamford School
Southfields House, Stamford,
Lincolnshire PE9 2BQ
Tel: 01780 750300
Headmaster: Mr Nick Gallop
Age range: B11–18 years
(boarding from 11)

Viking School
140 Church Road North, Skegness,
Lincolnshire PE25 2QJ
Tel: 01754 765749
Principal: Ms Laura Middlebrook
Age range: 3–11 years

Witham Hall Preparatory School
Witham-on-the-Hill, Stamford,
Lincolnshire PE10 0JJ
Tel: +44(0)1778 590222
Headmaster: Mr William Austen
Age range: 4–13 years

Northamptonshire

Beachborough School
Westbury, Nr. Brackley,
Northamptonshire NN13 5LB
Tel: 01280 700071
Headmaster: Mr Christian Pritchard
Age range: 2–13 years
No. of pupils: 400
Fees: Day £3,190–£5,970

Bosworth Independent College
Bosworth Hall, 33-35 St Georges
Avenue, Northampton,
Northamptonshire NN2 6JA
Tel: 01604 239995
Principal: Mr Jason Lewis
Age range: 13–19 years

Laxton Junior School
East Road, Oundle,
Northamptonshire PE8 4BX
Tel: 01832 277275
Head: Mr Sam Robertson
Age range: 4–11 years

Maidwell Hall
Maidwell, Northampton,
Northamptonshire NN6 9JG
Tel: 01604 686234
Headmaster: Mr R A
Lankester MA, PGCE
Age range: 4–13 years
Fees: FB £27,966

Northampton High School GDST
Newport Pagnell Road,
Hardingstone, Northampton,
Northamptonshire NN4 6UU
Tel: 01604 765765
Headmistress: Adele O'Doherty
Age range: G2–18 years
No. of pupils: 600
Fees: Day £3,346–£4,918

OneSchool Global UK Northampton Campus
Billing Road East, Northampton,
Northamptonshire NN3 3LF
Tel: 01604 633819
Age range: 7–18 years

Oundle School
The Great Hall, New Street, Oundle,
Northamptonshire PE8 4GH
Tel: +44 (0)1832 277122
Head of School: Mrs Sarah Kerr-Dineen
Age range: 11–18 years

Overstone Park School
Overstone Park,
Overstone, Northampton,
Northamptonshire NN6 0DT
Tel: 01604 643787
Principal: Mrs M F Brown
BA(Hons), PGCE
Age range: 2–18 years

Pitsford School
Pitsford Hall, Pitsford, Northampton,
Northamptonshire NN6 9AX
Tel: 01604 880306
Headteacher: Dr Craig Walker
Age range: 3–18 years
Fees: Day £8,751–£15,183

Quinton House School
Upton Hall, Upton, Northampton,
Northamptonshire NN5 4UX
Tel: 01604 752050
Headteacher: Mr Tim Hoyle
Age range: 2–18 years
No. of pupils: 390
Fees: Day £8,040–£11,985

Spratton Hall
Smith Street, Spratton,
Northamptonshire NN6 8HP
Tel: 01604 847292
Head Master: Mr Simon Clarke
Age range: 4–13 years
No. of pupils: 380
Fees: Day £10,725–£16,275

St Peter's School
52 Headlands, Kettering,
Northamptonshire NN15 6DJ
Tel: 01536 512066
Headteacher: Mr Mark Thomas
Age range: 3–11 years

Wellingborough School
London Road, Wellingborough,
Northamptonshire NN8 2BX
Tel: 01933 222427
Headmaster: Mr A N Holman
Age range: 3–18 years

Winchester House School
High Street, Brackley,
Northamptonshire NN13 7AZ
Tel: 01280 702483
Head: Ms Antonia Lee
Age range: 3–13 years
(boarding from 7)

Nottinghamshire

Colston Bassett Preparatory School
School Lane, Colston
bassett, Nottingham,
Nottinghamshire NG12 3FD
Tel: 01949 81118
Headteacher: Mrs C Newcombe
Age range: 4–11 years

Coteswood House Pre-school & Day Nursery
19 Thackeray's Lane, Woodthorpe,
Nottingham, Nottinghamshire NG5 4HT
Tel: 01159 676551
Age range: 2–5 years

Fig Tree Primary School
30 Bentinck Road, Nottingham,
Nottinghamshire NG7 4AF
Tel: 01159 788152
Headteacher: Mrs Nabeela Hussain
Age range: 5–11 years

Highfields School
London Road, Newark,
Nottinghamshire NG24 3AL
Tel: 01636 704103
Headteacher: Mrs Sarah H Lyons
Age range: 2–11 years

Hollygirt School
Elm Avenue, Nottingham,
Nottinghamshire NG3 4GF
Tel: 0115 958 0596
Head of School: Dr. Helen Barsham
Age range: 3–16 years

Jamia Al-Hudaa Residential College
Forest House, Berkeley Avenue,
Mapperley Park, Nottingham,
Nottinghamshire NG3 5TT
Tel: 01159 690800
Principal: Raza ul-Haq Siakhvy
Age range: 11–19 years

Nottingham Girls' High School GDST
9 Arboretum Street, Nottingham,
Nottinghamshire NG1 4JB
Tel: 01159 417663
Head: Miss Julie Keller
Age range: G3–18 years

Nottingham High School
Waverley Mount, Nottingham,
Nottinghamshire NG7 4ED
Tel: 01159 786056
Headmaster: Mr Kevin Fear BA
Age range: 4–18 years

OneSchool Global UK Nottingham Campus
Wellington Street, Long
Eaton, Nottingham,
Nottinghamshire NG10 4HR
Tel: 0115 973 3568
Age range: 7–18 years

Plumtree School
Church Hill, Plumtree, Nottingham,
Nottinghamshire NG12 5ND
Tel: 0115 937 5859
Head Teacher: Phil Simpson
Age range: 3–11 years

Salterford House School
Salterford Lane, Calverton,
Nottingham, Nottinghamshire
NG14 6NZ
Tel: 01159 652127
Head: Ms Kimberley Venables
Age range: 3–11 years

Saville House School
11 Church Street, Mansfield
Woodhouse, Mansfield,
Nottinghamshire NG19 8AH
Tel: 01623 904418
Headteacher: Ms Claire King
Age range: 3–11 years

St Joseph's School
33 Derby Road, Nottingham,
Nottinghamshire NG1 5AW
Tel: 01159 418356
Head Teacher: Mr Ashley Crawshaw
Age range: 1–11 years

The Iona School
310 Sneinton Dale, Nottingham,
Nottinghamshire NG3 7DN
Tel: 01159 415295
Chair of College: Mr Rob Strafford
Age range: 3–11 years

The Orchard School
South Leverton, Retford,
Nottinghamshire DN22 0DJ
Tel: 01427 880395
Head Teacher: Mrs Sandra
Fox BA, PGCE
Age range: 5–16 years

Trent College and The Elms
Derby Road, Long Eaton, Nottingham,
Nottinghamshire NG10 4AD
Tel: 0115 8494949
Head: Mr Bill Penty
Age range: 0–18 years
No. of pupils: 1121
Fees: Day £14,994–£18,789

Wellow House School
Wellow, Newark,
Nottinghamshire NG22 0EA
Tel: 01623 861054
Headmistress: Ms Kirsty Lamb
Age range: 3–13 years

Worksop College
Cuthbert's Avenue, Worksop,
Nottinghamshire S80 3AP
Tel: 01909 537100
Headmaster: Dr John Price
Age range: 11–18 years

Worksop College, Ranby House
Retford, Nottinghamshire DN22 8HX
Tel: 01777 703138
Headmaster: Mr David Thorpe
Age range: 3–11 years

Rutland

Brooke Priory School
Station Approach, Oakham,
Rutland LE15 6QW
Tel: 01572 724778
Headmaster: Mr Duncan Flint
Age range: 2–11 years

OAKHAM SCHOOL
For further details see p.110
Chapel Close, Oakham,
Rutland LE15 6DT
Tel: 01572 758758
Email: admissions@
oakham.rutland.sch.uk
Website:
www.oakham.rutland.sch.uk
Headmaster: Mr Henry
Price MA (Oxon)
Age range: 10–18 years
No. of pupils: 1040 VIth376
Fees: Day £6,580–£8,140
FB £10,100–£13,550

Uppingham School
Uppingham, Rutland LE15 9QE
Tel: +44 (0)1572 822216
Headmaster: Dr Richard Maloney
Age range: 13–18 years

Greater London

*See also East (D333) for schools in Essex and Hertfordshire; South-East (D377) for schools in Kent and Surrey

KEY TO SYMBOLS
- ⊕ *Boys' school*
- ⊛ *Girls' school*
- ⊕ *International school*
- 16⁺ *Tutorial or sixth form college*
- Ⓐ *A levels*
- ⊕ *Boarding accommodation*
- £ *Bursaries*
- ⒾⒷ *International Baccalaureate*
- ✐ *Learning support*
- 16⁺ *Entrance at 16+*
- ⊕ *Vocational qualifications*
- ⒾⒶⓅⓈ *Independent Association of Preparatory Schools*
- ⒽⓂⒸ *The Headmasters' & Headmistresses' Conference*
- ⒾⓈⒶ *Independent Schools Association*
- ⒼⓈⒶ *Girls' School Association*
- ⒷⓈⒶ *Boarding Schools' Association*
- Ⓢ *Society of Heads*

Unless otherwise indicated, all schools are coeducational day schools. Single-sex and boarding schools will be indicated by the relevant icon.

Essex

Al-Noor Primary School
619-629 Green Lane, Goodmayes,
Ilford, Essex IG3 9RP
Tel: 020 8597 7576
Headteacher: Mrs Someera Butt
Age range: 4–11 years

Avon House Preparatory School
490 High Road, Woodford
Green, Essex IG8 0PN
Tel: 020 8504 1749
Headteacher: Mrs Amanda Campbell
Age range: 3–11 years
No. of pupils: 268
Fees: Day £3,530–£3,950

Bancroft's School
High Road, Woodford
Green, Essex IG8 0RF
Tel: 020 8505 4821
Head: Mr Simon Marshall MA, PGCE
(Cantab), MA, MPhil (Oxon)
Age range: 7–18 years
Ⓐ Ⓔ ✎ ⑯

Beehive Preparatory School
233 Beehive Lane, Redbridge,
Ilford, Essex IG4 5ED
Tel: 020 8550 3224
Head Teacher: Mr Jamie Gurr
Age range: 2–11 years

Braeside School
130 High Road, Buckhurst
Hill, Essex IG9 5SD
Tel: 020 8504 1133
Headmistress: Ms Chloe Moon
Age range: 2–16 years

Chigwell School
High Road, Chigwell, Essex IG7 6QF
Tel: 020 8501 5700
Headmaster: Mr M E Punt
M.A. M.Sc. P.G.C.E.
Age range: 4–18 years
🏤 Ⓐ 🏛 Ⓔ ✎ ⑯

Daiglen School
68 Palmerston Road, Buckhurst
Hill, Essex IG9 5LG
Tel: 020 8504 7108
Headteacher: Mrs P Dear
Age range: 3–11 years
✎

Eastcourt Independent School
1-5 Eastwood Road, Goodmayes,
Ilford, Essex IG3 8UW
Tel: 020 8590 5472
Headmistress: Mrs Christine
Redgrave BSc(Hons), DipEd, MEd
Age range: 3–11 years
No. of pupils: 220
Fees: Day £2,600

**Gidea Park Preparatory
School & Nursery**
2 Balgores Lane, Gidea Park,
Romford, Essex RM2 5JR
Tel: 01708 740381
Head of School: Mr Callum Douglas
Age range: 2–11 years
No. of pupils: 100
Fees: Day £10,775
✎

**Guru Gobind Singh
Khalsa College**
Roding Lane, Chigwell, Essex IG7 6BQ
Tel: 020 8559 9160
Principal: Mr Amarjit Singh
Toor BSc(Hons), BSc, BT
Age range: 3–19 years

Immanuel School
Havering Grange, Havering
Road, Romford, Essex RM1 4HR
Tel: 01708 764449
Principal: Ms Sarah Williams
Age range: 3–16 years

Loyola Preparatory School
103 Palmerston Road, Buckhurst
Hill, Essex IG9 5NH
Tel: 020 8504 7372
Headmistress: Mrs K R Anthony
Age range: B3–11 years
No. of pupils: 200
Fees: Day £11,085
🏃 Ⓔ ✎

Oakfields Preparatory School
Harwood Hall, Harwood Hall Lane,
Upminster, Essex RM14 2YG
Tel: 01708 220117
Headmistress: Katrina Carroll
Age range: 2–11 years
No. of pupils: 202
Fees: Day £10,296–£11,121

Oaklands School
6-8 Albion Hill, Loughton,
Essex IG10 4RA
Tel: 020 8508 3517
Headmistress: Ms Sue Belej
Age range: 2–11 years

Park School for Girls
20-22 Park Avenue, Ilford, Essex IG1 4RS
Tel: 020 8554 2466
Head Teacher: Mrs Catherine Redfern
Age range: G4–16 years
🏃 ⑯

St Aubyn's School
Bunces Lane, Woodford
Green, Essex IG8 9DU
Tel: 020 8504 1577
Headmaster: Mr Leonard
Blom BEd(Hons) BA NPQH
Age range: 3–13 years
✎

**St Mary's Hare Park
School & Nursery**
South Drive, Gidea Park,
Romford, Essex RM2 6HH
Tel: 01708 761220
Headteacher: Mr Ludovic Bernard
Age range: 2–11 years

**The Ursuline Preparatory
School Ilford**
2-4 Coventry Road, Ilford, Essex IG1 4QR
Tel: 020 8518 4050
Acting Headteacher: Mrs
Lorraine Pereira
Age range: 3–11 years

**Woodford Green
Preparatory School**
Glengall Road, Woodford
Green, Essex IG8 0BZ
Tel: 020 8504 5045
Headmaster: Mr J P Wadge
Age range: 3–11 years
No. of pupils: 385
Fees: Day £3,725
Ⓔ ✎

Hertfordshire

Lyonsdown School
3 Richmond Road, New Barnet,
Barnet, Hertfordshire EN5 1SA
Tel: 020 8449 0225
Head: Mrs Rittu Hall
Age range: G3–11 years
No. of pupils: 180
Fees: Day £3,681–£11,766
🏃 ✎

Mount House School
Camlet Way, Hadley Wood,
Barnet, Hertfordshire EN4 0NJ
Tel: 020 8449 6889
Head: Mrs Sarah Richardson
Age range: 11–18 years
✎ ⑯

Susi Earnshaw Theatre School
The Bull Theatre, 68 High Street,
Barnet, Hertfordshire EN5 5SJ
Tel: 020 8441 5010
Headteacher: Ms Julia Hammond
Age range: 9–16 years
Ⓔ

The Royal Masonic School for Girls
Rickmansworth Park, Rickmansworth,
Hertfordshire WD3 4HF
Tel: 01923 773168
Headmaster: Mr Kevin Carson
M.Phil (Cambridge)
Age range: B2–4 years G2–18 years
🏃 🏤 🏛 Ⓔ ✎ ⑯

Kent

Ashgrove School
116 Widmore Road,
Bromley, Kent BR1 3BE
Tel: 020 8460 4143
Head of School: Dr Patricia Ash
Age range: 3–11 years

Babington House School
Grange Drive, Chislehurst, Kent BR7 5ES
Tel: 020 8467 5537
Headmaster: Mr Tim Lello
MA, FRSA, NPQH
Age range: 3–18 years
No. of pupils: 439

Benedict House Preparatory School
1-5 Victoria Road, Sidcup,
Kent DA15 7HD
Tel: 020 8300 7206
Headteacher: Mr Craig Wardle
Age range: 3–11 years

Bickley Park School
14 & 24 Page Heath Lane,
Bickley, Bromley, Kent BR1 2DS
Tel: 020 8467 2195
Head of School: Ms Tammy Howard
Age range: B2–13 years G2–4 years

Bishop Challoner School
228 Bromley Road, Shortlands,
Bromley, Kent BR2 0BS
Tel: 020 8460 3546
Headteacher: Mr Mark
Wallace BA (Hons), MBA
Age range: 3–18 years

Breaside Preparatory School
41-43 Orchard Road,
Bromley, Kent BR1 2PR
Tel: 020 8460 0916
Executive Principal: Mrs Karen A
Nicholson B.Ed, NPQH, Dip EYs
Age range: 2–11 years
No. of pupils: 376
Fees: Day £11,580–£13,494

Bromley High School GDST
Blackbrook Lane, Bickley,
Bromley, Kent BR1 2TW
Tel: 020 8781 7000/1
Head: Mrs A M Drew
BA(Hons), MBA (Dunelm)
Age range: G4–18 years

Darul Uloom London
Foxbury Avenue, Perry Street,
Chislehurst, Kent BR7 6SD
Tel: 020 8295 0637
Principal: Mufti Muhammed
Kamil Sheikh
Age range: B11–19 years

Farringtons School
Perry Street, Chislehurst, Kent BR7 6LR
Tel: 020 8467 0256
Head: Mr David Jackson
Age range: 3–18 years
No. of pupils: 700 VIth100
Fees: Day £16,260 WB £27,120 FB £34,050

Merton Court Preparatory School
38 Knoll Road, Sidcup, Kent DA14 4QU
Tel: 020 8300 2112
Headmaster: Mr Dominic
Price BEd, MBA
Age range: 3–11 years
No. of pupils: 320
Fees: Day £3,095–£4,675

St Christopher's The Hall School
49 Bromley Road, Beckenham,
Kent BR3 5PA
Tel: 020 8650 2200
Headteacher: Mr Tom Carter
Age range: 3–11 years

St David's Prep
Justin Hall, Beckenham Road,
West Wickham, Kent BR4 0QS
Tel: 020 8777 5852
Head Teacher: Ms Julia Foulger
Age range: 3–11 years

West Lodge School
36 Station Road, Sidcup, Kent DA15 7DU
Tel: 020 8300 2489
Head Teacher: Mr Robert Francis
Age range: 3–11 years

Wickham Court School
Layhams Road, West
Wickham, Kent BR4 9HW
Tel: 020 8777 2942
Principal: Ms Lisa Harries
Age range: 3–11 years

Middlesex

ACS Hillingdon International School
108 Vine Lane, Hillingdon,
Uxbridge, Middlesex UB10 0BE
Tel: +44 (0) 1895 259771
Head of School: Mr Martin Hall
Age range: 4–18 years

Alpha Preparatory School
21 Hindes Road, Harrow,
Middlesex HA1 1SH
Tel: 020 8427 1471
Headmaster: Mr Pádraic Fahy
Age range: 3–11 years

Ashton House School
50-52 Eversley Crescent,
Isleworth, Middlesex TW7 4LW
Tel: 020 8560 3902
Headteacher: Mrs Angela Stewart
Age range: 3–11 years

Buckingham Preparatory School
458 Rayners Lane, Pinner,
Harrow, Middlesex HA5 5DT
Tel: 020 8866 2737
Head of School: Mrs Sarah Hollis
Age range: B3–11 years

Buxlow Preparatory School
5/6 Castleton Gardens, Wembley,
Middlesex HA9 7QJ
Tel: 020 8904 3615
Headteacher: Mr D May
Age range: 2–11 years

Edgware Jewish Girls – Beis Chinuch
296 Hale Lane, Edgware,
Middlesex HA8 8NP
Tel: 020 8905 4376
Headteacher: Mr M Cohen
Age range: G3–11 years

Halliford School
Russell Road, Shepperton,
Middlesex TW17 9HX
Tel: 01932 223593
Headmaster: Mr James Davies BMus
(Hons) LGSM FASC ACertCM PGCE
Age range: B11–18 years G16–18 years
No. of pupils: 450
Fees: Day £19,200

Hampton Prep and Pre-Prep School
Gloucester Road, Hampton,
Middlesex TW12 2UQ
Tel: 020 8979 1844
Headmaster: Mr Tim Smith
Age range: B3–11 years G3–7 years

Hampton School
Hanworth Road, Hampton,
Middlesex TW12 3HD
Tel: 020 8979 5526
Headmaster: Mr Kevin
Knibbs MA (Oxon)
Age range: B11–18 years

Harrow School
5 High Street, Harrow on the
Hill, Middlesex HA1 3HP
Tel: 020 8872 8000
Head Master: Mr Alastair Land
Age range: B13–18 years

Holland House School
1 Broadhurst Avenue, Edgware,
Middlesex HA8 8TP
Tel: 020 8958 6979
Headteacher: Mrs Emily Brown
Age range: 4–11 years
No. of pupils: 147

Jack & Jill Family of Schools
20 First Cross Road, Twickenham,
Middlesex TW2 5QA
Tel: 03333 444630
Age range: B2–4 years G2–11 years

Kew House School
Kew House, 6 Capital Interchange
Way, London, Middlesex TW8 0EX
Tel: 0208 742 2038
Headmaster: Mr Will Williams
Age range: 11–18 years
No. of pupils: 576
Fees: Day £7,674
Ⓐ 🖉 16⃝

Lady Eleanor Holles
Hanworth Road, Hampton,
Middlesex TW12 3HF
Tel: 020 8979 1601
Head of School: Mrs Heather Hanbury
Age range: G7–18 years
No. of pupils: 970
Fees: Day £21,738
🏃 Ⓐ £ 🖉 16⃝

Lady Nafisa School
Inglenook, Sipson Road, Sipson,
West Drayton, Middlesex UB7 0JG
Tel: 02087 070001
Headteacher: Ms Fouzia Butt
Age range: G11–16 years
🏃

Menorah Foundation School
Abbots Road, Edgware,
Middlesex HA8 0QS
Tel: 020 8906 9992
Headteacher: Karen Kent
Age range: B11–21 years

Merchant Taylors' School
Sandy Lodge, Northwood,
Middlesex HA6 2HT
Tel: 01923 820644
Head Master: Mr S J
Everson MA (Cantab)
Age range: B11–18 years
🏃 🖉 16⃝

Newland House School
Waldegrave Park, Twickenham,
Middlesex TW1 4TQ
Tel: 020 8865 1234
Head of School: Mr Chris Skelton
Age range: 3–13 years

North London Collegiate School
Canons, Canons Drive, Edgware,
Middlesex HA8 7RJ
Tel: +44 (0)20 8952 0912
Headmistress: Mrs Sarah Clark
Age range: G4–18 years
No. of pupils: 1080
Fees: Day £5,956–£7,049
🏃 🎾 Ⓐ £ IB 16⃝

Northwood College for Girls GDST
Maxwell Road, Northwood,
Middlesex HA6 2YE
Tel: 01923 825446
Head of School: Mrs Rebecca Brown
Age range: G3–18 years
No. of pupils: 844
🏃 Ⓐ 🖉 16⃝

Oak Heights
2-3 Red Lion Court, Alexandra Road,
Hounslow, Middlesex TW3 1JS
Tel: 020 8577 1827
Head: Mr S Dhillon
Age range: 11–16 years

Orley Farm School
South Hill Avenue, Harrow,
Middlesex HA1 3NU
Tel: 020 8869 7600
Headmaster: Mr Tim Calvey
Age range: 4–13 years
🖉

Quainton Hall School & Nursery
91 Hindes Road, Harrow,
Middlesex HA1 1RX
Tel: 020 8515 9500
Headmaster: S Ford BEd
(Hons), UWE Bristol
Age range: 3–11 years
Fees: Day £11,850–£13,050

Radnor House
Pope's Villa, Cross Deep,
Twickenham, Middlesex TW1 4QG
Tel: +44 (0)20 8891 6264
Head: Mr Darryl Wideman
MA Oxon, PGCE
Age range: 9–18 years
🎾 16⃝

Reddiford School
36-38 Cecil Park, Pinner,
Middlesex HA5 5HH
Tel: 020 8866 0660
Headteacher: Mrs J Batt CertEd, NPQH
Age range: 3–11 years

Regent College London
Regent House, 167 Imperial Drive,
Harrow, Middlesex HA2 7HD
Tel: +44 (0)20 3870 6666
Co-Principals: Dr Selva Pankaj
& Mrs Tharshiny Pankaj
Age range: 14–24 years
16⃝ 16⃝

Roxeth Mead School
Buckholt House, 25 Middle Road,
Harrow, Middlesex HA2 0HW
Tel: 020 8422 2092
Co-Headteachers: Mrs Suzanne
Goodwin & Mrs Sarah Mackintosh
Age range: 0–7 years

St Catherine's Prep
Cross Deep, Twickenham,
Middlesex TW1 4QJ
Tel: 020 8891 2898
Headmistress: Mrs Johneen
McPherson MA
Age range: G4–11 years
No. of pupils: 102
Fees: Day £12,480–£13,470
🏃

ST CATHERINE'S SCHOOL
For further details see p.124
Cross Deep, Twickenham,
Middlesex TW1 4QJ
Tel: 020 8891 2898
Email: info@stcatherineschool.co.uk
Website:
www.stcatherineschool.co.uk
Headmistress: Mrs Johneen
McPherson MA
Age range: G5–18 years
No. of pupils: 434
Fees: Day £13,395–£16,875
🏃 🎾 Ⓐ £ 🖉 16⃝

St Christopher's School
71 Wembley Park Drive,
Wembley, Middlesex HA9 8HE
Tel: 020 8902 5069
Head of School: Mr Jonathan Coke
Age range: 2–11 years

ST HELEN'S COLLEGE
For further details see p.122
Parkway, Hillingdon, Uxbridge,
Middlesex UB10 9JX
Tel: 01895 234371
Email: info@sthelenscollege.com
Website: www.sthelenscollege.com
Head: Ms Shirley Drummond
BA, PGCert, MLDP, FCCT
Age range: 2–11 years
No. of pupils: 380
Fees: Day £10,560–£13,020
🖉

St Helen's School
Eastbury Road, Northwood,
Middlesex HA6 3AS
Tel: +44 (0)1923 843210
Headmistress: Mrs Alice Lucas
Age range: G3–18 years
No. of pupils: 1150
🏃 🎾 16⃝

St John's School
Potter Street Hill, Northwood,
Middlesex HA6 3QY
Tel: 020 8866 0067
Headmaster: Mr Sean Robinson
Age range: B3–13 years
🏃

St Martin's School
40 Moor Park Road, Northwood,
Middlesex HA6 2DJ
Tel: 01923 825740
Headmaster: Mr S Dunn BEd (Hons)
Age range: B3–13 years
🏃 🖉

St. John's Senior School
North Lodge, The Ridgeway,
Enfield, Middlesex EN2 8BE
Tel: +44 (0)20 8366 0035
Head Teacher: Mr A Tardios
Age range: 11–18 years

Tashbar of Edgware
Mowbray Road, Edgware,
Middlesex HA8 8JL
Age range: B3–11 years
🏃

**The Hall Pre-Preparatory
School & Nursery**
The Grange Country House,
Rickmansworth Road, Northwood,
Middlesex HA6 2RB
Tel: 01923 822807
Headmistress: Mrs S M Goodwin
Age range: 0–7 years

The John Lyon School
Middle Road, Harrow on the
Hill, Middlesex HA2 0HN
Tel: 020 8515 9443
Head: Miss Katherine Haynes
BA, MEd, NPQH
Age range: 11–18 years
No. of pupils: 600
Ⓐ £ 🖉 16⃝

The Mall School
185 Hampton Road, Twickenham,
Middlesex TW2 5NQ
Tel: 0208 977 2523
Headmaster: Mr D C Price BSc, MA
Age range: B4–11 years
🏃 🖉

The St Michael Steiner School
Park Road, Hanworth Park,
London, Middlesex TW13 6PN
Tel: 0208 893 1299
Age range: 3–18 years
🖉

Twickenham Preparatory School
Beveree, 43 High Street, Hampton,
Middlesex TW12 2SA
Tel: 020 8979 6216
Headmaster: Mr Oliver Barrett
Age range: B4–13 years G4–11 years

Surrey

Al-Khair School
109-117 Cherry Orchard Road,
Croydon, Surrey CR0 6BE
Tel: 020 8662 8664
Headteacher: Mrs Aisha Chaudhry
Age range: 2–16 years

Broomfield House School
Broomfield Road, Kew Gardens,
Richmond, Surrey TW9 3HS
Tel: 020 8940 3884
Head of School: Ms Susie Byers
Age range: 3–11 years

Cambridge Tutors College
Water Tower Hill, Croydon,
Surrey CR0 5SX
Tel: 020 8688 5284/7363
Principal: Dr Chris Drew
Age range: 14–23 years

Canbury School
Kingston Hill, Kingston upon
Thames, Surrey KT2 7LN
Tel: 020 8549 8622
Headmistress: Ms Carolyn Yates
Age range: 11–18 years

Collingwood School
3 Springfield Road, Wallington,
Surrey SM6 0BD
Tel: 020 8647 4607
Headmaster: Mr Leigh Hardie
Age range: 3–11 years

Croydon High School GDST
Old Farleigh Road, Selsdon, South
Croydon, Surrey CR2 8YB
Tel: 02082 607543
Head: Ms Annabel Davies
Age range: G3–18 years

Cumnor House School for Boys
168 Pampisford Road, South
Croydon, Surrey CR2 6DA
Tel: 020 8645 2614
Head of School: Miss Emma Edwards
Age range: B4–13 years
No. of pupils: 423
Fees: Day £3,880–£4,655

Cumnor House School for Girls
1 Woodcote Lane, Purley,
Surrey CR8 3HB
Tel: 020 8668 0050
Head of School: Mrs
Amanda McShane
Age range: G4–11 years

Date Valley School Trust
Mitcham Court, Cricket Green,
Mitcham, Surrey CR4 4LB
Tel: +44 (0)20 8648 4647
Headteacher: Neena Lone
Age range: 3–11 years

Educare Small School
12 Cowleaze Road, Kingston
upon Thames, Surrey KT2 6DZ
Tel: 020 8547 0144
Head Teacher: Mrs E Steinthal
Age range: 3–11 years

ELMHURST SCHOOL
For further details see p.114
44-48 South Park Hill Road, South
Croydon, Surrey CR2 7DW
Tel: 020 8688 0661
Email: admissions@
elmhurstschool.net
Website: www.elmhurstschool.net
Head of School: Mrs Sara Marriott
Age range: B3–11 years
No. of pupils: 140
Fees: Day £3,680–£4,290

Falcons Prep Richmond
41 Kew Foot Road, Richmond,
Surrey TW9 2SS
Tel: 020 8948 9490
Headmistress: Ms Olivia Buchanan
Age range: B3–13 years

Holy Cross Preparatory School
George Road, Kingston upon
Thames, Surrey KT2 7NU
Tel: 020 8942 0729
Headteacher: Mrs S Hair BEd(Hons)
Age range: G3–11 years

Homefield Preparatory School
Western Road, Sutton, Surrey SM1 2TE
Tel: 0208 642 0965
Headmaster: Mr John Towers
Age range: B4–13 years
No. of pupils: 350
Fees: Day £6,345–£13,650

KEW COLLEGE PREP
For further details see p.116
24-26 Cumberland Road,
Kew, Surrey TW9 3HQ
Tel: 020 8940 2039
Email: enquiries@kewcollege.com
Website: www.kewcollege.com
Head: Mrs Jane Bond
BSc, MA(Ed), PGCE
Age range: 3–11 years
No. of pupils: 284

Kew Green Preparatory School
Layton House, Ferry Lane, Kew
Green, Richmond, Surrey TW9 3AF
Tel: 020 8948 5999
Headmistress: Mrs N Gibson
Age range: 4–11 years
No. of pupils: 273
Fees: Day £6,304

KING'S HOUSE SCHOOL
For further details see p.118
68 King's Road, Richmond,
Surrey TW10 6ES
Tel: 020 8940 1878
Email: admissions@
kingshouseschool.org
Website: www.kingshouseschool.org
Head: Mr Mark Turner
BA, PGCE, NPQH
Age range: B3–13 years G3–4 years
No. of pupils: 425
Fees: Day £2,720–£6,530

Kingston Grammar School
70 London Rd, Kingston upon
Thames, Surrey KT2 6PY
Tel: 020 8546 5875
Head: Mr Stephen Lehec
Age range: 11–18 years

LALEHAM LEA SCHOOL
For further details see p.120
29 Peaks Hill, Purley, Surrey CR8 3JJ
Tel: 020 8660 3351
Email: secretary@lalehamlea.co.uk
Website: www.lalehamlea.co.uk
Headteacher: Ms K Barry
Age range: 3–11 years
No. of pupils: 131
Fees: Day £9,576

Marymount London
George Road, Kingston upon
Thames, Surrey KT2 7PE
Tel: +44 (0)20 8949 0571
Headmistress: Mrs Margaret Giblin
Age range: G11–18 years
No. of pupils: 260
Fees: Day £27,250 WB
£44,180 FB £46,130

Oakwood Independent School
Godstone Road, Purley,
Surrey CR8 2AN
Tel: 020 8668 8080
Headmaster: Mr Ciro Candia
BA(Hons), PGCE
Age range: 3–11 years
No. of pupils: 176
Fees: Day £9,030–£9,840
ⓔ

Old Palace of John Whitgift School
Old Palace Road, Croydon,
Surrey CR0 1AX
Tel: 020 8688 2027
Head: Mrs. C Jewell
Age range: G3–18 years
No. of pupils: 650
Fees: Day £3,300–£5,536
ⓐ Ⓐ ⓔ ⑯

Old Vicarage School
46-48 Richmond Hill, Richmond,
Surrey TW10 6QX
Tel: 020 8940 0922
Headmistress: Mrs G D Linthwaite
Age range: G3–11 years
No. of pupils: 200
Fees: Day £5,200
ⓐ ✏

Park Hill School
8 Queens Road, Kingston upon
Thames, Surrey KT2 7SH
Tel: 020 8546 5496
Headmaster: Mr Alistair Bond
Age range: 2–11 years
No. of pupils: 100
Fees: Day £10,440
✏

Rokeby School
George Road, Kingston upon
Thames, Surrey KT2 7PB
Tel: 020 8942 2247
Head: Mr J R Peck
Age range: B4–13 years
ⓐ ✏

Royal Russell Junior School
Coombe Lane, Croydon,
Surrey CR9 5BX
Tel: 020 8651 5884
Junior School Headmaster: Mr
James C Thompson
Age range: 3–11 years
No. of pupils: 300
Fees: Day £11,160–£14,220

Royal Russell School
Coombe Lane, Croydon,
Surrey CR9 5BX
Tel: 020 8657 3669
Headmaster: Christopher Hutchinson
Age range: 11–18 years
ⓐ Ⓐ 🏛 ⓔ ✏ ⑯

Seaton House School
67 Banstead Road South,
Sutton, Surrey SM2 5LH
Tel: 020 8642 2332
Headmistress: Mrs Debbie Morrison
Higher Diploma in Education (RSA)
Age range: B3–5 years G3–11 years
No. of pupils: 164
Fees: Day £10,188

Shrewsbury House School
107 Ditton Road, Surbiton,
Surrey KT6 6RL
Tel: 020 8399 3066
Executive Head: Ms Joanna Hubbard
MA BA(Hons) PGCE PGDipSEN
Age range: B7–13 years
ⓐ ✏

St David's School
23/25 Woodcote Valley Road,
Purley, Surrey CR8 3AL
Tel: 020 8660 0723
Headmistress: Cressida Mardell
Age range: 3–11 years
No. of pupils: 167
Fees: Day £6,375–£10,650
ⓔ ✏

St James Senior Boys School
Church Road, Ashford, Surrey TW15 3DZ
Tel: 01784 266930
Headmaster: Mr David Brazier
Age range: B11–18 years
No. of pupils: 403 VIth65
Fees: Day £18,930
ⓐ Ⓐ Ⓐ ⓔ ✏ ⑯

STAINES PREPARATORY SCHOOL
For further details see p.126
3 Gresham Road, Staines-upon-
Thames, Surrey TW18 2BT
Tel: 01784 450909
Email: admissions@
stainesprep.co.uk
Website: www.stainesprep.co.uk
Head of School: Ms Samantha
Sawyer B.Ed (Hons), M.Ed, NPQH
Age range: 3–11 years
No. of pupils: 298
Fees: Day £11,250–£13,500
ⓔ ✏

Surbiton High School
13-15 Surbiton Crescent, Kingston
upon Thames, Surrey KT1 2JT
Tel: 02085 465245
Principal: Mrs Rebecca Glover
Age range: B4–11 years G4–18 years
ⓐ Ⓐ ⓔ ✏ ⑯

Sutton High School GDST
55 Cheam Road, Sutton,
Surrey SM1 2AX
Tel: 020 8642 0594
Headmistress: Mrs Katharine Crouch
Age range: G3–18 years
No. of pupils: 600 VIth60
Fees: Day £10,095–£17,043
ⓐ Ⓐ ⓔ ✏ ⑯

The Cedars School
Coombe Road, Lloyd Park,
Croydon, Surrey CR0 5RD
Tel: 020 8185 7770
Headmaster: Robert Teague Bsc (Hons)
Age range: B11–18 years
ⓐ

The Royal Ballet School
White Lodge, Richmond,
Surrey TW10 5HR
Tel: 020 8392 8440
Artistic Director: Christopher Powney
Age range: 11–19 years
(boarding from 11)
🏛

The Study School
57 Thetford Road, New
Malden, Surrey KT3 5DP
Tel: 020 8942 0754
Head of School: Mrs Donna
Brackstone-Drake
Age range: 3–11 years
No. of pupils: 134
Fees: Day £4,860–£11,388

Trinity School
Shirley Park, Croydon, Surrey CR9 7AT
Tel: 020 8656 9541
Head: Alasdair Kennedy MA (Cantab)
Age range: B10–18 years G16–18 years
No. of pupils: 1007
Fees: Day £16,656
ⓐ Ⓐ ⓔ ✏ ⑯

Unicorn School
238 Kew Road, Richmond,
Surrey TW9 3JX
Tel: 020 8948 3926
Headmaster: Mr Kit Thompson
Age range: 3–11 years
Fees: Day £7,170–£13,170
ⓔ ✏

Westbury House
80 Westbury Road, New
Malden, Surrey KT3 5AS
Tel: 020 8942 5885
Age range: 3–11 years
Fees: Day £4,860–£11,115

WHITGIFT SCHOOL
For further details see p.128
Haling Park, South Croydon,
Surrey CR2 6YT
Tel: +44 20 8633 9935
Email: admissions@whitgift.co.uk
Website: www.whitgift.co.uk
Headmaster: Mr Christopher Ramsey
Age range: B10–18 years
No. of pupils: 1550
Fees: Day £22,269 WB
£35,973 FB £43,629
ⓐ Ⓐ Ⓐ 🏛 ⓔ Ⓑ ✏ ⑯

London

KEY TO SYMBOLS

- ⊕ Boys' school
- ⊕ Girls' school
- ⊕ International school
- 16 Tutorial or sixth form college
- Ⓐ A levels
- ⊕ Boarding accommodation
- £ Bursaries
- IB International Baccalaureate
- ⊘ Learning support
- 16 Entrance at 16+
- ⊕ Vocational qualifications
- IAPS Independent Association of Preparatory Schools
- HMC The Headmasters' & Headmistresses' Conference
- ISA Independent Schools Association
- GSA Girls' School Association
- BSA Boarding Schools' Association
- S Society of Heads

Unless otherwise indicated, all schools are coeducational day schools. Single-sex and boarding schools will be indicated by the relevant icon.

Central London

CATS London
43-45 Bloomsbury Square,
London WC1A 2RA
Tel: 02078 411580
Principal: Mario Di Clemente
Age range: 15–24 years
ⓐ Ⓐ ⓛ £ 16+

Charterhouse Square School
40 Charterhouse Square,
London EC1M 6EA
Tel: 020 7600 3805
Age range: 3–11 years

CITY OF LONDON SCHOOL
For further details see p.134
Queen Victoria Street,
London EC4V 3AL
Tel: 020 3680 6300
Email: admissions@
cityoflondonschool.org.uk
Website:
www.cityoflondonschool.org.uk
Head: Mr A R Bird MSc
Age range: B10–18 years
No. of pupils: 950 VIth250
Fees: Day £21,057
ⓕ Ⓐ £ 🖉 16+

City of London School for Girls
St Giles' Terrace, Barbican,
London EC2Y 8BB
Tel: 020 7847 5500
Headmistress: Mrs E Harrop
Age range: G7–18 years
No. of pupils: 725
ⓕ Ⓐ £ 🖉 16+

Dallington School
8 Dallington Street, Islington,
London EC1V 0BW
Tel: 020 7251 2284
Head: Linda Kiernan
Age range: 3–11 years
No. of pupils: 81
Fees: Day £11,490–£14,490

École Jeannine Manuel – London
43-45 Bedford Square,
London WC1B 3DN
Tel: 020 3829 5970
Head of School: Pauline Prévot
Age range: 3–18 years
No. of pupils: 585
Fees: Day £20,760
ⓐ £ Ⓑ

Italia Conti Academy of Theatre Arts
Italia Conti House, 23 Goswell
Road, London EC1M 7AJ
Tel: 020 7608 0047
Director: Chris White
Age range: 10–21 years
16+ Ⓐ 16+

ST PAUL'S CATHEDRAL SCHOOL
For further details see p.170
2 New Change, London EC4M 9AD
Tel: 020 7248 5156
Email: admissions@spcs.
london.sch.uk
Website: www.spcslondon.com
Headmaster: Simon Larter-
Evans BA (Hons), PGCE, FRSA
Age range: 4–13 years
No. of pupils: 270
Fees: Day £5,348–£5,759 FB £3,235
ⓛ £ 🖉

The Lyceum School
65 Worship Street, London EC2A 2DU
Tel: +44 (0)20 7247 1588
Headmistress: Mrs Hilary Wyatt
Age range: 3–11 years

East London

Al-Falah Primary School
48 Kenninghall Road,
Hackney, London E5 8BY
Tel: 020 8985 1059
Headteacher: Mr M A Hussain
Age range: 5–11 years

Al-Mizan School
46 Whitechapel Road, London E1 1JX
Tel: 020 7650 3070
Head: Mr Askor Ali
Age range: B7–11 years

Azhar Academy
235A Romford Road, Forest
Gate, London E7 9HL
Tel: 020 8534 5959
Headteacher: Mrs R Rehman
Age range: G11–16 years
No. of pupils: 189
ⓕ

Beis Trana Girls' School
186 Upper Clapton Road,
London E5 9DH
Tel: 020 8815 8000
Head of School: Mrs M Shmaya
Age range: G3–16 years
ⓕ

Chingford House Nursery
22 Marlborough Road, Waltham
Forest, London E4 9AL
Tel: 02085 272902
Age range: 6 months–5 years

Faraday Prep School
Old Gate House, 7 Trinity Buoy
Wharf, London E14 0JW
Tel: 020 8965 7374
Head Teacher: Lucas Motion
Age range: 4–11 years
No. of pupils: 100
Fees: Day £3,981
£

Forest School
College Place, Snaresbrook,
London E17 3PY
Tel: 020 8520 1744
Warden: Mr Cliff Hodges
Age range: 4–18 years
Ⓐ £ 🖉 16+

Gatehouse School
Sewardstone Road, Victoria
Park, London E2 9JG
Tel: 020 8980 2978
Head of School: Mrs Sevda Corby
Age range: 3–11 years
No. of pupils: 489
Fees: Day £4,130–£4,353
🖉

Grangewood Independent School
Chester Road, Forest
Gate, London E7 8QT
Tel: 020 8472 3552
Headteacher: Mrs B A Roberts
B.Ed (Hons); PG Cert (SEN)
Age range: 2–11 years
No. of pupils: 71
Fees: Day £5,157–£6,751
🖉

Hyland House School
Holcombe Road, Tottenham,
, London N17 9AD
Tel: 0208 520 4186
Head Teacher: Mrs Gina Abbequaye
Age range: 3–11 years
Fees: Day £2,520

London East Academy
46 Whitechapel Road, London E1 1JX
Tel: 020 7650 3070
Headteacher: Askor Ali
Age range: B11–18 years
ⓕ Ⓐ

Lubavitch House School (Junior Boys)
135 Clapton Common, London E5 9AE
Tel: 020 8800 1044
Head: Mr R Leach
Age range: B5–11 years
No. of pupils: 101
ⓕ

Madani Girls School
Myrdle Street, London E1 1HL
Tel: 020 7377 1992
Headteacher: Muhammad S. Rahman
Age range: G11–18 years
ⓕ

Normanhurst School
68-74 Station Road, Chingford,
London E4 7BA
Tel: 020 8529 4307
Headmistress: Mrs Jacqueline Job
Age range: 2–16 years

Pillar Box Montessori Nursery & Pre-Prep School
107 Bow Road, London E3 2AN
Tel: 020 8980 0700
Director: Lorraine Redknapp
Age range: 0–5 years
Fees: Day £12,000

Quwwat-ul Islam Girls School
16 Chaucer Road, Forest
Gate, London E7 9NB
Tel: 020 8548 4736
Headteacher: Ms Shazia Member
Age range: G4–11 years
ⓕ

River House Montessori School
Great Eastern Enterprise 3,
Millharbour, London E14 9XP
Tel: 02075 389886
Principal: Ms Sarah Greenwood
Age range: 3–16 years
🖉

Snaresbrook Preparatory School
75 Woodford Road, South
Woodford, London E18 2EA
Tel: 020 8989 2394
Head of School: Mr Ralph Dalton
Age range: 3–11 years
Fees: Day £8,922–£11,934
🖉

Talmud Torah Machzikei Hadass School
1 Belz Terrace, Clapton, London E5 9SN
Tel: 020 8800 6599
Headteacher: Rabbi C Silbiger
Age range: B3–16 years
ⓕ

Winston House Preparatory School
140 High Road, London E18 2QS
Tel: 020 8505 6565
Head Teacher: Mrs Marian Kemp
Age range: 3–11 years

North London

Annemount School
18 Holne Chase, Hampstead
Garden Suburb, London N2 0QN
Tel: 020 8455 2132
Principal: Mrs G Maidment
BA(Hons), MontDip
Age range: 2–7 years

Avenue Pre-Prep & Nursery School
2 Highgate Avenue, Highgate,
London N6 5RX
Tel: 020 8348 6815
Principal: Mrs. Mary Fysh
Age range: 2–8 years

Beis Chinuch Lebonos Girls School
Woodberry Down Centre,
Woodberry Down, London N4 2SH
Tel: 020 88097 737
Age range: G2–16 years

Beis Malka Girls School
93 Alkham Road, London N16 6XD
Tel: 020 8806 2070
Age range: G2–16 years

Beis Rochel D'Satmar Girls School
51-57 Amhurst Park, London N16 5DL
Tel: 020 8800 9060
Headmistress: Mrs E Katz
Age range: G2–18 years

Bnois Jerusalem School
79-81 Amhurst Park, London N16 5DL
Tel: 020 8211 7136
Age range: G3–16 years

Bobov Primary School
87-90 Egerton Road, London N16 6UE
Tel: 020 8809 1025
Headmaster: Mr Chaim Weissman
Age range: B3–13 years

Channing School
The Bank, Highgate, London N6 5HF
Tel: 020 8340 2328
Head: Mrs B M Elliott
Age range: G4–18 years

Dwight School London
6 Friern Barnet Lane, London N11 3LX
Tel: 020 8920 0600
Head: Chris Beddows
Age range: 2–18 years

Finchley & Acton Yochien School
6 Hendon Avenue, Finchley,
London N3 1UE
Tel: 020 8343 2191
Headteacher: J Tanabe
Age range: 2–6 years
No. of pupils: 145

Grange Park Preparatory School
13 The Chine, Grange Park,
Winchmore Hill, London N21 2EA
Tel: 020 8360 1469
Headteacher: Miss F Rizzo
Age range: G4–11 years
No. of pupils: 90
Fees: Day £10,300–£10,378

Greek Secondary School of London
22 Trinity Road, London N22 8LB
Tel: +44 (0)20 8881 9320
Headteacher: Nikos Kazantzakis
Age range: 13–18 years

Highgate
North Road, Highgate, London N6 4AY
Tel: 020 8340 1524
Head Master: Mr A S Pettitt MA
Age range: 3–18 years
No. of pupils: 1541 VIth312
Fees: Day £18,165–£20,970

Highgate Junior School
Cholmeley House, 3 Bishopswood
Road, London N6 4PL
Tel: 020 8340 9193
Principal: Mr S M James BA
Age range: 7–11 years
Fees: Day £19,230

Highgate Pre-Preparatory School
7 Bishopswood Road, London N6 4PH
Tel: 020 8340 9196
Principal: Mrs Diane Hecht
Age range: 3–7 years
No. of pupils: 150
Fees: Day £18,165

Keble Prep
Wades Hill, Winchmore
Hill, London N21 1BG
Tel: 020 8360 3359
Headmaster: Mr P Gill BA (Hons)
Age range: B4–13 years

Kerem School
Norrice Lea, London N2 0RE
Tel: 020 8455 0909
Head Teacher: Miss Alyson Burns
Age range: 3–11 years
Fees: Day £9,435

Lubavitch House School (Senior Girls)
107-115 Stamford Hill, Hackney,
London N16 5RP
Tel: 020 8800 0022
Headmaster: Rabbi Shmuel Lew FRSA
Age range: G11–18 years
No. of pupils: 102
Fees: Day £3,900

NORFOLK HOUSE SCHOOL
For further details see p.158
10 Muswell Avenue, Muswell
Hill, London N10 2EG
Tel: +44 (0)2088 834584
Email: office@
norfolkhouseschool.org
Website:
www.norfolkhouseschool.org
Headteacher: Mr Tej Lander
Age range: 2–11 years

North London Grammar School
110 Colindeep Lane, Hendon,
London NW9 6HB
Tel: 0208 205 0052
Headteacher: Mr Fatih Adak
Age range: 7–18 years

North London Rudolf Steiner School
1-3 The Campsbourne, London N8 7PN
Tel: 020 8341 3770
Age range: 0–7 years
No. of pupils: 40

Palmers Green High School
Hoppers Road, Winchmore
Hill, London N21 3LJ
Tel: 020 8886 1135
Headmistress: Mrs Wendy Kempster
Age range: G3–16 years
No. of pupils: 300
Fees: Day £5,880–£15,930

Pardes House Primary School
Hendon Lane, Finchley, London N3 1SA
Tel: 020 8343 3568
Headteacher: Rabbi J Sager
MA, B.Ed, NPQH, FCCT
Age range: B4–11 years

Phoenix Academy
85 Bounces Road, Edmonton,
London N9 8LD
Tel: 020 8887 6888
Headteacher: Mr Paul Kelly
Age range: 5–18 years
No. of pupils: 19

ROSEMARY WORKS INDEPENDENT SCHOOL
For further details see p.168
1 Branch Place, London N1 5PH
Tel: 02077 393950
Email: info@rosemaryworks.com
Website: www.rosemaryworks.com
Headteacher: Ms Amanda
Parker NPQH, MPhil
Age range: 3–11 years

Salcombe Preparatory School
224-226 Chase Side, Southgate,
London N14 4PL
Tel: 020 8441 5356
Headmistress: Mrs Sarah-Jane
Davies BA(Hons) QTS MEd
Age range: 3–11 years
No. of pupils: 250
Fees: Day £11,673

Shakhsiyah School, London
1st Floor, 277 St Ann's Road,
London N15 5RG
Tel: 020 8802 8651
Head Teacher: Mrs Foziya Reddy
Age range: 3–14 years

St Paul's Steiner School
1 St Paul's Road, Islington,
London N1 2QH
Tel: 020 7226 4454
College of Teachers: College
of Teachers
Age range: 2–14 years
No. of pupils: 136

Sunrise Nursery, Stoke Newington
1 Cazenove Road, Stoke Newington, Hackney, London N16 6PA
Tel: 020 8806 6279
Principal: Didi Ananda Manika
Age range: 15 months–5 years

Sunrise Primary School
55 Coniston Road, Tottenham, London N17 0EX
Tel: 020 8806 6279 (Office); 020 8885 3354 (School)
Head: Mrs Mary-Anne Lovage MontDipEd, BA
Age range: 2–11 years
No. of pupils: 30
Fees: Day £5,550

Talmud Torah Chaim Meirim School
26 Lampard Grove, London N16 6XB
Tel: 020 8806 0898
Principal: Rabbi S Hoffman
Age range: B4–13 years

Talmud Torah Yetev Lev School
111-115 Cazenove Road, London N16 6AX
Tel: 020 8806 3834
Age range: B2–11 years

Tawhid Boys School
21 Cazenove Road, London N16 6PA
Tel: 020 8806 2999
Headteacher: Mr Usman Mapara
Age range: B10–15 years
No. of pupils: 115

Tayyibah Girls School
88 Filey Avenue, Hackney, London N16 6JJ
Tel: 020 8880 0085
Headmistress: Mrs N B Qureishi MSc
Age range: G5–18 years

The Children's House School Nursery
77 Elmore Street, London N1 3AQ
Tel: 020 7354 2113
Head of School: Salima Keshavjee
Age range: 2–4 years
Fees: Day £3,060–£5,020

The Children's House Upper School
King Henry's Walk, London N1 4PB
Tel: 020 7249 6273
Head of School: Kate Orange
Age range: 4–7 years
Fees: Day £5,310

The Gower School Nursery
18 North Road, Islington, London N7 9EY
Tel: 020 7700 2445
Principal: Miss Emma Gowers
Age range: 3 months–5 years

The Gower School Primary
10 Cynthia Street, Barnsbury, London N1 9JF
Tel: 020 7278 2020
Principal: Miss Emma Gowers
Age range: 4–11 years

TTTYY School
14 Heathland Road, London N16 5NH
Tel: 020 8802 1348
Head of School: Rabbi A Friesel
Age range: B2–13 years

Vita et Pax School
Priory Close, Southgate, London N14 4AT
Tel: 020 8449 8336
Headteacher: Miss Gillian Chumbley
Age range: 3–11 years
Fees: Day £9,360

Yesodey Hatorah Senior Girls' School
Egerton Road, London N16 6UB
Tel: 020 8826 5500
Acting Head Teacher: Mrs C Neuberger
Age range: 3–16 years
No. of pupils: 920

North-West London

Al-Sadiq & Al-Zahra Schools
134 Salusbury Road, London NW6 6PF
Tel: 020 7372 7706
Headteacher: Dr M Movahedi
Age range: 4–16 years

Arnold House School
1 Loudoun Road, St John's Wood, London NW8 0LH
Tel: 020 7266 4840
Headmaster: Mr Giles F Tollit
Age range: B3–13 years

Barnet Hill Academy
10A Montagu Road, Hendon, London NW4 3ES
Tel: 02034112660
Principal: Mr Alim Shaikh MA, PGCE, MPhil, NPQH
Age range: B3–11 years G3–16 years
Fees: Day £3,000

Beis Soroh Schneirer
Arbiter House, Wilberforce Road, London NW9 6AX
Tel: 020 8201 7771
Head of School: Mrs Sonia Mossberg
Age range: G2–11 years

Belmont, Mill Hill Preparatory School
The Ridgeway, London NW7 4ED
Tel: 020 8906 7270
Headmaster: Mr Leon Roberts MA
Age range: 7–13 years
No. of pupils: 550
Fees: Day £19,560

Beth Jacob Grammar School for Girls
Stratford Road, Hendon, London NW4 2AT
Tel: 020 8203 4322
Headteacher: Mrs M Gluck
Age range: G11–17 years

Brampton College
Lodge House, Lodge Road, Hendon, London NW4 4DQ
Tel: 020 8203 5025
Principal: Mr Bernard Canetti
Age range: 15–19 years

Brondesbury College for Boys
8 Brondesbury Park, London NW6 7BT
Tel: 020 8830 4522
Headteacher: Mr Amzad Ali
Age range: B11–16 years
No. of pupils: 93

Collège Français Bilingue de Londres
87 Holmes Road, Kentish Town, , London NW5 3AX
Tel: 020 7993 7400
Head of School: Mr David Gassian
Age range: 3–15 years
No. of pupils: 700

DEVONSHIRE HOUSE PREPARATORY SCHOOL
For further details see p.136
2 Arkwright Road, Hampstead, London NW3 6AE
Tel: 020 7435 1916
Email: enquiries@dhprep.co.uk
Website: www.devonshirehouseschool.co.uk
Headmistress: Mrs S. Piper BA(Hons)
Age range: B2–13 years G2–11 years
No. of pupils: 543
Fees: Day £9,870–£20,475

Francis Holland School, Regent's Park, NW1
Clarence Gate, Ivor Place, Regent's Park, London NW1 6XR
Tel: 020 7723 0176
Head of School: Mrs Katharine Woodcock
Age range: G11–18 years
No. of pupils: 556 VIth120
Fees: Day £22,890

Goodwyn School
Hammers Lane, Mill Hill, London NW7 4DB
Tel: 020 8959 3756
Principal: Struan Robertson
Age range: 3–11 years
No. of pupils: 193
Fees: Day £5,436–£11,943

Grimsdell, Mill Hill Pre-Preparatory School
Winterstoke House, Wills Grove, Mill Hill, London NW7 1QR
Tel: 020 8959 6884
Head: Mrs Kate Simon BA, PGCE
Age range: 3–7 years
No. of pupils: 188
Fees: Day £15,095

Hampstead Fine Arts College
Centre Studios, 41-43 England's Lane, London NW3 4YD
Tel: +44 (0)207 586 0312
Principal: Ms Candida Cave
Age range: 13–19 years

Hampstead Hill Pre-Prep & Nursery School
St Stephen's Hall, Pond Street, Hampstead, London NW3 2PP
Tel: 020 7435 6262
Principal: Mrs Andrea Taylor
Age range: 2–7+ years

HEATHSIDE SCHOOL HAMPSTEAD
For further details see p.148
84a Heath Street, Hampstead,
London NW3 1DN
Tel: +44 (0)20 3058 4011
Email: info@
heathsideschoolhampstead.com
Website: www.
heathsideschoolhampstead.com
Headteacher: Katherine Vintiner
Age range: 2–13 years
No. of pupils: 230
Fees: Day £17,642–£19,974

Hendon Prep School
20 Tenterden Grove, Hendon,
London NW4 1TD
Tel: 020 8203 7727
Age range: 2–11 years
No. of pupils: 165
Fees: Day £6,975–£15,600

Hereward House School
14 Strathray Gardens, Hampstead,
London NW3 4NY
Tel: 020 7794 4820
Headmaster: Mr P Evans
Age range: B4–13 years
Fees: Day £15,615–£16,065

ICS LONDON
For further details see p.150
7B Wyndham Place,
London W1H 1PN
Tel: +44 (0)20 729 88800
Email: admissions@ics.uk.net
Website: www.icschool.co.uk
Head of School: David Laird
Age range: 3–19 years
No. of pupils: 175
Fees: Day £19,770–£28,920

IRIS School
100 Carlton Vale, London NW6 5HE
Tel: 020 7372 8051
Headteacher: Mr Seyed Abbas Hosseini
Age range: 6–16 years

Islamia Girls' High School
129 Salusbury Road, London NW6 6PE
Tel: 020 7372 3472
Headteacher: Mrs Fawziah Islam
Age range: G11–16 years
Fees: Day £6,900

Lyndhurst House Prep School
24 Lyndhurst Gardens, Hampstead,
London NW3 5NW
Tel: 020 7435 4936
Head of School: Mr Andrew
Reid MA (Oxon)
Age range: B4–13 years
No. of pupils: 125
Fees: Day £18,360–£20,790

Maple Walk Prep School
62A Crownhill Road, London NW10 4EB
Tel: 020 8963 3890
Head Teacher: Claire Murdoch
Age range: 4–11 years
No. of pupils: 190
Fees: Day £3,866

Maria Montessori Institute
26 Lyndhurst Gardens, Hampstead,
London NW3 5NW
Tel: 020 7435 3646
Director of Training & School: Mrs Lynne
Lawrence BA, Mont Int Dip(AMI)
Age range: 2–12 years
No. of pupils: 50
Fees: Day £5,580–£13,560

**Maria Montessori School
– Hampstead**
26 Lyndhurst Gardens, Hampstead,
London NW3 5NW
Tel: +44 (0)20 7435 3646
Director of School: Miss L Kingston
Age range: 2–12 years
No. of pupils: 100
Fees: Day £6,270–£13,560

Mill Hill School
The Ridgeway, Mill Hill Village,
London NW7 1QS
Tel: 020 8959 1176
Head: Mrs Jane Sanchez
BSc (Hons) PGCE
Age range: 13–18 years
(boarding from 13)
No. of pupils: 876 VIth312
Fees: Day £21,987 WB £31,140 FB £36,900

Naima Jewish Preparatory School
21 Andover Place, London NW6 5ED
Tel: 020 7328 2802
Headmaster: Mr Bill Pratt
Age range: 3–11 years

Nancy Reuben Primary School
Finchley Lane, Hendon,
London NW4 1DJ
Tel: 020 82025646
Head: Anthony Wolfson
Age range: 3–11 years
No. of pupils: 207

**NORTH BRIDGE HOUSE NURSERY
AND PRE-PREP HAMPSTEAD**
For further details see p.160
8 Netherhall Gardens,
London NW3 5RR
Tel: 020 7428 1520
Head of School: Mrs
Christine McLelland
Age range: 2–7 years
No. of pupils: 190

**NORTH BRIDGE HOUSE NURSERY
AND PRE-PREP WEST HAMPSTEAD**
For further details see p.160
85-87 Fordwych Rd, London NW2 3TL
Tel: 020 7428 1520
Head of School: Mrs
Christine McLelland
Age range: 2–7 years

**NORTH BRIDGE HOUSE PREP
SCHOOL REGENT'S PARK**
For further details see p.160
1 Gloucester Avenue,
London NW1 7AB
Tel: 020 7428 1520
Head of School: Mr James Stenning
Age range: 7–13 years
No. of pupils: 385
Fees: Day £18,960–£20,520

**NORTH BRIDGE HOUSE
SENIOR CANONBURY**
For further details see p.160
6-9 Canonbury Place,
Islington, London N1 2NQ
Tel: 020 7428 1520
Head of School: Mr Brendan Pavey
Age range: 11–18 years
No. of pupils: 220
Fees: Day £19,230–£21,735

**NORTH BRIDGE HOUSE
SENIOR HAMPSTEAD**
For further details see p.160
65 Rosslyn Hill, London NW3 5UD
Tel: 020 7428 1520
Email: admissionsenquiries@
northbridgehouse.com
Website:
www.northbridgehouse.com
Executive Headteacher: Mr
Brendan Pavey
Age range: 2–18 years
No. of pupils: 1400
Fees: Day £8,676–£23,148

Rainbow Montessori School
13 Woodchurch Road,
Hampstead, London NW6 3PL
Tel: 020 7328 8986
Head Mistress: Maggy Miller MontDip
Age range: 2–5 years

Saint Christina's School
25 St Edmunds Terrace, Regent's
Park, London NW8 7PY
Tel: 020 7722 8784
Headteacher: Miss J Finlayson
Age range: 3–11 years
No. of pupils: 224
Fees: Day £13,500

Sarum Hall School
15 Eton Avenue, London NW3 3EL
Tel: 020 7794 2261
Headteacher: Victoria Savage
Age range: G3–11 years
No. of pupils: 184

**South Hampstead
High School GDST**
3 Maresfield Gardens, London NW3 5SS
Tel: 020 7435 2899
Head of School: Mrs V Bingham
Age range: G4–18 years
No. of pupils: 900
Fees: Day £15,327–£18,654

**Southbank International
School – Hampstead**
16 Netherhall Gardens,
London NW3 5TH
Tel: 020 7243 3803
Principal: Shirley Harwood
Age range: 3–11 years
No. of pupils: 210

London: ENGLAND

D357

St Christopher's School
32 Belsize Lane, Hampstead,
London NW3 5AE
Tel: 020 7435 1521
Head: Emma Crawford-Nash
Age range: G4–11 years
No. of pupils: 235
Fees: Day £14,700

St John's Wood Pre-Preparatory School
St Johns Hall, Lords Roundabout,
London NW8 7NE
Tel: 020 7722 7149
Principal: Adrian Ellis
Age range: 3–7 years

St Margaret's School
18 Kidderpore Gardens,
Hampstead, London NW3 7SR
Tel: 020 7435 2439
Principal: Mr M Webster BSc, PGCE
Age range: G4–16 years
No. of pupils: 156
Fees: Day £12,591–£14,589

St Martin's School
22 Goodwyn Avenue, Mill
Hill, London NW7 3RG
Tel: 020 8959 1965
Head Teacher: Mrs Samantha Mbah
Age range: 3–11 years
No. of pupils: 90
Fees: Day £7,800

St Mary's School Hampstead
47 Fitzjohn's Avenue, Hampstead,
London NW3 6PG
Tel: 020 7435 1868
Head Teacher: Mrs Harriet Connor-Earl
Age range: G2 years 9 months–11 years
No. of pupils: 300
Fees: Day £9,060–£16,740

St Nicholas School
22 Salmon Street, London NW9 8PN
Tel: 020 8205 7153
Headmaster: Mr Matt Donaldson
BA (Hons), PGCE, PGDip (Surv)
Age range: 3 months–11 years

St. Anthony's School for Boys
90 Fitzjohn's Avenue, Hampstead,
London NW3 6NP
Tel: 020 7431 1066
Head of School: Mr Richard
Berlie MA (Cantab)
Age range: B2–13 years G2–4 years
No. of pupils: 280

St. Anthony's School for Girls
Ivy House, 94-96 North End
Road, , London NW11 7SX
Tel: 020 3869 3070
Head of School: Mr Donal Brennan
Age range: G2–11 years
No. of pupils: 85
Fees: Day £18,000

The Academy School
3 Pilgrims Place, Rosslyn Hill,
Hampstead, London NW3 1NG
Tel: 020 7435 6621
Headteacher: Mr Garth
Evans BA (Lond)
Age range: 6–13 years

The American School in London
One Waverley Place, London NW8 0NP
Tel: 020 7449 1221
Head: Robin Appleby
Age range: 4–18 years
No. of pupils: 1350
Fees: Day £27,050–£31,200

The Cavendish School
31 Inverness Street, Camden
Town, London NW1 7HB
Tel: 020 7485 1958
Headmistress: Miss Jane Rogers
Age range: G3–11 years
No. of pupils: 260
Fees: Day £15,300

The Hall School
23 Crossfield Road, Hampstead,
London NW3 4NU
Tel: 020 7722 1700
Headmaster: Mr Chris Godwin
Age range: B4–13 years

The King Alfred School
Manor Wood, North End
Road, London NW11 7HY
Tel: 020 8457 5200
Head: Robert Lobatto MA (Oxon)
Age range: 4–18 years
No. of pupils: 670

The Mount, Mill Hill International
Milespit Hill, London NW7 2RX
Tel: +44 (0)20 3826 33
Head of School: Ms Sarah Bellotti
Age range: 13–17 years
No. of pupils: 80
Fees: Day £27,000 WB
£37,500 FB £44,250

The Mulberry House School
7 Minster Road, West Hampstead,
London NW2 3SD
Tel: 020 8452 7340
Headteacher: Ms Victoria
Playford BA Hons, QTS
Age range: 2–7 years
No. of pupils: 223

The Village Prep School
2 Parkhill Road, Belsize Park,
London NW3 2YN
Tel: 020 7485 4673
Head of School: Ms
Morven MacDonald
Age range: G2–11 years

Torah Vodaas
Brent Park Road, West Hendon
Broadway, London NW9 7AJ
Tel: 020 3670 4670
Head of School: Rabbi Y Feldman
Age range: B2–11 years

Trevor-Roberts School
55-57 Eton Avenue, London NW3 3ET
Tel: 020 7586 1444
Headmaster: Simon Trevor-Roberts BA
Age range: 5–13 years
Fees: Day £14,700–£16,200

**University College School
Hampstead (UCS) Junior**
11 Holly Hill, Hampstead,
London NW3 6QN
Tel: 020 7435 3068
Headmaster: Mr Lewis Hayward
Age range: B7–11 years

**University College School
Hampstead (UCS) Pre-Prep**
36 College Crescent, Hampstead,
London NW3 5LF
Tel: 020 7722 4433
Headmistress: Ms Zoe Dunn
Age range: B4–7 years

**University College School
Hampstead (UCS) Senior**
Frognal, Hampstead, London NW3 6XH
Tel: 020 7435 2215
Headteacher: Mr Mark J Beard
Age range: B11–18 years G16–18 years

Wentworth College
6-10 Brentmead Place,
London NW11 9LH
Tel: 02084 588524
Principal: Manuel Guimaraes
Age range: 14–19 years

South-East London

Alleyn's School
Townley Road, Dulwich,
London SE22 8SU
Tel: 020 8557 1500
Head of School: Jane Lunnon
Age range: 4–18 years

Blackheath High School GDST
Vanbrugh Park, Blackheath,
London SE3 7AG
Tel: 020 8853 2929
Head: Mrs Carol Chandler-Thompson
BA (Hons) Exeter, PGCE Exeter
Age range: G3–18 years
No. of pupils: 780

Blackheath Prep
4 St Germans Place, Blackheath,
London SE3 0NJ
Tel: 020 8858 0692
Head: Alex Matthews
Age range: 3–11 years
No. of pupils: 385

Colfe's Junior School
Horn Park Lane, Lee, London SE12 8AW
Tel: 020 8463 8240
Head: Ms C Macleod
Age range: 3–11 years
No. of pupils: 355
Fees: Day £13,230–£13,995

Colfe's School
Horn Park Lane, Lee, London SE12 8AW
Tel: 020 8852 2283
Head: Mr R F Russell MA(Cantab)
Age range: 3–18 years
No. of pupils: 1120

DLD College London
199 Westminster Bridge
Road, London SE1 7FX
Tel: +44 (0)20 7935 8411
Age range: 14–19 years
No. of pupils: 375
Fees: Day £25,500–£33,000
FB £20,085–£28,830

Dulwich College
Dulwich Common, London SE21 7LD
Tel: 020 8693 3601
Master: Dr J A F Spence
Age range: B0–18 years
Fees: Day £21,672 WB
£42,408 FB £45,234

Dulwich College Kindergarten & Infants School
Eller Bank, 87 College Road,
London SE21 7HH
Tel: 020 8693 1538
Head: Mrs Miranda Norris
Age range: 3 months–7 years
No. of pupils: 251

Dulwich Prep London
42 Alleyn Park, Dulwich,
London SE21 7AA
Tel: 020 8766 5500
Head Master: Miss Louise Davidson
Age range: B3–13 years
(boarding from 8) G3–5 years
👤🏫✏️

Eltham College
Grove Park Road, Mottingham,
London SE9 4QF
Tel: 0208 857 1455
Headmaster: Guy Sanderson
Age range: 7–18 years
No. of pupils: 911 VIth199
Ⓐ💷16

Greenwich Steiner School
Woodlands, 90 Mycenae Road,
Blackheath, London SE3 7SE
Tel: 020 8858 4404
Age range: 3–14 years
No. of pupils: 180
Fees: Day £7,310–£8,100
💷

Heath House Preparatory School
37 Wemyss Road, Blackheath,
London SE3 0TG
Tel: 020 8297 1900
Head Teacher: Mrs Sophia
Laslett CertEd PGDE
Age range: 3–11 years
No. of pupils: 125
Fees: Day £13,485–£14,985
💷✏️

Herne Hill School
The Old Vicarage, 127 Herne
Hill, London SE24 9LY
Tel: 020 7274 6336
Headteacher: Mrs Ngaire Telford
Age range: 2–7 years
No. of pupils: 296
Fees: Day £6,225–£14,955

James Allen's Girls' School
144 East Dulwich Grove,
Dulwich, London SE22 8TE
Tel: 020 8693 1181
Head of School: Mrs Sally-
Anne Huang MA, MSc
Age range: G4–18 years
No. of pupils: 1075
👤Ⓐ💷16

Kings Kids Christian School
100 Woodpecker Road,
Newcross, London SE14 6EU
Tel: 020 8691 5813
Headteacher: Mrs M Okenwa
Age range: 5–11 years

London Christian School
40 Tabard Street, London SE1 4JU
Tel: 02031 306430
Head Teacher: Miss Nicola
Collett-White
Age range: 3–11 years

Marathon Science School
1-9 Evelyn Street, Surrey
Quays, London SE8 5RQ
Tel: +44 (0)20 7231 3232
Headteacher: Mr Uzeyir Onur
Age range: B11–16 years
No. of pupils: 67
👤🏫

Oakfield Preparatory School
125-128 Thurlow Park Road, West
Dulwich, London SE21 8HP
Tel: 020 8670 4206
Head of School: Mrs Moyra Thompson
Age range: 2–11 years
No. of pupils: 310
Fees: Day £12,324

Octavia House School, Kennington
214b Kennington Road,
London SE11 6AU
Tel: 020 3651 4396 (option 3)
Assistant Principal: Ms Knight
Age range: 14–16 years

Octavia House School, Vauxhall
Vauxhall Street, London SE11 5LG
Tel: 020 3651 4396 (option 1)
Vice Principal: Mr Ward
Age range: 5–11 years

Octavia House School, Walworth
Larcom Street, London SE17 1RT
Tel: 020 3651 4396 (option 2)
Assistant Principal: Mr Dickens
Age range: 11–14 years

Riverston School
63/69 Eltham Road, Lee,
London SE12 8UF
Tel: 020 8318 4327
Headmaster: Mr David A T Ward MA
Age range: 9 months–19 years

Rosemead Preparatory School & Nursery, Dulwich
70 Thurlow Park Road, London SE21 8HZ
Tel: 020 8670 5865
Headmaster: Mr Phil Soutar
Age range: 2–11 years
No. of pupils: 366
Fees: Day £10,272–£11,286
💷✏️

St Dunstan's College
Stanstead Road, London SE6 4TY
Tel: 020 8516 7200
Headmaster: Mr Nicholas Hewlett
Age range: 3–18 years
No. of pupils: 870
🌐Ⓐ💷16

St Olave's Preparatory School
106 Southwood Road, New
Eltham, London SE9 3QS
Tel: 020 8294 8930
Headteacher: Miss Claire
Holloway BEd, QTS
Age range: 3–11 years
No. of pupils: 220
Fees: Day £10,848–£12,300
✏️

Sydenham High School GDST
15 & 19 Westwood Hill, London SE26 6BL
Tel: 020 8557 7004
Headmistress: Mrs
Katharine Woodcock
Age range: G4–18 years
No. of pupils: 665
👤Ⓐ💷16

The Pointer School
19 Stratheden Grove, Blackheath,
London SE3 7TH
Tel: 020 8293 1331
Headmaster: Mr Adam M Greenwood
BSc (Hons), PGCE, GCGI, MBA
Age range: 3–11 years

The Villa School & Nursery
54 Lyndhurst Grove, Peckham,
London SE15 5AH
Tel: 020 7703 6216
Head Teacher: Louise Maughan
Age range: 2–7 years

South-West London

Al-Risalah Secondary School
145 Upper Tooting Road,
London SW17 7TJ
Tel: 020 8767 6057
Executive Principal: Suhayl Lee
Age range: 11–16 years

Beechwood Nursery School
55 Leigham Court Road,
Streatham, London SW16 2NJ
Tel: 020 8677 8778
Age range: 0–5 years

Bertrum House Nursery
290 Balham High Road,
London SW17 7AL
Tel: 020 8767 4051
Age range: 2–5 years
✏️

Broomwood Hall Lower School
50 Nightingale Lane, London SW12 8TE
Tel: 020 8682 8840
Head: Miss Jo Townsend
Age range: 4–8 years
No. of pupils: 320
Fees: Day £5,820

Broomwood Hall Upper School
68-74 Nightingale Lane,
London SW12 8NR
Tel: 020 8682 8810
Head: Mrs Louisa McCafferty
Age range: G8–13 years
No. of pupils: 250
Fees: Day £7,140
👤✏️

Cameron Vale School
4 The Vale, Chelsea, London SW3 6AH
Tel: 020 7352 4040
Headmistress: Mrs Bridget Saul
Age range: 4–11 years
Fees: Day £19,305
💷✏️

Centre Academy London
92 St John's Hill, Battersea,
London SW11 1SH
Tel: 020 7738 2344
Head of School: Mrs. Kas Lee-Douglas
Age range: 9–19 years
🌐✏️16

Collingham College
23 Collingham Gardens,
London SW5 0HL
Tel: +44 (0)20 7244 7414
Principal: Ms Sally Powell
Age range: 14–19 years
16Ⓐ

Dolphin School
106 Northcote Road,
London SW11 6QW
Tel: 020 7924 3472
Head Teacher: Mr S Gosden
Age range: 2–11 years
No. of pupils: 162
Fees: Day £12,885–£14,085
💷✏️

Donhead Preparatory School
33 Edge Hill, Wimbledon,
London SW19 4NP
Tel: 020 8946 7000
Headmaster: Mr P J J Barr
Age range: B4–11 years
👤✏️

EATON HOUSE BELGRAVIA
For further details see p.142
3-5 Eaton Gate, London SW1W 9BA
Tel: 0203 917 5050
Email: admissions@
eatonhouseschools.com
Website:
www.eatonhouseschools.com
Headteacher: Mr Huw May
Age range: B2–11 years G2–4 years
No. of pupils: 320

**EATON HOUSE THE MANOR
BOYS' SCHOOL**
For further details see p.144
58 Clapham Common North
Side, London SW4 9RU
Tel: 0203 917 5050
Email: admissions@
eatonhouseschools.com
Website:
www.eatonhouseschools.com
Head of Prep: Mrs Sarah Segrave
Age range: B2–13 years G2–4 years
No. of pupils: 510

**EATON HOUSE THE MANOR
GIRLS' SCHOOL**
For further details see p.146
58 Clapham Common North
Side, London SW4 9RU
Tel: 0203 917 5050
Email: admissions@
eatonhouseschools.com
Website:
www.eatonhouseschools.com
Headteacher: Mrs Claire Fildes
Age range: B2–4 years G2–11 years
No. of pupils: 260

Eaton Square Prep School
55-57 Eccleston Square,
London SW1V 1PP
Tel: +44 (0)20 7931 9469
Head of School: Ms Trish Watt
Age range: 4–11 years

Ecole Charles De Gaulle – Wix
Clapham Common North
Side, London SW4 0AJ
Tel: +44 20 7738 0287
Headteacher: Mr Blanchard
Age range: 5–11 years
No. of pupils: 100

École Primaire Marie D'Orliac
60 Clancarty Road, London SW6 3AA
Tel: +44 (0)20 7736 5863
Director: Mr Blaise Fenart
Age range: 4–11 years

Emanuel School
Battersea Rise, London SW11 1HS
Tel: 020 8870 4171
Headmaster: Mr Robert Milne
Age range: 10–18 years
No. of pupils: 1050
Fees: Day £20,145

Eveline Day & Nursery Schools
14 Trinity Crescent, Upper
Tooting, London SW17 7AE
Tel: 020 8672 4673
Headmistress: Ms Eveline Drut
Age range: 3 months–11 years
No. of pupils: 80
Fees: Day £13,859

Falcons School for Girls
11 Woodborough Road,
Putney, London SW15 6PY
Tel: 020 8992 5189
Headmistress: Ms Sara Williams-Ryan
Age range: G4–11 years
Fees: Day £7,800–£15,705

Falkner House
19 Brechin Place, South
Kensington, London SW7 4QB
Tel: 02073 734501
Headteachers: Mrs Flavia
Rogers & Mrs Eleanor Dixon
Age range: 3–11 years

Finton House School
171 Trinity Road, London SW17 7HL
Tel: 020 8682 0921
Head of School: Mr Ben Freeman
Age range: 4–11 years
No. of pupils: 300
Fees: Day £15,378–£15,588

**Francis Holland School,
Sloane Square, SW1**
39 Graham Terrace, London SW1W 8JF
Tel: 020 7730 2971
Head: Mrs Lucy Elphinstone
MA(Cantab)
Age range: G4–18 years
No. of pupils: 520 VIth70
Fees: Day £17,760–£20,085

Garden House School
Boys' School & Girls' School,
Turk's Row, London SW3 4TW
Tel: 020 7730 1652
Boys' Head: Mr Christian
Warland BA(Hons), LLB.
Age range: 3–11 years
No. of pupils: 490
Fees: Day £17,700–£22,800

Glendower School
86/87 Queen's Gate, London SW7 5JX
Tel: 020 7370 1927
Headmistress: Mrs Sarah
Knollys BA, PGCE
Age range: G4–11+ years
No. of pupils: 206
Fees: Day £19,200

Hall School Wimbledon
17, The Downs, Wimbledon,
London SW20 8HF
Tel: 020 8879 9200
Headmaster: Mr. A Hammond
Age range: 5–18 years
No. of pupils: 160
Fees: Day £4,570–£6,140

Harrodian
Lonsdale Road, London SW13 9QN
Tel: 020 8748 6117
Headmaster: Mr James R Hooke
Age range: 4–18 years
No. of pupils: 1023
Fees: Day £5,000–£8,000

Hill House
17 Hans Place, Chelsea,
London SW1X 0EP
Tel: 020 7584 1331
Headmaster: Mr Richard Townend
Age range: 4–13 years
No. of pupils: 600
Fees: Day £15,000–£18,600

Hornsby House School
Hearnville Road, Balham,
London SW12 8RS
Tel: 020 8673 7573
Headmaster: Mr Edward Rees
Age range: 4–11 years

Hurlingham School
122 Putney Bridge Road,
Putney, London SW15 2NQ
Tel: 02081 030706
Headmaster: Mr Simon Gould
Age range: 4–11 years

Ibstock Place School
Clarence Lane, London SW15 5PY
Tel: 020 8876 9991
Head of School: Mr Christopher Wolsey
Age range: 4–18 years
No. of pupils: 990
Fees: Day £5,870–£7,450

KENSINGTON PARK SCHOOL
For further details see p.152
40-44 Bark Place, Bayswater,
London W2 4AT
Tel: +44 (0)20 7616 4400
Email: admissions@kps.co.uk
Website: www.kps.co.uk
Headmaster: Mr Stephen Mellor
Age range: 11–18 years

Kensington Prep School
596 Fulham Road, London SW6 5PA
Tel: 0207 731 9300
Head of School: Mrs Caroline
Hulme-McKibbin
Age range: G4–11 years
No. of pupils: 289
Fees: Day £17,193

King's College School
Southside, Wimbledon
Common, London SW19 4TT
Tel: 020 8255 5300
Head: Dr Anne Cotton
Age range: B7–18 years G16–18 years
No. of pupils: 1479

Knightsbridge School
67 Pont Street, Knightsbridge,
London SW1X 0BD
Tel: +44 (0)20 7590 9000
Head of School: Ms Shona Colaço
Age range: 3–16 years

L'Ecole de Battersea
Trott Street, Battersea, London SW11 3DS
Tel: 020 7371 8350
Principal: Mrs F Brisset
Age range: 3–11 years
No. of pupils: 250
Fees: Day £4,745

L'Ecole des Petits
2 Hazlebury Road, Fulham,
London SW6 2NB
Tel: 020 7371 8350
Principal: Mrs F Brisset
Age range: 3–6 years
No. of pupils: 120
Fees: Day £4,615

London Steiner School
9 Weir Road, Balham, London SW12 0LT
Tel: 0208 772 3504
Age range: 3–14 years

**Lycée Français Charles
de Gaulle de Londres**
35 Cromwell Road, London SW7 2DG
Tel: 020 7584 6322
Headteacher: Didier Devilard
Age range: 3–18 years
No. of pupils: 3450
Fees: Day £7,066–£14,782

**Mander Portman Woodward
– MPW London**
90-92 Queen's Gate, London SW7 5AB
Tel: 020 7835 1355
Principal: Mr John Southworth BSc MSc
Age range: 14–19 years
No. of pupils: 600
Fees: Day £10,252

More House School
22-24 Pont Street, Knightsbridge,
London SW1X 0AA
Tel: 020 7235 2855
Head: Ms Faith Hagerty
Age range: G11–18 years
No. of pupils: 140
Fees: Day £7,250

NEWTON PREP
For further details see p.156
149 Battersea Park Road,
London SW8 4BX
Tel: 020 7720 4091
Email: enquiries@newtonprep.co.uk
Website:
www.newtonprepschool.co.uk
Headmistress: Mrs Alison
Fleming BA, MA Ed, PGCE
Age range: 3–13 years
No. of pupils: 646
Fees: Day £10,575–£22,395

Northcote Lodge
26 Bolingbroke Grove, London SW11 6EL
Tel: 020 8682 8888
Head: Mr Clive Smith-Langridge
Age range: B8–13 years
No. of pupils: 260
Fees: Day £7,140

Northwood Senior
3 Garrad's Road, London SW16 1JZ
Tel: 020 8161 0301
Head: Mrs Susan Brooks
Age range: 11–16 years
Fees: Day £7,140

Oliver House Preparatory School
7 Nightingale Lane, London SW4 9AH
Tel: 020 8772 1911
Headteacher: Mr Rob Farrell
Age range: 3–11 years
No. of pupils: 144
Fees: Day £6,600–£15,090

Parkgate House School
80 Clapham Common North
Side, London SW4 9SD
Tel: +44 (0)20 7350 2461
Principal: Miss Catherine Shanley
Age range: 2–11 years
No. of pupils: 220
Fees: Day £5,940–£15,600

Parsons Green Prep School
1 Fulham Park Road, Fulham,
London SW6 4LJ
Tel: 02073 719009
Head: Dr Pamela Edmonds
Age range: 4–11 years

**Prince's Gardens
Preparatory School**
10–13 Prince's Gardens,
London SW7 1ND
Tel: 0207 591 4622
Headmistress: Mrs Alison Melrose
Age range: 3–11 years

PROSPECT HOUSE SCHOOL
For further details see p.164
75 Putney Hill, London SW15 3NT
Tel: 020 8246 4897
Email: info@prospecths.org.uk
Website: www.prospecths.org.uk
Headmaster: Mr Michael
Hodge BPED(Rhodes) QTS
Age range: 3–11 years
No. of pupils: 310
Fees: Day £9,954–£20,742

Putney High School GDST
35 Putney Hill, London SW15 6BH
Tel: 020 8788 4886
Headmistress: Mrs Suzie
Longstaff BA, MA, PGCE
Age range: G4–18 years
No. of pupils: 976 VIth150

QUEEN'S GATE SCHOOL
For further details see p.166
133 Queen's Gate, London SW7 5LE
Tel: 020 7589 3587
Email: registrar@queensgate.org.uk
Website: www.queensgate.org.uk
Principal: Miss Amy Wallace MA
MPhil (Cantab), PGCE (Oxon)
Age range: G4–18 years
No. of pupils: 500 VIth81

Redcliffe School Trust Ltd
47 Redcliffe Gardens, Chelsea,
London SW10 9JH
Tel: 020 7352 9247
Head: Sarah Lemmon
Age range: 3–11 years
Fees: Day £6,660–£17,730

Sinclair House Preparatory School
59 Fulham High Street,
Fulham, London SW6 3JJ
Tel: 0207 736 9182
Principal: Mrs Carlotta T M O'Sullivan
Age range: 2–11 years
No. of pupils: 120
Fees: Day £5,280–£17,025

**St Mary's Summerstown
Montessori**
46 Wimbledon Road, Tooting,
London SW17 0UQ
Tel: 020 8947 7359
Head: Liz Maitland NNEB, RSH, MontDip
Age range: 18 months–5 years
No. of pupils: 30
Fees: Day £1,300

St Paul's Juniors
St Paul's School, Lonsdale
Road, London SW13 9JT
Tel: 020 8748 3461
Head of School: Maxine Shaw
Age range: B7–13 years

St Paul's School
Lonsdale Road, Barnes,
London SW13 9JT
Tel: 020 8748 9162
High Master: Ms Sally-Anne Huang
Age range: B13–18 years

St Philip's School
6 Wetherby Place, London SW7 4NE
Tel: 020 7373 3944
Headmaster: Mr Wulffen-Thomas
Age range: B7–13 years

**Streatham & Clapham
High School GDST**
42 Abbotswood Road,
London SW16 1AW
Tel: 020 8677 8400
Headmaster: Dr Millan Sachania
Age range: G3–18 years
No. of pupils: 603 VIth70
Fees: Day £10,431–£19,743

Sussex House School
68 Cadogan Square, London SW1X 0EA
Tel: 020 7584 1741
Headmaster: Mr N P Kaye
MA(Cantab), ACP, FRSA, FRGS
Age range: B8–13 years

Swedish School
82 Lonsdale Road, London SW13 9JS
Tel: 020 8741 1751
Head of School: Ms. Jenny
Abrahamsson
Age range: 3–18 years

Thames Christian College
Wye Street, Battersea,
London SW11 2HB
Tel: 020 7228 3933
Executive Head: Stephen
Holsgrove PhD
Age range: 11–16 years
No. of pupils: 120
Fees: Day £15,780

**THE HAMPSHIRE
SCHOOL, CHELSEA**
For further details see p.172
15 Manresa Road, Chelsea,
London SW3 6NB
Tel: +44 (0)2073 527077
Email: info@
thehampshireschoolchelsea.co.uk
Website: www.
thehampshireschoolchelsea.co.uk
Headteacher: Mr Richard Lock
Age range: 3–11 years

The Laurels School
126 Atkins Road, Clapham,
London SW12 0AN
Tel: 020 8674 7229
Headmistress: Linda Sanders BA
Hons (Bristol), MA (Madrid)
Age range: G11–18 years

THE MERLIN SCHOOL
For further details see p.174
4 Carlton Drive, London SW15 2BZ
Tel: 020 8788 2769
Email: admissionenquiries@
merlinschool.net
Website: www.merlinschool.net
Headteacher: Miss Violet McConville
Age range: 4–8 years
No. of pupils: 130
Fees: Day £5,510

The Montessori Pavilion – The Kindergarten School
Vine Road, Barnes, London SW13 0NE
Tel: 07554 277 746
Headmistress: Ms Georgina Dashwood
Age range: 3–8 years
No. of pupils: 50

The Norwegian School
28 Arterberry Road, Wimbledon,
London SW20 8AH
Tel: 020 8947 6617
Head: Mr Ivar Chavannes
Age range: 3–16 years

The Roche School
11 Frogmore, London SW18 1HW
Tel: 020 8877 0823
Headmistress: Mrs Vania Adams
BA(Hons), PGCE, MA
Age range: 2–11 years
No. of pupils: 274
Fees: Day £15,600–£16,290

The Rowans School
19 Drax Avenue, Wimbledon,
London SW20 0EG
Tel: 020 8946 8220
Head Teacher: Mrs. Joanna Hubbard
MA BA (Hons) PGCE QTS PGDipSEN
Age range: 3–8 years
Fees: Day £7,905–£13,170

The Study Preparatory School
Wilberforce House, Camp
Road, Wimbledon Common,
London SW19 4UN
Tel: 020 8947 6969
Head of School: Miss Vicky
Ellis BSc (Hons), QTS, MA
Age range: G4–11 years
No. of pupils: 320
Fees: Day £4,925

The White House Preparatory School & Woodentops Kindergarten
24 Thornton Road, London SW12 0LF
Tel: 020 8674 9514
Principal: Mrs. Mary McCahery
Age range: 2–11 years
Fees: Day £4,436–£4,740

Thomas's Preparatory School – Battersea
28-40 Battersea High Street,
London SW11 3JB
Tel: 020 7978 0900
Head: Simon O'Malley
Age range: 4–13 years
No. of pupils: 547
Fees: Day £18,747–£20,868

Thomas's Preparatory School – Clapham
Broomwood Road, London SW11 6JZ
Tel: 020 7326 9300
Headmaster: Mr Philip Ward BEd(Hons)
Age range: 4–13 years
No. of pupils: 647
Fees: Day £17,262–£19,518

Thomas's Preparatory School – Fulham
Hugon Road, London SW6 3ES
Tel: 020 7751 8200
Head: Miss Annette Dobson
BEd(Hons), PGCertDys
Age range: 4–11 years
Fees: Day £17,880–£20,016

Tower House School
188 Sheen Lane, London SW14 8LF
Tel: 020 8876 3323
Head: Mr Gregory Evans
Age range: B4–13 years

URSULINE PREPARATORY SCHOOL
For further details see p.176
18 The Downs, Wimbledon,
London SW20 8HR
Tel: 020 8947 0859
Email: headteachersoffice@
ursulineprep.org
Website: www.ursulineprep.org
Head Teacher: Mrs Caroline
Molina BA (Hons)
Age range: B3–4 years G3–11 years
No. of pupils: 145

WANDSWORTH PREPARATORY SCHOOL
For further details see p.178
The Old Library, 2 Allfarthing
Lane, London SW18 2PQ
Tel: +44 (0)2088 704133
Email: office@wandsworthprep.com
Website:
www.wandsworthprep.com
Headteacher: Ms Laura Nike
Age range: 4–11 years

Westminster Abbey Choir School
Dean's Yard, London SW1P 3NY
Tel: 0207 654 4918
Headmaster: Mr Peter Roberts
Age range: B7–10 years

Westminster Cathedral Choir School
Ambrosden Avenue, London SW1P 1QH
Tel: 020 7798 9081
Headmaster: Mr Neil McLaughlan
Age range: B4–13 years

Westminster School
Little Dean's Yard, Westminster,
London SW1P 3PB
Tel: 020 7963 1000
Head Master: Dr Gary Savage
Age range: B13–18 years G16–18 years

Westminster Tutors
86 Old Brompton Road, South
Kensington, London SW7 3LQ
Tel: 020 7584 1288
Principal: Joe Mattei
Age range: 14+ years
No. of pupils: VIth40
Fees: Day £4,000–£25,000

Westminster Under School
27 Vincent Square, London SW1P 2NN
Tel: 020 7821 5788
Master: Mrs C J Jefferson
Age range: B7–13 years

Willington Prep
Worcester Road, Wimbledon,
London SW19 7QQ
Tel: 020 8944 7020
Head of School: Mr Keith Brown
Age range: 3–11 years
No. of pupils: 220

Wimbledon Common Preparatory
113 Ridgway, Wimbledon,
London SW19 4TA
Tel: 020 8946 1001
Head Teacher: Mrs Tracey Buck
Age range: B4–8 years
No. of pupils: 160
Fees: Day £13,185

Wimbledon High School GDST
Mansel Road, Wimbledon,
London SW19 4AB
Tel: 020 8971 0900
Headmistress: Mrs Jane Lunnon
Age range: G4–18 years
No. of pupils: 900 VIth155
Fees: Day £14,622–£18,810

West London

Abercorn School
38 Portland Place, London W1B 1LS
Tel: 020 7100 4335
Headmaster: Mr Christopher
Hammond
Age range: 2–13 years

Albemarle Independent College
18 Dunraven Street, Mayfair,
London W1K 7FE
Tel: 02074 097273
Co-Principals: Beverley
Mellon & James Eytle
Age range: 14–19 years

ArtsEd Day School & Sixth Form
14 Bath Road, Chiswick, London W4 1LY
Tel: 020 8987 6666
Headteacher: Mr Adrian Blake
Age range: 11–18 years

Ashbourne Independent Sixth Form College
17 Old Court Place, Kensington, London W8 4PL
Tel: 020 7937 3858
Principal: Mr Michael Kirby MSc, BApSc, MInstD
Age range: 13–19 years
16 Ⓐ £

Avenue House School
70 The Avenue, Ealing, London W13 8LS
Tel: 020 8998 9981
Headteacher: Mr J Sheppard
Age range: 3–11 years
No. of pupils: 135
Fees: Day £11,250

Bales College
742 Harrow Road, Kensal Town, London W10 4AA
Tel: 020 8960 5899
Principal: William Moore
Age range: 11–19 years
No. of pupils: 90
Fees: Day £11,550–£12,750

BASSETT HOUSE SCHOOL
For further details see p.132
60 Bassett Road, Notting Hill, London W10 6JP
Tel: 020 8969 0313
Email: info@bassetths.org.uk
Website: www.bassetths.org.uk
Headmistress: Mrs Kelly Gray
Age range: 3–11 years
No. of pupils: 120
Fees: Day £9,954–£20,742

Bute House Preparatory School for Girls
Bute House, Luxemburg Gardens, London W6 7EA
Tel: 020 7603 7381
Head of School: Ms Sian Bradshaw
Age range: G4–11 years

Chepstow House School
108a Lancaster Road, London W11 1QS
Tel: 0207 243 0243
Headteacher: Angela Barr
Age range: 2–11 years

Chiswick & Bedford Park Prep School
Priory House, Priory Avenue, London W4 1TX
Tel: 020 8994 1804
Head of School: Ms Henrietta Adams
Age range: B3–7+ years G3–11 years

Clifton Lodge School
8 Mattock Lane, Ealing, London W5 5BG
Tel: 020 8579 3662
Head of School: Mr Michael Belsito
Age range: 3–11 years
No. of pupils: 130
Fees: Day £13,650–£16,305

Connaught House School
47 Connaught Square, London W2 2HL
Tel: 020 7262 8830
Principal: Mrs V Hampton
Age range: 4–11 years
No. of pupils: 75
Fees: Day £16,650–£18,300

David Game College
31 Jewry Street, London EC3N 2ET
Tel: 02072 216665
Principal: D T P Game MA, MPhil
Age range: 13–22 years

DURSTON HOUSE
For further details see p.138
12-14 Castlebar Road, Ealing, London W5 2DR
Tel: 020 8991 6530
Email: info@durstonhouse.org
Website: www.durstonhouse.org
Headmaster: Mr Giles Entwisle
Age range: B4–13 years
No. of pupils: 326
Fees: Day £4,470–£5,720

EALING INDEPENDENT COLLEGE
For further details see p.140
83 New Broadway, Ealing, London W5 5AL
Tel: 020 8579 6668
Email: admissions@ealingindependentcollege.com
Website: www.ealingindependentcollege.com
Headteacher: Allan Cairns
Age range: 13–19 years
No. of pupils: 96

Eaton Square Senior School
106 Piccadilly, Mayfair, London W1J 7NL
Tel: +44 (0)20 7491 7393
Head of School: Ms Caroline Townshend
Age range: 11–18 years

Ecole Francaise Jacques Prevert
59 Brook Green, London W6 7BE
Tel: 020 7602 6871
Headteacher: Delphine Gentil
Age range: 4–11 years

Fulham School
1-3 Chesilton Road, London SW6 5AA
Tel: 020 8154 6751
Pre-Prep & Nursery Head: Di Steven
Age range: 3–18 years
No. of pupils: 650
Fees: Day £18,420–£21,567

Godolphin and Latymer School
Iffley Road, Hammersmith, London W6 0PG
Tel: +44 (0)20 8741 1936
Head Mistress: Dr Frances Ramsey
Age range: G11–18 years
No. of pupils: 800
Fees: Day £23,085

Great Beginnings Montessori Nursery
39 Brendon Street, London W1H 5JE
Tel: 020 7258 1066
Head: Mrs Wendy Innes
Age range: 2–6 years

Greek Primary School of London
3 Pierrepoint Road, Acton, London W3 9JR
Tel: 020 899 26156
Primary School Head Teacher: Mrs Despoina Kyriakidou BA, MA, QTS
Age range: 1–11 years

Halcyon London International School
33 Seymour Place, , London W1H 5AU
Tel: +44 (0)20 7258 1169
Director: Mr Barry Mansfield
Age range: 11–18 years

Harvington School
20 Castlebar Road, Ealing, London W5 2DS
Tel: 020 8997 1583
Headmistress: Mrs Anna Evans
Age range: B3–4 years G3–11 years
No. of pupils: 140
Fees: Day £6,525–£12,615

Hawkesdown House School Kensington
27 Edge Street, Kensington, London W8 7PN
Tel: 020 7727 9090
Headmistress: Mrs S Gillam BEd (Cantab)
Age range: 2–8 years
No. of pupils: 100
Fees: Day £4,725–£21,120

Heathfield House School
Heathfield Gardens, Chiswick, London W4 4JU
Tel: 020 8994 3385
Headteacher: Mrs Goodsman
Age range: 4–11 years
No. of pupils: 197
Fees: Day £2,471–£3,676

Holland Park Pre Prep School and Day Nursery
5, Holland Road, Kensington, London W14 8HJ
Tel: 020 7602 9066/020 7602 9266
Head Mistress: Mrs Kitty Mason
Age range: 3 months–8 years
No. of pupils: 39
Fees: Day £9,180–£18,120

Instituto Español Vicente Cañada Blanch
317 Portobello Road, London W10 5SZ
Tel: +44 (0) 20 8969 2664
Principal: Carmen Pinilla Padilla
Age range: 4–19 years

International School of London (ISL)
139 Gunnersbury Avenue, London W3 8LG
Tel: +44 (0)20 8992 5823
Principal: Mr Richard Parker
Age range: 3–18 years
No. of pupils: 500
Fees: Day £19,000–£26,300

King Fahad Academy
Bromyard Avenue, Acton, London W3 7HD
Tel: 020 8743 0131
Director General: Dr Tahani Aljafari
Age range: 3–19 years

La Petite Ecole Francaise
73 Saint Charles Square, London W10 6EJ
Tel: +44 208 960 1278
Principal: Mme Marjorie Lacassagne
Age range: 3–11 years

Latymer Prep School
36 Upper Mall, Hammersmith, London W6 9TA
Tel: 020 7993 0061
Principal: Ms Andrea Rutterford B.Ed (Hons)
Age range: 7–11 years
No. of pupils: 165
Fees: Day £18,330

Latymer Upper School
King Street, Hammersmith,
London W6 9LR
Tel: 020862 92024
Head: Mr D Goodhew MA(Oxon)
Age range: 11–18 years
No. of pupils: 1400
Fees: Day £6,945
Ⓐ £ ◯ 16·

Le Herisson
River Court Methodist
Church, Rover Court Road,
Hammersmith, London W6 9JT
Tel: 020 8563 7664
Director: Maria Frost
Age range: 2–6 years
Fees: Day £8,730–£8,970
◯

L'Ecole Bilingue
St David's Welsh Church, St Mary's
Terrace, London W2 1SJ
Tel: 020 7224 8427
Headteacher: Ms Veronique Ferreira
Age range: 3–11 years
No. of pupils: 68
Fees: Day £9,960–£10,770

Leiths School of Food & Wine
16-20 Wendell Road, Shepherd's
Bush, London W12 9RT
Tel: 020 8749 6400
Age range: 17+ years
16·

LLOYD WILLIAMSON
SCHOOL FOUNDATION
For further details see p.154
12 Telford Road, London W10 5SH
Tel: 020 8962 0345
Email: admin@lws.org.uk
Website: www.lloydwilliamson.co.uk
Co-Principals: Ms Lucy Meyer
& Mr Aaron Williams
Age range: 4 months–16 years
Fees: Day £18,000
◯

London Welsh School Ysgol Gymraeg Llundain
Hanwell Community Centre,
Westcott Crescent, London W7 1PD
Tel: 020 8575 0237
Lead Teacher: Mrs Rachel King
Age range: 3–11 years

Maida Vale School
18 Saltram Crescent, London W9 3HR
Tel: 020 4511 6000
Headmaster: Steven Winter
Age range: 11–18 years
No. of pupils: 121
Fees: Day £7,674

Norland Place School
162-166 Holland Park Avenue,
London W11 4UH
Tel: 020 7603 9103
Headmaster: Mr Patrick Mattar MA
Age range: B4–8 years G4–11 years
Fees: Day £16,107–£18,072
Ⓐ ◯

Notting Hill & Ealing High School GDST
2 Cleveland Road, West
Ealing, London W13 8AX
Tel: (020) 8799 8400
Headmaster: Mr Matthew Shoults
Age range: G4–18 years
Ⓐ Ⓐ £ 16·

Notting Hill Preparatory School
95 Lancaster Road, London W11 1QQ
Tel: 020 7221 0727
Head of School: Mrs Sarah Knollys
Age range: 4–13 years
No. of pupils: 370
Fees: Day £7,130
£ ◯

ORCHARD HOUSE SCHOOL
For further details see p.162
16 Newton Grove, Bedford
Park, London W4 1LB
Tel: 020 8742 8544
Email: info@orchardhs.org.uk
Website: www.orchardhs.org.uk
Headmaster: Mr Kit Thompson
Age range: 3–11 years
No. of pupils: 273
Fees: Day £10,158–£21,159

Pembridge Hall School
18 Pembridge Square, London W2 4EH
Tel: 020 7229 0121
Headmaster: Mr Henry Keighley-Elstub
Age range: G4–11 years
Ⓐ

Portland Place School
56-58 Portland Place, London W1B 1NJ
Tel: 0207 307 8700
Headmaster: Mr David Bradbury
Age range: 10–16 years
Ⓐ ◯

Queen's College
43-49 Harley Street, London W1G 8BT
Tel: 020 7291 7000
Principal: Mr Richard Tillet
Age range: G11–18 years
Ⓐ 16·

Queen's College Preparatory School
61 Portland Place, , London W1B 1QP
Tel: 020 7291 0660
Headmistress: Mrs Laura Hall
Age range: G4–11 years
Ⓐ

Ravenscourt Park Preparatory School
16 Ravenscourt Avenue, London W6 0SL
Tel: 020 8846 9153
Headmaster: Mr Carl Howes
MA (Cantab), PGCE (Exeter)
Age range: 4–11 years
No. of pupils: 409
Fees: Day £6,304
◯

Ray Cochrane Beauty School
118 Baker Street, London W1U 6TT
Tel: 02033 896888
Heads of Education: Xubin
Yuan & Eleonora Androva
Age range: 16+ years
16· 16· ✿

Southbank International School – Kensington
36-38 Kensington Park
Road, London W11 3BU
Tel: +44 (0)20 7243 3803
Principal: Siobhan McGrath
Age range: 3–18 years
Ⓐ IB ◯

Southbank International School – Westminster
63-65 Portland Place, London W1B 1QR
Tel: 020 7243 3803
Principal: Dr Paul Wood
Age range: 11–19 years
Ⓐ IB ◯ 16·

St Augustine's Priory
Hillcrest Road, Ealing, London W5 2JL
Tel: 020 8997 2022
Headteacher: Mrs Sarah
Raffray M.A., N.P.Q.H
Age range: B3–4 years G3–18 years
No. of pupils: 485
Fees: Day £11,529–£16,398
Ⓐ Ⓐ ◯ 16·

St Benedict's School
54 Eaton Rise, Ealing, London W5 2ES
Tel: 020 8862 2000
Headmaster: Mr A Johnson BA
Age range: 3–18 years
No. of pupils: 1073 VIth203
Fees: Day £13,995–£18,330
Ⓐ £ ◯ 16·

St James Preparatory School
Earsby Street, London W14 8SH
Tel: 020 7348 1777
Headmistress: Mrs Catherine
Thomlinson BA(Hons)
Age range: 3–11 years
Fees: Day £16,425–£17,910
£

St James Senior Girls' School
Earsby Street, London W14 8SH
Tel: 020 7348 1777
Headmistress: Mrs Sarah Labram BA
Age range: G11–18 years
No. of pupils: 295 VIth67
Fees: Day £20,100
Ⓐ Ⓐ £ ◯ 16·

St Paul's Girls' School
Brook Green, London W6 7BS
Tel: 020 7603 2288
High Mistress: Mrs Sarah Fletcher
Age range: G11–18 years
No. of pupils: 778
Fees: Day £25,887–£27,831
Ⓐ Ⓐ £ ◯ 16·

Sylvia Young Theatre School
1 Nutford Place, London W1H 5YZ
Tel: 020 7258 2330
Principal: Sylvia Young OBE
Age range: 10–16 years
16· £ ◯

Tabernacle School
32 St Anns Villas, Holland
Park, London W11 4RS
Tel: 020 7602 6232
Headteacher: Mrs P Wilson
Age range: 3–16 years
Fees: Day £6,500–£9,500

The Falcons Pre-Preparatory School for Boys
2 Burnaby Gardens, Chiswick,
London W4 3DT
Tel: 020 8747 8393
Head of School: Ms Liz McLaughlin
Age range: B2–7 years G2–4 years
Fees: Day £7,500–£15,705
Ⓐ ◯

The Japanese School
87 Creffield Road, Acton,
London W3 9PU
Tel: 020 8993 7145
Age range: 6–16 years

**Thomas's Preparatory
School – Kensington**
17-19 Cottesmore Gardens,
London W8 5PR
Tel: 020 7361 6500
Headmistress: Miss Joanna Ebner
MA, BEd(Hons)(Cantab), NPQH
Age range: 4–11 years
Fees: Day £20,526–£21,789
£ ✐

Wetherby Preparatory School
Bryanston Square, London W1H 2EA
Tel: 020 7535 3520
Headmaster: Mr Nick Baker
Age range: B8–13 years
⚇

Wetherby Pre-Preparatory School
11 Pembridge Square, London W2 4ED
Tel: 020 7727 9581
Headmaster: Mr Mark Snell
Age range: B2–8 years
⚇ ✐

Wetherby Senior School
100 Marylebone Lane,
London W1U 2QU
Tel: 020 7535 3530
Headmaster: Mr David Lawrence
Age range: B11–18 years
Fees: Day £22,995
⚇

Young Dancers Academy
25 Bulwer Street, London W12 8AR
Tel: 020 8743 3856
Head: Mrs K Williams
Age range: 11–16 years
Fees: Day £12,237–£12,690

North-East

KEY TO SYMBOLS

- (�) Boys' school
- (♀) Girls' school
- (🌐) International school
- (16) Tutorial or sixth form college
- (A) A levels
- (🏛) Boarding accommodation
- (£) Bursaries
- (IB) International Baccalaureate
- (✎) Learning support
- (16) Entrance at 16+
- (🎓) Vocational qualifications
- (IAPS) Independent Association of Preparatory Schools
- (HMC) The Headmasters' & Headmistresses' Conference
- (ISA) Independent Schools Association
- (GSA) Girls' School Association
- (BSA) Boarding Schools' Association
- (S) Society of Heads

Unless otherwise indicated, all schools are coeducational day schools. Single-sex and boarding schools will be indicated by the relevant icon.

Durham

**BARNARD CASTLE
SENIOR SCHOOL**
For further details see p.182
Barnard Castle, Durham DL12 8UN
Tel: +44 (0)1833 696030
Email: admissions@
barneyschool.org.uk
Website:
www.barnardcastleschool.org.uk
Headmaster: Mr Tony Jackson
Age range: 4–18 years
No. of pupils: 736
Fees: Day £7,626–£15,498
FB £22,362–£31,659

Delta Independent School
Parliament Street, Consett,
Durham DH8 5DH
Tel: 01207 502680
Principal: Ms Helen Daglish
Age range: 13–16 years

Durham High School for Girls
Farewell Hall, South Road,
Durham DH1 3TB
Tel: 0191 384 3226
Headmistress: Mrs Simone Niblock
Age range: G3–18 years
No. of pupils: 347

Durham School
Quarryheads Lane, Durham DH1 4SZ
Tel: +44 (0)191 731 9270
Headmaster: Mr Kieran McLaughlin
Age range: 11–18 years

The Chorister School (Bow)
South Road, Durham DH1 3LS
Tel: 0191 731 9270
Head of School: Ms Sally Harrod
Age range: 3–7 years

The Chorister School (Cathedral)
The College, Durham DH1 3EL
Tel: +44 (0)191 731 9270
Head of School: Ms Sally Harrod
Age range: 7–11 years

The Independent Grammar School: Durham
Claypath, Durham DH1 1RH
Tel: 07984 619739
Principal: Mr Chris Gray
Age range: 4–13 years

Northumberland

Longridge Towers School
Longridge Towers, Berwick-upon-
Tweed, Northumberland TD15 2XQ
Tel: 01289 307584
Headmaster: Mr Jonathan Lee
Age range: 3–19 years
No. of pupils: 313

Mowden Hall School
Newton, Stocksfield,
Northumberland NE43 7TP
Tel: 01661 842147
Head: Ms Kate Martin
Age range: 3–13 years

Stockton-on-Tees

Red House School
36 The Green, Norton,
Stockton-on-Tees TS20 1DX
Tel: 01642 553370
Head: Dr Rebecca Ashcroft
Age range: 3–16 years

Teesside High School
The Avenue, Eaglescliffe,
Stockton-on-Tees TS16 9AT
Tel: 01642 782095
Head of School: Mrs K Mackenzie
Age range: 3–18 years

Yarm School
The Friarage, Yarm, Stockton-
on-Tees TS15 9EJ
Tel: 01642 786023
Head of School: Dr Huw Williams
Age range: 3–18 years

Tyne & Wear

Argyle House School
19-20 Thornhill Park, Sunderland,
Tyne & Wear SR2 7LA
Tel: 01915 100726
Headteacher: Mr. Chris Johnson
Age range: 3–16 years

Dame Allan's Boys' School
Fowberry Crescent, Fenham,
Newcastle upon Tyne,
Tyne & Wear NE4 9YJ
Tel: 01912 750608
Head of School: Mr P Wildsmith
Age range: B11–16 years

Dame Allan's Girls' School
Fowberry Crescent, Fenham,
Newcastle upon Tyne,
Tyne & Wear NE4 9YJ
Tel: 01912 750608
Head of School: Mrs E Fiddaman
Age range: G11–16 years

Dame Allan's Junior School & Nursery
Hunters Road, Spital Tongues,
Newcastle upon Tyne, Tyne
& Wear NE2 4NG
Tel: 01912 750608
Headteacher: Mr Geoff Laidler
Age range: 3–11 years

Dame Allan's Sixth Form
Fowberry Crescent, Fenham,
Newcastle upon Tyne,
Tyne & Wear NE4 9YJ
Tel: 01912 750608
Head of School: Mr P Terry
Age range: 16–18 years

**Gateshead Jewish
Boarding School**
10 Rydal Street, Gateshead,
Tyne & Wear NE8 1HG
Tel: 01914 771431
Age range: B10–16 years
ⓐ

Gateshead Jewish Primary School
18-22 Gladstone Terrace,
Gateshead, Tyne & Wear NE8 4EA
Tel: 01914 772154
Age range: B5–11 years
ⓐ

**Newcastle High School
for Girls GDST**
Tankerville Terrace, Jesmond,
Newcastle upon Tyne,
Tyne & Wear NE2 3BA
Tel: 01912 016511
Head: Mr Michael Tippett
Age range: G3–18 years
ⓐ Ⓐ £ ✎ 16ᐟ

Newcastle Preparatory School
6 Eslington Road, Jesmond, Newcastle
upon Tyne, Tyne & Wear NE2 4RH
Tel: 01912 811769
Head of School: Ms Fiona Coleman
Age range: 3–11 years
✎

Newcastle School for Boys
30 West Avenue, Gosforth, Newcastle
upon Tyne, Tyne & Wear NE3 4ES
Tel: 01912 559300
Headmaster: Mr David Tickner
Age range: B3–18 years
ⓐ Ⓐ £ ✎ 16ᐟ

**OneSchool Global UK York
(Springwell) Campus**
60 Peareth Hall Road, Springwell,
Gateshead, Tyne & Wear NE9 7NT
Tel: 01904 663300
Age range: 7–18 years

Royal Grammar School
Eskdale Terrace, Newcastle upon
Tyne, Tyne & Wear NE2 4DX
Tel: 01912 815711
Headmaster: Mr Geoffrey Stanford
Age range: 7–18 years
Ⓐ £ ✎ 16ᐟ

Westfield School
Oakfield Road, Gosforth, Newcastle
upon Tyne, Tyne & Wear NE3 4HS
Tel: 01912 553980
Headmaster: Mr Neil Walker
Age range: G3–18 years
ⓐ 🌐 16ᐟ

D370

North-West

KEY TO SYMBOLS

- 🕆 *Boys' school*
- 🕆 *Girls' school*
- 🌐 *International school*
- ⑯ *Tutorial or sixth form college*
- Ⓐ *A levels*
- 🏫 *Boarding accommodation*
- £ *Bursaries*
- ⒾⒷ *International Baccalaureate*
- ✎ *Learning support*
- ⑯ *Entrance at 16+*
- 🎓 *Vocational qualifications*
- ⒾⒶⓅⓈ *Independent Association of Preparatory Schools*
- ⒽⓂⒸ *The Headmasters' & Headmistresses' Conference*
- ⒾⓈⒶ *Independent Schools Association*
- ⒼⓈⒶ *Girls' School Association*
- ⒷⓈⒶ *Boarding Schools' Association*
- Ⓢ *Society of Heads*

Unless otherwise indicated, all schools are coeducational day schools. Single-sex and boarding schools will be indicated by the relevant icon.

Cheshire

Abbey Gate College
Saighton Grange, Saighton,
Chester, Cheshire CH3 6EN
Tel: 01244 617352
Head: Mr Craig Jenkinson
Age range: 4–18 years
Ⓐ Ⓔ 🖊 ⑯

Alderley Edge School for Girls
Wilmslow Road, Alderley
Edge, Cheshire SK9 7QE
Tel: 01625 583028
Head of School: Ms Nicola Smillie
Age range: G2–18 years
🚺 Ⓐ Ⓔ ⒾⒷ 🖊 ⑯

BEECH HALL SCHOOL
For further details see p.186
Beech Hall Drive, Tytherington,
Macclesfield, Cheshire SK10 2EG
Tel: 01625 422192
Email: secretary@
beechhallschool.org
Website: www.beechhallschool.org
Headmaster: Mr James Allen
Age range: 6 months–16 years
🖊

**Bowdon Preparatory
School for Girls**
Ashley Road, Bowdon,
Altrincham, Cheshire WA14 2LT
Tel: 0161 928 0678
Headmistress: Mrs Helen Gee
Age range: G3–11 years
🚺

BRABYNS PREPARATORY SCHOOL
For further details see p.188
34-36 Arkwright Road, Marple,
Stockport, Cheshire SK6 7DB
Tel: 0161 427 2395
Email: admin@
brabynsprepschool.co.uk
Website:
www.brabynsprepschool.co.uk
Headteacher: Mrs Lindsay McKenna
Age range: 2–11 years
Fees: Day £1,974–£2,719
Ⓔ 🖊

Cransley School
Belmont Hall, Belmont Road,
Great Budworth, Northwich,
Cheshire CW9 6HN
Tel: 01606 891747
Head of School: Mr Richard Pollock
LL.B, PGCE, PG Dip (RNCM)
Age range: 4–16 years
🖊

Greater Grace Christian School
Church Lane, Backford,
Chester, Cheshire CH2 4BE
Tel: 01244 851797
Age range: 5–18 years

**Green Meadow
Independent School**
Robson Way, Lowton, Warrington,
Cheshire WA3 2RD
Tel: 01942 671138
Head of School: Mrs S Green
Age range: 3–14 years

Greenbank Preparatory School
64 Heathbank Road, Cheadle
Hulme, Stockport, Cheshire SK8 6HU
Tel: 0161 485 3724
Head of School: Mr Malcolm Johnson
Age range: 6 months–11 years
No. of pupils: 283
Fees: Day £9,480
Ⓔ 🖊

Hale Preparatory School
Broomfield Lane, Hale,
Cheshire WA15 9AS
Tel: 0161 928 2386
Headmaster: Mr J F Connor
Age range: 4–11 years

Lady Barn House School
Schools Hill, Cheadle, Cheshire SK8 1JE
Tel: 0161 428 2912
Head of School: Ms Louise Higson
Age range: 3–11 years
No. of pupils: 479
Ⓔ 🖊

**OneSchool Global UK
Northwich Campus**
Hartford Manor, Greenbank Lane,
Northwich, Cheshire CW8 1HW
Tel: 01606 210320
Age range: 7–18 years

Pownall Hall School
Carrwood Road, Pownall Park,
Wilmslow, Cheshire SK9 5DW
Tel: 01625 523141
Headmaster: Mr David Goulbourn
Age range: 6 months–11 years
🖊

Terra Nova School
Jodrell Bank, Holmes Chapel,
Crewe, Cheshire CW4 8BT
Tel: 01477 571251
Headmaster: Mr Paul Campbell
Age range: 2–13 years
(boarding from 8)
🏫 Ⓔ 🖊

The Firs School
45 Newton Lane, Upton,
Chester, Cheshire CH2 2HJ
Tel: 01244 322443
Head Teacher: Miss Rosemary Evans
Age range: 2–11 years
🖊

The Grange School
Bradburns Lane, Hartford,
Northwich, Cheshire CW8 1LU
Tel: 01606 533431
Senior Head: Dr Lorraine Earps
Age range: 4–18 years
Ⓐ Ⓔ 🖊 ⑯

The Hammond School
Mannings Lane, Chester,
Cheshire CH2 4ES
Tel: 01244 305350
Principal: Ms Jennifer Roscoe
Age range: 11–19+ years
🎭 🏫 Ⓔ 🖊 ⑯

The King's School in Macclesfield
Alderley Road, Prestbury,
Cheshire SK10 4SP
Tel: 01625 260000
Headmaster: Mr Jason Slack
Age range: 3–18 years
Ⓔ 🖊 ⑯

The King's School, Chester
Wrexham Road, Chester,
Cheshire CH4 7QL
Tel: 01244 689500
Headmaster: Mr George Hartley
Age range: 4–18 years
Ⓔ 🖊 ⑯

The Queen's School
City Walls Road, Chester,
Cheshire CH1 2NN
Tel: 01244 312078
Headmistress: Mrs Sue
Wallace-Woodroffe
Age range: G4–18 years
No. of pupils: 450
🚺 Ⓐ Ⓔ ⑯

The Ryleys School
Ryleys Lane, Alderley Edge,
Cheshire SK9 7UY
Tel: 01625 583241
Headteacher: Mrs Julia Langford
Age range: 1–11 years
🖊

Wilmslow Preparatory School
Grove Avenue, Wilmslow,
Cheshire SK9 5EG
Tel: 01625 524246
Headteacher: Mr Bradley
Lavagna-Slater
Age range: 3–11 years
Ⓔ 🖊

Yorston Lodge Prep School
18 St John's Road, Knutsford,
Cheshire WA16 0DP
Tel: 01565 746 841
Headmistress: Mrs Janet Dallimore
Age range: 3–11 years

Cumbria

Austin Friars School
Etterby Scaur, Carlisle,
Cumbria CA3 9PB
Tel: 01228 528042
Headmaster: Mr Matt Harris
Age range: 3–18 years
Ⓐ £ 🖉 ⑯

Casterton, Sedbergh Preparatory School
Casterton, Kirkby Lonsdale,
Cumbria LA6 2SG
Tel: 01524 279200
Headmaster: Mr Will Newman
BA(Ed) Hons MA
Age range: 3–13 years
🏫 £ 🖉

Hunter Hall School
Frenchfield, Penrith, Cumbria CA11 8UA
Tel: 01768 891291
Head Teacher: Mrs Donna Vinsome
Age range: 3–11 years
🖉

LIME HOUSE SCHOOL
For further details see p.196
Holm Hill, Dalston, Carlisle,
Cumbria CA5 7BX
Tel: 01228 710225
Email: office@
limehouseschool.co.uk
Website:
www.limehouseschool.co.uk
Headteacher: Mr Andy Guest
Age range: 7–18 years
No. of pupils: 170
🏫 Ⓐ 🏫 £ 🖉 ⑯

For further details see p.196

Sedbergh School
Station Road, Sedbergh,
Cumbria LA10 5HG
Tel: 015396 20535
Headmaster: Mr Dan Harrison
Age range: 3–19 years
🏫 Ⓐ 🏫 £ 🖉 ⑯

St Bees School
Wood Lane, St Bees,
Cumbria CA27 0DS
Tel: 01946 828000
Headmaster: Mr Robin Silk
Age range: 11–18 years
🏫

Windermere School
Patterdale Road, Windermere,
Cumbria LA23 1NW
Tel: 015394 46164
Headmaster: Mr Thomas Hill
Age range: 3–18 years
(boarding from 7)
No. of pupils: 350
Fees: Day £18,855 WB
£31,740 FB £32,985
🏫 Ⓐ £ IB ⑯

Greater Manchester

Abbey College Manchester
5-7 Cheapside, Off King
Street, Manchester, Greater
Manchester M2 4WG
Tel: 0161 817 2700
Principal: Mr Chris Randell
Age range: 15–21 years
🏫 ⑯ Ⓐ 🏫 🖉 ⑯

Abbotsford Preparatory School
211 Flixton Road, Urmston, Manchester,
Greater Manchester M41 5PR
Tel: 0161 748 3261
Head of School: Mrs Catherine
Howard B.Ed(Hons)
Age range: 4 months–11 years

Altrincham Preparatory School
Marlborough Road, Bowdon,
Altrincham, Greater
Manchester WA14 2RR
Tel: 0161 928 3366
Headmaster: Mr N J Vernon
Age range: B2–11 years
🏃 🖉

Beech House School
184 Manchester Road, Rochdale,
Greater Manchester OL11 4JQ
Tel: 01706 646309
Principal: Mr Kevin Sartain
Age range: 2–16 years
🖉

Beis Ruchel Girls School
87 Devonshire Street, Salford,
Manchester, Greater
Manchester M7 4AE
Tel: 01617 951830
Age range: G2–16 years
🏃

Bnos Yisroel School
Leicester Road, Salford, Manchester,
Greater Manchester M7 4DA
Tel: 01617 923896
Headmaster: Rabbi R Spitzer
Age range: G3–16 years
🏃

Bolton School
Chorley New Road, Bolton,
Greater Manchester BL1 4PA
Tel: 01204 840201
Heads of School: Mr Philip
Britton & Miss Sue Hincks
Age range: 0–18 years
Fees: Day £9,966–£12,462
Ⓐ £ 🖉 ⑯

Branwood Preparatory School
Stafford Road, Monton,
Eccles, Manchester, Greater
Manchester M30 9HN
Tel: 0161 789 1054
Headmaster: Mr Andrew Whittell
Age range: 3–11 years
🖉

Bridgewater School
Drywood Hall, Worsley Road,
Worsley, Manchester, Greater
Manchester M28 2WQ
Tel: 0161 794 1463
Head Teacher: Mrs JAT Nairn
CertEd(Distinction)
Age range: 3–18 years
No. of pupils: 452
Ⓐ £ ⑯

Bury Catholic Preparatory School
Arden House, 172 Manchester Road,
Bury, Greater Manchester BL9 9BH
Tel: 0161 797 5804
Acting Headteacher: Miss H Farrow
Age range: 3–11 years
🖉

Bury Grammar Schools
Tenterden Street, Bury, Greater
Manchester BL9 0HN
Tel: 0161 696 8600
Headmistress: Mrs J Anderson
Age range: 3–18 years
🖉

Cheadle Hulme School
Claremont Road, Cheadle Hulme,
Cheadle, Greater Manchester SK8 6EF
Tel: 0161 488 3330
Head: Mr Neil Smith
Age range: 3–18 years
🖉 ⑯

Chetham's School of Music
Long Millgate, Manchester,
Greater Manchester M3 1SB
Tel: 0161 834 9644
Joint Principals: Nicola
Smith & Tom Redmond
Age range: 8–18 years
No. of pupils: 300
🏫 Ⓐ 🏫 🖉 ⑯

Clarendon Cottage School
Ivy Bank House, Half Edge Lane,
Eccles, Manchester, Greater
Manchester M30 9BJ
Tel: 0161 950 7868
Head of School: Miss E Bagnall
Age range: 3–11 years
🖉

Clevelands Preparatory School
425 Chorley New Road, Bolton,
Greater Manchester BL1 5DH
Tel: 01204 843898
Head of School: Mr Keith Cahillane
Age range: 2–11 years

Covenant Christian School
The Hawthorns, 48 Heaton
Moor Road, Stockport, Greater
Manchester SK4 4NX
Tel: 0161 432 3782
Head: Dr Roger Slack
Age range: 5–16 years

Darul Uloom Al Arabiya Al Islamiya (Darul Uloom Bury)
Holcombe Hall, Holcombe, Bury,
Greater Manchester BL8 4NG
Tel: 01706 826106
Head: Mr Mohammed Mulla
Age range: B11–23 years
🏃 🏫

Darul Uloom Al Jamiatul Islamiyah (Darul Uloom Bolton)
Mount St Joseph's Convent, Willows Lane, Bolton, Greater Manchester BL3 4HF
Tel: 01204 62622
Head of School: Irfan Ibrahim
Age range: B11–25 years

Farrowdale House Preparatory School
Farrow Street, Shaw, Oldham, Greater Manchester OL2 7AD
Tel: 01706 844533
Headteacher: Miss Z. N. Campbell BA (Hons) PGCE
Age range: 3–11 years

FOREST PARK PREPARATORY SCHOOL
For further details see p.190
Lauriston House, 27 Oakfield, Sale, Greater Manchester M33 6NB
Tel: 0161 973 4835
Email: office@forestparkprep.co.uk
Website: www.forestparkprep.co.uk
Headteacher: Mr Nick Tucker
Age range: 3–11 years

FOREST PREPARATORY SCHOOL
For further details see p.192
Moss Lane, Timperley, Altrincham, Greater Manchester WA15 6LJ
Tel: 0161 980 4075
Email: enquiries@forestschool.co.uk
Website: www.forestschool.co.uk
Headmaster: Mr Graeme Booth
Age range: 2–11 years

Hulme Hall Grammar School
Beech Avenue, Stockport, Greater Manchester SK3 8HA
Tel: 0161 485 3524
Headmaster: Mr Dean Grierson
Age range: 2–16 years
No. of pupils: 200
Fees: Day £2,840–£3,300

Kassim Darwish Grammar School for Boys
Hartley Hall, Alexandra Road South, Manchester, Greater Manchester M16 8NH
Tel: 0161 8607676
Executive Headteacher: Mrs M Mohamed
Age range: B11–16 years

King of Kings School
142 Dantzic Street, Manchester, Greater Manchester M4 4DN
Tel: 0161 834 4214
Headteacher: Mrs Brenda Lewis
Age range: 3–18 years

Lord's School
Green Lane, Bolton, Greater Manchester BL3 2EF
Tel: 01204 523731
Headteacher: Mrs Anne Ainsworth
Age range: 7–18 years

Loreto Preparatory School
Dunham Road, Altrincham, Greater Manchester WA14 4GZ
Tel: 0161 928 8310
Headteacher: Mrs Anne Roberts
Age range: G3–11 years

Madrasatul Imam Muhammad Zakariya
Keswick Street, Bolton, Greater Manchester BL1 8LX
Tel: 01204 384434
Headteacher: Mrs Amena Sader
Age range: G11–19 years

Manchester High School for Girls
Grangethorpe Road, Manchester, Greater Manchester M14 6HS
Tel: 0161 224 0447
Head Mistress: Mrs Helen F Jeys
Age range: G4–18 years
No. of pupils: 1000

Manchester Islamic Grammar School for Girls
55 High Lane, Chorlton, Manchester, Greater Manchester M21 9FA
Tel: 0161 881 2127
Headmistress: Mrs Mona Mohamed
Age range: G11–16 years

Manchester Junior Girls School
64 Upper Park Road, Salford, Greater Manchester M7 4JA
Tel: 0161 740 0566
Head of School: Mrs Hannah Ehrentreu
Age range: G3–13 years

Manchester Muslim Preparatory School
551 Wilmslow Road, Withington, Manchester, Greater Manchester M20 4BA
Tel: 0161 445 5452
Headteacher: Ms D Ghafori-Kanno
Age range: 3–11 years

Mechinoh School
13 Upper Park Road, Salford, Greater Manchester M7 4HY
Tel: 0161 7959275
Head of School: Rabbi N Baddiel
Age range: B11–16 years

Moor Allerton Preparatory School
131 Barlow Moor Road, West Didsbury, Manchester, Greater Manchester M20 2PW
Tel: 0161 445 4521
Headmistress: Ms Kathryn Unsworth
Age range: 6 months–11 years

Oholei Yosef Yitzchok (OYY) Lubavitch Boys School
4 Upper Park Road, Salford, Greater Manchester M7 4HL
Tel: 01617 400923
Head of School: Mendel Cohen
Age range: 5–16 years

Oholei Yosef Yitzchok (OYY) Lubavitch Girls School
460 Bury New Road, Park Lane, Salford, Greater Manchester M7 4LH
Tel: 01617 050483
Head of School: Mrs Avigail Di Veroli
Age range: G2–17 years

Oldham Hulme Grammar School
Chamber Road, Oldham, Greater Manchester OL8 4BX
Tel: 0161 624 4497
Principal: Mr CJD Mairs
Age range: 3–18 years

Prestwich Preparatory School
St Margaret's Building, 400 Bury Old Road, Prestwich, Manchester, Greater Manchester M25 1PZ
Tel: 0161 773 1223
Headmistress: Miss P Shiels
Age range: 2–11 years

Rochdale Islamic Academy Boys School (RIAB)
36 Taylor Street, Rochdale, Greater Manchester OL12 0HX
Tel: 01706 347344
Head of School: Mr Arshad Ashraf
Age range: B11–16 years

Rochdale Islamic Academy Girls School (RIAG)
Greenbank Road, Rochdale, Greater Manchester OL12 0HZ
Tel: 01706 710184
Head of School: Mr Arshad Ashraf
Age range: G11–16 years

St Ambrose Preparatory School
Hale Barns, Altrincham, Greater Manchester WA15 0HF
Tel: 0161 903 9193
Headmaster: F J Driscoll
Age range: 3–11 years

St. Bede's College
Alexandra Park, Manchester, Greater Manchester M16 8HX
Tel: 0161 226 3323
Headteacher: Mrs Sandra Pike
Age range: 3–18 years

Stella Maris School
St. John's Road, Heaton Mersey, Stockport, Greater Manchester SK4 3BR
Tel: 0161 432 0532
Headteacher: Mrs N Johnson
Age range: 3–11 years

Stockport Grammar School
Buxton Road, Stockport, Greater Manchester SK2 7AF
Tel: 0161 456 9000
Headmaster: Dr Paul Owen
Age range: 3–18 years

Tashbar of Manchester
20 Upper Park Road, Salford, Greater Manchester M7 4HL
Tel: 01617 208254
Head of School: Rabbi David Hammond
Age range: B3–12 years

Teenage Works
Partington House, Partington Street, Failsworth, Manchester, Greater Manchester M35 9RD
Tel: 0161 222 8168
Head of School: Ms Louise Hodson
Age range: 11–18 years

The Chadderton Preparatory Grammar School
Broadway, Chadderton, Oldham, Greater Manchester OL9 0AD
Tel: 0161 620 6570
Headteacher: Mrs Caroline Greenwood
Age range: 2–11 years

The Manchester Grammar School
Old Hall Lane, Fallowfield, Manchester, Greater Manchester M13 0XT
Tel: 0161 224 7201
High Master: Dr Martin Boulton
Age range: B7–18 years

Trinity Christian School
Birbeck Street, Off High Street, Stalybridge, Greater Manchester SK15 1SH
Tel: 0161 303 0674
Head: Mr Michael Stewart
Age range: 3–16 years

Withington Girls' School
100 Wellington Road, Fallowfield, Manchester, Greater Manchester M14 6BL
Tel: 0161 224 1077
Headmistress: Mrs S J Haslam BA
Age range: G7–18 years

Isle of Man

King William's College
Castletown, Isle of Man IM9 1TP
Tel: +44 (0)1624 820110
Principal: Mr Joss Buchanan
Age range: 11–18 years
No. of pupils: 380
Fees: Day £19,745–£26,395
FB £32,740–£39,390

The Buchan School
Westhill, Arbory Road, Castletown, Isle of Man IM9 1RD
Tel: +44 (0)1624 820110
Head of School: Mrs Janet Billingsley Evans
Age range: 2–11 years

Lancashire

Abrar Academy
34-36 Garstang Road, Preston, Lancashire PR1 1NA
Tel: 01772 82 87 32
Head of School: Mr A Chowdhury
Age range: B11–21 years

AKS Lytham
Clifton Drive South, Lytham St Annes, Lancashire FY8 1DT
Tel: 01253 784100
Headmaster: Mr David Harrow
Age range: 0–18 years

Al Islah Girls High School
108 Audley Range, Blackburn, Lancashire BB1 1TF
Tel: 01254 261573
Headteacher: Ms Nikhat Pardesi
Age range: G11–16 years

Ashbridge Independent School
Lindle Lane, Hutton, Preston, Lancashire PR4 4AQ
Tel: 01772 619900
Headteacher: Ms Karen Mehta
Age range: 0–11 years

Highfield Priory School
58 Fulwood Row, Fulwood, Preston, Lancashire PR2 5RW
Tel: 01772 709624
Headteacher: Jeremy M Duke
Age range: 2–11 years
No. of pupils: 210
Fees: Day £8,370

Islamiyah Girls High School
Willow Street, Blackburn, Lancashire BB1 5NQ
Tel: 01254 661259
Interim Head Teacher: Salma Patel
Age range: G11–16 years

Jamea Al Kauthar
Ashton Road, Lancaster, Lancashire LA1 5AJ
Tel: +44 (0)1524 389898
Age range: G11–18 years
(boarding from 11)

Jamiatul Ilm Wal Huda
15 Moss Street, Blackburn, Lancashire BB1 5JT
Tel: 01254 673105
Principal: Mr Abdus-Samad Ahmed
Age range: B11–25 years

Lancaster Steiner School
Lune Road, Lancaster, Lancashire LA1 5QU
Tel: 01524 381876
Principal: Patricia Williams
Age range: 0–11 years

Markazul Uloom
Park Lee Road, Blackburn, Lancashire BB2 3NY
Tel: 01254 581569
Head of School: Mr Sajid Bargit
Age range: B11–16 years

Moorland School
Ribblesdale Avenue, Clitheroe, Lancashire BB7 2JA
Tel: 01200 423833
Headteacher: Mrs. Deborah Frost
Age range: 3 months–18 years (boarding from 7)

Oakhill School & Nursery
Wiswell Lane, Whalley, Clitheroe, Lancashire BB7 9AF
Tel: 01254 823546
Principal: Ms Jane Buttery BA (Hons) NPQH
Age range: 0–16 years

OneSchool Global UK Lancaster Campus
Melling Road, Hornby, Lancashire LA2 8LH
Tel: 01524 222159
Age range: 7–18 years

Scarisbrick Hall School
Southport Road, Scarisbrisk, Ormskirk, Lancashire L40 9RQ
Tel: 01704 841151
Headmaster: Mr J Shaw
Age range: 0–18 years

St Joseph's Park Hill School
Padiham Road, Burnley,
Lancashire BB12 6TG
Tel: 01282 455622
Headteacher: Mrs Maria Whitehead
Age range: 3–11 years

St Pius X Catholic Preparatory School
Oak House, 200 Garstang Road,
Fulwood, Preston, Lancashire PR2 8RD
Tel: 01772 719937
Headmaster: Mr Patrick Gush
Age range: 2–11 years

St. Annes College Grammar School
293 Clifton Drive South, Lytham
St Annes, Lancashire FY8 1HN
Tel: +44 (0)1253 725815
Head of School: S R Welsby
Age range: 2–18 years

Stonyhurst College
Stonyhurst, Clitheroe,
Lancashire BB7 9PZ
Tel: 01254 827073
Headmaster: Mr John
Browne BA LLB MBA
Age range: 3–18 years
No. of pupils: 801
Fees: Day £21,750 WB £31,500
FB £36,600–£39,300

The Alternative School
Suite 4a, Ribble Court, 1 Mead Way,
Padiham, Lancashire BB12 7NG
Tel: 01282 851800
Head of School: Ms Kirsty Swierkowski
Age range: 5–18 years

Westholme School
Wilmar Lodge, Meins Road,
Blackburn, Lancashire BB2 6QU
Tel: 01254 506070
Principal: Dr Richard Robson
Age range: 4–18 years

Merseyside

Auckland College
65-67 Parkfield Road, Aigburth,
Liverpool, Merseyside L17 4LE
Tel: 01517 270083
Headteacher: Miss Stephanie Boyd
Age range: 3–16 years

Avalon School
Caldy Road, West Kirby, Wirral,
Merseyside CH48 2HE
Tel: 01516 256993
Headteacher: Ms Joanna Callaway
Age range: 2–11 years

Birkenhead School
58 Beresford Road, Oxton,
Wirral, Merseyside CH43 2JD
Tel: 01516 524014
Headmaster: Mr Paul Vicars
Age range: 3 months–18 years

Carleton House Preparatory School
145 Menlove Avenue, Liverpool,
Merseyside L18 3EE
Tel: 01517 220756
Headteacher: Mrs Sandy Coleman
Age range: 3–11 years

Christian Fellowship School
Overbury Street, Edge Hill,
Liverpool, Merseyside L7 3HL
Tel: 01517 091642
Head Teacher: Mrs R Boulton
(BA Tons, PGCE)
Age range: 0–16 years

Prenton Preparatory School
12 Mount Pleasant, Oxton,
Wirral, Merseyside CH43 5SY
Tel: 01516 523182
Headteacher: Mr M Jones
BSC Hons, PGCE
Age range: 2–11 years

St. Mary's College
Everest Road, Crosby, Liverpool,
Merseyside L23 5TW
Tel: 01519 243926
Principal: Mr Michael Kennedy Bsc, MA
Age range: 0–18 years

Stanfield Preparatory School
Liverpool Road, Crosby, Liverpool,
Merseyside L23 0QP
Tel: 01519 499400
Headmistress: Miss E Lynan
Age range: 4–11 years

The Belvedere Preparatory School
23 Belvidere Road, Princes Park,
Aigburth, Liverpool, Merseyside L8 3TF
Tel: 01514 711137
Headmistress: Miss Clare Burnham
Age range: 3–11 years

The Merchant Taylors' Boys' School
Liverpool Road, Crosby, Liverpool,
Merseyside L23 0QP
Tel: 01519 499400
Headmaster: Mr David Wickes
Age range: B11–18 years

The Merchant Taylors' Girls' School
Liverpool Road, Crosby, Liverpool,
Merseyside L23 0QP
Tel: 01519 499400
Headmistress: Mrs Claire Tao
Age range: G11–18 years

Tower College
Mill Lane, Rainhill, Prescot,
Merseyside L35 6NE
Tel: 01514 264333
Head of School: Ms Andrea Bingley
Age range: 3 months–16 years

South-East

*See also Greater London (D347)
for schools in Kent and Surrey

KEY TO SYMBOLS
- ⚤ *Boys' school*
- ⚤ *Girls' school*
- 🌐 *International school*
- 16 *Tutorial or sixth form college*
- Ⓐ *A levels*
- 🏫 *Boarding accommodation*
- £ *Bursaries*
- IB *International Baccalaureate*
- ✎ *Learning support*
- 16 *Entrance at 16+*
- 🎓 *Vocational qualifications*
- IAPS *Independent Association of Preparatory Schools*
- HMC *The Headmasters' & Headmistresses' Conference*
- ISA *Independent Schools Association*
- GSA *Girls' School Association*
- BSA *Boarding Schools' Association*
- S *Society of Heads*

*Unless otherwise indicated, all schools are coeducational day schools.
Single-sex and boarding schools will be indicated by the relevant icon.*

Berkshire

Alder Bridge Steiner-Waldorf School
Bridge House, Mill Lane, Padworth,
Reading, Berkshire RG7 4JU
Tel: 0118 971 4471
Head of School: Lucia Dimarco
Age range: 3–14 years

Bradfield College
Bradfield, Berkshire RG7 6AU
Tel: 0118 964 4516
Headmaster: Dr Christopher Stevens
Age range: 13–18 years
No. of pupils: 820
Fees: Day £32,280 FB £40,350
(icons)

Caversham Preparatory School
16 Peppard Road, Caversham,
Reading, Berkshire RG4 8JZ
Tel: 01189 478 684
Head of School: Mrs Naomi Williams
Age range: 3–11 years

Claires Court Junior Boys
Ridgeway, The Thicket,
Maidenhead, Berkshire SL6 3QE
Tel: 01628 327400
Head of Juniors: Ms Leanne Kirby
Age range: B4–11 years
(icons)

**Claires Court Nursery,
Girls and Sixth Form**
1 College Avenue, Maidenhead,
Berkshire SL6 6AW
Tel: 01628 327500
Head of Juniors: Ms Leanne Kirby
Age range: B16–18 years G2–18 years
(icons)

Claires Court Senior Boys
Ray Mill Road East, Maidenhead,
Berkshire SL6 8TE
Tel: 01628 327600
Head of Senior Boys: Mr James Wilding
Age range: B11–16 years
(icons)

Crosfields School
Shinfield Road, Reading,
Berkshire RG2 9BL
Tel: 0118 987 1810
Headmaster: Mr Craig Watson
Age range: 3–16 years

**Deenway Montessori School
& Unicity College**
3-5 Sidmouth Street, Reading,
Berkshire RG1 4QX
Tel: 0118 9574737
Headmaster: Mr Munawar Karim
LL.B (Hons), M.A, Mont. Dip.
Age range: 3–18+ years
(icon)

Dolphin School
Waltham Road, Hurst, Reading,
Berkshire RG10 0FR
Tel: 0118 934 1277
Headmaster: Mr Adam Hurst
Age range: 3–13 years
(icons)

EAGLE HOUSE SCHOOL
For further details see p.218
Sandhurst, Berkshire GU47 8PH
Tel: 01344 772134
Email: info@eaglehouseschool.com
Website:
www.eaglehouseschool.com
Headmaster: Mr A P N
Barnard BA(Hons), PGCE
Age range: 3–13 years
No. of pupils: 388
Fees: Day £13,035–
£20,385 FB £27,390
(icons)

Elstree School
Woolhampton Hill, Woolhampton,
Reading, Berkshire RG7 5TD
Tel: 01189 713302
Headmaster: Mr Sid Inglis
B.A. (Hons), P.G.C.E.
Age range: 3–13 years
No. of pupils: 270
(icons)

Eton College
Windsor, Berkshire SL4 6DW
Tel: +44 (0)1753 370 611
Head Master: Mr Simon Henderson MA
Age range: B13–18 years
No. of pupils: 1342
Fees: FB £44,094
(icons)

Eton End School
35 Eton Road, Datchet,
Slough, Berkshire SL3 9AX
Tel: 01753 541075
Head of School: Mrs Sophie Banks MEd
Age range: 3–11 years
No. of pupils: 244
Fees: Day £10,266–£13,119
(icons)

Heathfield School
London Road, Ascot, Berkshire SL5 8BQ
Tel: 01344 898343
Head of School: Ms Sarah Wilson
Age range: G11–18 years
(boarding from 11)
Fees: Day £7,840–£8,000
FB £12,650–£12,950
(icons)

Hemdean House School
Hemdean Road, Caversham,
Reading, Berkshire RG4 7SD
Tel: 0118 947 2590
Head Teacher: Mrs Helen Chalmers
Age range: 3–11 years
(icons)

Herries Preparatory School
Dean Lane, Cookham
Dean, Berkshire SL6 9BD
Tel: 01628 483350
Headteacher: Mr Robert Grosse
Age range: 3–11 years
(icon)

Highfield Preparatory School
2 West Road, Maidenhead,
Berkshire SL6 1PD
Tel: 01628 624918
Headteacher: Mrs Joanna Leach
Age range: B2–7 years G2–11 years
(icons)

Holme Grange School
Heathlands Road, Wokingham,
Berkshire RG40 3AL
Tel: 0118 978 1566
Headteacher: Mrs Claire Robinson
BA (Open) PGCE NPQH
Age range: 3–16 years
No. of pupils: 660
Fees: Day £10,665–£16,140
(icons)

Lambrook School
Winkfield Row, Nr Ascot,
Berkshire RG42 6LU
Tel: 01344 882717
Headmaster: Mr Jonathan Perry
Age range: 3–13 years
No. of pupils: 600
(icons)

Leighton Park School
Shinfield Road, Reading,
Berkshire RG2 7ED
Tel: 0118 987 9600
Head: Mr Matthew L S Judd BA, PGCE
Age range: 11–18 years
No. of pupils: 520
(icons)

Long Close School
Upton Court Road, Upton,
Slough, Berkshire SL3 7LU
Tel: 01753 520095
Headteacher: Miss K Nijjar
BA (Hons), Med, MA
Age range: 2–16 years
No. of pupils: 329
(icons)

Luckley House School
Luckley Road, Wokingham,
Berkshire RG40 3EU
Tel: 0118 978 4175
Head: Mrs Areti Bizior
Age range: 11–18 years
(icons)

Ludgrove
Wokingham, Berkshire RG40 3AB
Tel: 0118 978 9881
Head of School: Mr Simon Barber
Age range: B8–13 years
(icons)

LVS Ascot
London Road, Ascot, Berkshire SL5 8DR
Tel: 01344 882770
Principal: Mrs Christine Cunniffe
BA (Hons), MMus, MBA
Age range: 4–18 years
No. of pupils: 800
Fees: Day £12,915–£19,335
FB £27,585–£33,975
(icons)

Meadowbrook Montessori School
Malt Hill, Warfield, Berkshire RG42 6JQ
Tel: 01344 890869
Director of Education: Ms Serena Gunn
Age range: 4–11 years

Newbold School
Popeswood Road, Binfield,
Bracknell, Berkshire RG42 4AH
Tel: 01344 421088
Headteacher: Mrs Jaki Crissey
MA, BA, PGCE Primary
Age range: 3–11 years

**OneSchool Global UK
Reading Campus (Primary)**
401 Old Whitley Wood Lane,
Reading, Berkshire RG2 8QA
Tel: 0118 931 2938
Age range: 7–11 years

**OneSchool Global UK
Reading Campus (Senior)**
The Quad, 14 Arkwright Road,
Reading, Berkshire RG2 0LU
Tel: 03000 700421
Age range: 11–18 years

Our Lady's Preparatory School
The Avenue, Crowthorne,
Wokingham, Berkshire RG45 6PB
Tel: 01344 773394
Headmaster: Mr Michael Stone
Age range: 3 months–11 years
(icon)

Padworth College
Sopers Lane, Reading,
Berkshire RG7 4NR
Tel: 0118 983 2644
Principal: Lorraine Atkins
Age range: 14–19 years
🌍Ⓐ🏫£16·

Pangbourne College
Pangbourne, Reading,
Berkshire RG8 8LA
Tel: 0118 984 2101
Headmaster: Thomas J C Garnier
Age range: 11–18 years
No. of pupils: 458
Fees: Day £6,300–£8,540 WB
£8,210–£11,510 FB £9,050–£12,680
🌍Ⓐ🏫£✎16·

Papplewick School
Windsor Road, Ascot, Berkshire SL5 7LH
Tel: 01344 621488
Headmaster: Mr Tom Bunbury
Age range: B6–13 years
♂🏫

Queen Anne's School
6 Henley Road, Caversham,
Reading, Berkshire RG4 6DX
Tel: 0118 918 7300
Head: Ms Elaine Purves
Age range: G11–18 years
(boarding from 11)
No. of pupils: G450
Fees: Day £8,370 FB £13,590
♀🌍Ⓐ🏫£✎16·

Reading Blue Coat School
Holme Park, Sonning Lane, Sonning,
Reading, Berkshire RG4 6SU
Tel: 0118 944 1005
Headmaster: Mr Peter Thomas
Age range: B11–18 years G16–18 years
♂Ⓐ£✎16·

Reddam House Berkshire
Bearwood Road, Sindlesham,
Wokingham, Berkshire RG41 5BG
Tel: +44 (0)118 974 8300
Principal: Mr Rick Cross
Age range: 3 months–18 years
No. of pupils: 650
Fees: Day £12,000–£19,248 WB
£27,981–£32,244 FB £29,526–£33,789
🌍Ⓐ🏫£✎16·

Shakhsiyah School, Slough
Cippenham Lodge, Cippenham
Lane, Slough, Berkshire SL1 5AN
Tel: 01753 518 000
Head Teacher: Mrs Tahreem Sabir
Age range: 3–11 years

St Andrew's School
Buckhold, Pangbourne,
Reading, Berkshire RG8 8QA
Tel: 0118 974 4276
Head Master: Ed Graham
Age range: 3–13 years
(boarding from 7)
Fees: Day £3,890–£6,525
🏫✎

St Bernard's Preparatory School
Hawtrey Close, Slough, Berkshire SL1 1TB
Tel: 01753 521821
Headteacher: Mrs A Verma
Age range: 2–11 years
✎

St Edward's Prep
64 Tilehurst Road, Reading,
Berkshire RG30 2JH
Tel: 0118 957 4342
Headteacher: Mr Jonathan Parsons
Age range: 3–11 years

St George's Ascot
Wells Lane, Ascot, Berkshire SL5 7DZ
Tel: 01344 629900
Headmistress: Mrs Liz Hewer
MA (Hons) (Cantab) PGCE
Age range: G11–18 years
(boarding from 11)
♀🌍Ⓐ🏫£✎16·

St George's School Windsor Castle
Windsor Castle, Windsor,
Berkshire SL4 1QF
Tel: 01753 865553
Head Master: Mr W Goldsmith
BA (Hons), FRSA, FCCT
Age range: 3–13 years
🏫✎

**St John's Beaumont
Preparatory School**
Priest Hill, Old Windsor, Berkshire SL4 2JN
Tel: 01784 494 053
Headmaster: Mr G E F Delaney
BA(Hons), PGCE, MSc
Age range: B3–13 years
No. of pupils: 240
Fees: Day £3,540–£6,820 FB £10,415
♂🏫£✎

St Joseph's College
Upper Redlands Road,
Reading, Berkshire RG1 5JT
Tel: 0118 966 1000
Head of School: Mrs Laura Stotesbury
Age range: 3–18 years
Ⓐ£✎16·

St Mary's School Ascot
St Mary's Road, Ascot, Berkshire SL5 9JF
Tel: 01344 296614
Headmistress: Mrs Danuta Staunton
Age range: G11–18 years
(boarding from 11)
♀🌍Ⓐ🏫£✎16·

St Piran's School
Gringer Hill, Maidenhead,
Berkshire SL6 7LZ
Tel: 01628 594300
Headmaster: Mr Sebastian Sales
Age range: 2–11 years
✎

Sunningdale School
Dry Arch Road, Sunningdale,
Berkshire SL5 9PY
Tel: 01344 620159
Headmaster: Tom Dawson MA, PGCE
Age range: B7–13 years
♂🏫✎

THE ABBEY SCHOOL
For further details see p.260
Kendrick Road, Reading,
Berkshire RG1 5DZ
Tel: 0118 987 2256
Email: admissions@theabbey.co.uk
Website: www.theabbey.co.uk
Head: Mr Will le Fleming
Age range: G3–18 years
No. of pupils: 1000
Fees: Day £13,185–£19,830
♀🌍Ⓐ🏫£IB✎16·

The King's House School, Windsor
King's House, 77A Frances Road,
Windsor, Berkshire SL4 3AQ
Tel: 01753 834850
Headteacher: Mrs Lyndsey Harding
Age range: 3–11 years

The Marist Preparatory School
King's Road, Sunninghill,
Ascot, Berkshire SL5 7PS
Tel: 01344 624291
**Vice Principal Prep
Phase:** Mrs Jane Gow
Age range: G2–11 years
♀✎

The Marist School
King's Road, Sunninghill,
Ascot, Berkshire SL5 7PS
Tel: 01344 624291
Principal: Ms Jo Smith
Age range: G2–18 years
♀Ⓐ16·

THE ORATORY PREP SCHOOL
For further details see p.264
Great Oaks, Goring Heath,
Reading, Berkshire RG8 7SF
Tel: 0118 984 4511
Email: office@oratoryprep.co.uk
Website: www.oratoryprep.co.uk
Headteacher: Mr Andrew De Silva
Age range: 2–13 years
(boarding from 7)
No. of pupils: 330
Fees: Day £3,600–£6,200
FB £7,790–£9,050
🏫✎

The Oratory School
Woodcote, Reading, Berkshire RG8 0PJ
Tel: 01491 683500
Head Master: Mr Joe Smith
BA(Hons), MEd, PGCE
Age range: 11–18 years
🌍Ⓐ🏫£✎16·

The Vine Christian School
Three Mile Cross Church,
Basingstoke Road, Three Mile Cross,
Reading, Berkshire RG7 1HF
Tel: 0118 988 6464
Head of School: Mrs René Esterhuizen
Age range: 3–18 years

Trinity Christian School
11 Glebe Road, Reading,
Berkshire RG2 7AG
Tel: 0118 336 0477
Head of School: Mr Nigel Steele
Age range: 4–11 years

UPTON HOUSE SCHOOL
For further details see p.268
115 St Leonard's Road,
Windsor, Berkshire SL4 3DF
Tel: 01753 862610
Email: registrar@uptonhouse.org.uk
Website: www.uptonhouse.org.uk
Head: Mrs Rhian Thornton BA
(Hons) NPQH LLE PGCE
Age range: 2–11 years
No. of pupils: 299
Fees: Day £3,383–£5,615

**Waverley Preparatory
School & Day Nursery**
Waverley Way, Finchampstead,
Wokingham, Berkshire RG40 4YD
Tel: 0118 973 1121
Principal: Mr Guy Shore
Age range: 3 months–11 years

WELLINGTON COLLEGE
For further details see p.270
Duke's Ride, Crowthorne,
Berkshire RG45 7PU
Tel: +44 (0)1344 444000
Email: admissions@
wellingtoncollege.org.uk
Website:
www.wellingtoncollege.org.uk
Master: Mr James Dahl
Age range: 13–18 years
No. of pupils: 1100 VIth485
Fees: Day £32,940–
£35,760 FB £45,090

Buckinghamshire

Gayhurst School
Bull Lane, Gerrards Cross,
Buckinghamshire SL9 8RJ
Tel: 01753 969538
Headmaster: Gareth R A Davies
Age range: 3–11 years

**International School of
Creative Arts (ISCA)**
Framewood Road, Wexham,
Buckinghamshire SL2 4QS
Tel: +44 (0)1753 208820
Head of School: Mr Robert Hunter
Age range: 15–19 years
No. of pupils: 85

MALTMAN'S GREEN SCHOOL
For further details see p.232
Maltmans Lane, Gerrards Cross,
Buckinghamshire SL9 8RR
Tel: 01753 883022
Email: registrar@
maltmansgreen.com
Website: www.maltmansgreen.com
Headmistress: Mrs Jill Walker
BSc (Hons), MA Ed, PGCE
Age range: G2–11 years
No. of pupils: 315
Fees: Day £2,595–£5,700

St Mary's School
94 Packhorse Road, Gerrards
Cross, Buckinghamshire SL9 8JQ
Tel: 01753 883370
Head of School: Mrs Patricia Adams
Age range: G3–18 years

Teikyo School UK
Framewood Road, Wexham,
Buckinghamshire SL2 4QS
Tel: 01753 663711
Age range: 15–18 years

Thorpe House School
Oval Way, Gerrards Cross,
Buckinghamshire SL9 8QA
Tel: 01753 882474
Headmaster: Mr Nicholas Pietrek
Age range: B4–16 years

East Sussex

Annan The Froebel School
Lewes Road, Easons Green,
Uckfield, East Sussex TN22 5RE
Tel: 01825 841410
Principal: Ms Debby Hunter
Age range: 2–11 years

Bartholomews Tutorial College
22-23 Prince Albert Street,
Brighton, East Sussex BN1 1HF
Tel: 01273 205965/205141
Age range: 14+ years
No. of pupils: 40
Fees: Day £22,000

Battle Abbey School
High Street, Battle, East Sussex TN33 0AD
Tel: 01424 772385
Headmaster: Mr David Clark
BA, M Phil (Cantab)
Age range: 3 months–18
years (boarding from 11)

Bede's Prep School
Duke's Drive, Eastbourne,
East Sussex BN20 7XL
Tel: +44 (0)1323 734222
Age range: 3 months–13
years (boarding from 9)

Bede's Senior School
Upper Dicker, Hailsham,
East Sussex BN27 3QH
Tel: +44 (0)1323 843252
Age range: 13–18 years
(boarding from 13)

Brighton & Hove Montessori School
67 Stanford Avenue, Brighton,
East Sussex BN1 6FB
Tel: 01273 702485
Headteacher: Mrs Daisy
Cockburn AMI, MontDip
Age range: 2–12 years

Brighton College
Eastern Road, Brighton,
East Sussex BN2 0AL
Tel: 01273 704200
Head Master: Richard Cairns
Age range: 3–18 years

**BRIGHTON COLLEGE NURSERY,
PRE-PREP & PREP SCHOOL**
For further details see p.204
Walpole Lodge, Walpole Road,
Brighton, East Sussex BN2 0EU
Tel: 01273 704343
Email: prepadmissions@
brightoncollege.net
Website:
www.brightoncollege.org.uk
Headmaster: Mr Ant Falkus
Age range: 3–13 years
No. of pupils: 512
Fees: Day £4,400–£7,430

Brighton Girls GDST
Montpelier Road, Brighton,
East Sussex BN1 3AT
Tel: 01273 280280
Head: Ms Rosie McColl
Age range: G4–18 years

Buckswood School
Broomham Hall, Rye Road, Guestling,
Hastings, East Sussex TN35 4LT
Tel: 01424 813 813
Co-Principals: Michael
Shaw & Kevin Samson
Age range: 10–19 years

CLAREMONT SCHOOL
For further details see p.212
Bodiam, Nr Robertsbridge,
East Sussex TN32 5UJ
Tel: 01580 830396
Email: enquiries@
claremontschool.co.uk
Website:
www.claremontschool.co.uk
Age range: 3 months–18
years (boarding from 10)

Darvell School
Darvell, Brightling Road,
Robertsbridge, East Sussex TN32 5DR
Tel: 01580 883300
Age range: 6–14 years

Didac School
16 Trinity Trees, Eastbourne,
East Sussex BN21 3LE
Tel: +44 1323 417276
Age range: 16–18 years

Eastbourne College
Old Wish Road, Eastbourne,
East Sussex BN21 4JX
Tel: 01323 452323 (Admissions)
Headmaster: Mr Tom
Lawson MA (Oxon)
Age range: 13–18 years

**Greenfields Independent
Day & Boarding School**
Priory Road, Forest Row,
East Sussex RH18 5JD
Tel: +44 (0)1342 822189
Executive Head: Mr. Jeff Smith
Age range: 2–18 years
(boarding from 10)

Lancing Prep Hove
The Droveway, Hove,
East Sussex BN3 6LU
Tel: 01273 503452
Headmistress: Mrs Kirsty Keep BEd
Age range: 3–13 years

Lewes Old Grammar School
140 High Street, Lewes,
East Sussex BN7 1XS
Tel: 01273 472634
Headmaster: Mr Robert Blewitt
Age range: 3–18 years

Mayfield School
The Old Palace, Mayfield,
East Sussex TN20 6PH
Tel: 01435 874642
Head: Ms Antonia Beary MA,
MPhil (Cantab), PGCE
Age range: G11–18 years
(boarding from 11)
No. of pupils: 405
Fees: Day £7,750 FB £12,250

Michael Hall School
Kidbrooke Park, Priory Road, Forest
Row, East Sussex RH18 5JA
Tel: 01342 822275
Head of School: Emmeline Hawker
Age range: 0–19 years

Roedean School
Roedean Way, Brighton,
East Sussex BN2 5RQ
Tel: 01273 667500
Headmaster: Mr. Oliver Bond
BA(Essex), PGCE, NPQH
Age range: G11–18 years
(boarding from 11)
No. of pupils: 675 VIth155
Fees: Day £5,670–£7,415 WB
£10,030–£11,185 FB £10,990–£13,305

Sacred Heart School
Mayfield Lane, Durgates,
Wadhurst, East Sussex TN5 6DQ
Tel: 01892 783414
Headteacher: Ms Johanna Collyer
Age range: 2–11 years

**SKIPPERS HILL MANOR
PREPARATORY SCHOOL**
For further details see p.250
Five Ashes, Mayfield, East
Sussex TN20 6HR
Tel: 01825 830234
Email: info@skippershill.com
Website: www.skippershill.com
Headmaster: Mr Phillip Makhouli
Age range: 2–13 years
Fees: Day £2,932–£5,062

St Andrew's Prep
Meads Street, Eastbourne,
East Sussex BN20 7RP
Tel: 01323 733203
Headmaster: Tom Gregory
BA(Hons), PGCE
Age range: 9 months–13 years
No. of pupils: 374

St Christopher's School
33 New Church Road, Hove,
East Sussex BN3 4AD
Tel: 01273 735404
Head of School: Ms Elizabeth Lyle
Age range: 4–13 years

The Brighton Waldorf School
Roedean Road, Brighton,
East Sussex BN2 5RA
Tel: 01273 386300
School Director: Mr Damian Mooncie
Age range: 0–16 years

The Drive Prep School
101 The Drive, Hove, East
Sussex BN3 6GE
Tel: 01273 738444
Head Teacher: Mrs S Parkinson
CertEd, CertPerfArts
Age range: 7–16 years

The Montessori Place
45 Cromwell Road, Hove,
East Sussex BN3 3ER
Tel: 01273 773 764
Head of School: Mr Rob Gueterbock
Age range: 15 months–18 years

Vinehall
Robertsbridge, East Sussex TN32 5JL
Tel: 01580 880413
Headmaster: Joff Powis
Age range: 2–13 years
No. of pupils: 220
Fees: Day £10,350–£19,290 WB
£22,575–£23,100 FB £24,525–£25,125

Windlesham School
190 Dyke Road, Brighton,
East Sussex BN1 5AA
Tel: 01273 553645
Headmaster: Mr John Ingrassia
Age range: 3–11 years

Hampshire

Alton School
Anstey Lane, Alton,
Hampshire GU34 2NG
Tel: 01420 82070
Headmaster: Mr Karl Guest
Age range: 0–18 years
No. of pupils: 400

Ballard School
Fernhill Lane, New Milton,
Hampshire BH25 5SU
Tel: 01425 626900
Headmaster: Mr Andrew McCleave
Age range: 2–16 years
No. of pupils: 451
Fees: Day £3,015–£5,550

**Bedales Prep, Dunhurst &
Pre-Prep, Dunannie**
Alton Road, Steep, Petersfield,
Hampshire GU32 2DR
Tel: 01730 300200 / 01730 300400
**Head of Bedales Prep,
Dunhurst:** Mr Colin Baty
Age range: 3–13 years

Bedales School
Church Road, Steep, Petersfield,
Hampshire GU32 2DG
Tel: 01730 300100
Head of School: Mr Will Goldsmith
Age range: 13–18 years

Boundary Oak School
Roche Court, Wickham Road,
Fareham, Hampshire PO17 5BL
Tel: 01329 280955
Executive Headmaster: Mr James
Polansky MA (Cantab) PGCE
Age range: 2–16 years
No. of pupils: 348
Fees: Day £9,195–£14,886 WB
£16,155–£21,078 FB £18,144–£23,067

Brockwood Park School
Brockwood Park, Bramdean,
Alresford, Hampshire SO24 0LQ
Tel: +44 (0)1962 771744
Principal: Mr Antonio Autor
Age range: 14–19 years

CHURCHER'S COLLEGE
For further details see p.208
Petersfield, Hampshire GU31 4AS
Tel: 01730 263033
Email: admissions@
churcherscollege.com
Website:
www.ChurchersCollege.com
Headmaster: Mr Simon
Williams , MA, BSc
Age range: 3–18 years
Fees: Day £11,535–£17,265

Daneshill School
Stratfield Turgis, Basingstoke,
Hampshire RG27 0AR
Tel: 01256 882707
Head of School: Jim Massey
Age range: 2–13 years
No. of pupils: 303
Fees: Day £11,550–£15,615

Ditcham Park School
Ditcham Park, Petersfield,
Hampshire GU31 5RN
Tel: 01730 825659
Headmaster: Mr Graham
Spawforth MA, MEd
Age range: 2–16 years

DURLSTON COURT
For further details see p.216
Becton Lane, Barton-on-Sea, New
Milton, Hampshire BH25 7AQ
Tel: 01425 610010
Email: registrar@durlstoncourt.co.uk
Website: www.durlstoncourt.co.uk
Headmaster: Mr Richard May
Age range: 2–16 years
(Year 9 from 2023)
No. of pupils: 260

Embley
Embley Park, Romsey,
Hampshire SO51 6ZE
Tel: 01794 512206
Headteacher: Mr Cliff Canning
Age range: 2–18 years
No. of pupils: 600
Fees: Day £9,165–£17,004 WB
£29,310 FB £9,598–£33,636

Farleigh School
Red Rice, Andover,
Hampshire SP11 7PW
Tel: 01264 710766
Headmaster: Fr Simon Everson
Age range: 3–13 years
No. of pupils: 460

Farnborough Hill
Farnborough Road, Farnborough,
Hampshire GU14 8AT
Tel: 01252 545197
Head: Mrs A Neil BA, MEd, PGCE
Age range: G11–18 years

Forres Sandle Manor
Fordingbridge, Hampshire SP6 1NS
Tel: 01425 653181
Head of School: Mr Robert Tasker
Age range: 2–16 years
No. of pupils: 145

Glenhurst School
16 Beechworth Road, Havant,
Hampshire PO9 1AX
Tel: 023 9248 4054
Age range: 3 months–5 years

**Grantham Farm Montessori
School & The Children's House**
Grantham Farm, Baughurst,
Tadley, Hampshire RG26 5JS
Tel: 0118 981 5821
Head Teacher: Ms Emma Wetherley
Age range: 2–7 years

Highfield and Brookham Schools
Highfield Lane, Liphook,
Hampshire GU30 7LQ
Tel: 01428 728000
Headteachers: Mr Phillip Evitt MA
(Hons), PGCE & Mrs Sophie Baber
BA (Hons), PGCE, PG Cert
Age range: 2–13 years
No. of pupils: 448

Hurst Lodge School
Yateley Hall, Firgrove Road,
Yateley, Hampshire GU46 6HJ
Tel: 01252 227002
Principal: Ms Victoria Smit
Age range: 4–19 years

Inwoods Small School
Brockwood Park, Bramdean,
Alresford, Hampshire SO24 0LQ
Tel: +44 (0)1962 771065
Age range: 5–11 years

KING EDWARD VI SCHOOL
For further details see p.226
Wilton Road, Southampton,
Hampshire SO15 5UQ
Tel: 023 8070 4561
Email: registrar@kes.hants.sch.uk
Website: kes.school
Head Master: Mr N T Parker
Age range: 11–18 years
No. of pupils: 965
Fees: Day £18,645

Kingscourt School
182 Five Heads Road, Catherington,
Hampshire PO8 9NJ
Tel: 023 9259 3251
Head of School: Amanda Bembridge
Age range: 3–11 years
No. of pupils: 158
Fees: Day £2,856

Lord Wandsworth College
Long Sutton, Hook,
Hampshire RG29 1TA
Tel: 01256 862201
Head of School: Mr Adam Williams
Age range: 11–18 years

Mayville High School
35-37 St Simon's Road, Southsea,
Portsmouth, Hampshire PO5 2PE
Tel: 023 9273 4847
Headteacher: Mrs Rebecca Parkyn
Age range: 2–16 years

Meoncross School
Burnt House Lane, Stubbington,
Fareham, Hampshire PO14 2EF
Tel: 01329 662182
Headmaster: Mr Mark Cripps
Age range: 2–16 years
No. of pupils: 405
Fees: Day £8,736–£12,576

Moyles Court School
Moyles Court, Ringwood,
Hampshire BH24 3NF
Tel: 01425 472856
Headmaster: Mr Richard Milner-Smith
Age range: 2–16 years

Portsmouth High School GDST
Kent Road, Southsea, Portsmouth,
Hampshire PO5 3EQ
Tel: 023 9282 6714
Headmistress: Mrs Jane
Prescott BSc NPQH
Age range: G3–18 years
No. of pupils: 500
Fees: Day £2,574–£4,800

Prince's Mead School
Worthy Park House, Kings Worthy,
Winchester, Hampshire SO21 1AN
Tel: 01962 888000
Headmaster: Mr Peter Thacker
Age range: 3–11 years

Ringwood Waldorf School
Folly Farm Lane, Ashley, Ringwood,
Hampshire BH24 2NN
Tel: 01425 472664
Age range: 3–18 years

Rookwood School
Weyhill Road, Andover,
Hampshire SP10 3AL
Tel: 01264 325900
Headmaster: Mr A Kirk-Burgess
BSc, PGCE, MSc (Oxon)
Age range: 2–18 years
(boarding from 7)

Salesian College
119 Reading Road, Farnborough,
Hampshire GU14 6PA
Tel: 01252 893000
Headmaster: Mr Gerard Owens
Age range: B11–18 years G16–18 years

SHERBORNE HOUSE SCHOOL
For further details see p.244
39 Lakewood Road, Chandlers Ford,
Eastleigh, Hampshire SO53 1EU
Tel: 02380 252440
Email: info@sherbornehouse.co.uk
Website:
www.sherbornehouse.co.uk
Headmaster: Mr Mark Beach
Age range: 6 months–11 years

SHERFIELD SCHOOL
For further details see p.246
South Drive, Sherfield-on-Loddon,
Hook, Hampshire RG27 0HU
Tel: 01256 884800
Email: admissions@
sherfieldschool.co.uk
Website: www.sherfieldschool.co.uk
Headmaster: Mr Nick Brain
BA(Hons), PGCE, MA, NPQH
Age range: 3 months–18
years (boarding from 9)
No. of pupils: 625

St John's College
Grove Road South, Southsea,
Portsmouth, Hampshire PO5 3QW
Tel: 023 9281 5118
Head of School: Mrs Mary Maguire
Age range: 4–18 years

St Neot's School
St Neot's Road, Eversley,
Hampshire RG27 0PN
Tel: 0118 9739650
Headmaster: Mr Jonathan Slot
Age range: 2–13 years

St Nicholas' School
Redfields House, Redfields
Lane, Church Crookham,
Fleet, Hampshire GU52 0RF
Tel: 01252 850121
Headmistress: Dr O Wright
PhD, MA, BA Hons, PGCE
Age range: B3–7 years G3–16 years

St Swithun's Prep
Alresford Road, Winchester,
Hampshire SO21 1HA
Tel: 01962 835750
Head of School: Mr Jonathan Brough
Age range: B3–4 years G3–11 years
No. of pupils: 186

ST SWITHUN'S SCHOOL
For further details see p.254
Alresford Road, Winchester,
Hampshire SO21 1HA
Tel: 01962 835700
Email: office@stswithuns.com
Website: www.stswithuns.com
Head of School: Jane
Gandee MA(Cantab)
Age range: G11–18 years
No. of pupils: 505 VIth137
Fees: Day £22,794 FB £38,340

Stockton House School
Stockton Avenue, Fleet,
Hampshire GU51 4NS
Tel: 01252 616323
Early Years Manager: Mrs
Jenny Bounds BA EYPS
Age range: 2–5 years

**STROUD SCHOOL, KING
EDWARD VI PREPARATORY**
For further details see p.258
Highwood House, Highwood Lane,
Romsey, Hampshire SO51 9ZH
Tel: 01794 513231
Email: registrar@stroud-kes.org.uk
Website: stroud.kes.school
Headmistress: Mrs Rebecca Smith
Age range: 3–13 years
Fees: Day £4,060–£6,515

The Gregg Prep School
17-19 Winn Road, Southampton,
Hampshire SO17 1EJ
Tel: 023 8055 7352
Headteacher: Mr M Pascoe
Age range: 4–11 years

The Gregg School
Townhill Park House, Cutbush Lane,
Southampton, Hampshire SO18 3RR
Tel: 023 8047 2133
Headteacher: Mrs S Sellers
Age range: 11–16 years

The King's School
Lakesmere House, Allington Lane,
Fair Oak, Eastleigh, Southampton,
Hampshire SO50 7DB
Tel: 023 8060 0986
Headteacher: Mrs Heather Bowden
Age range: 4–16 years

The New Forest Small School
1 Southampton Road, Lyndhurst,
Hampshire SO43 7BU
Tel: 02380 284415
Headteacher: Ms Maz Wilberforce
Age range: 3–16 years

The Pilgrims' School
3 The Close, Winchester,
Hampshire SO23 9LT
Tel: 01962 854189
Head: Dr Sarah Essex
Age range: B4–13 years

The Portsmouth Grammar School
High Street, Portsmouth,
Hampshire PO1 2LN
Tel: +44 (0)23 9236 0036
Age range: 2–18 years

Thorngrove School
The Mount, Highclere, Newbury,
Hampshire RG20 9PS
Tel: 01635 253172
Headmaster: Mr Adam King
Age range: 2–13 years

Twyford School
Twyford, Winchester,
Hampshire SO21 1NW
Tel: 01962 712269
Headmaster: Mr Andrew Harvey
Age range: 2–13 years

Walhampton
Walhampton, Lymington,
Hampshire SO41 5ZG
Tel: 01590 613300
Head: Mr Jonny Timms
Age range: 2–13 years
(boarding from 7)

West Hill Park School
St Margaret's Lane, Titchfield,
Hampshire PO14 4BS
Tel: 01329 842356
Headmaster: Mr Chris Ward
Age range: 3–13 years

Winchester College
College Street, Winchester,
Hampshire SO23 9NA
Tel: 01962 621100
Headmaster: Dr. T R Hands
Age range: B13–18 years
(boarding from 13)

Yateley Manor School
51 Reading Road, Yateley,
Hampshire GU46 7UQ
Tel: 01252 405500
Headmaster: Mr Robert Upton
Age range: 3–13 years

Isle of Wight

**Priory School of Our
Lady of Walsingham**
Beatrice Avenue, Whippingham,
Isle of Wight PO32 6LP
Tel: 01983 861222
Headmaster: Mr Edmund Matyjaszek
Age range: 4–18 years
No. of pupils: 170
Fees: Day £6,900–£9,990

RYDE SCHOOL WITH UPPER CHINE
For further details see p.240
Queen's Road, Ryde, Isle
of Wight PO33 3BE
Tel: 01983 562229
Email: admissions@rydeschool.net
Website: www.rydeschool.org.uk
Headmaster: Mr Will Turner
Age range: 2–18 years
(boarding from 10)
No. of pupils: 795
Fees: Day £2,780–£4,970 WB
£9,600–£9,765 FB £10,780–£10,945

Kent

Ashford School
East Hill, Ashford, Kent TN24 8PB
Tel: +44 (0)1233 625171
Head: Mr Michael Hall
Age range: 3 months–18 years (boarding from 11)
No. of pupils: 916 VIth127
Fees: Day £10,815–£18,294 WB £26,775 FB £38,778

Beech Grove School
Forest Drive, Nonington, Dover, Kent CT15 4FB
Tel: 01304 843 707
Headteacher: Timothy Maas
Age range: 6–18 years

Beechwood School
12 Pembury Road, Tunbridge Wells, Kent TN2 3QD
Tel: 01892 532747
Headmaster: Mr Justin Foster-Gandey
Age range: 3–18 years

Benenden School
Cranbrook, Kent TN17 4AA
Tel: 01580 240592
Headmistress: Ms Samantha Price
Age range: G11–18 years (boarding from 11)

BETHANY SCHOOL
For further details see p.202
Curtisden Green, Goudhurst, Cranbrook, Kent TN17 1LB
Tel: 01580 211273
Email: registrar@bethanyschool.org.uk
Website: www.bethanyschool.org.uk
Headmaster: Mr Francie Healy BSc, HDipEd, NPQH
Age range: 11–18 years
No. of pupils: 346 VIth77
Fees: Day £18,795–£20,760 WB £29,175–£32,205 FB £31,455–£35,400

Bronte School
7 Pelham Road, Gravesend, Kent DA11 0HU
Tel: 01474 533805
Headmistress: Ms Emma Wood
Age range: 4–11 years

Bryony School
Marshall Road, Rainham, Gillingham, Kent ME8 0AJ
Tel: 01634 231511
Head of School: Mrs N Gee
Age range: 2–11 years

CATS Canterbury
68 New Dover Road, Canterbury, Kent CT1 3LQ
Tel: +44 (0)1227866540
Principal: Severine Collins
Age range: 14–21 years
No. of pupils: 450
Fees: Day £17,370–£27,990 FB £13,230–£19,140

Chartfield School
45 Minster Road, Westgate on Sea, Kent CT8 8DA
Tel: 01843 831716
Head & Proprietor: Miss L P Shipley
Age range: 3–11 years

Cobham Hall School
Brewers Road, Cobham, Kent DA12 3BL
Tel: 01474 823371
Headteacher: Mrs Wendy Barrett
Age range: G11–18 years (boarding from 11)
No. of pupils: 150
Fees: Day £6,804–£8,246 FB £10,279–£12,831

Dover College
Effingham Crescent, Dover, Kent CT17 9RH
Tel: 01304 205969
Head of School: Mr Simon Fisher
Age range: 3–18 years

Dulwich Prep Cranbrook
Coursehorn, Cranbrook, Kent TN17 3NP
Tel: 01580 712179
Headmaster: Mr Paul David BEd(Hons)
Age range: 2–16 years

Earlscliffe
29 Shorncliffe Road, Folkestone, Kent CT20 2NB
Tel: +44 (0)1303 253951
Director: Mr Tim Fish
Age range: 15–19 years

Elliott Park School
18-20 Marina Drive, Minster, Sheerness, Kent ME12 2DP
Tel: 01795 873372
Head Teacher: Ms Samantha Dolman
Age range: 3–11 years

Fosse Bank School
Mountains, Noble Tree Road, Hildenborough, Tonbridge, Kent TN11 8ND
Tel: 01732 834212
Headmistress: Miss Alison Cordingley
Age range: 2–11 years

Gad's Hill School
Gravesend Road, Higham, Rochester, Kent ME3 7PA
Tel: 01474 822366
Headmaster: Mr Paul Savage
Age range: 3–16 years

Haddon Dene School
57 Gladstone Road, Broadstairs, Kent CT10 2HY
Tel: 01843 861176
Headmistress: Mrs Joanne Parpworth
Age range: 3–11 years

Hilden Grange School
62 Dry Hill Park Road, Tonbridge, Kent TN10 3BX
Tel: 01732 352706
Headmaster: Mr J Withers BA(Hons)
Age range: 3–13 years
No. of pupils: 311

Hilden Oaks Preparatory School & Nursery
38 Dry Hill Park Road, Tonbridge, Kent TN10 3BU
Tel: 01732 353941
Head of School: Mrs. K Joiner
Age range: 3 months–11 years

Holmewood House School
Barrow Lane, Langton Green, Tunbridge Wells, Kent TN3 0EB
Tel: 01892 860000
Head of School: Mrs Ruth O'Sullivan
Age range: 3–13 years
No. of pupils: 450

Kent College Pembury
Old Church Road, Pembury, Tunbridge Wells, Kent TN2 4AX
Tel: +44 (0)1892 822006
Head of School: Miss Katrina Handford
Age range: G3–18 years (boarding from 8)
No. of pupils: 500
Fees: Day £22,575 WB £28,200 FB £35,700

KENT COLLEGE, CANTERBURY
For further details see p.224
Whitstable Road, Canterbury, Kent CT2 9DT
Tel: +44 (0)1227 763 231
Email: admissions@kentcollege.co.uk
Website: www.kentcollege.com
Head of Kent College: Mr Mark Turnbull
Age range: 3 months–18 years (boarding from 8 years)
No. of pupils: 818
Fees: Day £3,855–£6,932 FB £9,326–£12,883

KING'S SCHOOL ROCHESTER
For further details see p.230
Satis House, Boley Hill, Rochester, Kent ME1 1TE
Tel: 01634 888555
Email: admissions@kings-rochester.co.uk
Website: www.kings-rochester.co.uk
Principal: Mr B Charles
Age range: 3–18 years
No. of pupils: 638 VIth101
Fees: Day £3,770–£7,175 FB £8,175–£11,775

Lorenden Preparatory School
Painter's Forstal, Faversham, Kent ME13 0EN
Tel: 01795 590030
Head of School: Mr Richard McIntosh
Age range: 3–11 years
No. of pupils: 122
Fees: Day £3,085–£4,485

Marlborough House School
High Street, Hawkhurst, Kent TN18 4PY
Tel: 01580 753555
Head: Mr Eddy Newton
Age range: 2–13 years
No. of pupils: 250
Fees: Day £9,165–£18,690

NORTHBOURNE PARK SCHOOL
For further details see p.236
Betteshanger, Deal, Kent CT14 0NW
Tel: 01304 611215
Email: admissions@northbournepark.com
Website: www.northbournepark.com
Headmaster: Mr Sebastian Rees BA(Hons), PGCE, NPQH
Age range: 2–13 years (boarding from 7)
No. of pupils: 188
Fees: Day £9,243–£17,607 WB £22,161 FB £25,659

OneSchool Global UK Maidstone Campus
Heath Road, Maidstone, Kent ME17 4HT
Tel: 03000 700 507
Age range: 7–18 years

Radnor House, Sevenoaks
Combe Bank Drive,
Sevenoaks, Kent TN14 6AE
Tel: 01959 563720
Head of School: Mr Fraser Halliwell
Age range: 2–18 years

Rochester Independent College
254 St Margaret's Banks,
Rochester, Kent ME1 1HY
Tel: +44 (0)163 482 8115
Head of School: Mr Alistair Brownlow
Age range: 11–18 years

Rose Hill School
Coniston Avenue, Tunbridge
Wells, Kent TN4 9SY
Tel: 01892 525591
Head: Ms Emma Neville
Age range: 3–13 years

Russell House School
Station Road, Otford,
Sevenoaks, Kent TN14 5QU
Tel: 01959 522352
Headmaster: Mr Craig McCarthy
Age range: 2–11 years

Sackville School
Tonbridge Road, Hildenborough,
Tonbridge, Kent TN11 9HN
Tel: 01732 838888
Headteacher: Ms Leoni Ellis
Age range: 11–18 years

Saint Ronan's School
Water Lane, Hawkhurst, Kent TN18 5DJ
Tel: 01580 752271
Headmaster: Mr William
Trelawny-Vernon BSc(Hons)
Age range: 3–13 years

Sevenoaks Preparatory School
Godden Green, Sevenoaks,
Kent TN15 0JU
Tel: 01732 762336
Headmaster: Mr Luke Harrison
Age range: 2–13 years

Sevenoaks School
High Street, Sevenoaks, Kent TN13 1HU
Tel: +44 (0)1732 455133
Head of School: Mr Jesse R
Elzinga AB MSt FCCT
Age range: 11–18 years
No. of pupils: 1164
Fees: Day £25,020–£28,413
FB £39,960–£43,353

Solefield School
Solefields Road, Sevenoaks,
Kent TN13 1PH
Tel: 01732 452142
Headmistress: Ms Helen McClure
Age range: B4–13 years

Somerhill
Tonbridge, Kent TN11 0NJ
Tel: 01732 352124
Principal: Mr Duncan Sinclair
Age range: 2–13 years

Spring Grove School
Harville Road, Wye, Kent TN25 5EZ
Tel: 01233 812337
Head of School: Mrs Therésa Jaggard
Age range: 2–11 years
No. of pupils: 226
Fees: Day £9,459–£13,290

St Andrew's School
24-28 Watts Avenue, Rochester,
Medway, Kent ME1 1SA
Tel: 01634 843479
Principal: Mrs E Steinmann-Gilbert
Age range: 2–11 years

St Edmund's School
St Thomas Hill, Canterbury,
Kent CT2 8HU
Tel: 01227 475601
Head: Mr Edward O'Connor MA
(Cantab), MPhil (Oxon), MEd (Cantab)
Age range: 2–18 years
(boarding from 11)
No. of pupils: 602

St Faith's Prep
5 The Street, Ash, Canterbury,
Kent CT3 2HH
Tel: 01304 813409
Headmaster: Mr Lawrence Groves
Age range: 2–11 years

ST LAWRENCE COLLEGE
For further details see p.252
College Road, Ramsgate,
Kent CT11 7AE
Tel: 01843 572931
Email: admissions@slcuk.com
Website: www.slcuk.com
Head of College: Mr Barney Durrant
Age range: 3–18 years
No. of pupils: 585
Fees: Day £8,394–£18,558
FB £29,454–£38,952

St Michael's Preparatory School
Otford Court, Row Dow, Otford,
Sevenoaks, Kent TN14 5RY
Tel: 01959 522137
Head: Mr Nik Pears
Age range: 2–13 years

Steephill School
Off Castle Hill, Fawkham,
Longfield, Kent DA3 7BG
Tel: 01474 702107
Head: Mr John Abbott
Age range: 3–11 years

Sutton Valence Preparatory School
Church Road, Chart Sutton,
Maidstone, Kent ME17 3RF
Tel: 01622 842117
Head: Miss C Corkran
Age range: 2–11 years

Sutton Valence School
North Street, Sutton Valence,
Kent ME17 3HL
Tel: 01622 845200
Headmaster: Mr James A Thomas
MA (Cantab) MA (London) NPQH
Age range: 11–18 years
(boarding from 11)
No. of pupils: 557

The Granville School
2 Bradbourne Park Road,
Sevenoaks, Kent TN13 3LJ
Tel: 01732 453039
Headmistress: Mrs Louise
Lawrance B. Prim. Ed. (Hons)
Age range: B3–4 years G3–11 years

The Junior King's School, Canterbury
Milner Court, Sturry,
Canterbury, Kent CT2 0AY
Tel: 01227 714000
Head of School: Ms Emma Károlyi
Age range: 3–13 years

The King's School, Canterbury
Lattergate Office, 25 The Precincts,
Canterbury, Kent CT1 2ES
Tel: 01227 595501
Head of School: Ms Jude Lowson
Age range: 13–18 years

The Mead School
16 Frant Road, Tunbridge
Wells, Kent TN2 5SN
Tel: 01892 525837
Headmistress: Ms Catherine
Openshaw
Age range: 3–11 years

THE NEW BEACON SCHOOL
For further details see p.262
Brittains Lane, Sevenoaks,
Kent TN13 2PB
Tel: 01732 452131
Email: admin@newbeacon.org.uk
Website: www.newbeacon.org.uk
Headmaster: Mr Mike Piercy
Age range: B3–13 years G3–4 years
No. of pupils: 350

Tonbridge School
High Street, Tonbridge, Kent TN9 1JP
Tel: 01732 304297
Headmaster: Mr James
Priory MA (Oxon)
Age range: B13–18 years
No. of pupils: 798
Fees: Day £33,636 FB £44,835

Walthamstow Hall School
Holly Bush Lane, Sevenoaks,
Kent TN13 3UL
Tel: 01732 451334
Headmistress: Miss Stephanie Ferro
Age range: G3–18 years

Wellesley House
114 Ramsgate Road,
Broadstairs, Kent CT10 2DG
Tel: 01843 862991
Headmaster: Mr G D Franklin
Age range: 2–13 years

Surrey

Aberdour School
Brighton Road, Burgh Heath,
Tadworth, Surrey KT20 6AJ
Tel: +44 (0)1737 354119
Headmaster: Mr S. D. Collins
Age range: 2–11 years
No. of pupils: 343
Fees: Day £4,710–£16,272

ACS Cobham International School
Heywood, Portsmouth Road,
Cobham, Surrey KT11 1BL
Tel: +44 (0) 1932 867251
Head of School: Mr Barnaby Sandow
Age range: 2–18 years

ACS Egham International School
London Road, Egham, Surrey TW20 0HS
Tel: +44 (0) 1784 430800
Head of School: Mr Jeremy Lewis
Age range: 4–18 years

Aldro School
Lombard Street, Shackleford,
Godalming, Surrey GU8 6AS
Tel: 01483 810266
Headmaster: Mr Chris Carlier
Age range: 7–13 years

Amesbury School
Hazel Grove, Hindhead,
Surrey GU26 6BL
Tel: 01428 604322
Head of School: Mr Jonathan Whybrow
Age range: 2–13 years

Banstead Preparatory School
Sutton Lane, Banstead, Surrey SM7 3RA
Tel: 01737 363601
Head of School: Mr Jon Chesworth
Age range: 2–11 years

Barfield School
Guildford Road, Runfold,
Farnham, Surrey GU10 1PB
Tel: 01252 782271
Headmaster: Mr Andy Boyle
Age range: 2–11 years

Barrow Hills School
Roke Lane, Witley, Godalming,
Surrey GU8 5NY
Tel: +44 (0)1428 683639
Headmaster: Mr Philip Oldroyd
Age range: 2–13 years
No. of pupils: 216
Fees: Day £16,785

Belmont School
Pasturewood Road, Holmbury St
Mary, Dorking, Surrey RH5 6LQ
Tel: 01306 730852
Headmistress: Mrs Helen Skrine
BA, PGCE, NPQH, FRSA
Age range: 3–16 years
No. of pupils: 200

Bishopsgate School
Bishopsgate Road, Englefield
Green, Egham, Surrey TW20 0YJ
Tel: 01784 432109
Headmaster: Mr R Williams
Age range: 3–13 years
No. of pupils: 370

Box Hill School
London Road, Mickleham,
Dorking, Surrey RH5 6EA
Tel: 01372 373382
Headmaster: Cory Lowde
Age range: 11–18 years
No. of pupils: 425
Fees: Day £20,820 WB £30,480

Caterham School
Harestone Valley Road,
Caterham, Surrey CR3 6YA
Tel: 01883 343028
Headmaster: Mr C. W.
Jones MA(Cantab)
Age range: 3–18 years

Charterhouse
Godalming, Surrey GU7 2DX
Tel: +44 (0)1483 291501
Head: Dr Alex Peterken
Age range: B13–18 years (boarding
from 13) G16–18 years
No. of pupils: 895

Chinthurst School
52 Tadworth Street, Tadworth,
Surrey KT20 5QZ
Tel: 01737 812011
Head: Miss Catherine Trundle
Age range: 3–11 years

City of London Freemen's School
Ashtead Park, Ashtead, Surrey KT21 1ET
Tel: +44 (0)1372 822400
Headmaster: Mr Roland J. Martin
Age range: 7–18 years

**CLAREMONT FAN
COURT SCHOOL**
For further details see p.210
Claremont Drive, Esher,
Surrey KT10 9LY
Tel: 01372 473794
Email: admissions@
claremont.surrey.sch.uk
Website:
www.claremontfancourt.co.uk
Head: Mr William Brierly
Age range: 2–18 years
No. of pupils: 1100

Coworth Flexlands School
Valley End, Chobham, Surrey GU24 8TE
Tel: 01276 855707
Head of School: Miss Nicola Cowell
Age range: B2–7 years G2–11 years
No. of pupils: 120

CRANLEIGH SCHOOL
For further details see p.214
Horseshoe Lane, Cranleigh,
Surrey GU6 8QQ
Tel: +44 (0) 1483 273666
Email: admissions@cranleigh.org
Website: www.cranleigh.org
Headmaster: Mr Martin
Reader MA, MPhil, MBA
Age range: 7–18 years
(including Prep School)
No. of pupils: 683 VIth256
Fees: Day £35,175 FB £42,720

Cranmore School
Epsom Road, West Horsley,
Surrey KT24 6AT
Tel: 01483 280340
Headmaster: Mr Barry Everitt
Age range: 2–18 years

Danes Hill School
Leatherhead Road, Oxshott,
Surrey KT22 0JG
Tel: 01372 842509
Head of School: Mrs Maxine Shaw
Age range: 3–13 years
No. of pupils: 725
Fees: Day £6,981–£20,340

Danesfield Manor School
Rydens Avenue, Walton-on-
Thames, Surrey KT12 3JB
Tel: 01932 220930
Head Teacher: Mrs Jo Smith
Age range: 2–11 years

Downsend School
1 Leatherhead Road,
Leatherhead, Surrey KT22 8TJ
Tel: 01372 372197
Headmaster: Mr Ian Thorpe
Age range: 2–16 years
No. of pupils: 792
Fees: Day £11,970–£17,985

Duke of Kent School
Peaslake Road, Ewhurst,
Surrey GU6 7NS
Tel: 01483 277313
Head: Mrs Sue Knox BA(Hons) MBA MEd
Age range: 3–16 years
No. of pupils: 316
Fees: Day £2,740–£6,540

Dunottar School
High Trees Road, Reigate,
Surrey RH2 7EL
Tel: 01737 761945
Headmaster: Mr Mark Tottman
Age range: 11–18 years

Edgeborough
84 Frensham Road, Frensham,
Farnham, Surrey GU10 3AH
Tel: 01252 792495
Headmaster: Mr Daniel Cox
Age range: 2–13 years
(boarding from 7)
No. of pupils: 370

Epsom College
College Road, Epsom, Surrey KT17 4JQ
Tel: 01372 821000
Head of School: Ms Emma Pattison
Age range: 11–18 years
(boarding from 13)

Essendene Lodge School
Essendene Road, Caterham,
Surrey CR3 5PB
Tel: 01883 348349
Headteacher: Mrs K Ali
Age range: 2–11 years

Ewell Castle School
Church Street, Ewell, Epsom,
Surrey KT17 2AW
Tel: 020 8393 1413
Principal: Mr Silas Edmonds
Age range: 3–18 years
No. of pupils: 670
Fees: Day £5,382–£18,141
Ⓐ Ⓔ ➷ 16

Feltonfleet School
Byfleet Road, Cobham, Surrey KT11 1DR
Tel: 01932 862264
Headmistress: Mrs Shelley Lance
Age range: 3–13 years
(boarding from 7)
No. of pupils: 492
🏫 Ⓔ ➷

Frensham Heights
Rowledge, Farnham, Surrey GU10 4EA
Tel: 01252 792561
Head: Mr Rick Clarke
Age range: 3–18 years
(boarding from 11)
👥 Ⓐ 🏫 Ⓔ ➷ 16

Glenesk School
Ockham Road North, East
Horsley, Surrey KT24 6NS
Tel: 01483 282329
Headmistress: Mrs Sarah Bradley
Age range: 2–7 years
No. of pupils: 100
Fees: Day £11,658–£13,176
Ⓔ ➷

GORDON'S SCHOOL
For further details see p.222
West End, Woking, Surrey GU24 9PT
Tel: 01276 858084
Email: registrar@gordons.school
Website: www.gordons.school
Head Teacher: Andrew Moss MEd
Age range: 11–18 years
No. of pupils: 938 VIth317
Fees: Day £9,081 WB
£18,222 FB £19,446
Ⓐ 🏫 Ⓔ ➷ 16

Greenfield School
Old Woking Road, Woking,
Surrey GU22 8HY
Tel: 01483 772525
Headmistress: Mrs. Tania Botting MEd
Age range: 6 months–11 years
No. of pupils: 335
Ⓔ ➷

Guildford High School
London Road, Guildford,
Surrey GU1 1SJ
Tel: 01483 561440
Headmistress: Mrs F J Boulton BSc, MA
Age range: G4–18 years
👥 Ⓐ Ⓔ 16

Hall Grove School
London Road, Bagshot,
Surrey GU19 5HZ
Tel: 01276 473059
Principal: Mr Alastair Graham
Age range: 3–13 years
(boarding from 8)
🏫

Halstead Preparatory School
Woodham Rise, Woking,
Surrey GU21 4EE
Tel: 01483 772682
Head: Mrs S Maher BSc
Age range: G2–11 years
👥 ➷

Hampton Court House
Hampton Court Road, East
Molesey, Surrey KT8 9BS
Tel: +44 (0)20 8943 0889
Headteacher: Dr Adrian Rainbow
Age range: 3 months–18 years
No. of pupils: 300
Fees: Day £14,637–£20,895
Ⓐ

Hazelwood School
Wolf's Hill, Limpsfield, Oxted,
Surrey RH8 0QU
Tel: 01883 712194
Head: Mrs Lindie Louw
Age range: 3 months–13 years
➷

Hoe Bridge School
Hoe Place, Old Woking Road,
Woking, Surrey GU22 8JE
Tel: 01483 760018
Headmaster: Mr C Webster
MA BSc (Hons) PGCE
Age range: 2–16 years
➷

Hurtwood House
Holmbury St Mary, Dorking,
Surrey RH5 6NU
Tel: 01483 279000
Principal: Mr Cosmo Jackson
Age range: 16–18 years
No. of pupils: 360
Fees: Day £29,748 FB £44,622
16 Ⓐ 🏫

KING EDWARD'S WITLEY
For further details see p.228
Petworth Road, Godalming,
Surrey GU8 5SG
Tel: 01428 686735
Email: admissions@kesw.org
Website: www.kesw.org
Head: Mrs Joanna Wright
Age range: 11–18 years
No. of pupils: 440
👥 Ⓐ 🏫 Ⓔ IB ➷ 16

Kingswood House School
56 West Hill, Epsom, Surrey KT19 8LG
Tel: 01372 723590
Headmaster: Mr Duncan
Murphy BA (Hons), MEd, FRSA
Age range: 4–16 years
No. of pupils: 250
Ⓔ ➷

Lingfield College
Racecourse Road, Lingfield,
Surrey RH7 6PH
Tel: 01342 832407
Headmaster: Mr R Bool B.A. Hons, MBA
Age range: 2–18 years
No. of pupils: 935
Fees: Day £11,250–£21,801
Ⓐ Ⓔ ➷ 16

Little Downsend Ashtead
Ashtead Lodge, 22 Oakfield
Road, Ashtead, Surrey KT21 2RE
Tel: 01372 385439
Head of School: Ms Vanessa Conlan
Age range: 2–6 years
➷

Little Downsend Epsom
Epsom Lodge, 6 Norman Avenue,
Epsom, Surrey KT17 3AB
Tel: 01372 385438
Head of School: Ms Vanessa Conlan
Age range: 2–6 years
➷

Little Downsend Leatherhead
13 Epsom Road, Leatherhead,
Surrey KT22 8ST
Tel: 01372 385437
Head of School: Ms Vanessa Conlan
Age range: 2–6 years
➷

Longacre School
Hullbrook Lane, Shamley Green,
Guildford, Surrey GU5 0NQ
Tel: 01483 893225
Head of School: Mr Matthew Bryan
MA(Cantab.), MA(Oxon.), MSc, FRSA
Age range: 2–11 years
No. of pupils: 267
Fees: Day £11,355–£17,250
Ⓔ ➷

Lyndhurst School
36 The Avenue, Camberley,
Surrey GU15 3NE
Tel: 01276 22895
Head: Mr A Rudkin BEd(Hons)
Age range: 3–11 years
No. of pupils: 126
Ⓔ ➷

**MANOR HOUSE SCHOOL,
BOOKHAM**
For further details see p.234
Manor House Lane, Little Bookham,
Leatherhead, Surrey KT23 4EN
Tel: 01372 457077
Email: admin@
manorhouseschool.org
Website:
www.manorhouseschool.org
Headteacher: Ms Tracey
Fantham BA (Hons) MA NPQH
Age range: B2–6 years G2–16 years
No. of pupils: 300
Fees: Day £9,747–£18,315
👥 Ⓔ ➷

Micklefield School
10 Somers Road, Reigate,
Surrey RH2 9DU
Tel: 01737 224212
Head: Mr R Ardé
Age range: 3–11 years
No. of pupils: 210
Fees: Day £10,965–£13,935
Ⓔ ➷

Milbourne Lodge School
Arbrook Lane, Esher, Surrey KT10 9EG
Tel: 01372 462737
Head: Mrs Judy Waite
Age range: 4–13 years
No. of pupils: 276
Fees: Day £13,695–£17,205
Ⓔ

Notre Dame School
Cobham, Surrey KT11 1HA
Tel: 01932 869990
Head of Seniors: Mrs Anna King
MEd, MA (Cantab), PGCE
Age range: B2–7 years G2–18 years
No. of pupils: 600
👥 Ⓐ Ⓔ ➷ 16

Oakhyrst Grange School
160 Stanstead Road,
Caterham, Surrey CR3 6AF
Tel: 01883 343344
Headmaster: Mr Alex Gear
Age range: 4–11 years
No. of pupils: 152
Fees: Day £1,472–£3,414

OneSchool Global UK Hindhead Campus
Tilford Road, Hindhead,
Surrey GU26 6SJ
Tel: 01428 601800
Age range: 7–18 years

OneSchool Global UK Kenley Campus
Victor Beamish Avenue,
Kenley, Surrey CR3 5FX
Tel: 01883 338634
Age range: 7–18 years

PARKSIDE SCHOOL
For further details see p.238
The Manor, Stoke d'Abernon,
Cobham, Surrey KT11 3PX
Tel: 01932 862749
Email: office@parkside-school.co.uk
Website: www.parkside-school.co.uk
Headteacher: Ms Nicole Janssen
Age range: B2–13 years G2–4 years
No. of pupils: 270

Prior's Field
Priorsfield Road, Godalming,
Surrey GU7 2RH
Tel: 01483 810551
Age range: G11–18 years
(boarding from 11)
No. of pupils: 450
Fees: Day £18,900 FB £30,825

Reed's School
Sandy Lane, Cobham, Surrey KT11 2ES
Tel: 01932 869001
Headmaster: Mr Mark Hoskins BA MA MSc
Age range: B11–18 years (boarding from 11) G16–18 years

Reigate Grammar School
Reigate Road, Reigate, Surrey RH2 0QS
Tel: 01737 222231
Headmaster: Mr Shaun Fenton MA (Oxon) MEd (Oxon)
Age range: 11–18 years
No. of pupils: 969 VIth262
Fees: Day £19,140–£19,350

Reigate St Mary's Prep & Choir School
Chart Lane, Reigate, Surrey RH2 7RN
Tel: 01737 244880
Headmaster: Mr Marcus Culverwell MA
Age range: 2–11 years

RGS Prep
Maori Road, Guildford, Surrey GU1 2EL
Tel: 01483 880650
Head of School: Mr Toby Freeman-Day
Age range: B3–11 years
Fees: Day £15,999

Ripley Court School
Rose Lane, Ripley, Surrey GU23 6NE
Tel: 01483 225217
Headmistress: Ms Aislinn Clarke
Age range: 3–13 years

Rowan Preparatory School
6 Fitzalan Road, Claygate,
Surrey KT10 0LX
Tel: 01372 462627
Headmistress: Mrs Susan Clarke BEd, NPQH
Age range: G2–11 years
No. of pupils: 317
Fees: Day £11,526–£15,294

Royal Alexandra and Albert School
Gatton Park, Reigate, Surrey RH2 0TD
Tel: 01737 649 000
Headmaster: Mr Mark Dixon
Age range: 7–18 years

Royal Grammar School, Guildford
High Street, Guildford, Surrey GU1 3BB
Tel: 01483 880600
Headmaster: Dr J M Cox BSc, PhD
Age range: B11–18 years
No. of pupils: 940
Fees: Day £19,035

Rydes Hill Preparatory School
Rydes Hill House, Aldershot Road,
Guildford, Surrey GU2 8BP
Tel: 01483 563160
Headmistress: Mrs Sarah Norville
Age range: B3–7 years G3–11 years
No. of pupils: 180
Fees: Day £3,006–£4,565

Shrewsbury House Pre-Preparatory School
22 Milbourne Lane, Esher,
Surrey KT10 9EA
Tel: 01372 462781
Head: Mr Jon Akhurst BA (Hons) PGCE
Age range: 3–7 years
Fees: Day £6,225–£13,740

SIR WILLIAM PERKINS'S SCHOOL
For further details see p.248
Guildford Road, Chertsey,
Surrey KT16 9BN
Tel: 01932 574900
Email: reg@swps.org.uk
Website: www.swps.org.uk
Head: Mr C C Muller
Age range: G11–18 years
No. of pupils: 600
Fees: Day £6,246

St Catherine's, Bramley
Station Road, Bramley,
Guildford, Surrey GU5 0DF
Tel: 01483 899609
Headmistress: Alice Phillips
Age range: G4–18 years
(boarding from 11)
Fees: Day £9,240–£18,885 FB £31,125

St Christopher's School
6 Downs Road, Epsom, Surrey KT18 5HE
Tel: 01372 721807
Headteacher: Mrs A C Thackray MA, BA(Hons)
Age range: 3–7 years
No. of pupils: 137
Fees: Day £10,485

St Edmund's School
Portsmouth Road, Hindhead,
Surrey GU26 6BH
Tel: 01428 604808
Headmaster: Mr A J Walliker MA(Cantab), MBA, PGCE
Age range: 2–16 years

St George's College
Weybridge Road, Addlestone,
Weybridge, Surrey KT15 2QS
Tel: 01932 839300
Headmistress: Mrs Rachel Owens
Age range: 11–18 years
No. of pupils: 909 VIth250
Fees: Day £17,655–£20,100

St George's Junior School
Thames Street, Weybridge,
Surrey KT13 8NL
Tel: 01932 839400
Head Master: Mr Antony Hudson MA (CANTAB), PGCE, NPQH
Age range: 3–11 years
No. of pupils: 644
Fees: Day £5,640–£14,640

St Hilary's School
Holloway Hill, Godalming,
Surrey GU7 1RZ
Tel: 01483 416551
Headmistress: Mrs Jane Whittingham BEdCert, ProfPracSpLD
Age range: 2–11 years
No. of pupils: 250
Fees: Day £10,092–£14,850

St Ives School
Three Gates Lane, Haslemere,
Surrey GU27 2ES
Tel: 01428 643734
Headteacher: Kay Goldsworthy
Age range: 2–11 years

St John's School
Epsom Road, Leatherhead,
Surrey KT22 8SP
Tel: 01372 373000
Head of School: Mrs Rowena Cole
Age range: 11–18 years
(boarding from 11)
No. of pupils: 840
Fees: Day £22,500–£25,560 WB £32,441

St Teresa's Effingham (Preparatory School)
Effingham, Surrey RH5 6ST
Tel: 01372 453456
Headteacher: Ms Sarah Conrad
Age range: B2–4 years G2–11 years

St Teresa's Effingham (Senior School)
Effingham, Surrey RH5 6ST
Tel: +44 (0)1372 452037
Headmistress: Ms Claire McShane
Age range: G11–18 years
(boarding from 11)

ST. ANDREW'S SCHOOL
For further details see p.256
Church Hill House, Horsell,
Woking, Surrey GU21 4QW
Tel: 01483 760943
Email: admissions@st-
andrews.woking.sch.uk
Website:
www.st-andrews.woking.sch.uk
Headmaster: Mr D Fitzgerald
Age range: 3–13 years
No. of pupils: 310
Fees: Day £4,392–£17,280

**TASIS The American
School in England**
Coldharbour Lane, Thorpe,
Surrey TW20 8TE
Tel: +44 (0)1932 582316
Head of School: Mr Bryan Nixon
Age range: 3–18 years
(boarding from 12)
No. of pupils: 620
Fees: Day £12,770–£27,430 FB £50,850

The Hawthorns School
Pendell Court, Bletchingley,
Redhill, Surrey RH1 4QJ
Tel: 01883 743048
Head of School: Mr Adrian Floyd
Age range: 2–13 years

THE ROYAL SCHOOL, HASLEMERE
For further details see p.266
Farnham Lane, Haslemere,
Surrey GU27 1HQ
Tel: 01428 605805
Email: admissions@
royal.surrey.sch.uk
Website: www.royal-school.org
Head: Mrs Pippa Smithson
BA (Hons), PGCE, MEd
Age range: 6 weeks–18
years (boarding from 11)
No. of pupils: 315
Fees: Day £3,681–£6,414
WB £9,435 FB £10,731

Tormead School
27 Cranley Road, Guildford,
Surrey GU1 2JD
Tel: 01483 575101
Headmistress: Mrs Christina Foord
Age range: G4–18 years
No. of pupils: 760 VIth120
Fees: Day £8,385–£15,915

Warlingham Park School
Chelsham Common,
Warlingham, Surrey CR6 9PB
Tel: 01883 626844
Headmaster: Mrs S S Buist
Age range: 2–11 years
No. of pupils: 96
Fees: Day £4,230–£8,565

WESTON GREEN SCHOOL
For further details see p.272
Weston Green Road, Thames
Ditton, Surrey KT7 0JN
Tel: 020 8398 2778
Email: info@
westongreenschool.org.uk
Website:
www.westongreenschool.org.uk
Head Teacher: Mrs Sarah
Evans BA Hons, NPQH
Age range: 2–11 years
No. of pupils: 195

Woldingham School
Marden Park, Woldingham,
Surrey CR3 7YA
Tel: 01883 349431
Head of School: Dr James Whitehead
Age range: G11–18 years
(boarding from 11)
No. of pupils: 626
Fees: Day £23,160–£25,365
FB £34,170–£42,330

Woodcote House School
Snows Ride, Windlesham,
Surrey GU20 6PF
Tel: 01276 472115
Headmaster: Mr D.M.K. Paterson
Age range: B7–13 years

Yehudi Menuhin School
Stoke Road, Stoke d'Abernon,
Cobham, Surrey KT11 3QQ
Tel: 01932 864739
Interim Head: Richard Tanner
Age range: 7–19 years
No. of pupils: 80 VIth36
Fees: FB £34,299

West Sussex

Ardingly College
College Road, Ardingly, Haywards
Heath, West Sussex RH17 6SQ
Tel: +44 (0)1444 893320
Headmaster: Mr Ben Figgis
Age range: 13–18 years

**Ardingly College
Preparatory School**
College Road, Haywards Heath,
West Sussex RH17 6SQ
Tel: +44 (0)1444 893320
Head of Prep School: Mr Harry Hastings
Age range: 2–13 years

Brambletye
Brambletye, East Grinstead,
West Sussex RH19 3PD
Tel: 01342 321004
Headmaster: Will Brooks
Age range: 2–13 years

BURGESS HILL GIRLS
For further details see p.206
Keymer Road, Burgess Hill,
West Sussex RH15 0EG
Tel: 01444 241050
Email: admissions@
burgesshillgirls.com
Website: burgesshillgirls.com
Head of School: Lars Fox
Age range: B2–4 years G2–18 years
No. of pupils: 557 VIth70
Fees: Day £9,825–£22,410
FB £34,560–£39,900

Christ's Hospital
Horsham, West Sussex RH13 0LJ
Tel: 01403 211293
Head Teacher: Mr Simon Reid
Age range: 11–18 years
No. of pupils: 900
Fees: Day £18,510–£23,310 FB £35,850

Conifers School
Egmont Road, Midhurst,
West Sussex GU29 9BG
Tel: 01730 813243
Headmistress: Mrs Emma Smyth
Age range: 2–13 years
No. of pupils: 104
Fees: Day £7,350–£9,750

Copthorne Prep School
Effingham Lane, Copthorne,
West Sussex RH10 3HR
Tel: 01342 712311
Headmaster: Mr Chris Jones
Age range: 2–13 years
No. of pupils: 340
Fees: Day £9,750–£16,740
WB £20,400 FB £25,500

Cottesmore School
Buchan Hill, Pease Pottage,
West Sussex RH11 9AU
Tel: 01293 520648
Head: T F Rogerson
Age range: 4–13 years
No. of pupils: 170
Fees: Day £3,199–£4,267 FB £9,095

Cumnor House Sussex
London Road, Danehill, Haywards
Heath, West Sussex RH17 7HT
Tel: 01825 790347
Headmaster: Mr Fergus Llewellyn
Age range: 2–13 years
(boarding from 11)

Dorset House School
The Manor, Church Lane, Bury,
Pulborough, West Sussex RH20 1PB
Tel: 01798 831456
Headmaster: Mr Matt Thomas
Med BA Ed (Hons) (Exeter) FRGS
Age range: 4–13 years
No. of pupils: 140
Fees: Day £9,315–£18,945
WB £1,258–£4,488

FARLINGTON SCHOOL
For further details see p.220
Strood Park, Horsham,
West Sussex RH12 3PN
Tel: 01403 254967
Email: office@farlingtonschool.com
Website: www.farlingtonschool.com
Headmaster: Mr James Passam
Age range: 4–18 years
No. of pupils: 340
Fees: Day £2,050–£6,350
WB £10,500 FB £11,300

Great Ballard School
Eartham House, Eartham, Nr
Chichester, West Sussex PO18 0LR
Tel: 01243 814236
Head of School: Mr Matt King
Age range: 2–16 years
No. of pupils: 136
Fees: Day £8,580–£16,200

Great Walstead School
East Mascalls Lane, Lindfield,
Haywards Heath, West Sussex RH16 2QL
Tel: 01444 483528
Headmaster: Mr Chris Calvey
Age range: 2–13 years
No. of pupils: 345
Fees: Day £2,895–£5,550

Handcross Park School
Handcross, Haywards Heath,
West Sussex RH17 6HF
Tel: 01444 400526
Headmaster: Mr Richard Brown
Age range: 2–13 years
No. of pupils: 339
Fees: Day £3,230–£6,360 WB
£5,370–£7,480 FB £6,030–£8,130

Hurstpierpoint College
College Lane, Hurstpierpoint,
West Sussex BN6 9JS
Tel: 01273 833636
Headmaster: Mr. Tim Manly
Age range: 4–18 years

Lancing College
Lancing, West Sussex BN15 0RW
Tel: 01273 452213
Head Master: Mr Dominic T Oliver MPhil
Age range: 13–18 years
No. of pupils: 550 VIth255
Fees: Day £8,190 FB £11,995

Lancing Prep Worthing
Broadwater Road, Worthing,
West Sussex BN14 8HU
Tel: 01903 201123
Head: Mrs Heather Beeby
Age range: 2–13 years

Oakwood Preparatory School
Chichester, West Sussex PO18 9AN
Tel: 01243 575209
Headteacher: Mrs Clare Bradbury
Age range: 2–11 years
No. of pupils: 275
Fees: Day £3,170–£5,110

Our Lady of Sion School
Gratwicke Road, Worthing,
West Sussex BN11 4BL
Tel: 01903 204063
Headmaster: Mr Steven Jeffery
Age range: 3–18 years
No. of pupils: 410
Fees: Day £8,640–£13,575

Pennthorpe School
Church Street, Horsham,
West Sussex RH12 3HJ
Tel: 01403 822391
Headmistress: Alexia Bolton
Age range: 2–13 years
No. of pupils: 362
Fees: Day £2,070–£16,605

Rikkyo School in England
Guildford Road, Rudgwick,
Horsham, West Sussex RH12 3BE
Tel: 01403 822107
Headmaster: Mr Roger Munechika
Age range: 10–18 years
No. of pupils: 116
Fees: FB £15,000–£21,600

SEAFORD COLLEGE
For further details see p.242
Lavington Park, Petworth,
West Sussex GU28 0NB
Tel: 01798 867392
Email: headmasterpa@seaford.org
Website: www.seaford.org
Headmaster: J P Green MA BA
Age range: 5–18 years
No. of pupils: 943 VIth264
Fees: Day £11,880–£24,630
WB £24,735–£33,345 FB £38,070

Shoreham College
St Julians Lane, Shoreham-by-
Sea, West Sussex BN43 6YW
Tel: 01273 592681
Headmaster: Mr R Taylor-West
Age range: 3–16 years
No. of pupils: 375
Fees: Day £9,750–£15,150

Slindon College
Slindon House, Slindon, Arundel,
West Sussex BN18 0RH
Tel: 01243 814320
Head Teacher: Mr Mark Birkbeck
Age range: B8–18 years
(boarding from 11)

**Sompting Abbotts
Preparatory School**
Church Lane, Sompting,
West Sussex BN15 0AZ
Tel: 01903 235960
Principal: Mrs P M Sinclair
Age range: 2–13 years

Steyning Grammar School
Shooting Field, Steyning,
West Sussex BN44 3RX
Tel: +44 (0)1903 814555
Headteacher: Mr Nick Wergan
Age range: 11–18 years
No. of pupils: 1975
Fees: WB £9,100 FB £11,100

The Prebendal School
52-55 West Street, Chichester,
West Sussex PO19 1RT
Tel: 01243 772220
Headteacher: Mrs L Salmond Smith
Age range: 3–13 years
No. of pupils: 181
Fees: Day £8,160–£15,495 WB
£18,975–£20,100 FB £22,290

Westbourne House School
Coach Road, Chichester,
West Sussex PO20 2BH
Tel: 01243 782739
Headmaster: Mr Martin Barker
Age range: 2–13 years

Windlesham House School
London Road, Washington,
Pulborough, West Sussex RH20 4AY
Tel: 01903 874701
Head of School: Ben Evans
Age range: 4–13 years
No. of pupils: 280

Worth School
Paddockhurst Road, Turners Hill,
Crawley, West Sussex RH10 4SD
Tel: +44 (0)1342 710200
Head Master: Stuart McPherson
Age range: 11–18 years
No. of pupils: 580 VIth222
Fees: Day £15,960–£23,730
FB £21,210–£33,690

South-West

KEY TO SYMBOLS
- Boys' school
- Girls' school
- International school
- Tutorial or sixth form college
- A levels
- Boarding accommodation
- Bursaries
- International Baccalaureate
- Learning support
- Entrance at 16+
- Vocational qualifications
- Independent Association of Preparatory Schools
- The Headmasters' & Headmistresses' Conference
- Independent Schools Association
- Girls' School Association
- Boarding Schools' Association
- Society of Heads

Unless otherwise indicated, all schools are coeducational day schools. Single-sex and boarding schools will be indicated by the relevant icon.

Bath & North-East Somerset

Bath Academy
27 Queen Square, Bath, Bath & North-East Somerset BA1 2HX
Tel: 01225 334577
Principal: Mr Tim Naylor
Age range: 14–19+ years

Downside School
Stratton-on-the-Fosse, Radstock, Bath, Bath & North-East Somerset BA3 4RJ
Tel: 01761 235100
Head Master: Mr Andrew Hobbs
Age range: 11–18 years
No. of pupils: 360
Fees: Day £18,705–£22,200 FB £28,245–£37,905

King Edward's Junior School
North Road, Bath, Bath & North-East Somerset BA2 6JA
Tel: 01225 464218
Head of School: Mr Greg Taylor
Age range: 7–11 years

King Edward's Pre-Prep & Nursery School
Weston Lane, Bath, Bath & North-East Somerset BA1 4AQ
Tel: 01225 421681
Head of School: Ms Jayne Gilbert
Age range: 3–7 years

King Edward's Senior & Sixth Form School
North Road, Bath, Bath & North-East Somerset BA2 6HU
Tel: 01225 464313
Head of School: Mr Martin J Boden
Age range: 11–18 years

Kingswood School
Lansdown Road, Bath, Bath & North-East Somerset BA1 5RG
Tel: 01225 734200
Headmaster: Mr Andrew Gordon-Brown
Age range: 9 months–18 years

Monkton Prep School
Church Road, Combe Down, Bath, Bath & North-East Somerset BA2 7ET
Tel: 01225 831200
Head: Mrs Catherine Winchcombe
Age range: 2–13 years (boarding from 7)
No. of pupils: 305

Monkton Senior School
Monkton Combe, Bath, Bath & North-East Somerset BA2 7HG
Tel: 01225 721133
Principal: Mr Chris Wheeler
Age range: 13–18 years (boarding from 13)
No. of pupils: 372 VIth140
Fees: Day £20,880–£21,945 WB £30,945 FB £34,110–£35,010

Prior Park College
Ralph Allen Drive, Bath, Bath & North-East Somerset BA2 5AH
Tel: +44 (0)1225 835353
Headmaster: Mr Ben Horan
Age range: 11–18 years

Royal High School Bath, GDST
Lansdown Road, Bath, Bath & North-East Somerset BA1 5SZ
Tel: +44 (0)1225 313877
Head: Mrs Kate Reynolds
Age range: G3–18 years (boarding from 11)
No. of pupils: 580
Fees: Day £5,041–£5,262 FB £11,234–£11,809

The Paragon School
Lyncombe House, Lyncombe Vale, Bath, Bath & North-East Somerset BA2 4LT
Tel: 01225 310837
Head of School: Ms Rosie Allen
Age range: 3–11 years

Bristol

Badminton School
Westbury Road, Westbury-on-Trym, Bristol BS9 3BA
Tel: 0117 905 5200
Headmistress: Mrs Rebecca Tear BSc, MA, PGCE
Age range: G3–18 years (boarding from 9)

Bristol Grammar School
University Road, Bristol BS8 1SR
Tel: 0117 973 6006
Headmaster: Mr Jaideep Barot
Age range: 4–18 years

Bristol International College
Torwood House, 8 Durdham Park, Redland, Bristol BS6 6XA
Tel: +44 (0)117 374 4888
CEO & Principal: Mr John Milne
Age range: 14–18 years

Bristol Steiner School
Redland Hill House, Redland, Bristol BS6 6UX
Tel: 0117 933 9990
Acting Head Teacher: Lorraine Swords
Age range: 3–11 years
No. of pupils: 128
Fees: Day £7,977

Carmel Christian School
817A Bath Road, Brislington, Bristol BS4 5NL
Tel: 0117 977 5678
Head of School: Ms Joanne Collins
Age range: 3–5 years

Cleve House School
254 Wells Road, Knowle, Bristol BS4 2PN
Tel: 0117 9777218
Head of School: Ms Clare Fraser
Age range: 2–11 years

Clifton College
32 College Road, Clifton, Bristol BS8 3JH
Tel: 0117 315 7000
Head of College: Dr Tim Greene MA DPhil
Age range: 13–18 years (boarding from 13)

Clifton College Preparatory School
The Avenue, Clifton, Bristol BS8 3HE
Tel: +44 (0)117 315 7502
Head of Preparatory School: Mr Jim Walton
Age range: 2–13 years (boarding from 8)

Clifton High School
College Road, Clifton, Bristol BS8 3JD
Tel: 0117 973 0201
Head of School: Mr Matthew Bennett
Age range: 3–18 years

Collegiate School, Bristol
Stapleton, Bristol BS16 1BJ
Tel: 0117 965 5207
Headmaster: Mr Jeremy McCullough
Age range: 3–18 years
No. of pupils: 816
Fees: Day £8,055–£14,625

Ecole Française de Bristol
Stanton Road, Southmead, Bristol BS10 5SJ
Tel: +44 (0)117 9692410
Age range: 3–16 years

Fairfield School
Fairfield Way, Backwell, Bristol BS48 3PD
Tel: 01275 462743
Headmistress: Mrs Lesley Barton
Age range: 2–11 years

Gracefield Preparatory School
266 Overndale Road,
Fishponds, Bristol BS16 2RG
Tel: 0117 956 7977
Headteacher: Mr J Gunter
Age range: 4–11 years

Queen Elizabeth's Hospital
Berkeley Place, Clifton, Bristol BS8 1JX
Tel: 0117 930 3040
Head: Mr Rupert Heathcote
Age range: B7–18 years G16–18 years

Redmaids' High Junior School
Grange Court Road, Westbury-
on-Trym, Bristol BS9 4DP
Tel: 0117 962 9451
Headteacher: Mrs Lisa
Brown BSc (Hons)
Age range: G7–11 years

**Redmaids' High School
Senior & Sixth Form**
Westbury Road, Westbury-
on-Trym, Bristol BS9 3AW
Tel: 0117 962 2641
Head: Mr Paul Dwyer
Age range: G11–18 years

The Downs Preparatory School
Wraxall, Bristol BS48 1PF
Tel: 01275 852008
Head: Ms Debbie Isaachsen
Age range: 4–13 years

Tockington Manor School
Washingpool Hill Road,
Tockington, Bristol BS32 4NY
Tel: 01454 613229
Headmaster: Mr Stephen Symonds
Age range: 2–13 years

Torwood House School
8 Durdham Park, Redland,
Bristol BS6 6XA
Tel: 01179 736620
Head Teacher: Mrs Dionne
Seagrove B.Ed, M.Ed
Age range: 0–11 years

Cornwall

Polwhele House School
Truro, Cornwall TR4 9AE
Tel: 01872 273011
Head of School: Mrs Hilary Mann
Age range: 3–13 years

St Joseph's School
15 St Stephen's Hill, Launceston,
Cornwall PL15 8HN
Tel: 01566 772580
Head Teacher: Mr Oliver Scott
Age range: 4–16 years

St. Piran's School
14 Trelissick Road, Hayle,
Cornwall TR27 4HY
Tel: 01736 752612
Headteacher: Mrs Lucy Draycott
Age range: 4–16 years

Truro High School for Girls
Falmouth Road, Truro, Cornwall TR1 2HU
Tel: 01872 272830
Headmistress: Mrs Sarah Matthews
Age range: G4–18 years
(boarding from 9)

Truro School
Trennick Lane, Truro, Cornwall TR1 1TH
Tel: 01872 272763
Head of School: Mr Andy Johnson
Age range: 3–18 years

Devon

Abbey School
Hampton Court, St Marychurch,
Torquay, Devon TQ1 4PR
Tel: 01803 327868
Principal: Mrs Sylvia Greinig
Age range: 0–11 years

Blundell's Preparatory School
Milestones House, Blundell's Road,
Tiverton, Devon EX16 4NA
Tel: 01884 252393
Head Master: Mr Andrew
Southgate BA Ed (Hons)
Age range: 3–11 years

Blundell's School
Tiverton, Devon EX16 4DN
Tel: 01884 252543
Head: Mr Bart Wielenga BComm,
Natal & Johannesburg, BEd
Age range: 11–18 years

Exeter Cathedral School
The Chantry, Palace Gate,
Exeter, Devon EX1 1HX
Tel: 01392 255298
Headmaster: James Featherstone
Age range: 3–13 years
No. of pupils: 266
Fees: Day £2,823–£4,623 FB £2,722

Exeter School
Victoria Park Road, Exeter,
Devon EX2 4NS
Tel: 01392 307080
Head: Ms Louise Simpson
Age range: 7–18 years
No. of pupils: 944
Fees: Day £12,120–£14,700

Fletewood School
88 North Road East, Plymouth,
Devon PL4 6AN
Tel: 01752 663782
Headteacher: Mrs R Gray
Age range: 3–11 years

King's School
Hartley Road, Mannamead,
Plymouth, Devon PL3 5LW
Tel: 01752 771789
Head of School: Mrs Clare Page
Age range: 8 months–11 years

KINGSLEY SCHOOL
For further details see p.276
Northdown Road, Bideford,
Devon EX39 3LY
Tel: 01237 426200
Email: admissions@
kingsleyschoolbideford.co.uk
Website:
www.kingsleyschoolbideford.co.uk
Headteacher: Mr Robert Pavis
Age range: 0–18 years
(boarding from 9)
No. of pupils: 395
Fees: Day £2,180 WB £6,135 FB £8,775

Mount Kelly
Parkwood Road, Tavistock,
Devon PL19 0HZ
Tel: +44 (0)1822 813100
Head of School: Mr. Guy Ayling
Age range: 3–18 years

**OneSchool Global UK
Plymouth Campus**
Foulston Avenue, Plymouth,
Devon PL5 1HL
Tel: 01752 363290
Age range: 7–18 years

Park School
Park Road, Dartington Hall,
Totnes, Devon TQ9 6EQ
Tel: 01803 864588
Headteacher: Arnet Donkin
Age range: 3–12 years

Plymouth College
Ford Park, Plymouth, Devon PL4 6RN
Tel: 01752 505100
Headteacher: Mrs Jo Hayward
Age range: 3–18 years
No. of pupils: 569

Sands School
48 East Street, Ashburton,
Devon TQ13 7AX
Tel: 01364 653666
Age range: 11–17 years

Shebbear College
Shebbear, Beaworthy, Devon EX21 5HJ
Tel: 01409 282000
Head: Ms Caroline Kirby
Age range: 4–18 years

South Devon Steiner School
Hood Manor, Buckfastleigh Road,
Dartington, Totnes, Devon TQ9 6AB
Tel: 01803 897377
Education Manager: Jeff van Zyl
Age range: 3–19 years

**St Christopher's Prep
School & Nursery**
Mount Barton, Staverton,
Devon TQ9 6PF
Tel: 01803 762202
Headmistress: Mrs Alexandra Cottell
Age range: 3–11 years

St John's School
Broadway, Sidmouth, Devon EX10 8RG
Tel: 01395 513984
Head of School: Mr Bryan Kane
Age range: 2–18 years
(boarding from 8)

St Peter's Preparatory School
Harefield, Lympstone,
Exmouth, Devon EX8 5AU
Tel: 01395 272148
Head: Mrs Charlotte Johnston
Age range: 3–13 years

St Wilfrid's School
25-29 St David's Hill, Exeter,
Devon EX4 4DA
Tel: 01392 276171
Headteacher: Mr Ross Bovingdon
Age range: 3–16 years

Stover School
Stover, Newton Abbot,
Devon TQ12 6QG
Tel: +44 (0)1626 354505
Headmaster: Mr R W D Notman
Age range: 3–18 years

The Maynard School
Denmark Road, Exeter, Devon EX1 1SJ
Tel: 01392 273417
Headmistress: Mrs Liz Gregory
Age range: G4–18 years

The New School
The Avenue, Exminster,
Exeter, Devon EX6 8AT
Tel: 01392 496122
Head: Mr Daniel Ayling
Age range: 3–7 years
No. of pupils: 71
Fees: Day £8,676–£8,934

Trinity School
Buckeridge Road, Teignmouth,
Devon TQ14 8LY
Tel: 01626 774138
Headmaster: Mr Lawrence Coen
Age range: 3–18 years
(boarding from 9)

West Buckland School
Barnstaple, Devon EX32 0SX
Tel: 01598 760000
Headmaster: Mr Phillip Stapleton
Age range: 3–18 years

Dorset

**Bournemouth Collegiate
School (BCS Prep)**
40 St. Osmund's Road, Lower
Parkstone, Poole, Dorset BH14 9JY
Tel: 01202 714110
Head of School: Miss Kay Smith
Age range: 2–11 years
No. of pupils: 267
Fees: Day £7,365–£12,075

**Bournemouth Collegiate
School (BCS Senior)**
College Road, Southbourne,
Bournemouth, Dorset BH5 2DY
Tel: 01202 436550
Head of School: Mr Russell Slatford
Age range: 11–18 years
No. of pupils: 402
Fees: Day £15,240 WB
£28,740 FB £32,090

Bryanston Prep
Durweston, Blandford, Dorset DT11 0PY
Tel: 01258 452065
Head of School: Mr Will Lockett
Age range: 3–13 years

Bryanston School
Blandford Forum, Dorset DT11 0PX
Tel: 01258 484633
Head: Richard Jones
Age range: 3–18 years
No. of pupils: 806
Fees: Day £33,525 FB £40,890

Canford School
Canford Magna, Wimborne,
Dorset BH21 3AD
Tel: 01202 841254
Headmaster: Mr B A M Vessey MA, MBA
Age range: 13–18 years

Castle Court School
Knoll Lane, Corfe Mullen,
Wimborne, Dorset BH21 3RF
Tel: 01202 694438
Headmaster: Mr Luke Gollings
Age range: 2–13 years

Clayesmore School
Blandford Road, Iwerne
Minster, Dorset DT11 8LL
Tel: 01747 813111
Head of School: Mrs Jo Thomson
Age range: 3–18 years

Dumpton School
Deans Grove House, Deans Grove,
Wimborne, Dorset BH21 7AF
Tel: 01202 883818
Headmaster: Mr Christian Saenger
Age range: 2–13 years

Hanford School
Child Okeford, Blandford
Forum, Dorset DT11 8HN
Tel: 01258 860219
Headmaster: Mr Rory Johnston
Age range: G7–13 years
(boarding from 7)

Leweston Prep School
Sherborne, Dorset DT9 6EN
Tel: 01963 210790
Head of School: Ms Alanda Phillips
Age range: 0–11 years

Leweston Senior School
Sherborne, Dorset DT9 6EN
Tel: 01963 210691
Head of School: Mr John
Paget-Tomlinson
Age range: 11–18 years

Milton Abbey School
Blandford Forum, Dorset DT11 0BZ
Tel: 01258 880484
Head: Judith Fremont-Barnes
Age range: 13–18 years

Park School
43 Queens Park South Drive,
Bournemouth, Dorset BH8 9BJ
Tel: 01202 396640
Headteacher: Mrs Melanie Dowler
Age range: 3 months–11 years

Port Regis
Motcombe Park, Shaftesbury,
Dorset SP7 9QA
Tel: 01747 857800
Headmaster: Mr Titus Mills
Age range: 2–13 years
(boarding from 7)

Sherborne Girls
Bradford Road, Sherborne,
Dorset DT9 3QN
Tel: 01935 812245
Headmistress: Dr Ruth Sullivan
BSc, PGCE, MSc, PhD
Age range: G11–18 years
(boarding from 11)

Sherborne International
Newell Grange, Newell,
Sherborne, Dorset DT9 4EZ
Tel: +44 (0)1935 814743
Principal: Mr Tim Waters MA
(Oxon), MSc (Oxon)
Age range: 8–17 years

Sherborne Preparatory School
Acreman Street, Sherborne,
Dorset DT9 3NY
Tel: 01935 812097
Head: Ms Natalie Bone
Age range: 3–13 years
(boarding from 7)

Sherborne School
Abbey Road, Sherborne, Dorset DT9 3LF
Tel: +44 (0)1935 812249
Headmaster: Dr Dominic
Luckett BA, DPhil, FRSA,FHA
Age range: B13–18 years

St Martin's School
15 Stokewood Road,
Bournemouth, Dorset BH3 7NA
Tel: 01202 292011
Headteacher: Ms Laura Richards
Age range: 4–11 years

Sunninghill Preparatory School
South Court, South Walks Road,
Dorchester, Dorset DT1 1EB
Tel: 01305 262306
Acting Head: Mrs Nancy Sewed
Age range: 3–13 years

Talbot Heath
Rothesay Road, Talbot Woods,
Bournemouth, Dorset BH4 9NJ
Tel: 01202 761881
Senior School Head: Mrs A
Holloway MA (Oxon) PGCE
Age range: G3–18 years
(boarding from 11)

Talbot House Preparatory School
8 Firs Glen Road, Talbot Park,
Bournemouth, Dorset BH9 2LR
Tel: 01202 510348
Headteacher: Mrs Emma Haworth
Age range: 3–11 years

Somerset

All Hallows Preparatory School
Cranmore Hall, Shepton
Mallet, Somerset BA4 4SF
Tel: 01749 881600
Headmaster: Dr Trevor Richards
Age range: 3–13 years

Chard School
Fore Street, Chard, Somerset TA20 1QA
Tel: 01460 63234
Headteacher: Ms Katie Hill
Age range: 4–11 years

Hazlegrove Prep School
Hazlegrove House, Sparkford,
Somerset BA22 7JA
Tel: +44 (0)1963 442606
Headmaster: Mr Mark White MA (Hons)
Age range: 2–13 years
No. of pupils: 364
Fees: Day £3,076–£6,237
FB £7,235–£9,232

King's Bruton
The Plox, Bruton, Somerset BA10 0ED
Tel: 01749 814200
Headmaster: Mr I S Wilmshurst MA
Age range: 13–18 years
No. of pupils: 360
Fees: Day £24,723 FB £35,568

King's College
South Road, Taunton, Somerset TA1 3LA
Tel: 01823 328200
Headmaster: Mr Michael Sloan
Age range: 13–18 years

King's Hall School
Kingston Road, Taunton,
Somerset TA2 8AA
Tel: 01823 285920
Head: Mr Justin Chippendale
Age range: 2–13 years
No. of pupils: 310
Fees: Day £8,850–£18,750

Millfield Preparatory School
Edgarley Hall, Glastonbury,
Somerset BA6 8LD
Tel: 01458 832446
Headmaster: Dan Thornburn
Age range: 2–13 years
No. of pupils: 434

Millfield School
Butleigh Road, Street,
Somerset BA16 0YD
Tel: 01458 442291
Headmaster: Mr Gavin Horgan
Age range: 13–18 years
No. of pupils: 1301
Fees: Day £27,165 FB £41,355

Perrott Hill
North Perrott, Crewkerne,
Somerset TA18 7SL
Tel: 01460 72051
Headmaster: Mr Alex McCullough
Age range: 3–13 years

Queen's College
Trull Road, Taunton, Somerset TA1 4QS
Tel: +44 (0)1823 272559
Head of College: Mr Julian Noad
Age range: 3 months–18 years

Sidcot School
Oakridge Lane, Winscombe,
Somerset BS25 1PD
Tel: 01934 843102
Headmaster: Iain Kilpatrick
BA MEd FRSA
Age range: 3–18 years
(boarding from 11)
No. of pupils: 603
Fees: Day £2,900–£6,510
FB £9,830–£12,030

Springmead Preparatory
School & Nursery
13 Castle Corner, Beckington,
Frome, Somerset BA11 6TA
Tel: 01373 831555
Headteacher: Ms Sally Cox
Age range: 3–11 years

Taunton School
Staplegrove Road, Taunton,
Somerset TA2 6AD
Tel: +44 (0)1823 703703
**Headmaster, Taunton
School:** Mr. James Johnson
Age range: 0–18 years
No. of pupils: 1000

Wellington School
South Street, Wellington,
Somerset TA21 8NT
Tel: 01823 668800
Headmaster: Mr Eugene du Toit
Age range: 3–18 years

Wells Cathedral School
The Liberty, Wells, Somerset BA5 2ST
Tel: +44 (0)1749 834200
Head Master: Mr Alastair Tighe
Age range: 2–18 years

West Midlands

KEY TO SYMBOLS

- 🛈 Boys' school
- 🛈 Girls' school
- 🛈 International school
- 16: Tutorial or sixth form college
- Ⓐ A levels
- 🛈 Boarding accommodation
- £ Bursaries
- Ⓑ International Baccalaureate
- 🛈 Learning support
- 16: Entrance at 16+
- 🛈 Vocational qualifications
- Ⓘ Independent Association of Preparatory Schools
- ⒽⓂⒸ The Headmasters' & Headmistresses' Conference
- Ⓘ Independent Schools Association
- ⒼⓈⒶ Girls' School Association
- ⒷⓈⒶ Boarding Schools' Association
- Ⓢ Society of Heads

Unless otherwise indicated, all schools are coeducational day schools. Single-sex and boarding schools will be indicated by the relevant icon.

Herefordshire

Hereford Cathedral School
The Old Deanery, The Cathedral Close, Hereford, Herefordshire HR1 2NG
Tel: 01432 363 500
Headmaster: Dr Michael Gray Gray
Age range: 3–18 years
🖊 16+

Lucton School
Lucton, Herefordshire HR6 9PN
Tel: 01568 782000
Headmaster: Mr David Bicker-Caarten
Age range: 6 months–18 years (boarding from 7)
No. of pupils: 300
Fees: Day £7,500–£14,250 WB £24,345–£28,695 FB £35,130
🐎 Ⓐ 🏛 £ 🖊 16+

Shropshire

Adcote School for Girls
Little Ness, Shrewsbury, Shropshire SY4 2JY
Tel: 01939 260202
Headmistress: Mrs Diane Browne
Age range: G7–18 years (boarding from 7)
Fees: Day £9,141–£14,838 FB £19,618–£38,100
🚹 🐎 🏛 £ 🖊 16+

Bedstone College
Bedstone, Bucknell, Shropshire SY7 0BG
Tel: 01547 530303
Headmaster: Mr Toby Mullins
Age range: 4–18 years
🐎 🏛 £ 🖊 16+

Birchfield School
Albrighton, Wolverhampton, Shropshire WV7 3AF
Tel: 01902 372534
Headmistress: Sarah Morris
Age range: 4–16 years
No. of pupils: 142
Fees: Day £7,500–£11,000
£ 🖊

Castle House School
Chetwynd End, Newport, Shropshire TF10 7JE
Tel: 01952 567600
Headteacher: Mr Ian Sterling
Age range: 2–11 years
🖊

Concord College
Acton Burnell Hall, Acton Burnell, Shrewsbury, Shropshire SY5 7PF
Tel: +44 (0)1694 731631
Principal: Dr Michael R Truss
Age range: 13–18 years
No. of pupils: 600
Fees: Day £16,200 FB £48,900
🐎 Ⓐ 🏛 £ 🖊 16+

ELLESMERE COLLEGE
For further details see p.284
Ellesmere, Shropshire SY12 9AB
Tel: 01691 622321
Email: registrar@ellesmere.com
Website: www.ellesmere.com
Head of School: Mr Brendan Wignall MA, FRSA, MCMI
Age range: 7–18 years (boarding from 12)
No. of pupils: 600
Fees: Day £6,960 WB £9,035 FB £12,655
🐎 Ⓐ 🏛 £ IB 🖊 16+

Moor Park
Richards Castle, Ludlow, Shropshire SY8 4DZ
Tel: 01584 876 061
Headmaster: Mr Charles G O'B Minogue
Age range: 0–13 years
No. of pupils: 214
Fees: Day £2,225–£6,215 FB £7,700–£9,225
🏛 £ 🖊

Moreton Hall
Weston Rhyn, Oswestry, Shropshire SY11 3EW
Tel: +44 (0)1691 773671
Principal: Mr George Budd
Age range: 11–18 years
🚹 🐎 🏛

Moreton Hall Prep
Weston Rhyn, Oswestry, Shropshire SY11 3EW
Tel: 01691 776028
Head: Mr John Bond
Age range: 6 months–11 years
No. of pupils: 150
Fees: Day £10,650–£15,135 FB £24,570
🐎 🏛 £ 🖊 16+

Oswestry School
Upper Brook Street, Oswestry, Shropshire SY11 2TL
Tel: +44 (0)1691 655711
Headmaster: Mr Peter Middleton
Age range: 4–18 years
🐎 🏛 🖊 16+

Packwood Haugh School
Ruyton XI Towns, Shrewsbury, Shropshire SY4 1HX
Tel: 01939 260217
Headmaster: Mr Robert Fox
Age range: 4–13 years
🏛 🖊

Prestfelde Preparatory School
London Road, Shrewsbury, Shropshire SY2 6NZ
Tel: 01743 245400
Head of School: Mrs F Orchard
Age range: 3–13 years
🏛 🖊

Shrewsbury High School GDST
32 Town Walls, Shrewsbury, Shropshire SY1 1TN
Tel: 01743 494000
Headteacher: Ms Jo Sharrock
Age range: G4–18 years
🚹 🖊 16+

SHREWSBURY SCHOOL
For further details see p.288
The Schools, Shrewsbury, Shropshire SY3 7BA
Tel: 01743 280552
Email: admissions@shrewsbury.org.uk
Website: www.shrewsbury.org.uk
Headmaster: Mr. Leo Winkley
Age range: 13–18 years
No. of pupils: 845
Fees: Day £27,930 FB £42,210
🐎 Ⓐ 🏛 £ 🖊 16+

St Winefride's RC Independent School
Belmont, Shrewsbury, Shropshire SY1 1TE
Tel: 01743 369883
Headteacher: Mrs E Devey
Age range: 3–11 years
🖊

The Old Hall School
Stanley Road, Wellington, Shropshire TF1 3LB
Tel: 01952 223117
Headmaster: Mr Martin Stott
Age range: 4–11 years
No. of pupils: 232
Fees: Day £8,850–£13,920
£ 🖊

Wrekin College
Wellington, Shropshire TF1 3BH
Tel: +44 (0)1952 265600
Headmaster: Mr Tim Firth
Age range: 11–18 years
🐎 🏛 🖊 16+

Staffordshire

Abbotsholme School
Rocester, Uttoxeter,
Staffordshire ST14 5BS
Tel: 01889 590217
Head of School: Mr Simon Ruscoe-Price
Age range: 2–18 years
No. of pupils: 285
Fees: Day £8,985–£22,485 WB
£18,525–£27,450 FB £24,585–£33,750

Chase Grammar School
Convent Close, Cannock,
Staffordshire WS11 0UR
Tel: +44 (0)1543 501800
Principal: Mr Michael Hartland
Age range: 2–19 years

Denstone College
Uttoxeter, Staffordshire ST14 5HN
Tel: 01889 590484
Head of School: Miss Lotte Tulloch
Age range: 4–18 years
(boarding from 7)
No. of pupils: 735
Fees: Day £11,007–£17,253 WB
£20,682–£23,259 FB £20,682–£32,409

**EDENHURST PREPARATORY
SCHOOL**
For further details see p.282
Westlands Avenue, Newcastle-
under-Lyme, Staffordshire ST5 2PU
Tel: 01782 619348
Email: office@edenhurst.co.uk
Website: www.edenhurst.co.uk
Headteacher: Mr Michael Hibbert
Age range: 3 months–11 years
Fees: Day £3,019–£3,655

Lichfield Cathedral School
The Palace, The Close, Lichfield,
Staffordshire WS13 7LH
Tel: 01543 306170
Head: Mrs Susan E Hannam
BA (Hons) MA PGCE
Age range: 2–18 years

Maple Hayes Hall School
Abnalls Lane, Lichfield,
Staffordshire WS13 8BL
Tel: 01543 264387
Principal: Dr N E Brown MSc, BA, MINS,
MSCMe, AFBPsS, CPsychol, FRSA, CSci
Age range: 7–17 years

Newcastle under Lyme School
Mount Pleasant, Newcastle-under-
Lyme, Staffordshire ST5 1DB
Tel: 01782 631197
Headmaster: Mr Michael
Getty BA, NPQH
Age range: 3–18 years
No. of pupils: 879 VIth152
Fees: Day £3,152–£4,330

St Joseph's Preparatory School
Rookery Lane, Trent Vale, Stoke-
on-Trent, Staffordshire ST4 5RF
Tel: 01782 417533
Headteacher: Mr D Hood
BA (Joint Hons), PGCE
Age range: 3–11 years

St. Dominic's Grammar School
32 Bargate Street, Brewood,
Staffordshire ST19 9BA
Tel: 01902 850248
Headmaster: Mr Peter
McNabb BSc Hons, PGCE
Age range: 4–18 years

St. Dominic's Priory School Stone
37 Station Road, Stone,
Staffordshire ST15 8ER
Tel: +44 (0)1785 814181
Headteacher: Mrs Rebecca Harrison
Age range: 3–16 years

Stafford Grammar School
Burton Manor Road, Stafford,
Staffordshire ST18 9AT
Tel: 01785 249752
Headmaster: Mr L H Thomas
Age range: 3–18 years
No. of pupils: 422
Fees: Day £11,013–£13,464

Yarlet School
Yarlet, Stafford, Staffordshire ST18 9SU
Tel: 01785 286568
Headmaster: Mr I Raybould BEd(Hons)
Age range: 2–13 years

Warwickshire

Arnold Lodge School
15-17 Kenilworth Road, Leamington
Spa, Warwickshire CV32 5TW
Tel: 01926 778050
Headmaster: Mr David Preston
Age range: 4–18 years

Bilton Grange Preparatory School
Dunchurch, Rugby,
Warwickshire CV22 6QU
Tel: 01788 810217
Headmaster: Mr Gareth Jones
Age range: 3–13 years
(boarding from 8)

Crackley Hall School
St Joseph's Park, Kenilworth,
Warwickshire CV8 2FT
Tel: 01926 514444
Headmaster: Mr Rob Duigan
Age range: 4–11 years

King's High School
Banbury Road, Warwick,
Warwickshire CV34 6YE
Tel: 01926 494485
Head Master: Dr Stephen Burley
Age range: G11–18 years

OneSchool Global UK
Atherstone Campus
Long Street, Atherstone,
Warwickshire CV9 1AE
Tel: 01827 721751
Age range: 7–18 years

Princethorpe College
Leamington Road, Princethorpe,
Rugby, Warwickshire CV23 9PX
Tel: 01926 634200
Headmaster: Mr Ed Hester
Age range: 11–18 years

Rugby School
Lawrence Sheriff Street, Rugby,
Warwickshire CV22 5EH
Tel: +44 (0)1788 556216
Head Master: Mr Gareth Parker-Jones
Age range: 13–18 years
(boarding from 13)

Stratford Preparatory School
Church House, Old Town, Stratford-
upon-Avon, Warwickshire CV37 6BG
Tel: 01789 297993
Head of School: Ms Tracey Woodcock
Age range: 2–11 years

The Crescent School
Bawnmore Road, Bilton, Rugby,
Warwickshire CV22 7QH
Tel: 01788 521595
Headmaster: Mr J.P. Thackway
B.A.Hons, P.G.C.E.
Age range: 4–11 years

The Croft Preparatory School
Alveston Hill, Loxley Road, Stratford-
upon-Avon, Warwickshire CV37 7RL
Tel: 01789 293795
Headmaster: Mr Marcus Cook
Age range: 3–11 years

The Kingsley School
Beauchamp Hall, Beauchamp
Avenue, Leamington Spa,
Warwickshire CV32 5RD
Tel: 01926 895358
Headteacher: Mr James Mercer-Kelly
Age range: B3–11 years G3–18 years

Twycross House Pre-Preparatory
School (The Hollies)
The Green, Twycross (Near
Atherstone), Warwickshire CV9 3PQ
Tel: 01827 880725
Age range: 4–8 years

Twycross House School
The Green, Twycross (Near
Atherstone), Warwickshire CV9 3PQ
Tel: 01827 880651
Headmaster: Mr S D Assinder
Age range: 8–18 years
(16)

Warwick Preparatory School
Banbury Road, Warwick,
Warwickshire CV34 6PL
Tel: 01926 491545
Headmistress: Ms Hellen Dodsworth
Age range: B3–7 years G3–11 years

Warwick School
Myton Road, Warwick,
Warwickshire CV34 6PP
Tel: 01926 776400
Head Master: Mr James Barker
Age range: B7–18 years

West Midlands

Abu Bakr Girls School
Shelly Campus, Scarborough Road,
Walsall, West Midlands WS2 9TY
Tel: 01922 612361
Acting Head Teacher: Moulana
M Luqman
Age range: G4–16 years

Al Ameen Primary School
Stanfield House, 447 Warwick
Way, Tyseley, Birmingham,
West Midlands B11 2JR
Tel: 0121 706 3322
Head Teacher: Maulana
Mohammed Aminur Rahman
Age range: 3–11 years

Al Huda Girls School
74-76 Washwood Heath Road, Saltley,
Birmingham, West Midlands B8 1RD
Tel: 01213 288999
Head of School: Asif Jawaid
Age range: G11–16 years

Al-Burhan Grammar School
Spring Road Centre, 258 Spring
Road, Tyseley, Birmingham,
West Midlands B11 3DW
Tel: 01214 405454
Headteacher: Dr Mohammad
Nasrullah BSc MSc PhD
Age range: G11–16 years

Al-Furqan Primary School
Reddings Lane, Tyseley, Birmingham,
West Midlands B11 3EY
Tel: 01217 772222
Executive Head Teacher: Ms
Susan Barratt
Age range: 4–11 years

Bablake School
Coundon Road, Coventry,
West Midlands CV1 4AU
Tel: 02476 271200
Headmaster: Mr Andrew Wright
Age range: 3–18 years

**Birchfield Independent
Girls' School**
30 Beacon Hill, Aston, Birmingham,
West Midlands B6 6JU
Tel: 01213 277707
Head Teacher: Ms Rehana Mogra
Age range: G11–17 years

**Darul Uloom Islamic High School
(Darul Uloom Birmingham)**
521-527 Coventry Road, Small Heath,
Birmingham, West Midlands B10 0LL
Tel: 0121 688 6507
Head of School: Ustaadh Azharul Islam
Age range: B11–16 years

Edgbaston High School for Girls
Westbourne Road, Edgbaston,
Birmingham, West Midlands B15 3TS
Tel: 01214 545831
Headmistress: Mrs Clare Macro
Age range: G2–18 years
No. of pupils: 880
Fees: Day £3,106–£4,695

Elmfield Rudolf Steiner School
14 Love Lane, Stourbridge,
West Midlands DY8 2EA
Tel: 01384 394633
Age range: 3–17 years

Elmhurst Ballet School
249 Bristol Road, Edgbaston,
Birmingham, West Midlands B5 7UH
Tel: +44 (0)1214 726655
Principal: Ms Jessica Ward
Age range: 11–19 years
(boarding from 11)

Emmanuel School (Walsall)
36 Wolverhampton Road, Walsall,
West Midlands WS2 8PR
Tel: 01922 635810
Head Teacher: Mr Jonathan
Swain BA PGCE
Age range: 3–16 years

Eversfield Preparatory School
Warwick Road, Solihull,
West Midlands B91 1AT
Tel: 0121 705 0354
Headmaster: Mr Robert A
Yates MA, BA, PGCE, LPSH
Age range: 3–11 years
No. of pupils: 335
Fees: Day £8,410–£12,300

Green Heath School
43-51 Whitmore Road, Small Heath,
Birmingham, West Midlands B10 0NR
Tel: 0121 213 1171
Head of School: Mr Z Khan
Age range: 11–19 years

Green Oak Academy
11-15 Woodstock Road, Moseley,
Birmingham, West Midlands B13 9BB
Tel: 01214 496690
Head Teacher: Dr Razia Ghani
Age range: G11–16 years

Greenfields Primary School
472 Coventry Road, Small Heath,
Birmingham, West Midlands B10 0UG
Tel: 01217 724567
Headteacher: Mr Matthew Williams
Age range: 5–11 years

Hallfield School
48 Church Road, Edgbaston,
Birmingham, West Midlands B15 3SJ
Tel: 0121 454 1496
Head Master: Mr Keith Morrow
Age range: 3 months–13 years

Hamd House School
The Custard House, 29-43 Blake Lane,
Birmingham, West Midlands B9 5QT
Tel: +44 (0)1217 713030
Age range: 5–16 years

Highclare School
10 Sutton Road, Erdington,
Birmingham, West Midlands B23 6QL
Tel: 01213 737400
Headmaster: Dr Richard Luker
Age range: 2–18 years

Hydesville Tower School
25 Broadway North, Walsall,
West Midlands WS1 2QG
Tel: 01922 624374
Headteacher: Mrs Raj Samra
Age range: 3–16 years
No. of pupils: 289
Fees: Day £9,738–£13,758

**Jamia Islamia Birmingham
School & College**
Fallows Road, Sparkbrook,
Birmingham, West Midlands B11 1PL
Tel: 01217 726400
Headteacher: Monzoor
Hussain NPQH PGCE Bsc
Age range: 11–18 years

**King Edward VI High
School for Girls**
Edgbaston Park Road, Birmingham,
West Midlands B15 2UB
Tel: 01214 721834
Principal: Mrs Kirsty von Malaisé
Age range: G11–18 years

King Edward's School
Edgbaston Park Road, Birmingham,
West Midlands B15 2UA
Tel: 01214 721672
Chief Master: Dr Katy Ricks
Age range: B11–18 years
No. of pupils: 876
Fees: Day £5,175

King Henry VIII Preparatory School
Warwick Road, Coventry,
West Midlands CV3 6AQ
Tel: 02476 271160
Headmaster: Mr J. Holtby
Age range: 3–11 years

King Henry VIII School
Warwick Road, Coventry,
West Midlands CV3 6AQ
Tel: 02476 271111
Headmaster: Mr Philip
Dearden BA (Hons), MA Ed
Age range: 11–18 years

Kingswood School
St James Place, Shirley, Solihull,
West Midlands B90 2BA
Tel: 01217 447883
Headmaster: Mr Rob Luckham
BSc(Hons), PGCE
Age range: 2–16 years

Lambs Christian School
113 Soho Hill, Hockley, Birmingham,
West Midlands B19 1AY
Tel: 01215 543790
Headteacher: Mrs Patricia Ekhuenelo
Age range: 3–11 years

Lote Tree Primary
643 Foleshill Road, Coventry,
West Midlands CV6 5JQ
Tel: 02476 261803
Headteacher: Ms Mariam Ashique
Age range: 2–11 years

**MANDER PORTMAN
WOODWARD – MPW
BIRMINGHAM**
For further details see p.286
16-18 Greenfield Crescent,
Edgbaston, Birmingham,
West Midlands B15 3AU
Tel: 0121 454 9637
Email: birmingham@mpw.ac.uk
Website: www.mpw.ac.uk
Principal: Mr Mark Shingleton
Age range: 14–19 years

Mayfield Preparatory School
Sutton Road, Walsall, West
Midlands WS1 2PD
Tel: 01922 624107
Headmaster: Mr Matthew Draper
Age range: 2–11 years

Newbridge Preparatory School
51 Newbridge Crescent,
Tettenhall, Wolverhampton,
West Midlands WV6 0LH
Tel: 01902 751088
Headmistress: Mrs Sarah Fisher
Age range: B2–7 years G2–11 years

Norfolk House School
4 Norfolk Road, Edgbaston,
Birmingham, West Midlands B15 3PS
Tel: 01214 547021
Susannah: Ms Susannah Palmer
Age range: 3–11 years

Pattison School
86-90 Binley Road, Coventry,
West Midlands CV3 1FQ
Tel: 024 7645 5031
Head of School: Mr Graeme Delaney
Age range: 2–18 years

Priory School
39 Sir Harry's Road, Edgbaston,
Birmingham, West Midlands B15 2UR
Tel: 0121 440 4103
Headmaster: Mr J Cramb
Age range: 6 months–18 years

Rosslyn School
1597 Stratford Road, Hall Green,
Birmingham, West Midlands B28 9JB
Tel: 01217 442743
Head of School: Mrs Irina Jones
Age range: 11 months–11 years

Ruckleigh School
17 Lode Lane, Solihull, West
Midlands B91 2AB
Tel: 01217 052773
Headmaster: Mr Dominic Smith
Age range: 3–11 years

Solihull School
Warwick Road, Solihull,
West Midlands B91 3DJ
Tel: 01217 050958
Head of Senior School: Mr
Sean A Morgan
Age range: 3–18 years

St George's School, Edgbaston
31 Calthorpe Road, Edgbaston,
Birmingham, West Midlands B15 1RX
Tel: 01216 250398
Head of School: Mr Gary
Neal BEd (Hons)
Age range: 3–18 years

TETTENHALL COLLEGE
For further details see p.290
Wood Road, Tettenhall,
Wolverhampton, West
Midlands WV6 8QX
Tel: 01902 751119
Email: admissions@tettcoll.co.uk
Website:
www.tettenhallcollege.co.uk
Headteacher: Mr
Christopher McAllister
Age range: 2–18 years
(boarding from 10)
No. of pupils: 440

The Blue Coat School
Somerset Road, Edgbaston,
Birmingham, West Midlands B17 0HR
Tel: 01214 106800
Headmaster: Mr N G Neeson
Age range: 3–11 years

**THE ROYAL SCHOOL,
WOLVERHAMPTON**
For further details see p.292
Penn Road, Wolverhampton,
West Midlands WV3 0EG
Tel: +44 (0)1902 341230
Email: info@theroyal.school
Website: theroyalschool.co.uk
Principal: Mr Mark Heywood
Age range: 4–19 years
(boarding from 11)
No. of pupils: 1476
Fees: FB £14,580

The Shrubbery School
Walmley Ash Road, Walmley, Sutton
Coldfield, West Midlands B76 1HY
Tel: 01213 511582
Head Teacher: Mrs Amanda Lees
Age range: 3–11 years

WEST HOUSE SCHOOL
For further details see p.294
24 St James's Road, Edgbaston,
Birmingham, West Midlands B15 2NX
Tel: 0121 440 4097
Email: secretary@
westhouseprep.com
Website: www.westhouseprep.com
Headmaster: Mr Alistair M J
Lyttle BA(Hons), PGCE, NPQH
Age range: B6 months–11
years G6 months–4 years
No. of pupils: 350
Fees: Day £2,200–£4,226

Wolverhampton Grammar School
Compton Road, Wolverhampton,
West Midlands WV3 9RB
Tel: 01902 421326
Head: Mr Alex Frazer
Age range: 4–18 years

Worcestershire

Abberley Hall School
Abberley Hall, Worcester,
Worcestershire WR6 6DD
Tel: 01299 896275
Headmaster: Mr Jonnie Besley
Age range: 2–13 years

Bowbrook House School
Peopleton, Pershore,
Worcestershire WR10 2EE
Tel: 01905 841242
Headteacher: Mr C D Allen BSc(Hons)
Age range: 3–16 years
Fees: Day £5,775–£11,388

Bromsgrove Preparatory School
Old Station Road, Bromsgrove,
Worcestershire B60 2BU
Tel: 01527 579600
Headmistress: Jacqui Deval-Reed
Age range: 7–13 years
Fees: Day £11,640–£15,105 WB
£17,685–£21,390 FB £24,240–£29,895

Bromsgrove Pre-preparatory & Nursery School
Avoncroft House, Hanbury Road,
Bromsgrove, Worcestershire B60 4JS
Tel: 01527 579679 (Ext:204)
Age range: 2–7 years

Bromsgrove School
Worcester Road, Bromsgrove,
Worcestershire B61 7DU
Tel: +44 (0)1527 579679
Headmaster: Peter Clague
Age range: 13–18 years
No. of pupils: 1300
Fees: Day £17,940 WB £26,610 FB £40,155

Heathfield Knoll School
Wolverley, Kidderminster,
Worcestershire DY10 3QE
Tel: 01562 850204
Head of School: Mr. L. G. Collins
B.Sc.(Hons), M.A.,P.G.C.E.
Age range: 3 months–16 years
No. of pupils: 223
Fees: Day £9,045–£14,283

King's Hawford
Lock Lane, Claines, Worcester,
Worcestershire WR3 7SD
Tel: 01905 451292
Head of School: Ms Jennie Phillips
Age range: 2–11 years
No. of pupils: 270
Fees: Day £2,661–£4,789

King's St Alban's
Mill Street, Worcester, WR1 2NJ
Tel: 01905 354906
Head of School: Mr Richard Chapman
Age range: 2–11 years
No. of pupils: 182
Fees: Day £2,538–£4,593

King's Worcester
5 College Green, Worcester,
Worcestershire WR1 2LL
Tel: 01905 721700
Headteacher: Mr Gareth Doodes
Age range: 11–18 years
No. of pupils: 896
Fees: Day £4,850

Madinatul Uloom Islamic College
Butts Lane, Stone, Kidderminster,
Worcestershire DY10 4BH
Tel: 01562 66894
The Head: Head
Age range: B11–24 years
No. of pupils: 200

Madresfield Early Years Centre
Hayswood Farm, Madresfield,
Malvern, Worcestershire WR13 5AA
Tel: 01684 574378
Head: Mrs A Bennett M.B.E.
Age range: 1–5 years
No. of pupils: 216
Fees: Day £5,800–£6,500

Malvern College
College Road, Malvern,
Worcestershire WR14 3DF
Tel: +44 (0)1684 581515
Headmaster: Keith Metcalfe
MA (Cantab)
Age range: 13–18 years
No. of pupils: 660

Malvern St James Girls' School
15 Avenue Road, Great Malvern,
Worcestershire WR14 3BA
Tel: 01684 892288
Headteacher: Mrs Olivera
Raraty BA PGCE
Age range: G4–18 years
(boarding from 7)

RGS Dodderhill
Crutch Lane, Droitwich,
Worcestershire WR9 0BE
Tel: 01905 778290
Headmistress: Mrs Sarah Atkinson
Age range: B2–11 years G2–16 years
No. of pupils: 190
Fees: Day £6,870–£11,700

RGS Springfield
Springfield, Britannia Square,
Worcester, Worcestershire WR1 3DL
Tel: 01905 24999
Headmistress: Mrs Laura Brown
Age range: 2–11 years
No. of pupils: 140
Fees: Day £8,160–£12,546

RGS The Grange
Grange Lane, Claines, Worcester,
Worcestershire WR3 7RR
Tel: 01905 451205
Headmaster: Mr Gareth Hughes
Age range: 2–11 years

River School
Oakfield House, Rose Bank,
Worcester, Worcestershire WR3 7ST
Tel: 01905 457047
Headteacher: Mr Adrian Parsonage
Age range: 2–16 years

The Downs Malvern
Colwall, Malvern,
Worcestershire WR13 6EY
Tel: 01684 544100
Headmaster: Mr Alastair Cook
Age range: 3–13 years
Fees: Day £7,107–£17,076 WB
£12,882–£19,890 FB £14,640–£22,602

The Elms
Colwall, Malvern,
Worcestershire WR13 6EF
Tel: 01684 540344
Headmaster: Mr Chris Hattam
Age range: 3–13 years
No. of pupils: 200
Fees: Day £8,085–£19,500
FB £24,000–£24,480

The Royal Grammar School Worcester
Upper Tything, Worcester,
Worcestershire WR1 1HP
Tel: 01905 613391
Headmaster: Mr John Pitt
Age range: 11–18 years
No. of pupils: 764
Fees: Day £13,080

Winterfold House
Chaddesley Corbett, Kidderminster,
Worcestershire DY10 4PW
Tel: 01562 777234
Headmistress: Mrs Denise
Toms BA (Hons) QTS, NPQH
Age range: 3 months–13 years

Yorkshire & Humberside

KEY TO SYMBOLS

- 🚹 *Boys' school*
- 🚺 *Girls' school*
- 🌐 *International school*
- 16 *Tutorial or sixth form college*
- Ⓐ *A levels*
- 🏫 *Boarding accommodation*
- £ *Bursaries*
- IB *International Baccalaureate*
- 🖊 *Learning support*
- 16 *Entrance at 16+*
- *Vocational qualifications*
- IAPS *Independent Association of Preparatory Schools*
- HMC *The Headmasters' & Headmistresses' Conference*
- ISA *Independent Schools Association*
- GSA *Girls' School Association*
- BSA *Boarding Schools' Association*
- S *Society of Heads*

Unless otherwise indicated, all schools are coeducational day schools.
Single-sex and boarding schools will be indicated by the relevant icon.

East Riding of Yorkshire

Froebel House School
5 Marlborough Avenue, Kingston upon Hull, East Riding of Yorkshire HU5 3JP
Tel: 01482 342272
Head Teacher: Mr A Roberts M.Ed BA Hons PGCE
Age range: 4–11 years

Hessle Mount School
Jenny Brough Lane, Hessle, East Riding of Yorkshire HU13 0JZ
Tel: 01482 643371
Principal: Miss Sarah Cutting
Age range: 3–8 years

Hymers College
Hymers Avenue, Kingston upon Hull, East Riding of Yorkshire HU3 1LW
Tel: 01482 343555
Headmaster: Mr Justin Stanley
Age range: 8–18 years

Tranby
Tranby Croft, Anlaby, Kingston upon Hull, East Riding of Yorkshire HU10 7EH
Tel: 01482 657016
Headmistress: Mrs Alex Wilson BA (Surrey) PGCE (Cantab) MA (London)
Age range: 3–18 years
No. of pupils: 576

North Yorkshire

St Peter's 13-18
Clifton, York, North Yorkshire YO30 6AB
Tel: 01904 527300
Head Master: Mr Jeremy Walker
Age range: 13–18 years

St Peter's 2-8
Clifton, York, North Yorkshire YO30 6AB
Tel: 01904 527361
Head of School: Mr Phil Hardy
Age range: 2–8 years

St Peter's 8-13
Queen Anne's Road, York, North Yorkshire YO30 7WA
Tel: 01904 527416
Head of School: Mr Andy Falconer
Age range: 8–13 years

Ampleforth College
York, North Yorkshire YO62 4ER
Tel: 01439 766000
Head: Mr Robin Dyer
Age range: 11–18 years

Ashville College
Green Lane, Harrogate, North Yorkshire HG2 9JP
Tel: +44 (0)1423 566358
Head: Mrs Rhiannon Wilkinson
Age range: 2–18 years

Aysgarth School
Newton le Willows, Bedale, North Yorkshire DL8 1TF
Tel: 01677 450240
Head of School: Mr Rob Morse
Age range: B3–13 years (boarding from 8) G3–8 years

Belmont Grosvenor School
Swarcliffe Hall, Birstwith, Harrogate, North Yorkshire HG3 2JG
Tel: 01423 771029
Acting Headteacher: Mrs E Shea
Age range: 0–11 years

Bootham Junior School
Rawcliffe Lane, York, North Yorkshire YO30 6NP
Tel: 01904 655021
Head: Mrs Helen Todd
Age range: 3–11 years
Fees: Day £2,430–£3,630

Bootham School
York, North Yorkshire YO30 7BU
Tel: 01904 623261
Head: Mr Chris Jeffery BA, FRSA
Age range: 11–18 years

Brackenfield School
128 Duchy Road, Harrogate, North Yorkshire HG1 2HE
Tel: 01423 508558
Headteacher: Mr Joe Masterson
Age range: 2–11 years

Chapter House Preparatory School
Thorpe Underwood Hall, Ouseburn, York, North Yorkshire YO26 9SS
Tel: 01423 33 33 30
Head Teacher: Mrs Karen Kilkenny BSc
Age range: 3 months–10 years

Cundall Manor School
Cundall, North Yorkshire YO61 2RW
Tel: 01423 360200
Headmaster: Mr Christopher James-Roll
Age range: 2–16 years (boarding from 7)
Fees: Day £10,785–£17,805 WB £22,395–£23,115

Fyling Hall School
Robin Hood's Bay, Whitby, North Yorkshire YO22 4QD
Tel: 01947 880353
Headmaster: Mr. Steven Allen
Age range: 4–18 years

Giggleswick Junior School
Settle, North Yorkshire BD24 0DG
Tel: 01729 893100
Headmaster: Mr Sam Hart
Age range: 2–11 years
No. of pupils: 98
Fees: Day £9,195–£14,505 WB £23,175 FB £24,000

Giggleswick School
Settle, North Yorkshire BD24 0DE
Tel: 01729 893000
Headmaster: Mr Sam Hart
Age range: 11–18 years
No. of pupils: 341
Fees: Day £17,850–£24,000 WB £26,205–£34,005 FB £27,450–£37,128

Harrogate Ladies' College
Clarence Drive, Harrogate, North Yorkshire HG1 2QG
Tel: 01423 504543
Principal: Mrs Sylvia Brett
Age range: G11–18 years (boarding from 11)

Highfield Prep School
Clarence Drive, Harrogate, North Yorkshire HG1 2QG
Tel: 01423 537060
Head: Mr James Savile
Age range: 2–11 years

POCKLINGTON SCHOOL
For further details see p.298
West Green, Pocklington, York, North Yorkshire YO42 2NJ
Tel: 01759 321200
Email: admissions@pocklingtonschool.com
Website: www.pocklingtonschool.com
Headmaster: Mr Toby Seth MA (Cantab)
Age range: 2–18 years
No. of pupils: 775 VIth180
Fees: Day £17,127 WB £27,321 FB £31,434

QUEEN ETHELBURGA'S COLLEGIATE
For further details see p.300
Thorpe Underwood Hall, Ouseburn, York, North Yorkshire YO26 9SS
Tel: 01423 33 33 30
Email: admissions@qe.org
Website: www.qe.org
Principal: Dan Machin
Age range: 3–19 years (boarding from 7)
No. of pupils: 1400

Queen Margaret's School
Escrick Park, York, North Yorkshire YO19 6EU
Tel: 01904 727600
Head: Ms Sue Baillie
Age range: G11–18 years (boarding from 11)

Queen Mary's School
Baldersby Park, Topcliffe, Thirsk,
North Yorkshire YO7 3BZ
Tel: 01845 575000
Head: Carole Cameron
Age range: B4–7 years G4–16
years (boarding from 7)

Scarborough College
Filey Road, Scarborough,
North Yorkshire YO11 3BA
Tel: +44 (0)1723 360620
Headmaster: Mr Guy Emmett
Age range: 3–18 years
(boarding from 11)
No. of pupils: 484
Fees: Day £8,022–£15,741
FB £24,528–£32,277

Terrington Hall
Terrington, York, North
Yorkshire YO60 6PR
Tel: 01653 648227
Headmaster: Mr. Simon Kibler
Age range: 3–13 years

The Mount School York
Dalton Terrace, York, North
Yorkshire YO24 4DD
Tel: 01904 667500
Principal: Mr David Griffiths
Age range: G3–18 years
(boarding from 11)

The Read School
Drax, Selby, North Yorkshire YO8 8NL
Tel: 01757 618248
Head: Ms Ruth Ainley
Age range: 4–18 years
(boarding from 8)

Wharfedale Montessori School
Bolton Abbey, Skipton, North
Yorkshire BD23 6AN
Tel: 01756 710452
Age range: 6 months–11 years

York Steiner School
Danesmead, Fulford Cross, York,
North Yorkshire YO10 4PB
Tel: 01904 654983
Headteacher: Ms Annabel Gibb
Age range: 0–14 years

North-East Lincolnshire

OneSchool Global UK
Ridgeway Campus
Ridge Way, Scunthorpe, North-
East Lincolnshire DN17 1BS
Tel: 03300 552611
Age range: 7–18 years

St Martin's Preparatory School
63 Bargate, Grimsby, North-
East Lincolnshire DN34 5AA
Tel: 01472 878907
Age range: 2–11 years

St. James School
22 Bargate, Grimsby, North-
East Lincolnshire DN34 4SY
Tel: 01472 503260
Headmistress: Ms Trudy Harris
Age range: 11–18 years

The Children's House
Station Road, Stallingborough,
North-East Lincolnshire DN41 8AJ
Tel: 01472 886000
Headteacher: Ms Theresa Ellerby
Age range: 4–11 years

South Yorkshire

Al-Mahad-Al-Islam School
1 Industry Road, Sheffield,
South Yorkshire S9 5FP
Tel: 01142 431224
Headteacher: Mrs Juwairiah Khan
Age range: G11–17 years

Bethany School
Finlay Street, Sheffield,
South Yorkshire S3 7PS
Tel: 0114 272 6994
Head of School: Mr David Charles
B.Eng. (Hons) (Sheffield) PGCE
Age range: 4–16 years

Birkdale School
4 Oakholme Road, Sheffield,
South Yorkshire S10 3DH
Tel: 01142 668408
Head of School: Mr Peter Harris
Age range: B4–18 years G16–18 years

Hill House School
6th Avenue, Auckley, Doncaster,
South Yorkshire DN9 3GG
Tel: +44 (0)1302 776300
Headmaster: Mr David Holland
Age range: 3–18 years

Mylnhurst Preparatory
School & Nursery
Button Hill, Woodholm Road, Ecclesall,
Sheffield, South Yorkshire S11 9HJ
Tel: 0114 2361411
Headmistress: Mrs Hannah
Cunningham
Age range: 3–11 years

Sheffield Girls' GDST
10 Rutland Park, Sheffield,
South Yorkshire S10 2PE
Tel: 01142 660324
Head: Mrs Nina Gunson
Age range: G4–18 years

Sycamore Hall Preparatory School
1 Hall Flat Lane, Balby, Doncaster,
South Yorkshire DN4 8PT
Tel: 01302 856800
Headmistress: Miss Jane Spencer
Age range: 3–11 years

Westbourne School
60 Westbourne Road, Sheffield,
South Yorkshire S10 2QT
Tel: 01142 660374
Headmaster: Mr John B Hicks MEd
Age range: 3–16 years

West Yorkshire

Ackworth School
Pontefract Road, Ackworth,
Pontefract, West Yorkshire WF7 7LT
Tel: 01977 233 600
Headteacher: Mr. Anton
Maree BA Rhodes (HDE)
Age range: 2–18 years
No. of pupils: 510
Fees: Day £3,000–£4,935
FB £8,436–£10,692

Al Mu'min Primary School
Clifton St, Bradford, West
Yorkshire BD8 7DA
Tel: 01274 488593
Headteacher: Mr M M Azam
Age range: 4–11 years
No. of pupils: 102

Al-Furqaan Preparatory School
Drill Hall House, Bath Street,
Dewsbury, West Yorkshire WF13 2JR
Tel: 01924 453 661
Head of School: Ms
Shaheda Ughratdar
Age range: 2–11 years

Bradford Christian School
Livingstone Road, Bolton Woods,
Bradford, West Yorkshire BD2 1BT
Tel: 01274 532649
Headmaster: P J Moon BEd(Hons)
Age range: 4–16 years
Fees: Day £2,460–£4,440

Bradford Grammar School
Keighley Road, Bradford,
West Yorkshire BD9 4JP
Tel: 01274 542492
Headmaster: Dr Simon Hinchliffe
Age range: 6–18 years
No. of pupils: VIth266

Brontë House School
Apperley Bridge, Bradford,
West Yorkshire BD10 0NR
Tel: 0113 250 2811
Head: Mrs Sarah Chatterton
Age range: 2–11 years
No. of pupils: 312
Fees: Day £9,765–£12,978

Crystal Gardens
38-40 Greaves Street, Bradford,
West Yorkshire BD5 7PE
Tel: 01274 575400
Headteacher: Rashta Bibi
Age range: 4–11 years

**Dale House Independent
School & Nursery**
Ruby Street, Carlinghow, Batley,
West Yorkshire WF17 8HL
Tel: 01924 422215
Headmistress: Mrs S M G
Fletcher BA, CertEd
Age range: 2–11 years

**Darul Uloom Dawatul Imaan
(Darul Uloom Bradford)**
Harry Street, Off Wakefield Road,
Bradford, West Yorkshire BD4 9PH
Tel: 01274 402233
Headteacher: Moulana
Abdurrahman Kayat Sahib
Age range: B11–25 years

Eternal Light Secondary School
Christopher Street, Off Little Horton
Lane, Bradford, West Yorkshire BD5 9DH
Tel: 01274 501597
Headteacher: Mr Yusuf Collector
Age range: B11–15 years
No. of pupils: 91

Fulneck School
Fulneck, Pudsey, Leeds,
West Yorkshire LS28 8DS
Tel: +44 (0)113 257 0235
Principal: Ms Francine Smith
Age range: 3–18 years
(boarding from 11)

Gateways School
Leeds Road, Harewood, Leeds,
West Yorkshire LS17 9LE
Tel: 0113 2886345
Headmistress: Dr Tracy Johnson
Age range: B2–15 years G2–18 years
No. of pupils: 430
Fees: Day £9,270–£14,865

Ghyll Royd School and Pre-School
Greystone Manor, Ilkley Road, Burley in
Wharfedale, West Yorkshire LS29 7HW
Tel: 01943 865575
Headteacher: Mr David
Martin BA MA PGCE
Age range: 2–11 years
No. of pupils: 100
Fees: Day £3,200

Hipperholme Grammar School
Bramley Lane, Hipperholme,
Halifax, West Yorkshire HX3 8JE
Tel: 01422 202256
Headteacher: Mr Nicholas James
Age range: 11–16 years
Fees: Day £10,410–£13,002

Huddersfield Grammar School
Royds Mount, Luck Lane, Marsh,
Huddersfield, West Yorkshire HD1 4QX
Tel: 01484 424549
Headmistress: Mrs Donna Holmes
Age range: 3–16 years
No. of pupils: 546
Fees: Day £9,009–£11,103

Institute of Islamic Education
South Street, Savile Town, Dewsbury,
West Yorkshire WF12 9NG
Tel: 01924 485712/01924 455762
Principal: Mr Mohamed Aswat
Age range: B11–25 years
No. of pupils: 184

**Islamic Tarbiyah
Preparatory School**
Ambler Street, Bradford,
West Yorkshire BD8 8AW
Tel: 01274 490462
Headteacher: Mr S A Nawaz
Age range: 5–10 years

**Jaamiatul Imaam Muhammad
Zakaria School**
Thornton View Road, Clayton,
Bradford, West Yorkshire BD14 6JX
Tel: 01274 882007
Headteacher: Mrs Z Hajee
Age range: G11–16 years
No. of pupils: 416

Lady Lane Park School
Lady Lane, Bingley, West
Yorkshire BD16 4AP
Tel: 01274 551168
Headmaster: Mr Nigel Saunders
Age range: 2–11 years
No. of pupils: 150
Fees: Day £8,016

Leeds Menorah School
399 Street Lane, Leeds, West
Yorkshire LS17 6JQ
Tel: 0113 2697709
Age range: 3–16 years

M A Institute
Lumb Lane, Bradford, West
Yorkshire BD8 7RZ
Tel: 01274 395454
Age range: B11–16 years
No. of pupils: 68

Madni Academy
40-42 Scarborough Street, Savile Town,
Dewsbury, West Yorkshire WF12 9AY
Tel: 01924 500335
Headmistress: Mrs S A Mirza
Age range: G3–18 years

Mill Cottage Montessori School
Wakefield Road, Brighouse,
West Yorkshire HD6 4HA
Tel: 01484 400500
Principal: Ailsa Nevile
Age range: 0–11 years

Moorfield School
Wharfedale Lodge, 11 Ben Rhydding
Road, Ilkley, West Yorkshire LS29 8RL
Tel: 01943 607285
Headmistress: Mrs Tina Herbert
Age range: 2–11 years
No. of pupils: 110
Fees: Day £10,395

Moorlands School
Foxhill, Weetwood Lane, Leeds,
West Yorkshire I S16 5PF
Tel: 0113 2785286
Headteacher: Miss J Atkinson
Age range: 2–11 years
No. of pupils: 149
Fees: Day £8,985–£10,566

Netherleigh & Rossefield School
Parsons Road, Heaton, Bradford,
West Yorkshire BD9 4AY
Tel: 01274 543162
Headteacher: Miss A Leary
Age range: 2–11 years

New Horizon Community School
Newton Hill House, Newton Hill Road,
Leeds, West Yorkshire LS7 4JE
Tel: 0113 262 4001
Acting Head: Qudisia Butt
Age range: G11–16 years
No. of pupils: 87
Fees: Day £1,800

Olive Secondary School
Byron Street, Bradford, West
Yorkshire BD3 0AD
Tel: +44+ (0)1274 725005 /
+44 (0)1274 725013
Headteacher: Mr Amjad Mohammed
Age range: 11–18 years
No. of pupils: 115
Fees: Day £2,075

OneSchool Global UK
York Campus
Bishopthorpe Road, York,
West Yorkshire YO23 2QA
Tel: 01904 663300
Age range: 7–18 years

Paradise Primary School
1 Bretton Street, Dewsbury,
West Yorkshire WF12 9BB
Tel: 01924 439803
Headteacher: Mrs Hafsa Patel
Age range: 2–11 years
No. of pupils: 217

Queen Elizabeth Grammar
School (Junior School)
158 Northgate, Wakefield,
West Yorkshire WF1 3QY
Tel: 01924 373821
Acting Head: Mr M Shevill
BEd MSc FCCT
Age range: B4–11 years
(symbol)

Queen Elizabeth Grammar
School (Senior School)
154 Northgate, Wakefield,
West Yorkshire WF1 3QX
Tel: 01924 373943
Acting Head: Mr Martin
Shevill BEd MSc FCCT
Age range: B11–18 years
(symbols)

Queenswood School
Queen Street, Morley, Leeds,
West Yorkshire LS27 9EB
Tel: 0113 2534033
Headteacher: Mrs J A Tanner
MMus, BA, FTCL, ARCO
Age range: 4–11 years
Fees: Day £6,000–£6,447

Richmond House School
170 Otley Road, Leeds, West
Yorkshire LS16 5LG
Tel: 0113 2752670
Headteacher: Mrs Helen Stiles
Age range: 3–11 years
No. of pupils: 219
Fees: Day £5,850–£9,150
(symbols)

RISHWORTH SCHOOL
For further details see p.302
Oldham Road, Sowerby Bridge,
Halifax, West Yorkshire HX6 4QA
Tel: 01422 822217
Email: admissions@
rishworth-school.co.uk
Website:
www.rishworth-school.co.uk
Head: Dr Anthony Wilkins
Age range: 3–18 years
(boarding from 11)
(symbols)

Silcoates School
Wrenthorpe, Wakefield,
West Yorkshire WF2 0PD
Tel: 01924 291614
Headmaster: Chris Wainman MA
Age range: 4–18 years
(symbols)

The Branch Christian School
Dewsbury Revival Centre,
West Park Street, Dewsbury,
West Yorkshire WF13 4LA
Tel: +44 (0)1924 452511
Head of School: Jo Holt
Age range: 3–16 years
No. of pupils: 26
(symbol)

THE FROEBELIAN SCHOOL
For further details see p.304
Clarence Road, Horsforth,
Leeds, West Yorkshire LS18 4LB
Tel: 0113 2583047
Email: office@froebelian.co.uk
Website: www.froebelian.com
Head Teacher: Mrs Catherine
Dodds BEd (Hons), PGCE
Age range: 3–11 years
No. of pupils: 160
Fees: Day £5,850–£8,700
(symbols)

The Gleddings School
Birdcage Lane, Savile Park,
Halifax, West Yorkshire HX3 0JB
Tel: 01422 354605
School Director: Mrs Jill Wilson CBE
Age range: 3–11 years
No. of pupils: 191
Fees: Day £3,555–£5,910

The Grammar School at Leeds
Alwoodley Gates, Harrogate Road,
Leeds, West Yorkshire LS17 8GS
Tel: 0113 2291552
Principal: Mrs Sue Woodroofe
Age range: 3–18 years
No. of pupils: 2120 VIth418
Fees: Day £9,441–£13,788
(symbols)

The Mount School
3 Binham Road, Edgerton,
Huddersfield, West Yorkshire HD2 2AP
Tel: 01484 426432
Head of School: Mr Euan Burton-Smith
Age range: 3–11 years
No. of pupils: 115
Fees: Day £8,070
(symbol)

Wakefield Girls' High
School (Junior School)
2 St John's Square, Wakefield,
West Yorkshire WF1 2QX
Tel: 01924 374577
Head: Ms Heidi-Jayne Boyes BSc (Hons)
Age range: G4–11 years
(symbols)

Wakefield Girls' High
School (Senior School)
Wentworth Street, Wakefield,
West Yorkshire WF1 2QS
Tel: 01924 372490
Head: Ms Heidi-Jayne Boyes BSc (Hons)
Age range: G11–18 years
(symbols)

Wakefield Grammar Pre-
Preparatory School
Margaret Street, Wakefield,
West Yorkshire WF1 2DG
Tel: 01924 231627
Age range: 3–7 years

Wakefield Independent School
The Nostell Centre, Doncaster
Road, Nostell, Wakefield,
West Yorkshire WF4 1QG
Tel: 01924 865757
Headmistress: Mrs K E Caryl
Age range: 3–16 years

Westville House School
Carter's Lane, Middleton, Ilkley,
West Yorkshire LS29 0DQ
Tel: 01943 608053
Headteacher: Mrs Nikki
Hammond BA(Hons) PGCE
Age range: 3–11 years
(symbol)

Woodhouse Grove School
Apperley Bridge, Bradford,
West Yorkshire BD10 0NR
Tel: 0113 250 2477
Headmaster: Mr James Lockwood
Age range: 11–18 years
No. of pupils: 751 VIth200
Fees: Day £14,490–£14,694
FB £30,555–£30,720
(symbols)

Northern Ireland

KEY TO SYMBOLS

- ⚲ *Boys' school*
- ⚲ *Girls' school*
- 🌐 *International school*
- 16 *Tutorial or sixth form college*
- Ⓐ *A levels*
- ♟ *Boarding accommodation*
- £ *Bursaries*
- Ⓘ *International Baccalaureate*
- ✎ *Learning support*
- 16 *Entrance at 16+*
- ✿ *Vocational qualifications*
- (IAPS) *Independent Association of Preparatory Schools*
- (HMC) *The Headmasters' & Headmistresses' Conference*
- (ISA) *Independent Schools Association*
- (GSA) *Girls' School Association*
- (BSA) *Boarding Schools' Association*
- S *Society of Heads*

Unless otherwise indicated, all schools are coeducational day schools.
Single-sex and boarding schools will be indicated by the relevant icon.

County Antrim

Ballymoney Independent Christian School
55 Market Street, Ballymoney, County Antrim BT53 6ED
Tel: 028 2766 3402
Principal: Mrs J Boyd
Age range: 3–11 years

Belfast Royal Academy
5-17 Cliftonville Road, Belfast, County Antrim BT14 6JL
Tel: 028 9074 0423
Principal: Mrs Hilary Woods
Age range: 11–18 years
Ⓐ 16+

Bloomfield Collegiate School
Astoria Gardens, Upper Newtownards Road, Belfast, County Antrim BT5 6HW
Tel: 028 90 471214
Principal: Mr G Greer
Age range: G11–18 years

Campbell College
Belmont Road, Belfast, County Antrim BT4 2ND
Tel: 028 9076 3076
Headmaster: Mr Robert Robinson
Age range: B11–18 years

Campbell College Junior School
Belmont Road, Belfast, County Antrim BT4 2ND
Tel: 028 9076 3076
Head of Junior School: Miss Andrea Brown
Age range: B3–11 years G3–4 years

Dominican College
38 Fortwilliam Park, Belfast, County Antrim BT15 4AQ
Tel: 028 90 370298
Principal: Ms Lynda Catney
Age range: G11–18 years

Hunterhouse College
Upper Lisburn Road, Finaghy, Belfast, County Antrim BT10 0LE
Tel: 028 9061 2293
Principal: Mr Andrew Gibson MA, DipEd, PQH
Age range: G11–18 years

Inchmarlo
Cranmore Park, Belfast, County Antrim BT9 6JR
Tel: 028 9038 1454
Headteacher: Mrs A Morwood
Age range: B4–11 years

Methodist College
1 Malone Road, Belfast, County Antrim BT9 6BY
Tel: 028 9020 5205
Principal: Mr Scott Naismith
Age range: 4–18 years

Newtownabbey Independent Christian school
307-309 Ballyclare Road, Glengormley, Newtownabbey, County Antrim BT36 4TQ
Tel: 028 9084 4937
Principal: Mrs L McClung
Age range: 4–18 years

Royal Belfast Academical Institution
College Square East, Belfast, County Antrim BT1 6DL
Tel: 028 9024 0461
Principal: Ms Janet Williamson
Age range: B11–18 years

St Mary's Christian Brothers' Grammar School
147a Glen Road, Belfast, County Antrim BT11 8NR
Tel: 028 9029 4000
Head of School: Mrs Siobhan Kelly
Age range: B11–19 years

Victoria College Belfast
2A Cranmore Park, Belfast, County Antrim BT9 6JA
Tel: 028 9066 1506
Principal: Mrs Karen Quinn
Age range: G3–19 years

County Armagh

Portadown Independent Christian School
Levaghery Gardens, Portadown, County Armagh BT63 5EQ
Tel: 028 3833 6733
Principal: Miss Diane Haffey
Age range: 3–16 years

The Royal School, Armagh
College Hill, Armagh, County Armagh BT61 9DH
Tel: 02837 522807
Headmaster: Mr Graham G W Montgomery
Age range: 4–18 years (boarding from 8)

County Down

Bangor Grammar School
84 Gransha Road, Bangor, County Down BT19 7QU
Tel: 028 91 473734
Headteacher: Mrs E P Huddleson
Age range: B11–18 years

Bangor Independent Christian School
277A Clandeboye Road, Bangor, County Down BT19 1AA
Tel: 028 9145 0240
Headteacher: Miss Anna Priestley
Age range: 3–16 years

Harmony Christian School
17-19 Main Street, Ballynahinch, County Down BT24 8DH
Tel: 028 9756 3487
Principal: Mrs Leanne Woods
Age range: 4–18 years

Holywood Steiner School
34 Croft Road, Holywood, County Down BT18 0PR
Tel: 028 9042 8029
Headteacher: Mr Peter Chambers
Age range: 3–17 years

Mourne Independent Christian School
5 Carrigenagh Road, Kilkeel, County Down BT34 4NE
Tel: 028 417 62712
Principal: Mrs H Campbell
Age range: 4–16 years

OneSchool Global UK Newry Campus
22 Rampart Road, Newry, County Down BT34 2QU
Tel: 02830 260777
Age range: 7–18 years

Rockport School
15 Rockport Road, Craigavad, Holywood, County Down BT18 0DD
Tel: 028 9042 8372
Headmaster: Mr George Vance
Age range: 3–18 years

County Londonderry

Coleraine Grammar School
23-33 Castlerock Road, Coleraine, County Londonderry BT51 3LA
Tel: 028 7034 4331
Headmaster: Dr David Carruthers
Age range: 11–18 years

OneSchool Global UK Knockloughrim Campus
23 Rocktown Road, Knockloughrim, County Londonderry BT45 8QE
Tel: 02879 645191
Age range: 7–18 years

County Tyrone

Clogher Valley Independent Christian School
150 Ballagh Road, Fivemiletown, County Tyrone BT75 0QP
Tel: 028 89521851
Principal: Mrs R Carscadden
Age range: 4–16 years

Kilskeery Independent Christian School
19 Old Junction Road, Kilskeery, Omagh, County Tyrone BT78 3RN
Tel: 028 89 561 560
Principal: Mrs Pamela Foster
Age range: 4–18 years

The Royal School, Dungannon
2 Ranfurly Road, Dungannon, County Tyrone BT71 6EG
Tel: 02887 722710
Headmaster: Dr David Burnett
Age range: 11–18 years (boarding from 11)

Scotland

KEY TO SYMBOLS

- ⚤ Boys' school
- ⚤ Girls' school
- 🌐 International school
- 16- Tutorial or sixth form college
- Ⓐ A levels
- ⚑ Boarding accommodation
- £ Bursaries
- IB International Baccalaureate
- ✎ Learning support
- 16+ Entrance at 16+
- Vocational qualifications
- IAPS Independent Association of Preparatory Schools
- HMC The Headmasters' & Headmistresses' Conference
- ISA Independent Schools Association
- GSA Girls' School Association
- BSA Boarding Schools' Association
- S Society of Heads

Unless otherwise indicated, all schools are coeducational day schools. Single-sex and boarding schools will be indicated by the relevant icon.

Aberdeen

Albyn School
17-23 Queen's Road,
Aberdeen AB15 4PB
Tel: 01224 322408
Headmaster: Mr Stefan Horsman
Age range: 2–18 years
Ⓐ Ⓔ ✎ 16+

International School of Aberdeen
Pitfodels House, North Deeside Road,
Pitfodels, Cults, Aberdeen AB15 9PN
Tel: 01224 730300
Head of School: Mr Nick Little
Age range: 3–18 years
🌐 Ⓔ ⒾⒷ ✎ 16+

Robert Gordon's College
Schoolhill, Aberdeen AB10 1FE
Tel: 01224 646346
Head of College: Mr
Robin Macpherson
Age range: 3–18 years
Ⓔ ✎ 16+

St Margaret's School for Girls
17 Albyn Place, Aberdeen AB10 1RU
Tel: +44 (0)1224 584466
Headmistress: Miss Anna Tomlinson
Age range: B3–5 years G3–18 years
🏃 Ⓔ ✎ 16+

Aberdeenshire

**OneSchool Global UK
Caledonia (North) Campus**
Millden, Balmedie,
Aberdeenshire AB23 8YY
Tel: 01259 303030
Age range: 7–18 years

Angus

Lathallan School
Brotherton Castle, Johnshaven,
Montrose, Angus DD10 0HN
Tel: 01561 362220
Headmaster: Mr Richard Toley
Age range: 6 months–18 years
🏛 Ⓔ ✎ 16+

Argyll & Bute

Lomond School
10 Stafford Street, Helensburgh,
Argyll & Bute G84 9JX
Tel: +44 (0)1436 672476
Principal: Mrs Johanna Urquhart
Age range: 3–18 years
No. of pupils: 320
Fees: Day £9,200–£12,750
WB £22,150 FB £29,650
🌐 🏛 Ⓔ ⒾⒷ ✎ 16+

Borders

St. Mary's School
Abbey Park, Melrose, Borders TD6 9LN
Tel: 01896 822517
Headmaster: Mr Liam Harvey
Age range: 2–13 years
🏛 Ⓔ ✎

Clackmannanshire

Dollar Academy
Dollar, Clackmannanshire FK14 7DU
Tel: 01259 742511
Rector: Mr Ian Munro
Age range: 4–18 years
(boarding from 10)
No. of pupils: 1340
Fees: Day £10,899–£14,571 WB
£28,197–£31,869 FB £30,051–£33,723
🌐 🏛 ✎ 16+

**OneSchool Global UK
Caledonia (South) Campus**
The Pavillions, Stirling Road, Alloa,
Clackmannanshire FK10 1TA
Tel: 01259 303030
Age range: 7–18 years

Dundee

High School of Dundee
Euclid Crescent, Dundee DD1 1HU
Tel: 01382 202921
Rector: Mrs Lise Hudson
Age range: 3–18 years
No. of pupils: 1000
Fees: Day £9,618–£13,650
Ⓔ ✎ 16+

East Lothian

Belhaven Hill School
Belhaven Road, Dunbar,
East Lothian EH42 1NN
Tel: 01368 862785
Headmaster: Mr. Olly Langton
Age range: 5–13 years
🏛 ✎

Loretto Junior School
North Esk Lodge, 1 North High Street,
Musselburgh, East Lothian EH21 6JA
Tel: 0131 653 4570
Headmaster: Mr Andrew Dickenson
Age range: 3–12 years
🏛 Ⓔ ✎

LORETTO SCHOOL
For further details see p.308
Pinkie House, Linkfield Road,
Musselburgh, East Lothian EH21 7RE
Tel: +44 (0)131 653 4455
Email: admissions@loretto.com
Website: www.loretto.com
Head of School: Dr.
Graham R. W. Hawley
Age range: 3–18 years
No. of pupils: 520
Fees: Day £2,933–£8,385
FB £8,020–£12,315
🌐 Ⓐ 🏛 Ⓔ ✎ 16+

The Compass School
West Road, Haddington,
East Lothian EH41 3RD
Tel: 01620 822642
Headmaster: Mr Mark Becher
MA(Hons), PGCE
Age range: 3–12 years
✎

Edinburgh

Basil Paterson School & College
65/66 Queen Street, Edinburgh EH2 4NA
Tel: 01312 253802
Age range: 14–16+ years
16+ Ⓐ ✎

Cargilfield School
45 Gamekeeper's Road,
Edinburgh EH4 6HU
Tel: 0131 336 2207
Headmaster: Mr. Robert Taylor
Age range: 3–13 years
🏛 Ⓔ ✎

Clifton Hall School
Newbridge, Edinburgh EH28 8LQ
Tel: 0131 333 1359
Headmaster: Mr R Grant
Age range: 3–18 years
Ⓔ ✎ 16+

Edinburgh Montessori Arts School
18N Liberton Brae, Edinburgh EH16 6AE
Tel: 0131 600 0123
Principal: Ms Emma Rattigan
Age range: 1–18 years

Edinburgh Steiner School
60-64 Spylaw Road,
Edinburgh EH10 5BR
Tel: 0131 337 3410
Age range: 2–18 years
No. of pupils: 380
Ⓔ ✎ 16+

ESMS Junior School
11 Queensferry Terrace,
Edinburgh EH4 3EQ
Tel: +44 (0)131 311 1111
Head of School: Mr Mike Kane
Age range: 3–11 years
🏛 ✎

Fettes College
Carrington Road, Edinburgh EH4 1QX
Tel: +44 (0)131 332 2281
Head of School: Mrs Helen Harrison
Age range: 13–18 years
🌐 Ⓐ 🏛 Ⓔ ⒾⒷ ✎ 16+

Fettes College Preparatory School
East Fettes Avenue, Edinburgh EH4 1DL
Tel: +44 (0)131 332 2976
Headmaster: Mr A A Edwards
Age range: 7–13 years

George Heriot's School
Lauriston Place, Edinburgh EH3 9EQ
Tel: 0131 229 7263
Principal: Mr Gareth Warren
Age range: 3–18 years

George Watson's College
69-71 Colinton Road,
Edinburgh EH10 5EG
Tel: 0131 446 6000
Principal: Mr Melvyn Roffe
Age range: 3–18 years

Mannafields Christian School
Unit B12, St Margaret's House, 151
London Road, Edinburgh EH7 6AE
Tel: 131516 3221
Age range: 5–14 years

Merchiston Castle School
294 Colinton Road, Edinburgh EH13 0PU
Tel: 0131 312 2200
Headmaster: Mr Jonathan Anderson
Age range: B7–18 years
(boarding from 7)
No. of pupils: 400
Fees: Day £15,330–£26,040
FB £22,080–£35,880

Regius School
69a Whitehill Street, Newcraighall,
Edinburgh EH21 8QZ
Tel: 0131 669 2913
Age range: 5–14 years

St George's School for Girls
Garscube Terrace, Edinburgh EH12 6BG
Tel: 0131 311 8000
Head: Mrs Alex Hems
Age range: B3–5 years G3–18
years (boarding from 10)

St Mary's Music School
Coates Hall, 25 Grosvenor
Crescent, Edinburgh EH12 5EL
Tel: 0131 538 7766
Headteacher: Dr Kenneth Taylor
BSc Hons, PhD, PGCE, PG Dip
Age range: 9–19 years

Stewart's Melville College
Queensferry Road, Edinburgh EH4 3EZ
Tel: +44 (0)131 311 1000
Head of School: Mr Anthony Simpson
Age range: B12–18 years

The Edinburgh Academy
42 Henderson Row, Edinburgh EH3 5BL
Tel: 0131 556 4603
Rector: Barry Welsh
Age range: 2–18 years

The Mary Erskine School
Ravelston, Edinburgh EH4 3NT
Tel: +44 (0)131 347 5700
Head of School: Ms Kirsty Nicholson
Age range: G12–18 years
(boarding from 12)

Fife

St Leonards School
The Pends, St Andrews, Fife KY16 9QJ
Tel: 01334 472126
Head: Mr Simon Brian
Age range: 5–18 years
No. of pupils: 590
Fees: Day £10,726–£17,374
FB £26,289–£40,954

Glasgow

Belmont House School
Sandringham Avenue, Newton
Mearns, Glasgow G77 5DU
Tel: 0141 639 2922
Principal: Mr Melvyn D Shanks
BSc, DipEd, MInstP, CPhys, SQH
Age range: 3–18 years

Fernhill School
Fernbrae Avenue, Burnside,
Rutherglen, Glasgow G73 4SG
Tel: 0141 634 2674
Head Teacher: Mr Mark Donnelly
Age range: 2–18 years

Hutchesons' Grammar School
21 Beaton Road, Glasgow G41 4NW
Tel: 0141 423 2933
Rector: Mr Colin Gambles
BSc (Hons) PGCE
Age range: 3–18 years

Kelvinside Academy
33 Kirklee Road, Glasgow G12 0SW
Tel: 0141 357 3376
Rector: Mr Daniel J Wyatt BA (Ed) Hons
Age range: 3–18 years

Olivewood Primary School
81 Lister Street, Glasgow G4 0BZ
Age range: 5–11 years

St Aloysius' College
45 Hill Street, Glasgow G3 6RJ
Tel: 0141 332 3190
Head Master: Mr Matthew Bartlett
MA (Cantab), PGCE, NLE, NPQH
Age range: 3–18 years

**The Glasgow Academy,
Kelvinbridge**
Colebrooke Street, Kelvinbridge,
Glasgow G12 8HE
Tel: 0141 334 8558
Rector: Mr Matthew K
Pearce BA (Dunelm)
Age range: 3–18 years

The Glasgow Academy, Milngavie
Mugdock Road, Milngavie,
Glasgow G62 8NP
Tel: 0141 956 3758
Rector: Mr Matthew K
Pearce BA (Dunelm)
Age range: 3–8 years

The Glasgow Academy, Newlands
54 Newlands Road, Newlands,
Glasgow G43 2JG
Tel: 0141 632 0736
Rector: Mr Matthew K
Pearce BA (Dunelm)
Age range: 3–8 years

The High School of Glasgow
637 Crow Road, Glasgow G13 1PL
Tel: 0141 954 9628
Rector: Mr John O'Neill
Age range: 3–18 years

Moray

Drumduan School
Clovenside Road, Forres,
Moray IV36 2RD
Tel: + 44 (0)1309 676300
Principal Teacher: Krzysztof
Zajaczkowski
Age range: 3–18 years

Gordonstoun
Elgin, Moray IV30 5RF
Tel: 01343 837837
Principal: Ms Lisa Kerr BA
Age range: 4–18 years

Perth & Kinross

Ardvreck School
Crieff, Perth & Kinross PH7 4EX
Tel: 01764 653112
Headmistress: Mrs Ali Kinge
Age range: 3–13 years
(boarding from 7)
🏫 £ ✎

Craigclowan Preparatory School
Edinburgh Road, Perth,
Perth & Kinross PH2 8PS
Tel: 01738 626310
Head of School: John Gilmour
Age range: 3–13 years
No. of pupils: 212
Fees: Day £4,950
£ ✎

Glenalmond College, Perth
Glenalmond, Perth, Perth
& Kinross PH1 3RY
Tel: 01738 842000
Warden: Dr Michael Alderson
Age range: 12–18 years
🌍 Ⓐ 🏫 £ ✎ 16+

Kilgraston School
Bridge of Earn, Perth, Perth
& Kinross PH2 9BQ
Tel: 01738 812257
Head: Mrs Dorothy MacGinty
Age range: B5–12 years G5–18
years (boarding from 8)
👧 🌍 Ⓐ 🏫 £ ✎ 16+

Morrison's Academy
Ferntower Road, Crieff,
Perth & Kinross PH7 3AN
Tel: 01764 653885
Rector: Mr A J McGarva
Age range: 2–18 years
£ ✎ 16+

Strathallan School
Forgandenny, Perth, Perth
& Kinross PH2 9EG
Tel: 01738 812546
Headmaster: Mr Mark Lauder MA Hons
Age range: 7–18 years
No. of pupils: 545
Fees: Day £16,092–£25,452
FB £26,649–£38,199
🌍 Ⓐ 🏫 £ ✎ 16+

Perthshire

Queen Victoria School
Dunblane, Perthshire FK15 0JY
Tel: 01786 822288
Head: Donald Shaw BSc(Hons) PGCE
Age range: 11–18 years
🌍 🏫 ✎ 16+

Al-Qalam Primary & High School
Ben Nevis Road, Paisley,
Renfrewshire PA2 7LA
Tel: 014123 72236
Executive Head: Mr Shoeb Sarguroh
Age range: 5–14 years

Cedars School of Excellence
31 Ardgowan Square, Greenock,
Renfrewshire PA16 8NJ
Tel: 01475 723905
Interim Head: Ms Jennifer Offord
Age range: 5–18 years
✎

St Columba's School
Duchal Road, Kilmacolm,
Renfrewshire PA13 4AU
Tel: 01505 872238
Rector: Ms Victoria J. Reilly
Age range: 3–18 years
✎ 16+

South Ayrshire

Wellington School
Carleton Turrets, 1 Craigweil Road,
Ayr, South Ayrshire KA7 2XH
Tel: 01292 269321
Head: Mr S Johnson MA
(Cantab) PGCE
Age range: 3–18 years
£ ✎ 16+

South Lanarkshire

Hamilton College
Bothwell Road, Hamilton,
South Lanarkshire ML3 0AY
Tel: 01698 282700
Headteacher: Mr Richard Charman
Age range: 2–18 years
No. of pupils: 400
Fees: Day £8,985–£12,588
£ ✎ 16+

Stirling

Fairview International School, Bridge of Allan
52 Kenilworth Road, Bridge
of Allan, Stirling FK9 4RY
Tel: +44 (0)1786 231952
Headteacher: Mr David Hicks
Age range: 5–18 years
IB

Wales

KEY TO SYMBOLS

- ⚤ *Boys' school*
- ⚤ *Girls' school*
- 🌐 *International school*
- 16 *Tutorial or sixth form college*
- Ⓐ *A levels*
- 🏛 *Boarding accommodation*
- £ *Bursaries*
- IB *International Baccalaureate*
- ✎ *Learning support*
- 16 *Entrance at 16+*
- 🌐 *Vocational qualifications*
- IAPS *Independent Association of Preparatory Schools*
- HMC *The Headmasters' & Headmistresses' Conference*
- ISA *Independent Schools Association*
- GSA *Girls' School Association*
- BSA *Boarding Schools' Association*
- S *Society of Heads*

Unless otherwise indicated, all schools are coeducational day schools. Single-sex and boarding schools will be indicated by the relevant icon.

Cardiff

Cardiff Sixth Form College
1-3 Trinity Court, 21-27 Newport
Road, , Cardiff CF24 0AA
Tel: +44 (0)29 2049 3121
Principal: Mr Gareth Collier
Age range: 15–18 years

Carmarthenshire

Llandovery College
Queensway, Llandovery,
Carmarthenshire SA20 0EE
Tel: +44(0)1550 723000
Warden: Mr Dominic Findlay
Age range: 4–18 years

St. Michael's School
Bryn, Llanelli, Carmarthenshire SA14 9TU
Tel: 01554 820325
Headmaster: Mr Benson Ferrari
Age range: 3–18 years

Clwyd

Rydal Penrhos Preparatory School
Pwllycrochan Avenue, Colwyn
Bay, Clwyd LL29 7BT
Tel: +44 (0)1492 530 381
Head of School: Mrs Lucy Davies
Age range: 2–11 years

Rydal Penrhos Senior School
Pwllycrochan Avenue, Colwyn
Bay, Clwyd LL29 7BT
Tel: +44 (0)1492 530155
Head of School: Mr Phil Sutton
Age range: 11–18 years

St David's College
Gloddaeth Hall, Llandudno,
Clwyd LL30 1RD
Tel: 01492 875974
Headmaster: Mr Andrew Russell
Age range: 9–19 years
(boarding from 9)

Denbighshire

Fairholme Preparatory School
The Mount, Mount Road, St.
Asaph, Denbighshire LL17 0DH
Tel: 01745 583 505
Principal: Mrs E Perkins MA(Oxon)
Age range: 3–11 years

Myddelton College
Peakes Lane, Denbigh,
Denbighshire LL16 3EN
Tel: +44 174 547 2201
Head Teacher: Mr Andrew Allman
Age range: 4–18 years

Ruthin School
Mold Road, Ruthin,
Denbighshire LL15 1EE
Tel: 01824 702543
Interim Head: Ms Sue Frencham
Age range: 11–18 years

Glamorgan

Cardiff Academy
Harlech Court, Bute Terrace,
Cardiff, Glamorgan CF10 2FE
Tel: 02920 318 318
Principal: Mrs Caroline Williams
Age range: 16–19 years

Cardiff Montessori School
Golden Gate, 73 Ty Glas
Avenue, Llanishen, Cardiff,
Glamorgan CF14 5DX
Tel: 02920 567311
Head of School: Ms Esma Izzidien
Age range: 2–12 years

Cardiff Muslim Primary School
Merthyr Street, Cathays, Cardiff,
Glamorgan CF24 4JL
Tel: 029 2034 2040
Headteacher: Sakhawat Ali
Age range: 4–11 years

Cardiff Steiner School
Hawthorn Road West, Llandaff North,
Cardiff, Glamorgan CF14 2FL
Tel: 029 2056 7986
Age range: 3–18 years

Ely Presbyterian Church School
4-6 Archer Road, Cardiff,
Glamorgan CF5 4FR
Tel: 02920 596410
Headteachers: Mrs Julia Haines
& Stephanie Williams
Age range: 3–16 years

Ffynone House School
36 St James's Crescent, Swansea,
Glamorgan SA1 6DR
Tel: 01792 464967
Headteacher: Mr Michael Boulding
Age range: 11–18 years

Howell's School, Llandaff GDST
Cardiff Road, Llandaff, Cardiff,
Glamorgan CF5 2YD
Tel: 029 2056 2019
Principal: Mrs Sally Davis BSc
Age range: B16–18 years G3–18 years

Kings Monkton School
6 West Grove, Cardiff,
Glamorgan CF24 3XL
Tel: 02920 482854
Principal: Mr Paul Norton
Age range: 3–18 years

Oakleigh House School
38 Penlan Crescent, Uplands,
Swansea, Glamorgan SA2 0RL
Tel: 01792 298537
Headmistress: Mrs Rhian
Ferriman BA(Hons)Ed, MEd
Age range: 2–11 years

OneSchool Global UK Swansea Campus
Sway Road, Morriston, Swansea,
Glamorgan SA6 6JA
Tel: 01792 581221
Age range: 7–18 years

St Clare's School
Newton, Porthcawl,
Glamorgan CF36 5NR
Tel: 01656 782509
Head of School: Helen Hier
Age range: 2–18 years
No. of pupils: 250
Fees: Day £6,753–£11,799

St John's College, Cardiff
College Green, Old St Mellons,
Cardiff, Glamorgan CF3 5YX
Tel: 029 2077 8936
Headteacher: Mr Shaun
Moody BA (Hons) PGCE
Age range: 3–18 years

The Cathedral School, Llandaff
Cardiff Road, Llandaff, Cardiff,
Glamorgan CF5 2YH
Tel: 029 2056 3179
Head: Ms Clare Sherwood
Age range: 3–18 years

Ummul Mumineen Academy
142 Penarth Road, Grangetown,
Cardiff, Glamorgan CF11 6NJ
Tel: 02920 220 383
Age range: 8–16 years

WESTBOURNE SCHOOL
For further details see p.312
Hickman Road, Penarth,
Glamorgan CF64 2AJ
Tel: 029 2070 5705
Email: admissions@
westbourneschool.com
Website:
www.westbourneschool.com
Headteacher: Dr GW Griffiths
BSc, PhD, ARCS, PGCE
Age range: 2–18 years
No. of pupils: 351
Fees: Day £8,520–£14,975
FB £35,850–£37,950

Gwynedd

Bangor Independent School
The Old Canonry, 39 Ffordd Gwynedd,
Bangor, Gwynedd LL57 1DT
Tel: 01248 354635
Headteacher: Mr Paul Gash
Age range: 3–11 years

St Gerard's School
Ffriddoedd Road, Bangor,
Gwynedd LL57 2EL
Tel: 01248 351656
Head Teacher: Mr Campbell Harrison
Age range: 4–18 years
No. of pupils: 143
Fees: Day £7,695–£11,655

Treffos School
Llansadwrn, Nr. Menai Bridge, Isle
of Anglesey, Gwynedd LL59 5SD
Tel: 01248 712322
Headmaster: Dr S. Humphreys
Age range: 3–11 years

Monmouthshire

Llangattock School Monmouth
Llangattock-Vibon-Avel, Monmouth,
Monmouthshire NP25 5NG
Tel: 01600 772 213
Principal: Ms Rosemary Whaley
Age range: 2–19 years

Monmouth Prep School
Hadnock Road, Monmouth,
Monmouthshire NP25 3NG
Tel: 01600 715930
Age range: 3–11 years
(boarding from 7)

Monmouth School for Boys
Almshouse Street, Monmouth,
Monmouthshire NP25 3XP
Tel: 01600 713143
Age range: B11–18 years
(boarding from 11)

Monmouth School for Girls
Hereford Road, Monmouth,
Monmouthshire NP25 5XT
Tel: 01600 711100
Age range: G11–18 years
(boarding from 11)

Rougemont School
Llantarnam Hall, Malpas Road,
Newport, Monmouthshire NP20 6QB
Tel: 01633 820800
Headmaster: Mr Robert Carnevale
Age range: 3–18 years

Pembrokeshire

Castle School Pembrokeshire
Glenover House, Scarrowscant Lane,
Haverfordwest, Pembrokeshire SA61 1ES
Tel: 01437 558010
Director: Ms Harriet Harrison
Age range: 3–18 years

Nant-y-Cwm Steiner School
Llanycefn, Clunderwen,
Pembrokeshire SA66 7QJ
Tel: +44 (0)1437 563640
Age range: 3–14 years

Redhill High School
Clynderwen House, Clynderwen,
Pembrokeshire SA66 7PN
Tel: 01437 211003
Headmaster: Mr Alun Millington
Age range: 11–18 years

Redhill Preparatory School
The Garth, St David's
Road, Haverfordwest,
Pembrokeshire SA61 2UR
Tel: 01437 762472
Head Teacher: Mr Adrian Thomas
Age range: 0–11 years

Powys

Christ College
Brecon, Powys LD3 8AF
Tel: 01874 615440
Head: Mr Gareth Pearson
Age range: 7–18 years
No. of pupils: 370
Fees: Day £9,582–£19,584
FB £19,431–£34,419

**OneSchool Global UK
Newtown Campus**
Sarn, Newtown, Powys SY16 4EJ
Tel: 01686 670152
Age range: 7–18 years

Vale of Glamorgan

UWC Atlantic
St Donat's Castle, St Donat's, Llantwit
Major, Vale of Glamorgan CF61 1WF
Tel: +44 (0)1446 799000
Principal: Naheed Bardai
Age range: 16–19 years
No. of pupils: 350

Examinations and qualifications

Common Entrance

What is Common Entrance?

The Common Entrance examinations are used in UK independent schools (and some independent schools overseas) for transfer from junior to senior schools at the ages of 11+ and 13+. They were first introduced in 1904 and are internationally recognised as being a rigorous form of assessment following a thorough course of study. The examinations are produced by the Independent Schools Examinations Board and backed by HMC (Headmasters' and Headmistresses' Conference), GSA (Girls' Schools Association), and IAPS (Independent Association of Prep Schools) which together represent the leading independent schools in the UK, and many overseas.

Common Entrance is not a public examination as, for example, GCSE, and candidates may normally be entered only in one of the following circumstances:

a) they have been offered a place at a senior school subject to their passing the examination, or

b) they are entered as a 'trial run', in which case the papers are marked by the junior school concerned

Candidates normally take the examination in their own junior or preparatory schools, either in the UK or overseas.

How does Common Entrance fit into the progression to GCSEs?

Rapid changes in education nationally and internationally have resulted in regular reviews of the syllabuses for all the Common Entrance examinations. Reviews of the National Curriculum, in particular, have brought about a number of changes, with the Board wishing to ensure that it continues to set high standards. It is also a guiding principle that Common Entrance should be part of the natural progression from 11-16, and not a diversion from it.

Common Entrance at 11+

At 11+, the examination consists of papers in English, mathematics and science. It is designed so that it can be taken by candidates either from independent preparatory schools or by candidates from schools in the maintained sector or overseas who have had no special preparation. The examination is normally taken in January for entrance to senior schools in the following September.

Common Entrance at 13+

At 13+, most candidates come from independent preparatory schools. The compulsory subjects are English, mathematics and science. Papers in French, geography, German, Classical Greek, history, Latin, religious studies and Spanish are also available and candidates usually offer as many subjects as they can. In most subjects, papers are available at more than one level to cater for candidates of different abilities. There are three examination sessions each year, with the majority of candidates sitting in the summer prior to entry to their senior schools in September.

Marking and grading

The papers are set centrally but the answers are marked by the senior school for which a candidate is entered. Mark schemes are provided by the Board but senior schools are free to set their own grade boundaries. Results are available within two weeks of the examinations taking place.

Pre-Testing and the ISEB Common Pre-Tests

A number of senior independent schools 'pre-test' pupils for entry, prior to them taking their main entrance examinations at a later date. Usually, these pre-tests take place when a pupil is in Year 6 or Year 7 of his or her junior school and will then be going on to sit Common Entrance in Year 8. The tests are designed to assess a pupil's academic potential and suitability for a particular senior school so that the child, the parents and the school know well in advance whether he/she is going to be offered a place at the school, subject to a satisfactory performance in the entrance examinations. The tests enable senior schools to manage their lists and help to ensure that pupils are not entered for examinations in which they are unlikely to be successful. In short, it reduces uncertainty for all concerned.

Pre-tests may be written specifically for the senior school for which the candidate is entered but a growing number of schools are choosing to use the Common Pre-Tests provided by the Independent Schools Examinations Board. These online tests are usually taken in the candidate's own junior school and one of their main advantages is that a pupil need sit the tests only once, with the results then made available to any senior school which wishes to use them. The multiple-choice tests cover verbal reasoning, non-verbal reasoning, English and mathematics, with the results standardised according to the pupil's age when they are taken. Further information is available on the ISEB website at www.iseb.co.uk.

Parents are advised to check the entrance requirements for senior schools to see if their child will be required to sit a pre-test.

Further information

Details of the Common Entrance examinations and how to register candidates are available on the ISEB website www.iseb.co.uk. Copies of past papers and a wide range of textbooks and other resources can be purchased from Galore Park Publishing Ltd at www.galorepark.co.uk. Support materials are also available from Hodder Education and other publishers; see the Resources section of the ISEB website for details.

Independent Schools Examinations Board
Endeavour House, Crow Arch Lane,
Ringwood, Hampshire BH24 1HP

Telephone: 01425 470555
Email: enquiries@iseb.co.uk
Web: www.iseb.co.uk

7+ Entrance Exams

What is the 7+?
The 7+ is the descriptive name given to the entrance exams set by an increasing number of independent schools for pupils wishing to gain admission into their Year 3.

7+ entrance exams may be simply for admission into a selective preparatory school, which will then prepare the child for Common Entrance exams to gain a place at senior school. Alternatively, the 7+ can be a route into a school with both prep and senior departments, therefore often effectively bypassing the 11+ or 13+ Common Entrance exams.

The Independent Schools Examinations Board provides Common Entrance examinations and assessments for pupils seeking entry to independent senior schools at 11+ and 13+, but there is as yet no equivalent for the 7+. The testing is largely undertaken by the individual schools, although some schools might commission the test from external agencies. Many schools in the incredibly competitive London area offer entrance exams at 7+ and some share specimen papers on their website to clarify what 7+ children will face.

Who sits the 7+?
The 7+ is sat by Year 2 children, who may be moving from a state primary school or a stand-alone pre-prep school to an independent prep school (although many prep schools now have their own pre-prep department, with a cohort of children poised to pass into Year 3 there).

Registration for 7+ entrance exams usually closes in the November of Year 2, with the exams then sat in January or February, for entry that September.

How is the 7+ assessed?
Written exam content will be primarily English and maths based, whilst spelling, dictation, mental arithmetic and more creative skills may be assessed verbally on a one-to-one basis. Group exercises are also sometimes used to look at a child's initiative and their ability to work with others.

Schools will not only be looking for academic potential, but also good citizens and a mixture of personalities to produce a well-rounded year group. For this reason, children are often asked to attend an interview. Some schools interview all candidates, whilst others may call back a limited number with good test results. They will be looking for a child's ability to look an adult in the eye and think on their feet, but also simply to show some spark and personality.

After the assessments, children will be told if they have been successful in gaining a firm place, or a place on a waiting list.

Further Information
As the 7+ is not centrally regulated, it is best for parents to seek accurate admissions and testing information direct from the schools in which they are interested. In addition to a school's facilities and ethos, choosing a school for admission at 7+ will probably also involve whether the school has a senior department and if not, the prep school's record in gaining its students places at target senior schools.

Experienced educational consultants may be able to help parents decide which independent prep school is best suited for their child, based on their personality, senior school ambitions and academic potential. Many parents enlist the help of tutors to prepare children for the 7+, if only to reduce the fear of the unknown in these very young children. This is achieved by teaching them the required curriculum, what to expect on their test and interview days, and giving them the opportunity to practice tackling the type of assessments they will face.

The Pre-Senior Baccalaureate

What is the Pre-Senior Baccalaureate?
The Pre-Senior Baccalaureate (PSB) is part of the Learning Skills Trust (LST) which operates 2 frameworks of study. The PSB is designed for Years 2 – 8 and the Skills Development Framework (SDF) for Years 9 – 11. The frameworks focus on the active development and assessment of 6 core skills: Communication, Collaboration, Leadership, Independence, Reviewing and Improving and Thinking and Learning. Member schools promote the core skills across all areas of school life, and provide guidance for pupils in progressing these skills, which are seen as essential for developing capable and balanced adults, able to make the most of the opportunities of a fast-changing world. A strong but appropriate knowledge base compliments this, with the use of focused tutoring, pastoral care and Well Being programmes.

Schools do not work to a prescribed curriculum and the emphasis is upon promoting an independent approach which works for each individual school. There are subject INSET days for LST school staff annually, supported by specialist colleagues, to ensure that work done in LST schools compliments the demands of education at higher levels.

The development of skills is recognised as essential by the Independent Schools Inspectorate (ISI), and recent ISI reports on PSB schools highlight the excellent contribution the PSB has in schools achieving excellence.

Assessment
The PSB has a 10-point scale for all subjects studied with a compulsory spine covering: English, Maths, Science, Modern Languages, The Humanities, Art, Design Technology, Music, Sport and PE with each pupil additionally completing a cross curricular project - The Pre-Senior Project Qualification. Optional subjects are agreed with schools, but these must be supported by a scheme of work clearly identifying

appropriate core skills which are assessed on a narrative scale. The 10-point scale cross references both ISEB and National Curriculum assessment levels. Pupils moving on to senior school do so via individual senior school pre-testing arrangements, the award of the PSB certificate, core ISEB papers or a combination of the above.

The SDF is a commitment to enable students across 3 years to experience authentic interdisciplinary experiences through extended project work. Schools have freedom to work within the framework and adapt it to their specific setting and existing programmes can be adapted to the SDF. The assessment of core skills is across all aspects of school life and not focused on academic subjects, which have their own particular demands. Time is given for students to reflect on the development of core skills, progression academically and contributions more widely to school life. A particular emphasis is given to the successful transition to independent study and away from closed learning tasks assessed on knowledge retention rather than student reflection.

Membership categories

All schools join as Partner Members and progress to full membership following an audit.

Affiliated membership is for schools that have developed their own skills-based approach, in line with LST principles; staff can participate in training opportunities and the Heads of Affiliated Schools join committee meetings as guests.

Membership of the above categories is dependent upon strong ISI reports, the development of a skills-based curriculum, with skills clearly identified in schemes of work, and excellent teaching.

Foundation membership is for organisations that actively support the LST by providing funding which enables the charity to invest in research, IT, etc. They also provide staff for meetings and conferences and offer a valuable perspective on the operation of the charity.

Further details

The LST is an entirely independent charity overseen by a Board of Trustees who have expertise in both primary and secondary education. Details of the LST can be found on the website – psbacc.org – together with contact details for the Operations Manager who can provide further details on request. .

General Certificate of Secondary Education (GCSE)

What are the GCSE qualifications?

GCSE qualifications were first introduced in 1986 and are the principal means of assessment at Key Stage 4 across a range of academic subject areas. They command respect and have status not only in the UK but worldwide.

Main features of the GCSE

There are four unitary awarding organisations for GCSEs in England (see 'Awarding organisations and examination dates' section, p437). WJEC and CCEA also offer GCSE qualifications in Wales and Northern Ireland. Each examining group designs its own specifications but they are required to conform to set criteria. For some aspects of the qualification system, the exam boards adopt common ways of working. When the exam boards work together in this way they generally do so through the Joint Council of Qualifications (JCQ). The award of a grade is intended to indicate that a candidate has met the required level of skills, knowledge and understanding.

New, reformed GCSEs have been introduced in recent years. Assessment in these reformed GCSEs consists primarily of formal examinations taken at the end of the student's two-year course. Other types of assessment, non-exam assessment (NEA), is used where there are skills and knowledge which cannot be assessed through exams. Ofqual have set the percentage of the total marks that will come from NEA.

The reformed GCSEs feature new and more demanding content, as required by the government and developed by the exam boards. Courses are designed for two years of study (linear assessment) and no longer divided into different modules.

Exams can only be split into 'foundation tier' and 'higher tier' if one exam paper does not give all students the opportunity to show their knowledge and their abilities.

Such tiering is only available in maths, science and modern foreign languages; other subjects do not have tiers. Resit opportunities will only be available each November in English language and maths, and then only for students who have turned 16 by the 31st of August in the year of the November assessment.

Summer 2022 marked the return of GCSE exams for the first time since 2019. Exams in 2020 and 2021 were replaced by alternatives due to constraints imposed following the pandemic. Grades were awarded through teachers' assessments based on mock exams, coursework and other available evidence.

Grading

The basic principle that exam boards follow when setting grade boundaries is that if the group of students (the cohort) taking a qualification in one year is of similar ability to the cohort in the previous year then the overall results (outcomes) should be comparable.

The reformed exams taken in summer 2017 were the first to show a new grading system, with the A* to G grades being phased out.

The grading system is 9 to 1, with 9 being the top grade. Ofqual says this allows greater differentiation between students. It expects that broadly the same proportion of students will achieve a grade 4 and above as those who achieved a grade C and above, that broadly the same proportion of students will achieve a grade 7 and above as those who achieved a grade A and above. There are three anchor points between the new grading system and the old one: the bottom of the new 1 grade is the same as the bottom of the old G grade, the bottom of the new 4 grade is the bottom of the old C grade, and the bottom of the 7 grade is the same as the bottom of the old A grade. Grade 9 will be set using the tailored approach formula in the first award.

Grades 2, 3, 5 and 6 will be awarded arithmetically so that the grade boundaries are equally spaced in terms of marks from neighbouring grades.

The government's definition of a 'strong pass' is set at grade 5 for reformed GCSEs. A grade 4 – or 'standard pass' – will continue to be a level 2 achievement. The DfE does not expect employers, colleges or universities to raise the bar to a grade 5 if a grade 4 would meet their requirements.

Can anyone take GCSE qualifications?

GCSEs are intended mainly for 16-year-old pupils, but are open to anyone of any age, whether studying full-time or part-time at a school, college or privately. There are no formal entry requirements.

Students normally study up to ten subjects over a two-year period. Short course GCSEs are available in some subjects (including PE and religious studies) – these include half the content of a full GCSE, so two short course GCSEs are equivalent to one full GCSE.

The English Baccalaureate

The English Baccalaureate (EBacc) is a school performance measure. It allows people to see how many pupils get a grade C or above (current grading) in the core academic subjects at Key Stage 4 in any government-funded school.

Progress 8 and Attainment 8

Progress 8 aims to capture the progress a pupil makes from the end of primary school to the end of secondary school. It is a type of value added measure, which means that pupils' results are compared to the actual achievements of other pupils with the same prior attainment.

The new performance measures are designed to encourage schools to offer a broad and balanced curriculum with a focus on an academic core at Key Stage 4, and reward schools for the teaching of all their pupils, measuring performance across 8 qualifications. Every increase in every grade a pupil achieves will attract additional points in the performance tables.

Progress 8 will be calculated for individual pupils solely in order to calculate a school's Progress 8 score, and there will be no need for schools to share individual Progress 8

scores with their pupils. Schools should continue to focus on which qualifications are most suitable for individual pupils, as the grades pupils achieve will help them reach their goals for the next stage of their education or training.

Attainment 8 will measure the achievement of a pupil across 8 qualifications including mathematics (double weighted) and English (double weighted), 3 further qualifications that count in the English Baccalaureate (EBacc) measure and 3 further qualifications that can be GCSE qualifications (including EBacc subjects) or any other non-GCSE qualification on the DfE approved list.

General Certificate of Education (GCE) Advanced level (A level)

Typically, A level qualifications are studied over a two-year period. There are no lower or upper age limits. Schools and colleges usually expect students aged 16-18 to have obtained grade 5s (A*-C in the old criteria) in five subjects at GCSE level before taking an advanced level course. This requirement may vary between centres and according to which specific subjects are to be studied. Mature students may be assessed on different criteria as to their suitability to embark on the course.

GCE Qualifications

Over the past few years, AS level and A level qualifications have been in a process of reform. New subjects have been introduced gradually, with the first wave taught from September 2015. Subjects that have not been reformed are no longer be available for teaching.

GCE qualifications are available at two levels: the Advanced Subsidiary (AS), which is generally delivered over one year and is seen as half an A level; and the A level (GCE). Nearly 70 titles are available, covering a wide range of subject areas, including humanities, sciences, language, business, arts, mathematics and technology.

One of the major reforms is that AS level results no longer count towards an A level in England (they previously counted for 50%). The two qualifications are linear, with AS assessments typically taking place after one year and A levels after two.

Some GCE AS and A levels, particularly the practical ones, contain a proportion of coursework. All GCE A levels that contain one or more types of assessment will have an element of synoptic assessment that tests students' understanding of the whole specification. GCE AS are graded A-E and A levels are graded A*-E.

Overall the amount of coursework at A level has been reduced in the reforms. In some subjects, such as the sciences, practical work will not contribute to the final A level but will be reported separately in a certificate of endorsement. In the sciences, students will do at least 12 practical activities, covering apparatus and techniques. Exam questions about practical work will make up at least 15% of the total marks for the qualification and students will be assessed on their knowledge, skills and understanding of practical work.

Summer 2022 marked the return of exams for the first time since 2019. Exams in 2020 and 2021 were replaced by alternatives due to constraints imposed following the pandemic. Grades were awarded through teachers' assessments based on mock exams, coursework and other available evidence

Cambridge International AS & A Level

Cambridge International AS & A Level is an internationally benchmarked qualification, taught in over 130 countries worldwide. It is typically for learners aged 16 to 19 years who need advanced study to prepare for university. It was created specifically for an international audience and the content has been devised to suit the wide variety of schools worldwide and avoid any cultural bias.

Cambridge International A Level is typically a two-year course, and Cambridge International AS Level is typically one year. Some subjects can be started as a Cambridge International AS Level and extended to a Cambridge International A Level. Students can either follow a broad course of study, or specialise in one particular subject area.

Learners use Cambridge International AS & A Levels to gain places at leading universities worldwide, including the UK, Ireland, USA, Canada, Australia, New Zealand, India, Singapore, Egypt, Jordan, South Africa, the Netherlands, Germany and Spain. In places such as the US and Canada,

good grades in carefully chosen Cambridge International A Level subjects can result in up to one year of university course credit.

Assessment options:

Cambridge International AS & A Levels have a linear structure with exams at the end of the course. Students can choose from a range of assessment options:

Option 1: take Cambridge International AS Levels only. The Cambridge International AS Level syllabus content is half a Cambridge International A Level.

Option 2: staged assessment, which means taking the Cambridge International AS Level in one exam session and the Cambridge International A Level at a later session. However, this route is not possible in all subjects.

Option 3: take all Cambridge International A Level papers in the same examination session, usually at the end of the course.

Grades and subjects

Cambridge International A Levels are graded from A* to E. Cambridge International AS Levels are graded from A to E.

Subjects: available in 55 subjects including accounting, Afrikaans, Afrikaans – first language (AS only), Afrikaans language (AS only), applied information and communication technology, Arabic, Arabic language (AS only), art and design, biology, business, chemistry, Chinese, Chinese language (AS only), classical studies, computing, design and technology, design and textiles, digital media & design, divinity, economics, English language, English literature, environmental management, food studies, French, French language (AS only), French literature (AS only), general paper, geography, German, German language (AS only), Global Perspectives & Research, Hindi, Hindi language (AS only), Hindi literature (AS only), Hinduism, history, Islamic studies, Japanese language (AS only), English language and literature (AS only), law, Marathi, Marathi language (AS only), marine science, mathematics, further mathematics, media studies, music, physical education, physical science, physics, Portuguese, Portuguese language (AS only), Portuguese literature (AS only), psychology, sociology, Spanish, Spanish

first language (AS only), Spanish language (AS only), Spanish literature (AS only), Tamil, Tamil language (AS only), Telugu, Telugu language (AS only), thinking skills, travel and tourism, Urdu, Urdu language (AS only).
Website: www.cambridgeinternational.org/alevel

Cambridge IGCSE

Cambridge IGCSE is the world's most popular international qualification for 14 to16 year olds. It develops skills in creative thinking, enquiry and problem solving, in preparation for the next stage in a student's education. Cambridge IGCSE is taken in over 150 countries, and is widely recognised by employers and higher education institutions worldwide.

Cambridge IGCSE is graded from A*-G. In the UK, Cambridge IGCSE is accepted as equivalent to the GCSE. It can be used as preparation for Cambridge International A & AS Levels, UK A and AS levels, IB or AP and in some instances entry into university. Cambridge IGCSE First Language English and Cambridge IGCSE English Language qualifications are recognised by a significant number of UK universities as evidence of competence in the language for university entrance.

Subjects: available in over 70 subjects including accounting, Afrikaans – first language, Afrikaans – second language, agriculture, Arabic – first language, Arabic – foreign language, art and design, Baha Indonesia, Bangladesh studies, biology, business studies, chemistry, child development, Chinese – first language, Chinese – second language, Chinese (Mandarin) – foreign language, computer studies, Czech – first language, design and technology, development studies, drama, Dutch – first language, Dutch – foreign language, economics, English – additional language, English – first language, English – literature, English – second language, enterprise, environmental management, food and nutrition, French – first language, French – foreign language, geography, German – first language, German – foreign language, global perspectives, Greek – foreign language, Hindi as a second language, Italian – foreign language, history, India studies, Indonesian – foreign language, information and communication technology, IsiZulu as a second language, Japanese – first language, Japanese – foreign language, Kazakh as a second language, Korean (first language), Latin, Malay – first language, Malay – foreign language, mathematics, mathematics – additional, international mathematics, music, Pakistan studies, physical education, physical science, physics, Portuguese – first language, Portuguese – foreign language, religious studies, Russian – first language, science – combined, sciences – co-ordinated (double), sociology, Spanish – first language, Spanish – foreign language, Spanish – literature, Thai – first language, travel and tourism, Turkish – first language, Urdu – second language, world literature.
Website: www.cambridgeinternational.org/igcse

Edexcel International GCSEs

Pearson's Edexcel International GCSEs are academic qualifications aimed at learners aged 14 to 16. They're equivalent to a UK General Certificate of Secondary Education (GCSE), and are the main requirement for Level 3 studies, including progression to GCE AS or A levels, BTECs or employment. International GCSEs are linear qualifications, meaning that students take all of the exams at the end of the course. They are available at Level 1 (grades 3-1) and Level 2 (grades 9-4). There are currently more than 100,000 learners studying Edexcel International GCSEs, in countries throughout Asia, Africa, Europe, the Middle East and Latin America. Developed by subject specialists and reviewed regularly, many of Pearson's Edexcel International GCSEs include specific international content to make them relevant to students worldwide.

Pearson's Edexcel International GCSEs were initially developed for international schools. They have since become popular among independent schools in the UK, but are not approved for use in UK state schools.

OCR Free Standing Maths Qualifications (FSMQ)

Aimed at those students wishing to acquire further qualifications in maths, specifically additional mathematics and foundations of advanced mathematics (MEI). Further UCAS points can be earned upon completion of the advanced FSMQ in additional mathematics.

AQA Certificate in Mathematical Studies (Core Maths)

This Level 3 qualification has been available since September 2015. It is designed for students who achieved a Grade 4 or above at GCSE and want to continue studying Maths. The qualification carries UCAS points equivalent to an AS level qualification.

AQA Certificate in Further Maths

This level 2 qualification has been designed to provide stretch and challenge to the most able mathematicians. This will be best suited to students who either already have, or are expected to achieve the top grades in GCSE Mathematics and are likely to progress to A level Mathematics and Further Mathematics.

Scottish qualifications

Information supplied by the Scottish Qualifications Authority

In Scotland, qualifications are awarded by the Scottish Qualifications Authority (SQA), the national accreditation and awarding body. A variety of qualifications are offered in schools, including:

- National Qualifications (National Units, National Courses, Skills for Work Courses and Scottish Baccalaureates)

- National Qualification Group Awards (National Certificates and National Progression Awards)

- Awards

National Qualifications cover subjects to suit everyone's interests and skills – from Chemistry to Construction, History to Hospitality, and Computing to Care.

Qualifications in the Scottish qualifications system sit at various levels on the Scottish Credit and Qualifications Framework (SCQF). There are 12 levels on the SCQF and each level represents the difficulty of learning involved. Qualifications in schools span SCQF levels 1 to 7.

National Qualifications (NQ)

National Qualifications are among the most important types of qualification in Scotland.

National Qualifications range from SCQF levels 1 to 7 and include National Units, National Courses, Skills for Work Courses, Scottish Baccalaureates and National Qualification Group Awards.

They are taught in the senior phase of secondary school and they are also offered in colleges, and by some training providers.

They are designed to help young people to demonstrate the skills, knowledge and understanding they have developed at school or college and enable them to prepare for further learning, training and employment.

National Courses

National Courses are available in over 60 subjects, at the following levels: National 2 (SCQF level 2), National 3 (SCQF level 3), National 4 (SCQF level 4), National 5 (SCQF level 5), Higher (SCQF level 6), and Advanced Higher (SCQF level 7).

National 2, National 3 and National 4 courses consist of units and unit assessments, which are internally assessed by teachers and lecturers, and quality assured by SQA. Students complete the unit assessments during class time. National 4 courses also include an Added Value Unit assessment that assesses students' performance across the whole course. This is usually in the form of an assignment, performance, practical activity or class test. National 2 to National 4 courses are not graded but are assessed as pass or fail.

National 5, Higher and Advanced Higher courses do not include units. They involve a course assessment that takes place at the end of the course. For most subjects, the course assessment is a combination of one or more formal exams and one or more coursework assessments (such as an assignment, performance, project or practical activity). SQA marks all exams and the majority of coursework. In some subjects, coursework is internally assessed by the teacher or lecturer and quality assured by SQA, while performances and practical activities may be subject to visiting assessment by an SQA examiner.

National 5, Higher and Advanced Higher courses are graded A to D or 'no award'.

National Units

National Units are the building blocks of National 2 to National 4 Courses and National Qualification Group Awards. They are also qualifications in their own right and can be done on an individual basis — such as National 1 qualifications, which are standalone units. Units are normally designed to take 40 hours of teaching to complete and each one is assessed by completing a unit assessment. Over 3500 National Units are available, including National Literacy and Numeracy Units, which assess students' literacy and numeracy skills.

Freestanding units are also available at SCQF levels 5, 6 and 7 and can be taken on an individual basis.

Skills for Work Courses

Skills for Work courses are designed to introduce students to the demands and expectations of the world of work. They are available in a variety of areas such as construction, hairdressing and hospitality. The courses involve a strong element of learning through involvement in practical and vocational activities, and develop knowledge, skills and experience that are related to employment. They consist of units and unit assessments, which are internally assessed by teachers and lecturers, and quality assured by SQA. Skills for Work courses are not graded but are assessed as pass or fail. They are available at National 4, National 5 and Higher levels (SCQF levels 4 to 6) and are often delivered in partnership between schools and colleges.

Scottish Baccalaureates

Scottish Baccalaureates consist of a coherent group of Higher and Advanced Higher qualifications, with the addition of an interdisciplinary project. They are available in four subject areas: Expressive Arts, Languages, Science and Social Sciences. The interdisciplinary project is marked and awarded at Advanced Higher level (SCQF level 7). It provides students with a platform to apply their knowledge in a realistic context, and to demonstrate initiative, responsibility and independent working. Aimed at high-achieving sixth year students, the Scottish Baccalaureate encourages personalised, in-depth study and interdisciplinary learning in their final year of secondary school.

National Qualification Group Awards

National Certificates (NCs) and National Progression Awards (NPAs) are referred to as National Qualification Group Awards. These qualifications provide students preparing for work with opportunities to develop skills that are sought after by employers. They are available at SCQF levels 2 to 6.

NCs prepare students for employment, career development or progression to more advanced study at HNC/HND level. They are available in a range of subjects, including: Sound Production, Technical Theatre, and Child, Health and Social Care.

NPAs develop specific skills and knowledge in specialist vocational areas, including Journalism, Architecture and Interior Design, and Legal Services. They link to National Occupational Standards, which are the basis of Scottish Vocational Qualifications (SVQs) and are taught in partnership between schools, colleges, employers and training providers.

Awards

SQA Awards provide students with opportunities to acquire skills, recognise achievement and promote confidence through independent thinking and positive attitudes, while motivating them to be successful and participate positively in the wider community.

A variety of different awards are offered at a number of SCQF levels and cover subjects including leadership, employability and enterprise. These awards are designed to recognise the life, learning and work skills that students gain from taking part in activities both in and out of school, such as sports, volunteering and fundraising.

For more information on SQA and its portfolio of qualifications, visit www.sqa.org.uk

SVQs (Scotland)

Scottish Vocational Qualifications (SVQs) are work-based qualifications that demonstrate someone can do their job well and to the national standards for their sector. There are over 500 SVQs that cover many occupations in Scotland – from forestry to IT, management to catering, and from journalism to construction. Experts from industry, commerce and education produce SVQs based on national standards.

Many people study for SVQs in the workplace while carrying out their day-to-day role. Each SVQ unit defines one aspect of a job and what it is to be competent in that aspect of the job. Learners can work through one unit at a time, or gather evidence for several units at the same time. There are no formal written exams, instead learners collect and submit evidence, usually from their own work. They are assessed by an SVQ assessor and the assessment can take place at the learner's place of work, at college or through a training provider.

Find out more at www.sqa.org.uk/svq

Additional and Alternative

Cambridge Primary

Cambridge Primary is typically for learners aged 5 to 11 years. It develops learner skills and understanding in 10 subjects: English as a first or second language, mathematics, science, art & design, digital literacy, music, physical education, Cambridge Global Perspectives and ICT. The flexible curriculum frameworks include optional assessment tools to help schools monitor learners' progress and give detailed feedback to parents. At the end of Cambridge Primary, schools can enter students for Cambridge Primary Checkpoint tests which are marked in Cambridge.
Website: www.cambridgeinternational.org/primary

Cambridge ICT Starters introduces learners, typically aged 5 to 14 years, to the key ICT applications they need to achieve computer literacy and to understand the impact of technology on our daily lives. It can be taught and assessed in English or Spanish.

Cambridge Lower Secondary

Cambridge Lower Secondary is typically for learners aged 11 to 14 years. It develops learner skills and understanding in 10 subjects: English, English as a second language, mathematics, science, art & design, digital literacy, music, physical education, Cambridge Global Perspectives and ICT, and includes assessment tools. At the end of Cambridge Lower Secondary, schools can enter students for Cambridge Lower Secondary Checkpoint tests which are marked in Cambridge and provide an external international benchmark for student performance.
Website: www.cambridgeinternational.org/lowersecondary

European Baccalaureate (EB)

Not to be confused with the International Baccalaureate (IB) or the French Baccalaureate, this certificate is available in European schools and recognised in all EU countries.

To obtain the baccalaureate, a student must obtain a minimum score of 50%, which is made up from: coursework, oral participation in class and tests (50%); five written examinations (35%) – mother-tongue, first foreign language and maths are compulsory for all candidates; three oral examinations (15%) – mother tongue and first foreign language are compulsory (history or geography may also be compulsory here, dependant on whether the candidate has taken a written examination in these subjects).

Subjects taught in different languages have the same syllabi, regardless of the language, and the same is valid for examinations – the content is simply translated into different languages. In case of languages, the syllabi vary, but nevertheless, they are harmonized and the examinations have to follow an agreed structure. The EB has been specifically designed to meet, at the very least, the minimum qualification requirements of each member state.

Study for the EB begins at nursery stage (age 4) and progresses through primary (age six) and on into secondary school (age 12).

Syllabus
Languages: Bulgarian, Czech, Danish, Dutch, English, Estonian, Finnish, Finnish as a second national language, French, Gaelic as other national language German, Greek, Hungarian, Italian, Latvian, Lithuanian, Maltese as other national language, Polish, Portuguese, Romanian, Slovak, Slovenian, Spanish, Swedish, Swedish for Finnish pupils.

Literary: art education, non-confessional ethics, geography, ancient Greek, history, human sciences, Latin, music, philosophy, physical education.

Sciences: biology, chemistry, economics, ICT, mathematics, physics.
For more information, contact:
Office of the Secretary-General of the European Schools
Rue de la Science 23, B-1040 Bruxelles
Tel: +32 2295 3745; Fax: +32 2298 6298
Website: www.eursc.eu

The International Baccalaureate (IB)

The International Baccalaureate (IB) offers four challenging and high quality educational programmes for a worldwide community of schools, aiming to develop internationally minded people who, recognizing their common humanity and shared guardianship of the planet, help to create a better, more peaceful world.

The IB works with schools around the world (both state and privately funded) that share the commitment to international education to deliver these programmes.

Schools that have achieved the high standards required for authorization to offer one or more of the IB programmes are known as IB World Schools. There are over half a million students attending almost 5000 IB World Schools in over 150 countries and this number is growing annually.

The Primary Years, Middle Years and Diploma Programmes share a common philosophy and common characteristics. They develop the whole student, helping students to grow intellectually, socially, aesthetically and culturally. They provide a broad and balanced education that includes science and the humanities, languages and mathematics, technology and the arts. The programmes teach students to think critically, and encourage them to draw connections between areas of knowledge and to use problem-solving techniques and concepts from many disciplines. They instil in students a sense of responsibility towards others and towards the environment. Lastly, and perhaps most importantly, the programmes give students an awareness and understanding of their own culture and of other cultures, values and ways of life.

A fourth programme called the IB Career-related Programme (CP) became available to IB World Schools from September 2012. All IB programmes include:
- A written curriculum or curriculum framework
- Student assessment appropriate to the age range
- Professional development and networking opportunities for teachers
- Support, authorization and programme evaluation for the school

The IB Primary Years Programme

The IB Primary Years Programme (PYP), for students aged three to 12, focuses on the development of the whole child as an inquirer, both in the classroom and in the world outside. It is a framework consisting of five essential elements (concepts, knowledge, skills, attitude, action) and guided by six trans-disciplinary themes of global significance, explored using knowledge and skills derived from six subject areas (language, social studies, mathematics, science and technology, arts, and personal, social and physical education) with a powerful emphasis on inquiry-based learning.

The most significant and distinctive feature of the PYP is the six trans-disciplinary themes. These themes are about issues that have meaning for, and are important to, all of us. The programme offers a balance between learning about or through the subject areas, and learning beyond them. The six themes of global significance create a trans-disciplinary framework that allows students to 'step up' beyond the confines of learning within subject areas:
- Who we are
- Where we are in place and time
- How we express ourselves
- How the world works
- How we organize ourselves
- Sharing the planet

The PYP exhibition is the culminating activity of the programme. It requires students to analyse and propose solutions to real-world issues, drawing on what they have learned through the programme. Evidence of student development and records of PYP exhibitions are reviewed by the IB as part of the programme evaluation process.

Assessment is an important part of each unit of inquiry as it both enhances learning and provides opportunities for students to reflect on what they know, understand and can do. The teacher's feedback to the students provides the guidance, the tools and the incentive for them to become more competent, more skilful and better at understanding how to learn.

The IB Middle Years Programme (MYP)

The Middle Years Programme (MYP), for students aged 11 to 16, comprises eight subject groups:
- Language acquisition
- Language and literature
- Individuals and societies
- Sciences
- Mathematics
- Arts
- Physical and health education
- Design

The MYP requires at least 50 hours of teaching time for each subject group in each year of the programme. In years 4 and 5, students have the option to take courses from six of the eight subject groups within certain limits, to provide greater flexibility in meeting local requirements and individual student learning needs.

Each year, students in the MYP also engage in at least one collaboratively planned interdisciplinary unit that involves at least two subject groups.

MYP students also complete a long-term project, where they decide what they want to learn about, identify what they already know, discovering what they will need to know to complete the project, and create a proposal or criteria for completing it

The MYP aims to help students develop their personal understanding, their emerging sense of self and their responsibility in their community.

The MYP allows schools to continue to meet state, provincial or national legal requirements for students with access needs. Schools must develop an inclusion/special educational needs (SEN) policy that explains assessment access arrangements, classroom accommodations and curriculum modification that meet individual student learning needs.

The IB Diploma Programme (IBDP)

The IB Diploma Programme, for students aged 16 to 19, is an academically challenging and motivating curriculum of international education that prepares students for success at university and in life beyond studies.

DP students choose at least one course from six subject groups, thus ensuring depth and breadth of knowledge and experience in languages, social studies, the experimental sciences, mathematics, and the arts. With more than 35 courses to choose from, students have the flexibility to further explore and learn subjects that meet their interest. Out of the six courses required, at least three and not more than four must be taken at higher level (240 teaching hours), the others at standard level (150 teaching hours). Students can take examinations in English, French or Spanish.

In addition, three unique components of the programme – the DP core – aim to broaden students' educational experience and challenge them to apply their knowledge and skills. The DP core – the extended essay (EE), theory of knowledge (TOK) and creativity, activity, service (CAS) – are compulsory and central to the philosophy of the programme.

The IB uses both external and internal assessment to measure student performance in the DP. Student results are determined by performance against set standards, not by each student's position in the overall rank order. DP assessment is unique in the way that it measures the extent to which students have mastered advanced academic skills not what they have memorized. DP assessment also encourages an international outlook and intercultural skills, wherever appropriate.

The IB diploma is awarded to students who gain at least 24 points out of a possible 45 points, subject to certain minimum levels of performance across the whole programme and to satisfactory participation in the creativity, activity, and service requirement.

Recognized and respected by leading universities globally, the DP encourages students to be knowledgeable, inquiring, caring and compassionate, and to develop intercultural understanding, open-mindedness and the attitudes necessary to respect and evaluate a range of viewpoints.

The IB Career Related Programme (IBCP)

The IB Career-related Programme, for students aged 16 to 19, offers an innovative educational framework that combines academic studies with career-related learning. Through the CP, students develop the competencies they need to succeed in the 21st century. More importantly, they have the opportunity to engage with a rigorous study programme that genuinely interests them while gaining transferable and lifelong skills that prepares them to pursue higher education, apprenticeships or direct employment.

CP students complete four core components – language development, personal and professional skills, service learning and a reflective project – in order to receive the International Baccalaureate Career-related Programme Certificate. Designed to enhance critical thinking and intercultural understanding, the CP core helps students develop the communication and personal skills, as well as intellectual habits required for lifelong learning.

Schools that choose to offer the CP can create their own distinctive version of the programme and select career pathways that suit their students and local community needs. The IB works with a variety of CRS providers around the world and schools seeking to develop career pathways with professional communities can benefit from our existing collaborations. All CRS providers undergo a rigorous curriculum evaluation to ensure that their courses align with the CP pedagogy and meet IB quality standards. The flexibility to meet the needs, backgrounds and contexts of learners allows CP schools to offer an education that is relevant and meaningful to their students.

Launched in 2012, there are 250 CP schools. Many schools with the IB Diploma Programme (DP) and the Middle Years Programme (MYP) have chosen the CP as an alternative IB pathway to offer students. CP schools often report that the programme has helped them raise student aspiration, increase student engagement and retention and encouraged learners to take responsibility for their own actions, helping them foster high levels of self-esteem through meaningful achievements.

For more information on IB programmes, visit: www.ibo.org
Africa, Europe, Middle East IB Global Centre,
Churchillplein 6, The Hague, 2517JW, The Netherlands
Tel: +31 (0)70 352 6000
Email: support@ibo.org

Pearson Edexcel Mathematics Awards

Pearson's Edexcel Mathematics Awards are small, stand-alone qualifications designed to help students to develop and demonstrate proficiency in different areas of mathematics. These Awards enable students to focus on understanding key concepts and techniques, and are available across three subjects, including: Number and Measure (Levels 1 and 2), Algebra (Levels 2 and 3) and Statistical Methods (Levels 1, 2 and 3).

Designed to build students' confidence and fluency; the Awards can fit into the existing programme of delivery for mathematics in schools and colleges, prepare students for GCSE and/or GCE Mathematics, and to support further study in other subjects, training or the workplace. They offer a choice of levels to match students' abilities, with clear progression between the levels. These small, 60-70 guided learning hour qualifications are assessed through one written paper per level. Each qualification is funded and approved for pre-16 and 16-18 year old students in England and in schools and colleges in Wales.

Projects

Extended Project Qualification (EPQ)

AQA, OCR, Pearson and WJEC offer the Extended Project Qualification, which is a qualification aimed at developing a student's research and independent learning skills. The EPQ can be taken as a stand-alone qualification, and it is equivalent to half an A level in UCAS points (but only a third of performance points).

Students complete a research based written report and may produce an artefact or a practical science experiment as part of their project.

Cambridge International Project Qualification (IPQ)

Cambridge International is offering a new standalone project-based qualification, which can be taken alongside Cambridge International AS & A levels. Students complete a 5000-word research project on a topic of their choice. The qualification is assessed by Cambridge International.

For more information, go to www.cambridgeinternational.org/advanced

Entry level and basic skills

Entry Level Qualifications

If you want to take GCSE or NVQ Level 1 but have not yet reached the standard required, then entry level qualifications are for you as they are designed to get you started on the qualifications ladder.

Entry level qualifications are available in a wide range of areas. You can take an entry level certificate in most subjects where a similar GCSE exists. There are also vocational entry level qualifications – some in specific areas like retail or catering and others where you can take units in different work-related subjects to get a taster of a number of career areas. Also available are entry level certificates in life skills and the basic skills of literacy and numeracy.

Anyone can take an entry level qualification – your school or college will help you decide which qualification is right for you.

Entry level qualifications are flexible programmes so the time it takes to complete will vary according to where you study and how long you need to take the qualification.

Subjects available include: Art and Design, Computer Science, English, Geography, History, Latin, Mathematics, Physical Education and Science.

Functional Skills

Functional Skills are qualifications in English and maths that equip learners with the basic practical skills required in everyday life, education and the workplace. They are available at Entry Level, Level 1 and Level 2. Functional Skills are identified as funded 'stepping stone' qualifications to English and maths GCSE for post-16 learners who haven't previously achieved a grade 3 in these subjects. There are part of apprenticeship completion requirements.

Vocational qualifications

Applied Generals/Level 3 Certificates

Applied General qualifications are available in a wide range of subjects, they are a real alternative to A level support progression to further study or employment aimed at students aged 16-18.

Developed together with teachers, schools, colleges and higher education institutions, they help learners to develop knowledge and skills.

A mixture of assessment types means learners can apply their knowledge in a practical way. An integrated approach creates a realistic and relevant qualification for learners.

AQA Technical Award

AQA's Technical Award is a practical, vocational Level 1/2 qualification for 14- to 16-year-olds to take alongside GCSEs.

The Technical Award in Performing Arts provides an introduction to life and work, equipping learners with the practical, transferable skills and core knowledge needed to progress to further general or vocational study, including Level 3 qualifications, employment or apprenticeships.

Learners are assessed on doing rather than knowing through the project-based internal assessments, where they can apply their knowledge to practical tasks. There are two internally assessed units worth 30% each, and an externally assessed exam worth 40%.

The last time schools can enter for this qualification will be summer 2023, and there will be no resit opportunity.

BTECs

BTEC Level 2 First qualifications

ie BTEC Level 2 Diplomas, BTEC Level 2 Extended Certificates, BTEC Level 2 Certificates and BTEC Level 2 Award.

BTEC Firsts are Level 2 introductory work-related programmes covering a wide range of vocational areas including business, engineering, information technology, health and social care, media, travel and tourism, and public services.

Programmes may be taken full or part-time. They are practical programmes that provide a foundation for the knowledge and skills you will need in work. Alternatively, you can progress onto a BTEC National qualification, Applied GCE A level or equivalent.

There are no formal entry requirements and they can be studied alongside GCSEs. Subjects available include: Agriculture, Animal Care, Applied Science, Art and Design, Business, Children's Care, Learning and Development, Construction, Countryside and the Environment, Engineering, Fish Husbandry, Floristry, Health and Social care, Horse Care, Horticulture, Hospitality, IT, Land-based Technology, Business, Creative Media Production, Music, Performing Arts, Public Services, Sport, Travel and Tourism, and Vehicle Technology.

BTEC Foundation Diploma in Art and Design (QCF)

For those students preparing to go on to higher education within the field of art and design. This diploma is recognised as one of the best courses of its type in the UK, and is used in preparation for degree programmes. Units offered include researching, recording and responding in art and design, media experimentation, personal experimental studies, and a final major project.

BTEC Nationals

ie BTEC Level 3 Extended Diplomas (QCF), BTEC Level 3 Diplomas (QCF), BTEC Level 3 Subsidiary Diplomas (QCF), BTEC Level 3 Certificates (QCF)

BTEC National programmes are long-established vocational programmes. They are practical programmes that are highly valued by employers. They enable you to gain the knowledge and skills that you will need in work, or give you the choice to progress on to a BTEC Higher National, a Foundation Degree or a degree programme.

BTEC Nationals, which hold UCAS points cover a range of vocationally specialist sectors including child care, children's play, learning and development, construction, art and design, aeronautical engineering, electrical/electronic engineering, IT, business, creative and media production, performing arts, public services, sport, sport and exercise sciences and applied science. The programmes may be taken full- or part-time, and can be taken in conjunction with NVQs and/or functional skills units at an appropriate level.

There are no formal entry requirements, but if you have any of the following you are likely to be at the right level to study a BTEC national qualification.

- a BTEC Level 2 First qualification
- GCSEs – at grades A*-C in several subjects
- Relevant work experience

There are also very specialist BTEC Nationals, such as Pharmaceutical Science and Blacksmithing and Metalworking.

BTEC Higher Nationals

Known as HNDs and HNCs – ie BTEC Level 5 HND Diplomas (QCF) and BTEC Level 4 HNC Diplomas (QCF)

BTEC HNDs and HNCs are further and higher education qualifications that offer a balance of education and vocational training. They are available in over 40 work-related subjects such as Graphic Design, Business, Health and Social Care, Computing and Systems Development, Manufacturing Engineering, Hospitality Management, and Public Services.

BTEC higher national courses combine study with hands-on work experience during your course. Once completed, you can use the skills you learn to begin your career, or continue on to a related degree course.

HNDs are often taken as a full-time course over two years but can also be followed part-time in some cases.

HNCs are often for people who are working and take two years to complete on a part-time study basis by day release, evenings, or a combination of the two. Some HNC courses are done on a full-time basis. There are no formal entry requirements, but if you have any of the following you are likely to be at the right academic level:

- at least one A level
- a BTEC Level 3 National qualification
- level 3 NVQ

BTEC specialist and professional qualifications

These qualifications are designed to prepare students for specific and specialist work activities. These are split into two distinct groups:

- Specialist qualifications (entry to Level 3)
- Professional qualifications (Levels 4-7)

Cambridge Nationals

Cambridge Nationals from exam board OCR are vocationally-related qualifications that take an engaging, practical and inspiring approach to learning and assessment.

They are industry-relevant, geared to key sector requirements and very popular with schools and colleges because they suit such a broad range of learning styles and abilities.

Cambridge Nationals are available in: Child Development, Creative iMedia, Engineering Design, Engineering Manufacture, Enterprise and Marketing, Health and Social Care, ICT, Information Technologies, Principles in Engineering and Engineering Business, Sport Science, Sport Studies, Systems Control in Engineering. They are joint Level 1 and 2 qualifications aimed at students aged 14-16 in full-time study.

Cambridge Technicals

OCR's Cambridge Technicals are practical and flexible vocationally-related qualifications, offering students in-depth study in a wide range of subjects, including business, health and social care, IT, sport, art and design, digital media, applied science, performing arts and engineering.

Cambridge Technicals are aimed at young people aged 16-19 who have completed Key Stage 4 of their education and want to study in a more practical, work-related way.

Cambridge Technicals are available at Level 2 and Level 3, and carry UCAS points at Level 3.

NVQs

NVQs reward those who demonstrate skills gained at work. They relate to particular jobs and are usefully taken while you are working. Within reason, NVQs do not have to be completed in a specified amount of time. They can be taken by full-time employees or by school and college students with a work placement or part-time job that enables them to develop the appropriate skills. There are no age limits and no special entry requirements.

NVQs are organised into levels, based on the competencies required. Levels 1-3 are the levels most applicable to learners within the 14-19 phase. Achievement of Level 4 within this age group will be rare. See the OCR website for further information.

Occupational Studies (Northern Ireland)

Targeted at learners working towards and at Level 1 and 2 in Key Stage 4 within the Northern Ireland curriculum. For further information see the CCEA website.

OCR Vocational Qualifications

These are available at different levels and different sizes. Levels 1-3 are the levels most applicable to learners within the 14-19 phase. The different sizes are indicated with the use of Award, Certificate and Diploma in the qualification title and indicate the number of hours it typically takes to complete the qualification.

Vocational qualifications are assessed according to each individual specification, but may include practical assessments and/or marked assessments. They are designed to provide evidence of a student's relevant skills and knowledge in their chosen subject. These qualifications can be used for employment or as a path towards further education. See the OCR website for further details.

SVQs (Scotland)

Scottish Vocational Qualifications (SVQs) are work-based qualifications that demonstrate someone can do their job well and to the national standards for their sector. There are over 500 SVQs that cover many occupations in Scotland – from forestry to IT, management to catering, and from journalism to construction. Experts from industry, commerce and education produce SVQs based on national standards.

Many people study for SVQs in the workplace while carrying out their day-to-day role. Each SVQ unit defines one aspect of a job and what it is to be competent in that aspect of the job. Learners can work through one unit at a time, or gather evidence for several units at the same time. There are no formal written exams, instead learners collect and submit evidence, usually from their own work. They are assessed by an SVQ assessor and the assessment can take place at the learner's place of work, at college or through a training provider.

Find out more at www.sqa.org.uk/svq

Awarding organisations and examination dates

Awarding organisations and examination dates

In England there are four awarding organisations, each offering GCSEs, AS and A levels (Eduqas offers only reformed qualifications in England, whereas WJEC offers in England, Wales, Northern Ireland and independent regions). There are separate awarding organisations in Wales (WJEC) and Northern Ireland (CCEA). The awarding organisation in Scotland (SQA) offers equivalent qualifications.

This information was supplied by the awarding bodies and was accurate at the time of going to press. It is intended as a general guide only for candidates in the United Kingdom. Dates are subject to variation and should be confirmed with the awarding organisation concerned.

AQA

Qualifications offered:
GCSE
AS and A level
Foundation Certificate of Secondary Education (FCSE)
Entry Level Certificate (ELC)
Foundation and Higher Projects
Extended Project Qualification (EPQ)
Applied Generals/AQA Level 3 Certificates and Extended Certificates
Functional Skills
AQA Certificate
Technical Award

Other assessment schemes:
Unit Award Scheme (UAS)

Contact:
Email: eos@aqa.org.uk
Website: www.aqa.org.uk
Tel: 0800 197 7162 (8am–5pm Monday to Friday)
+44 161 696 5995 (Outside the UK)

Devas Street, Manchester M15 6EX
Stag Hill House, Guildford, Surrey GU2 7XJ
Windsor House, Cornwall Road, Harrogate, HG1 2PW
2nd Floor, Lynton House, 7–12 Tavistock Square, London, WC1H 9LT

CCEA – Council for the Curriculum, Examinations and Assessment

Qualifications offered:
GCSE
GCE AS/A level
Key Skills (Levels 1-4)
Entry Level Qualifications
Occupational Studies (Levels 1 & 2)
QCF Qualifications
Applied GCSE and GCE

Contact:
Email: info@ccea.org.uk
Website: www.ccea.org.uk

29 Clarendon Road, Clarendon Dock, Belfast, BT1 3BG
Tel: (028) 9026 1200

Eduqas

Eduqas, part of WJEC, offers Ofqual reformed GCSEs, AS and A levels to secondary schools and colleges. Our qualifications are available in England, Channel Islands, Isle of Man, Northern Ireland and to the independent sector in Wales (restrictions may apply).

Qualifications offered:
GCSE (9-1)
AS
A level
Level 3

Contact:
Email: info@wjec.co.uk
Website: www.eduqas.co.uk

Eduqas (WJEC CBAC Ltd),
245 Western Avenue, Cardiff, CF5 2YX
Telephone: 029 2026 5000

IB – International Baccalaureate

Qualification offered:
IB Diploma
IB Career-related Certificate

Contact:
Email: support@ibo.org
Website: www.ibo.org

IB Global Centre, The Hague, Churchillplein 6, 2517 JW, The Hague, The Netherlands
Tel: +31 70 352 60 00

IB Global Centre, Washington DC, 7501 Wisconsin Avenue, Suite 200 West Bethesda, Maryland 20814, USA
Tel: +1 301 202 3000

IB Global Centre, Singapore, 600 North Bridge Road, #21-01 Parkview Square, Singapore 188778
Tel: +65 6 579 5000

IB Global Centre, Cardiff, Peterson House, Malthouse Avenue, Cardiff Gate, Cardiff, Wales, CF23 8GL, UK
Email: reception@ibo.org
Tel: +44 29 2054 7777

International Baccalaureate Foundation Office, Route des Morillons 15, Grand-Saconnex, Genève, CH-1218, Switzerland
Tel: +41 22 309 2540

OCR – Oxford Cambridge and RSA Examinations – and Cambridge International

Qualifications offered by OCR or sister awarding organisation Cambridge Assessment International Education (Cambridge International) include:
GCSE
GCE AS/A level
IGCSE
International AS/A level
Extended Project
Cambridge International Project Qualification
Cambridge Pre-U
Cambridge Nationals
Cambridge Technicals
Functional Skills
FSMQ – Free Standing Maths Qualification
NVQ

Contact:
OCR
OCR Head Office, The Triangle Building, Shaftesbury Road, Cambridge, CB2 8EA
Website: www.ocr.org.uk
Tel: +44 1223 553998

Cambridge International
Website: www.cambridgeinternational.org
Email: info@cambridgeinternational.org
Tel: +44 1223 553554

Pearson

Qualifications offered:
Pearson's qualifications are offered in the UK but are also available through their international centres across the world. They include:
DiDA, CiDA
GCE A levels
GCSEs
Functional Skills
International GCSEs and Edexcel Certificates
ESOL (Skills for Life)
BTEC Enterprise qualifications
BTEC Entry Level, Level 1 and Level 1 Introductory
BTEC Firsts
BTEC Foundation Diploma in Art and Design
BTEC Industry Skills
BTEC International Level 3
BTEC Level 2 Technicals
BTEC Level 3 Technical Levels in Hospitality
BTEC Nationals
BTEC Specialist and Professional qualifications
BTEC Tech Awards
Higher Nationals
T Levels

Contact:
190 High Holborn, London WC1V 7BH

See website for specific contact details:
qualifications.pearson.com

SQA – Scottish Qualifications Authority

Qualifications offered:
National Qualifications (NQs): National 1 to National 5; Higher; Advanced Higher
Skills for Work; Scottish Baccalaureates
National Certificates (NCs)
National Progression Awards (NPAs)
Awards
Core Skills
Scottish Vocational Qualifications (SVQs)
Higher National Certificates and Higher National Diplomas (HNCs/HNDs)*

*SQA offers HNCs and HNDs to centres in Scotland. Outside of Scotland, the equivalent qualifications are the SQA Advanced Certificate and SQA Advanced Diploma.

Contact:
Email: customer@sqa.org.uk Tel: 0345 279 1000
Website: www.sqa.org.uk
Glasgow – The Optima Building, 58 Robertson Street, Glasgow, G2 8DQ
Dalkeith – Lowden, 24 Wester Shawfair, Dalkeith, Midlothian, EH22 1FD

WJEC

With over 65 years' experience in delivering qualifications, WJEC is the largest provider in Wales and a leading provider in England and Northern Ireland.

Qualifications offered:
GCSE
GCE A/AS
Functional Skills
Entry Level
Welsh Baccalaureate Qualifications
Essential Skills Wales
Wider Key Skills
Project Qualifications Principal Learning
Other general qualifications such as Level 1 and Level 2 Awards and Certificates including English Language, English Literature, Latin Language, Latin Language & Roman Civilisation and Latin Literature
QCF Qualifications

Contact:
Email: info@wjec.co.uk
Website: www.wjec.co.uk

245 Western Avenue, Cardiff, CF5 2YX
Tel: 029 2026 5000

Educational organisations

Educational organisations

Artsmark

Arts Council England's Artsmark was set up in 2001, and rounds are held annually.
All schools in England can apply for an Artsmark – primary, middle, secondary, special and pupil referral units, maintained and independent – on a voluntary basis. An Artsmark award is made to schools showing commitment to the full range of arts – music, dance, drama and art and design.
Tel: 0161 934 4317
Email: artsmark@artscouncil.org.uk
Website: www.artsmark.org.uk

Association for the Education and Guardianship of International Students (AEGIS)

AEGIS brings together schools and guardianship organisations to ensure and promote the welfare of international students. AEGIS provides accreditation for all reputable guardianship organisations.
AEGIS, The Wheelhouse, Bond's Mill Estate, Bristol Road, Stonehouse, Gloucestershire GL10 3RF.
Tel: 01453 821293
Email: info@aegisuk.net
Website: www.aegisuk.net

The Association of American Study Abroad Programmes (AASAP)

Established in 1991 to represent American study abroad programmes in the UK.
Contact: Kalyn Franke, AASAP/UK,
University of Maryland in London, Connaught Hall, 36-45 Tavistock Square, London WC1H 9EX
Email: info@aasapuk.org
Website: www.aasapuk.org

The Association of British Riding Schools (ABRS)

An independent body of proprietors and principals of riding establishments, aiming to look after their interests and those of the riding public and to raise standards of management, instruction and animal welfare.
Blenheim Business Centre, Smithers Hill, Shipley, West Sussex RH13 8PP.
Tel: 01403 741188
Email: office@abrs-info.org
Website: www.abrs-info.org

Association of Colleges (AOC)

Created in 1996 to promote the interest of further education colleges in England and Wales.
2-5 Stedham Place, London WC1A 1HU
Tel: 0207 034 9900
Email: enquiries@aoc.co.uk
Website: www.aoc.co.uk

Association of Governing Bodies of Independent Schools (AGBIS)

AGBIS supports and advises governing bodies of schools in the independent sector on all aspects of governance.
Registered charity No. 1108756
Association of Governing Bodies of Independent Schools, 3 Codicote Road, Welwyn, Hertfordshire AL6 9LY
Tel: 01438 840730
Email: enquiries@agbis.org.uk
Website: www.agbis.org.uk

Association of Employment and Learning Providers (AELP)

AELP's purpose is to influence the education and training agenda. They are the voice of independent learning providers throughout England.
Association of Employment and Learning Providers,
2nd Floor, 9 Apex Court, Bradley Stoke, Bristol, BS32 4JT
Tel: 0117 986 5389
Email: enquiries@aelp.org.uk
Website: www.aelp.org.uk

The Association of School and College Leaders (ASCL)

Formerly the Secondary Heads Association, the ASCL is a professional association for secondary school and college leaders.
Association of School and College Leaders, 2nd Floor, Peat House, 1 Waterloo Way, Leicester, LE1 6LP
Tel: 0116 299 1122
Fax: 0116 299 1123
Email: info@ascl.org.uk
Website: www.ascl.org.uk

Boarding Schools' Association (BSA)

For information on the BSA see editorial on page 35

The British Accreditation Council (BAC)

The British Accreditation Council (BAC) has now been the principal accrediting body for the independent further and higher education and training sector for over 30 years. BAC-accredited institutions in the UK now number more than 300, offering everything from website design to yoga to equine dentistry, as well as more standard qualifications in subjects such as business, IT, management and law. As well as our accreditation of institutions offering traditional teaching, BAC has developed a new accreditation scheme for providers offering online, distance and blended learning. Some students may also look to study outside the UK at one of the institutions holding BAC international accreditation.
Wax Chandlers' Hall 1st Floor, 6 Gresham Street, London, EC2V 7AD
Tel: 0300 330 1400
Email: info@the-bac.org
Website: www.the-bac.org

The British Association for Early Childhood Education (BAECE)

Promotes quality provision for all children from birth to eight in whatever setting they are placed. Publishes booklets and organises conferences for those interested in early years education and care. Registered charity Nos. 313082; SC039472
Early Education, Regus offices, 2 Victoria Square, St Albans AL1 3TF
Tel: 01727 884925
Email: office@early-education.org.uk
Website: www.early-education.org.uk

The Choir Schools' Association (CSA)

Represents 44 schools attached to cathedrals, churches and college chapels, which educate cathedral and collegiate choristers.
CSA Information Officer, 39 Bournside Road, Cheltenham, Gloucestershire, GL51 3AL
Tel: 07903 850597
Email: ian.jones@choirschools.org.uk
Website: www.choirschools.org.uk

CIFE

CIFE is the professional association for independent sixth form and tutorial colleges accredited by the British Accreditation Council (BAC), the Independent Schools Council or the DfE (Ofsted). Member colleges specialise in preparing students for GCSE and A level (AS and A2) in particular and university entrance in general.
The aim of the association is to provide a forum for the exchange of information and ideas, and for the promotion of best practice, and to safeguard adherence to strict standards of professional conduct and ethical propriety. Further information can be obtained from CIFE:
Tel: 0208 767 8666
Email: enquiries@cife.org.uk
Website: www.cife.org.uk

Council of British International Schools (COBIS)

COBIS is a membership association of British schools of quality worldwide and is committed to a stringent process of quality assurance for all its member schools. COBIS is a member of the Independent Schools Council (ISC) of the United Kingdom.
COBIS, 55–56 Russell Square, Bloomsbury, London WC1B 4HP
Tel: 020 3826 7190
Email: pa@cobis.org.uk
Website: www.cobis.org.uk

Council of International Schools (CIS)

CIS is a not-for-profit organisation committed to supporting its member schools and colleges in achieving and delivering the highest standards of international education. CIS provides accreditation to schools, teacher and leader recruitment and best practice development. CIS Higher Education assists member colleges and universities in recruiting a diverse profile of qualified international students.
Schipholweg 113, 2316 XC Leiden, The Netherlands.
Tel: +31 71 524 3300
Email: info@cois.org
Website: www.cois.org

Dyslexia Action (DA)

A registered, educational charity (No. 268502), which has established teaching and assessment centres and conducts teacher-training throughout the UK. The aim of the institute is to help people with dyslexia of all ages to overcome their difficulties in learning to read, write and spell and to achieve their potential.
Dyslexia Action Training and Guild, Centurion House, London Road, Staines-upon-Thames TW18 4AX
Tel: 01784 222 304
Email: trainingcourses@dyslexiaaction.org.uk
Website: www.dyslexiaaction.org.uk

European Association for International Education (EAIE)

A not-for-profit organisation aiming for internationalisation in higher education in Europe. It has a membership of over 1800.
PO Box 11189, 1001 GD Amsterdam, The Netherlands
Tel: +31 20 344 5100
Fax: +31 20 344 5119
Email: info@eaie.org
Website: www.eaie.org

ECIS (European Collaborative for International Schools)

ECIS is a membership organisation which provides services to support professional development, good governance and leadership in international schools.
24 Greville Street,
London, EC1N 8SS
Tel: 020 7824 7040
Email: ecis@ecis.org
Website: www.ecis.org

The Girls' Day School Trust (GDST)

The Girls' Day School Trust (GDST) is one of the largest, longest-established and most successful groups of independent schools in the UK, with 4000 staff and over 20,000 students between the ages of 3 and 18. As a charity that owns and runs a family of 25 schools in England and Wales, it reinvests all its income into its schools for the benefit of the pupils. With a long history of pioneering innovation in the education of girls, the GDST now also educates boys in some of its schools, and has two coeducational sixth form colleges. Registered charity No. 306983
10 Bressenden Place, London, SW1E 5DH
Tel: 020 7393 6666
Email: info@wes.gdst.net
Website: www.gdst.net

Girls' Schools Association (GSA)

For information on the GSA see editorial on page 36

The Headmasters' and Headmistresses' Conference (HMC)

For information on the HMC see editorial on page 37

Human Scale Education (HSE)

An educational reform movement aiming for small education communities based on democracy, fairness and respect. Registered charity No. 1000400
Email: contact@hse.org.uk
Website: www.humanscaleeducation.com

The Independent Association of Prep Schools (IAPS)

For further information about IAPS see editorial on page 38

The Independent Schools Association (ISA)

For further information about ISA see editorial on page 39

The Independent Schools' Bursars Association (ISBA)

Exists to support and advance financial and operational performance in independent schools. The ISBA is a charitable company limited by guarantee. Company No. 6410037; registered charity No. 1121757
Bluett House, Unit 11–12 Manor Farm, Cliddesden, nr Basingstoke, Hampshire RG25 2JB
Tel: 01256 330369
Email: isbaoffice@theisba.org.uk
Website: www.theisba.org.uk

The Independent Schools Council (ISC)

The Independent Schools Council exists to promote choice, diversity and excellence in education; the development of talent at all levels of ability; and the widening of opportunity for children from all backgrounds to achieve their potential. Its 1280 member schools educate more than 500,000 children at all levels of ability and from all socioeconomic classes. Nearly a third of children in ISC schools receive help with fees. The Governing Council of ISC contains representatives from each of the eight ISC constituent associations listed below. See also page 34.

Members:
Association of Governing Bodies of Independent Schools (AGBIS)
Girls' Schools Association (GSA)
Headmasters' and Headmistresses' Conference (HMC)
Independent Association of Prep Schools (IAPS)
Independent Schools Association (ISA)
Independent Schools Bursars' Association (ISBA)
The Society of Heads

The council also has close relations with the BSA, COBIS, SCIS and WISC.

First Floor, 27 Queen Anne's Gate,
London, SW1H 9BU
Tel: 020 7766 7070
Fax: 020 7766 7071
Email: research@isc.co.uk
Website: www.isc.co.uk

The Independent Schools Examinations Board (ISEB)

Details of the Common Entrance examinations are obtainable from:
Independent Schools Examinations Board,
Endeavour House, Crow Arch Lane, Ringwood BH24 1HP
Tel: 01425 470555
Email: enquiries@iseb.co.uk
Website: www.iseb.co.uk
Copies of past papers can be purchased from Galore Park: www.galorepark.co.uk

International Baccalaureate (IB)

For full information about the IB see full entry on page 429.

International Schools Theatre Association (ISTA)

International body of teachers and students of theatre, run by teachers for teachers. Registered charity No. 1050103
Lakeside Offices, The Old Cattle Market, Coronation Park, Helston, Cornwall, TR13 0SR
Tel: 01326 560398
Email: office@ista.co.uk
Website: www.ista.co.uk

Maria Montessori Institute (MMI)

Authorised by the Association Montessori Internationale (AMI) to run their training course in the UK. Further information is available from:
26 Lyndhurst Gardens, Hampstead, London NW3 5NW
Tel: 020 7435 3646
Email: info@mariamontessori.org
Website: www.mariamontessori.org

The National Association of Independent Schools & Non-Maintained Schools (NASS)

A membership organisation working with and for special schools in the voluntary and private sectors within the UK. Registered charity No. 1083632
PO Box 705, York YO30 6WW
Tel/Fax: 01904 624446
Email: krippon@nasschools.org.uk
Website: www.nasschools.org.uk

National Day Nurseries Association (NDNA)

A national charity that aims to promote quality in early years. Registered charity No. 1078275
NDNA, National Early Years Enterprise Centre, Longbow Close, Huddersfield, West Yorkshire HD2 1GQ
Tel: 01484 407070
Fax: 01484 407060
Email: info@ndna.org.uk
Website: www.ndna.org.uk

3 Connaught House, Riverside Business Park, Benarth Road, Conwy, LL32 8UB
Tel: 01824 707823
Email: wales@ndna.org.uk

NDNA Scotland, The Mansfield Traquair Centre, 15 Mansfield Place, Edinburgh EH3 6BB
Tel: 0131 516 6967
Email: scotland@ndna.org.uk

National Foundation for Educational Research (NFER)

NFER is the UK's largest independent provider of research, assessment and information services for education, training and children's services. Its clients include UK government departments and agencies at both national and local levels. NFER is a not-for-profit organisation and a registered charity No. 313392
Head Office, The Mere, Upton Park, Slough, Berkshire SL1 2DQ
Tel: 01753 574123
Fax: 01753 691632
Email: enquiries@nfer.ac.uk
Website: www.nfer.ac.uk

Potential Plus UK

Potential Plus UK is an independent charity that supports the social, emotional and learning needs of children with high learning potential of all ages and backgrounds. Registered charity No. 313182
Potential Plus UK, The Open University, Vaughan Harley Building Ground Floor, Walton Hall, Milton Keynes, MK7 6AA
Tel: 01908 646433
Email: amazingchildren@potentialplusuk.org
Website: www.potentialplusuk.org

Round Square

An international group of schools formed in 1967 following the principles of Dr Kurt Hahn, the founder of Salem School in Germany, and Gordonstoun in Scotland. The Round Square, named after Gordonstoun's 17th century circular building in the centre of the school, now has more than 100 member schools. Registered charity No. 327117
Round Square, First Floor, Morgan House, Madeira Walk, Windsor SL4 1EP
Tel: 01474 709843
Website: www.roundsquare.org

Royal National Children's SpringBoard Foundation

On 1 July 2017 the Royal National Children's Foundation (RNCF) merged with The SpringBoard Bursary Foundation to create the Royal National Children's SpringBoard Foundation ('Royal SpringBoard'). The newly merged charity gives life-transforming bursaries to disadvantaged and vulnerable children from across the UK.
Buckingham Suite, 7 Grosvenor Gardens,
London SW1W 0BD
Tel: 020 3405 3630
Email: admin@royalspringboard.org.uk
Website: www.royalspringboard.org.uk

School Fees Independent Advice (SFIA)

For further information about SFIA, see editorial on page 32

Schools Music Association of Great Britain (SMA)

The SMA is a national 'voice' for music in education. It is now part of the Incorporated Society of Musicians Registered charity No. 313646
Website: www.ism.org/sma

Scottish Council of Independent Schools (SCIS)

Representing more than 70 independent, fee-paying schools in Scotland, the Scottish Council of Independent Schools (SCIS) is the foremost authority on independent schools in Scotland and offers impartial information, advice and guidance to parents. Registered charity No. SC018033
1 St Colme Strret, Edinburgh EH3 6AA
Tel: 0131 556 2316
Email: info@scis.org.uk
Website: www.scis.org.uk

Society of Education Consultants (SEC)

The Society is a professional membership organisation that supports management consultants who specialise in education and children's services. The society's membership includes consultants who work as individuals, in partnerships or in association with larger consultancies.
SEC, Bellamy House, 13 West Street, Cromer NR27 9HZ
Tel: 0330 323 0457
Email: administration@sec.org.uk
Website: www.sec.org.uk

The Society of Heads

For full information see editorial on page 40

State Boarding Forum (SBF)

For full information about the SBF see editorial on page 35

Steiner Waldorf Schools Fellowship (SWSF)

Representing Steiner education in the UK and Ireland, the SWSF has member schools and early years centres in addition to interest groups and other affiliated organisations. Member schools offer education for children within the normal range of ability, aged 3 to 18. Registered charity No. 295104
35 Park Rd, London NW1 6XT
Tel: 020 4524 9933
Email: admin@steinerwaldorf.org
Website: www.steinerwaldorf.org

Support and Training in Prep Schools (SATIPS)

SATIPS aims to support teachers in the independent and maintained sectors of education. Registered charity No. 313688
7 Lakeside, Overstone Park, Northampton, Northamptonshire, NN6 0QS
Website: www.satips.org

The Tutors' Association

The Tutors' Association is the professional body for tutoring and wider supplementary education sector in the UK. Launched in 2013, they have over 1,300 members, including Individual and Corporate Members representing some 30,000 tutors throughout the UK.
Tel: 01628 306108
Email: info@thetutorsassociation.org.uk
Website: www.thetutorsassociation.org.uk

UCAS (Universities and Colleges Admissions Service)

UCAS is the organisation responsible for managing applications to higher education courses in England, Scotland, Wales and Northern Ireland. Registered charity Nos. 1024741 and SC038598
Rosehill, New Barn Lane,
Cheltenham, Gloucestershire GL52 3LZ
Tel: 0371 468 0 468
Website: www.ucas.com

UKCISA – The Council for International Student Affairs

UKCISA is the UK's national advisory body serving the interests of international students and those who work with them. Registered charity No. 1095294
Website: www.ukcisa.org.uk

United World Colleges (UWC)

UWC was founded in 1962 and their philosophy is based on the ideas of Dr Kurt Hahn (see Round Square Schools). Registered charity No. 313690.
UWC International, Third Floor, 55 New Oxford Street, London, WC1A 1BS, UK
Tel: 020 7269 7800
Fax: 020 7405 4374
Email: info@uwcio.uwc.org
Website: www.uwc.org

World-Wide Education Service of CfBT Education Trust (WES)

A leading independent service which provides home education courses worldwide.
Waverley House, Penton,
Carlisle, Cumbria CA6 5QU
Tel: 01228 577123
Email: office@weshome.com
Website: www.weshome.com

Glossary

ACETS   Awards and Certificates in Education

AEA   Advanced Extension Award

AEB   Associated Examining Board for the General Certificate of Education

AEGIS   Association for the Education and Guardianship of International Students

AGBIS   Association of Governing Bodies of Independent Schools

AHIS   Association of Heads of Independent Schools

AJIS   Association of Junior Independent Schools

ALP   Association of Learning Providers

ANTC   The Association of Nursery Training Colleges

AOC   Association of Colleges

AP   Advanced Placement

ASCL   Association of School & College Leaders

ASL   Additional and Specialist Learning

ATI   The Association of Tutors Incorporated

AQA   Assessment and Qualification Alliance/Northern Examinations and Assessment Board

BA   Bachelor of Arts

BAC   British Accreditation Council for Independent Further and Higher Education

BAECE   The British Association for Early Childhood Education

BD   Bachelor of Divinity

BEA   Boarding Educational Alliance

BEd   Bachelor of Education

BLitt   Bachelor of Letters

BPrimEd   Bachelor of Primary Education

BSA   Boarding Schools' Association

BSc   Bachelor of Science

BTEC   Range of work-related, practical programmes leading to qualifications equivalent to GCSEs and A levels awarded by Edexcel

Cantab   Cambridge University

CATSC   Catholic Association of Teachers in Schools and Colleges

CCEA   Council for the Curriculum, Examination and Assessment

CDT   Craft, Design and Technology

CE   Common Entrance Examination

CEAS   Children's Education Advisory Service

CertEd   Certificate of Education

CIE   Cambridge International Examinations

CIFE   Conference for Independent Education

CIS   Council of International Schools

CISC   Catholic Independent Schools' Conference

CLAIT   Computer Literacy and Information Technology

CNED   Centre National d'enseignement (National Centre of long distance learning)

COBIS   Council of British International)

CSA	The Choir Schools' Association	INSET	In service training	PGCE	Post Graduate Certificate in Education
CST	The Christian Schools' Trust	ISA	Independent Schools Association	PhD	Doctor of Philosophy
DfE	Department for Education (formerly DfES and DCFS)	ISBA	Independent Schools' Bursars' Association	PL	Principal Learning
		ISCis	Independent Schools Council information service	PNEU	Parents' National Education Union
DipEd	Diploma of Education	ISC	Independent Schools Council	PYP	Primary Years Programme
DipTchng	Diploma of Teaching	ISEB	Independent Schools Examination Board	QCA	Qualifications and Curriculum Authority
EAIE	European Association for International Education	ISST	International Schools Sports Tournament	QCF	Qualifications and Credit Framework
ECIS	European Council of International Schools	ISTA	International Schools Theatre Association	RSIS	The Round Square Schools
EdD	Doctor of Education	ITEC	International Examination Council	SAT	Scholastic Aptitude Test
Edexcel	GCSE Examining group, incorporating Business and Technology Education Council (BTEC) and University of London Examinations and Assessment Council (ULEAC)	JET	Joint Educational Trust	SATIPS	Support & Training in Prep Schools/Society of Assistant Teachers in Prep Schools
		LA	Local Authority		
		LISA	London International Schools Association	SBSA	State Boarding Schools Association
		MA	Master of Arts	SCE	Service Children's Education
EFL	English as a Foreign Language	MCIL	Member of the Chartered Institute of Linguists	SCIS	Scottish Council of Independent Schools
ELAS	Educational Law Association	MEd	Master of Education	SCQF	Scottish Credit and Qualifications Framework
EPQ	Extended Project qualification	MIoD	Member of the Institute of Directors	SEC	The Society of Educational Consultants
ESL	English as a Second Language	MLitt	Master of Letters	SEN	Special Educational Needs
FCoT	Fellow of the College of Teachers (TESOL)	MSc	Master of Science	SFCF	Sixth Form Colleges' Forum
FEFC	Further Education Funding Council	MusD	Doctor of Music	SFIA	School Fees Insurance Agency Limited
FRSA	Fellow of the Royal Society of Arts	MYP	Middle Years Programme	SFIAET	SFIA Educational Trust
FSMQ	Free-Standing Mathematics Qualification	NABSS	National Association of British Schools in Spain	SMA	Schools Music Association
GCE	General Certificate of Education	NAGC	National Association for Gifted Children	SoH	The Society of Heads
GCSE	General Certificate of Secondary Education	NAHT	National Association of Head Teachers	SQA	Scottish Qualifications Authority
GDST	Girls' Day School Trust	NAIS	National Association of Independent Schools	STEP	Second Term Entrance Paper (Cambridge)
GNVQ	General National Vocational Qualifications	NASS	National Association of Independent Schools & Non-maintained Special Schools	SVQ	Scottish Vocational Qualifications
GOML	Graded Objectives in Modern Languages			SWSF	Steiner Waldorf Schools Fellowship
GSA	Girls' Schools Association	NDNA	National Day Nurseries Association	TABS	The Association of Boarding Schools
GSVQ	General Scottish Vocational Qualifications	NEASC	New England Association of Schools and Colleges	TISCA	The Independent Schools Christian Alliance
HMC	Headmasters' and Headmistresses' Conference			TOEFL	Test of English as a Foreign Language
HMCJ	Headmasters' and Headmistresses' Conference Junior Schools	NFER	National Federation of Educational Research	UCAS	Universities and Colleges Admissions Service for the UK
		NPA	National Progression Award		
HNC	Higher National Certificate	NQ	National Qualification	UCST	United Church Schools Trust
HND	Higher National Diploma	NQF	National Qualifications Framework	UKLA	UK Literacy Association
IAPS	Independent Association of Prep Schools	NQT	Newly Qualified Teacher	UKCISA	The UK Council for International Education
IB	International Baccalaureate	NVQ	National Vocational Qualifications	UWC	United World Colleges
ICT	Information and Communication Technology	OCR	Oxford, Cambridge and RSA Examinations	WISC	World International Studies Committee
IFF	Inspiring Futures Foundation (formerly ISCO)	OLA	Online Language Assessment for Modern Languages	WJEC	Welsh Joint Education Committee
IGCSE	International General Certificate of Secondary Education			WSSA	Welsh Secondary Schools Association
		Oxon	Oxford		

Index

455